MARK TWAIN SPEAKING

MARK TWAIN SPEAKING

Edited by Paul Fatout

UNIVERSITY OF IOWA PRESS

Library of Congress Cataloging in Publication Data

Clemens, Samuel Langhorne, 1835–1910.
Mark Twain speaking.

Bibliography: p.
I. Fatout, Paul. II. Title.
PS1302.F3 1976 815′.4 76–15986
ISBN 0–87745–056–0

University of Iowa Press, Iowa City 52242

Printed in the United States of America

For permission to use copyrighted material, acknowledgment is made to Harper & Row for the following from *Mark Twain's Speeches* (1923): "On Speech-Making Reform," "On After-Dinner Speaking," "On Adam," "Advice to Youth," "Speech," "Turncoats," "A Tribute," "Yale College Speech," "On Foreign Critics," "Introducing Doctor Van Dyke," and from pp. xv–xvi of the Introduction by Albert Bigelow Paine; for "His Grandfather's Old Ram" from *Mark Twain in Eruption;* and for excerpts from *Mark Twain's Autobiography, The Love Letters of Mark Twain, Mark Twain's Notebook,* and *My Father Mark Twain.*

For permission to use unpublished Mark Twain items, acknowledgment is made to the Mark Twain Company for the following manuscripts: "Bishop Speech," "On the Three Great Laws to be Observed in the Treatment of Bright's Disease," "Christening Yarn," "Speech Introducing Winston Churchill," "De Woman Wid De Gold'n Arm," "Lecture Notes for 'Innocents,'" and an untitled MS on printers and printing; for autobiographical dictations of December 28, 1906, "The Long Clam"; August 28, 1906, Fellowcraft Club; and August 28, 1906, Speech-making Experiment; for excerpts on General Grant and Vienna from Notebooks 15 and 32; for revisions of "Punch, Brothers, Punch," *The Stolen White Elephant* (1882), and part of Chapter XVI of *Huckleberry Finn,* Tauchnitz ed. (1885); and the first paragraph of Mark Twain's letter to the New York Press Club, June 1, 1869.

Mark Twain at "Stormfield," Redding, Connecticut. A holograph note accompanying the photograph reads, "From home of Laura Frazier (Becky Thatcher—of Mark Twain fame) & was among her things & was taken on her trip to Stormfield in 1908 (picture was taken by her or by her daughter at that time)." The photograph is in the Special Collections section of The University of Iowa Libraries, a gift of Philip Adler.

Mark Twain Speaking

For JOHN C. GERBER

Contents

Introduction xv
Acknowledgments xxix
Selection of Texts xxx
Abbreviations xxx

1 Presentation Speech 1
2 Sandwich Islands Lecture 4
3 Concluding Remarks 16
4 Address to the Czar 18
5 Woman—The Pride of Any Profession 20
6 Pilgrim Life 23
7 Introductory Remarks 25
8 The American Vandal Abroad 27
9 Concluding Remarks 37
10 The Reliable Contraband 38
11 Artemus Ward Lecture 41
12 Roughing It Lecture 48
13 On Governor James W. Nye 64
14 *Aldine* Dinner 65
15 Savage Club 69
16 Whitefriars Club 72
17 Meeting of Americans 74
18 The Ladies 78
19 The Guests 82
20 Introducing the Reverend Charles Kingsley 83
21 Massachusetts Press Association 85
22 Curtain Speech 87
23 Insurance Dinner 89
24 Curtain Speech 92
25 Spelling Match 94
26 Republican Mass Meeting 97
27 The Weather of New England 100
28 Curtain Speech 103
29 Putnam Phalanx 106
30 Whittier Birthday Dinner 110

31	Bayard Taylor Dinner	116
32	Anglo-American Club	120
33	Stanley Club	122
34	Stomach Club	125
35	Introducing General Hawley	128
36	Army of the Tennessee Reunion	130
37	The Babies	131
38	Holmes Breakfast	134
39	Welcome to General Grant	136
40	Republican Rally	138
41	Funeral Oration	146
42	Papyrus Club	148
43	Army of the Potomac Reunion	151
44	De Woman Wid De Gold'n Arm	155
45	Montreal Dinner	157
46	New England Society	162
47	Fréchette Dinner	166
48	Saturday Morning Club	169
49	New England Society	173
50	Introducing George W. Cable	176
51	On Adam	178
52	Wheelmen	181
53	Turncoats	182
54	Mugwump Rally	186
55	Mock Oration on the Dead Partisan	188
56	On Speech-Making Reform	190
57	Actors Fund Fair	194
58	Huck Saves Jim	195
59	The Compositor	200
	Rejected Version of Typothetae Speech	204
60	Remarks on Copyright	206
61	Our Children	210
62	Yankee Smith of Camelot	211
63	Introducing Henry M. Stanley	214
64	Stationers Board of Trade	216
65	An Author's Soldiering	219
66	Daly's Theatre	222
67	Army and Navy Club	225
68	Post-Prandial Oratory	230
69	Yale Alumni Association	235
70	Introducing Nye and Riley	238
71	The Long Clam	240
72	The Grand Tour—1. The Sandwich Islands	244

73	Fellowcraft Club	247
74	The Humorist on the Copyright Question	251
75	The Christening Yarn	254
76	Curtain Speech	256
77	On Foreign Critics	257
78	National Wholesale Druggists Association	261
79	Robert A. Pryor Dinner	263
80	Lotos Club	265
81	Brander Matthews Dinner	269
82	Advice	271
83	Cramp's Shipyard	274
84	Curtain Speech	276
85	Morals Lecture	279
86	Interview	287
87	His Grandfather's Old Ram	289
88	Yorick Club	292
89	Australian Institute of Journalists	298
90	Savage Club	302
91	Commemoration Luncheon	305
92	Punch, Brothers, Punch	308
93	Interview	312
94	Die Schrecken der Deutschen Sprache	314
95	Jubilee of the Hungarian Press	319
96	Savage Club	321
97	Authors Club	322
98	Whitefriars Club	324
99	New Vagabonds Club	330
100	The Day We Celebrate	333
101	Remarks on Copyright	335
102	Literature	337
103	The Drama	338
104	Reading Room Opening	340
105	Travelogue	342
106	Galveston Orphans Bazaar	344
107	Woman's Press Club	346
108	Lotos Club	349
109	New York Press Club	353
110	Society of American Authors	356
111	The Disappearance of Literature	358
112	Public Education Association	360
113	Our City	363
114	Introducing Winston S. Churchill	367
115	Causes of Our Present Municipal Corruption	370

116	Hebrew Technical School for Girls	374
117	University Settlement Society	377
118	Lincoln Celebration	381
119	Remarks on Osteopathy	384
120	New York Senate	389
121	Training That Pays	390
122	Lotos Club	392
123	Poughkeepsie Eastman Club	395
124	University Club	398
125	Missouri Society	401
126	Speech-Making Experiment	403
127	Edmund Burke on Croker and Tammany	404
128	Two Political Speeches	414
129	Mock Eulogy of Tammany	415
130	Good Citizenship Association	418
131	Lotos Club	420
132	Scotch Humor	423
133	Yale Alumni Association	426
134	Society of Medical Jurisprudence	429
135	Hannibal High School Graduation	431
136	University of Missouri Commencement	435
137	Harbor Boat Christening	440
138	Eugene Field Commemoration	442
139	Speech on Art	443
140	Lotos Club	447
141	Sixty-seventh Birthday Dinner	453
142	Seventieth Birthday Dinner	462
143	Benefit Matinee for Russian Sufferers	468
144	Society of Illustrators	472
145	Tuskegee Institute Meeting	478
146	Manhattan Dickens Fellowship	482
147	Ends of the Earth Club	485
148	Introducing Dr. Henry Van Dyke	487
149	West Side Branch Y.M.C.A.	492
150	Barnard College Reception	495
151	Freundschaft Society	503
152	New York State Association for the Blind	506
153	Women's University Club Reception	511
154	Club A Dinner	513
155	Robert Fulton Monument Association	515
156	San Francisco Relief Meeting	519
157	Billiards Exhibition	520
158	Associated Press	522

159 Concert Debut of Clara Clemens 528
160 Interview 530
161 Remarks on Copyright 533
162 Burlesque Temperance Lecture 541
163 Reminiscences of Longfellow and Others 543
164 Curtain Speech 546
165 Actors Fund Fair 548
166 Government House, Annapolis 550
167 Interview 554
168 Royal Garden Party 556
169 Our Guest 558
170 Lord Mayor's Dinner 564
171 The Day We Celebrate 567
172 Savage Club 572
173 Lord Mayor's Dinner, Liverpool 577
174 Interview 585
175 Fulton Day 587
176 Bishop Speech 590
177 Curtain Speech 596
178 Associated Societies of Engineers 597
179 Pleiades Club 600
180 Lotos Club 603
181 Pilgrims Club 612
182 Garrison Children, Bermuda 616
183 Interview 617
184 Humorists and Cartoonists 619
185 Curtain Speech 620
186 C.C.N.Y. Dedication 621
187 Associated Alumni of C.C.N.Y. 623
188 American Booksellers Association 626
189 Queen Victoria—an American Tribute 628
190 Opening of the Mark Twain Library 630
191 New York Postgraduate Medical School 631
192 Lotos Club 637
193 Henry H. Rogers Dinner 640
194 William Travers Jerome Dinner 643
195 Misses Tewksbury's School Graduation 645

Mark Twain Speaking: *A Chronology* 647

Index 681

Introduction

Sam Clemens, just turned twenty, made his first speech, an impromptu, at a printers' banquet in Keokuk on January 17, 1856. It was a tentative approach to a long career as lecturer and dinner speaker, as advocate of causes, and introducer at meetings charitable and political. By late middle age he was a veteran in demand for all sorts of occasions, from formal dinners to fund-raising campaigns. During the last decade of his life, as world citizen of international fame, he was regarded as an authoritative spokesman on all human affairs, so great an attraction that his presence at a function assured its success.

Public speaking, for which he had a remarkable aptitude, was a popular variety of nineteenth-century mass entertainment, and of education and culture. By the end of the Civil War almost every town of any size had a young men's literary society, which arranged a course of six or eight lectures by visiting speakers during a season that ran from about October to March. In hundreds of communities audiences trudged to town hall or opera house, come fair weather or foul, to be informed and improved.

A heavy demand for talkers created a corps of itinerants who gave much of their time to lecturing as a profession. Stalwarts of this guild were Wendell Phillips, a fiery agitator; John B. Gough, a magnificent thunderer against the evils of the demon rum; Henry Ward Beecher, a verbal wizard who evoked laughter and tears; Anna E. Dickinson, an emotional orator on society and politics; and Petroleum V. Nasby (David Ross Locke), a favorite funny man. These blue-ribbon performers received more invitations than they could accept.

On call were many other speakers of varied talents, such as Robert G. Ingersoll, Horace Greeley, the Reverend T. De Witt Talmage, Theodore Tilton, George William Curtis, Robert Collyer, Josh Billings (Henry Wheeler Shaw), Josiah Holland, George Francis Train, Paul B. Du Chaillu, and P. T. Barnum. Earnest ladies stumped for women's rights: Susan B. Anthony, Elizabeth Cady Stanton, Mary A. Livermore, Julia Ward Howe, Matilda Joslyn Gage, Victoria Woodhull. Some espoused general culture with the aid of feminine charm: Kate Field, known as "The Rose of the Rostrum"; Lillian Edgarton, "The Pearl of the Platform"; Olive Logan, "The Lily of the Lyceum."

Trundling from town to town, pundits, preachers, professors, writers, and showmen discussed topics moral, philosophical, historical, literary, and political. "The Coming Girl," "Modern Society," "Muscle and Good Cheer," "Hours With the British Poets," "Nature and Art," "Whither Are We Drifting?": such titles suggest the range of a lyceum course. Small-town people generally expected a lecture to be grave and edifying. They preferred the sonorous periods of a traditional orator like Edward Everett, with plenty of roaring and thumping thrown in. Villagers who grumbled over paying fifty cents to hear a speaker felt swindled by a discourse that seemed frivolous or unspectacular. City crowds were less provincial, more tolerant, more ready to laugh at flippancy and wit. Mark Twain discovered these differences. He was happier joking a diversified audience in New York or Pittsburgh than he was trying to overcome the dour disapproval of rural citizens.

He reached the platform by accident, he said, and it may be so. When he returned to California from the Sandwich Islands in August 1866, hard up and casting about for some enterprise promising ready cash, he was prevailed upon to schedule a lecture on the Islands, at an admission price of one whole dollar. According to his own story, as told in *Roughing It,* he was dubious of his ability to interest an audience, fearful of failure. Yet a boisterously approving crowd filled Maguire's Opera House, and next day only the minor carping of a few critics marred the high praise of the press. If he had really questioned his speaking skill, the San Francisco debut removed uncertainty. From that time forth he confidently went ahead, assured of his competence.

Exhilarated by a promising start, he took his lecture on tour for several weeks among mining towns of California and Nevada. In the East by January 1867, he gave variants of the same lecture in the Midwest during the spring of that year, then made his first New York City appearance at Cooper Union on May 6, having a good time before a house filled by papering with complimentary tickets. After the *Quaker City* excursion he wrote a talk about his foreign travels, entitled "Pilgrim Life," which he delivered in San Francisco on his return there in April 1868, then in a few other towns on a brief swing through California and Nevada mining country. By the time he was ready for the eastern lyceum circuit he was a fairly well-seasoned platformer of some forty performances, chiefly before western audiences.

In the fall of 1868 he signed on for a tour of states in the East and Middle West. For this jaunt he wrote "The American Vandal Abroad," which was mainly a transcript of material shortly to appear in *The Innocents Abroad.* Entering the eastern arena as a little-known newcomer facing sharp competition from veteran speakers, Mark Twain ingratiated himself with most of his listeners, but serious-minded people had reservations about his levity. Many were disconcerted by his low, drawling voice, also by his conversational manner devoid of rhetorical flourishes and dramatic gestures.

Nevertheless, a gratifying number of invitations induced a second tour for the season of 1869–70, for which he reverted to his standby under the title of "Our Fellow Savages of the Sandwich Islands." At this time, *The Innocents Abroad* having become a best-seller, he was an object of interest as a personality and as a successful author whom people flocked in to see as well as hear—some croakers maintaining that he wrote better than he talked. Soon after the end of the tour he married Olivia Langdon on February 2, 1870. Then, settling down in Buffalo as part owner of the *Express,* he announced firmly that his speaking days were over.

That ultimatum was as meaningless as periodic notices announcing positively the last farewell performance of a famous actress or singer. Unable to resist the lure of the platform, he went trouping again for several months in 1871–72. This tour was his most chaotic and least successful. Starting with a lecture clumsily entitled "Reminiscences of Some Uncommonplace Characters Whom I Have Chanced to Meet"—which he believed was sure to "fetch" an audience—he soon found that it failed to fetch anybody. Hastily improvising a talk on the life and humor of Artemus Ward, he discovered that this number did not please either; critics complained of unoriginality and stale jokes. Still, he continued to use both lectures until, about midseason, he hit his stride with a third one made of western material that would appear in his forthcoming book, *Roughing It.*

Disgusted by the spotty season, he again announced that he was through forever with the platform. Yet in London late in 1873 he gave the Sandwich Islands talk for two weeks, followed by two weeks of "Roughing It"; these appearances were managed by the English impresario, George Dolby. Mark Twain puzzled and charmed British audiences at the Queen's Concert Rooms in Hanover Square, and attracted full houses at Liverpool and Leicester.

After that sortie his perennial threat of retiring became a temporary reality as he stayed off the circuit for a number of years, although occasionally giving benefit lectures and programs of readings that marked a change in his technique. Instead of presenting a more or less coherent discourse on a single topic like the Sandwich Islands, he told a series of anecdotes. In a continually enlarging repertoire were the ghost story of the Golden Arm, the Mexican plug encounter out of *Roughing It,* Baker and the Blue Jays, the Jumping Frog, King Sollermun, Grandfather's Old Ram, and other familiars he worked up as he went along.

He used the anecdotal method on a long tour with George W. Cable in 1884–85, under the management of Major James B. Pond. Sensing the absurdity of periodic retirements and reappearances, Mark Twain explained to a New York audience, as reported by the *Sun,* November 19, 1884: "They say lecturers and burglars never reform. I don't know how it is with burglars—it is so long now since I had intimate relations with those people—but it is quite true of lecturers. They never reform. Lecturers and readers say they are going to leave the platform, never to return. They mean it, they mean it. But there comes, in time, an overpowering temptation to come out on the platform and give truth and morality one more lift. You can't resist." He underlined his nonresistance when he told a reporter for the Baltimore *American:* "I love the platform, and I would like to live on it but I cannot be traveling about all the time."

The tour with Cable was by turns sunny and stormy: Mark Twain exhilarated by lively audiences, depressed by glum houses that did not respond; enjoying the companionship of Cable, yet enraged by his fundamentalist piety and Sabbatarianism. Mark Twain was not an easy man to associate with, nor was he happy when he shared the limelight with anybody.

After that exhausting experience he might never have undertaken another speaking tour had not the failure of his publishing company and the Paige typesetter plunged him deeply into debt in 1894. To repay creditors, he contracted for a lecturing tour that took him around the world in 1895–96. Speaking in a number of towns in the United States and Canada on a leisurely progress to Vancouver, B.C., he then set out across the Pacific for engagements in the principal cities of Australia, New Zealand, Ceylon, India, Mauritius, and South Africa. Again he was the storyteller, casually reeling off anecdotes intended to entertain. They succeeded. The trip was a triumph: full houses, laughing and cheering, lavish attention everywhere. The returns liquidated about one-third of the debt.

Age and recurrent illness made the long journey taxing, but he looked forward to a tour in Britain and another in the United States. These plans were cancelled by the death of his daughter, Susy, in August 1896. Thereafter he was no longer a traveling speaker, although he had become so famous a platformer that he could have named his own price. Pond made tempting offers: $50,000 for 125 nights, $10,000 for ten nights. Mark Twain declined them all. He reached the point of refusing pay for any speaking performance, preferring, he said, the gratis platform that allowed him freedom to say what he pleased.

During the years when he was a traveling lecturer, he was also called upon for after-dinner speaking, which came to play a large part in his life. In his day a dinner in honor of an eminent guest was an important full-dress occasion, conducted according to an established pattern. Staged at a club or a great hotel like the Waldorf-Astoria or a famous restaurant like Delmonico's, it began about 7:30 P.M. with six or eight courses accompanied by appropriate wines, menu cards generally printed in French and often elaborately decorated. The unhurried pace allowed time, between courses, for diners to stroll around visiting each other's tables, or for performers to entertain with songs and vaudeville acts.

Then, when coffee and liqueurs had arrived, the program went on to toasts, eight or ten of them, sometimes more, every toast calling for a bumper of champagne. Unscheduled talks were against the rules. Anybody not on the toast list who tried to make a speech stood a good chance of being heckled or shouted down. The festivities, usually prolonged until well after midnight, required stamina that merits our admiration.

Women were such a rarity at these affairs that if any lady sat among the gentlemen, the papers reported the fact as news. If there was a gallery, a feminine contingent might gather there to listen to the speeches, but as a rule a banquet was for men only. Mark Twain believed that women at a dinner meant failure for a speaker because they were too timid to show their feelings, and their presence made the men timid, too. As a satisfactory crowd he cited the 850 male convicts of the Elmira Reformatory, where he occasionally performed as reader and storyteller. Preferable to mixed company was a stag dinner audience, which gave a speaker latitude by permitting ribaldry, an opportunity of which he took advantage once in a while. Not often, however, and neither did other speakers. Although steady winebibbing was routine, a banquet did not degenerate to a boozy session of bawdy stories. Toasts, always paying compliments to the chief guest, were usually dignified, sometimes pedestrian, generally earnest, occasionally stirring. When given by veterans like Mark Twain, Joseph H. Choate, Chauncey Depew, St. Clair McKelway, Thomas B. Reed, William Dean Howells, and other accomplished speakers, responses were eloquent, entertaining, and witty.

Mark Twain called banqueting an insane recreation, about as tiring as ditchdigging. During a preliminary half hour everybody stood around bandying inane remarks. Then they marched into the dining hall, which at once resounded with a loud buzz of talk and clatter of tableware, the noise often augmented by orchestra music that intensified the strain of trying to make conversation heard above the hubbub. Nothing could equal such a tumult, he said, but hell on a Sunday night. The long progression of toasts might not get under way until half past nine or later, and afterward the banqueter could creep home at a dead hour numb of body and fuzzy of mind.

Banqueting was a rigorous pastime. Nevertheless, from the late 1860s almost to the end of his life Mark Twain was a resolute diner-out who reveled in that insane recreation, weathering long dinner sessions with a gusto that became more marked as the evening wore on. In his notebooks are a great many dates of dinners for distinguished guests, in addition to memoranda about select parties, at all of which the eating and drinking and talking went on for hours. Until past the age of seventy he was capable of one or two formal banquets a week, besides private dinners, luncheons, receptions and soirées that filled a good many of his days with a tight schedule of engagements: e.g., in his notebook for 1900, when he was in London, one entry reminds him of a luncheon at 1:30, a tea at 4:30, another tea at 5:30, a dinner at 7:30, and some affair at 11:30 P.M. If there was a midnight supper, then dancing until 4 A.M., he stayed. For him, bedtime came only when there was no other place to go and nobody left to talk to.

Fond though he was of being the center of attention at a grand dinner attended by several hundred gentlemen resplendent in white ties and aglow with good fellowship and champagne, he also relished the small company of congenial spirits who dined safely beyond reach of prying newsmen. Sometimes he accepted an invitation only on condition that the press be excluded. He had no grudge against reporters, but he knew that, however faithfully they reproduced the words of a speech, any version published in the hard light of the morning after failed to catch inflection, rhythm, emphasis, and facial expressions—what he called the unspoken implications and soul of the delivery—not to speak of the exhilarating banquet atmosphere, redolent of Havana cigars and vintage bouquet. As he said in one of his own speeches, seeing the thing in the paper, "You do not recognize the corpse. You wonder if this is really that gay and handsome creature of the evening before. You look him over and find that he certainly is those very remains. Then you want to bury him. You wish you could bury him privately."

His contemporaries testify that the speaker in person gave the words vitality. Speeches that seem vapid in print, trivial or commonplace, had flair when Mark Twain's voice and mannerisms made them come alive. Paine spoke for a large majority when he said in his introduction to *MTS* (23): "Not to have heard Mark Twain is to have missed much of the value of his utterance. He had immeasurable magnetism and charm . . . . No one could resist him—probably nobody ever tried to do so."

As a talker he was willing and tireless. Invitations arrived in a steady stream: to dinners for ambassadors, philanthropists, touring noblemen, prominent actors, clerical dignitaries and financial tycoons, important persons literary and governmental, the President of the United States; to meetings on behalf of causes civic and humanitarian; to a wide variety of affairs from a royal garden party at Windsor to a convention of the International Sunshine Society, deliberations of the Organizaton for the Prevention of Unnecessary Noise, Human Race Club, Campfire Club, Little Mothers' Aid Association, American Civic Alliance, Bibliophile Society, Peace Society, and many other groups in New York City or scattered around the country from Hoboken to the Great Divide. Declining most of the invitations, he nevertheless accepted a good many. Requested to say a few words, he always complied, and he was offended if not asked. At a dinner for Prince Henry of Prussia in 1902, he was incensed because he was not only omitted from the toast list, but also shunted away from the speakers' table to an insignificant place among the ordinary diners.

For years he kept pace with such stalwart banqueters as General Horace Porter, General Sherman, Laurence Hutton, F. Hopkinson Smith, Frank Lawrence, Melville Stone, Richard Watson Gilder, Bishop Potter, George Harvey, and others whose names regularly appeared on the rosters of those present. Among the dependables, Mark Twain had top priority. His presence at a dinner or any other occasion, and the probability of a speech by him, assured a large audience as certainly as Caruso's name in the cast of an opera packed the house at the Metropolitan.

Modifying the banquet routine as age crept up on him, he conserved energy by skipping the dining part, and arriving only when the speech-making was about to begin. Usually the chief guest spoke first, a vulnerable position because he had no chance to talk back to anybody. Mark Twain, who seldom missed an opportunity to talk back, considered the last place on the program a post of honor because it meant that that speaker was good enough to make the crowd stay to the end, but he also liked to be number three or four on the list. Then he could pick up points from previous speakers and leave early if the doings were uninteresting.

The chairman was a key man who was largely responsible for the sprightliness or dullness of the evening. Mark Twain, who kept a box score on toastmastering talent, had such high standards that few earned a rating of excellent. He once told a reporter that a dinner chairman was usually an ass, and he gloomily observed that nine times out of ten a banquet committee perversely chose a toastmaster who had no qualifications for the job.

The chairman's opening speech of welcome, interspersed with complimentary references to the guest of honor, went far to set the tone for the evening. If the chairman was experienced but heavy-minded, not very imaginative, he was likely to be too stodgy to arouse enthusiasm. If he was amateurish, he might begin by confessing that he was no speaker, then prove it by a lame, apologetic performance of false starts, half-hearted jokes, and fumbling sentences that depressed everybody. Inadequacy could become contagious. It might spread to other speakers, even to old stagers, throw them off their stride and slow down the whole affair.

The successful chairman was a competent speaker able to think on his feet, a man having some gift for lively riposte and a well-turned phrase, as well as enough mental agility to improvise and to keep the pace spirited. Skillful toastmasters were not common, even in New York. Howells was a good one, as were Brander Matthews, Melville Stone, Colonel Harvey, Frank Lawrence, and Mark Twain himself. A chairman, he said, should not be stiff or clumsy, and he was obligated to furnish texts for speakers, a text being a statement that offered a take-off point for discussion or, preferably, rebuttal. Although expected to compliment the guest of honor, he should add something, almost anything, to counteract unmitigated praise, which Mark Twain considered cruel and stupid because it put the guest in such an embarrassing position that he could say nothing in reply. Mark Twain relished ingenious insults, which gave him an opening for back talk.

In scattered notes on speech-making, which he thought of compiling as a banqueter's handbook, but never did, he set down instructions for those on the toast list. One rule was that anybody scheduled for a speech should write it and memorize it. Then he should deliver it with an air of confidence, trying not to show distress by fidgety distractions like wadding up his napkin while he talked, or fiddling with a coat button or pushing wine glasses around. Since a banquet was a social event, not a forum for debating momentous questions, or an arena for political propaganda, a speech there involved nothing of grave consequence. The chief obligation of the speaker was to interest his listeners, to enliven them if he could, certainly not to bore them or exasperate them.

A dinner audience, not content with a makeshift performance, tested a speaker's mettle. Men for whom banqueting was a way of life were given to firm judgments on the ability of those who spoke.

Accustomed to hearing toasts proposed by the most accomplished members of the after-dinner guild, the gentlemen who lifted their glasses were inclined to be critical of the mediocre talker. They would not show their disapproval rudely, but the forced laughter that greeted his jokes and the thin applause when he sat down let him know that he was not a success.

Mark Twain was both annoyed and amused by an inept speaker who had not prepared himself, and who was handicapped by scant grace of manner and language. Still, he was more compassionate than scornful of the novice so unnerved by standing before an audience that he could only mumble incoherently—a predicament that must have seemed unbelievable to a fluent talker like Mark Twain. One incompetent he found entertaining was the vacant-minded fellow who frantically repeated himself as he groped for words. In dinner speeches, Mark Twain sometimes parodied that kind of floundering: "Mr. President and gentlemen—I thank you most heartily—I, that is, I—I am happy in being considered worthy to—to—," and so on. A good mimic, assuming the role of the stammering amateur, he could delight an audience with an imitation of confusion.

His approach to speech-making was professional. There was nothing offhand about his concern for a craft to which he gave his best attention as lifelong student of the spoken word. He was a conscious artist, alert to nuances, sensitive to meaning and arrangement of words, and persistent in attempts to make speech serve his purposes. The long-since rejected estimate of Mark Twain, the writer, as a "divine amateur" is an equally inaccurate judgment of the man as talker.

His way of speaking, whether on the lecture platform or in the banquet hall, was so nonchalant, so remote from stylized elocution or resounding oratory that audiences believed he spoke extempore. As if taking part in a living room conversation, he drawled lazily along like a clever improvisor inventing a monologue on the spur of the moment. Lounging casually if there was something to lean on, he seldom moved, used few gestures, and maintained a solemn countenance that was almost severe. Trained upon the audience like a battery were the piercing eyes that became most penetrating when the speaker was most witty.

His unorthodox technique puzzled listeners accustomed to the attitudinizing of the declamatory style, the clangor of the spellbinder, and the lectern-pounding of the fist-shaker. When he was on the lecture circuit, some critics, misled by careless stance and indolent delivery, took him to task for failure to prepare.

He did prepare, did not extemporize. Methodically following his own instructions, he wrote his talks, laboriously memorized them—he said he needed at least four days to work up an impromptu speech—then gave them so skillfully that they sounded like improvisations. Familiar with the ruses of studied artlessness that conceals art, he used them like an actor, as he explains in *MTE* (224): "fictitious hesitancies for the right word, fictitious unconscious pauses, fictitious unconscious side remarks, fictitious unconscious embarrassments, fictitious unconscious emphasis placed upon the wrong word with a deep intention back of it"—all of those fictitious additions having been written into his manuscript. An invaluable attribute was the voice: sometimes dryly unemphatic or rasping like an unrosined bow, then resonant, ranging through a gamut of tones.

Superbly equipped by nature and by attention to manner and devices, he fascinated listeners, who did not know that what seemed to be spontaneity was an illusion created by painstaking workmanship. After the hilarious "Babies" speech at the Chicago reunion of the Army of the Tennessee in 1879, General Sherman exclaimed, *MTL* (1:371): "Lord bless you, my boy, I don't know how you do it—it's a secret that's beyond me—but it was great—give me your hand again." Mark Twain tells us how he did it: by schooling himself for a speaking assignment like an actor for every performance of a play, then estimating the temper of his audience as cannily as an adroit lawyer sizing up a jury.

In *MTN* (236), he reminds himself that "Drill is the valuable thing. Drill—drill—*drill*—that is the precious thing. For, from drill comes the automatic, and few things in this world are well done until they can *do themselves.*" To the end of his speaking career he drilled: on inflection, tempo, phrasing, emphasis, and those fictitious accompaniments that made the performance seem spontaneous. In his notebooks many fragments of speeches and stories show his untiring search for the best combination of words, for proper pace and most telling detail.

Much interested in the effect of pauses, he experimented with timing to make them precisely right, and remarked upon the failure of other speakers to use this asset. Clergymen, he observed, often destroyed the stately beauty of the Lord's Prayer by racing headlong through it, as if believing that the faster they said it the sooner it would be answered. Considering the pause an eloquent silence that achieved an effect beyond the power of words, he broke the silence at the peak of emotion reflected in the faces before him. A fraction of a second either way might be needed to make an audience shout with laughter or jump as one man with a shock of surprise.

Rehearsing orally, he knew the length of his speech to the minute, hence never made the common mistake of running overtime.

People did not glance furtively at their watches while Mark Twain was speaking. He tried to teach his method to other speakers, like Howells, but without much success. As he said in one of his dinner speeches, a man should try out his remarks "on a plaster cast, or an empty chair, or any other appreciative object that will keep quiet until the speaker has got his matter and his delivery limbered up," but they seldom learned the useful discipline of oral rehearsal.

Banqueters did not seem to mind staying up late listening to a number of speakers, nor did they object to a long speech if it were well done. Still, by a sort of tacit agreement, a toast was supposed to be reasonably brief, not longer than twelve to fifteen minutes. Mark Twain disapproved of a speaker—particularly a colorless speaker—who said, "I must not detain you longer," or "Just one more word and I am done," then detained the suffering audience by many more words that carried him far beyond his allotted time. Among notes for the abortive banqueter's handbook, one recommends a brass band sounding off on signal to halt a stupefying talker who droned on and on.

In what was called a reading, he sharply distinguished between the written word and the spoken. Having heard Dickens read from his own works in 1868, Mark Twain had assumed that the performer merely walked on with a book, then read from it. But he discovered to his surprise that printed pieces did not read easily aloud because they were too literary, too stiff for effective speech. Hence, he said, *MTE* (216), "they have to be limbered up, broken up, colloquialized, and turned into the common forms of unpremeditated talk—otherwise they will bore the house, not entertain it." Besides, a man with his nose in a book could not keep an eye on the audience, as he always wanted to do. After what he called a few "ghastly" trials with a book on the tour of 1884–85, he laid it aside and never thereafter carried a text to the platform. He had the actor's point of view that, in telling a story without book, the narrator made the tale more convincing by himself becoming the characters in it.

Doggedly he rehearsed a repertoire of stories by talking them off until they lost their literary formality. Revising parts of his own books—*Huckleberry Finn* and others—he was like a detached stranger limbering up his own narratives. The acme of his study was the discovery that he needed only to remember the outline of a story, then fill in with detail invented on the spot. The method permitted continual variation, which was one of Mark Twain's great assets as a storyteller. He spun the same old yarns again and again, but by introducing new circumstances each time, perhaps subtly changing the emphasis, he made an old story seem fresh. The filling-in scheme also allowed him to hasten the denouement if the audience showed signs of flagging attention, and to delay it when the faces expressed ever-mounting interest.

It was far from his intention to make anybody tired of listening. He wanted people always to be emotionally alert, figuratively coming to him for more, never receding to the apathy of surfeit. If he ever bored anybody, the dissenter's complaint is not on record, the prevailing opinion being that Mark Twain was the best storyteller extant. Richard Watson Gilder's comment in *The Outlook* (December 3, 1904) may serve as a general verdict: "I have heard stories told by him which were either largely improvisations, or rehearsals, or studied performances, on public occasions and before private audiences of three or four or more, and always with the same spirit, originality, dramatic completeness, artistic finish, and sustained and surprising humor—i.e., a humor continually inventive of new surprises."

The speaking performances in this edition reveal, by variety of tone and subject, something of Mark Twain's craftmanship. A large part of his technique—perhaps the larger part—does not show in print: change of pace, shadings of emphasis, sentences left unfinished because the audience anticipated his point, ability to gauge the temper of an audience. It was a sensitive pulse-taking, indicated by reporters' interpolations of "[Laughter]" and "[Applause]." Sometimes the words alone seem neither striking enough nor funny enough to justify applause or laughter, but his way of saying them invoked the cheers and brought down the house. If blessed with natural talent not possessed by everybody, he yet brought to the task a student's industry and an artist's imagination, both of which are powerful aids to the gifted.

His speeches show that fondness for foolery and the tall tale were with him from start to finish, and an abiding attention to the entertainment of his audience. Yet the substance is rarely entirely frivolous. Sense underlies nonsense, irony is apparent from the beginning, humor may be only a thin veil for astute criticism, and his point of view is sometimes clairvoyantly modern.

When he often referred to himself as a teacher, he was more serious than humorous. Again and again he strikes that note: "I cannot keep from talking even at the risk of being instructive"; "I have been a teacher all my life, and never got a cent for teaching"; the remark on his seventieth birthday, when "you stand unafraid and unabashed upon your seven-terraced summit and look down and teach—unrebuked"; and the sardonic maxim, "It is noble to teach oneself; it is nobler still to teach others—and less trouble."

Appeals on behalf of honest government, the plight of the poor, the blind, the Negro, the maltreated, scorn of sham and hypocrisy and corruption: all show the moral earnestness of the teacher, even of the preacher, as he also called himself, meriting throughout his life the title of Moralist of the Main. His earnestness, even when camouflaged by humor, shows likewise the sanity and vigor of Mark Twain, the strong feeling for justice and humanitarianism that make him, notwithstanding perplexing contradictions of his paradoxical character, a compelling personality, memorable not only as a writer or talker, but also as a man.

The words without the speaker put us under a handicap impossible to overcome. The solemn demeanor, the modulations of voice, the easy shift from moods gay to grave, the actor's mannerisms: all contributed to a presentation often described as "inimitable." Because he and his contemporaries are no longer on the stage, the word only vaguely suggests qualities beyond exposition and beyond recovery. Intimations of the inimitable should be on call somewhere in the reader's imagination when he considers *Mark Twain Speaking.*

ACKNOWLEDGMENTS

Thanks to the Iowa State University Press for permission to use parts of the "Morals Lecture" and "Roughing It Lecture" from *The Trouble Begins at Eight;* and to Cyril Clemens for permission to use the "Lecture on Art" from *Mark Twain the Letter Writer.* For suggestions, information and inspiration, assistance bibliographical, textual, photographic and otherwise, I am grateful to: John C. Gerber, University of Iowa; Frederick Anderson, Henry Nash Smith and others, the Mark Twain Papers, University of California, Berkeley; the staff of the Newspaper Room, University of California; John Barr Tompkins and staff, Bancroft Library, University of California; the late Franklin Meine, Chicago; fellow Twainians Walter Blair, Edgar Branch, John Tuckey, Louis Budd, Howard Baetzhold, and Leon Dickinson; and William J. Whalen, Purdue University Editor. For generous aid I am indebted to helpful people in many libraries: State Historical Society of Missouri; Houghton Library, Harvard; Yale University Library; New York Public Library; Alderman Library, University of Virginia; York, Maine, Public Library; Edward Laurence Doheny Memorial Library, St. John's Seminary, Camarillo, California; Emory University Library; Alexander Turnbull Library, Wellington, New Zealand; State Library of Victoria, Australia; Public Library of South Australia, Adelaide; City of Sydney, Australia, Public Library; Public Library, Bloemfontein, South Africa; State Library, Pretoria, South Africa; University of Natal Library, Durban, South Africa; Purdue University Library; West Lafayette, Indiana, Public Library. Librarians are invaluable. I have never met one who begrudged assistance, whether in the Library of Congress or the small one-room library of a faraway village. Finally, a special citation is due my wife, Roberta, who not only endured the ups and downs of much travel to California and elsewhere, but also put up with the clutter and clatter of a long editorial job that seemed to go on interminably during a hot dry summer. For her, a special Salud!

P.F.

SELECTION OF TEXTS

The editor soon realized, with dismay, that he could not be certain of exactly what Mark Twain said on any occasion. No electronic gear recorded the words precisely as they were spoken. In the absence of such modern devices, no text can be regarded as authoritative.

A manuscript might appear to have some claim to reliability, as it represents what Mark Twain intended to say. Yet, though he wrote his speeches and memorized them, he was not a pedestrian learner who committed them word for word. Once on his feet and talking, he was likely to depart from the script by introducing new detail or turns of phrase, and he generally added comments suitable to a particular event. Hence, a manuscript is not more trustworthy than any other text.

Manuscript versions often differ from those in newspapers and anthologies, and all of them usually differ from each other. To single out the correct one from among four or five variants, sometimes more, poses an insoluble problem. Therefore, the best parts of available texts, or what seemed to be the most Twainian parts, have been combined into composite versions. Conjecture has played a part in the process, together with attention to vernacular style, which he was more likely to use than a formal manner of speaking. This method, it is hoped, may catch something of the spirit and tone of Mark Twain, along with much that he probably said.

ABBREVIATIONS

Alta	San Francisco *Alta California*
Courant	Hartford, Connecticut, *Courant*
CTrib	Chicago *Tribune*
Eloquence(R)	*Modern Eloquence.* 4 Vols. Ed. Thomas B. Reed. Philadelphia, 1903.
Eloquence(T)	*Modern Eloquence.* 15 Vols. Ed. Ashley H. Thorndike. New York, 1928.
LLMT	*The Love Letters of Mark Twain.* Ed. Dixon Wecter. New York, 1949.

Lotos *After Dinner Speeches at the Lotos Club.* Arranged by John Elderkin, Chester A. Lord, Charles W. Price. New York, 1911.

MS Manuscript

MTA *Mark Twain's Autobiography.* 2 Vols. Ed. Albert Bigelow Paine. New York, 1924.

MTB Albert Bigelow Paine. *Mark Twain: A Biography.* 4 Vols. New York, 1912.

MTE *Mark Twain in Eruption.* Ed. Bernard DeVoto. New York, 1940.

MTL *Mark Twain's Letters.* 2 Vols. Ed. Albert Bigelow Paine. New York, 1917.

MTP The Mark Twain Papers, University of California, Berkeley.

MTN *Mark Twain's Notebook.* Ed. Albert Bigelow Paine. New York, 1935.

MTS(10) *Mark Twain's Speeches.* Compiled by F. A. Nast. With an Introduction by William Dean Howells. New York, 1910.

MTS(23) *Mark Twain's Speeches.* With an Introduction by Albert Bigelow Paine, and an Appreciation by William Dean Howells. New York, 1923.

NY*Trib* New York *Tribune*

Sketches Mark Twain. *Sketches New and Old.* New York, 1903.

Times New York *Times*

Trouble Fred W. Lorch. *The Trouble Begins at Eight.* Ames, Iowa, 1966.

TS Typescript

World New York *World*

· 1 ·

To defend San Francisco against possible enemy attack during the Civil War, the War Department loaded the new monitor Camanche, *in sections, aboard the* Aquila, *which sailed on a voyage around the Horn in May 1863. The day after the* Aquila *arrived in San Francisco in November, she sank at her pier. Efforts to raise her were unsuccessful until the Navy Department sent out a salvage crew headed by Captain Israel J. Merritt and including Major Edward C. Perry, a military engineer late of the Union Army. Rigging a cofferdam, they salvaged the dismantled* Camanche, *which was reassembled on shore and some months later launched with great fanfare. The* Aquila *was also refloated. For his aid in achieving these feats, Major Perry was honored on the occasion at which Mark Twain delivered the speech below.*

For an informative account of the salvaging and attendant circumstances, see: Edgar M. Branch, "Major Perry and the Monitor Camanche: *An Early Mark Twain Speech,"* American Literature *39, no. 2 (May 1967):170–79.*

Presentation Speech

Maguire's Opera House, San Francisco, June 12, 1864

Major Perry: Permit me, sir, on the part of your countless friends, the noble sons of the forest—the Diggers, the Pi-Utes, the Washoes, the Shoshones, and the numberless and nameless tribes of aborigines that roam the deserts of the Great Basin to the eastward of the snowy mountains further north—to present you this costly and beautiful *cane,* reared under their own eyes, and fashioned by their own inspired hands. The red men whom I represent, although visibly black from the wear and tear of outdoor life, from contact with the impurities of the earth, and from the absence of soap and their natural indifference to water, admire the unblemished virtue and the spotless integrity which they find in you; albeit these dusty savages are arrayed in rabbit skins and their princely blood is food for the very vermin they cherish and protect, they still respect you, because your repugnance to graybacks—either in the way of food or society—and your antipathy to the skins of wild beasts as raiment, is bold, undisguised and honest; finally, although these dingy warriors see no blood upon your hands, no human bones about your neck, no scalps suspended from your belt, they behold in you a brave whom they delight to honor—for they see you, in fancy, on the warpath in the three fights on the Bull's Run field; again in the historic seven-days' struggle before Richmond; and again sweeping down the lines with McClellan, in the fire and smoke and thunder of battle at Antietam, with a wound in your leg and blood in your eye! and they honor you as they would a High-you-muck-a-muck of many tribes, with crimson blankets and a hundred squaws. I am charged to say to you, that if you will visit the campoodies of the nomads of the desert, you shall fare sumptuously upon crickets and grasshoppers and the fat of the land; the skin of the wild coyote shall be your bed, and the daughters of the chiefs shall serve you.

Receive the cane kindly—cherish it in memory of your savage friends in San Francisco, and bear in mind always the lesson it teaches: its head is formed of a human hand clasping a fish—the hand will cling to the fish through good or evil fortune, until one or the other is destroyed. And the moral it teaches is this: When you undertake a thing, stick to it through storm and sunshine; never flinch—never yield an inch—never give up—*hold your grip* till you bust!

You have been a citizen of San Francisco four months, Major Perry; you came to raise the *Aquila,* with Captain Merritt, and you did it, and did it well—she rides at anchor in the bay. You held your grip. The consciousness of your success will be half your reward—and the other half will be duly paid in greenbacks by the government. Your labors finished, you are now about to leave us tomorrow for your old home across the seas, and we are here to bid you God speed and a safe voyage.

In the name of Winnemucca, War Chief of the Pi-Utes; Sioux-Sioux, Chief of the Washoes; Buckskin Joe, Chief of the Pitt Rivers; Buffalo Jim, Chief of the Bannocks; Washakee, Grand Chief of the Shoshones; and further, in the names of the lordly chiefs of all the swarthy tribes that breathe the free air of the hills and plains of the Pacific Coast, I salute you. Behold! they stand before you—thirsty.

Text / "Presentation Speech," *Alta,* June 13, 1864. The text is accompanied by a news story, which says in part: "The presentation speech was written upon a parchment seven feet long, by three and a half feet in width, and magnificently illuminated, and while it was being read by Mark Twain, Esq., of Virginia City, the entire audience was dissolved in tears." The words, which Branch surmises were written by Mark Twain, suggest that the occasion was bibulously hilarious.

Major Perry / He enlisted in the Fifteenth New York Infantry on June 17, 1861. His regiment, which became the Fifteenth New York Volunteer Engineers, was part of the Army of the Potomac, under command of General George B. McClellan, in the Peninsula Campaign of 1862. Perry, commissioned major in November of that year, and cited for gallant service at West Point, New Bridge, and Yorktown, was mustered out on June 25, 1863.

cane / According to the *Alta,* "The cane weighs something less than twelve pounds, and might have been copied from Emperor Norton's." Joshua Abraham Norton was a celebrated San Francisco eccentric who proclaimed himself Emperor of the United States and Protector of Mexico. San Franciscans were very fond of him and his two faithful dogs, Bummer and Lazarus.

graybacks / Civil War slang for body lice, also for Confederate soldiers.

campoodies / From the Piute "campo," a camp, an Indian village. In *Innocents Abroad,* vol. 2, chap. 24, Mark Twain says that the Palestinian village of Endor, a dismal place of "Dirt, degradation, and savagery," is "worse than an Indian *campoodie.*"

Captain Merritt / Israel John Merritt (1829–1911) of New York City: inventor, wrecker and expert salvager. He invented and in 1865 patented the pontoon for raising sunken vessels, a device that revolutionized the salvage business. The "Captain" was a courtesy title.

greenbacks / Legal tender notes first issued by the federal government in 1862 to defray the cost of the war. Because the government suspended specie payment, the notes rapidly depreciated, sometimes being worth only thirty-five cents on the dollar. Specie payment was resumed in 1879.

·2·

The many versions of the Sandwich Islands lecture evolved from Mark Twain's four months' visit to Hawaii in 1866 and his twenty-five letters from there published in the Sacramento Union. *Continually varying his delivery, he used the Islands as a lecture topic more often than any other: almost one hundred times in the United States and England, usually announcing the title as "Our Fellow Savages of the Sandwich Islands."*

Sandwich Islands Lecture

First Given in San Francisco, October 2, 1866; Intermittently Thereafter Until December 8, 1873

Ladies and gentlemen: The next lecture in this course will be delivered this evening, by Samuel L. Clemens, a gentleman whose high character and unimpeachable integrity are only equalled by his comeliness of person and grace of manner. And I am the man! I was obliged to excuse the chairman from introducing me, because he never compliments anybody and I knew I could do it just as well.

The Sandwich Islands will be the subject of my lecture—when I get to it—and I shall endeavor to tell the truth as nearly as a newspaper man can. If I embellish it with a little nonsense, that makes no difference; it won't mar the truth; it is only as the barnacle ornaments the oyster by sticking to it. That figure is original with me! I was born back from tidewater and don't know as the barnacle *does* stick to the oyster.

Unfortunately, the first object I ever saw in the Sandwich Islands was a repulsive one. It was a case of Oriental leprosy, of so dreadful a nature that I have never been able to get it out of my mind since. I don't intend that it shall give a disagreeable complexion to this lecture at all, but inasmuch as it was the first thing I saw in those islands, it naturally suggested itself when I proposed to talk about the islands. It is a very hard matter to get a disagreeable object out of one's memory. I discovered that a good while ago. When I made that funeral excursion in the *Quaker City* they showed me some very interesting objects in a cathedral, and I expected to recollect every one of them—but I didn't.

I forgot every one of them—except one—and that I remembered because it was unpleasant. It was a curious piece of ancient sculpture. They don't know where they got it nor how long they have had it. It is a stone figure of a man without any skin—a freshly skinned man showing every vein, artery and tissue. It was the heaviest thing, and yet there was something fascinating about it. It looked so natural; it looked as if it was in pain, and you know a freshly skinned man would naturally look that way. He would unless his attention was occupied with some other matter. It was a dreadful object, and I have been sorry many a time since that I ever saw that man. Sometimes I dream of him, sometimes he is standing by my bedpost, sometimes he is stretched between the sheets, touching me—the most uncomfortable bedfellow I ever had.

I can't get rid of unpleasant recollections. Once when I ran away from school I was afraid to go home at night, so I crawled through a window and laid down on a lounge in my father's office. The moon shed a ghastly light in the room, and presently I descried a long, dark mysterious shape on the floor. I wanted to go and touch it—but I didn't—I restrained myself—I didn't do it. I had a good deal of presence of mind—tried to go to sleep—kept thinking of it. By and by when the moonlight fell upon it, I saw that it was a dead man lying there with his white face turned up in the moonlight. I never was so sick in all my life. I never wanted to take a walk so bad! I went away from there. I didn't hurry—simply went out of the window—and took the sash along with me. I didn't need the sash, but it was handier to take it than to leave it. I wasn't scared, but I was a good deal agitated. I have never forgotten that man. He had fallen dead in the street and they brought him in there to try him, and they brought him in guilty, too.

But I am losing time; what I have been saying don't bear strictly on the Sandwich Islands, but one reminiscence leads to another, and I am obliged to bring myself down in this way, on account of that unpleasant thing that I first saw there. It is not safe to come to any important matter in an entirely direct way. When a young gentleman is about to talk to a young lady about matrimony he don't go straight at it. He begins by talking about the weather. I have done that many a time.

My next remarks will refer to the Sandwich Islands. Now if an impression has gotten abroad in the land that the Sandwich Islands are in South America, that is the error I wish to attack; that is the error I wish to combat. To cut the matter short the Sandwich Isles are 2,000 miles southwest from San Francisco, but why they were put away out there in the middle of the Pacific, so far away from any place and in such an inconvenient locality, is no business of ours—it was the work of providence and is not open to question. The subject is a good deal like many others we should like to inquire into, such as, what mosquitoes were made for, etc., but under the circumstances we naturally feel a delicacy about doing it.

The islands are a dozen in number and their entire area is not greater I suppose than that of Rhode Island and Connecticut combined. They are of volcanic origin, of volcanic construction I should say. There is not a spoonful of legitimate dirt in the whole group, unless it has been imported. Eight of the islands are inhabited, and four of them are entirely girdled with a belt of mountains comprising the most productive sugar lands in the world. The sugar lands in Louisiana are considered rich, and yield from 500 to 1,700 pounds per acre. A two-hundred-acre crop of wheat in the States is worth twenty or thirty thousand dollars; a two-hundred-acre crop of sugar in these islands is worth two hundred thousand dollars. You could not do that in this country unless you planted it with stamps and reaped it in bonds. I could go on talking about the sugar interest all night—and I have a notion to do it. But I will spare you. It is very interesting to those who are interested in it, but I'll drop it now. You will find it all in the Patent Office reports, and I can recommend them as the most placid literature in the world.

These islands were discovered some eighty or ninety years ago by Captain Cook, though another man came very near discovering them before, and he was diverted from his course by a manuscript found in a bottle. He wasn't the first man who has been diverted by suggestions got out of a bottle. When these islands were discovered the population was about 400,000, but the white man came and brought various complicated diseases, and education, and civilization, and all sorts of calamities, and consequently the population began to drop off with commendable activity. Forty years ago they were reduced to 200,000, and the educational and civilizing facilities being increased they dwindled down to 55,000, and it is proposed to send a few more missionaries and finish them. It isn't the education or civilization that has settled them; it is the imported diseases, and they have all got the consumption and other reliable distempers, and to speak figuratively, they are retiring from business pretty fast. When they pick up and leave we will take possession as lawful heirs.

There are about 3,000 white people in the islands; they are mostly Americans. In fact they are the kings of the Sandwich Islands; the monarchy is not much more than a mere name. These people stand as high in the scale of character as any people in the world, and some of them who were born and educated in those islands don't even know what vice is. A Kanaka or a native is nobody unless he has a princely income of $75 annually, or a splendid estate worth $100. The country is full of office-holders and office-seekers; there are plenty of such noble patriots. Of almost any party of three men, two would be office-holders and one an office-seeker. In a little island half the size of one of the wards of St. Louis, there are lots of noblemen, princes and men of high degree, with grand titles, holding big offices, receiving immense salaries—such as ministers of war, secretaries of the navy, secretaries of state and ministers of justice. They make a fine display of uniforms, and are very imposing at a funeral. That's the country for a petty hero to go to, he would soon have the conceit taken out of him. There are so many of them that a nobleman from any other country would be nobody. They only lionize their own people, and therefore they lionize everybody.

In color, the natives are a rich, dark brown—a sort of black and tan. A very pleasing tint. The tropical sun and the easy-going ways inherited from their ancestors, have made them rather idle, but they are not vicious at all, they are good people. The native women in the rural districts wear a loose, magnificent curtain calico garment, but the men don't. Upon great occasions the men wear an umbrella, or some little fancy article like that—further than this they have no inclination toward gorgeousness of attire.

In the old times the king was absolute, his person was sacred, and if even the shadow of a common Kanaka fell upon him the Kanaka had to die. There was no help for him. Whatever the king tabooed it was death to touch or speak of. After the king, came the high priests who sacrificed human victims; after them came the great feudal chiefs, and then the common Kanakas, who were the slaves of all, and wretchedly oppressed. Away down at the bottom of this pyramid were the women, the abject slaves of the whole party. They did all the work and were cruelly mistreated. It was death for a woman to sit at table with her husband, or to eat of the choice fruits of the islands at any time. They seemed to have had a sort of dim knowledge of what came of women eating fruit in the Garden of Eden and they didn't feel justified in taking any more chances. And it is wisdom—unquestionably it is wisdom. Adam wasn't strict enough. Eve broke the *taboo,* and hence comes all this trouble. Can't be too particular about fruit—with women.

They were a rusty set all round—those Kanakas. By and by the American missionaries came and they struck off the shackles from the whole race, breaking the power of the kings and chiefs. They set the common man free, elevated his wife to a position of equality, and gave a spot of land to each to hold forever. The missionaries taught the whole nation to read and write with facility, in the native tongue. I don't suppose there is today a single uneducated person above eight years of age in the Sandwich Islands. It is the best educated country in the world, I believe, not excepting portions of the United States. That has all been done by the American missionaries. And in a large degree it was paid for by the American Sunday school children with their pennies. We all took part in it. True, the system gave opportunities to bad boys. Many a bad boy acquired the habit of confiscating pennies of the missionary cause. But it is one of the proudest recollections of my life that I never did that—at least not more than once or twice. I know that I contributed. I have had nearly $2 invested there for thirty years. But I don't mind it. I don't care for the money if it has been doing good. I don't say this in order to show off, but just mention it as a gentle, humanizing fact that may possibly have a benevolent and beneficent effect upon some members of this audience.

These natives are very hospitable people indeed—very hospitable. If you want to stay a few days and nights in a native's cabin you can stay and welcome. They will do everything they possibly can to make you comfortable. They will feed you on baked dog, or poi, or raw fish, or raw salt pork, fricasseed cats—all the luxuries of the season. Everything the human heart can desire, they will set before you. Perhaps, now, this isn't a captivating feast at first glance, but it is offered in all sincerity, and with the best motives in the world, and that makes any feast respectable whether it is palatable or not. But if you want to trade, that's quite another matter—that's business! And the Kanucker is ready for you. He is a born trader, and he will swindle you if he can. He will lie straight through, from the first word to the last. Not such lies as you and I tell, but gigantic lies, lies that awe you with their grandeur, lies that stun you with their imperial impossibility. He will sell you a molehill at the market price of a mountain, and will lie it up to an altitude that will make it cheap at the money. If he is caught, he slips out of it with an easy indifference that has an unmistakable charm about it.

One peculiarity of these Kanakas is that nearly every one of them has a dozen mothers—not natural ones—I haven't got down yet where I can make such a statement as that—but adopted mothers. They have a custom of calling any woman mother they take a liking to—no matter what her color or politics—and it is possible for one native to have a thousand mothers if his affections are liberal and stretchy, and most of them are. This custom breeds some curious incidents. A California man went down there and opened a sugar plantation. One of his hands came and said he wanted to bury his mother. He gave him permission. Shortly after he came again with the same request. "I thought you buried her last week," said the gentleman. "This is another one," said the native. "All right," said the gentleman, "go and plant her." Within a month the man wanted to bury some more mothers. "Look here," said the planter, "I don't want to be hard on you in your affliction, but it appears to me that your stock of mothers holds out pretty well. It interferes with business, so clear out, and never come back until you have buried every mother you have in the world."

They are an odd sort of people, too. They can die whenever they want to. That's a fact. They don't mind dying any more than a jilted Frenchman does. When they take a notion to die they die, and it don't make any difference whether there is anything the matter with them or not, and they can't be persuaded out of it. When one of them makes up his mind to die, he just lays down and is just as certain to die as though he had all the doctors in the world hold of him. A gentleman in Hawaii asked his servant if he wouldn't like to die and have a big funeral. He said yes, and looked happy, and the next morning the overseer came and said, "That boy of yours laid down and died last night and said you were going to give him a fine funeral."

They are very fond of funerals. Big funerals are their main weakness. Fine grave clothes, fine funeral appointments, and a long procession are things they take a generous delight in. Years ago a Kanaka and his wife were condemned to be hanged for murder. They received the sentence with manifest satisfaction because it gave an opening for a funeral, you know. It makes but little difference to them whose it is; they would as soon attend their own funeral as anybody else's. This couple were of consequence, and had landed estates. They sold every foot of ground they had and laid it out in fine clothes to be hung in. And the woman appeared on the scaffold in a white satin dress and slippers and feathers of gaudy ribbon, and the man was arrayed in a gorgeous vest, blue clawhammer coat and brass buttons, and white kid gloves. As the noose was adjusted around his neck, he blew his nose with a grand theatrical flourish, so as to show his embroidered white handkerchief. I never, never knew of a couple who enjoyed hanging more than they did.

They are very fond of dogs, these people—not the great Newfoundland or the stately mastiff, but a species of little mean, contemptible cur that a white man would condemn to death on general principles. There is nothing attractive about these dogs—there is not a handsome feature about them, unless it is their bushy tails. A friend of mine said if he had one of these dogs he would cut off the tail and throw the rest of the dog away. They feed this dog, pet him, take ever so much care of him, and then cook and eat him. I couldn't do that. I would rather go hungry for two days than devour an old personal friend in that way; but many a white citizen of those islands throws aside his prejudices and takes his dinner off one of those puppies—and after all it is only our cherished American sausage with the mystery removed.

A Kanaka will eat anything he can bite—a live fish, scales and all, which must be rather annoying to the fish, but the Kanaka doesn't mind that. It used to be said that the Kanakas were cannibals, but that was a slander. They didn't eat Captain Cook—or if they did, it was only for fun. There was one instance of cannibalism. A foreigner, from the South Pacific Islands, set up an office and did eat a good many Kanakas. He was a useful citizen, but had strong political prejudices and used to save up a good appetite for just before election, so that he could thin out the Democratic vote.

At this point in my lecture, in other cities, I usually illustrate cannibalism, but I am a stranger here and don't feel like taking liberties. Still, if any one in the audience will lend me an infant, I will illustrate the matter. But it is of no consequence—it don't matter. I know children have become scarce and high, owing to the inattention they have received since the women's rights movement began. I will leave out that part of my program, though it is very neat and pleasant. Yet it is not necessary. *I* am not hungry.

Well, that foreign cannibal after a while got tired of Kanakas—as most anybody would—and thought he would like to try white man with onions. So he captured and devoured a tough old whaleship captain, but it was the worst thing he ever did. Of course, he could no more digest that old whaler than a keg of nails. There is no telling how much he suffered, with this sin on his conscience and the whaler on his stomach. He lingered for a few days and then died. Now I don't believe this story myself, and have only told it for its moral. You don't appear to see the moral; but I know there is a moral in it, because I have told it thirty or forty times, and never got a moral out of it yet!

With all these excellent and hospitable ways these Kanakers have some cruel instincts. They will put a live chicken in the fire just to see it hop about. In the olden times they used to be cruel to themselves. They used to tear their hair and burn their flesh, shave their heads, knock out an eye or a couple of front teeth, when a great person or a king died—just to testify to their sorrow, and if their grief was so sore that they couldn't possibly bear it, they would go out and scalp their neighbor, or burn his house down. It was an excellent custom, too, for it gave every one a good opportunity to square up old grudges. Pity we didn't have it here! They would also kill an infant now and then—bury him alive sometimes; but the missionaries have annihilated infanticide—for my part I can't see why.

The ladies of the Sandwich Islands have a great many pleasant customs which I don't know but we might practice with profit here. The women all ride like men. I wish to introduce that reform in this country. Our ladies ought, by all means to ride like men, these sidesaddles are so dangerous. When women meet each other in the road, they run and kiss and hug each other, and they don't blackguard each other behind each other's backs. I would like to introduce that reform, also. I don't suppose our ladies do it. But they might. But I believe I am getting on dangerous ground. I won't pursue that any further.

These people do nearly everything wrong end first. They buckle the saddle on the right side which is the wrong side; they mount a horse from the wrong side; they turn out on the wrong side to let you go by; they use the same word to say "good-by" and "good morning"; they use "yes" when they mean "no"; the women smoke more than the men do; when they beckon to you to come toward them they always motion in the opposite direction; the only native bird that has handsome feathers has only two, and they are under its wings instead of on top of its head; frequently a native cat has a tail only two inches long and has got a knot tied in the end of it; the native duck lives on the dry tops of mountains 5,000 feet high; the natives always stew chickens instead of baking them; they dance at funerals and sing a dismal heartbroken dirge when they are happy; and with atrocious perverseness they wash your shirts with a club and iron them with a brickbat. In their playing of the noble American game of "seven-up," that's a game, well, I'll explain that by and by. Some of you, perhaps, know all about it, and the rest must guess—but, in their playing of that really noble and intellectual game the dealer deals to his right instead of to his left, and what is insufferably worse—the ten always takes the ace! Now, such abject ignorance as that is reprehensible, and, for one, I am glad the missionaries have gone there.

Now, you see what kind of voters you will have if you take those islands away from these people as we are pretty sure to do some day. They will do everything wrong end first. They will make a deal of trouble here too. Instead of fostering and encouraging a judicious system of railway speculation, and all that sort of thing, they will elect the most incorruptible men to Congress. Yes, they will turn everything upside down.

In Honolulu they are the most easy-going people in the world. Some of our people are not acquainted with their customs. They started a gas company once, and put the gas at $13 a thousand feet. They only took in $16 the first month. They all went to bed at dark. They are an excellent people. I speak earnestly. They do not even know the name of some of the vices in this country. A lady called on a doctor. She wanted something for general debility. He ordered her to drink porter. She called him again. The porter had done her no good. He asked her how much porter she had taken. She said a tablespoonful in a tumbler of water. I wish we could import such blessed ignorance into this country. They don't do much drinking there. When they have paid the tax for importing the liquor they have got nothing left to purchase the liquor with. They are very innocent and drink anything that is liquid—kerosene, turpentine, hair oil. In one town, on a Fourth of July, an entire community got drunk on a barrel of Mrs. Winslow's soothing syrup.

The chief glory of the Sandwich Islands is their great volcano. The volcano of Kee-law-ay-oh is 17,000 feet in diameter, and from 700 to 800 feet deep. Vesuvius is nowhere. It is the largest volcano in the world; shoots up flames tremendously high. You witness a scene of unrivaled sublimity, and witness the most astonishing sights. When the volcano of Kee-law-ay-oh broke through a few years ago, lava flowed out of it for twenty days and twenty nights, and made a stream forty miles in length, till it reached the sea, tearing up forests in its awful fiery path, swallowing up huts, destroying all vegetation, rioting through shady dells and sinuous cañons. Amidst this carnival of destruction, majestic columns of smoke ascended and formed a cloudy murky pall overhead. Sheets of green, blue, lambent flames were shot upward, and pierced the vast gloom, making all sublimely grand.

The natives are indifferent to volcanic terrors. During the progress of an eruption they ate, drank, bought, sold, planted, builded, apparently indifferent to the roar of consuming forests, the startling detonations, the hissing of escaping steam, the rending of the earth, the shivering and melting of gigantic rocks, the raging and dashing of the fiery waves, the bellowings and unearthly mutterings coming up from a burning deep. They went carelessly on, amid the rain of ashes, sand, and fiery scintillations, gazing vacantly at the ever-varying appearance of the atmosphere, murky, black, livid, blazing, the sudden rising of lofty pillars of flame, the upward curling of ten thousand columns of smoke, and their majestic roll in dense and lurid clouds. All these moving phenomena were regarded by them as the fall of a shower or the running of a brook; while to others they were as the tokens of a burning world, the departing heavens, and a coming judge. There! I'm glad I've got that volcano off my mind.

I once knew a great, tall gawky country editor, near Sacramento, to whom I sent an ode on the sea, starting it with "The long, green swell of the Pacific." The country editor sent back a letter and stated I couldn't fool him, and he didn't want any base insinuations from me.

He knew who I meant when I wrote the "long, green swell of the Pacific."

There is one thing characteristic of the tropics that a stranger must have, whether he likes it or not, and that is the boo-hoo fever. Its symptoms are nausea of the stomach, severe headache, backache and bellyache, and a general utter indifference whether school keeps or not. You can't be a full citizen of the Sandwich Islands unless you have had the boo-hoo fever. You will never forget it. I remember a little boy who had it once there. A New Yorker asked him if he was afraid to die. He said, "No; I am not afraid to die of anything, except the boo-hoo fever."

The climate of these islands is delightful, it is beautiful. In Honolulu the thermometer stands at about 80 or 82 degrees pretty much all the year round—don't change more than 12 degrees in twelve months. In the sugar districts the thermometer stands at 70 and does not change at all. Any kind of thermometer will do—one without any quicksilver is just as good. Eighty degrees by the seashore, and 70 degrees farther inland, and 60 degrees as you ascend the slope of the mountain, and as you go higher 50 degrees, 40, 30, and ever decreasing in temperature, till you get to the top, where it's so cold that you can't speak the truth. I know, for I've been there! The climate is wonderfully healthy, for white people in particular, so healthy that white people venture on the most reckless imprudence. They get up too early; you can see them as early as half-past seven in the morning, and they attend to all their business, and keep it up till sundown. It don't hurt 'em, don't kill 'em, and yet it ought to do so. I have seen it so hot in California that greenbacks went up to 142 in the shade.

These Sandwichers believe in a superstition that the biggest liars in the world have got to visit the islands some time before they die. They believe that because it is a fact—you misunderstand—I mean that when liars get there they stay there. They have several specimens they boast of. They treasure up their little perfections, and they allude to them as if the man was inspired—from below. They had a man among them named Morgan. He never allowed anyone to tell a bigger lie than himself, and he always told the last one too. When someone was telling about the natural bridge in Virginia, he said he knew all about it, as his father had helped to build it. Someone was bragging of a wonderful horse he had. Morgan told them of one he had once. While out riding one day a thundershower came on and chased him for eighteen miles, and never caught him. Not a single drop of rain dropped onto his horse, but his dog was swimming behind the wagon the whole of the way.

Once, when the subject of mean men was being discussed, Morgan told them of an incorporated company of mean men. They hired a poor fellow to blast rock for them. He drilled a hole four feet deep, put in the powder, and began to tamp it down around the fuse. I know all about tamping, as I have worked in a mine myself. The crowbar struck a spark and caused a premature explosion and that man and his crowbar shot up into the air, and he went higher and higher, till he didn't look bigger than a boy, and he kept on going higher and higher, until he didn't look bigger than a dog, and he kept on going higher and higher, until he didn't look bigger than a bee, and then he went out of sight; and presently he came in sight again, looking no bigger than a bee, and he came further and further, until he was as big as a dog, and further and further and further, until he was as big as a boy, and he came further and further, until he assumed the full size and shape of a man, and he came down and fell right into the same old spot and went to tamping again. And would you believe it—concluded Morgan—although that poor fellow was not gone more than fifteen minutes, yet that mean company docked him for loss of time.

The land that I have tried to tell you about lies out there in the midst of the watery wilderness, in the very heart of the almost soilless solitudes of the Pacific. It is a dreamy, beautiful, charming land. I wish I could make you comprehend how beautiful it is. It is a land that seems ever so vague and fairy-like when one reads about it in books, peopled with a gentle, indolent, careless race.

It is Sunday land. The land of indolence and dreams, where the air is drowsy and things tend to repose and peace, and to emancipation from the labor, and turmoil, and weariness, and anxiety of life.

Text / Composite, based upon: "Mark Twain at the Mercantile Library Hall," St. Louis *Democrat,* March 28, 1867; "Mark Twain's Lecture," Providence, Rhode Island, *Press,* November 10, 1869; "Mark Twain's Lecture," *Courant,* November 24, 1869; "Mark Twain's Lecture," New Haven, Connecticut, *Morning Journal,* December 28, 1869; "Our Fellow Savages of the Sandwich Islands," Portland, Maine, *Transcript,* January 1, 1870; "Our Fellow Savages of the Sandwich Islands," Troy, New York, *Times,* January 12, 1870; "Mark Twain, What He Knows About the Sandwich Islands," Brooklyn *Eagle,* February 8, 1873; "Cracking Jokes," London *Once a Week,* n.s., no. 306 (November 8, 1873):402–5; "The Sandwich Islands," *Eloquence*(R), 4:253–59, and *Eloquence*(T), 13:133–39; "From Mark Twain's First Lecture," *MTB,* 4:1601–3.

introduction / To circumvent local chairmen who introduced him with lavish praise and labored jokes, Mark Twain adopted the practice of introducing himself with an extravagant eulogy of his own accomplishments. One reporter, attempting to capture in print the inflated substance and slow delivery, represented them thus: "Ladies and gentlemen: I—have—lectured—many—years—and—in—many—towns—large—and—small. I have traveled—north—south—east—and—west. I—have—met—many—great—men: *very*—great—men. But—I—have—never—yet—in—all—my—travels—met—the—president—of—a—*country*—lyceum—who—could—introduce—me—to—an—audience—with—that—*distinguished*—consideration—which—my *merits* deserve." See Joel Benton, "Reminiscences of Eminent Lecturers," *Harper's New Monthly Magazine* 96, no. 574 (March 1898):610.

Captain Cook / James Cook (1728–79). British navigator and explorer. On a voyage in search of the Northwest Passage he came upon the islands in 1778. He named them Sandwich Islands after the earl of Sandwich, first lord of the Admiralty.

Kanaka / A Polynesian word meaning "man," formerly applied to Hawaiian natives and to other South Pacific islanders.

poi / A favorite Hawaiian food made of taro root mixed into a paste and allowed to ferment. Mark Twain said, St. Louis *Democrat,* March 28, 1867: "Eating poi will cure a drunkard. In order to like poi you must get used to it. It smells a good deal worse than it tastes, and it tastes a good deal worse than it looks."

Kee-law-ay-oh / Kilauea, an active volcano on the slope of Mauna Loa. An altitude of 4,000 feet and a circumference of eight miles make it one of the largest and most spectacular craters in the world.

· 3 ·

After taking "The Sandwich Islands" on a tour of California and Nevada mining towns in the autumn of 1866, Mark Twain returned to San Francisco, where he gave a farewell lecture before sailing for the East a few days later. His concluding remarks, below, were a formal leave-taking, couched in oratorical language more conventional than he generally used. Press and public united in wishing him well.

Concluding Remarks

Congress Hall, San Francisco, December 10, 1866

My Friends and Fellow Citizens: I have been treated with extreme kindness and cordiality by San Francisco, and I wish to return my sincerest thanks and acknowledgments. I have also been treated with marked and unusual generosity, forbearance and good-fellowship, by my ancient comrades, my brethren of the press—a thing which has peculiarly touched me, because long experience in the service has taught me that we of the press are slow to praise but quick to censure each other, as a general thing—wherefore, in thanking them I am anxious to convince them, at the same time, that they have not lavished their kind offices upon one who cannot appreciate or is insensible to them.

I am now about to bid farewell to San Francisco for a season, and to go back to that common home we all tenderly remember in our waking hours and fondly revisit in dreams of the night—a home which is familiar to my recollection, but will be an unknown land to my unaccustomed eyes. I shall share the fate of many another longing exile who wanders back to his early home to find gray hairs where he expected youth, graves where he looked for firesides, grief where he had pictured joy—everywhere change!—remorseless change where he had heedlessly dreamed that desolating Time had stood still!—to find his cherished anticipations a mockery, and to drink the lees of disappointment instead of the beaded wine of a hope that is crowned with its fruition!

And while I linger here upon the threshold of this, my new home, to say to you, my kindest and my truest friends, a warm good-by and an honest peace and prosperity attend you, I accept the warning that mighty changes will have come over this home also when my returning feet shall walk these streets again.

I read the signs of the times and I, that am no prophet, behold the things that are in store for you. Over slumbering California is stealing the dawn of a radiant future! The great China Mail Line is established, the Pacific Railroad is creeping across the continent, the commerce of the world is about to be revolutionized. California is Crown Princess of the new dispensation! She stands in the center of the grand highway of the nations; she stands midway between the Old World and the New, and both shall pay her tribute. From the Far East and from Europe, multitudes of stout hearts and willing hands are preparing to flock hither; to throng her hamlets and villages; to till her fruitful soil; to unveil the riches of her countless mines; to build up an empire on these distant shores that shall shame the bravest dreams of her visionaries. From the opulent lands of the Orient, from India, from China, Japan, the Amoor; from tributary regions that stretch from the Arctic circle to the equator, is about to pour in upon her the princely commerce of a teeming population of four hundred and fifty million souls. Half the world stands ready to lay its contributions at her feet! Has any other state so brilliant a future? Has any other city a future like San Francisco?

This straggling town shall be a vast metropolis; this sparsely populated land shall become a crowded hive of busy men; your waste places shall blossom like the rose and your deserted hills and valleys shall yield bread and wine for unnumbered thousands; railroads shall be spread hither and thither and carry the invigorating blood of commerce to regions that are languishing now; mills and workshops, yea, and *factories* shall spring up everywhere, and mines that have neither name nor place today shall dazzle the world with their affluence. The time is drawing on apace when the clouds shall pass away from your firmament, and a splendid prosperity shall descend like a glory upon the whole land!

I am bidding the old city and my old friends a kind, but not a sad farewell, for I know that when I see this home again, the changes that will have been wrought upon it will suggest no sentiment of sadness; its estate will be brighter, happier and prouder a hundred fold than it is this day. This is its destiny, and in all sincerity I can say, So mote it be!

Text / "Mark Twain's Farewell," *Alta*, December 15, 1866.

desolating Time / The solemn words give the impression of a Rip Van Winkle returning home after a very long absence. When Mark Twain visited his family in Missouri in the spring of 1867, he had been away not quite six years.

Pacific Railroad / Under construction at the time, the first transcontinental railroad was formed by the Union Pacific road extending its line west from Omaha, and the Central Pacific (later part of the Southern Pacific) moving east from Sacramento. They met at Promontory, Utah, in 1869.

· 4 ·

When the Quaker City *excursionists were invited to call upon the Czar of Russia, they appointed a committee to draft an address: T. D. Crocker, A. N. Sanford, Colonel Kinney, William Gibson, and Mark Twain, chairman. The chairman wrote the address, which was read by the American Consul for Odessa. Mark Twain said of his assignment,* MTB, *1:333–34: "That job is over. Writing addresses to emperors is not my strong suit. However, if it is not as good as it might be it doesn't signify—the other committeemen ought to have helped me write it; they had nothing to do, and I had my hands full."*

Address to the Czar

Yalta, Russia, August 25, 1867

Your Imperial Majesty: We are a handful of private citizens of America, traveling simply for recreation, and unostentatiously, as becomes our unofficial state, and therefore we have no excuse to tender for presenting ourselves before your Majesty, save the desire of offering our grateful acknowledgments to the lord of a realm which, through good and evil report, has been the steadfast friend of the land we love so well.

We could not presume to take a step like this, did we not know well that the words we speak here, and the sentiments wherewith they are freighted, are but the reflex of the thoughts and feelings of all our

16299

countrymen, from the green hills of New England to the shores of the far Pacific. We are few in number, but we utter the voice of a nation!

One of the brightest pages that has graced the world's history since written history had birth, was recorded by your Majesty's hand when it loosed the bonds of twenty million serfs; and Americans can but esteem it a privilege to do honor to a ruler who has wrought so great a deed. The lesson that was taught us then, we have profited by, and are free in truth, today, even as we were before in name. America owes much to Russia—is indebted to her in many ways—and chiefly for her unwavering friendship in seasons of our greatest need. That that friendship may still be hers in times to come, we confidently pray; that she is and will be grateful to Russia and to her sovereign for it, we know full well; that she will ever forfeit it by any premeditated, unjust act, or unfair course, it were treason to believe.

Text / Composite, based upon: TS, Notebook 18, August 11–October 1867, MTP; "Address to the Czar," *MTB*, 1:333.

·5·

In 1867–68, when Mark Twain was briefly a secretary for William M. Stewart, senator from Nevada, he became known in Washington as a lively writer and entertaining talker. At the Correspondents dinner, responding to the twelfth toast, to "Woman," he was a great success with an audience of journalists and politicos. Mark Twain said in an Alta *letter, February 19, 1868: "I think the women of San Francisco ought to send me a medal, or a doughnut, or something, because I had them chiefly in mind in this eulogy."*

Woman—The Pride of Any Profession and the Jewel of Ours

Newspaper Correspondents Club Banquet, Washington, D.C., January 11, 1868

Mr. President: I do not know why I should have been singled out to receive the greatest distinction of the evening—for so the office of replying to the toast to woman has been regarded in every age. I do not know why I have received this distinction, unless it be that I am a trifle less homely than the other members of the club. But be this as it may, Mr. President, I am proud of the position, and you could not have chosen anyone who would have accepted it more gladly, or labored with a heartier good will to do the subject justice, than I—because, sir, I love the sex. I love *all* the women, sir, irrespective of age or color.

Human intelligence cannot estimate what we owe to woman, sir. She sews on our buttons; she mends our clothes; she ropes us in at the church fairs; she confides in us; she tells us whatever she can find out about the little private affairs of the neighbors; she gives us good advice—and plenty of it; she gives us a piece of her mind, sometimes, and sometimes all of it; she soothes our aching brows; she bears our children—ours as a general thing. In all the relations of life, sir, it is but a just and a graceful tribute to woman to say of her that she is a brick.

Wheresoever you place woman, sir—in whatever position or estate—she is an ornament to that place she occupies, and a treasure to the world. Look at the noble names of history! Look at Cleopatra!—look at Desdemona!—look at Florence Nightingale!—look at Joan of Arc!—look at Lucretia Borgia! Well, suppose we let Lucretia slide. Look at Joyce Heth!—look at Mother Eve! You need not look at her unless you want to, but Eve was ornamental, sir—particularly before the fashions changed!

I repeat, sir, look at the illustrious names of history! Look at the Widow Machree!—look at Lucy Stone!—look at Elizabeth Cady Stanton!—look at George Francis Train! And, sir, I say it with bowed head and deepest veneration, look at the mother of Washington! She raised a boy that could not tell a lie—*could not tell a lie!* But he *never had any chance.* It might have been different if he had belonged to the Washington Newspaper Correspondents Club.

I repeat, sir, that in whatever position you place a woman she is an ornament to society and a treasure to the world. As a sweetheart, she has few equals and no superiors; as a cousin, she is convenient; as a wealthy grandmother with an incurable distemper, she is precious; as a wet nurse, she has no equal among men!

What, sir, would the people of this earth be, without woman? They would be scarce, sir—almighty scarce. Then let us cherish her—let us protect her—let us give her our support, our encouragement, our sympathy—ourselves, if we get a chance.

But, jesting aside, Mr. President, woman is lovable, gracious, kind of heart, beautiful—worthy of all respect, of all esteem, of all deference. Not any here will refuse to drink her health right cordially in this bumper of wine, for each and every one of us has personally known, and loved, and honored, the very best one of them all—his own mother!

Text / Composite, based upon: "Annual Banquet of the Correspondents' Club," Washington *Evening Star,* January 13, 1868; "Woman—an Opinion," *MTS*(10):104–6; *MTS*(23):31–33.

Florence Nightingale / (1820–1910). British nurse and philanthropist. Known as "The Lady With the Lamp," she is best remembered for establishing sanitary hospital procedures, routing entrenched British officialdom during the Crimean War (1854), then serving as advisor during the American Civil War and the Franco-Prussian War. She was the first woman to receive Britain's Order of Merit (1907).

Lucretia Borgia / Lucrezia Borgia (1480–1519). A daughter of Pope Alexander VI, she is generally thought of as an assassin who disposed of victims by undetectable poisons. Some modern historians contend, however, that she was merely the passive agent of her father and of the real villain of the family, her Machiavellian brother, Cesare.

Joyce Heth / (ca. 1788–1836). A Negro exhibited by P. T. Barnum as the 160-year-old nurse of George Washington.

Lucy Stone / Lucy Blackwell Stone (1818–93). American feminist. She was an anti-slavery lecturer and coorganizer of the American Woman's Suffrage Association. Although married to Dr. Henry B. Blackwell, she insisted on keeping her maiden name.

Elizabeth Cady Stanton / (1815–1902). American crusader for temperance, anti-slavery, and woman's suffrage. She was first president of the National Woman's Suffrage Association (1869) and president of the American Woman's Suffrage Association (1890). Conservatives regarded her as a dangerous radical because of her belief that women should control their own property, and that drunkenness and brutality were grounds for divorce.

George Francis Train / (1829–1904). American entrepreneur. Involved in grandiose financial and political schemes, he espoused the Paris Commune and the Fenians, and once announced himself as an independent candidate for president. He lectured on bizarre subjects, was in and out of jail, and wrote voluminously, cultivating a reputation for eccentricity as a self-styled "Champion Crank." Mark Twain's including him among well-known women was an allusion to Train's voluble defense of feminism.

·6·

Mark Twain returned to California for a stay of three months in the spring of 1868. He was writing his first book, The Innocents Abroad, *based on more than fifty travel letters he had sent to the* Alta *during the* Quaker City *excursion to Europe and the Holy Land in 1867. From the same material he composed a lecture, which he delivered twice in San Francisco, then in most of the towns on the tour route of 1866. The excerpt given here is, conjecturally, a fragment of that lecture. No complete text exists, but much of it probably went into another lecture, "The American Vandal Abroad," which he wrote for his first tour of the eastern lyceum circuit in 1868–69.*

Pilgrim Life

Platt's Hall, San Francisco, April 14–15, 1868; Tour of California and Nevada, April 17–30, 1868

In conclusion I will observe that even galloping as we did about the world, we learned something. The lesson of the Excursion was a good one. It taught us that foreign countries are excellent to travel in, but that the best country to live in is America, after all. We found no soap in the hotels of Europe, and they charged us for candles we never burned. We saw no ladies anywhere that were as beautiful as our own ladies here at home and especially in this audience. We saw none anywhere that dressed with such excellent taste as do our ladies at home here. I am not a married man, but—but—I would like to be. I only mention it in the most casual way, though, and—do not mean anything—anything personal by it. We saw no government on the other side *like our own*—not *just* like our own. The Sultan's was a little like it. One of his great officers came into office without a cent, and went out in a few years and built himself a palace worth three million. It brought tears to my eyes in that far foreign land—it was so like home. The Sultan confiscated it. He said he liked to see a man prosper, but he didn't like to see him get wealthy on two thousand a year and no perquisites.

We saw no energy in the capitals of Europe like the tremendous energy of New York, and we saw no place where intelligence and enterprise were so widely diffused as they are here in our country. We saw nowhere any architectural achievement that was so beautiful to the eye as the national capitol of America, at Washington, and we saw nowhere any building that was—that was—just like our own Washington Monument. We saw no people anywhere so self-denying, and patriotic and prompt in collecting their salaries as our own members of Congress. We saw nothing in Europe, Asia or Africa to make us wish to live there, and when the voyage was done (and it was a very, very pleasant one, take it altogether) we were glad to get back to our own country where moral and religious freedom prevail—where politicians are incorruptible—where accident policies are cheap and where the chances to get your money back are good on all the railroads.

Ah, I had rather live here than in Turkey—in Constantinople, with its beggars, its dogs, its ugly overpraised mosques, its Sultan, who has 800 wives, and yet isn't happy. It is a perfectly *unanswerable* argument against matrimony. If a man can't be happy with 800 wives, what chance is there for him with only *one?* None in the world. People tell me that it makes a man happy to have a woman love him—and I used to be innocent enough to believe it before I went to Constantinople. Theorizing is all very well, but facts and figures are better. If the love of just one woman could make a man so happy, what ought to be the natural result if he had the love of 800 of them? Why he just simply couldn't *stand* so much bliss, that is all. He couldn't live through it. Such a deluge of deliciousness as that would be bound to swamp him. He couldn't contain all that sweetness any more than a one-gallon jug could contain 800 gallons of sugar house molasses. Sentiment is all very well, but sentiment can't stand the test of mathematics. Travel hath made me wise—and I warn the youth of ——— to beware of matrimony. It is a delusion and a snare. I have seen it under its most favorable aspect, and I ought to know whereof I speak. It is my deliberate judgment that a man—that a man—wouldn't be happy with forty *thous*and wives! The Sultan of Turkey talked to me like a father. He saw that I sympathized with him, and he opened his heart and told me all his troubles. He said, "Why, Governor, you can't imagine the expense and the bother that all those women cost me—why it isn't fifteen minutes ago, since my ugliest wife, and she is a spectacle to look at, No. 642—I have forgotten her other name—was in here trying to get me to buy her $100,000 worth of jewelry. Oh, an ugly woman hasn't got any effrontery, you know, and another one, No. 422, came right after her with a black eye, she'd had a fight with No. 764 and got the worst of it. And then," he said, "this great fat regiment of wives . . . . [The MS breaks off here.]

Text / Lecture notes for "Innocents," TS of incomplete MS, Webster Collection, MTP.

Washington Monument / A satirical reference to the unfinished structure. The cornerstone was laid on July 4, 1848, but work soon stopped, and the monument remained a sawed-off stump for more than thirty years, finally being completed by army engineers in 1885.

I warn the youth of ——— / Mark Twain filled the blank with the name of the town he was speaking in.

Sultan of Turkey / The unfinished yarn about the Sultan's wives is a forerunner of Johnson's report on the household of Brigham Young in chapter 15 of *Roughing It.*

· 7 ·

To advertise his lecture on "The Oldest of the Republics, Venice Past and Present," Mark Twain published in San Francisco papers fictitious letters of protest from prominent people, hotel managers, the clergy, board of aldermen, fraternal organizations, and "1500 in the Steerage," all of whom begged him not to lecture. "There is a limit," they said, "to human endurance." A curt note from the chief of police advised him to leave town. Mark Twain, affecting indignation, rejected their appeal, and referred to the hoax in his introductory remarks.

Introductory Remarks

Mercantile Library, San Francisco, July 2, 1868

Ladies and gentlemen: If anyone in San Francisco has a just right this evening to feel gratified—more, to feel proud—it is I, who stand before you. The compliment of your attendance here I thoroughly appreciate. It is a greater compliment than I really deserve, perhaps—but for that matter I have always been rather better treated in San Francisco than I actually deserved. I am willing to say that. I appreciate your attendance here tonight all the more because there was such a widespread, such a furious, such a determined opposition to my lecturing upon this occasion. Pretty much the entire community wrote petitions imploring me *not* to lecture—to forebear—to have compassion upon a persecuted people. I never had such a unanimous call to—to—to leave, before. But I resisted, and am here; and I am glad that I am privileged to address a full house, instead of having to pour out this cataract of wisdom upon empty benches. I do not exactly propose to *instruct* you this evening, but rather to tell you a good many things which you have known very well before, no doubt, but which may have grown dim in your memories—for the multifarious duties and annoyances of daily life are apt to drive from our minds a large part of what we learn, and that knowledge is of little use which we cannot recall. So I simply propose to refresh your memories. I trust this will be considered sufficient apology for making this lecture somewhat didactic. I don't know what didactic means, but it is a good, high-sounding word, and I wish to use it, meaning no harm whatever.

Text / *Alta,* July 3, 1868. The full text of the lecture has not survived.

·8·

For his first lyceum tour, Mark Twain again turned to the Quaker City *excursion of 1867. He said he "smouched" the lecture from his forthcoming book,* Innocents Abroad, *and he also incorporated material from "Pilgrim Life" and "Venice." Since none of his spoken performances was a set piece repeated verbatim each time he gave it, he added embellishments and varied the phrasing as the fancy struck him on the road. The zigzag itinerary of the tour took him to forty-two towns and cities in eight states of the East and Middle West.*

The American Vandal Abroad

Lyceum Season: November 17, 1868–March 3, 1869

I am to speak of the American Vandal this evening, but I wish to say in advance that I do not use the term in derision, or apply it as a reproach, but I use it because it is convenient and duly and properly modified it best describes the roving, independent, free-and-easy character of that class of traveling Americans who are *not* elaborately educated, cultivated, and refined, and gilded and filigreed with the ineffable graces of the first society. The best class of our countrymen who go abroad keep us well posted about their doings in foreign lands, but their brethren Vandals cannot sing their own praises or publish their adventures.

The American Vandal goes everywhere and is always at home everywhere. He attempts to investigate the secrets of the harems; he views the rock where Paul was let down in a basket, and seriously asks where the basket is. He will choke himself to death trying to smoke a Turkish pipe and swears it is good. He will go into ecstasics over the insufferable horrors of the Turkish bath, though he is thinking the while that he may never come out alive. He learns to ride a camel. He packs his trunk with figs and other little vegetables. He looks picturesque when beholding Rome from the dome of St. Peter's. His soul is full of admiration. He rises above earthly cares. He is proud and looks proud. His countenance is beaming. He does not fail to let the public know that he is an American. This is not a fault. It is commendable. I have seen him in the company of kings and queens, lords and popes. He is always self-possessed, always untouched, unabashed—even in the presence of the Sphinx.

The American Vandal gallops over England, Scotland, Spain and Switzerland, and finally brings up in Italy. He thinks it is the proper thing to visit Genoa, the stately old City of Palaces, whose vast marble edifices almost meet together over streets so narrow that three men can hardly walk abreast in them and so crooked that a man generally comes out of them about the same place he went in at. He only stays in Genoa long enough to see a few celebrated things and get some fragments of stone from the house Columbus was born in—for your genuine Vandal is an intolerable and incorrigible relic-gatherer. It is estimated that if all the fragments of stone brought from Columbus's house by travelers were collected together they would suffice to build a house 14,000 feet long and 16,000 feet high and I suppose they would.

Next he hurries to Milan and takes notes of the Grand Cathedral: (for he is always taking notes). Oh, I remember Milan and the noble Cathedral well enough—that marble miracle of enchanting architecture. I remember how we entered and walked about its vast spaces and among its huge columns, gazing aloft at the monster windows all aglow with brilliantly colored scenes in the life of the Savior and his followers. And I remember the sideshows and curiosities there, too. The guide showed us a coffee-colored piece of sculpture which he said was considered to have come from the hand of Phidias, since it was not possible that any other man, of any epoch, could have copied nature with such faultless accuracy. The figure was that of a man without a skin; with every vein, artery, muscle, every fibre and tendon and tissue of the human frame, represented in minute detail. It looked natural because it looked somehow *as if it were in pain.* A skinned man *would be likely to look that way*—unless his attention were occupied by some other matter. It was a hideous thing, and yet there was a fascination about it somewhere. I am very sorry I saw it, because I shall *always* see it now. I shall dream of it, sometimes. I shall dream that it is resting its corded arms on the bed's head and looking down on me with its dead eyes; I shall dream that it is stretched between the sheets with me and touching me with its exposed muscles and its stringy cold legs.

They have many holy relics in the Cathedral of Milan. The priest showed us two of St. Paul's fingers and one of St. Peter's; and a bone of Judas Iscariot—it was a black one—and bones and little vessels of blood of St. John, St. Mark and several other of the disciples. They keep these relics in vials, in a glass case, and have them labeled as we often see geological specimens. And they showed us a handkerchief in which the Savior had left the impression of his face (we saw another in Rome afterward), and a piece of the stone the angels rolled away from the door of the Holy Sepulchre (we saw the whole of the stone afterward in Jerusalem)—and a part of the real crown of thorns (we saw a whole one at Notre Dame in Paris)—and a fragment of the purple robe worn by the Savior, a nail from the True Cross and a picture of the Virgin and Child painted by the veritable hand of St. Luke. In every cathedral into which the American Vandal wanders, all over Europe, and especially Italy, he finds repetitions of these same relics—until finally he becomes so accustomed to them, and so attached to them that a cathedral that hasn't a pretended splinter of the Cross, or piece of a saint or fragment of a martyr to show, has no charm for *him.* I knew one of these gentry—a simple-minded, innocent Vandal, he was and very vulgar—who had a perfect *passion* for these things. Whenever he went into a great cathedral—when everybody was going into ecstasies over the grand architecture and paintings and such things, he'd beckon to a priest and say, "Here, friend, stuffy, trot out your relics!" He didn't mean any disrespect but that was his way, you know.

The Vandal goes to see the ancient and most celebrated painting in the world, "The Last Supper"—we all know it in engravings: the disciples all sitting on [one] side of a long plain table, and Christ with bowed head in the center—all the last suppers in the world are copied from this painting. It is so damaged now, by the wear and tear of three hundred years that the figures can hardly be distinguished. The Vandal goes to see this picture, which all the world praises—looks at it with a critical eye and says it's a perfect old nightmare of a picture and he wouldn't give forty dollars for a million like it—(and I share his opinion), and then he is done with Milan.

He paddles around the Lake of Como for a few days, and then takes the cars. He is bound for Venice, the oldest and the proudest and the princeliest Republic that ever graced the earth. We put on a good many airs with our little infant Republic of a century's growth, but we grow modest when we stand before this gray, old, imperial city that was a haughty, invincible, magnificent Republic for fourteen hundred years! The Vandal is bound for Venice! He has a long, weary ride of it, but just as the day is closing he hears someone shout, "*Venice!*" and puts his head out of the window, and sure enough, afloat on the placid sea, a league away, lies the great city with its towers and domes and steeples drowsing in a golden mist of sunset!

Have you been to Venice—and seen the winding canals, and the stately edifices that border them all along, ornamented with the quaint devices and sculptures of a former age?—and have you seen the great

Cathedral of St. Mark's—and the Giant's Staircase—and the famous Bridge of Sighs—and the great Square of St. Mark's—and the ancient pillar, with the winged lion of St. Mark that stands on it, whose story and whose origin are a mystery—and the Rialto, where Shylock used to loan money on human flesh and other collateral?—And have you seen the gondolas and heard the romantic gondolier sing—as only the romantic gondolier *can* sing—according to the romances? *I* have heard the romantic gondoliers sing—we had just entered Venice at eight in the evening and were floating away toward the hotel. We were poking dismally around in the shadows among long rows of towering untenanted buildings, and were very sad and disheartened and disappointed—for *this* was not the Venice we had expected. It was at such a time as this that this ragged, barefooted guttersnipe turned up and began to sing, true to the traditions of his race.

I stood it for about five minutes—and then I said:

"Look here, Roderigo Gonzales Michael Angelo—Smith—I'm a pilgrim and I'm a stranger, but I'm not going to stand any such caterwauling as that! If this thing goes on one of us has got [to] take water. It is enough that my cherished dreams of Venice have been blighted forever, without taxing *your* talents to make the matter worse. Another yelp out of you and overboard you go!"

I had begun to feel that the old Venice of song and story had departed forever. But I was too hasty. In a few minutes we swept gracefully out into the Grand Canal, and under the mellow moonlight the Venice of poetry and romance stood revealed. Right from the water's edge rose stately palaces of marble; gondolas were gliding swiftly hither and thither and disappearing suddenly through unsuspected gates and alleys; ponderous stone bridges threw their shadows athwart the glittering waves. There was life and motion everywhere, and yet everywhere there was a hush, a stealthy sort of stillness, that was suggestive of secret enterprises of bravoes and of lovers; and clad half in moonbeams and half in mysterious shadows, the grim old mansions of the Republic seemed to have an expression about them of having an eye out for just such enterprises as these at that moment. Music came stealing over the waters—Venice was complete.

The gondola is an institution. But it seems queer—ever so queer—this thing of a boat doing duty as a private carriage. In Venice we see business men come to the front door, portly fellows, with their portliness gauged according to their incomes, step into a *gondola,* instead of a street car, and go off down town to the counting-house. We see young ladies, out visiting, stand on the stoop, and laugh, chatter, and flirt their fans, and kiss good-by, and say, "Come *soon,*

Maria—now *do*—you've been just as mean as ever you *could*—and mother's dying to see you, and so's the poodle and the cat and everybody—and Oh, we've moved into the new house, and Oh it's such a *love* of a place—so convenient to the post office, and the church, and the Y.M.C.A.—and we do have such fishing and such carrying on and *such* swimming matches in the back yard—Oh you *must* come—no distance at all—and if you go down through by St. Mark's and the Bridge of Sighs and out through the alley and come up by Santa Maria del Frari, and into the Grand Canal, there isn't a *bit* of current—now *do* come, Sally Maria—by-bye!" and then the little humbug trips down the steps, jumps into the gondola—says under her breath, "Disagreeable old thing I hope she *won't* come!"—goes skimming away around the corner, and the other girl slams the street door and says, "Well, that infliction's over, anyway—but I suppose I've *got* to go and see her—tiresome, stuck-up thing!"

Ah, human nature is just the same, all over the world—and *girls* are just the same everywhere—the girls in Venice are just like the girls in Cleveland—*they* wear their dresses cut bias—certainly—and put the most gorgeous gussets on 'em, and gores and all that sort of thing—and wad up their hair behind so bewitchingly and prop it up with a crupper—and *they* keep a pet kangaroo so as they can see how to do the Grecian Bend right. Ah the girls in Venice are precisely like the girls in Pittsburgh—a Venice girl is as *much like* a Pittsburgh girl as—as—as one *blessed* angel is like another! (That was a close place—but I rubbed through.)

And we see the diffident young man, *mild* of moustache, *affluent* of hair, *indigent* of brain, *elegant* of costume, drive up in his gondola to *her* father's mansion—tell his hackman to—*bail out* and wait—start fearfully up the steps and meet the *old man* right on the threshold!—hear him ask what street the new British bank is in—as if *that* were what he came for—and then bounce into his boat and scurry away with his coward heart in his boots!—see him come sneaking around the corner again directly, with a corner of the gondola curtain open toward the old gentleman's disappearing gondola—and then out scampers his Susan with a flock of little Italian endearments fluttering from her lips and goes to drive with him in the watery avenues away down toward the Rialto.

We see the ladies go out shopping, in the most natural way, and flit from street to street, and from store to store, just in the good old fashion, except that they leave the gondola instead of a private carriage waiting for them a couple of hours at the curbstone—waiting while they make the nice young clerks pull down tons and tons of silks and velvets and bombazine and bobbinett and moire antiques and solferino and all those splendid fabrics—and then they buy a paper of pins and go paddling up the canal to confer a portion of their disastrous patronage on the other stores. And they always have their purchases *sent home* just in the good old way. Ah, human nature is *very* much the same all over the world—and it was *so* like my dear native home to see a lady buy ten cents' worth of blue ribbon and—have it sent home in a scow. Ah, these little touches of nature move one almost to tears in those far-off foreign lands! Human nature is just the same all over the world. Blessed Woman—her ways are ways of pleasantness and all her paths are peace.

I love the whole sex—my own mother was a woman.

And we see little girls and boys go out for an airing, with their nurses, in the gondola—when they've been good and haven't stolen any jam, nor told any lies they couldn't substantiate. *I* never had any trouble about going out for an airing, when *I* was young—because I never stole jam—when I could get my little brother to steal it for me—and I always made it a point to be just as particular about telling a lie as if I were telling the truth. I'd rather have a sound judgment than *talent.*

And we see staid families, with prayer book and beads, enter the gondola, dressed in their Sunday best, and float solemnly away to church.

At midnight we see the theater break up and discharge its swarm of chattering youth and beauty, hear the cries of the hackman-gondoliers and behold the struggling crowd jump aboard the black multitude of boats and go skimming down the moonlit avenues—we see them branching off, here and there and disappearing up divergent streets; we hear the faint sounds of laughter, of shouted farewells floating up out of the distance—and then, the strange pageant being gone, we have lonely stretches of glittering water, of stately buildings, of blotting shadows, of weird stone faces creeping into the moonlight, of deserted bridges, of motionless boats at anchor—and over all broods that mysterious stillness, that stealthy quiet, that befits so well this old dreaming Venice! [Opposite this passage in the MS is a marginal note by Mark Twain: "Very slow."]

Our Vandals hurried away from Venice and scattered abroad everywhere. You could find them breaking specimens from the dilapidated tomb of Romeo and Juliet at Padua—and infesting the picture galleries of Florence—and risking their necks on the Leaning Tower of Pisa—and snuffing sulphur fumes on the summit of Vesuvius—and burrowing among the exhumed wonders of Herculaneum and Pompeii—and you might see them with spectacles on and blue cotton umbrellas under their arms benignantly contemplating Rome from the venerable arches of the Coliseum.

And finally we sailed from Naples, and in due time anchored before the Piraeus, the seaport of Athens in Greece. But the quarantine was in force, and so they set a guard of soldiers to watch us and would not let us go ashore. However, I and three other Vandals took a boat, and muffled the oars, and slipped ashore at 11:30 at night, and dodged the guard successfully. Then we made a wide circuit around the slumbering town, avoiding all roads and houses—for they'd about as soon hang a body as not for violating the quarantine laws in those countries. We got around the town without any accident, and then struck out across the Attic Plain, steering straight for Athens—over rocks and hills, and brambles and everything—with Mt. Helicon for a landmark. And so we tramped five or six miles. The Attic Plain is a mighty uncomfortable plain to travel in, even if it *is* so historical. The armed guards got after us three times and flourished their gleaming gun barrels in the moonlight, because they thought we were stealing grapes occasionally—and the fact is we *were*—for we found by and by that the brambles that tripped us up so often were grape vines—but these people in the country didn't know that we were quarantine blockade-runners, and so they only scared us and jawed Greek at us, and let us go, instead of arresting us.

We didn't care about Athens particularly, but we wanted to see the famous Acropolis and its ruined temples, and we did. We climbed the steep hill of the Acropolis about one in the morning and tried to storm that grand old fortress that had scorned the battles and sieges of three thousand years. We had the garrison out, mighty quick—four Greeks—and we bribed them to betray the citadel and unlock the gates. In a moment we stood in the presence of the noblest ruins we had ever seen—the most elegant, the most graceful, the most imposing. The renowned Parthenon towered above us, and about us were the wreck of what were once the snowy marble Temples of Hercules and a second Minerva, and another whose name I have forgotten. Most of the Parthenon's grand columns are still standing, but the roof is gone.

As we wandered down the marble paved length of this mighty temple, the scene was strangely impressive. Here and there in lavish profusion were gleaming white statues of men and women, propped against blocks of marble, some of them armless, some without legs, others headless—but all looking mournful and sentient, and startlingly human! They rose up and confronted the midnight intruder on every side—they stared at him with stony eyes from unlooked-for nooks and recesses; they peered at him over fragmentary heaps far down the desolate corridors; they barred his way in the midst of the broad forum, and solemnly pointed with handless arms the way from the sacred fane; and through the roofless temple the moon looked down and banded the floor and darkened the scattered fragments and broken statues with the slanting shadows of the columns!

What a world of ruined sculpture was about us! Stood up in rows—stacked up in piles—scattered broadcast over the wide area of the Acropolis—were hundreds of crippled statues of all sizes and of the most exquisite workmanship; and vast fragments of marble that once belonged to the entablatures, covered with bas-reliefs representing battles and sieges, ships of war with three and four tiers of oars, pageants and processions—everything one could think of.

We walked out into the grass-grown, fragment-strewn court beyond the Parthenon. It startled us, every now and then, to see a stony white face stare suddenly up at us out of the grass with its dead eyes. The place seemed alive with ghosts. We half expected to see the Athenian heroes of twenty centuries ago glide out of the shadows and steal into the old temple they knew so well and regarded with such boundless pride.

The full moon was riding high in the cloudless heavens, now. We sauntered carelessly and unthinkingly to the edge of the lofty battlements of the citadel, and looked down—and lo, a vision! And *such* a vision! Athens by moonlight! All the beauty in all the world combined could not rival it! The prophet that thought the splendors of the New Jerusalem were revealed to him, surely saw this instead. It lay in the level plain right under our feet—all spread abroad like a picture—and we looked down upon it as we might have looked from a balloon. We saw no semblance of a street, but every house, every window, every clinging vine, every projection, was as distinct and sharply marked as if the time were noonday; and yet there was no glare, no glitter, nothing harsh or repulsive—the silent city was flooded with the mellowest light that ever streamed from the moon, and seemed like some living creature wrapped in peaceful slumber. On its further side was a little temple whose delicate pillars and ornate front glowed with a rich lustre that chained the eye like a spell; and nearer by the palace of the King reared its creamy walls out of the midst of a great garden of shrubbery that was flecked all over with a random shower of amber lights—a spray of golden sparks that lost their brightness in the glory of the moon and glinted softly upon the sea of dark foliage like the pallid stare of the milky way! Overhead the stately columns, majestic still in their ruin—under foot the dreaming city—in the distance the silver sea—not on the broad earth is there another picture half so beautiful!

We got back to the ship safely, just as the day was dawning. We had walked upon pavements that had been pressed by Plato, Aristotle, Demosthenes, Socrates, Phocion, Euclid, Xenophon, Herodotus, Diogenes, and a hundred others of deathless fame, and were satisfied. We got to stealing grapes again on the way back, and half a dozen rascally guards with muskets and pistols captured us and marched us in the center of a hollow square nearly to the sea—till we were well beyond all the graperies. Military escort—ah, I never traveled in so much state in all my life.

I leave the Vandal here. I have not time to follow *him* further— nor *our* Vandals to Constantinople and Smyrna and the Holy Land, Egypt, the Islands of the Sea and to Russia and his visit to the Emperor. But I wish I *could* tell of that visit of our gang of *Quaker City* Vandals to the grandest monarch of the age, America's stanch, old, steadfast Friend, Alexander II, Autocrat of Russia!

The Emperor is a man of noble presence—tall and spare—has a kind blue eye—looks great and *good* and every inch an Emperor. It was a novel sensation to stand in the presence of this man, chatting easily and pleasantly like an ordinary mortal, and so simply dressed—yet whose slightest word is law to 70,000,000 of human beings!—who could open his lips and ships would fly through the waves, locomotives would speed over the plains, couriers would hurry from village to village, a hundred telegraphs would flash the word to the four corners of an Empire that stretches its vast proportions over a seventh part of the habitable globe, and a countless multitude of men would spring to do his bidding! If this man sprained his ankle, a million miles of telegraph would carry the news over mountains—valleys—under the trackless sea—and ten thousand newspapers would prate of it; if he were grievously ill, all the nations would know it before the sun rose again—if he dropped lifeless where he stood, the effect might be felt in the furthest lands of Christendom! Yet where I stood, worm of the dust as I am, I could have overturned this god—I could have knocked this colossus down with *my* feeble fist—but I restrained myself.

If there is a moral to this lecture it is an injunction to all Vandals to *travel.* I am glad the American Vandal *goes* abroad. It does him good. It makes a better *man* of him. It rubs out a multitude of his old unworthy biases and prejudices. It aids his religion for it enlarges his charity and his benevolence and it broadens his views of men and things; it deepens his generosity and his compassion for the failings and shortcomings of his fellow creatures. Contact with men of various nations and many creeds, teaches him that there are *other* people in the world besides his own little clique, and other opinions as worthy of attention and respect as his own. He finds that he and *his* are not the most momentous matters in the universe. Cast into trouble and misfortune in strange lands and being mercifully cared for by those he never saw before, he begins to learn the best lesson of all—that one which culminates in the conviction that God puts *something* good and something lovable in every man His hands create—that the world is *not* a cold, harsh, cruel prison-house, stocked with all manner of selfishness and hate and wickedness. It *liberalizes* the Vandal to travel—you never saw a bigoted, opinionated, stubborn, narrow-minded, self-conceited, *almighty mean man* in your life but he had stuck in one place since he was born and thought God made the world and dyspepsia and bile for *his* especial comfort and satisfaction. So I say, *by all means,* let the American Vandal *go on* traveling, and let no man discourage him. Remember.

Our Vandals in the *Quaker City* will never regret their pilgrimage—they learned something—matters that were useful—other matters that were only pleasant. Much that they learned, much that they saw, much that they heard, they will forget—but still a store of softly-tinted images will remain in their memories—and float through their reveries and dreams for many and many a year to come. They will remember *some*thing.

Text / Composite, based upon: "Vandals," TS of incomplete MS, MTP; "The American Vandal," *MTS*(23):21–30; Cleveland *Herald,* November 18, 1868; Chicago *Republican,* January 8, 1869; Peoria *Daily Transcript,* January 12, 1869.

just like the girls in Cleveland / Cleveland was the first stop on the 1868–69 tour. Mark Twain undoubtedly substituted the name of whatever subsequent town he was speaking in. See following note.

as much like a Pittsburgh girl as . . . one *blessed angel* / Pittsburgh was the second stop on the tour. When he spoke in Elmira, the third stop, where Olivia Langdon was in the audience, the reference to a blessed angel was not merely a manner of speaking.

Cast into trouble and misfortune in strange lands / Possibly an allusion to his own experience in Damascus, where he was laid low by what he called "a violent attack of cholera, or cholera morbus." Commenting on his feud with the religious vagaries of the pilgrims, he remarks: "And did I not overhear Church, another pilgrim, say he did not care who went or who stayed, *he* would stand by me till I walked out of Damascus on my own feet or was carried out in a coffin, if it was a year?" See *The Innocents Abroad,* vol. 2, chaps. 8, 20.

· 9 ·

On the lyceum tour of 1868–69, Cleveland was a focal point because it was the home of Mrs. Mary Mason Fairbanks, who had been a correspondent for the Cleveland Herald *on the* Quaker City *excursion. On shipboard she had undertaken to tutor the wild humorist of the Pacific slope on refinement of manners and of writing, and had kept a critical eye on him thereafter. He accepted her instruction gratefully, or seemed to, called her "Mother," and made her his confidante, sending her progress reports on his impetuous courtship of Olivia Langdon of Elmira, New York. It was at the request of Mother Fairbanks that he gave the "Vandals" as a benefit lecture for a Cleveland orphanage, concluding with an appeal for liberal donations.*

Concluding Remarks

Protestant Orphan Asylum Benefit, Case Hall, Cleveland, January 22, 1869

Ladies and gentlemen: I am well aware of the fact that it would be a most gigantic fraud for you to pay a dollar each to hear my lecture. But you pay your dollar to the orphan asylum and have the lecture thrown in! So if it is not worth anything it does not cost you anything! There is no expense connected with this lecture. Everything is done gratuitously and you have the satisfaction of knowing that all you have paid goes for the benefit of the orphans. I understand that there are to be other entertainments given week after next for the same object, the asylum being several thousand dollars in debt, and I earnestly recommend you all to attend them and not let your benevolence stop with this lecture. There will be eating to be done. Go there and eat, and eat, and keep on eating and *pay as you go.* The proprietors of the skating rink have generously offered to donate to the asylum the proceeds of one evening, to the amount of a thousand dollars, and when that evening comes, go and skate. I do not know whether you can all skate or not, but go and try! If you break your necks it will be no matter; it will be to help the orphans.

Don't be afraid of giving too much to the orphans, for however much you give you have the easiest part of the bargain. Some persons have to take care of those sixty orphans and they have to wash them.

Orphans have to be washed! And it's no small job either for they have only one wash tub and it's a slow business. They can't wash but one orphan at a time! They have to be washed in the most elaborate detail, and by the time they get through with the sixty, the original orphan has to be washed again. Orphans won't stay washed! I've been an orphan myself for twenty-five years and I know this to be true. There is a suspicion of impurity and imposition about many ostensibly benevolent enterprises, but there is no taint of reproach upon this for the benefit of those little waifs upon the sea of life and I hope your benevolence will not stop here. In conclusion I thank you for the patience and fortitude with which you have listened to me.

Text / Cleveland *Leader,* January 23, 1869.
your benevolence / The press reported that the benefit lecture yielded $807.

· 10 ·

By 1869 Mark Twain was well started on the way to the eminence he later achieved as an after-dinner speaker. He had embarked on a banqueting career that became more strenuous as he became more famous, and that continued almost to the end of his life. For some unknown reason, however, he did not attend the dinner of the New York Press Club to respond to the toast to the "Reliable Contraband," given below. Although he said he intended to deliver the speech "extemporaneously," it was read by proxy.

The Reliable Contraband

New York Press Club Dinner, Delmonico's, June 5, 1869

Mr. President and gentlemen: I thank you most heartily—I, that is I—I am happy in being considered worthy to—to—in truth, gentlemen, I am unprepared to make a speech—this call is entirely unexpected, I assure you—I did not expect it—that is, I did not expect to be called upon—if I had expected to be called upon I would have prepared myself, but not ex—being, as I may say, entirely unprepared and not expecting it, it is entirely unexpected to me, and I am entirely unprepared. But I thank you very kindly, I assure you. However, at this moment a thought occurs to me. I will offer a sentiment, and preface it with a few subsequent remarks which I hope to be able to make in the interim, if the theme shall chance to suggest to me anything to say. I beg that you will fill your ———

(*Private memorandum*—To recollect to take notice, at this point, whether these fellows are drinking out of gourds, goblets, jugs, or what they *are* drinking out of, and so not make any stupid blunder and spoil the effect of the speech.)

and join me in a toast:

To One whose eminent Services in time of great national peril we gratefully acknowledge—whose memory we revere—whose death we deplore—the journalist's truest friend, the late "Reliable Contraband."

Mr. President and gentlemen: It is my painful duty to mar these festivities with the announcement of the death of one who was dear to us all—our tried and noble friend, the "Reliable Contraband." To the world at large this event will bring no sorrow, for the world never comprehended him, never knew him as we did, never had such cause to love him—but unto *us* the calamity brings unutterable anguish, for it heralds the loss of one whose great heart beat for us alone, whose tireless tongue vibrated in our interest only, whose fervent fancy wrought its miracles solely for our enrichment and renown.

In his time, what did he not do for us? When marvels languished and sensation dispatches grew tame, who was it that laid down the shovel and the hoe and came with healing on his wings? The Reliable Contraband. When armies fled in panic and dismay, and the great cause seemed lost beyond all hope of succor, who was it that turned the tide of war and gave victory to the vanquished? The Reliable Contraband. When despair hung its shadows about the hearts of the people and sorrow sat upon every face, who was it that braved every danger to bring cheering and incomprehensible news from the front? The Reliable Contraband. Who took Richmond the first time? The Reliable Contraband. Who took it the second time? The Reliable Contraband. Who took it *every* time until the last, and then felt the bitterness of hearing a nation applaud the man more who took it once than that greater man who had taken it six times before? The Reliable Contraband. When we needed a bloodless victory, whom did we look to win it? The Reliable Contraband. When we needed news to make the people's bowels yearn and their knotted and combined locks to stand on end like quills upon the fretful porcupine, whom did we look to to fetch it? The Reliable Contraband. When we needed *any* sort or description of news, upon *any* sort or description of subject, who was it that stood always ready to steal a horse and bring that news along? The Reliable Contraband.

My friends, he was the faithfullest vassal that ever fought, bled and lied in the glorious ranks of journalism. Thunder and lightning never stopped him—annihilated railroads never delayed him—the telegraph never overtook him—military secrecy never crippled his knowledge—strategic feints never confused his judgment— cannon balls couldn't kill him--clairvoyance couldn't find him—Satan himself couldn't catch him! His information comprised all knowledge, possible and impossible—his imagination was utterly boundless--his capacity to make mighty statements and so back them up as to make an inch of truth cover an acre of ground without appearing to stretch or tear, was a thing that appalled even the most unimpressible with its awful grandeur.

The Reliable Contraband is no more. Born of the war, and a necessity of the war and of the war only, he watched its progress, took note of its successes and reverses, manufactured and recorded the most thrilling features of its daily history, and then when it died his great mission was fulfilled, his occupation gone, and he died likewise. No journalist here present can lay his hand upon his heart and say he had not cause to love this faithful creature over whose unsentient form we drop these unavailing tears—for no journalist among us all can lay his hand upon his heart and say he ever lied with such pathos, such unction, such exquisite symmetry, such sublimity of conception and such felicity of execution as when he did it through and by the inspiration of this regally gifted marvel of mendacity, the lamented "*Reliable Contraband.*" Peace to his ashes!

Text / Mark Twain to the New York Press Club, June 1, 1869, Clifton Waller Barrett Library of the University of Virginia Library, Charlottesville. Published, except for the introductory paragraph, as "Mark Twain's Eulogy on 'The Reliable Contraband,'" *Packard's Monthly* 2, no. 7 (July 1869):220–21.

Reliable Contraband / During the Civil War a contraband was a Negro slave who fled to Union lines or remained in territory occupied by Union troops. "Reliable Contraband" was newspaper jargon for a real or imaginary source of war news, generally the latter. The term was roughly synonymous with "rumor."

I am unprepared to make a speech / Mark Twain was never, or almost never, unprepared. His so-called "extemporaneous" speeches were carefully rehearsed before delivery. The stumbling introduction above is an excellent example of a confusion that was merely assumed. He wrote the whole sequence, then gave it verisimilitude by simulated hesitancy and stammering repetition, matching spoken uncertainty with visible signs of pretended distress.

their knotted and combined locks, etc. / A free adaptation of lines from *Hamlet* (1.5), in which the ghost of Hamlet's father says he could unfold a tale of horror that would make "Thy knotted and combined locks to part / And each particular hair to stand on end / Like quills upon the fretful porpentine."

· 11 ·

The lyceum season of 1871–72 was a stormy one for Mark Twain. He began with a lecture burdened by the top-heavy title of "Reminiscences of Some Uncommonplace Characters Whom I Have Chanced to Meet." When it was unfavorably received by several audiences at the outset, he hastily wrote a new lecture about Artemus Ward, just one of the uncommonplace characters. He delivered this lecture a number of times in the East and Middle West, never satisfied with it, continually revising, continually vexed by a mixed response that varied from the stern disapproval of small towns to the occasional praise of metropolitan critics. For the last third of the tour he composed yet another lecture, using material from his new book, Roughing It, *and with this one regained some of the ground lost in earlier failures. The season was so plagued with ups and downs, many more downs than usual, that he characterized it as "detestable."*

Artemus Ward Lecture

Lecture Season, 1871–72

Ladies and gentlemen: I ask leave to introduce to you the lecturer of the evening, Mr. Charles F. Clemens, otherwise known as "Mark Twain," a gentleman, I may say, whose devotion to science, aptness in philosophy, historical accuracy, and love of—truth are in perfect harmony with his majestic and imposing appearance. I—ah—refer—ah—indirectly to—to myself! It is not, I know, customary to introduce a lecturer after having the amount of advertising that

I have had; but as the management desired that the introduction should be made, I preferred making it myself, being sure by this means of getting in all the—facts!

My lecture is about Artemus Ward, who was one of the great humorists of our age. When I first started out on this missionary tour it was my intention to touch in my lecture upon a number of other uncommonplace characters I have met—Bunyan, Martin Luther, Milton and a few others; but I find that to mention all these old fellows, the companions of my childish hours, takes a great deal too much time, and, therefore, I confine myself to the single great man whom I have named. It is my purpose to show that Artemus Ward was America's greatest humorist, not manufactured or bogus, but a born humorist, and I will give you a skeleton outline—I have not time for more—of his life. In this outline I shall not load you down with historic facts to such an extent that you will be unable to get home with them, nor will I even make for you any of my philosophical deductions. This last promise is, on my part, a sacrifice, for I admire my philosophical deductions as I admire few other things on earth. Strange as it may seem, I have always found that the effect produced by them upon an audience was that of intense and utter exasperation.

Artemus Ward was a humorist from the cradle to the grave. We cannot, indeed, go back to his cradle, but very early in life we find him perpetrating a witticism. The circumstances were these: When Artemus Ward was very young he and a companion got hold of a pack of cards and learned to play euchre. Artemus was perfectly fascinated with the game and played it as often as he had an opportunity; but it had to be done on the sly, and he had to hide his cards from his parents. So, when he was looking around for a place to hide them, the boys thought the safest place where they could put the cards was in the pocket of the minister's black gown, under the very aegis of the church. I don't know what aegis means, but it's a good word and I suppose it's all right. Well, the old minister was called on to baptize a convert, and as he went down into the water wearing the gown, the cards began to come up to the surface and float off. The boys who were on the bank watching, though in great fear, kept their eyes on the cards. As it happened there came up first two bowers and three aces. Of course the boys were thrashed, and an old aunt of Artemus' proceeded to lecture him on the enormity of his crime. "Why," said she, "just imagine how the poor man must have felt when he saw the cards coming up! I should have thought he would have fainted, and I don't see how he got out." "Well," said Artemus, "I don't see how he could help going out on such a hand."

Artemus Ward's real name, as most of you are probably aware, was

Charles F. Browne. He was born in Waterford, Maine, in 1834. His personal appearance was not like that of most Maine men. He looked like a glove-stretcher. His hair, red, and brushed well forward at the sides, reminded one of a divided flame. His nose rambled on aggressively before him, with all the strength and determination of a cow-catcher, while his red moustache—to follow out the simile—seemed not unlike the unfortunate cow. He was of Puritan descent, and prided himself not a little on being derived from that stern old stock of people, who had left their country and home for the sake of having freedom on a foreign shore to enjoy their own religion, and, at the same time, to prevent other folks from enjoying theirs. I don't know whether it is treasonable to speak in this way about those reverend old chaps, the Pilgrim Fathers. I am a Puritan Father myself, at least I am descended from one. One of my ancestors cut a conspicuous figure in the "Boston massacre," fighting first on one side and then on the other. He wasn't a man to stand foolin' around while a massacre was goin' on. Why, to hear our family talk, you'd think that not a man named anything but Twain was in that massacre—and when you came to hear all about it, you'd wish that such was the case. Then I had another ancestor in the battle of Bunker Hill. He was everything, that ancestor of mine was—killed, wounded and missing. He was a prompt, businesslike fellow, and to make sure of being the last of the three he did it first of all—did it well, too—he was prompt that way—before a shot was fired. Why, I could stand here for a week and tell you of my distinguished ancestors, and I think I'll do it. On second thoughts I think I won't, but go back to my subject.

Ward never had any regular schooling; he was too poor to afford it, for one thing, and too lazy to care for it for another. He had an intense ingrained dislike for work of any kind; he even objected to see other people work, and on one occasion went so far as to submit to the authorities of a certain town an invention to run a treadmill by steam. Such a notion could not have originated with a hard-hearted man. Ward was a dutiful man, and his first act, when money began to come in on him from his lectures, was to free from encumbrance the old homestead in his native town and settle it upon his aged mother.

Besides having wit, and brilliant scintillations of happy fancies, Artemus possessed genuine humor. He once took an old Queen Anne musket and loaded it according to directions given by a hired man. The directions were, to put in a handful of powder or so, a handful of bullets or so, a handful of nails or so. Ward did as he was told, only he had to take out a few of the bullets to make room for the nails. The gun being loaded, the boy went into the woods to shoot it off, but, soon as his hand got to the trigger, his courage failed, and finally he came home with the gun unfired, and handed it in that state to his father. The father sighted a sapling and let drive. The result was a small earthquake.

Old Mr. Ward was laid up for a week. The senile gentleman, upon recovering, asked his son to come forward. He questioned him about the loading of the fowling piece—why he didn't make a report. The precocious youth replied he supposed that the gun would report for itself, and so it did. That was enough.

While still young he apprenticed himself to a printer in Skowhegan. Artemus was pleased with the place, and used often to pronounce the name, it reminded him so much of the names of old Spain and Portugal, because it was so different.

About the age of sixteen he went to Boston, and got on "Mrs. Partington's" *Carpet Bagger*. Then it was that he wrote his first piece, and dropped it stealthily into the office, and how proud he felt next day, when they gave it to him to set up; then he commenced to write and write generally. He touched everything. He even wrote a column of a scientific essay, entitled "Iz Cats Useful?" and sent it to the Smithsonian Institute. He tired of settled life and poor pay in Boston and wandered off over the country to better his fortune, obtaining a position in Cleveland as a reporter at $12 a week. It was while in Cleveland that he wrote his first badly spelled article, signing it "Artemus Ward." He did not think much of it at the time of writing it, but it gave him a start that speedily sent him to the top of the ladder without touching a single rung.

Here he made himself well known in his particular line. Alluding to a very slow railroad, he said that the railroad was a breeder of injustice. He told of a convict who was started to the jail at the end of the road, but got so old while going he did not answer the description when he got there. Speaking of this same road, he once told the conductor the cow-catcher should be at the other end—there the danger lay. "You can't," said he, "overtake a cow, but what's to hinder one walking in the back door and biting the passengers?"

The wit of Mr. Ward was very lively. He was a great humorist, nevertheless. True, he must not be compared with Holmes or Lowell. These men have a refinement that he did not possess; but this does not detract from the great showman's ability to create fun for the million.

The flood tide of his popularity soon bore Artemus to New York, where for a time he infused new life into the columns of *Vanity Fair,* a comic journal published in that city. The quickening was but for a time, and the paper had already entered upon that rapid decline which every American comic journal seems destined to, even in its early youth. Artemus watched *Vanity Fair* in its death agonies, saw it expire, and said above its grave that he had always been of the opinion that an occasional joke improved a comic paper.

Some of the best things attributed to Artemus Ward were not his. Indeed, his celebrated expression, "It would be ten dollars in Jeff Davis's pocket if he had never been born," I found in an English author, who wrote some fifty years ago. Pounds were substituted for dollars, and some other name appeared in the place of Jeff Davis. Again, in one of his lectures Ward used to say that to be attached to anything did not argue good feeling toward it, for he knew of a horse being attached to a dray and yet being down on that dray. A western journalist told me that this witticism was not original with Artemus Ward, but that he himself was the author of it.

But, in spite of this, Ward must not be regarded as a plagiarist. It is possible for a man to write what he thinks is a creation, but which is in fact only a memory; and it is also possible for two minds at different times to happen on the same idea. Holmes bears witness to this in the *Autocrat of the Breakfast Table.* I myself have written what I thought was my own—have imagined that I have created something clever and really good, and found out afterwards that the whole thing had been filched from me years and years before by Josephus.

The idea of lecturing then occurred to Artemus. The success of this new employment, although not great at first, soon exceeded his most sanguine expectations, and he adopted it as a permanent profession. The lectures which Ward delivered with so much success all over the country were without form or consistence or sequence. His first one he called "The Babes in the Wood," but "My Seven Grandmothers"—the name he originally intended to give it—would have been equally appropriate for anything there was in the lecture. At Christmas time, in 1861, he opened his "Babes" in New York and subsequently in California and elsewhere. His profits during that season amounted to something like $30,000 or $40,000—a very considerable sum for that day, but a gas fitter on the New York courthouse does better than that now. His success as a lecturer depended even more on the manner than on the matter.

His inimitable way of pausing and hesitating, of gliding in a moment from seriousness to humor without appearing to be conscious of so doing, cannot be reproduced, so that many of his best things read flat and tame in consequence. It was unkind to report him. There was more in his pauses than in his words. And so no reporter's pen could do him justice.

Having lectured for three months in California, Artemus went over to England, and opened with his panorama in Egyptian Hall, London, and lectured to the nobility as well as common people. His success was so great that he threatened at one time to compel the Royal Family to remain away from his exhibition. Some of the pictures in his exhibition were most wretchedly painted. Of one of the pictures, that of some impossible animal, he assured his audience that some of the greatest artists in the city came to the hall every morning before daybreak, with lanterns, to inspect it. "They say they never saw anything like it before, and hope they never will again." He was always tender-footed in matters of criticism. He said that some people found fault and slurred at him for not saying things like Edward Everett. "Why are they so one-sided?" he asked; "Edward Everett ought to be slurred some, I think, because he can't make a speech like me."

In England Ward was heartily received, and his efforts to please were very successful, but the climate of cold and fog seemed to have the effect of eating away his life, and although he struggled hard he had to relinquish his vocation. He lectured until his health was in such condition that he was nightly attended by his physician at the theater. One night in January, four years ago, the people found the doors of Egyptian Hall closed against them. When he knew that he must die, his only desire was to get home, but this was denied him. He got as far as Southampton, but his physician peremptorily forbade his attempting the sea voyage, and at Southampton, on the 6th of March, 1867, in the thirty-fourth year of his age, he died. Death at any time is sad, but under such circumstances as these it wrings the sigh of pity from every heart.

ARTEMUS WARD

Is he gone to the land of no laughter,
This man that made mirth for us all?
Proves death but a silence hereafter
From the sounds that delight or appall?
Once closed, have the lips no more duty,
No more pleasure the exquisite ears;
Has the heart done o'erflowing with beauty,
As the eyes have with tears?

Nay, if aught be sure, what can be surer
Than that Earth's good decays not with Earth?
And of all the heart's springs none are purer,
Than the springs of the fountain of mirth.
He that sounds them has pierced the heart's hollows,
The place where tears are and sleep;

For the foam-flakes that dance in life's shallows
Are wrung from life's deep.

He came with a heart full of gladness,
From the glad-hearted world of the West,
Won our laughter, but not with mere madness,
Spake and joked with us, not in mere jest;
For the pain in our hearts lingered after,
When the merriment dies from our ears,
And those that were loudest in laughter
Are silent in tears.

Ladies and gentlemen, my subject made it necessary for me to allude to death, at all times solemn, and never to be approached with levity. As this is the case, I think it more conducive to your and my own self-respect to stop here than to end my remarks by a flippant or ill-timed jest or jibe. Thanking you all very kindly for your presence and marks of approbation, I bid you a good-night.

Text / Composite, based upon: " 'Mark Twain' on 'Artemus Ward,' " Hartford *Times,* November 9, 1871; "Mark Twain," Philadelphia *Inquirer,* November 21, 1871; "Mark Twain," Philadelphia *Press,* November 21, 1871; "Mark Twain's Lecture," Reading, Pennsylvania, *Times and Dispatch,* November 25, 1871; "Mark Twain on Artemus Ward," Albany *Evening Journal,* November 29, 1871; "Mark Twain," Toledo *Blade,* December 12, 1871; "Mark Twain Lectures About Artemus Ward," Logansport, Indiana, *Democratic Pharos,* December 20, 1871; "Artemus Ward," *Trouble,* 297–304.

Charles F. Clemens / After Ward's given names, Charles Farrar. Sometimes he introduced himself as "Samuel B." Clemens.

"Mrs. Partington's" Carpet Bagger / The Boston *Carpet Bag* was a weekly in which Sam Clemens's sketch, "The Dandy Frightening the Squatter," was published on May 1, 1852, when Artemus Ward was a compositor there. The editor, Benjamin Penhallow Shillaber (1814–90), created the character of Mrs. Partington, who was noted for malapropisms. Two collections of her remarks are *Life and Sayings of Mrs. Partington* (1854), and *Partingtonian Patchwork* (1873).

Edward Everett / (1794–1865). American Unitarian clergyman and public official. A versatile man, he was at various times pastor of

Boston's Brattle Street Church, professor of Greek at Harvard, governor of Massachusetts, ambassador to England, president of Harvard, and secretary of state. He had a great reputation as a public speaker of the formal sort. According to *McGuffey's Sixth Reader,* "He is celebrated as an elegant and forceful writer, and a chaste orator."

"Is he gone to the land of no laughter" / This poem, by James Rhoades, was published in the London *Spectator* on March 9, 1867, soon after the death of Ward in Southampton. It was a late addition to the lecture, put in after a number of Mark Twain's performances had been sharply criticized. All reports agree that he impressed his audiences by reading the verses eloquently.

· 12 ·

For the last eight weeks of the lyceum season of 1871–72, Mark Twain used "Roughing It," which was much more favorably received than his two previous lectures on this tour. It was also successful in London, where he delivered it for two weeks in December 1873, then in Leicester and Liverpool under the title, "Roughing It On the Silver Frontier."

Roughing It Lecture

Lecture Season, 1871–72; England, 1873

Ladies and gentlemen: By request of the chairman of the committee, who has been very busy, and is very tired, I suppose, I ask leave to introduce to you the lecturer of the evening, Mr. Clemens, otherwise Mark Twain, a gentleman whose great learning, whose historical accuracy, whose devotion to science, and whose veneration for the truth, are only equaled by his high moral character and his majestic presence. I refer in these vague and general terms to myself. I am a little opposed to the custom of ceremoniously introducing a lecturer to an audience, partly because it seems to me that it is not entirely necessary where a man has been pretty well advertised, and partly because it makes a lecturer feel uncomfortably awkward. But where it is necessary I would much rather make it myself. Then I can get in all the facts.

But it is not really the introduction that I care for—I don't care about that—that don't discommode me—but it's the compliments that sometimes go with it. That's what *hurts.* It would hurt anybody. The idea of a young lady being introduced into society as the sweetest singer or the finest conversationalist! You might as well knock her in the head at once. She could not say a word the rest of the evening. I never had but one public introduction that seemed to me just exactly the thing—an introduction brimful of grace. Why, it was a sort of inspiration. And yet the man who made it wasn't acquainted with me; but he was sensible to the backbone, and he said to me: "Now you don't want any compliments?" I said he was exactly right, I *didn't* want any compliments. And when he introduced me he said, "Ladies and gentlemen, I shan't fool away any unnecessary time in this introduction. I don't know anything about this man; at least I know only two things: one is, that he has never been in the penitentiary; and the other is, I don't know why." Such an introduction as that puts a man at his ease right off.

Now when I first started out on this missionary expedition, I had a lecture which I liked very well, but by and by I got tired of telling that same old stuff over and over again, and then I got up another lecture, and after that another one, and I am tired of that; so I just thought tonight I would try something fresh, if you are willing. I don't suppose you care what a lecturer talks about if he only tells the truth—at intervals. Now I have got a book in press (it will be out pretty soon), over 600 octavo pages, and illustrated after the fashion of the *Innocents Abroad.* Terms—however I am not around canvassing for the work. I should like to talk a little of that book to you tonight. It is very fresh in my mind, as it is not more than three months since I wrote it. Say thirty or forty pages—or if you prefer it the whole 600.

Ten or twelve years ago, I crossed the continent from Missouri to California, in the old overland stagecoach, a good while before the Pacific Railway was built. Over 1,900 miles. It was a long ride, day and night, through sagebrush, over sand and alkali plains, wolves and Indians, starvation and smallpox—everything to make the journey interesting. Had a splendid time, a most enjoyable pleasure trip, in that old stagecoach. We were bound for Nevada, which was then a brand-new Territory nearly or about as large as the state of Ohio. It was a desolate, barren, sterile, mountainous, unpeopled country, sagebrush and deserts of alkali. You could scarcely cast your eye in any direction but your gaze would be met by one significant object, and that was the projecting horns of a dried shrunken carcass of an ox, preaching eloquent sermons of the hardships suffered by those emigrants, where a soil refused to clothe its nakedness, except now and then a little rill (or, as you might call it, a river) goes winding through the plain. Such is the Carson River, which clothes the valley with refreshing and fragrant hay fields. However, hay is a scant crop, and with all the importations from California the price of that article has never come under $300 a ton. In the winter the price reaches $800, and once went up to $1,200 per ton, and then the cattle were turned out to die, and it is hardly putting the figures too strong to say that the valleys were paved with the remains of these cattle.

It is a land where the winters are long and rigorous, where the summers are hot and scorching, and where not a single drop of rain ever falls during eleven tedious months; where it never thunders, and never lightens; where no river finds its way to the sea, or empties its waters into the great lakes that have no perceptible outlet, and whose surplus waters are spirited through mysterious channels down into the ground. A territory broad and ample, but which has not yet had a population numbering 80,000, yet a country that produced $20,000,000 of silver bullion in the year 1863, and produces $12,000,000 to $16,000,000 every year, yet the population has fallen away until now it does not number more than 15,000 or 18,000. Yet that little handful of people vote just as strongly as they do anywhere, are just as well represented in the Senate of the United States as Michigan, or the great state of New York with her 3,000,000 or 4,000,000 of people. That is equality in representation.

I spoke of the sagebrush. That is a particular feature of the country out there. It's an interesting sort of shrub. You see no other sort of vegetable, and clear from Pike's Peak to California's edge, the sagebushes stand from three to six feet apart, one vast greenish-gray sea of sagebrush. It was the emigrant's fast friend, his only resource for fuel. In its appearance it resembles a venerable live oak with its rough bark and knotty trunk, everything twisted and dwarfed, covered with its thick foliage. I think the sagebrush are beautiful—one at a time is, anyway. Of course, when you see them as far as the eye can reach, seven days and a half in the week, it is different. I am not trying to get up an excitement over sagebrush, but there are many reasons why it should have some mention from an appreciative friend.

I grant you that as a vegetable for table use sagebrush is a failure. Its leaves taste like our ordinary sage; you can make sage tea of it, but anybody in this audience who has ever been a boy, or a girl, or both, in a country where doctors were scarce and measles and grandmothers plenty, don't hanker after sage tea. And yet after all there was a manifest Providence in the creation of sagebrush, for it is food for the mules and donkeys, and therefore many emigrant trains are enabled to pull through with their loads where ox teams would lie down and die of starvation. That a mule will eat sagebrush don't prove much, because I know a mule will eat anything. He don't give the toss-up of a copper between oysters, lead pipe, brick dust, or even patent office reports. He takes whatever he can get most of.

In our journey we kept climbing and climbing for I don't know how many days and nights. At last we reached the highest eminence—the extreme summit of the great range of the Rocky Mountains, and entered the celebrated South Pass. Now the South Pass is more suggestive of a straight road than a suspension bridge hung in the clouds, though in one place it suggests the latter. One could look below him on the diminishing crags and cañons lying down, down, down, away to the vague plain below, with a crooked thread in it which was the road, and tufts of feathers in it which were trees—the whole country spread out like a picture, sleeping in the sunlight, and darkness stealing over it, blotting out feature after feature under the frown on a gathering storm—not a film or shadow to mar the spectator's gaze. I could watch that storm break forth down there; could see the lightnings flash, the sheeted rain drifting along the canon's side, and hear the thunder crash upon crash, reverberating among a thousand rocky cliffs. This is a familiar experience to traveling people. It was a miracle of sublimity to a boy like me, who could hardly say that he had ever been away from home a single day in his life before.

We visited Salt Lake City in our journey. Carson City, the capital of Nevada, had a wild harum-scarum population of editors, thieves, lawyers, in fact all kinds of blacklegs. Its desperadoes, gamblers, and silver miners were armed to the teeth, every one of them dressed in the roughest kind of costumes, which looked strange and romantic to me and I was fascinated.

Everybody rode horseback in that town. I never saw such magnificent horsemanship as that displayed in Carson streets every day, and I did envy them, though I was not much of a horseman. But I had soon learned to tell a horse from a cow, and was burning with impatience to learn more. I was determined to have a horse and ride myself. Whilst this thought was rankling in my mind, the auctioneer came scouring through the plaza on a black beast, that was humped like a dromedary, and fearfully homely. He was going at "twenty, twenty-two-two dollars, for horse, saddle, and bridle."

A man standing near me—whom I didn't know—but who turned out to be the auctioneer's brother, noticed the wistful look in my eye, and observed that that was a remarkable horse to be going at such a price, let alone the saddle and bridle. I said I had half a notion to bid. "Now," he says, "I know that horse. I know him well. You are a stranger, I take it. You might think he is an American horse, but he is not anything of the kind. He is a Mexican plug—that's what he is—a genuine Mexican plug," but there was something else about that man's way of saying it, that made me just determined that I would own a genuine Mexican plug—if it took every cent I had. And I said, "Has he any other advantages?" He hooked his forefinger in the pocket of my army shirt, and led me to one side, and in a low tone so that no one else could hear said, "Sh! don't say a word! He can outbuck any horse in America; he can outbuck any horse in the world." Just then the auctioneer came along. "Twenty-four, twenty-four dollars, for the horse, saddle, and bridle." I said, "Twenty-seven!" "Sold!"

I took the genuine Mexican plug, paid for him, put him in a livery stable, let him get something to eat, and get rested, and then in the afternoon I brought him out in the plaza, and some of the citizens held him by the head, and others held him down to the earth by the tail, and I got on him. As soon as those people let go he put all his feet in a bunch together, let his back sag down, and then he arched it up suddenly, and shot me one hundred and eighty yards; and I came down again, straight down, and lighted in the saddle, and went up again. And when I came down the next time I lit on his neck, and seized him, and slid back into the saddle, and held on. Then he raised himself straight up in the air on his hind feet, and just walked around awhile, like a member of Congress, and then he came down and went up the other way, and just walked around on his hands, just as a schoolboy would. Then he came down on all fours again with the same old process of shooting me up in the air, and the third time I went up I heard a man say, "Oh, don't he buck!" So that was "bucking." I was very glad to know it. Not that I was enjoying it, but then I had been taking a general sort of interest in it, and had naturally desired to know what the name of it was. And whilst I was up somebody hit the horse a whack with a strap, and when I came down again the genuine bucker was gone.

While this performance was going on, a sympathizing crowd had gathered around, and one of them remarked to me, "Stranger, you have been taken in. That's a genuine Mexican plug," and another one says, "Think of it! You might have bought an American horse, used to all kinds of work, for a very little more money." Well I didn't want to talk. I didn't have anything to say. I was so jolted up, so internally, externally and eternally mixed up, gone all to pieces. I put my hand on my forehead, and the other on my stomach; and if I had been the owner of sixteen hands I could have found a place for every one of them.

Now if you would see the noblest, loveliest inland lake in the world, you should go to Lake Tahoe. It is just on the boundary line between California and Nevada. I have seen some of the world's celebrated lakes and they bear no comparison with Tahoe. There it is, a sheet of perfectly pure, limpid water, lifted up 6,300 feet above the sea—a vast oval mirror framed in a wall of snow-clad mountain peaks, above the common world. Solitude is king, and in that realm calm silence is brooding always. It is the home of rest and tranquillity and gives emancipation and relief from the griefs and plodding cares of life.

Could you but see the morning breaking there, gilding those snowy summits and then creeping gradually along the slopes until it sets the lake and woodlands free from mist, all agleam, you would see old Nature, the master artist, painting those dissolving views on the still water and finally grouping all these features into a complete picture. Every little dell, the mountains with their dome-turned pinnacles, the cataracts and drifting clouds, are all exquisitely photographed on the burnished surface of the lake, suffused with the softest and richest color.

This lake is ten miles from Carson City, and in company with a friend we used to foot it out there, taking along provisions and blankets—camp out on the lake shore two or three weeks at a time; not another human being within miles of us. We used to loaf about in the boat, smoke and read, sometimes play seven-up to strengthen the mind. It's a sinful game, but it's mighty nice. We'd just let the boat drift and drift wherever it wanted to. I can stand a deal of such hardship and suffering when I'm healthy. And the water was so wonderfully clear. Where it was eighty feet deep the pebbles on the bottom were just as distinct as if you held them in your hand; and in that clear white atmosphere it seemed as if the boat was drifting through the air. Out in the middle it was a deep dark indigo blue, and the official measurement made by the State Geologist of California shows it to be 1,525 feet deep in the center. You can imagine that it would take a great many churches and steeples piled one upon another before they would be perceptible above its surface. You might use up a great deal of ecclesiastical architecture in that way. Now, notwithstanding that lake is lifted so high among the clouds, surrounded by the everlasting snow-capped mountain peaks, with its surface higher than Mt. Washington in the East, and notwithstanding the water is pretty shallow around the edges, yet the coldest winter day in the recollection of humanity was never known to form ice upon its surface. It has no feeders but the little mountain rills, yet it never rises nor falls. Donner Lake, close by, freezes hard every winter. Why Lake Tahoe does not, is a question which no scientist has ever been able to explain.

If there are any consumptives here I urge them to go out there, renew their age, make their bodies hale and hearty, in the pure magnificent air of Lake Tahoe. If it don't cure them, I will bury them—I shall be glad to do it. I will give them a funeral that will be a comfort to them as long as they live. But it *will* cure them. I met a man there—he had been a man once—now he was nothing but a shadow and a very poor shadow at that—and that man had come there deliberately to die, and what a sickly failure he made of it! He was in dead earnest. He had heard that this air was easy and soothing to breathe, as God knows it is; and he had simply come out there to have what comfort he might whilst life ebbed away. And he had brought along a plan of his private graveyard, and pictures and drawings of different kinds of coffins and hearses, and such things; and he never did anything but sit around and study that graveyard, and figure at coffins, and such things, trying to make up his mind which kind he liked best, or which kind would be most becoming.

Well, I met that man three months afterward. He was chasing mountain sheep over mountains seven miles high, with a Sharps' rifle. He didn't get them, but he was chasing them just the same. He had used up his graveyard plans and things for wadding and had sent home for some more. Such a cure as that was! Why, when I first saw that man his clothes fitted him about as a circus tent fits the tent-pole; now they were snug to him; they stuck to him like postage stamps, and he weighed a ton. Yes, he weighed more than a ton, but I will throw in the odd ounces, I'm not particular about that, eleven I think it was. I know what I am talking about, for I took him to a hay scales and weighed him myself. A lot of us stood on there with him. But, really, that was a remarkable cure. I have exaggerated it a little. You might not have noticed it. But still it was a cure and a very remarkable one. I wish you would not heed my nonsense, but simply take note of my earnest word. I think if I could only persuade one invalid to go out there I should feel as if I had done one thing worth having accomplished. I am really sincere about that.

And if there is a sportsman in this audience, I say to him, shoulder your gun and go out there. It's the noblest hunting ground on earth. You can hunt there a year and never find anything—except mountain sheep; but you can't get near enough to shoot one. You can see plenty of them with a spyglass. Of course you can't shoot mountain sheep with a spyglass. It is our American Shamwah (I believe that is the way the word is pronounced—I don't know), with enormous horns, inhabiting the roughest mountain fastnesses, so exceedingly wild that it is impossible to get within rifle-shot of it. There was no other game in that country when I was there—except seven-up; though one can see a

California quail now and then—a proud, stately, beautiful bird, with a curved and graceful plume on top of its head. But you can't shoot one. You might as well try to kill a cast iron dog. They don't mind a mortal wound any more than a man would mind a scratch.

I had supposed in my innocence that silver mining was nice, easy business, and that of course silver lay around loose on the hillsides, and that all you had to do was to pick it up, and that you could tell it from any other substance on account of its brightness and its white metallic look. Then came my disappointment; for I found that silver was merely scattered through quartz rock. Gold is found in cement veins, in quartz veins, loosely mingled with the earth, in the sand in beds of rivers, but I never heard of any other house or home for silver to live in than quartz rock. This rock is of a dull whitish color faintly marked with blue veins. A fine powder of silver ore makes these blue veins and this yields $30 in bullion. A little dab of silver that I could crowd in my mouth came out of this 2,000 pounds of solid rock. I found out afterward that thirty-dollar rock was mighty profitable. Then they showed me some more rock which was a little more clouded, that was worth $50 a ton. The bluer and darker the rock the richer it was. Sometimes you could find it worth $400, $500, and $600 a ton. At rare intervals rock can be found that is worth $1,500 and $2,000 per ton, and at rarer intervals you would see a piece of quartz that had a mass of pure silver in its grip, large as a child's head—more than pure, because it always has a good deal of gold mixed up in its composition. The wire silver is Nature's aristocratic jewelry. The quartz crystallizes and becomes perfectly clear, just as clear and faultless as the diamond, and almost as radiant in beauty. Nature, down there in the depths of the earth, takes one of these quartz rocks, shapes a cavity, and right in its heart imprisons a delicate little coil of serpentine, pure white, aristocratic silver.

It was uphill work, this silver mining. There were plenty of mines, but it required a fortune to work one; for tons of worthless rock must be ground to powder to get at the silver. I was the owner of a hundred silver mines, yet I realized that I was the poorest man on earth. Couldn't sell to anybody; couldn't pay my board; so I had to go to work in a quartz mill at ten dollars a week. A nice place, truly, for the proprietor of a hundred silver mines! I was glad to get that berth, but I couldn't keep it. I don't know why; I was the most careful workman they ever had. They said so. I took more pains with my work than anybody else. I was shoveling sand—tailings as they call it. It is silver-bearing rock that has been ground up and worked over once. It is then saved and worked over again. I was so particular about it that I have sat still for one hour and a half and studied about the best way to shovel that sand. And if I couldn't cipher it out in my mind just so, I wouldn't go shoveling around recklessly—I would leave it alone until the next day. Many a time when I have been carrying sand from one pile to another, thirty or forty feet apart, I would get started with a pailful when a splendid idea would strike me and I would carry that sand right back and sit down and think about it. Like as not I would get so absorbed in it as to go to sleep. I almost always go to sleep when I am excited.

Why, I always knew there must be some tiptop, first-rate way to move that sand. At last I discovered it. I went to the boss, and told him that I had got just the thing, the very best and quickest way to get that sand from one pile to the other. And he says, "I'm awful glad to hear it." You never saw a man so uplifted as he was. It appeared to take a load off his breast—a load of sand, I suppose. And I said, "What you want now is a cast iron pipe about thirteen or fourteen feet in diameter, and, say, forty feet long. And you want to prop one end of that pipe up about thirty-five or forty feet off the ground. And then you want a revolving belt—just work it with the waste steam from the engine—a revolving belt with a revolving chair in it. I am to sit in that chair, and have a Chinaman down there to fill up the bucket with sand, and pass it up as I come around and I am just to soar up there and tilt it into that pipe, and there you are. It is as easy as rolling off a log." You never saw a man so overcome with admiration—so overwhelmed. Before he knew what he was about he discharged me. He said I had too much talent to be fooling away my time in a quartz mill.

If you will permit me, I would like to illustrate the ups and downs of fortune in the mining country with just a little personal experience of my own. I had a cabin mate by the name of Higbie—a splendid good fellow. One morning the camp was thrown into a fearful state of excitement, for the "Wide West" had struck a lead black with native silver and yellow with gold. The butcher had been dunning us a week or two. Higbie went up and brought a handful away and he sat studying and examining it, now and then soliloquizing in this manner: "That stuff never came out of the Wide West in the world." I told him it did, because I saw them hoist it out of the shaft. Higbie went away by himself, and came back in a couple of hours perfectly overcome with excitement. He came in, closed the door, went and looked out of the window to make sure there was nobody in the neighborhood, and said to me, "We are worth a million of dollars. The Wide West be hanged—that's a blind lead." Said I: "Higbie, are you *really* in earnest? Say it again: say it strong, Higbie." He replied: "Just as sure as I am standing here, it's a blind lead. We're rich." Poverty had vanished and we could buy that town and pay for it, and six more just like it. A blind lead is one that doesn't crop out above the ground like an ordinary quartz lead. The Wide West had simply tapped it in their shaft and we had discovered it. It belonged to us. It was our property and there wouldn't anybody in the camp dispute that fact. We took into partnership the foreman of the Wide West, and the Wide West had to stop digging. We were the lions of Esmeralda. People wanted to lend us money; other people wanted to sell us village lots on time; and the butcher brought us meat enough for a barbecue and went away without his pay.

Now there is a rule that a certain amount of work must be done on a new claim within the first ten days, or the claim is forfeited to anyone who may first take it up. Now I was called away to nurse an old friend who was dangerously ill at the Nine-Mile Ranch, and I just wrote a note and threw it into the window telling Higbie where I was gone. The fellow I went to nurse was an irascible sort of fellow, and while carrying him from the vapor bath I let my end of him fall, we had a quarrel and I started for home. When I reached there, I saw a vast concourse of people over at the claim and the thought struck me that we were richer than ever, probably worth two million certain. Presently I met Higbie looking like a ghost, and says I: "What on earth is the matter?" "Well," he says, "you didn't do the work on the mine. I depended on you. The foreman's mother dying in California, he didn't do the work, our claim is forfeited and we are ruined. We haven't a cent." We went home to the cabin. I looked down at the floor. There was my note, and beside it was a note from Higbie, telling me that he was going away to look for another mine which wouldn't have amounted to anything even if he had found it, in comparison with our claim.

It don't seem possible that there could be three as big fools in one small town, but we were there, and I was one of them. For once in my life I was absolutely a millionaire for just ten days by the watch. I was just ready to go into all kinds of dissipation and I am really thankful that this was a chapter in the history of my life, although at the time of course I did a great deal of weeping and gnashing my teeth. When I lost that million my heart was broken and I wanted to pine away and die, but I couldn't borrow money to live on while I did so, and I had to give that up. Everything appeared to go against me. Of course I might have suicided but that was kind of disagreeable.

I had written a few letters for the press, and just in the nick of time I received a letter from the Virginia City *Daily Enterprise* offering me $25 a week to go and be a reporter on that paper. I could hardly believe it, but this was no time for foolishness and I was in for anything. I never had edited anything, but if I had been offered the job of translating Josephus from the original Hebrew I should have taken it. If I had translated Josephus I would have thrown in as many jokes as I could for the money, and made him readable. I would have had a variety, if I had to write him all up new.

Well, I walked that 130 miles in pretty quick time and took the berth. Have you ever considered what straits reporters are sometimes pushed to in furnishing the public with news? Why, the first day items were so scarce, I couldn't find an item anywhere, and just as I was on the verge of despair, as luck would have it there came in a lot of emigrants with their wagon trains. They had been fighting with the Indians and got the worst of it. I got the names of their killed and wounded, and then by and by there was another train came in. They hadn't had any trouble and of course I was disappointed, but I did the best I could under the circumstances. I cross-questioned the boss emigrant and found that they were going right on through and wouldn't come back to make trouble, so I got his list of names and added to my killed and wounded, and I got ahead of all the other papers. I put that wagon train through the bloodiest Indian fight ever seen on the plains. They came out of that conflict covered with glory. The chief editor said he didn't want any better reporter than I was. I said: "You just bring on your Indians and fetch out your emigrants, leave me alone, and I will make the fur fly. I will hang a scalp on every sagebrush between here and the Missouri border."

That was all first-rate, but by and by items got low again and I was downhearted. I was miserable, because I couldn't strike an item. At last fortune favored me again. A couple of dear delightful desperadoes got into a row right before me and one of them shot the other. I stepped right up there and got the victim to give me his last words exclusively for the *Enterprise,* and I added some more to them so as to be sure to get ahead of the other papers, and then I turned to the desperado. Said I, "You are a stranger to me, sir, but you have done me a favor which I can never sufficiently thank you for. I shall ever regard you as a benefactor." And I asked him if he could lend me a half a dollar. We always borrowed a piece whenever we could—it was a public custom. The thought then struck me that I could raise a mob and hang on to the other desperado, but the officers got ahead of me and took him into custody. They were down on us and would always do any little mean thing like that, to spite us. And so I was fairly launched in literature, in the business of doing good. I love to do good. It is our duty. I think when a man does good all the time his conscience is so clear. I like to do right and be good, though there is a deal more fun in the other thing.

Now you see by my sort of experience a man may go to bed at night not worth a cent and wake up in the morning to find himself immensely wealthy, and very often he is a man who has a vast cargo of ignorance. To illustrate my point I will give you a story about a couple of those fresh nabobs whose names were Colonels Jim and Jack. Colonel Jim had seen considerable of the world, but Colonel Jack was raised down in the backwoods of Arkansas. These gentlemen after their good luck determined on a pleasure trip to New York; so they went to San Francisco, took a steamer, and in due time arrived in the great metropolis.

While passing along the street, Colonel Jack's attention was distracted by the hacks and splendid equipages he saw, and he says: "Well I've heard about these carriages all my life and I mean to have a ride in one. I don't care what it costs." So Colonel Jim stepped to the edge of the sidewalk and ordered a handsome carriage. Colonel Jack says: "No, you don't. None of your cheap turnouts for me. I'm here to have a good time, and money's no object. I'm going to have the best rig this country affords. You stop that yellow one there with the pictures on it." So they got into the empty omnibus and sat down. Colonel Jack says: "Well! ain't it gay? Ain't it nice? Windows and pictures and cushions, till you can't rest. What would the boys think of this if they could see us cut such a swell in New York? I wish they could see us. What is the name of this?" Colonel Jim told him it was a barouche.

After a while he poked his head out in front and said to the driver, "I say, Johnny, this suits *me.* We want this shebang all day. Let the horses go." The driver loosened the strap and passed his hand in for the fare. Colonel Jack, thinking that he wanted to shake hands, shook him heartily and said, "You understand me. You take care of me and I'll take care of you." He put a twenty-dollar gold piece into the driver's hand. The driver says, "I can't change that." Colonel Jack replied, "Put it into your pocket, I don't want any change. We're going to ride it out."

In a few minutes the bus stopped and a young lady got in. Colonel Jack stared at her. Pretty soon she got out her money to pay the driver. Colonel Jack says, "Put up your money, Miss; you're perfectly welcome to ride here just as long as you want to, but this barouche is chartered and we can't let you pay." Soon an old lady got in. Colonel Jack told her to "sit down. Don't be at all uneasy, everything is paid for and as free as if you were in your own turnout, but you can't pay a cent." Pretty soon two or three gentlemen got in, and ladies with children. Colonel Jack says, "Come right along. Don't mind us. Free blowout." By and by the crowd filled all the seats and were standing up, while the others climbed up on top. He nudged the Colonel Jim and says, "Colonel, what kind of cattle do they have here? If this don't bang anything I ever saw. Ain't they friendly, and so awful cool about it, but they ain't sociable." But I have related enough of that circumstance to illustrate the enormous simplicity of those unfledged biddies of fortune.

I reported on that morning newspaper three years, and it was pretty hard work. But I enjoyed its attractions. Reporting is the best school in the world to get a knowledge of human beings, human nature, and human ways. A nice, gentlemanly reporter—I make no references—is well treated by everybody. Just think of the wide range of his acquaintanceship, his experience of life and society. No other occupation brings a man into such familiar sociable relations with all grades and classes of people. The last thing at night—midnight—he goes browsing around after items among police and jailbirds, in the lockup, questioning the prisoners, and making pleasant and lasting friendships with some of the worst people on earth. And the very next evening he gets himself up regardless of expense, puts on all the good clothes his friends have got—goes and takes dinner with the Governor, or the Commander in Chief of the District, the United States Senator, and some more of the upper crust of society. He is on good terms with all of them, and is present at every public gathering, and has easy access to every variety of people. Why, I breakfasted almost every morning with the Governor, dined with the principal clergyman, and slept in the station house.

A reporter has to lie a little, of course, or they would discharge him. That is the only drawback to the profession. This is why I left it. I am different from Washington; I have a higher and grander standard of principle. Washington could not lie. I *can* lie but *won't*. Reporting is fascinating, but then it is distressing to have to lie so. Lying is bad—lying is very bad. Every individual in this house knows that by experience. I think that for a man to tell a lie when he can't make anything by it, is wrong.

When I finished reporting on that paper they made me chief editor. I lasted just a week. I edited that paper six days, and then I had five duels on my hands. I wouldn't have minded that if it had been the custom for those other people to challenge me. Then I would have simply declined with thanks. But it was not so. If you abused a man in the paper, if you called him names—they had no rights there such as we have—if the man didn't like it, you had to challenge him, and shoot him. Of course I didn't want to do this, but the publisher said it was the custom—society must be protected. If I could not do the duties of my position, he would have to hire somebody else.

I didn't mind the first three or four men; but the other man—I was after him. I knew he didn't want to fight, so I was going to make all the reputation out of him I could. He got touched at something I said about him—I don't know what it was now—I called him a thief, perhaps. He fought very shy of me at first, and so I plied him with bloodthirsty challenges all the more. At last he began to take an interest in this thing. It seemed as though he really was going to enter into it at last. All our boys were delighted at the prospect, but I was not. This was not a turn I was expecting in things.

I had taken for my second a fiery, peppery little fellow, named Steve, full of fight and anxious to have this thing fixed up right away. He took me over into a little ravine beyond the town to practice. It was the custom to fight with Colt's heavy revolvers at five steps. We borrowed a stable door for a mark from a gentleman who was absent. We set up that stable door, and then we propped a fence rail up against the middle to represent my antagonist, and put a squash on it to represent his head. He was a very light thin man, *very* thin—the poorest kind of material for a duel—you could not expect to do anything with a scattering shot at all. But he made a splendid line shot, and it was the line that I practiced on principally.

But there was no success about it. I could not hit the rail, and there was no need that I should hit the rail; the rail did not really represent him. It was a little too thin and narrow. But the squash was all right. Well, I could not hit the rail, and I could not hit the squash, and, finally, when I found I could not hit the door, either, I got a little discouraged. But when I noticed that I crippled one of the boys occasionally, I thought it was not so bad—I was dangerous with a pistol, but not reliable.

Finally we heard some shooting going on over in the other ravine. We knew what that meant. The other party was practicing. I didn't feel comfortable. They might straggle over the ridge, and see what was going on, and when they saw no bullet hole in the barn door, it would be too much encouragement for them. Just then a little bird, a little larger than a sparrow, lit on the sagebrush near by. Steve whipped out his revolver and shot its head off. The boys picked up the bird, and we were talking about it, when the other dueling party came over the ridge, and came down to see what was going on. When the second saw the bird he said, "How far off was that?" Steve said about thirty steps. "Who did that?" "Why, Twain, man, of course." "Did he, indeed! Can he do that often?" "Well, he can do that about four times in five."

I knew that little rascal was lying, but I didn't like to tell him so. I was one of those kind of men that don't like to be too frank or too familiar in a matter like that, so I didn't say anything. But it was a comfort to see those fellows' under jaws drop; to see them turn blue about the gills and look sick. They went off, and got their man, and took him home, and when I got home I found a little note from those parties, peremptorily declining the fight. How sore the boys were! How indignant they were! And so was I! But I was not distressed about it. I thought I could stand it, perhaps.

Well, I was out of that scrape, and I didn't want to get into any more of them. I turned the other four duels over to Steve, who wanted them. But when those people found out afterward that he did that shooting, he didn't get any good out of his duels. They wouldn't fight him.

All that was in my younger days, when I didn't know much—which I do now. I didn't know any better then, but now I am bitterly opposed to dueling. I think that dueling is immoral, and has a bad tendency, and I think it is every man's duty to frown down and discourage dueling. I do. I discourage it on all occasions. If a man were to challenge me now, I would go and take that man by the hand, and lead him to a quiet, private room—and kill him!

Ladies and gentlemen, after thanking you heartily for the attention you have given me this evening, I desire to wish you a very pleasant good night, and at the same time assure you earnestly that I have told nothing but the truth, and I have hardly exaggerated that.

Alternate Conclusion: following the story of Colonel Jack and Colonel Jim

When I told the chairman of the society this evening that I wanted to change my subject he said it was a little risky; he didn't know about it, but I pleaded so hard and said the only reason was I didn't want to talk that Artemus Ward lecture because it had been printed in the papers. I told him that I would put in a little scrap from the Artemus Ward lecture, just enough to cover the advertisement, and then I wouldn't be telling any lies. Besides, this anecdote had a moral to it. Well, that moral got him.

As nearly as I can cipher it out, the newspaper reporter has got us lecturers at a disadvantage. He can either make a synopsis or do most anything he wants to. He ought to be generous, and praise us or abuse us, but not print our speeches. Artemus Ward was bothered by a shorthand reporter, and he begged him not to do him the injustice to garble his speech. He says, "You can't take it all down as I utter it." The reporter said, "If you utter anything I can't take down I will agree not to print the speech." Along in the lecture he tipped the reporter a wink and he told the following anecdote. Whistle wherever the stars occur. If you can't, get somebody that can.

He said that several gentlemen were conversing in a hotel parlor and one man sat there who didn't have anything to say. By and by the gentlemen all went out except one of the number and the silent man. Presently the man reached out and touched the gentleman and says,

" * * I think, sir, I have seen you somewhere before. I am not * * sure where it was or * * when it was * * but I know I have * * seen you." The gentleman says, "Very likely; but what do you whistle for?" " * * I'll tell you all about it * * I used to stammer * * fearfully and I courted a * * girl and she wouldn't have me because I was afflicted with such an * * infirmity. I went to a doctor and * * he * * told me that every time I * * went to stammer * * that I must whistle, which I * * did, and it * * completely cured me. But don't you know that * * girl * * wouldn't have me at last, for she * * said that * * she wouldn't talk to a man that whistled as I did * * . She'd as soon hold a conversation with a wheelbarrow that wanted * * greasing."

Ladies and gentlemen: For three or four days I have had it in my mind to throw away that other lecture, but I never had the pluck to do it until tonight. The audience seemed to look friendly, and as I had been here before I felt a little acquainted. I thought I would make the venture. I sincerely thank you for the help you have given me, and I bid you good night.

Text / Composite, based upon: "Mark Twain," Chicago *Tribune,* December 18, 19, 24, 1871; "Mark Twain," Lansing *State Republican,* December 21, 1871; "Mark Twain," Columbus *Ohio State Journal,* January 6, 1872; "Mark Twain," Wheeling *Intelligencer,* January 11, 1872; "Roughing It," *Trouble:* 304–21.

a boy like me, who could hardly say that he had ever been away from home / From 1853 until the overland journey in 1861, Sam Clemens had spent more time away from home than he did in Hannibal. As a tramp printer he had visited New York, Philadelphia, and Cincinnati. As a Mississippi pilot he was familiar with St. Louis, New Orleans, and all the towns between.

Sharps' rifle / A breech-loading rifle named for the American inventor, Christian Sharps (1811–74). Also known as a "Beecher's Bible" because Henry Ward Beecher was involved in the project of furnishing rifles to Kansas emigrants in 1856.

Higbie / Calvin H. Higbie was a partner of Sam Clemens during his prospecting days in Aurora, Nevada, in 1862. According to *MTA,* 2:257, their residence was not a cabin but "a cotton-domestic lean-to at the base of a mountain." Mark Twain dedicated *Roughing It* to Higbie: "an honest man, a genial comrade, and a steadfast friend."

Esmeralda / A mining district about 100 miles south by west of Carson City, Nevada.

Steve / Stephen H. Gillis (1826–1912). He was a fellow reporter and crony of Mark Twain in Virginia City, a perpetrator of hoaxes, and probably the instigator of the abortive duel with James Laird, of the Virginia City *Union* in May 1864.

· 13 ·

When Mark Twain was preparing for his first New York lecture in Cooper Union in 1867, he expected James W. Nye, senator from Nevada and former territorial and state governor, to come from Washington to introduce the speaker. But Nye did not appear, offered no apology, and later said that he had never intended to do any favors for "a damned secessionist." Mark Twain, nursing a grudge against the governor, made a few unflattering remarks about him preliminary to a "Roughing It" lecture in New York in 1872.

On Governor Nye

Steinway Hall, New York, January 24, 1872

He was a real father to those poor Nevada Indians. He gave them, without regard to their sex or age, blankets and hoopskirts. You could see an Indian chief with a string of blacking boxes around his neck, and over his red blanket four or five of those hoopskirts, walking the streets as happy as a clam, with his hands sticking out of the slats. And yet, notwithstanding all the efforts and civilizing kindness of the good governor, those Indians didn't step out of their savage condition—they were just as degraded as if they had never seen a hoopskirt.

Text / "Mark Twain's Lecture," New York *Herald*, January 25, 1872.

hoopskirts / The apparently absurd allusion was based on fact. The San Rafael, California, *Marin County Journal* reported, August 10,

1861: "Gov. Nye brought some goods with him from New York for distribution among the Indians. Before starting out last Monday, the goods were overhauled and a fine assortment of hoops were found among the lot."

· 14 ·

The Aldine, *a monthly published in New York, called itself "A Typographic Art Journal." In April 1871, it published a picture and "An Autobiography" of Mark Twain. He said: "I was born November 30, 1835. I continue to live, just the same." The 1872 dinner, given by the publisher, James Sutton, and the editor, R. H. Stoddard, attracted such banqueting and literary lights as Schuyler Colfax, E. C. Stedman, George P. Putnam, and Bayard Taylor. Mark Twain's speech was reported to have been received with "shouts of laughter."*

Dinner Speech

The Aldine *Dinner, St. James Hotel, New York,*
Early February 1872

Gentlemen, I would rather address a "stag" dinner party than any other assemblage in the world, for the reason that when you make a point, those who have been listening always applaud, and those who have been talking to each other and did not hear it, applaud louder than anybody else, and if I only had a speech prepared for this occasion, I would take genuine delight in delivering it. But I got the notification to be present at this dinner this evening, at half-past eleven o'clock this morning to pay what I owe to the *Aldine* establishment; and I had to leave an hour after that in order that I might take the trip, so I had no opportunity to prepare a speech, and I am not one of those geniuses who can make a speech *impromptu.* I have made a great many happy impromptu speeches but I had time to prepare them.

Now, it is singular, and I suppose that, but for circumstances which happened when I was fourteen years of age, I might have rushed blindly into real impromptu speeches, and injured myself a good deal. This circumstance, which happened when I was fourteen years of age, has always protected me against anything of that kind, and it has led me to think a good deal. Now, I don't think a good deal, generally of what may probably be the moving springs of human nature. I put that in merely because it is a good expression. I mean it has led me to question in my own mind, what may probably have been the incidents in a man's life which have remained with him longest; whether they are important incidents or whether they are merely trivial ones. I have almost come to the conclusion that the things that stay longest by man, and shape his action in after life, are really things of trivial importance.

Now, I call your attention to the fact, in support of this argument, that Newton when he was—well, I don't know what he was doing now; I make no insinuations against Newton; I don't know what he was doing in the apple orchard, but you know he saw the apple fall, and that suggested the idea of the attraction of gravitation—I call your attention again to that expression and then again, one of the greatest inventors that ever lived—I am sorry for your instruction, I cannot tell his name—was led into this matter of gravitation by having to wait upon his mother while she was hearing confession, and, seeing the pendulum move back and forward—there was nothing else for him to contemplate—and that set him into this matter of looking at mechanics, and he invented a great many things—I don't know what they were, now it was trivial you know. And Galileo, loafing around in the Cathedral at Pisa, not knowing what he was there for, or how he was putting in his time, but he saw and took note of the gentle vibration of the chandelier to and fro, and through that invented the pendulum, which is understood to have made a revolution in mechanics, and I suppose it has. I take these learned things for granted.

All these are trivial matters, but they brought about vast results. Now the thing that made the deepest impression on my mind, and has lasted until this moment, was a matter itself essentially trivial. It occurred when I was a boy, and it has protected me, up to this time, against making a speech when I hadn't a speech prepared. It was a remark made by a friend. He said, "I could have ketched them cats if I had on a good ready." Now, at first glance, that don't appear to convey an idea, but it does, and the meat of it is this: don't do anything unless you are prepared to do it, therefore, until this moment, I never made a speech unless I had that speech all set down and ready.

This incident is of no consequence to you at all, and yet I never made a speech in my life unless I tried to inculcate a moral; unless I tried to convey instruction, and if I can make you better men than you are—it is not for me to say there is room for it, though I suppose there is. If I can make you wiser than you are, or if I can protect you in after life as I have been protected, let me do it here, even if I perish on the spot.

Now this thing occurs in this wise. As trivial as it is, it is a matter to be treasured, I think, and remembered. When I was fourteen, as I remarked before, I was living with my parents, who were very poor and correspondingly honest. We had a youth living with us by the name of Jim Wolfe. He was an excellent fellow, seventeen years old, and very diffident. He and I slept together—virtuously—and one very bitter winter's night, a cousin Mary of mine—she's married now and gone—gave what they called a candy pulling, in those days in the West, and they took the saucers of hot candy outside of the house into the snow, under a sort of old bower that came out from the eaves—it was a sort of an ell then, all covered with vines—to cool this hot candy in the snow, and they were all sitting around there, and in the meantime we were gone to bed; we were not invited to attend this party, we were too young. All these young ladies and gentlemen assembled there, and Jim and I were in bed. There was about four inches of snow on this ell, and our window looked out on to it, and it was frozen hard.

A couple of tomcats—it is possible one of them might have been of the other sex—were assembled on the chimney in the middle of this ell, and they were growling at a fearful rate, and switching their tails about and going on, and we couldn't sleep at all. Finally Jim said, "For two cents I'd go out and snake them cats off that chimney," so I said, "Of course you would"; well, he said, "Well, I would; I have a mighty good notion to do it"; says I, "Of course you have; certainly you have, you have a great notion to do it." I hoped he might try it, but I was afraid he wouldn't. Finally I did get his ambition up, and he raised the window and climbed out on that icy roof, with nothing on but his socks and a very short shirt. He went climbing along on all fours on the roof towards this chimney where the cats were. In the meantime these young ladies and gentlemen were enjoying themselves down under the eaves, and when Jim got almost to that chimney he made a pass at the cats, and his heels flew up and he shot down and crashed through those vines, and lit in the midst of the ladies and gentlemen, and sat down in those hot saucers of candy, and there was a general stampede, of course, and he came upstairs dropping pieces of chinaware and candy all the way up, and when he got up there—now, anybody in the world would have gone into profanity or something calculated to relieve the mind under such circumstances, but he didn't; he scraped the candy off his legs, nursed his blisters a little, and said, "I could have ketched them cats if I had on a good ready."

Now, I say this, that if the opportunity had so fallen out that I could have had ample opportunity to get up a speech, I could have gotten up a speech that would have sent you all—home—happy or otherwise; I could have gotten up a speech that would have done honor to this occasion and to me, but under the circumstances, I have had no opportunity, and I could not get up such a speech, but as long as you live, if you remember the circumstances at all, you will remember that if I had on a good ready, I would have caught these literary cats here present. Now, I won't bore you any further, but I will simply say that I am glad to be present here, glad to help to celebrate this occasion, the new era of enlarged prosperity for *The Aldine,* and also the calling to the editorial chair of a gentleman of culture like Mr. Stoddard, and I am glad to be able to sit with so bright a company as this, and hope you will excuse further remarks from yours truly.

Text / " 'Mark Twain' in New York," *The Buyers' Manual and Business Guide,* compiled by J. Price and C. S. Haley (San Francisco, 1872):74–76. Partially published as "Cats and Candy," *MTS* (10):262–64, the occasion is incorrectly identified.

Stoddard / Richard Henry Stoddard (1825–1903). American writer. He was reviewer for the New York *World* (1860–70), editor of *The Aldine* (1869–74), and literary editor of the New York *Mail and Express* (1880–1903). Among his books are *Poems* (1852), and *Recollections Personal and Literary* (1903).

· 15 ·

Mark Twain made his first trip to England in August 1872, going over to keep Roughing It *out of the hands of British pirates like John Camden Hotten, and also to take notes for a book on Britain, which he never wrote. He was received with lavish hospitality. Called the Belle of London, he was guest of honor at dinners of the Savage Club, Whitefriars Club, the Sheriffs of London, and the Lord Mayor, as well as at convivial gatherings in country homes and London town houses. He met men eminent in the arts and professions: Tom Hood, Robert Browning, Charles Reade, Henry Irving, Alexander Kinglake, Charles Kingsley, Henry M. Stanley, Stopford Brooke, Richard Monkton Milnes, and others. It was a heady experience for Mark Twain. He had received no such flattering attention back home, where conservative opinion regarded him as a wild westerner of erratic talent, a literary upstart not worthy of mention in the same breath as the Brahmins of New England. At the Savage Club dinner he was greeted with a roar of cheers. Moncure D. Conway, reporting the event, described him as "tall, thin, grave, with something of the look of a young divinity student fallen among worldlings."*

Dinner Speech

Savage Club, London, ca. September 22, 1872

Mr. Chairman and gentlemen, it affords me sincere pleasure to meet this distinguished club, a club which has extended its hospitalities and its cordial welcome to so many of my countrymen. I hope you will excuse these clothes. I am going to the theater; that will explain these clothes. I have other clothes than these. Judging human nature by what I have seen of it, I suppose that the customary thing for a stranger to do when he stands here is to make a pun on the name of this club, under the impression, of course, that he is the first man that that idea has occurred to. It is a credit to our human nature—not a blemish upon it; for it shows that underlying all our depravity (and God knows, and *you* know, we are depraved enough) and all our sophistication, and untarnished by them, there is a sweet germ of innocence and simplicity still. When a stranger says to me, with a glow of inspiration in his eye, some gentle innocuous little thing about

"Twain" and "one flesh," and all that sort of thing, I don't try to crush that man into the earth—no. I feel like saying: "Let me take you by the hand, sir; let me embrace you: I have not heard that pun for weeks." We *will* deal in palpable puns. We *will* call parties named "King" Your Majesty, and we will say to the Smiths that we think we have heard that name before somewhere. Such is human nature. We cannot alter this. It is God that made us so for some good and wise purpose. Let us not repine. But though I may seem strange, may seem eccentric, I mean to refrain from punning upon the name of this club, though I could make a very good one if I had time to think about it—a week.

I cannot express to you what entire enjoyment I find in this first visit to this prodigious metropolis of yours. Its wonders seem to me to be limitless. I go about as in a dream—as in a realm of enchantment—where many things are rare and beautiful, and all things are strange and marvelous. Hour after hour I stand—I stand spellbound, as it were—and gaze upon the statuary in Leicester Square. I visit the mortuary effigies of noble old Henry VIII, and Judge Jeffreys, and the preserved gorilla, and try to make up my mind which of my ancestors I admire the most. I go to that matchless Hyde Park and drive all *around* it, and then I start to enter it at the Marble Arch—and—am induced to "change my mind." It is a great benefaction—is Hyde Park. There, in his hansom cab, the invalid can go—the poor, sad child of misfortune—and insert his nose between the railings, and breathe the pure health-giving air of the country and of heaven. And if he is a swell invalid, who isn't obliged to depend upon parks for his country air, he can drive inside—if he owns his vehicle. I drive round and round Hyde Park, and the more I see of the edges of it the more grateful I am that the margin is extensive.

And I have been to the Zoological Gardens. What a wonderful place that is! I have never seen such a curious and interesting variety of wild animals in any garden before—except "Mabille." I never believed before that there were so many different kinds of animals in the world as you can find there—and I don't believe it yet. I have been to the British Museum. I would advise you to drop in there some time when you have nothing to do—for five minutes—if you have never been there. It seems to me the noblest monument that this nation has yet erected to her greatness. I say to her, our greatness—as a nation. True, she has built other monuments, and stately ones, as well; but these she has uplifted in honor of two or three colossal demigods who have stalked across the world's stage, destroying tyrants and delivering nations, and whose prodigies will still live in memories of men ages after their monuments shall have crumbled to dust—I refer to the Wellington and Nelson columns, and—the Albert Memorial.

The library at the British Museum I find particularly astounding. I have read there hours together, and hardly made an impression on it. I revere that library. It is the author's friend. I don't care how mean a book is, it always takes one copy. And then, every day that author goes there to gaze at that book, and is encouraged to go on in the good work. And what a touching sight it is of a Saturday afternoon to see the poor careworn clergymen gathered together in that vast reading room cabbaging sermons for Sunday!

You will pardon my referring to these things. Everything in this monster city interests me, and I cannot keep from talking, even at the risk of being instructive. People here seem always to express distances by parables. To a stranger it is just a little confusing to be so parabolic—so to speak. I collar a citizen, and I think I am going to get some valuable information out of him. I ask him how far it is to Birmingham, and he says it is twenty-one shillings and sixpence. Now, we know that don't help a man any who is trying to learn. I find myself down town somewhere, and I want to get some sort of idea of where I am—being usually lost when alone—and I stop a citizen and say: "How far is it to Charing Cross?" "Shilling fare in a cab," and off *he* goes. I suppose if I were to ask a Londoner how far it is from the sublime to the ridiculous, he would try to express it in coin.

But I am trespassing upon your time with these geological statistics and historical reflections. I will not longer keep you from your orgies. 'Tis a real pleasure for me to be here, and I thank you for it. The name of the Savage Club is associated in my mind with the kindly interest and the friendly offices which you lavished upon an old friend of mine who came among you a stranger, and you opened your English hearts to him and gave him welcome and a home—Artemus Ward. Asking that you will join me, I give you his memory.

Text / Moncure D. Conway, "Mark Twain in London," Cincinnati *Commercial,* October 10, 1872; reprinted in Cleveland *Herald,* October 19, 1872. Published as "About London," *MTS*(10):417–21; *MTS*(23):37–41. Both *MTS* texts are misdated.

Savage Club / Founded in 1855, it was a coterie of authors, actors, and bon vivants. Artemus Ward, who had made the club his London headquarters, had been a great favorite, and Mark Twain became equally esteemed. See Aaron Watson, *The Savage Club* (1907).

these clothes / Mark Twain was in full evening dress, white tie and tails. At a Savage Club dinner anybody who wore formal attire was likely to be vigorously ragged. Hence his explanation, which he gave in a meek apologetic voice.

statuary in Leicester Square / It was dilapidated. An equestrian statue of a king was minus head and limbs, and the horse was also incomplete.

Judge Jeffreys / George, first Baron Jeffreys of Wem (1648–89). British jurist. As Lord Chancellor of England, he was notorious for flagrant injustice during the trials, known as "Bloody Assizes," of defendants involved in the Monmouth rebellion of 1685.

that matchless Hyde Park / Public cabs were not admitted to Hyde Park—only fashionable private carriages.

"Mabille" / Jardin Mabille, Paris. It was a popular resort for dancing and other diversions, much frequented by women of easy virtue. In *Innocents Abroad,* Mark Twain says that he and his companions visited Jardin Mabille but did not stay long.

Albert Memorial / The audience appreciated the irony of equating Prince Albert with Wellington and Nelson.

· 16 ·

In a letter to Mother Fairbanks, Mark Twain said that his reception in Britain was like the homecoming of the prodigal son. Assuredly the latchstring was out everywhere for the entertaining American, who was the heir apparent of Artemus Ward, and the fatted calf awaited him wherever he went. Small wonder that he conceived a fondness for England, its people, its ways, and its landscape, that he never entirely lost thereafter.

Dinner Speech

Whitefriars Club, London, ca. October 1872

Gentlemen: I thank you very heartily, indeed, for this expression of kindness toward me. What I have done for England and civilization in the arduous affairs which I have engaged in—that is good—that is so smooth that I will say it again and again—what I have done for England and civilization in the arduous part I have performed I have done with a simple-hearted devotion and no hope of reward. I am proud, I am very proud, that it was reserved for me to find Dr. Livingstone, and for Mr. Stanley to get all the credit. I hunted for that man in Africa, all over seventy-five or one hundred parishes, thousands and thousands of miles in the wilds and deserts, all over the place, sometimes riding Negroes and sometimes traveling by rail. I didn't mind the rail or anything else, so that I didn't come in for the tar and feathers. I found that man at Ujiji—a place you may remember if you have ever been there—and it was a very great satisfaction that I found him just in the nick of time. I found that poor old man deserted by his niggers and by his geographers, deserted by all of his kind, except the gorillas—dejected, miserable, famishing, absolutely famishing; but he was eloquent. Just as I found him he had eaten his last elephant, and he said to me, "God knows where I shall get another." He had nothing to wear, except his venerable and honorable naval suit, and nothing to eat but his diary.

But I said to him, "It's all right, I have discovered you, and Stanley will be here by the four o'clock train, and will discover you officially, and then we will turn to and have a reg'lar good time." I said, "Cheer up, for Stanley has got corn, ammunition, glass beads, hymn books, whiskey and everything which the human heart can desire; he has got all kinds of valuables, including telegraph poles and a few cartloads of money. By this time, communication has been made with the land of Bibles and civilization, and property will advance." And then we surveyed all that country, from Ujiji, through Unanogo and other places, to Unyanyembe. I mention these names simply for your edification, nothing more—do not expect it—particularly as intelligence to the Royal Geographic Society. And then, having filled up the old man, we were all too full for utterance, and departed. We have since then feasted on honors.

Stanley has received a snuff box, and I have received considerable snuff; he has got to write a book and gather in the rest of the credit, and I am going to levy on the copyright and to collect the money. Nothing comes amiss to me—cash or credit; but, seriously, I do feel that Stanley is the chief man, and an illustrious one, and I do applaud him with all my heart. Whether he is an American or a Welshman by birth, or one, or both, matters not to me. So far as I am personally concerned, I am simply here to stay a few months, and to see English people and to learn English manners and customs, and to enjoy myself; so the simplest thing I can do, is to thank you for the toast you have honored me with, and for the remarks you have made, and to wish health and prosperity to the Whitefriars Club, and to sink down to my accustomed level.

Text / Composite, based upon: "On Stanley and Livingstone," *MTS*(10):154–56; *MTS*(23):133–34; San Jose, California, *Mercury,* October 10, 1872.

Dr. Livingstone / David Livingstone (1813–73). He was a Scottish missionary and traveler who made explorations in Africa.

Stanley / Henry Morton Stanley (1841–1904). British explorer. He accompanied the British expedition to Abyssinia (1868) as correspondent for the New York *Herald.* In 1869 Gordon Bennett, of the *Herald,* commissioned him to find Dr. Livingstone, who had set out to explore the lake region of South Africa, but had not been heard from for three years. After finding Livingstone at Ujiji, Stanley was honored by Queen Victoria, although his story, *How I Found Livingstone* (1871), was skeptically received in England.

Royal Geographic Society / A satirical allusion to Stanley's cool reception in England and his failure to conciliate the president of the Royal Geographic Society.

snuff box / Queen Victoria's gift to Stanley was a gold snuff box set with brilliants.

· 17 ·

In November 1872, Mark Twain, announcing that he had been called home, sailed for America where he spent the winter. In May 1873, returning to England with his family, he plunged again into the social whirl of luncheons, teas and banquets, adding to his list of distinguished acquaintances such notable Englishmen as Herbert Spencer, Wilkie Collins, Sir John Millais, and Anthony Trollope. Again he was called upon to respond to toasts at dinners.

After-Dinner Speech

Meeting of Americans, London, July 4, 1873

Mr. Chairman and ladies and gentlemen: I thank you for the compliment which has just been tendered me, and to show my appreciation of it I will not afflict you with many words. It is pleasant to celebrate in this peaceful way, upon this old mother soil, the anniversary of an experiment which was born of war with this same land so long ago, and wrought out to a successful issue by the devotion of our ancestors. It has taken nearly a hundred years to bring the English and Americans into kindly and mutually appreciative relations, but I believe it has been accomplished at last. It was a great step when the two last misunderstandings were settled by arbitration instead of cannon. It is another great step when England adopts our sewing machines without claiming the invention—as usual. It was another when they imported one of our sleeping cars the other day. And it warmed my heart more than I can tell, yesterday, when I witnessed the spectacle of an Englishman ordering an American sherry cobbler of his own free will and accord—and not only that, but with a great brain and level head, reminding the barkeeper not to forget the strawberries. With a common origin, a common literature, a common religion and common drinks, what is longer needful to the cementing of the two nations together in a permanent bond of brotherhood?

This is an age of progress, and ours is a progressive land. A great and glorious land, too—a land which has developed a Washington, a Franklin, a William M. Tweed, a Longfellow, a Motley, a Jay Gould, a Samuel C. Pomeroy, a recent Congress which has never had its equal—(in some respects) and a United States Army which conquered sixty Indians in eight months by tiring them out—which is much better than uncivilized slaughter, God knows. We have a criminal jury system which is superior to any in the world; and its efficiency is only marred by the difficulty of finding twelve men every day who don't know anything and can't read. And I may observe that we have an insanity plea that would have saved Cain. I think I can say, and say with pride, that we have some legislatures that bring higher prices than any in the world.

I refer with effusion to our railway system, which consents to let us live, though it might do the opposite, being our owners. It only destroyed 3,070 lives last year by collisions, and 27,260 by running over heedless and unnecessary people at crossings. The companies seriously regretted the killing of these 30,000 people, and went so far as to pay for some of them—voluntarily, of course, for the meanest of us would not claim that we possess a court treacherous enough to enforce a law against a railway company. But thank heaven the railway companies are generally disposed to do the right and kindly thing without compulsion. I know of an instance which greatly touched me at the time. After an accident the company sent home the remains of a dear, distant old relative of mine in a basket, with the remark, "Please state what figure you hold him at—and return the basket." Now there couldn't be anything friendlier than that.

But I must not stand here and brag all night. However, you won't mind a body bragging a little about his country on the Fourth of July. It is a fair and legitimate time to fly the eagle. I will say only one more word of brag—and a hopeful one. It is this. We have a form of government which gives each man a fair chance and no favor. With us no individual is born with a right to look down upon his neighbor and hold him in contempt. Let such of us as are not dukes find our consolation in that. And we may find hope for the future in the fact that as unhappy as is the condition of our political morality today, England has risen up out of a far fouler since the days when Charles II ennobled courtesans and all political place was a matter of bargain and sale. Be sure there is hope for us yet.

Footnote. At least the above is the speech which I was *going* to make; but our minister, General Schenck, presided, and after the blessing, got up and made a great long inconceivably dull harangue, and wound up by saying that inasmuch as speech-making did not seem to exhilarate the guests much, all further oratory would be dispensed with, during the evening, and we could just sit and talk privately to our elbow-neighbors and have a good sociable time. It is known that in consequence of that remark forty-four perfected speeches died in the womb. The depression, the gloom, the solemnity that reigned over the banquet from that time forth will be a lasting memory with many that were there. By that one thoughtless remark General Schenck lost forty-four of the best friends he had in England. More than one said that night, "And this is the sort of person that is sent to represent us in a great sister empire!"

Text / "After-Dinner Speech," MS, Willard S. Morse Collection, Yale University Library; published as "After-Dinner Speech," *Sketches:* 180–81; "Americans and the English," *MTS* (10):413–16; *MTS* (23):34–36. *Sketches* and *MTS* texts are misdated.

American sherry cobbler / The strawberries Mark Twain mentioned were evidently a refinement not common to our times. Modern formulas specify a tall drink made of sherry, shaved ice, powdered sugar, and citrus fruit, but say nothing about strawberries.

Tweed / William Marcy Tweed (1823–78). American political boss. Involved in corrupt deals with railroads and other profitable commodities, he was head of the notorious Tweed Ring that is said to have defrauded New York City of $30,000,000. Several times brought to trial, he eventually served one year of a twelve-year sentence and later died in the Ludlow Street jail.

Motley / John Lothrop Motley (1814–77). American historian and diplomat. A student of European history, he was United States minister to Austria (1861–67). Among his books are *The Rise of the Dutch Republic* (1856), and *The History of the United Netherlands* (1860–68).

Gould / Jay (originally Jason) Gould (1836–92). American financier. His devious operations with James Fisk and Daniel Drew, particularly with Erie Railroad stocks, were a national scandal. The attempt of this trio to corner the gold market precipitated the Black Friday panic of 1869. Gould was the symbol of greed and fraud, chiefly because his operations were more spectacular than lesser chicanery in an era of widespread corruption, business and political. His eldest daughter, Helen Miller Gould (1868–1938) became well known as a philanthropic apostle of good works, aiding needy students, endowing Y.M.C.A. branches, giving generously to hospitals, and sending Bibles to Mohammedan countries.

Pomeroy / Samuel Clarke Pomeroy (1816–91). American politician. Senator from the new state of Kansas, he was a radical anti-administration Republican. Suspected of bribery to win reelection in 1867, he was faced with evidence of bribery when he sought a third term. The disclosure ended his political career. Nevertheless, he was nominated for the presidency by the National Prohibition party in 1884.

our political morality / *The Gilded Age* (1873), by Mark Twain and Charles Dudley Warner, deals with political and corporate venality rampant after the Civil War. The character of the Honorable Abner Dilworthy, a corrupt Washington politician, is modeled after Senator Pomeroy, and the novel touches upon the Tweed Ring, bought legislatures, railroad swindles, and other scandals of our society. Henry Adams's novel, *Democracy* (1880), is an excoriating analysis of corrupt government, and his *Education* comments frequently on the smoggy moral climate of Washington. The darker pages of Walt Whitman's *Democratic Vistas* (1871) express dismay and indignation over the decay of principle and the breakdown of honesty. In the 1870s our political morality was indeed at a low ebb.

General Schenck / Robert Cumming Schenck (1809–90). American soldier and diplomat. Minister to Brazil (1851–53), he served in the Union Army during the Civil War and was ambassador to Great Britain (1871–76).

· 18 ·

In October 1873, Mark Twain gave the Sandwich Islands lecture for a week at the Queen's Concert Rooms in London and twice in Liverpool. Then he escorted his homesick family back to America, remained a few days, and reembarked for England. By late November he was again in London. Scheduled for three weeks of lectures on the Sandwich Islands, he changed to "Roughing It on the Silver Frontier" after the first week. Some British critics, affectionately recalling the popular Artemus Ward, were inclined to be skeptical about Mark Twain, but he won the approval of the general public. In off moments he resumed the program of sociability and after-dinner speaking.

The Ladies

209th Anniversary Festival of the Scottish Corporation of London, ca. November 1873

I am proud, indeed, of the distinction of being chosen to respond to this especial toast—to "The Ladies"—or to *Woman,* if you please, for that is the preferable term, perhaps; it is certainly the older, and therefore the more entitled to reverence. I have noticed and probably you may have noticed that the Bible, with that plain, blunt honesty which is such a conspicuous characteristic of the Scriptures, is always careful to never even refer to the illustrious mother of all mankind herself as a "lady," but speaks of her as a woman. It is odd but I think you will find that it is so. I am peculiarly proud of this honor, because I think that the toast to women is one which, by right and every rule of gallantry, should take precedence of all others—of the army, the navy, of even royalty itself perhaps, though the latter is not necessary in this day and in this land, for the reason that, tacitly, you do drink a broad general health to *all* good women when you drink the health of the Queen of England and the Princess of Wales.

I have in mind a poem, just now, which is familiar to you all, familiar to everybody. And what an inspiration that was (and how instantly the present toast recalls the verses to all our minds), where the most noble, the most gracious, the purest and sweetest of all poets says:

Woman! O woman—er—
Wom—

However, you remember the lines. And you remember *how* feelingly, how daintily, how almost imperceptibly the verses raise up before you, feature by feature, the ideal of a true and perfect woman; and how, as you contemplate the finished marvel, your homage grows into worship of the intellect that could create so fair a thing out of mere breath, mere words.

And you call to mind, now, as I speak, how the poet, with stern fidelity to the history of all humanity, delivers *this* beautiful child of his heart and his brain over to the trials and sorrows that must come to all, sooner or later, that abide in the earth; and how the pathetic story culminates in that apostrophe—so wild, so regretful, so full of mournful retrospection. The lines run thus:

Alas! Alas!—a—alas!
Alas!—alas!—

and so on. I do not remember the rest. But taken altogether, it seems to me that that poem is the noblest tribute to woman *that* human genius has ever brought forth—and I feel that if I were to talk hours I could not do my great theme completer or more graceful justice than I have now done in simply quoting that poet's matchless words.

The phases of the womanly nature are infinite in their variety. Take any type of woman, and you shall find in it something to respect, something to admire, something to love. And you shall find the whole world joining your heart and hand. Who was more patriotic than Joan of Arc? Who was braver? Who has given us a grander instance of self-sacrificing devotion? Ah! you remember, you remember well, what a throb of pain, what a great tidal wave of grief swept over us all when Joan of Arc fell at Waterloo. Who does not sorrow for the loss of Sappho, the sweet singer of Israel? Who among us does not *miss* the gentle ministrations, the softening influence, the humble piety, of Lucretia Borgia?

Who can join in the heartless libel that says woman is extravagant in dress, when he can look back and call to mind our simple and lowly Mother Eve arrayed in her modification of the Highland costume?

Sir, women have been soldiers, women have been painters, women have been poets. As long as language lives, the name of Cleopatra will live. And not because she conquered George III—but because she wrote those divine lines:

Let dogs delight to bark and bite,
For God hath made them so.

The story of the world is adorned with the names of illustrious ones of our own sex—some of them sons of St. Andrew, too—Scott, Bruce, Burns, the warrior Wallace, Ben Nevis, the gifted Ben Lomond, and the great new Scotchman, Ben Disraeli.

Out of the great plains of history tower whole mountain ranges of sublime women—the Queen of Sheba, Josephine, Semiramis, Sairey Gamp; the list is endless. But I will not call the mighty roll—the names rise up in your own memories at the mere suggestion, luminous with the glory of deeds that cannot die, hallowed by the loving worship of the good and the true of all epochs and all climes.

Suffice it for our pride and our honor that we in our day have added to it such names as those of Grace Darling and Florence Nightingale.

Woman is all that she should be—gentle, patient, long-suffering, *trust*ful, unselfish, full of generous impulses. It is her blessed mission to comfort the sorrowing, plead for the erring, encourage the faint of purpose, succor the distressed, uplift the fallen, befriend the friendless—in a word, afford the healing of her sympathies and a home in her heart for all the bruised and persecuted children of misfortune that knock at its hospitable door. And when I say, God bless her, there is none here present who has known the ennobling affection of a wife, or the steadfast devotion of a mother but in his heart will say, Amen!

Text / Composite, based upon: "The Ladies," MS, Henry W. and Albert A. Berg Collection, New York Public Library; "Mark Twain and the Ladies," London *Observer,* n.d., clipping, MTP; "The Ladies," *MTS*(10):94–98; *MTS*(23):42–45. The *MTS* texts are misdated.

"Let dogs delight," etc. / From *Divine Songs,* by Isaac Watts (1674–1748), British clergyman and hymn writer.

Ben Nevis / Mountain in west Scotland. It is the highest peak in Great Britain, altitude 4,406 feet.

Ben Lomond / Mountain on the east side of Loch Lomond, Scotland, altitude 3,192 feet.

Ben Disraeli / Benjamin Disraeli (1804–81), first earl of Beaconsfield. British statesman and writer. As a novelist he used fiction to advance the political ideas he hoped the conservative party would adopt. He was prime minister (1868, 1874–80); one of his memorable feats was the acquisition of the Suez Canal for England. At the time of Mark Twain's speech Disraeli had recently been made lord rector of Glasgow University.

Josephine / Marie Josephine Rose Tascher de la Pageria (1763–1814). She married Napoleon Bonaparte (1796), who divorced her (1809) because she had produced no heir. A great beauty, she was vain and extravagant, yet much admired for her pleasing manners, remarkable memory, and witty conversation.

Semiramis / A celebrated queen of Assyria (ca. 1250 B.C.). Legends represent her as the beautiful daughter of the fish-goddess, Derca-to, and as a warrior queen who built the city of Babylon, led campaigns against the Persians, Egyptians, Ethiopians, and Libyians, and became the Assyrian goddess, Istar. She was said to have had irresistible sexual charm.

Sairey Gamp / A fat old woman in Dickens's novel, *Martin Chuzzlewit,* "with a husky voice and a moist eye" and a fondness for the bottle.

Grace Darling / (1820–1910). British heroine. When the Forfarshire steamer was wrecked off Lovingstone Light, Farne Islands, on September 6, 1838, she went out in a small boat and rescued nine survivors who were clinging to a rock. For this feat a subscription of £700 was raised for her.

· 19 ·

In the speeches made abroad in the 1870s a recurrent note is that of amity between England and America, Mark Twain developing the theme with his usual blend of humor and seriousness. At an early stage of his public career he was rehearsing for the role he defined many years later as "self-appointed ambassador-at-large of the United States of America—without salary."

The Guests

St. Andrews Society Dinner, London, November 29, 1873

I feel singularly at home in this Scottish society. I have spent so much time in Scotland that everything connected with Scotland is familiar to me. Last summer I spent five weeks in that magnificent city of Edinburgh, resting. I needed rest, and I did rest. I did not know anybody. I did not take any letters of introduction at all. I simply rested and enjoyed myself. From my experience with the Scotch everything belonging to them is familiar, the language, the peculiarities of expression, even the technical things that are national, are simply household words with me. I remember when in Edinburgh I was nearly always taken for a Scotchman. Oh, yes! I had my clothes some part colored tartan, and rather enjoyed being taken for a Scotchman. I stuck a big feather in my cap too, and the people would follow me for miles. They thought I was a Highlander, and some of the best judges in Scotland said they had never seen a Highland costume like mine. What's more, one of those judges fined me for wearing it—out of mere envy, I suppose.

But any man may have a noble, good time in Scotland if they only think he's a native. For breakfast you may have oatmeal poultice—I beg pardon; I mean porridge. Then for dinner you have the fine Scotch game—the blackcock, the spatchcock, the woodcock, the moorcock.

I have simply to return my acknowledgments, and to apologize for not being able to make a speech; but give me fair play, and certainly I can make a speech that will astonish anybody, and nobody more than myself. My present position is a national one, if I may be regarded as representing the United States of America. On that side of the Atlantic there are 40,000,000 of people. They may be respectable, and I will say in conclusion that I do hope "A brother American" will soon cease to be simply a phrase meaning, but will by and by become a reality, when Great Britain and the citizens of America will be brethren indeed.

Text / "Mark Twain as a Scotchman," Lafayette, Indiana, *Courier*, January 14, 1874.

· 20 ·

After two lecture engagements in Liverpool in January 1874, Mark Twain sailed for home, and this time he remained there for a while. When Charles Kingsley came over for a lecture tour soon after, Mark Twain was delighted to introduce him to a Salem audience, also to entertain him and his wife for several days at the Clemens home in Hartford. Livy thought that the visitor was "a most wonderful man," and Mark Twain, too, admired his gentle character, but he was not enthusiastic about Kinglsey's novels.

Introducing the Reverend Charles Kingsley

Essex Institute, Salem, Massachusetts, ca. February 14, 1874

Ladies and gentlemen: I am here to introduce Mr. Charles Kingsley, the lecturer of the evening, and I take occasion to observe than when I wrote the book called *Innocents Abroad* I thought it was a volume which would bring me at once into intimate relation with the clergy. But I could bring evidence to show that from that day to this, this is the first time that I have ever been called upon to perform this pleasant office of vouching for a clergyman and give him a good unbiased start before an audience. Now that my opportunity has come at last, I am appointed to introduce a clergyman who needs no introduction to America.

And although I haven't been requested by the committee to endorse him, I volunteer that, because I think it is a graceful thing to do; and it is all the more graceful from being so unnecessary. But the most unnecessary thing I could do in introducing the Rev. Charles Kingsley would be to sound his praises to you, who have read his books and know his high merits as well as I possibly can, so I waive all that and simply say that in welcoming him cordially to this land of ours, I believe that I utter a sentiment which would go nigh to surprising him or possibly to deafen him, if I could concentrate in my voice the utterance of all those in America who feel that sentiment. And I am glad to say that this kindly feeling toward Mr. Kingsley is not wasted, for his heart is with America, and when he is in his own home the latchstring hangs on the outside of the door, for us. I know this from personal experience; perhaps that is why it has not been considered unfitting that I should perform this office in which I am now engaged. Now for a year, for more than a year, I have been enjoying the hearty hospitality of English friends in England, and this is a hospitality which is growing wider and freer every day toward our countrymen. I was treated so well there, so undeservedly well, that I should always be glad of an opportunity to extend to Englishmen the good offices of our people; and I do hope that the good feeling, the growing good feeling, between the old mother country and her strong, aspiring child will continue to extend until it shall exist over the whole great area of both nations. I have the honor to introduce to you the Rev. Charles Kingsley.

Text / *Eloquence*(R), 5:691–92. The text is misdated and the occasion incorrectly identified.

Charles Kingsley / (1819–75). British clergyman and writer. Canon of Westminster, Cambridge professor, and Christian Socialist, he was a writer of imaginative literature and of vigorous polemics against the Oxford Movement. He is best known for his novels of social import and adventure, among which are: *Alton Locke* (1850), *Hypatia* (1853), and *Westward Ho!* (1855).

his high merits / The irony here is that Mark Twain found no merit. His only comment on Kingsley as a novelist is a remark in a letter to Livy in 1869, *LLMT*:126, "Twichell gave me one of Kingsley's most tiresomest books—Hypatia—and I have tried to read it and can't. I'll try no more."

· 21 ·

The Twain-Kingsley reunion continued when both were guests at a Boston dinner of the Massachusetts Press Association. Kingsley was reported to have made "a short speech," then to have introduced Mark Twain.

Dinner Speech

Massachusetts Press Association, Boston,
February 17, 1874

Ladies and gentlemen: I don't know that I have the faculty inborn in Americans which Mr. Kingsley has called your attention to, but if I haven't it, I shall not take this occasion to confess it; and not having ever been to school I have not the faculty of declamation which the president speaks of. And as I only knew two hours ago that I was to be here, I have naturally come with no speech, because I never knew a man who could deliver an impromptu speech with only two hours to get it up in.

But the presence here of Mr. Kingsley—Canon Kingsley—his title canon has always been a puzzle to me—but his presence here suggests to me an episode of my own, recently, and as, under the old regime—I don't know what the old regime is, but it is something that used to exist before—when called upon, you had the privilege of telling an anecdote or singing a song. Never having sung a song, at least having never succeeded in singing a song, I am still perfectly willing to try now; but I am afraid it would be disagreeable to the audience, so I will tell an anecdote.

When I was crossing over from England the other day, there was a youth on board about sixteen years old, whose nationality I will not expose, who occupied his entire time eating, when there was anything to eat, and thinking about the next meal between times. I don't say he put his mind to it, for he didn't seem to have any mind. When sent out from the table he used to go up into the smoking cabin, and lie around there asking foolish questions. This boy never asked a question during the whole voyage that indicated the presence of knowledge of any kind whatever, and he came to be a perfect nuisance to everybody, and we tried all possible ways of crushing him and make him stop asking these questions.

But, as I said, Canon Kingsley reminds me of one occasion when I came up into the smoking room, in very ill humor—not in the humor a man ought to be in to listen patiently to silly questions. The question the boy began with was aggravating, because everybody knows that the first place a man goes to when he reaches London is Westminster Abbey, and the next place is Shakespeare's burial ground; and that this boy should ask me deliberately and with such innocence about him as he had, if, when I was in London, I went to Westminster Abbey. That is enough to make a man frantic.

I said, "What was it you said?" "When you were in London were you at Westminster Abbey?" "No," I said, "I stopped at Langham's Hotel." "But," he said, "it is not a hotel." "Well," I said, "what is it?" "Why, it is a church." I said, "A minute ago you said it was an abbey." "Well," he said, "it is an abbey and a church too." I said, "I don't know about that. You appear to be getting confused in your statements; how can it be an abbey and a church at the same time?"

There was another gentleman sitting there, whose nationality I will not mention, who said it was perfectly true that an abbey and the church were the same thing. I said I was much obliged to him, and asked him, "Where is this place, this church; is it in London?" "Oh yes!" he says, "of course it is in London. You know where the Parliament buildings are?" "Is it part of the Parliament?" "No," said he. "What has Parliament got to do with it?" I asked. "It has not got anything to do with it; the abbey is close by it." Said I, "Do you know how far Westminster Abbey is from Langham's Hotel, where I lived?" He said, "I suppose you know it is some distance." Said I, "Of course it is some distance." "Five or six miles," said he. "But," said I, "didn't you suppose I knew better than to get up early in the morning and travel four or five miles to church, when there were plenty of churches all around?" He said, "I didn't expect you to go to church." Said I, "What did you expect me to do?" He said, "Look at the monuments and things; monuments of everybody that has done anything and is dead. Their bodies are buried there." I said, "Do you mean to say that they actually take up the planks and bury men under the floor?" He said there were no planks there. I said, "Do they bury them right under the seats?" He said, "Of course they do." Said I, "Is that healthy?" "Well," he said, "I don't know whether it was healthy or not, they do it in all the churches." I said it was a curious custom, I had never heard of anything like it. If any of my friends were in Westminster Abbey I should not want people sitting around on their tombstones. He said, "You didn't hear the canon, then?" "I don't remember," said I; "I am a man of peace and don't know anything about artillery, anyway."

By this time the boy had not yet waked up, but the rest of the company which had gathered around had, and so we stopped the fun. As there is no moral to the anecdote, I won't attempt to put any to it. But, as I said, in the absence of having a speech to make to you, I thought I would simply tell an anecdote in honor of Canon Kingsley.

Text / "Mark Twain and Canon Kingsley," Boston *Advertiser,* n.d., reprinted in *Courant,* February 19, 1874.

· 22 ·

Of several plays written by the would-be playwright, Mark Twain, The Gilded Age *was the most successful. The New York opening was warmly received. President Grant went backstage to compliment John T. Raymond, playing the role of Colonel Sellers, and press notices, even in the* Atlantic Monthly, *were full of praise.*

Curtain Speech

Opening of The Gilded Age, *Park Theater, New York, September 16, 1874*

I thank you for the compliment of this call, and I will take advantage of it to say that I have written this piece in such a way that the jury can bring in a verdict of guilty or not guilty, just as they happen to feel about it. I have done this for this reason. If a play carries its best lesson by teaching what ought to be done in such a case, but is *not* done in real life, then the righteous verdict of guilty should appear; but if the best lesson may be conveyed by holding up the mirror and showing what *is* done every day in such a case but ought *not* to be done, then the satirical verdict of not guilty should appear. I don't know which is best, strict truth and satire, or a nice moral lesson void of both. So I leave my jury free to decide.

I am killing only one man in this tragedy now, and that is bad, for nothing helps out a play like bloodshed. But in a few days I propose to introduce the smallpox into the last act. And if that don't work I shall close with a general massacre.

I threw all my strength into the character of *Colonel Sellers,* hoping to make it a very strong tragedy part and pathetic. I think this gentleman *tries* hard to play it right and make it majestic and pathetic; but his *face* is against him. And his clothes! I don't think anybody can make a tragedy effect in that kind of clothes. But I suppose he thinks they are impressive. He is from one of the Indian reservations. Oh! I can see that he tries hard to make it solemn and awful and heroic, but really sometimes he almost makes me laugh. I meant that turnip dinner to be pathetic, for how more forcibly could you represent poverty and misery and suffering than by such a dinner, and of course if anything would bring tears to people's eyes *that* would; but this man eats those turnips as if they were the bread of life, and so of course the pathos is knocked clear out of the thing. But I think he will learn. He has an absorbing ambition to become a very great tragedian.

I hope you will overlook the faults in this play, because I have never written a play before, and if I am treated right maybe I won't offend again. I wanted to have some fine situations and spectacular effects in this piece, but I was interfered with. I wanted to have a volcano in a state of eruption, with fire and smoke and earthquakes, and a great tossing river of blood-red lava flowing down the mountain side, and have the hero of this piece come booming down that red-hot river in a cast iron canoe; but the manager wouldn't hear of it; he said there wasn't any volcano in Missouri—as if I am responsible for Missouri's poverty. And then he said that by the laws of nature the hero would burn up; his cast iron canoe wouldn't protect him. "Very well," I said, "put him in a patent fireproof safe and let him slide—all the more thrilling—and paint on it, 'This safe is from Herring's establishment,' same as you would on a piano, and you can pay the whole expense of the volcano just on the advertisement." But the manager objected, though he said heaps of pretty things—among others that I was an ass—and so I had to let the volcano go.

Text / *World,* September 17, 1874.

the jury can bring in a verdict / Mark Twain made his curtain speech at the end of the first act, in which Laura Hawkins (played by Gertrude Kellogg) had shot her seducer, Colonel George Selby (Milnes Levic), but had not been brought to trial. The foreman of the jury was William Gillette, a young man of Hartford who had defied the mores of his hometown by embarking on an actor's career with the aid of Mark Twain. In the play Gillette had one short line: "Not guilty."

this gentleman / John T. Raymond, stage name of John O'Brien (1836–87). American actor. Having been on the stage since 1853, he had built up a great reputation as a character actor who achieved comic effects by bizarre clothes, facial mobility, and bodily eccentricities. In *The Gilded Age,* he played the role of Colonel Mulberry Sellers as a comedy part, giving his performance, even his costume, an air of burlesque that did not please Mark Twain, whose remarks in the curtain speech were not entirely complimentary to his leading man. In *MTA* Raymond is characterized as great in humorous portrayal but otherwise as a selfish man, not very bright, often silly, and generally heartless.

· 23 ·

The guest of honor at the dinner noted below was described by the Courant, *October 16, 1874, as "the well known English insurance author. . . . in every respect a prominent insurance man." In the large crowd were officers of Hartford insurance companies, actuaries, medical examiners and others, including Mark Twain.*

Dinner Speech

Insurance Men's Banquet for Cornelius Walford,
Allyn House, Hartford, October 12, 1874

Gentlemen: I am glad, indeed, to assist in welcoming the distinguished guest of this occasion to a city whose fame as an insurance center has extended to all lands and given us the name of being a quadruple band of brothers working sweetly hand in hand—the Colt's Arms Company making the destruction of our race easy and convenient, our life insurance citizens paying for the victims when they pass away, Mr. Batterson perpetuating their memory with his stately monuments, and our fire insurance companies taking care of their hereafter. I am glad to assist in welcoming our guest—first, because he is an Englishman, and I owe a heavy debt of hospitality to certain of his fellow-countrymen; and secondly, because he is in sympathy with insurance, and has been the means of making many other men cast their sympathies in the same direction.

Certainly there is no nobler field for human effort than the insurance line of business—especially accident insurance. Ever since I have been a director in an accident insurance company I have felt that I am a better man. Life has seemed more precious. Accidents have assumed a kindlier aspect. Distressing special providences have lost half their horror. I look upon a cripple, now, with affection and interest—as an advertisement. I do not seem to care for poetry any more. I do not care for politics, even agriculture does not excite me. But to me, now, there is a charm about a railway collision that is unspeakable.

There is nothing more beneficent than accident insurance. I have seen an entire family lifted out of poverty and into affluence by the simple boon of a broken leg. I have had people come to me on crutches, with tears in their eyes, to bless this beneficent institution. In all my experience of life, I have seen nothing so seraphic as the look that comes into a freshly-mutilated man's face when he feels in his vest pocket with his remaining hand and finds his accident ticket all right. And I have seen nothing so sad as the look that came into another splintered customer's face, when he found he couldn't collect on a wooden leg.

I will remark here, by way of an advertisement, that the noble charity which we have named the Hartford Accident Insurance Company, is an institution which is peculiarly to be depended upon. A man is bound to prosper who gives it his custom. No man can take out a policy in it and not get crippled before the year is out. Now there was one indigent man who had been disappointed so often with other companies that he had grown disheartened, his appetite left him, he ceased to smile—said life was but a weariness. Three weeks ago I got him to insure with us, and now he is the brightest, happiest spirit in this land—has a good steady income and a stylish suit of new bandages every day, and travels around on a shutter.

I am informed by Mr. Charles E. Wilson, foreman of our patent leg and crutch factory—however, for further information on that head I will refer you to our other advertisements.

I will say, in conclusion, that my share of the welcome to our guest is none the less hearty because I talk so much nonsense, and I know that I can say the same for the rest of the speakers.

Text / Composite, based upon: "Grand Banquet to Mr. Cornelius Walford of England," *Courant,* October 16, 1874; "Speech on Accident Insurance," *Sketches:*229–30; "Accident Insurance—Etc.," *MTS*(10):249–51; *MTS*(23):80–82.

fame as an insurance center / The first Hartford insurance company was founded in 1810, and by the 1880s twenty large companies had been established there.

Mr. Batterson / James Goodwin Batterson (1823–1901). A Hartford dealer in granite and marble, he founded the Travelers Insurance Company (1863). He was a combination, not unusual in Hartford, of business man and culture seeker, having translated the *Iliad,* written poetry, studied law and geology, and collected paintings.

a director / Mark Twain was on the board of directors of the Hartford Accident Insurance Company, but what his duties were and how much attention he paid to the job do not appear.

Charles E. Wilson / He was president of the Hartford Accident Insurance Company.

· 24 ·

The Times *reported, December 24, 1874, that at the one hundredth performance of* The Gilded Age *the house "was literally crammed from pit to dome," and that, "in response to repeated calls for the author, Mr. Samuel L. Clemens, better known as Mark Twain, delivered an address, replete with humor in speech and gesture." After the New York run the play went on tour, earning about $900 a week and eventually netting some $70,000. When it came to Hartford in January 1875, Mark Twain, inducing prominent clergymen to attend the performance, was instrumental in breaking down local prejudice against the theater. See Kenneth R. Andrews,* Nook Farm *(Cambridge, 1950):97–98; also Marvin Felheim,* The Theater of Augustin Daly *(New York, 1956).*

Curtain Speech

One Hundredth Performance of The Gilded Age, *Park Theater, New York, December 23, 1874*

I thank you for this call, for it gives me an opportunity to testify my appreciation of the vast compliment which the metropolis has paid to Mr. Raymond and me in approving of our efforts to the very substantial extent of filling this house for us a hundred nights in succession. After such praise as this from the first city in the land it would be useless for me to try to pretend that we are not feeling a good deal "set up," so I shall not pretend anything of the kind. We feel a good deal vainer than anybody would want to confess. I learned through the newspapers that I was to make a speech here tonight, and so I went to work, as I always do, to try and do the very best I possibly could on this occasion. I was determined to do it; I went at it faithfully, but when I came to look critically into this matter I found that I shouldered a pretty heavy contract. I found I shouldered a very heavy contract because there is only one topic that is proper to be discussed on this platform at this time, and that is this play and these actors and all the success which this play has met. Very well, that is an excellent subject—for somebody else. It is right for an outsider, or for somebody not connected with the concern, but for me, the dramatist, to praise these actors of mine, to praise this play of mine, and this success of ours—that would not come gracefully from me. There would be a little egotism in it. Neither can I criticize and abuse the actors, for I don't want to. I could abuse the play, but I have better judgment, and I cannot praise these actors of mine right here in their hearing and before their faces, for that would make anybody with flesh and blood unhappy, and, indeed, to praise them would be like praising the members of my own family and glorifying the lady who does our washing. And the more I think of this matter, the more I see the difficulty of the position, until I find myself in a condition I once before experienced.

[*Times:* "Mr. Twain here recited from his published work, *Roughing It,* the sketch, 'A Genuine Mexican Plug.' "]

Through that adventure, through that misfortune I lost the faculty of speech; for twenty-four hours I was absolutely speechless, and this is the second time that that has occurred.

Text / "The One Hundredth Representation of 'The Gilded Age,' " *Times,* December 24, 1874.

· 25 ·

In the 1870s a spelling match was a social diversion as popular as charades, musical chairs, and taffy pulls. When the young people of the Hartford Asylum Hill Congregational Church put on a money-raising fair, the spelling match turned out to be the climax, filling the church with a crowd of spectators. Two teams of sixteen each competed under the leadership of Miss Blythe and the Reverend Joseph H. Twichell, Asylum Hill pastor, both captains enlisting some of Hartford's best known citizens. Mark Twain, on Miss Blythe's team, was one of the last to go down, failing on "chaldron," which he spelled "caldron." The Courant *reported, May 13, 1875: "Altogether the match proved very amusing, the Rev. Dr. Burton, Mr. Twichell and Mr. Clemens especially enlivening the evening by occasional comments. Speaker Durand and a large number of members of the legislature were among the spectators." The fair netted more than $600.*

Introductory Remarks

Spelling Match, Asylum Hill Congregational Church,
Hartford, May 12, 1875

Ladies and gentlemen: I have been honored with the office of introducing these approaching orthographical solemnities with a few remarks: The temperance crusade swept the land some time ago—that is, that vast portion of the land where it was needed—but it skipped Hartford. Now comes this new spelling epidemic, and this time *we* are stricken. So I suppose we needed the affliction. *I* don't say we needed it, for I don't see any use in spelling a word right—and never did. I mean I don't see any use in having a uniform and arbitrary way of spelling words. We might as well make all clothes alike and cook all dishes alike. Sameness is tiresome; variety is pleasing. I have a correspondent whose letters are always a refreshment to me, there is such a breezy unfettered originality about his orthography. He always spells Kow with a large K. Now that is just as good as to spell it with a small one. It is better. It gives the imagination a broader field, a wider scope. It suggests to the mind a grand, vague, impressive new kind of a cow.

Superb effects can be produced by variegated spelling. Now there is Blind Tom, the musical prodigy. He always spells a word according to the sound that is carried to his ear. And he is an enthusiast in orthography. When you give him a word, he shouts it out—puts all his soul into it. I once heard him called upon to spell orangutang before an audience. He said, "O, r-a-n-g, orang, g-e-r, ger, oranger, t-a-n-g, tang, orangger tang!" Now a body can respect an orangutang that spells his name in a vigorous way like that. But the feeble dictionary makes a mere kitten of him. In the old times people spelled just as they pleased. That was the right idea. You had two chances at a stranger then. You knew a strong man from a weak one by his ironclad spelling, and his handwriting helped you to verify your verdict.

Some people have an idea that correct spelling can be *taught*—and taught to anybody. That is a mistake. The spelling faculty is born in a man, like poetry, music, and art. It is a gift; it is a talent. People who have this gift in a high degree, only need to see a word once in print, and it is forever photographed upon their memory. They cannot forget it. People who haven't it must be content to spell more or less like—like thunder—and expect to splinter the dictionary wherever their orthographical lightning happens to strike. There are 114,000 words in the unabridged dictionary. I know a lady who can spell only 180 of them right. She steers clear of all the rest. She can't learn any more. So her letters always consist of those constantly recurring 180 words. Now and then, when she finds herself obliged to write upon a subject which necessitates the use of some other words, she—well, she don't write on that subject. I have a relative in New York who is almost sublimely gifted. She can't spell *any* word right. There is a game called Verbarium. A dozen people are each provided with a sheet of paper, across the top of which is written a long word like kaleidoscopical, or something like that, and the game is to see who can make up the most words out of that in three minutes, always beginning with the initial letter of that word. Upon one occasion the word chosen was cofferdam. When time was called everybody had built from five to twenty words except this young lady. She only had one word—calf. We all studied a moment and then said, "Why there is no l in cofferdam." Then we examined her paper. To the eternal honor of that uninspired, unconscious, sublimely independent soul be it said, she had spelt that word "caff!" If anybody here can spell calf any more sensibly than that, let him step to the front and take his milk.

Two prizes are offered for this evening's contest, one for the speller that holds out longest, and one for the speller that falls first. The first prize is a choice between Guizot's *History of France,* five octavo volumes, illustrated by De Neuvill, the London *Art Journal* for 1875, profusely illustrated with wood and steel; or a nosegay curiously painted upon slate—which picture is burned into the slate, and the surface is afterward beautifully polished. This ingenious sort of art is the invention of a New England lady. You can see fine specimens of it at Mr. Glazier's. I have been instructed not to reveal just yet what the prize is, which is to be given to that untrammeled spirit who shall succeed in sitting down first. The insurrection will now begin.

Text / "Spelling Match and Festival," *Courant,* May 13, 1875.

Blind Tom / A popular Negro pianist. A native of Georgia, somewhat retarded mentally, he was said to have played as well by the age of seven as he played later. He had a repertoire of hundreds of melodies, and disliked Sunday school music.

first prize / Mark Twain donated the first prize, which was won by Miss Stone, of Twichell's team. The runner-up was the Reverend Dr. Burton, who lost the championship when he failed to put the "e" in "calicoes."

spirit who shall succeed in sitting down first / The booby prize was a set of colored alphabet blocks and three volumes of government reports on agriculture and Credit Mobilier investigations. The winner was Judge Elisha Carpenter, who spelled "gizzard" with one "z."

· 26 ·

Taking a public political stand for the first time, Mark Twain presided at a Hartford Republican rally for Rutherford B. Hayes during the presidential campaign of 1876. The meeting had been preceded by a noisy torchlight parade of military companies, city band, Civil War veterans, and others. Hartford was strongly Republican, but not solidly so, for the marchers were spattered and thumped by mud and rocks flung by supporters of Samuel Tilden, Democratic candidate. When vote manipulation won a close election for Hayes, Mark Twain approved, but looking back years later, when he had become a political mugwump, he called the rigged victory "one of the Republican party's most cold-blooded swindles."

Political Speech

Republican Mass Meeting, Allyn Hall, Hartford, September 30, 1876

Ladies and gentlemen: I feel very greatly honored in being chosen to preside at this meeting. This employment is new to me. I never have taken any part in a political canvass before, except to vote. The tribe of which I am the humblest member—the literary tribe—is one which is not given to bothering about politics, but there are times when even the strangest departures are justified, and such a season, I take it, is the present canvass. Some one asked me the other day, why it was that nearly all the people who write books and magazines had lately come to the front and proclaimed their political preference, since such a thing had probably never occurred before in America; and why it was that almost all of this strange, new band of volunteers marched under the banner of Hayes and Wheeler. I think these people have come to the front mainly because they think they see at last a chance to make this government a good government; because they think they see a chance to institute an honest and sensible system of civil service which shall so amply prove its worth and worthiness that no succeeding President can ever venture to put his foot upon it. Our present civil system, born of General Jackson and the Democratic party, is so idiotic, so contemptible, so grotesque, that it would make the very savages of Dahomey jeer and the very gods of solemnity laugh.

We will not hire a blacksmith who never lifted a sledge. We will not hire a school teacher who does not know the alphabet. We will not have a man about us in our business life—in any walk of life, low or high—unless he has served an apprenticeship and can prove that he is capable of doing the work he offers to do. We even require a plumber to know something about his business, so that he shall at least know which side of a pipe is the inside. But when you come to our civil service, we serenely fill great numbers of our minor public offices with ignoramuses; we put the vast business of a custom house in the hands of a flathead who does not know a bill of lading from a transit of Venus, never having heard of either of them before. Under a Treasury appointment we pour oceans of money, and accompanying statistics, through the hands and brain of an ignorant villager who never before could wrestle with a two-weeks' wash bill without getting thrown. Under our consular system we send creatures all over the world who speak no language but their own, and even when it comes to that, go wading all their days through the blood of murdered tenses, and flourishing the scalps of mutilated parts of speech. When forced to it we order home a foreign ambassador who is frescoed all over with—with—with—indiscreetnesses, but we immediately send one in his place whose moral ceiling has a perceptible shady tint to it, and then he brays when we supposed he was going to roar.

We carefully train and educate our naval officers and military men, and we ripen and perfect their capabilities through long service and experience, and keep hold of these excellent servants through a just system of promotion. This is exactly what we hope to do with our civil service under Mr. Hayes. We hope and expect to sever that service as utterly from politics as is the naval and military service, and we hope to make it as respectable, too. We hope to make worth and capacity the sole requirements of the civil service, in the place of the amount of party dirty work the candidate has done.

By the time General Hawley has finished his speech, I think you will know why we, in this matter, put our trust in Hayes in preference to any other man.

I am not going to say anything about our candidates for state offices, because you know them, honor them, and will vote for them, but General Hawley, being comparatively a stranger, I will say a single word in commendation of him, and it will furnish one of the many reasons why I am going to vote for him for Congress. I ask you to look seriously and thoughtfully at just one almost incredible fact. General Hawley, in his official capacity as President of the Centennial Commission, has done one thing which you may not have heard commented upon, and yet it is one of the most astounding performances of this decade—an act almost impossible, perhaps, to any other public officer in this nation. General Hawley has taken as high as $121,000 gate money at the Centennial in a single day—and never stole a cent of it!

Text / Composite, based upon: "Mark Twain in Politics," *Times,* October 2, 1876; unidentified clipping, Scrapbook 1869–78, MTP.

Hayes / Rutherford Burchard Hayes (1822–93). American statesman. He was a Civil War veteran, brevetted major general of volunteers (1865). As nineteenth president of the United States (1877–81), he ended military occupation in Southern states and fostered civil service reform.

Wheeler / William Almon Wheeler (1819–87). American public man. He was Republican congressman from New York (1861–63, 1869–71), author of the Wheeler Compromise (1874) which adjusted difficulties in Louisiana, and vice-president of the United States (1877–81).

General Hawley / Joseph Roswell Hawley (1826–1905). American public man. A Civil War veteran, brevet major general of volunteers, he was governor of Connecticut (1866), became coeditor, with Charles Dudley Warner, of the *Courant* (1867), and was chairman of the Republican National Convention (1868). He served three terms in Congress, was president of the Centennial Commission (1876), and was senator from Connecticut (1881–1905).

· 27 ·

For the seventy-first annual dinner of the New England Society of New York the hall was decorated with flags and bouquets, the president's table with a floral design representing Plymouth Rock. Among the 200 banqueters were Mark Twain, the Reverend Edward Everett Hale, George William Curtis, the Reverend Richard S. Storrs, Joseph H. Choate, representatives of St. Andrews and St. Patrick's Societies, and Frederic Auguste Bartholdi, who became celebrated as sculptor of the Statue of Liberty. The Times *reported, December 23, 1876, that the affair was "one of the most brilliant celebrations of the kind that has ever been held in this city," and that the speeches were "full of earnestness, good feeling, good sense, and good wit."*

The Oldest Inhabitant—The Weather of New England

Seventy-first Annual Dinner, New England Society of New York, Delmonico's, December 22, 1876

Who can lose it and forget it?
Who can have it and regret it?
Be interposer 'twixt us *Twain.*
Merchant of Venice

Gentlemen: I reverently believe that the Maker who made us all, makes everything in New England—but the weather. I don't know who makes that, but I think it must be raw apprentices in the Weather Clerk's factory, who experiment and learn how in New England, for board and clothes, and then are promoted to make weather for countries that require a good article, and will take their custom elsewhere if they don't get it. There is a sumptuous variety about the New England weather that compels the stranger's admiration—and regret. The weather is always doing something there; always attending strictly to business; always getting up new designs and trying them on the people to see how they will go. But it gets through more business in spring than in any other season. In the spring I have counted one hundred and thirty-six different kinds of weather inside of four and twenty hours. It was I that made the fame and fortune of that man that had that marvelous collection of weather on exhibition at the Centennial that so astounded the foreigners. He was going to travel all over the world and get specimens from all the climes. I said, "Don't you do it; you come to New England on a favorable spring day." I told him what we could do, in the way of style, variety, and quantity. Well, he came, and he made his collection in four days. As to variety—why, he confessed that he got hundreds of kinds of weather that he had never heard of before. And as to quantity—well, after he had picked out and discarded all that was blemished in any way, he not only had weather enough, but weather to spare; weather to hire out; weather to sell; to deposit; weather to invest; weather to give to the poor.

The people of New England are by nature patient and forbearing; but there are some things which they will not stand. Every year they kill a lot of poets for writing about "Beautiful Spring." These are generally casual visitors, who bring their notions of spring from somewhere else, and cannot, of course, know how the natives feel about spring. And so, the first thing they know, the opportunity to inquire how they feel has permanently gone by.

Old Probabilities has a mighty reputation for accurate prophecy, and thoroughly well deserves it. You take up the papers and observe how crisply and confidently he checks off what today's weather is going to be on the Pacific, down South, in the Middle States, in the Wisconsin region; see him sail along in the joy and pride of his power till he gets to New England, and then—see his tail drop. *He* doesn't know what the weather is going to be like in New England. He can't any more tell than he can tell how many Presidents of the United States there's going to be next year. Well, he mulls over it, and by and by he gets out something about like this: Probable nor'-east to sou'-west winds, varying to the southard and westard and eastard and points between; high and low barometer, swapping around from place to place; probable areas of rain, snow, hail, and drought, succeeded or preceded by earthquakes, with thunder and lightning. Then he jots down this postscript from his wandering mind, to cover accidents: "But it is possible that the program may be wholly changed in the meantime."

Yes, one of the brightest gems in the New England weather is the dazzling uncertainty of it. There is only one thing certain about it, you are certain there is going to be plenty of weather—a perfect grand review; but you never can tell which end of the procession is going to move first. You fix up for the drought; you leave your umbrella in the house and sally out with your sprinkling pot, and ten to one you get drowned. You make up your mind that the earthquake is due; you stand from under, and take hold of something to steady yourself, and the first thing you know, you get struck by lightning. These are great disappointments. But they can't be helped. The lightning there is peculiar; it is so convincing! When it strikes a thing, it doesn't leave enough of that thing behind for you to tell whether—well, you'd think it was something valuable, and a Congressman had been there.

And the thunder. When the thunder commences to merely tune up, and scrape, and saw, and key up the instruments for the performance, strangers say, "Why, what awful thunder you have here!" But when the baton is raised and the real concert begins, you'll find that stranger down in the cellar, with his head in the ash barrel.

Now, as to the *size* of the weather in New England—lengthways, I mean. It is utterly disproportioned to the size of that little country. Half the time, when it is packed as full as it can stick, you will see that New England weather sticking out beyond the edges and projecting around hundreds and hundreds of miles over the neighboring states. She can't hold a tenth part of her weather. You can see cracks all about, where she has strained herself trying to do it.

I could speak volumes about the inhuman perversity of the New England weather, but I will give but a single specimen. I like to hear rain on a tin roof, so I covered part of my roof with tin, with an eye to that luxury. Well, sir, do you think it ever rains on the tin? No, sir; skips it every time.

Mind, in this speech I have been trying merely to do honor to the New England weather—no language could do it justice. But, after all, there are at least one of two things about that weather (or, if you please, effects produced by it) which we residents would not like to part with. If we hadn't our bewitching autumn foliage, we should still have to credit the weather with one feature which compensates for all its bullying vagaries—the ice storm—when a leafless tree is clothed with ice from the bottom to the top—ice that is as bright and clear as crystal; when every bough and twig is strung with ice beads, frozen dewdrops, and the whole tree sparkles, cold and white, like the Shah of Persia's diamond plume. Then the wind waves the branches, and the sun comes out and turns all those myriads of beads and drops to prisms, that glow and burn and flash with all manner of colored fires, which change and change again, with inconceivable rapidity, from blue to red, from red to green, and green to gold—the tree becomes a spraying fountain, a very explosion of dazzling jewels; and it stands there the acme, the climax, the supremest possibility in art or nature, of bewildering, intoxicating, intolerable magnificence! One cannot make the words too strong.

Month after month I lay up my hate and grudge against the New

England weather; but when the ice storm comes at last, I say: "There—I forgive you, now—the books are square between us, you don't owe me a cent; go, and sin no more; your little faults and foibles count for nothing—you are the most enchanting weather in the world!"

Text / Composite, based upon: "Forefathers' Day. Speech of Mr. Samuel L. Clemens," *Times,* December 23, 1876; "The Weather," *MTS*(10):59–63; *MTS*(23):53–57; "New England Weather," *Eloquence*(R):210–13; *Eloquence*(T):288–92; Mark Twain, "Speech on the Weather," *Tom Sawyer Abroad and Other Stories* (1896):402–6.

· 28 ·

In late 1876 Mark Twain and Bret Harte collaborated on a play, Ah Sin, *named after the Chinese laundryman of Harte's "Heathen Chinee." The play opened in Washington in May 1877, then, after revision, moved to New York in July, with Charles T. Parsloe in the title role. It was not a success, closing after five weeks of dwindling receipts. New York critics said that Mark Twain's curtain speech was more entertaining than the play, and the ironical overtones of his remarks suggest that he did not think highly of it either.*

Curtain Speech

Opening of Ah Sin, *Fifth Avenue Theatre, New York, July 31, 1877*

Ladies and gentlemen: In view of this admirable success, it is meet that I try to express to you our hearty thanks for the large share which your encouraging applause has had in producing this success. This office I take upon me with great pleasure. This is a very remarkable play. You may not have noticed it, but I assure you that it is so. The construction of this play was a work of great labor and research—and plagiarism. When the authors of this play began their work they were resolved that it should not lack blood-curdling disasters, accidents, calamities—for these things always help out a play. But we wanted them to be new ones, brilliant, unhackneyed. In a lucky moment, we hit upon the breaking down of a stage coach as being something perfectly fresh and appalling. It seemed a stroke of genius—an inspiration. We were charmed with it, so we naturally overdid it a little. Consequently, when the play was first completed, we found we had had that stage breakdown seven times in the first act. We saw that wouldn't do—the piece was going to be too stagy (I didn't notice that—that is very good). Yes, the critics and everybody would say this sort of thing argued poverty of invention. And, confidentially, it did resemble that, so of course we set to work and put some limitations upon that accident, and we threw a little variety into the general style of it, too. Originally the stage coach always came in about every seven minutes, and broke down at the footlights and spilt the passengers down among the musicians. You can see how monotonous that was—to the musicians. But we fixed all that. At present the stage coach only breaks down once, a private carriage breaks down once, and the horses of another carriage run away once. We could have left out one or two of these, but then we had the horses and vehicles on our hands and we couldn't afford to throw them away on a mere quibble. I am making this explanation in the hope that it will reconcile you to the repetition of that accident.

This play is more didactic than otherwise. For the instruction of the young we have introduced a game of poker in the first act. The game of poker is all too little understood in the higher circles of this country. Here and there you will find an ambassador that has some knowledge of the game, but you take the general average of the nation, and our ignorance ought to make us blush. Why, I have even known a clergyman—a liberal, cultivated, estimable, pure-hearted man, and a most excellent husband and father—who didn't value an ace full above two pair and a jack. Such ignorance as that is brutalizing. Whoever sees Mr. Parsloe in this piece sees as good and natural and consistent a Chinaman as he could see in San Francisco. I think his portrayal of the character reaches perfection. The whole purpose of the piece is to afford an opportunity for the illustration of this character. The Chinaman is going to become a very frequent spectacle all over America, by and by, and a difficult political problem, too. Therefore it seems well enough to let the public study him a little on the stage beforehand. The actors, the management, and the authors have done their best to begin this course of public instruction effectively this evening.

I will say only one more word about this remarkable play. It is this:

When this play was originally completed, it was so long, and so wide, and so deep (in places), and so comprehensive, that it would have taken two weeks to play it. And I thought this was a good feature. I supposed we could have a sign on the curtain, "To be continued," and it would be all right; but the manager said no, that wouldn't do; to play a play two weeks long would be sure to get us in trouble with the government because the Constitution of the United States says you shan't inflict cruel and inhuman punishments. So he set to work to cut it down, and cart the refuse to the paper mill. Now, that was a good thing. I never saw a play improve as this one did. The more he cut out of it, the better it got, right along. He cut out, and cut out, and cut out, and I do believe this would be one of the best plays in the world today if his strength had held out, and he could have gone on and cut out the rest of it. With this brief but necessary explanation of the plot and purpose and moral of this excellent work, I make my bow, repeat my thanks, and remark that the scissors have been repaired and the work of improvement will go on.

Text / Composite, based upon: "Fifth-Avenue Theatre," *Times*, August 1, 1877; Joseph Francis Daly, *The Life of Augustin Daly* (1917):234–36; De Lancy Ferguson, "Mark Twain's Lost Curtain Speeches," *South Atlantic Quarterly* 42 (July 1943):262–69.

· 29 ·

When the Ancient and Honorable Artillery Company of Massachusetts, oldest military organization in the nation, visited Hartford, it was greeted at the depot by the Putnam Phalanx and a thirteen-gun salute. Then there was a parade of marching groups, flags flying, and bands blaring. At a midday banquet, speeches by the governors of Massachusetts and Connecticut, several honorables, generals, and prominent citizens sounded notes of patriotism and invoked memories of General Israel Putnam and Bunker Hill. Mark Twain's speech varied somewhat from the pattern.

Dinner Speech

Putnam Phalanx Dinner for the Ancient and Honorable Artillery Company of Massachusetts, Allyn House, Hartford, October 2, 1877

I wouldn't have missed being here for a good deal. The last time I had the privilege of breaking bread with soldiers was some years ago, with the oldest military organization in England, the Ancient and Honourable Artillery Company of London, somewhere about its six-hundredth anniversary; and now I have enjoyed this privilege with its oldest child, the oldest military organization in America, the Ancient and Honorable Artillery Company of Massachusetts, on this your two hundred and fortieth anniversary. Fine old stock, both of you—and if you fight as well as you feed, God protect the enemy.

I did not assemble at the hotel parlors today to be received by a committee as a mere civilian guest; no, I assembled at the headquarters of the Putnam Phalanx, and insisted upon my right to be escorted to this place as one of the military guests. For I, too, am a soldier! I am inured to war. I have a military history. I have been through a stirring campaign, and there is not even a mention of it in any history of the United States or of the Southern Confederacy—to such lengths can the envy and the malignity of the historian go! I will unbosom myself here, where I cannot but find sympathy; I will tell you about it, and appeal through you to justice.

In the earliest summer days of the war, I slipped out of Hannibal,

Missouri, by night, with a friend, and joined a detachment of the rebel General Tom Harris's army (I find myself in a great minority here) up a gorge behind an old barn in Ralls County. Colonel Ralls, of Mexican War celebrity, swore us in. He made us swear to uphold the flag and Constitution of the United States, and to destroy every other military organization that we caught doing the same thing, which, being interpreted, means that we were to repel invasion. Well, you see, this mixed us. We couldn't really tell which side we were on, but we went into camp and left it to the God of Battles. For that was the term then. I was made Second Lieutenant and Chief Mogul of a company of eleven men, who knew nothing about war—nor anything, for we had no captain. My friend, who was nineteen years old, six feet high, three feet wide, and some distance through, and just out of the infant school, was made orderly sergeant. His name was Ben Tupper. He had a hard time. When he was mounted and on the march he used to go to sleep, and his horse would reach around and bite him on the leg, and then he would wake up and cry and curse, and want to go home. The other men pestered him a good deal, too. When they were dismounted they said they couldn't march in double file with him because his feet took up so much room. One night, when we were around the camp fire, some fellow on the outside in the cold said, "Ben Tupper, put down that newspaper: it throws the whole place into twilight, and casts a shadow like a blanket." Ben said, "I ain't got any newspaper." Then the other fellow said, "Oh, I see—'twas your ear!" We all slept in a corn crib, on the corn, and the rats were very thick. Ben Tupper had been carefully and rightly reared, and when he was ready for bed he would start to pray, and a rat would bite him on the heel, and then he would sit up and swear all night and keep everybody awake. He was town-bred and did not seem to have any correct idea of military discipline. If I commanded him to shut up, he would say, "Who was your nigger last year?" One evening I ordered him to ride out about three miles on picket duty, to the beginning of a prairie. Said he, "What!—in the night!—and them blamed Union soldiers likely to be prowling around there any time!" So he wouldn't go, and the next morning I ordered him again. Said he, "In the rain!—I think I see myself!" He didn't go. Next day I ordered him on picket duty once more. This time he looked hurt. Said he, "What! on Sunday?—you must be a damn fool!" Well, picketing might have been a very good thing, but I saw it was impracticable, so I dropped it from my military system.

We had a good enough time there at that barn, barring the rats and the mosquitoes and the rain. We levied on both parties impartially, and both parties hated us impartially. But one day we heard that the invader was approaching, so we had to pack up and move, of course, and within twenty-four hours he was coming again. So we moved again. Next day he was after us once more. Well, we didn't like it much, but we moved, rather than make trouble. This went on for a week or ten days more, and we saw considerable scenery. Then Ben Tupper lost patience. Said he, "War ain't what it's cracked up to be; I'm going home if I can't ever git a chance to sit down a minute. Why do these people keep us a-humpin' around so? Blame their skins, do they think this is an excursion?"

Some of the other town boys got to grumbling. They complained that there was an insufficiency of umbrellas. So I sent around to the farmers and borrowed what I could. Then they complained that the Worcestershire sauce was out. There was mutiny and dissatisfaction all around, and, of course, here came the enemy pestering us again—as much as two hours before breakfast, too, when nobody wanted to turn out, of course.

This was a little too much. The whole command felt insulted. I detached one of my aides and sent him to the brigadier, and asked him to assign us a district where there wasn't so much bother going on. The history of our campaign was laid before him, but instead of being touched by it, what did he do? He sent back an indignant message and said, "You have had a dozen chances inside of two weeks to capture the enemy, and he is still at large. [Well, we knew that!] Feeling bad? Stay where you are this time, or I will court-martial and hang the whole lot of you." Well, I submitted this brutal message to my battalion, and asked their advice. Said the orderly sergeant, "If Tom Harris wants the enemy, let him come and get him. I ain't got any use for my share, and who's Tom Harris anyway, I'd like to know, that's putting on so many frills? Why, I knew him when he wasn't nothing but a darn telegraph operator. Gentlemen, you can do as you choose; as for me, I've got enough of this sashaying around so's 't you can't get a chance to pray, because the time's all required for cussing. So off goes my war paint—you hear *me!*"

The whole regiment said, with one voice, "That's the talk for me." So there and then, on the spot, my brigade disbanded itself and tramped off home, with me at the tail of it. I hung up my own sword and returned to the arts of peace, and there were people who said I hadn't been absent from them yet. We were the first men that went into the service in Missouri; we were the first that went out of it anywhere. This, gentlemen, is the history of the part which my division took in the great rebellion, and such is the military record of its commander in chief, and this is the first time that the deeds of those warriors have been brought officially to the notice of mankind. Treasure these things in your hearts, and so shall the detected and truculent historians of this land be brought to shame and confusion. I ask you to fill your glasses and drink with me to the reverent memory of the orderly sergeant and those other neglected and forgotten heroes, my footsore and travel-stained paladins, who were first in war, first in peace, and were not idle during the interval that lay between.

Text / Composite, based upon: "Mark Twain's Speech," *Courant,* October 3, 1877; "Mark Twain's War Experiences," *Times,* October 7, 1877.

I am inured to war / Mark Twain's speech was a preview of "The Private History of a Campaign that Failed," first published in the *Century Magazine* 21, no. 2 (December 1885):193–204.

General Tom Harris's army / Brigadier General Thomas A. Harris commanded the Second Division, Missouri State Guard (1861).

· 30 ·

On the twentieth anniversary of the founding of the Atlantic Monthly, *the publishers gave a dinner to celebrate the seventieth birthday of John Greenleaf Whittier. The evening, though not devoid of decorous gayety, was rather solemn. As the Boston* Advertiser *put it next day, the presence of the guest of honor, as well as Emerson and Longfellow, "gave a reverent, almost holy, air to the place." Oliver Wendell Holmes was there, Warner, Howells, R. H. Stoddard, Thomas Wentworth Higginson, Charles Eliot Norton, and some fifty other* Atlantic *contributors. Speeches paid homage not only to Whittier, but also to the whole caste of New England literary Brahmins. Into this program of adulation Mark Twain, the wild westerner, injected a burlesque that was disrespectful of Emerson, Longfellow, and Holmes. The ensuing furor of indignation around Boston and elsewhere overwhelmed Mark Twain with a sense of guilt and made the occasion a traumatic experience. For the next thirty years he periodically reexamined the speech, his critical opinion swinging back and forth between admiration and distaste, his final verdict (1906) being entire approval. The best accounts of the affair and its consequences are Henry Nash Smith's "That Hideous Mistake of Poor Clemens's,"* Harvard Library Bulletin *9, no. 2 (Spring 1955):145–80; and "The California Bull and the Gracious Singers,"* Mark Twain: The Development of a Writer *(Cambridge, 1962).*

Dinner Speech

Atlantic Monthly *Dinner, Seventieth Birthday of John Greenleaf Whittier, Hotel Brunswick, Boston, December 17, 1877*

Mr. Chairman: This is an occasion peculiarly meet for the digging up of pleasant reminiscences concerning literary folk; therefore I will drop lightly into history myself. Standing here on the shore of the Atlantic and contemplating certain of its biggest literary billows, I am reminded of a thing which happened to me some fifteen years ago, when I had just succeeded in stirring up a little Nevadian literary ocean puddle myself, whose spume flakes were beginning to blow Californiawards. I started an inspection tramp through the southern mines of California. I was callow and conceited, and I resolved to try the virtue of my *nom de plume.* I very soon had an opportunity. I knocked at a miner's lonely log cabin in the foothills of the Sierras just at nightfall. It was snowing at the time. A jaded, melancholy man of fifty, barefooted, opened to me. When he heard my *nom de plume,* he looked more dejected than before. He let me in—pretty reluctantly, I thought—and after the customary bacon and beans, black coffee and a hot whiskey, I took a pipe. This sorrowful man had not said three words up to this time. Now he spoke up and said in the voice of one who is secretly suffering, "You're the fourth—I'm a-going to move." "The fourth what?" said I. "The fourth littery man that's been here in twenty-four hours—I'm a-going to move." "You don't tell me!" said I; "who were the others?" "Mr. Longfellow, Mr. Emerson and Mr. Oliver Wendell Holmes—dad fetch the lot!"

You can easily believe I was interested. I supplicated—three hot whiskies did the rest—and finally the melancholy miner began. Said he:

"They came here just at dark yesterday evening, and I let them in, of course. Said they were going to Yosemite. They were a rough lot—but that's nothing—everybody looks rough that travels afoot. Mr. Emerson was a seedy little bit of a chap—red-headed. Mr. Holmes was as fat as a balloon—he weighed as much as three hundred, and had double chins all the way down to his stomach. Mr. Longfellow was built like a prizefighter. His head was cropped and bristly—like as if he had a wig made of hair brushes. His nose lay straight down his face, like a finger, with the end joint tilted up. They had been drinking—I could see that. And what queer talk they used! Mr. Holmes inspected the cabin, then he took me by the buttonhole, and says he:

> Through the deep caves of thought
>   I hear a voice that sings:
> Build thee more stately mansions,
>   O my Soul!

"Says I, 'I can't afford it, Mr. Holmes, and moreover I don't want to.' Blamed if I liked it pretty well, either, coming from a stranger that way! However, I started to get out my bacon and beans, when Mr. Emerson came and looked on a while, and then *he* takes me aside by the buttonhole and says:

> Give me agates for my meat;
> Give me cantharides to eat;
> From air and ocean bring me foods,
> From all zones and latitudes.

"Says I, 'Mr. Emerson, if you'll excuse me, this ain't no hotel.' You see it sort of riled me—I warn't used to the ways of littery swells. But I went on a-sweating over my work, and next comes Mr. Longfellow and buttonholes me, and interrupts me. Says he:

> Honor be to Mudjekeewis!
> You shall hear how Pau-Puk-Kee-wis—

"But I broke in, and says I, 'Begging your pardon, Mr. Longfellow, if you'll be so kind as to hold your yawp for about five minutes, and let me get this grub ready, you'll do me proud.' Well, sir, after they'd filled up, I set out the jug. Mr. Holmes looks at it, and then he fires up all of a sudden and yells:

> Flash out a stream of blood-red wine!
> For I would drink to other days.

"By George, I was getting kind of worked up. I don't deny it, I was getting kind of worked up. I turns to Mr. Holmes, and says I, 'Looky here, my fat friend, I'm a-running this shanty, and if the court knows herself, you'll take whiskey straight or you'll go dry!' Them's the very words I said to him. Now I didn't want to sass such famous littery people, but you see they kind of forced me. There ain't nothing onreasonable 'bout me; I don't mind a passel of guests a-tread'n on my tail three or four times, but when it comes to *standin'* on it, it's different, and if the court knows herself, you'll take whiskey straight or you'll go dry! Well, between drinks they'd swell around the cabin and strike attitudes and spout. Says Mr. Longfellow:

> This is the forest primeval.

"Says Mr. Emerson:

> Here once the embattled farmers stood,
> And fired the shot heard round the world.

"Says I, 'Oh, blackguard the premises as much as you want to—it don't cost you a cent.' Well, they went on drinking, and pretty soon they got out a greasy old deck and went to playing cutthroat euchre at ten cents a corner—on trust. I begun to notice some pretty suspicious things. Mr. Emerson dealt, looked at his hand, shook his head, says:

> I am the doubter and the doubt—

and calmly bunched the hands and went to shuffling for a new layout. Says he:

> They reckon ill who leave me out;
> They know not well the subtle ways
> I keep. I pass, and deal *again!*

"Hang'd if he didn't go ahead and do it, too! Oh, he was a cool one. Well, in about a minute, things were running pretty tight, but all of a sudden I see by Mr. Emerson's eye that he judged he had 'em. He had already corralled two tricks, and each of the others one. So now he kind of lifts a little, in his chair, and says:

> I tire of globes and aces!
> Too long the game is played!

—and down he fetched a right bower. Mr. Longfellow smiles as sweet as pie, and says:

> Thanks, thanks to thee, my worthy friend,
> For the lesson thou has taught.

—and dog my cats if he didn't come down with *another* right bower! Well, sir, up jumps Holmes a-war whooping, as usual, and says:

> God help them if the tempest swings
> The pine against the palm!

—and I wish I may go to grass if he didn't swoop down with *another* right bower! Emerson claps his hand on his bowie, Longfellow claps his on his revolver, and I went under a bunk. There was going to be trouble; but that monstrous Holmes rose up, wobbling his double chins, and says he, 'Order, gentlemen; the first man that draws, I'll lay down on him and smother him!' All quiet on the Potomac, you bet you!

"They were pretty how-come-you-so now, and they begun to blow. Emerson says, 'The bulliest thing I ever wrote was "Barbara Frietchie." ' Says Longfellow, 'It don't begin with my "Biglow Papers." ' Says Holmes, 'My "Thanatopsis" lays over 'em both.' They mighty near ended in a fight. Then they wished they had some more company—and Mr. Emerson pointed at me and says:

> Is yonder squalid peasant all
> That this proud nursery could breed?

"He was a-whetting his bowie on his boot—so I let it pass. Well, sir, next they took it into their heads that they would like some music; so they made me stand up and sing 'When Johnny Comes Marching Home' till I dropped—at thirteen minutes past four this morning. That's what *I've* been through, my friend. When I woke at seven, they were leaving, thank goodness, and Mr. Longfellow had my only boots on, and his own under his arm. Says I, "Hold on there, Evangeline, what you going to do with *them?*" He says: 'Going to make tracks with 'em, because

Lives of great men all remind us
  We can make our lives sublime;
And departing, leave behind us
  Footprints on the sands of Time.

"As I said, Mr. Twain, you are the fourth in twenty-four hours—and I'm a-going to move—I ain't suited to a littery atmosphere."

I said to the miner, "Why, my dear sir, *these* were not the gracious singers to whom we and the world pay loving reverence and homage; these were imposters."

The miner investigated me with a calm eye for a while, then said he, "Ah—imposters, were they?—are *you?*" I did not pursue the subject; and since then I haven't traveled on my *nom de plume* enough to hurt. Such is the reminiscence I was moved to contribute, Mr. Chairman. In my enthusiasm I may have exaggerated the details a little, but you will easily forgive me that fault, since I believe it is the first time I have ever deflected from perpendicular fact on an occasion like this.

Text / Composite, based upon: MS, Willard S. Morse Collection, Yale University Library; Boston *Advertiser,* December 18, 1877; "Whittier," *Courant,* December 19, 1877; "The Story of a Speech," *MTS*(10):1–16; *MTS*(23):63–76; "A 'Littery' Episode," *Eloquence*(R), 1:214–18; *Eloquence*(T), 1:293–98.

Through the deep caves of thought / From Holmes's "The Chambered Nautilus" (1858).

Give me agates for my meat / From Emerson's "Mithridates" (1847).

Honor be to Mudjekeewis / From Canto 2, "The Four Winds," of Longfellow's *The Song of Hiawatha* (1855).

You shall hear how Pau-Puk-Kee-wis / From Canto 11, "Hiawatha's Wedding Feast," *The Song of Hiawatha.*

Flash out a stream of blood-red wine / From Holmes's "Mare Rubrum" (1858).

This is the forest primeval / Part of the first line of Longfellow's *Evangeline* (1845–47).

Here once the embattled farmers stood / From Emerson's "Concord Hymn" (1836).

I am the doubter and the doubt / From Emerson's "Brahma" (1857).

They reckon ill who leave me out / From stanza three of "Brahma."

They know not well the subtle ways / From the first stanza of "Brahma," misquoted. Emerson's words are: "They know not well the subtle ways / I keep, and pass, and turn again."

I tire of globes and aces / From Emerson's "Song of Nature" (1860), misquoted. The line is: "I tire of globes and races."

Thanks, thanks to thee, my worthy friend / From Longfellow's "The Village Blacksmith" (1840).

God help them if the tempest swings / From Holmes's "A Voice of the Loyal North" (1861).

they begun to blow / Mark Twain scrambled the authorship of the several poems. "Barbara Frietchie" (1863) was written by John G. Whittier, the "Biglow Papers" (1846–48, 1862–66) by James Russell Lowell, "Thanatopsis" (1817) by William Cullen Bryant.

Is yonder squalid peasant all / From Emerson's "Monadnoc" (1847).

When Johnny Comes Marching Home / This song, written in 1865 by Patrick Sarsfield Gilmore (1829–92), was very popular with Union soldiers who had been mustered out.

Lives of great men all remind us / From Longfellow's "A Psalm of Life" (1838).

· 31 ·

Shortly before Bayard Taylor sailed for Europe as United States minister to Germany, he was honored by a farewell dinner in New York. Two hundred gentlemen attended, and William Cullen Bryant presided. Among speakers other than Mark Twain were Howells, Warner, Mayor Ely, Edward Pierrepont, and W. W. Phelps. They remarked upon the government's extraordinary departure from custom in appointing an emissary who was not only a poet, but also a man who knew the language of the country.

Dinner Speech

Farewell Banquet for Bayard Taylor, Delmonico's, New York, April 4, 1878

Mr. Chairman: I had intended to make an address of some length here tonight, and in fact wrote out an impromptu speech, but have had no time to memorize it. I cannot make a speech on the moment, and therefore being unprepared I am silent and undone. However, I will say this much for the speech that I had written out—that it was a very good one, and I gave it away as I had no further use for it, and saw that I could not deliver it. Therefore I will ask the indulgence of the company here to let me retire without speaking. I will make my compliments to our honored friend, Mr. Taylor, but I will make them on board ship where I shall be a fellow passenger.

[The following is the speech Mark Twain had prepared.]

I have been warned—as, no doubt, have all among you that are inexperienced—that a dinner to our Ambassador is an occasion which demands, and even requires, a peculiar caution and delicacy in the handling of the dangerous weapon of speech. I have been warned to avoid all mention of international politics, and all criticisms, however mild, of countries with which we are at peace, lest such utterances embarrass our minister and our government in their dealings with foreign states. In a word, I have been cautioned to talk, but be careful not to say anything. I do not consider this a difficult task.

Now, it has often occurred to me that the conditions under which we live at the present day, with the revelations of geology all about us, viewing, upon the one hand, the majestic configurations of the silurian, oolitic, old red sandstone periods, and, upon the other, the affiliations, and stratifications, and ramifications of the prehistoric, post-pliocene, antepenultimate epochs, we are stricken dumb with amazed surprise, and can only lift up our hands and say with that wise but odious Frenchman: "It was a slip of the tongue, sir, and wholly unintentional—entirely unintentional." It would ill become me, upon an occasion like this, purposely to speak slightingly of a citizen of a country with whom we are at peace—and especially great and gracious France, whom God preserve! The subject, however, is a delicate one, and I will not pursue it.

But—as I was about to remark—cast your eye abroad, sir, for one pregnant moment over the vista which looms before you in the mighty domain of intellectual progression and contemplate the awe-compelling theory of the descent of man! Development, sir! Development! Natural selection! Correlation of the sexes! Spontaneous combustion!—what gulfs and whirlwinds of intellectual stimulus these magic words fling upon the burning canvas of the material universe of soul! Across the chasm of the ages we take the oyster by the hand and call him brother; and back, and still further back, we go, and breathe the germ we cannot see, and know, in him, our truer Adam! And as we stand, dazed, transfixed, exalted, and gaze down the long procession of life, marking how steadily, how symmetrically we have ascended, step by step, to our sublime estate and dignity of humanity—out of one lowly form into a little higher and a little higher forms—adding grace after every change—developing from tadpoles into frogs, frogs into fishes, fishes into birds, birds into reptiles, reptiles into Russians—I beg a million pardons, sir and gentlemen—it was a wholly innocent slip of the tongue, and due only to the excitement of debate—for far be it from me, on such an occasion as this, to cast a seeming slur upon a great nation with which we are at peace—a great and noble and Christian nation—whom God expand!

But, as I was about to remark, I maintain—and nothing can ever drive me from that position—that the contributions of the nineteenth century to science and the industrial arts are—are—but, of course they are. There is no need to dwell upon that. You look at it yourself. Look at steam! Look at the steamboat, look at the railway, look at the steamship! Look at the telegraph, which enables you to flash your thoughts from world to world, ignoring intervening seas. Look at the telephone, which enables you to speak into affection's remote ear the word that cheers, and into the ear of the foe the opinion which you ought not to risk at shorter range. Look at the sewing machine, look at the foghorn, look at the bell punch, look at the book agent. And, more than all, a thousand times, look at the last and greatest, the aerophone, which will enable Moody and Sankey to stand on the tallest summit of the Rocky Mountains and deliver their message to listening America!—and necessarily it will annul and do away with the pernicious custom of taking up a collection. Look at all these things, sir, and say if it is not a far prouder and more precious boon to have been born in the nineteenth century than in any century that went before it. Ah, sir, clothed with the all-sufficient grandeur of citizenship in the nineteenth century, even the wild and arid New Jerseyman might—a mistake, sir, a mistake, and entirely unintentional. Of all the kingdoms, principalities and countries with which it is our privilege to hold peaceful relations, I regard New Jersey as dearest to our admiration, nearest to our heart, the wisest and the purest among the nations. I retire the undiplomatic language, and beg your sympathy and indulgence.

But, as I was about to remark, it has always seemed to me—that is, of course, since I reached a reasoning age—that this much agitated question of future rewards and punishments was one upon which honest and sincere differences of opinion might exist; one individual, with more or less justice, leaning to the radical side of it, whilst another individual, with apparently equal justice, but with infinitely more common sense, more intelligence, more justification, leans to a bitter and remorseless detestation of the pitiless Prince of Perdition—a slip of the tongue, I do sincerely assure you—I beg you to let me withdraw that unintentional slur upon the character of that great and excellent personage with whom and whose country we are upon the closest and warmest terms, and who—it is no use, sir, I will sit down; I don't seem to have any knack at a diplomatic speech. I have probably compromised the country enough for the present.

Nonsense aside, sir, I am most sincerely glad to assist at this public expression of appreciation of Mr. Taylor's character, scholarship, and distinguished literary service. I am sure he was not merely one of the fittest men we had for the place, but the fittest. In so honoring him, our country has conspicuously honored herself.

Text / Composite, based upon: NY*Trib,* n.d., reprinted as "Bayard Taylor," *Courant,* April 6, 1878; "Mark Twain on the 19th Century," *Dick's Comic and Dialect Recitations* (1888):113–15.

Taylor / James Bayard Taylor (1825–78). American writer and traveler. A prolific writer of poetry, drama, and travel books, he published *Views Afoot* (1846), *Eldorado* (1850), *Poems of the Orient* (1855), a scholarly translation of Goethe's *Faust* (1870–71), and others. Wit and raconteur, he was a picturesque personality. Mark Twain characterized him as a genial and lovable man who was delighted with his appointment as United States envoy and minister plenipotentiary to Germany. Taylor died soon after assuming his duties in Berlin.

aerophone / A musical instrument in which sound is generated by a vibrating column of air, as in a trumpet or flute. Mark Twain apparently thought of it as something like a modern loudspeaker.

Moody and Sankey / Dwight Lyman Moody (1837–99) and Ira David Sankey (1840–1908). American revivalists. In the late nineteenth century they were a team of international evangelists who held revival meetings in the United States and England, Moody as exhorter, Sankey as musical director. They collaborated on *Gospel Hymns,* which became widely known. Moody founded in Chicago the Moody Bible Institute (1886), called "The West Point of Christian Service."

· 32 ·

In the spring of 1878 Mark Twain took his family abroad for a stay of some eighteen months. With wife and daughters settled in Germany, he and Twichell junketed for six weeks, professing to be on a walking trip but seldom walking. Then Twichell went home, and the Clemens family toured in France, Italy, and Switzerland, ending their foreign sojourn in England. There, in the familiar round of receptions and dinners, Mark Twain renewed old acquaintanceships and met other celebrities like Whistler, Henry James, Lewis Carroll, and Charles Darwin. Out of the European travels came A Tramp Abroad *(1880), in which some of the best parts are exaggerated accounts of adventures with Twichell.*

Dinner Speech

Anglo-American Club Banquet, Heidelberg, Germany, July 4, 1878

Gentlemen: Since I arrived, a month ago, in this old wonderland, this vast garden of Germany, my English tongue has so often proved a useless piece of baggage to me, and so troublesome to carry around, in a country where they haven't the checking system for luggage, that I finally set to work, last week, and learned the German language. Also! Es freut mich dass dies so ist, denn es muss, in ein hauptsächlich degree, höflich sein, dass man auf ein occasion like this, sein Rede in die Sprache des Landes worin he boards, aussprechen soll. Dafür habe ich, aus reinische Verlegenheit—no, Vergangenheit—no, I mean Höflichkeit—aus reinische Höflichkeit habe ich resolved to tackle this business in the German language, um Gottes willen! Also! Sie müssen so freundlich sein, und verzeih mich die interlarding von ein oder zwei Englischer Worte, hie und da, denn ich finde dass die deutsche is not a very copious language, and so when you've really got anything to say, you've got to draw on a language that can stand the strain.

Wenn aber man kann nicht meinem Rede verstehen, so werde ich ihm später dasselbe übersetz, wenn er solche Dienst verlangen wollen haben werden sollen sein hätte. (I don't know what wollen haben werden sollen sein hätte means, but I notice they always put it at the end of a German sentence—merely for general literary gorgeousness, I suppose.)

This is a great and justly honored day—a day which is worthy of the veneration in which it is held by the true patriots of all climes and nationalities—a day which offers a fruitful theme for thought and speech; und meinem Freunde—no, mein*en* Freund*en*—mein*es* Freund*es*—well, take your choice, they're all the same price; I don't know which one is right—also! ich habe gehabt worden gewesen sein, as Goethe says in his *Paradise Lost*—ich—ich—that is to say—ich—but let us change cars.

Also! Die Anblick so viele Grossbrittanischer und Amerikanischer hier zusammengetroffen in Brüderliche concord, ist zwar a welcome and inspiriting spectacle. And what has moved you to it? Can the terse German tongue rise to the expression of this impulse? Is it Freundschaftsbezeigungenstadtverodnetenversammlungenfamilieneigenthümlichkeiten? Nein, O nein! This is a crisp and noble word, but it fails to pierce the marrow of the impulse which has gathered this friendly meeting and produced diese Anblick—eine Anblick welche is gut zu sehen—gut für die Augen in a foreign land and a far country—eine Anblick solche als in die gewöhnliche Heidelberger phrase nennt man ein "schönes Aussicht!" Ja, freilich natürlich wahrscheinlich ebensowohl! Also! Die Aussicht auf dem Königsstuhl mehr grosserer ist, aber geistlische sprechend nicht so schön, lob' Gott! Because sie sind hier zusammengetroffen, in Brüderlichem concord, ein grossen Tag zu feiern, whose high benefits were not for one land and one locality only, but have conferred a measure of good upon all lands that know liberty today, and love it. Hundert Jahre vorüber, waren die Engländer und die Amerikaner Feinde; aber heute sind sie herzlichen Freunde, Gott sei Dank! May this good fellowship endure; may these banners here blended in amity so remain; may they never any more wave over opposing hosts, or be stained with blood which was kindred, is kindred, and always will be kindred, until a line drawn upon a map shall be able to say: "*This* bars the ancestral blood from flowing in the veins of the descendant!"

Text / "A Fourth of July Oration in the German Tongue, Delivered at a Banquet of the Anglo-American Club of Students by the Author of This Book," *A Tramp Abroad* (1907), Appendix D:283–84.

· 33 ·

From the first of March 1879 to early July the Clemens family was in France, which was not one of Mark Twain's favorite spots. He did not admire the French character, and of French society he clung to the stereotyped view that it was grossly immoral sexually. Dismal spring weather in Paris, damp and raw, did not improve his outlook. Besides, there seems to have been no lively round of social events, which he found stimulating. We do not hear of soirées or small gatherings at which he met eminent Frenchmen. When he assumed the familiar role of dinner speaker, as for the Stanley Club, it was apparently for an English-speaking audience.

Dinner Speech

Stanley Club, Paris, ca. April 1879

Mr. Ryan said to me just now that I'd got to make a speech. I said to Mr. Ryan, "The news came too late to save Roger McPherson." It is sad to know that some things always come too late, and when I look around upon this brilliant assembly I feel disappointed to think what a nice speech I might have made, what fine topics I might have found in Paris to speak about among these historic monuments, the architecture of Paris, the towers of Notre Dame, the caves, and other ancient things. Then I might have said something about the objects of which Paris folks are fond—literature, art, medicine, and adultery.

But the news came too late to save Roger McPherson! Perhaps you are not as well acquainted with McPherson as I am? Well, I'll explain who McPherson was. When we sailed from New York there came on board a man all haggard—a mere skeleton. He wasn't much of a man, he wasn't, and on the voyage we often heard him say to himself, "The news came too late to save Roger McPherson." I got interested, and I wanted to know about the man, so I asked him who was McPherson, and he said, "I'm McPherson; but the news came too late to save Roger McPherson."

"How too late?" I asked. "About three weeks too late," he replied: "I'll tell you how it happened: A friend of mine died, and they told me

I must take his body on the cars to his parents in Illinois. I said I'd do it, and they gave me a card with the address, and told me to go down to the depot and put it on a box I'd find there, have the box put on the baggage car, and go right along with it to Illinois. I found the box all right, and nailed the card on it, and put it on the cars; then I went in the depot and got a sandwich. I was walking around, eating my sandwich, and I passed by the baggage room, and there was my box, with a young man walking around, looking at it, and he had a card in his hand. I felt like going up to that young man, and saying, 'Stranger, that's my corpse.' But I didn't. I walked on, ate my sandwich, and when I looked in again the young man was gone; but there was that card nailed right on that box. I went and looked on that card. It was directed to Colonel Jenkins, Cleveland, Ohio. So I looked in the car, and there was my box all right.

"Just before the train started, a man came into the baggage car and laid a lot of limburger cheese down on my box; he didn't know what was in my box, you know, and I didn't know what was in his paper, but I found out later. It was an awful cold night, and after we started, the baggage master came in. He was a nice fellow, Johnson was, and he said, 'A man would freeze to death, out there; I'll make it all right.'

"So he shut all the doors and all the windows, built a roaring coal fire in the stove; then he took turns fixing the car and poking the fire, till I began to smell something and feel uncomfortable, so I moved as far away from my corpse as I could, and Johnson says to me, 'A friend of yours? Did he die lately? This year, I mean.' Says I, 'I'll fix it;' so I opened a window, and we took turns breathing the fresh air. After a while Johnson said, 'Let's smoke, I think that'll fix it.' So we lit our cigars and puffed a bit, but we got so sick that we let 'em go out again—it didn't do any good. We tried the air again. Says Johnson, 'He's in no trance, is he? There's doubt about some people being dead, but there's no doubt about him, is there? What did he die of?'

"We stopped at a station, and when we started off again Johnson came in with a bottle of disinfector, and says, 'I've got something now that'll fix it.' So he sprinkled it all around, over the box, the limburger, and over everything, but it wouldn't do, the smells didn't mix well. Johnson said, 'Just think of it. We've all got to die, all got to come to this.' Then we thought we'd move the box to one end of the car, so we stooped over it; I took one end and he took the other, but we couldn't get it far. Johnson says, 'We'll freeze to death if we stay out on the platform; we'll die if we stay in here.' So we took hold of it again; but Johnson, he couldn't stand it, he fell right over. I dragged him out on the platform, and the cold air soon brought him to, and we went in the car to get warm. 'What are we going to do?' asked Johnson, and he looked ill. 'We are sure to have typhoid fever and half a dozen other fevers. We're pizened, we are!'

"At last we thought it was better to go out on the platform. In an hour and a half I was taken off that platform stiff, nearly frozen to death. They put me to bed, and I had all them fevers that Johnson spoke about. You see the thing worked on my mind. It didn't do me no good to learn, three weeks later, that there had been a mistake—that my corpse had gone to Colonel Jenkins, Cleveland, and that I'd taken his box of rifles for decent burial to Illinois. The news came too late to save Roger McPherson—about three weeks too late." When I'm not prepared to speak, I always apologize, and that's the reason I've told you so much about Roger McPherson.

Text / "Too Late for Roger McPherson," *Times,* April 11, 1879. This yarn was first published as part of "Some Rambling Notes of an Idle Excursion," *The Stolen White Elephant* (1882). It appeared later as "The Invalid's Story," *In Defense of Harriet Shelley and Other Essays* (1892). The published versions are longer and more detailed than the speech.

· 34 ·

In Paris Mark Twain enjoyed the ribaldry of the Stomach Club, an unpublicized group that relished the belly laughs of bawdy humor. A few of his notebook entries imply that he was more than once a guest at these sub rosa sessions, one item observing that the funniest things are the forbidden ones. Another memorandum reminds him to make a collection of his "profane" pieces, but nothing came of it. Compared to the frankness of modern pornography, his contribution, below, appears remarkably restrained, almost decorous.

Some Thoughts on the Science of Onanism

Stomach Club Dinner, Paris, Spring 1879

My gifted predecessor has warned you against the "social evil—adultery." In his able paper he exhausted that subject; he left absolutely nothing more to be said on it. But I will continue his good work in the cause of morality by cautioning you against that species of recreation called self-abuse—to which I perceive that you are too much addicted. All great writers upon health and morals, both ancient and modern, have struggled with this stately subject; this shows its dignity and importance. Some of these writers have taken one side, some the other. Homer, in the second book of the *Iliad,* says with fine enthusiasm, "Give me masturbation or give me death!" Caesar, in his *Commentaries,* says, "To the lonely it is company; to the forsaken it is a friend; to the aged and impotent it is a benefactor; they that be penniless are yet rich, in that they still have this majestic diversion." In another place this excellent observer has said, "There are times when I perfer it to sodomy." Robinson Crusoe says, "I cannot describe what I owe to this gentle art." Queen Elizabeth said, "It is the bulwark of virginity." Cetewayo, the Zulu hero, remarked that "a jerk in the hand is worth two in the bush." The immortal Franklin has said, "Masturbation is the mother of invention." He also said, "Masturbation is the best policy." Michelangelo and all the other old Masters—old Masters, I will remark, is an abbreviation, a contraction—have used similar language. Michelangelo said to Pope Julius II, "Self-negation is noble, self-culture is beneficent, self-possession is manly, but to the truly great and inspiring soul they are poor and tame compared to self-abuse." Mr. Brown, here, in one of his latest and most graceful poems refers to it in an eloquent line which is destined to live to the end of time—"None know it but to love it, None name it but to praise."

Such are the utterances of the most illustrious of the masters of this renowned science, and apologists for it. The name of those who decry it and oppose it is legion; they have made strong arguments and uttered bitter speeches against it—but there is not room to repeat them here, in much detail. Brigham Young, an expert of incontestable authority, said, "As compared with the other thing, it is the difference between the lightning bug and the lightning." Solomon said, "There is nothing to recommend it but its cheapness." Galen said, "It is shameful to degrade to such bestial use that grand limb, that formidable member, which we votaries of science dub the 'Major Maxillary'—when they dub it at all—which is seldom. It would be better to decapitate the Major than to use him so. It would be better to amputate the *os frontis* than to put it to such a use." The great statistician, Smith, in his report to Parliament, says, "In my opinion, more children have been wasted in this way than in any other." It cannot be denied that the high authority of this art entitles it to our respect; but at the same time I think that its harmfulness demands our condemnation. Mr. Darwin was grieved to feel obliged to give up his theory that the monkey was the connecting link between man and the lower animals. I think he was too hasty. The monkey is the only animal, except man, that practices this science; hence he is our brother; there is a bond of sympathy and relationship between us. Give this ingenious animal an audience of the proper kind, and he will straightway put aside his other affairs and take a whet; and you will see by the contortions and his ecstatic expression that he takes an intelligent and human interest in his performance.

The signs of excessive indulgence in this destructive pastime are easily detectable. They are these: A disposition to eat, to drink, to smoke, to meet together convivially, to laugh, to joke, and tell indelicate stories—and mainly, a yearning to paint pictures. The results of the habit are: Loss of memory, loss of virility, loss of cheerfulness, loss of hopefulness, loss of character, and loss of progeny. Of all the various kinds of sexual intercourse, this has least to recommend it. As an amusement it is too fleeting; as an occupation it is too wearing; as a public exhibition there is no money in it. It is unsuited to the drawing room, and in the most cultured society it has long since been banished from the social board. It has at last, in our day of progress and improvement, been degraded to brotherhood with flatulence—among the best bred these two arts are now indulged only in private—though by consent of the whole company, when only males are present, it is still permissible, in good society, to remove the embargo upon the fundamental sigh.

My illustrious predecessor has taught you that all forms of the "social evil" are bad. I would teach you that some of those forms are more to be avoided than others; so, in concluding, I say, "If you *must* gamble away your lives sexually, don't play a Lone Hand too much." When you feel a revolutionary uprising in your system, get your Vendome Column down some other way—don't jerk it down.

Text / Composite, based upon: "Some Thoughts on the Science of Onanism," TS, MTP, of MS presumably extant but whereabouts unknown; *Some Thoughts on the Science of Onanism* (privately printed, January 1952).

Cetewayo / Also Cetywayo (ca. 1836–84). King of the Zulus. A great warrior, he defeated a British force at Isandhlwans, January 22, 1879. Later captured, he was taken to London, then reinstated as ruler (1883), but had to seek British protection.

None knew it but to love it / A modification of lines from Fitz-Greene Halleck (1790–1867), "On the Death of Joseph Rodman Drake": "None knew thee but to love thee, / Nor named thee but to praise."

Galen / Claudius Galenas Galen (ca. A.D. 130—ca. 200). Greek physician and philosopher. He was physician to the Emperor Marcus Aurelius and author of many works on medicine, logic, grammar, ethics, philosophy, and literature. Galen's work in medicine and physiology was standard until the sixteenth-seventeenth centuries, when it was superseded by the research of William Harvey and others.

Smith / Possibly Adam Smith (1723–90), a Scottish economist whose best known work is *The Wealth of Nations* (1776).

a yearning to paint pictures / A pleasantry aimed at the painters, American and European, who frequented gatherings of the Stomach Club. Perhaps a thrust specifically at Edwin Austin Abbey (1852–1911), an American painter with whom Mark Twain enjoyed trading jibes.

· 35 ·

Back home by late summer of 1879 and temporarily settled in Elmira, Mark Twain was promptly drafted as speaker for a local political meeting. The press reported a large turnout, a large part of the attraction undoubtedly being the announcement that he would be on the program.

Introducing General Hawley

Republican Meeting, Elmira, New York, October 16, 1879

I see I am advertised to introduce the speaker of the evening, General Hawley, of Connecticut, and I see it is the report that I am to make a political speech. Now, I must say this is an error. I wasn't constructed to make stump speeches, and on that head (politics) I have only this to say: First, see that you vote. Second, see that your neighbor votes. Lastly, see that yourself or neighbor don't scratch the ticket. General Hawley was President of the Centennial Commission. He was a gallant soldier in the war. He has been Governor of Connecticut, member of Congress, and was President of the convention that nominated Abraham Lincoln.

[General Hawley: "That nominated Grant."]

He says it was Grant, but I know better. He is a member of my church at Hartford and the author of "Beautiful Snow." Maybe he will deny that. It is not my province to enlarge upon matters generally. I am here simply to give him a character from his last place. As a fellow-townsman and dutiful citizen, I have a high respect for him; as a personal friend of years, I have the warmest regard for him; as a neighbor whose vegetable garden adjoins my own, why—why, I watch him. But that is nothing—we all do that with any neighbor. General Hawley is a man who keeps his promises; he is a man who always speaks the truth, and not only in private life but in politics; he is an editor who believes what he says in his own newspaper; as author of "Beautiful Snow," he has given us a poem which has added a new pang to winter. The public honor, public money, church property—anything and all things that are strictly public—are safe in his hands. I have watched him many a time, as the contribution box went by, and *I* never saw him take anything out of it. Would that we had more such men in politics. Charity, compassion, benevolence, are inborn in General Hawley; he never sends a tramp empty-handed from his door, but always gives him a letter of introduction to me. But above all and beyond all, it can be said with entire sincerity, that he is a square, honest man—a square, honest man in politics, think of that—and I will remark here, in confidence, that he occupies an almighty lonesome position.

General Hawley's public aspect is as creditable as his private one. As a member of Congress he has upheld our excellent President's hands; his voice and his vote have always been for the best good of his country; considerations of self have never influenced his policy; he has never backed down before a responsibility nor dodged one. As a citizen of the republic he is without reproach; in his faith in her institutions, in his pride in her greatness, in his affection for her and belief in her high destiny, he is an American of the Americans. As President of the Centennial Commission, he carried through and brought to a successful issue an enterprise which has borne the fame of our resources and industries to distant regions, and made our country a respected competitor in markets where her rivalry was of little moment before. As Governor of his state, he governed well and righteously; as a soldier he earned lasting praise and honor. His public trusts have been many, and never in the slightest did he prove unfaithful. Pure, honest, incorruptible, that is Joe Hawley. Such a man in politics is like a vase of attar of roses in a glue factory—it may modify the stench if it doesn't destroy it.

And now, in speaking thus highly of the speaker of the evening, I have not meant to flatter, but only to speak the plain and simple truth. I haven't said anything more of him than I would say of myself. Ladies and gentlemen, this is General Hawley.

Text / Composite, based upon: " 'The Innocents' in Elmira," *Times,* October 19, 1879; "Mark Twain," *Courant,* October 20, 1879.

"Beautiful Snow" / By John Whittaker Watson (1824–90), *Beautiful Snow and Other Poems* (1869): "O the snow, the beautiful snow, / Filling the sky and the earth below. / Over the house-tops, over the street, / Over the heads of the people you meet," and so on. The lines are still occasionally recited by broadcasters, particularly during the Christmas season.

· 36 ·

A reunion of the Army of the Tennessee in Chicago was a two-day outpouring of patriotic frenzy: clamorous bands, roaring cheers, dazzling gold braid, and thousands of Union veterans marching down Michigan Avenue. Mark Twain, the quasi-Confederate, was a favored visitor. For the meeting at Haverly's Theater, attended by an overflow audience of two thousand, the stage was set to represent a fort at Vicksburg. Mark Twain had a prominent place on the stage, along with two or three dozen Union generals and political bigwigs. When the house shouted for a speech from him, somebody yelled, "Tell us about Adam!" Caught off guard for once, he responded briefly.

Impromptu Speech

Thirteenth Reunion, Army of the Tennessee,
Haverly's Theater, Chicago, November 12, 1879

Ladies and gentlemen: I just within a moment heard General Sherman say to a gentleman sitting in my neighborhood that, if he would promise not to speak more than two minutes, he would let him get up. He didn't say that to me, and I judge, by his remarks to me, that he wouldn't allow me quite so much. But—is that loud enough?—I have not listened to a bad speech tonight, and I don't propose to be the one to furnish you with one; and I would, if I had time and permission go on and make an excellent speech. But I never was happy, never could make a good impromptu speech without several hours to prepare it.

Text / *CTrib,* November 13, 1879.

· 37 ·

The climax of the reunion was a grand banquet at the Palmer House. Attended by six hundred veterans, including Generals Grant, Sherman, Sheridan, Logan, Schofield, Pope, and other commanders, besides one admiral and a cluster of politicos, the affair went on almost all night. After an elaborate dinner–blue points, turtle soup, saddle of venison, buffalo steaks, truffle sauce, and so forth–aided by four kinds of wine, Roman Punch, and cognac, General Grant began the speech-making about half-past ten with a toast to "Our Country–Her Place Among the Nations." Then the band played the national anthem, and fireworks were set off in a miniature fort. Oratory and martial music continued for several hours. Mark Twain delivered the final toast, the fifteenth, about 3:30 A.M.*, standing on a table and pausing at the end of every sentence to allow laughter to subside. He considered "The Babies" one of his best dinner speeches–it fetched even the usually taciturn Grant. For his comments on the reunion, see his letters to Livy,* MTL, *1:370–73, and to Howells,* Mark Twain-Howells Letters, *eds. Henry Nash Smith and William Gibson (Harvard, 1960), 1:278–80.*

The Babies. As They Comfort Us in Our Sorrows, Let Us Not Forget Them in Our Festivities

Thirteenth Reunion Banquet, Army of the Tennessee,
Palmer House, Chicago, November 13, 1879

I like that. We haven't all had the good fortune to be ladies; we haven't all been generals, or poets, or statesmen; but when the toast works down to the babies, we stand on common ground, for we've all been babies. It is a shame that for a thousand years the world's banquets have utterly ignored the baby—as if *he* didn't amount to anything! If you gentlemen will stop and think a minute—if you will go back fifty or a hundred years, to your early married life, and recontemplate your first baby, you will remember that he amounted to a good deal, and even something over. You soldiers all know that when that little fellow arrived at family headquarters, you had to hand in your resignation. He took entire command. You became his lackey—his mere body servant, and you had to stand around, too. He was not a commander who made allowances for time, distance, weather, or anything else—you had to execute his order whether it was possible or not. And there was only one form of marching in his manual of tactics, and that was the double-quick. He treated you with every sort of insolence and disrespect, and the bravest of you didn't dare to say a word.

You could face the death storm at Donelson and Vicksburg, and give back blow for blow; but when he clawed your whiskers, and pulled your hair, and twisted your nose, you had to take it. When the thunders of war were sounding in your ears, you set your face toward the batteries, and advanced with steady tread; but, when he turned on the terrors of his war whoop, you advanced in the other direction—and mighty glad of the chance, too. When he called for soothing syrup, did you venture to throw out any side remarks about certain services being unbecoming an officer and a gentleman? No. You got up and *got* it. When he ordered his pap bottle, and it wasn't warm, did you talk back? Not you. You went to work and *warmed* it. You even descended so far in your menial office as to take a suck at that warm, insipid stuff yourself, just to see if it was right—three parts water to one of milk, a touch of sugar to modify the colic, and a drop of peppermint to kill those infernal hiccups. I can taste that stuff yet.

And how many things you learned, as you went along! Sentimental young folks still take stock in that beautiful old saying that when the baby smiles in his sleep, it is because the angels are whispering to him. Very pretty, but too thin—simply wind on the stomach, my friends! If the baby proposed to take a walk at the usual hour—half-past two in the morning—didn't you rise up promptly and remark—with a mental addition which wouldn't improve a Sunday school book *much*—that that was the very thing you were about to propose yourself? Oh, you were under good discipline. And as you went fluttering up and down the room in your undress uniform, you not only prattled undignified baby talk, but even tuned up your martial voices and tried to *sing!*—"Rock-a-by baby in the tree top," for instance. And what an affliction for the neighbors, too—for it isn't everybody within a mile around that likes military music at three in the morning. And when you had been keeping this sort of thing up two or three hours, and your little velvet-head intimated that nothing suited him like exercise and noise, and proposed to fight it out on that line if it took all night—what did you do? [When Mark Twain paused, voices shouted: "Go on!"] You simply *went* on till you dropped in the last ditch.

The idea that a *baby* doesn't amount to anything! Why, *one* baby is just a house and front yard full by itself. *One* baby can furnish more business than you and your whole Interior Department can attend to. He is enterprising, irrepressible, brim full of lawless activities. Do what you please, you can't make him stay on the reservation. Sufficient unto the day is one baby—as long as you are in your right mind don't you ever pray for twins. Twins amount to a permanent riot; and there ain't any real difference between triplets and an insurrection.

Yes, it was high time for a toastmaster to recognize the importance of the babies. Think what is in store for the present crop! Fifty years from now we shall all be dead—I trust—and then this flag, if it still survive—and let us hope it may—will be floating over a Republic numbering 200,000,000 souls, according to the settled laws of our increase; our present schooner of State will have grown into a political leviathan—a *Great Eastern*—and the cradled babies of today will be on deck. Let them be well trained, for we are going to leave a big contract on their hands. Among the three or four million cradles now rocking in the land are some which this nation would preserve for ages as sacred things, if we could know which ones they are. In one of these cradles the unconscious Farragut of the future is at this moment *teething*—think of it!—and putting in a world of dead earnest, unarticulated and perfectly justifiable profanity over it, too; in another, the future renowned astronomer is blinking at the shining Milky Way, with but a languid interest—poor little chap!—and wondering what has become of that other one they call the wet nurse; in another the future great historian is lying—and doubtless he will continue to lie until his earthly mission is ended; in another the future President is busying himself with no profounder problem of state than what the mischief has become of his hair so early, and in a mighty array of other cradles there are now some sixty thousand future office-seekers getting ready to furnish him occasion to grapple with that same old problem a second time.

And in still one more cradle, somewhere under the flag, the future illustrious Commander in Chief of the American armies is so little burdened with his approaching grandeurs and responsibilities as to be giving his whole strategic mind, at this moment, to trying to find out some way to get his own big toe into his mouth—an achievement which, meaning no disrespect, the illustrious guest of this evening turned *his* whole attention to some fifty-six years ago. And if the child is but a prophecy of the man, there are mighty few who will doubt that he *succeeded.*

Text / Composite, based upon: "Mark Twain. The Babies," *CTrib,* November 14, 1879; "Mark Twain," *The Grant Reception Monograph*

(1879):75–76; "Mark Twain on Babies," unidentified clipping, MTP; "The Babies" in the following: *Report of the Proceedings of the Society of the Army of the Tennessee, at the Thirteenth Annual Meeting* (1879):154–56; *MTS*(10):64–68; *MTS*(23):58–62; *Eloquence*(R), 1:218–21; *Eloquence*(T), 1:298–301.

Great Eastern / The largest steamship of the day: length 692 feet, beam 83 feet, displacement 27,000 tons. Her maiden voyage from Britain to New York occurred June 17–28, 1860. Although a failure as a transatlantic carrier, she held first place for size until the launching of the *Oceania* in 1899.

· 38 ·

The Atlantic Monthly, *doing the handsome thing by famous contributors, honored Oliver Wendell Holmes with a seventieth birthday breakfast. At this affair, which began about noon, a distinguished company assembled: Emerson, Whittier, Longfellow, Warner, George William Curtis, Stedman, Francis Parkman, and others. Mark Twain was one of the number. Still smarting over what he considered his outrageous performance at the Whittier dinner in 1877, he regarded the breakfast as an opportunity to atone. He insisted on speaking not later than third on the program to avoid the embarrassment he believed might otherwise affect him and disturb an audience wondering what new gaucheries the unpredictable humorist would perpetrate.*

Speech

Atlantic Monthly *Breakfast, Seventieth Birthday of Oliver Wendell Holmes, Boston, December 3, 1879*

I would have traveled a much greater distance than I have come to witness the paying of honors to Dr. Holmes; for my feeling toward him has always been one of peculiar warmth. When one receives a letter from a great man for the first time in his life, it is a large event to him, as all of you know by your own experience. You never can receive letters enough from famous men afterward to obliterate that one, or dim the memory of the pleasant surprise it was, and the gratification it gave you. Lapse of time cannot make it commonplace or cheap.

Well, the first great man who ever wrote me a letter was our guest—Oliver Wendell Holmes. He was also the first great literary man I ever stole anything from—and that is how I came to write to him and he to me. When my first book was new, a friend of mine said to me, "The dedication is very neat." Yes, I said, I thought it was. My friend said, "I always admired it, even before I saw it in *The Innocents Abroad.*" I naturally said, "What do you mean? Where did you ever see it before?" "Well, I saw it first some years ago as Doctor Holmes's dedication to his *Songs in Many Keys.*" Of course, my first impulse was to prepare this man's remains for burial, but upon reflection I said I would reprieve him for a moment or two and give him a chance to prove his assertion if he could. We stepped into a book store, and he did prove it. I had really stolen that dedication, almost word for word. I could not imagine how this curious thing had happened; for I knew one thing—that a certain amount of pride always goes along with a teaspoonful of brains, and that this pride protects a man from deliberately stealing other people's ideas. That is what a teaspoonful of brains will do for a man—and admirers had often told me that I had nearly a basketful—though they were rather reserved as to the size of the basket.

However, I thought the thing out, and solved the mystery. Two years before, I had been laid up a couple of weeks in the Sandwich Islands, and had read and reread Doctor Holmes's poems till my mental reservoir was filled up with them to the brim. The dedication lay on the top, and handy, so, by and by, I unconsciously stole it. Perhaps I unconsciously stole the rest of the volume, too, for many people have told me that my book was pretty poetical, in one way or another. Well, of course, I wrote Dr. Holmes and told him I hadn't meant to steal, and he wrote back and said in the kindest way that it was all right and no harm done; and added that he believed we all unconsciously worked over ideas gathered in reading and hearing, imagining they were original with ourselves. He stated a truth, and did it in such a pleasant way, and salved over my sore spot so gently and so healingly, that I was rather glad I had committed the crime, for the sake of the letter. I afterward called on him and told him to make perfectly free with any ideas of mine that struck him as being good protoplasm for poetry. He could see by that that there wasn't anything mean about me; and we got along right from the start.

I have met Dr. Holmes many times since; and lately he said—however, I am wandering wildly away from the one thing which I got on my feet to do; that is, to make my compliments to you, my fellow teachers of the great public, and likewise to say that I am right glad to see that Dr. Holmes is still in his prime and full of generous life; and as age is not determined by years, but by trouble and infirmities of mind and body, I hope it may be a very long time yet before anyone can truthfully say, "He is growing old."

Text / Composite, based upon: "Unconscious Plagiarism" in the following: *Eloquence*(R), 1:221–23; *Eloquence*(T), 1:301–3; *MTS*(10): 56–58; *MTS*(23):77–79. Both *MTS* texts are misdated.

· 39 ·

To give impetus to a Hartford Republican rally, ex-President Grant appeared in person. Mark Twain was one of a committee on arrangements that met the general in Boston, then escorted him to Hartford. After a great parade of five thousand marchers—bands, military companies, and dignitaries—a luncheon followed and a formal reception, at which Mark Twain delivered a speech of welcome.

Welcome to General Grant

Hartford, October 16, 1880

General Grant: I also am deputized to welcome you to the sincere and cordial hospitalities of Hartford, the city of the historic and revered Charter Oak, of which the most of this town is built. At first it was proposed to have only one speaker to welcome you, but this was changed, because it was feared that, considering the shortness of the crop of speeches this year, if anything occurred to prevent that speaker from delivering his speech you would feel disappointed.

By your example you have killed the hoary fashion of long speeches; and for this you deserve imperishable gratitude. We shall best honor you in honoring the lesson you have taught. As a soldier you proved yourself without a peer—and so we welcome you as the first soldier of the Republic; as President you inaugurated international arbitration—and so we welcome you as the first to lay the axe to the root of the trade of war, and as the pioneer in the march of the nations toward the last perfection of enlightened government, the substitution of reason for force in the settlement of controversies; and finally, as one who, being almost called—and yet not quite—to carry the standard of a great party for the third time, in a presidential campaign, has sunk the hero in the patriot, has cast aside all considerations of self, all pique, all narrow feeling, and has devoted his whole heart and the might of his great name to the cause of that party, and through it to the highest and best interest of the country, its progress and its civilization, we welcome you by the noblest of all the titles you have earned, that of First Citizen of the Republic.

I desire, at this point, to refer to your past history. By years of colossal labor and colossal achievement, you at last beat down a gigantic rebellion and saved your country from destruction. Then the country commanded you to take the helm of state. You preferred your great office of General of the Armies, and the rest and comfort which it afforded; but you loyally obeyed, and relinquished permanently the ample and well-earned salary of the generalship, and resigned your accumulating years to the chance mercies of a precarious existence.

By this present fatiguing progress through the land; by the sight of your honored face; by the wisdom of your words; and by the magic of your name, you are contributing a share whose magnitude cannot be overestimated, toward saving your country once more—this time from dishonor and shame, and from industrial disaster.

You are now a private citizen, but private employments are closed against you because your name would be used for speculative purposes, and you have refused to permit that. But your country will reward you, never fear. When Wellington won Waterloo, a battle about on a level with some dozen of your victories, sordid England tried to pay him for that service with wealth and grandeur; she made him a Duke, loaded him with minor and yet great and shining dignities, and gave him a sum of money equivalent, at present values, to $4,000,000.

If you had done and suffered for any other country what you have done and suffered for your own, you would have been affronted in the same sordid way; but thank God this vast and rich and mighty Republic is imbued to the core with a delicacy which will forever preserve her from so degrading a deserving man. Your country loves you, your country is proud of you, your country is grateful to you. Her praises, which have been ringing in your ears all these weeks and months, will never cease while the flag you saved continues to wave.

Your country stands ready, from this day forth, to testify her measureless love and pride and gratitude toward you, in every conceivable—inexpensive way. Welcome to Hartford, great soldier, honored statesman, unselfish citizen!

Text / Composite, based upon: TS, Notebook 15, July 26, 1880–December, 1881, pp. 11–13, MTP; NY*Trib*, October 17, 1880.

industrial disaster / Implying Republican belief in a high protective tariff and fear that a Democratic administration, by reducing or even abolishing tariffs, would bring ruin upon the country.

· 40 ·

During the final week of the presidential campaign of 1880, Hartford Republicans staged a great rally in the Opera House. The Courant *of October 27 reported an overflow crowd of fervent Garfield supporters, among whom were a number of Democrats. "It is to be hoped," the paper observed, that they "reaped some benefit from the political truths they heard." On the stage were solid citizens and veterans of the Hartford Wide Awake Club of 1860, displaying the transparency they had carried in torchlight processions twenty years before. The Second Ward Garfield Legion glee club entertained the gathering by singing "Garfield and Arthur, the People's Choice," "Same Old Crew," and other numbers. Warner made a speech, the Honorable Henry C. Robinson, and Mark Twain, who talked at greater length than usual. The* Courant *remarked that the audience was "held unbroken to the very close, at 10 o'clock."*

Political Speech

Republican Rally, Hartford Opera House, October 26, 1880

Friends say to me, "What do you mean by this?—you swore off from lecturing, years ago." Well, that is true; I did reform; and I reformed permanently, too. But *this* ain't a lecture; it is only a *speech*—nothing but a mere old cut-and-dried impromptu speech—and there's a great moral difference between a lecture and a speech, I can tell you. For when you deliver a lecture you get good pay, but when you make a speech you don't get a cent. You don't get anything at all from your own party, and you don't get anything out of the opposition but a noble, good supply of infamous episodes in your own private life which you hadn't heard of before—a scorching lot of facts about your private rascalities and scoundrelisms which is brand-new to you—all good enough stuff for by and by, when you get ready to write your autobiography, but of no immediate use to you, further than to show you what you *could* have become if you had attended strictly to business. I have never made but one political speech before this. That was years ago. I made a logical, closely-reasoned, compact, powerful argument against a discriminating and iniquitous tax which was about to be imposed by the opposition—I may say I made a most thoughtful, symmetrical and admirable argument; but a Michigan newspaper editor answered it—refuted it—utterly demolished it—by saying I was in the constant habit of horsewhipping my great grandmother. I should not have minded it so much—well, I don't know that I should have minded it at all—a little thing like that—if he had said I did it for her good; but when he said I merely did it for exercise, I felt that such a statement as that was almost sure to cast a shadow over my character. However, I don't mind these things particularly—it is the only intelligent and patriotic way of conducting a campaign. I don't mind what the opposition say of me, so long as they don't tell the truth about me; but when they descend to telling the truth about me, I consider that that is taking an unfair advantage. Why should we be bitter against each other?—such of us, of both parties, as are not ashamed of being Americans? But perhaps I have said enough by way of preface.

I am going to vote the Republican ticket, myself, from old habit, but what I am here for is to try to persuade you to vote the Democratic ticket; because if you throw the government of this country into the hands of the Republicans they will unquestionably kill that Wood tariff project. But if you throw this government into the hands of the Democrats, the Wood tariff project will become the law of the land, and every one of us will reap his share of the enormous benefits resulting from it. There will be nothing sectional about it—its wholesome generosities are as all-embracing as the broad and general atmosphere—the North, the South, the East, the West, will all have their portion of those benefactions. Consider the South's share, for instance. With a tariff "for revenue only," and no tariff for "protection," she will not be obliged to carry on a trade with us of the North and pay northern prices. No! She can buy of England, duty free, at far cheaper rates. The price of her cotton will remain as before, but the cost of producing will be vastly diminished, and the profit vastly increased. Wealth will pour in on her in such a deluge that she will not know what to do with the money. In time she will be able to buy and sell the North. Will the South cast a solid vote for the Wood tariff bill? I am glad to believe—yes, to know—that the South will stand by our Senator Eaton to a man, in this great and good cause.

And think of our share in the benefits of the Wood tariff. Some of our people sit up and cry all night for joy, when they think of them. They've raised the rivers here with their tears—joyful tears—and dissipated the malaria. And I wish they'd keep on crying—it is the only efficient sewerage we've ever had. Our first and chiefest benefit from the Wood tariff will be, that we shan't have any more factory smoke. Statistics on file in the War Department show that more people's eyes are injured by factory smoke in a year than by any other agent. Statistics—I've come loaded with statistics, for I've noticed that a man can't prove anything without statistics; no man can; Senator Eaton himself can't prove anything without statistics—or with them—whichever it is; I don't remember which it *is,* now, but I know it is one or the other of them, for I had it all thought out, once. Statistics—statistics—why statistics are more precious and useful than any other one thing in this world, except whiskey—I mean hymnbooks. This comes of trusting to inspiration instead of sticking to the cold text. A man can ruin himself that way making a public speech. Statistics in the Navy Department show that if the factory smoke were done away with, there would be a saving to the North, every year, of over $200,000 in diminished wash bills alone, and that the washerwoman who is today able to support her husband and children in free-handed plenty at the tub, would have to come down to wages that would not only benefit her health and strength by requiring her to work nights as well as days, but would enable you and me to fairly wallow in dissipations which are denied to us now by the grinding tyranny of the weekly wash bill. Statistics in the Interior Department show that factory smoke causes more profanity to the square mile than any other known agent, except the book agent.

Statistics in the Department of Justice show that with the departure of factory smoke the factory workmen would depart also, of necessity, they and their wives and children, and get what they need and what their honest hard work has earned for them, a good, long, soul-satisfying holiday. Nothing in the world to do but lie around in comfort and enjoy themselves. And while they were having holidays and a good time, the rest of the people would be vastly benefited, too, for occasionally when you needed a capable man to do some work for you, you could get him for half a dollar a day. You could have your pick and choice then, but you can't now, for there is more work and money than men; so they are in a position to come or not, just as they please; for a man can be as independent and as much his own master, free and untrammeled on *enough* as he can be on fifty thousand times enough. It is only when you cut him *below* enough that he ceases to be independent and can neither ante nor pass the buck as the prophet says—and so of course you raise him, and raise him, and raise him till you raise him *out* as the poet says—and it's no trick for you to do it, because you hold a flush against his two pair and a jack. I trust I make myself understood.

Yes, you can get men exceeding cheap, then, in the good time that is coming, when the Democratic tariff bill goes through; and our architecture will improve, too, for we shall have the stateliest kind of poorhouses all around and everywhere—they'll be so thick that the worst marksman here couldn't miss them with an old-fashioned Allen's revolver—and ten percent of the population will be in them, and just as comfortable and contented as angels. Why, you can even save on pew rent, then. Pew rent will go down to next to nothing, and the poorest sinner can have a place to sleep.

And real estate—think of that. You can buy a corner lot, then, for less than it costs you to buy a grave, now. Of course you'll *need* the grave more, then—but never mind that, that's a matter of *de*tail—you'll take which you please; I'm not trying to dictate—I'm only using the thing as an illustration. And you can build a house, then, cheaper than you can bury a man today—and there's more satisfaction in it, too—unless you can pick your man. You can keep a carriage then for less than it costs you to keep a wheelbarrow now. And bigamy—think of that! Bigamy will be cheaper then than monogamy is now. There's a million arguments—but I've only got all night to talk in, so I must leave most of them out.

The tyrannous unequal values of today will disappear; and real estate on the ground and real estate in a cart will be the same price—fifteen cents a cubic yard. And that is right—that is just. Try to make me believe there's *differences* in dirt—with *my* familiarity with it—that one kind of dirt is worth more than another kind—that even the *best* dirt is worth more than fifteen cents a yard? *No,* sir—*I* think it's *high.*

And in place of the confusion and noise of today, and the unsightly mud, the streets of the North will slumber in a soothing Sabbath calm, restful to the weary spirit, and be adorned with soft, rich carpets of grass, a solace to the eye and a satisfaction to the foot. The odious law which today deprives us of the improving, elevating, humanizing society of the tramp will be swept from the statute book by the tramp himself; for we shall all be tramps, then, and can outvote anything that can be devised to hamper us, and give the opposition long odds, too. Once more we shall see our old ragged tourists moving in eternal procession from house to house disdaining bread and demanding pie at the butt end of the club.

Immigration will cease, and emigration will take its place; and we shall all be benefited, because we shall pack up and go to countries where we can get fifty-five cents a day, and feed on meat four times a month.

And we can stretch forth a helping hand to revered old England in this her time of heavy distress. She was our enemy in the war days, and did all she could to injure us and cripple us and insult us; but she stands ready to be our friend now, and it is our duty and should be our pleasure to forgive and forget, and meet her with the kiss of love and peace; she is ready to be our friend—yes, more than ready; she is eager, she is anxious, to be our friend. And all she asks for this is that we shall pass the Wood tariff bill and so give her famishing factories a magnificent new lease of life and her whole people a rousing prosperity such as they have not known for years—a prosperity which will amply make up for all she is losing through her land troubles in Ireland—and by the generous might of the great Democratic party we *will* pass this bill, and fall weeping upon the grateful bosom of our old suffering mother land. We will say, "You fitted out pirates against us, but we forgive you; you cheated us out of one pirate after we had thrashed him in fair fight and had a just and righteous mortgage on him, but we forgive you; you connived secretly with Louis Napoleon for our overthrow, but we forgive you; you feasted and honored and sheltered our enemies, and obstructed our friends and sneered at them, but we forgive you; you have been the Irishman's hard master at home for seven hundred years, and you will be his hard master now in America, but no matter, he forgives you, and we forgive you—all and everything—and you shall have your Wood tariff bill which you urge upon us with an eloquence which moves even the unsentimental among us to say, 'Take our forges, take our factories, take our prosperities, take all we have, only say we are the one utterly loving, generous, forgiving, forgetting, magnanimous nation that graces the earth.' "

Yes, let her say that to us, and remove the troublesome factory smoke, and it is all we ask. For the one great central idea of this presidential battle is not which is the better man of the two; it is not war or peace; it is not religion; it is not sectional supremacy; it is not national honor, national glory—no, it is none of these, it is factory smoke. It all turns on factory smoke. Other matters are trifling, they are nothing. The supreme and only question is, who will rid us of the factory smoke? Only rid us of the factory smoke, and you rid us of everything else—and on top of it we win England's imperishable gratitude.

Now, I beseech you, lay aside all private selfishness, and mere considerations of bread and high wages, and go to the polls, vote the good old Democratic ticket, and clear this murky northern atmosphere of its all-pervading clouds of suffocating factory smoke. Then we will all knock off and have a good permanent holiday and a general good time. Vote your full strength for our three great and good Democratic standard bearers—English of Connecticut, English of Indiana, and the English on the other side of the water—for this fight is an English fight, pure and simple (all the family are in it), and there's nothing else to it. I would vote that ticket myself, but I have grown old in Republican sin, and it is too late to reform.

Now, I have spoken somewhat fantastically, but no matter, these fantastic trappings are hung around as solid and real a truth as anyone can utter. And it is a truth which not any of us can afford to whistle down the wind, or scoff at or ignore, or banish out of our minds unexamined and undigested—for in plain simple terms, it involves our actual *bread and meat,* and no amount of fine talk and cooked-up statistics can take away from it that stern and ominous fact. I will close these remarks with

A Fable

Once there was a community of happy and prosperous sparrows living in a pleasant wood, near a lake. In a wood on the other side of the lake, lived a community of cuckoos. You know, no doubt, the grasping and piratical habits of the cuckoo. Well, these cuckoos were always crossing the lake and trying to get a chance to lay their eggs in the sparrows' nests, so that the industrious sparrows would have to go to the trouble and expense of hatching and rearing their young for them. But there was a prohibitory protective tariff, which the cuckoos could not manage to get around. That is to say, there was a family of eagles living near the sparrows, and before a cuckoo could get in with her eggs, she had to pay a high duty—that is to say, the eagles ate her up, along with her eggs. That sort of a tariff had the effect of persuading the cuckoos to stay at home.

But by and by certain of the sparrows grew discontented and began to complain. They said: "This tariff is too exorbitant, it hampers our prosperity; what we need is a tariff for revenue only; this wood is pleasant, but if we had a Wood tariff it would be pleasanter; for then the cuckoos would come over, and eggs would be ever so much cheaper and plentier than they are now. Eggs would be dirt cheap, and we should all have just as many as we wanted."

This idea began to spread around, and pretty soon more than half of the sparrows were enthusiastic over it. So they went into power at the next election, and the first thing they did was to go forth in their strength and disable the eagles; that removed the protective tariff; then they passed their Wood tariff, with great rejoicings. Straightway, sure enough, the cuckoos swarmed over from the other side of the lake, flocked past the eagles' dismantled custom house, duty free, and laid their eggs in the sparrows' nests. The prophecy had come true; there was an abundance of eggs, and an apparent prodigious prosperity.

But things did not remain so bright. The sparrows found that they had to hatch out those eggs; a heavy job, but when it was done, they had a still heavier one before them, for they had to feed the little cuckoos, too, as well as their own little birds—for the cuckoo never helps—the cuckoo only furnishes the eggs, that is all—so the poor sparrows had to work double tides, and yet all the real profit went to the cuckoo tribe, for the little cuckoos were strong and voracious and they gobbled nine-tenths of every bite that came into the nest; wherefore they waxed stronger day by day, whilst the starving little sparrows waxed weaker and weaker. And at last the natural result came about—the powerful young cuckoos, seeing that they were boss of the situation, kicked the young sparrows out of the nests and took entire possession.

It was about this time that the community of sparrows rose up as one bird and remarked, "We are but mortal, we are but sparrows, and shall live to do many unwise things yet; but the next time anybody beguiles us with a 'tariff for revenue only,' he will have to get up at a particularly early hour in the morning."

Text / Composite, based upon: "Republican Rally," *Courant,* October 27, 1880; "Mark Twain Lifts His Voice," *Times,* October 27, 1880.

Wood tariff project / Fernando Wood (1812–81), Democratic congressman from New York (1863–65, 1867–81), prepared a comprehensive tariff bill (1878) to reduce import duties and to correct anomalies in the confusing tariff acts of the Civil War period. The bill had been killed two years before Mark Twain viewed with alarm.

Senator Eaton / William Wallace Eaton (1816–98). American legislator. Senator from Connecticut, he was a hard money Democrat, an advocate of tariff reform, and author of a bill to create a nonpartisan tariff commission.

Allen's revolver / Mark Twain describes the Allen in chapter 2 of *Roughing It:* "Simply drawing the trigger back, cocked and fired the pistol. As the trigger came back, the hammer would begin to rise and the barrel turn over, and presently down would drop the hammer, and away would speed the ball. To aim along the turning barrel and hit the thing aimed at was a feat which was probably never done with an 'Allen' in the world. . . . Sometimes all its six barrels would go off at once, and then there was no safe place in all the region round about, but behind it."

English of Connecticut / James Edward English (1812–90). American legislator. In Congress (1861), he was a War Democrat who supported Lincoln. He was governor of Connecticut (1867–69, 1870–71) and senator from Connecticut (1875–77).

English of Indiana / William Hayden English (1822–96). American legislator. A Democratic congressman from Indiana (1852–60), he opposed secession. In 1880 he was vice-presidential nominee on the Democratic ticket headed by Winfield Scott Hancock.

· 41 ·

Hartford Republicans celebrated the victory of their candidates, Garfield and Arthur, in a noisy session. Mark Twain disconcerted some listeners, however, by delivering a funeral oration in such a doleful voice that literal-minded people were slow to catch on.

Funeral Oration Over the Grave of the Democratic Party

Republican Jollification, Opera House, Hartford, November 2, 1880

There are occasions which are so solemn, so weighted with the deep concerns of life, that then even the licensed jester must lay aside his cap and bells and remember that he is a man and mortal; that even his light, butterfly career of folly has its serious seasons, and he cannot flee them or ignore them.

Such a time, my friends, is this, for we are in the near presence of one who is a passenger from this life, one whom we have known long and well, but shall know no more forever. About the couch of him who lies stricken are gathered those who hold him dear, and who await the coming of a great sorrow.

His breathing is faint, and grows fainter; his voice is become a whisper; his pulses scarcely record the languishing ebb and flow of the wasted current of life; his lips are pallid, and the froth of dissolution gathers upon them; his face is drawn; his cheeks are sunken; the roses are gone from them and ashes are in their place; his form is still; his feet are ice; his eyes are vacant; beaded sweat is on his brow; he picks at the coverlet with unconscious fingers; he "babbles o' green fields"; death's rattle is in his throat; his time is at hand.

With every breeze that comes to us out of the distances, near and far, from every segment of the wide horizon, there comes a voice heavy with mourning; and the burden of the mourning is, "The aged and stricken Democratic party is dying"; and the burden of the lament will be, "The mighty is fallen; the Democratic party is dead." And who and what is he that is dying and will presently be dead? A footsore political wanderer, a hoary political tramp, an itinerant poor actor familiar with many disguises, a butcher of many parts.

In the North he played "Protection" and "Hard Money." In the West he played "Protection," "Free Trade," "Hard Money," and "Soft Money," changing disguises and parts according to the exigencies of the occasion. In the South he played "Tariff for Revenue"; in the North and West he played "The Apostle of Freedom." In the South he played "The Assassin of Freedom," and mouthed the sacred shibboleths of liberty with cruel and bloody lips.

His latest and final appearance upon the nation's stage was in the new piece entitled "Forgery, a Farce," in which he was assisted by the whole strength of the company. It was a poor piece. It was indifferently played; so it failed, and he was hissed and abused by the audience. But he lies low now, and blame and praise are to him alike. The charitable will spare the one, the judicious will reserve the other.

Oh, friends! this is not a time for jests and levity, but a time for bended forms and uncovered heads, for we stand in the near presence of majestic death, a momentous and memorable death; a grisly and awful death. For it is a death from which there is no resurrection. Heaven bless us, one and all! Heaven temper the blow to the afflicted family. Heaven grant them a change of heart and a better life!

Text / "*Mark Twain,* Funeral Oration," *CTrib,* November 4, 1880.

"babbles o' green fields" / From Shakespeare's *Henry V* (2–3), the Hostess telling of the death of Falstaff: "for his nose was as sharp as a pen, and a' babbled of green fields." This famous emendation of the First Folio reading, "and a Table of greene fields," was made by Lewis Theobald in the eighteenth century.

"Forgery" / A reference to a letter said to have been written by Garfield, January 23, 1880, to H. L. Morey, of the Lynn, Massachusetts, Employers Union. First published in *Truth,* a New York scandal sheet, during the closing weeks of the campaign, it was widely reprinted. On the Chinese problem the letter says: "the question of employes is only a question of private and corporate economy, and individuals and companies have the right to buy labor where they can get it cheapest. We have a treaty with the Chinese government which should be religiously kept until its provisions are abrogated by the action of the general government, and I am not prepared to say that it should be abrogated until our great manufacturing interests are conserved in the matter of labor." This letter,

intended to discredit Garfield among American workingmen, was a forgery, allegedly perpetrated by one of the editors of *Truth*.

no resurrection / Mark Twain's pronouncement was premature. Indeed, he himself took part in reviving the Democratic party in the next presidential campaign of 1884.

· 42 ·

The Papyrus Club of Boston was composed chiefly of literary men and journalists. On Ladies Night, the gentlemen strove to provide something special for their feminine guests. Mark Twain was a good choice. The Times *reported, February 25, 1881: "The after-dinner features included the reading of a new and dainty poem, sent from London for the occasion, by James Russell Lowell, a finely drawn speech by E. P. Whipple, largely a eulogy of George Eliot, a speech by Mark Twain, and several short poems by members of the club–one by Robert Grant to the ladies, and another by John Boyle O'Reilly."*

Dinner Speech

Papyrus Club, Annual Ladies Night, Revere House, Boston, February 24, 1881

Ladies and gentlemen: I am perfectly astonished—a-s-t-o-n-i-s-h-e-d—ladies and gentlemen—astonished at the way history repeats itself. I find myself situated at this moment exactly and precisely as I was once before, years ago, to a jot, to a tittle—to a very hair. There isn't a shade of difference. It is the most astonishing coincidence that ever—but wait. I will tell you the former instance, and then you will see it for yourself.

Years ago I arrived one day at Salamanca, New York, eastward bound; must change cars there and take the sleeper train. There were crowds of people there, and they were swarming into the long sleeper train and packing it full, and it was a perfect purgatory of dust and confusion and gritting of teeth and soft, sweet, and low profanity. I asked the young man in the ticket office if I could have a sleeping section, and he answered "No!" with a snarl that shriveled me up like burned leather. I went off, smarting under this insult to my dignity, and asked another local official, supplicatingly, if I couldn't have some poor little corner somewhere in a sleeping car, and he cut me short with a venomous "No, you can't; every corner's full. Now, don't bother me any more." And he turned his back and walked off. My dignity was in a state now which cannot be described. I was so ruffled that—well, I said to my companion, "If these people knew who I am they—" but my companion cut me short there and said, "Don't talk such folly. If they did know who you are, do you suppose it would help your high mightiness to a vacancy in a train which has no vacancies it it? Ah, me! If you could only get rid of 148 pounds of your self-conceit, I would value the other pound of you above the national debt."

This did not improve my condition any to speak of, but just then I observed that the colored porter of a sleeping car had his eye on me. I saw his dark countenance light up. He whispered to the uniformed conductor, punctuating with nods and jerks toward me, and straightway this conductor came forward, oozing politeness from every pore, and said, "Can I be of any service to you? Will you have a place in the sleeper?" "Yes," I said, "and much obliged, too. Give me anything—anything will answer." He said, "We have nothing left but the big family stateroom, with two berths and a couple of armchairs in it, but it is entirely at your disposal. Here, Tom, take these satchels aboard."

Then he touched his hat and we and the colored Tom moved along. I was bursting to drop just one little remark to my companion, but I held in and waited. Tom made us comfortable in that sumptuous great apartment, and then said, with many bows and a perfect affluence of smiles, "Now, is dey anything you want, sah? 'Case you kin have jes' anything you wants. It don't make no difference what it is." I said, "Can I have some hot water and a tumbler at nine tonight—blazing hot, you know—about the right temperature for a hot Scotch punch?" "Yes, sah, dat you kin; you kin 'pen on it. I'll get it myse'f." "Good! Now that lamp is hung too high. Can I have a big coach candle fixed up just at the head of my bed, so that I can read comfortably?" "Yes, sah, you kin. I'll fix her up myse'f, an' I'll fix her so she'll burn all night, an' I'll see dat she does, too, 'case I'll keep my eye on her troo de do'. Yes, sah; an' you kin jes' call for anything you wants—it don't make no difference what it is—an' dish yer whole railroad'll be turned wrong end up an' inside out for to git it for you. Dat's so." And he disappeared.

Well, I tilted my head back, hooked my thumbs in my armholes, smiled a smile on my companion, and said gently, "Well, what do you say now?" My companion was not in a humor to respond—and didn't.

The next moment that smiling black face was thrust in at the crack of the door, and this speech followed: "Laws bless you, sah, I knowed you in a minute. I told de conductah so. Laws, I knowed you de minute I sot eyes on you." "Is that so, my boy? (handing him a quadruple fee); well, who am I?" "Jennul McClellan," and he disappeared again. My companion said vinegarishly, "Well, well! What do you say now?" Right there comes in the marvelous coincidence I mentioned a while ago, *viz.*, I was—speechless, and that is my condition now. Perceive it?

Text / Composite, based upon: "The Papyrus Club's Guests," *Times,* February 25, 1881; "Mistaken Identity" in the following: *MTS*(10):258–61; *MTS*(23):154–56; *Eloquence*(R), 1:223–25; *Eloquence*(T), 1:303–5.

a-s-t-o-n-i-s-h-e-d / Reporters sometimes attempted to illustrate Mark Twain's slow speech by spacing the words or the letters, an inadequate device but the best they could do in print. Mark Twain was annoyed when anybody called attention to his drawl, yet he himself made fun of it in his Monday Evening Club paper, "The Facts Concerning the Recent Carnival of Crime in Connecticut."

· 43 ·

When the Army of the Potomac gathered in Hartford for its twelfth reunion, Mark Twain was naturally on the program. He was in his element among a bevy of commanders–Generals Sherman, Porter, Miles, Sickles, Devens, Hawley, Burnside–and politicians, including two governors and Robert Todd Lincoln. Next day's Courant *reported an incidental occurrence: "While Mr. Clemens was speaking, a band came down the street and struck up 'Marching Through Georgia' in front of the hall. The remarks were interrupted. A voice in the hall started the words, others took it up, and the band finally joined in, producing a thrilling effect. Hardly had Mr. Clemens resumed when the outside band began 'Auld Lang Syne,' and grasping the situation, waved his hand in unison with the music, and the assemblage sang the words to the finish."*

The Benefit of Judicious Training

Twelfth Annual Reunion Banquet, Army of the Potomac, Allyn House, Hartford, June 8, 1881

"Let but the thoughtful civilian instruct the soldier in his duties, and the victory is sure." *Martin Farquhar Tupper on the Art of War.*

Mr. Chairman: I gladly join with my fellow townsmen in extending a hearty welcome to these illustrious generals and these war-scarred soldiers of the Republic. This is a proud day for us, and, if the sincere desire of our hearts has been fulfilled, it has not been an unpleasant day for them. I am in full accord, sir, with the sentiment of the toast—for I have always maintained, with enthusiasm, that the only wise and true way is for the soldier to fight the battle and the unprejudiced civilian to tell him how to do it. Yet when I was invited to respond to this toast and furnish this advice and instruction, I was almost as embarrassed as I was gratified; for I could bring to this great service but the one virtue of absence of prejudice and set opinion.

Still, but one other qualification was needed, and it was of only minor importance—I mean, knowledge of the subject—therefore, I was not disheartened, for I could acquire that, there being two weeks to spare. A general of high rank in this Army of the Potomac said two weeks was really more than I would need for the purpose—he had known people of my style who had learned enough in forty-eight hours to enable them to advise an army. Aside from the compliment, this was gratifying, because it confirmed an impression I had had before. He told me to go to the United States Military Academy at West Point, and said in his flowery, professional way that the cadets would "load me up." I went there and stayed two days, and his prediction proved correct. I make no boast on my own account—none; all I know about military matters I got from the gentlemen at West Point, and to them belongs the credit. They treated me with courtesy from the first; but when my mission was revealed, this mere courtesy blossomed into the warmest zeal. Everybody, officers and all, put down their work and turned their whole attention to giving me military information. Every question I asked was promptly and exhaustively answered. Therefore I feel proud to state that in the advice which I am about to give you, as soldiers, I am backed by the highest military authority in the land—yes, in the world, if an American does say it—West Point!

To begin, gentlemen. When an engagement is meditated, it is best to feel the enemy first. That is, if it is night; for, as one of the cadets explained to me, you do not need to feel him in the daytime, because you can see him then. I never should have thought of that, but it is true—perfectly true. In the daytime, the methods of procedure are various, but the best, it seems to me, is one which was introduced by General Grant. General Grant always sent an active young redoubt to reconnoiter and get the enemy's bearings. I got this from a high officer at the Point, who told me that he used to be a redoubt on General Grant's staff, and had done it often.

When the hour for the battle is come, move to the field with celerity—fool away no time. Under this head I was told of a favorite maxim of General Sheridan's. General Sheridan always said, "If the siege train isn't ready, don't wait—go by any train that's handy—to get there is the main thing." Now that is the correct idea. As you approach the field it is best to get out and walk. This gives you a better chance to dispose your forces judiciously for the assault. Get your artillery in position, and throw out stragglers to right and left to hold your lines of communication against surprise. See that every hod-carrier connected with a mortar battery is at his post. They told me at the Point that Napoleon despised mortar batteries, and never would use them; he said for real efficiency he wouldn't give a hatful of brickbats for a ton of mortar. However, that is all *he* knew about it.

Everything being ready for the assault, you want to enter the field with your baggage to the front. This idea was invented by our renowned guest, General Sherman. They told me General Sherman said the trunks and steamer chairs make a good protection for the soldiers; but that chiefly they attract the attention and rivet the interest of the enemy, and this gives you an opportunity to whirl the other end of the column around and attack him in the rear. I have given a good deal of study to this tactic since I learned about it, and it appears to me it is a rattling good idea. Never fetch on your reserves at the start. This was Napoleon's first mistake at Waterloo; next he assaulted with his bombproofs and ambulances and embrasures, when he ought to have used a heavier artillery; thirdly, he retired his right by *ricochet*—which uncovered his pickets—when his only possibility of success lay in doubling up his center, flank by flank, and throwing out his *chevaux-de-frise* by the left oblique to relieve the skirmish line and confuse the enemy—if such a maneuver would confuse him—and at West Point they said it would. It was about this time that the Emperor had two horses shot under him. How often you see the remark that General So-and-So, in such-and-such a battle, had two or three horses shot under him. General Burnside and many great European military men—as I was informed by a high artillery officer at West Point—have justly characterized this as a wanton waste of projectiles, and he impressed upon me a conversation held in the tent of the Prussian chiefs at Gravelotte, in the course of which our honored guest just referred to—General Burnside—observed that if you can't aim a horse so as to *hit* the general with it, shoot it *over* him and you may bag somebody on the other side, whereas a horse shot under a general does no sort of damage. I agree cordially with General Burnside, and heaven knows I shall rejoice to see the artillerists of this land and of all lands cease from this wicked and idiotic custom.

At West Point they told me of another mistake at Waterloo, namely, that the French were under fire from the beginning of the fight to the end of it—which was plainly a most effeminate and ill-timed attention to comfort, and a fatal and foolish diversion of military strength; for it probably took as many men to keep up the fires as it did to do the fighting. It would have been much better to have a small fire in the rear and let the men go there by detachments and get warm, and not try to warm up the whole army at once. All the cadets said that. An assault along the whole line was the one thing which would have restored Napoleon's advantage at this juncture; and he was actually rising in his stirrups to order it when a sutler burst at his side, and covered him with dirt and debris; and before he could recover his lost opportunity, Wellington opened a tremendous and devastating fire upon him from a monster battery of vivandieres, and the star of the great captain's glory set to rise no more. The cadet wept while he told me these mournful particulars.

When you leave a battlefield, always leave it in good order. Remove the wreck and rubbish and tidy up the place. However, in the case of a drawn battle, it is neither party's business to tidy up anything—you can leave the field looking as if the city government of New York had bossed the fight.

When you are traversing the enemy's country in order to destroy his supplies and cripple his resources, you want to take along plenty of camp followers—the more the better. They are a tremendously effective arm of the service, and they inspire in the foe the liveliest dread. A West Point professor told me that the wisdom of this was recognized as far back as Scripture times. He quoted the verse. He said it was from the new revision, and was a little different from the way it reads in the old one. I do not recollect the exact wording of it now, but I remember that it wound up with something about such-and-such a devastating agent being as "terrible as an army with bummers."

I believe I have nothing further to add but this: The West Pointers said a private should preserve a respectful attitude toward his superiors, and should seldom or never proceed so far as to offer suggestions to his general in the field. If the battle is not being conducted to suit him, it is better for him to resign. By the etiquette of war, it is permitted to none below the rank of newspaper correspondent to dictate to the general in the field.

Text / Composite, based upon: "Address of Mark Twain," *Society of the Army of the Potomac, Twelfth Annual Reunion* (1881):61–64; "Army of the Potomac Reunion," *Courant,* June 9, 1881; "Veterans of the Potomac," *Times,* June 9, 1881; "Speech of Samuel L. Clemens," *MTS*(23):98–103. The *MTS* text is incorrectly assigned to the thirteenth reunion.

Martin Farquhar Tupper / (1810–89). British writer. Author of popular Whig ballads, he became known as "The People's Poet Laureate" because of *Proverbial Philosophy,* published in four series (1839–76). This collection of moral reflections written in a doggerel sometimes almost metrical was so uninspired that it made the name of Tupper synonymous with banality and fatuousness.

"terrible as an army with bummers" / A modification of *The Song of Solomon* (6.4): "Thou art beautiful, O my love, as Tirzah, comely as Jerusalem, terrible as an army with banners." General Sherman's bummers were foragers who rounded up food for his army on its march to the sea. They also looted, destroyed property, and so harassed the populace that the song, "Marching Through Georgia," has ever since been anathema in the South.

· 44 ·

Mark Twain fashioned the ghost story of the Golden Arm out of a tale he had heard in childhood, told by old Uncle Dan'l in the flickering light of a kitchen fire. It became a standby on many programs. He enjoyed imitating the weird wailing of the wind, and experimenting with the pause before the explosive conclusion. As he says in "How to Tell a Story": "If I got it the right length precisely, I could spring the finishing ejaculation with effect enough to make some impressible girl deliver a startled little yelp and jump out of her seat–and that was what I was after." See also his letter to Joel Chandler Harris, Mark Twain to Uncle Remus, *Emory University Publications, series 7, no. 3 (Atlanta, 1953):10–12.*

De Woman wid de Gold'n Arm

Reading Selection, First Used About 1881 and Often Thereafter

Once upon a time, away long ago, there was a man and his wife that lived all alone in a house out in the middle of a big lonesome prairie. There wasn't anybody or any house or any trees for miles and miles and miles around. The woman had an arm that was gold—just pure solid gold from the shoulder all the way down. Well, by and by, one night, she died. It was in the middle of winter, and the wind was a-blowing, and the snow was a-drifting and the sleet was a-driving, and it was awful dark; but the man had to bury her; so he took her, and took a lantern, and went away off across the prairie and dug a grave; but when he was just going to put her in, he thought he would steal her golden arm, for he judged it couldn't ever be found out, and he was a powerful mean man. So then he cut it off, and buried her, and started back home. And he stumbled along, and plowed along, and the snow and the sleet swashed in his face so he had to turn his head one side, and could hardly get along at all; and the wind it kept a-crying, and a-wailing, and a-mourning, way off across the prairie, back there where the grave was, just so: *B-z-z-z-z-z* [imitating the rising and falling and complaining of the wintry night wind, through his teeth]. It seemed to him like it was a ghost crying and worrying about some trouble or another, and it made his hair stand up, and he was all trembling and shivering. The wind kept on going *Bzzz* and all of a sudden he caught his breath and stood still, and leaned his ear to listen. *B-z-z-z-z-z* goes the wind, but right along in the midst of that sound he hears some words, so faint and so far away off he can hardly make them out: *"W-h-e-r-e's m-y g-o-l-d-e-n a-a-a-rm? W-h-o's g-o-t m-y g-o-l-d-e-n a-a-a-rm?"* Down drops the lantern; and out it goes, and there he is, in that wide lonesome prairie, in the pitch dark and the storm. He started along again, but he could hardly pull one foot after the other; and all the way the wind was a-crying and the snow a-blowing, and the voice a-wailing, "W-h-e-r-e's m-y g-o-l-d-e-n a-a-a-rm? W-h-o's g-o-t m-y g-o-l-d-e-n a-a-a-arm?" At last he got home; and he locked the door, and bolted it, and chained it with a big log chain and put the chairs and things against it; and then he crept upstairs and got into bed and covered up his head and ears, and lay there a-shivering and a-listening. The wind it kept a-going *B-z-z-z-z,* and there was that voice again—away, *ever* so far away, out in the prairie. But it was a-coming—it was a-coming. Every time it said the words it was closer than it was before. By and by it was as close as the pasture; next it was as close as the branch; next it was this side the branch and right by the corn crib; next it was to the smokehouse; then it was right at the stile; then right in the yard; then it passed the ash hopper and was right at the door—right at the very door! "W-h-e-r-e's m-y g-o-l-d-e-n a-a-a-arm?" The man shook, and shook, and shivered. He don't hear the chain rattle, he don't hear the bolt break, he don't hear the door move—still next minute he hear something coming *p-a-t, p-a-t,* p-a-t, just as slow, and just as soft, up the stairs. It's right at the door, now: "W-h-e-r-e's m-y g-o-l-d-e-n a-a-a-arm?" Next it's right in the room: "W-h-o's g-o-t m-y g-o-l-d-e-n a-a-a-arm?" Then it's right up against the bed—then it's a-leaning down over the bed—then it's down right against his ear and a-whispering soft, so soft and dreadful: "W-h-e-r-e's m-y g-o-l-d-e-n a-a-a-arm? W-h-o's g-o-t m-y g-o-l-d-e-n a-a-a-arm?" [Then with a sudden fierce spring at the nearest auditor and a thunderous shout] "YOU *got it!*"

Text / "De Woman Wid De Gold'n Arm," MS, Emory University Library. Published in *Mark Twain to Uncle Remus:* 12–13; also, with variations, in "How to Tell a Story," and the *Youth's Companion,* October 3, 1895.

The wind it kept a-going, etc. / A marginal note on the MS says: "In the *telling,* the voice monotonously repeats, all through here."

· 45 ·

In Canada to apply for Canadian copyright on The Prince and the Pauper, *Mark Twain was feted by a group of parliamentarians, writers and businessmen, characterized by the Montreal* Gazette *(via* Courant, *December 13, 1881) as "devoted admirers of a great genius, who sought in a peculiarly English way to evince their appreciation of his literary peerage. The gathering was thoroughly representative of the intellectual and commercial greatness of Canada."*

Dinner Speech

Dinner for Mark Twain, Windsor Hotel, Montreal,
December 8, 1881

That a banquet should be given to me in this ostensibly foreign land and in this great city, and that my ears should be greeted by such complimentary words from such distinguished lips, are eminent surprises to me; and I will not conceal the fact that they are also deeply gratifying. I thank you, one and all, gentlemen, for these marks of favor and friendliness; and even if I have not really or sufficiently deserved them, I assure you that I do not any the less keenly enjoy and esteem them on that account.

When a stranger appears abruptly in a country, without any apparent business there, and at an unusual season of the year, the judicious thing for him to do is to explain. This seems peculiarly necessary in my case, on account of a series of unfortunate happenings here, which followed my arrival, and which I suppose the public have felt compelled to connect with that circumstance. I would most gladly explain if I could; but I have nothing for my defense but my bare word; so I simply declare, in all sincerity, and with my hand on my heart, that I never heard of that diamond robbery till I saw it in the morning paper; and I can say with perfect truth that I never saw that box of dynamite till the police came to inquire of me if I had any more of it. These are mere assertions, I grant you, but they come from the lips of one who was never known to utter an untruth, except for practice, and who certainly would not so stultify the traditions of an upright life as to utter one now, in a strange land, and in such a presence as this, when there is nothing to be gained by it and he does not need any practice. I brought with me to this city a friend—a Boston publisher—but, alas, even this does not sufficiently explain these sinister mysteries; if I had brought a Toronto publisher along the case would have been different. But no, possibly not; the burglar took the diamond studs, but left the shirt; only a *reformed* Toronto publisher would have left the shirt.

To continue my explanation, I did not come to Canada to commit crime—this time—but to prevent it. I came here to place myself under the protection of the Canadian law and secure a copyright. I have complied with the requirements of the law; I have followed the instructions of some of the best legal minds in the city, including my own, and so my errand is accomplished, at least so far as any exertions of mine can aid that accomplishment. This is rather a cumbersome way to fence and fortify one's property against the literary buccaneer, it is true; still, if it is effective, it is a great advance upon past conditions, and one to be correspondingly welcomed.

It makes one hope and believe that a day will come when, in the eye of the law, literary property will be as sacred as whiskey, or any other of the necessaries of life. In this age of ours, if you steal another man's label to advertise your own brand of whiskey with, you will be heavily fined and otherwise punished for violating that trademark; if you steal the whiskey without the trademark, you go to jail; but if you could prove that the whiskey was literature, you can steal them both, and the law wouldn't say a word. It grieves me to think how far more profound and reverent a respect the law would have for literature if a body could only get drunk on it. Still the world moves; the interests of literature upon our continent are improving; let us be content and wait.

We have with us here a fellow craftsman, born on our own side of the Atlantic, who has created an epoch in this continent's literary history—an author who has earned and worthily earned and received the vast distinction of being crowned by the Academy of France. This is honor and achievement enough for the cause and the craft for one decade, assuredly.

If one may have the privilege of throwing in a personal impression or two, I may remark that my stay in Montreal and Quebec has been exceedingly pleasant, but the weather has been a good deal of a disappointment. Canada has a reputation for magnificent winter weather, and has a prophet who is bound by every sentiment of honor and duty to furnish it; but the result this time has been a mess of characterless weather, which all right-feeling Canadians are probably ashamed of. Still, only the country is to blame; nobody has a right to blame the prophet, for this wasn't the kind of weather he promised.

Well, never mind, what you lack in weather you make up in the means of grace. This is the first time I was ever in a city where you couldn't throw a brick without breaking a church window. Yet I was told that you were going to build one more. I said the scheme is good, but where are you going to find room? They said, we will build it on top of another church and use an elevator. This shows that the gift of lying is not yet dead in the land.

I suppose one must come in the summer to get the advantages of the Canadian scenery. A cabman drove me two miles up a perpendicular hill in a sleigh and showed me an admirable snowstorm from the heights of Quebec. The man was an ass; I could have seen the snowstorm as well from the hotel window and saved my money. Still, I may have been the ass myself; there is no telling; the thing is all mixed up in my mind; but anyway there was an ass in the party; and I do suppose that wherever a mercenary cabman and a gifted literary character are gathered together for business, there is bound to be an ass in the combination somewhere. It has always been so in my experience; and I have usually been elected, too. But it is no matter; I would rather be an ass than a cabman, any time, except in summer-time; then, with my advantages, I could be both.

I saw the Plains of Abraham, and the spot where the lamented Wolfe stood when he made the memorable remark that he would rather be the author of Gray's "Elegy" than take Quebec. But why did he say so rash a thing? It was because he supposed there was going to be international copyright. Otherwise there would be no money in it. I was also shown the spot where Sir William Phipps stood when he said he would rather take a walk than take two Quebecs. And he took the walk. I have looked with emotion, here in your city, upon the monument which makes forever memorable the spot where Horatio Nelson did not stand when he fell. I have seen the cab which Champlain employed when he arrived overland at Quebec; I have seen the horse which Jacques Cartier rode when he discovered Montreal. I have used them both; I will never do it again. Yes, I have seen all the historical places; the localities have been pointed out to me where the scenery is warehoused for the season. My sojourn has been to my moral and intellectual profit; I have behaved with propriety and discretion; I have meddled nowhere but in the election. But I am used to voting, for I live in a town where, if you may judge by local prints, there are only two conspicuous industries—committing burglaries and holding elections—and I like to keep my hand in, so I voted a good deal here.

Where so many of the guests are French, the propriety will be recognized of my making a portion of my speech in the beautiful language in order that I may be partly understood. I speak French with timidity, and not flowingly—except when excited. When using that language I have often noticed that I have hardly ever been mistaken for a Frenchman, except, perhaps, by horses; never, I believe, by people. I had hoped that mere French construction—with English words—would answer, but this is not the case. I tried it at a gentleman's house in Quebec, and it would not work. The maid servant asked, "What would Monsieur?" I said, "Monsieur So-and-So, is he with himself?" She did not understand that either. I said, "He will desolate himself when he learns that his friend American was arrived, and he not with himself to shake him at the hand." She did not even understand that; I don't know why, but she didn't and she lost her temper besides. Somebody in the rear called out, "Qui est donc la?" or words to that effect. She said, "C'est un fou," and shut the door on me. Perhaps she was right; but how did she ever find that out? for she had never seen me before till that moment.

But, as I have already intimated, I will close this oration with a few sentiments in the French language. I have not ornamented them, I have not burdened them with flowers or rhetoric, for, to my mind, that literature is best and most enduring which is characterized by a noble simplicity: J'ai belle bouton d'or de mon oncle, mais je n'ai pas celui du charpentier. Si vous avez le fromage du brave menuisier, c'est bon; mais si vous ne l'avez pas, ne se desole pas, prenez le chapeau de drap noir de son beau frere malade. Tout a l'heure! Savoir faire! Qu'est ce que vous dit! Pate de fois gras! Revenons a nos moutons! Pardon, messieurs, pardonnez moi; essayant a parler la belle langue d'Ollendorf strains me more than you can possibly imagine. But I mean well, and I've done the best I could.

Text / Montreal *Gazette,* n.d., reprinted as "Mark Twain in Montreal" in *Courant,* December 13, 1881; and *Times,* December 10, 1881.

fellow craftsman / A reference to Louis Honoré Fréchette (1839–1908). Canadian poet, journalist, and parliamentarian. Known as poet laureate of Canada, he was a member of the Canadian Parliament and the editor of *La Patrie.* Among his books are *Mes Loires* (1862), *Les Ciseaux de Neige* (1880), and *Les Fleurs Boréalis* (1881). In 1877 he married Anne Howells, sister of William Dean Howells, and in 1897 he was made Companion of the Order of St. Michael and St. George by Queen Victoria.

Plains of Abraham / An elevated plain southwest of Quebec, it was the scene of the deciding battle of the French and Indian War, September 13, 1759.

Wolfe / James Wolfe (1727–59). British soldier. A major general commanding the expedition against Quebec, he led his army up to the Plains of Abraham and was killed in the battle. According to tradition, he made the remark about Gray's "Elegy" while in a boat crossing the river for a surprise attack.

Sir William Phipps / (1651–95). British colonial official. In 1690, commanding 32 ships and 2,200 men, he led an expedition against Montreal and Quebec but failed to take either city. He was governor of the Massachusetts Bay Colony (1692–94).

Champlain / Samuel de Champlain (1567?–1635). French explorer. One of the earliest travelers in North America, he founded Quebec (1608), and also penetrated country south of there and west as far as Lake Huron. He was instrumental in giving France a firm foothold in the New World.

Jacques Cartier / (1491–1557). French navigator. He explored the Gulf of St. Lawrence (1534), sailed up the St. Lawrence River to the site of present-day Montreal (1535), and made an unsuccessful attempt to colonize Canada (1541–42).

la belle langue d'Ollendorf / Ollendorf's System, devised by Heinrich Gottfried Ollendorf (1803–65), was a method of learning languages without a teacher. His manuals, stressing mastery of conversational forms, minimized grammatical rules.

· 46 ·

At the dinner of the New England Society of Philadelphia, Mark Twain was introduced as a man who, if not of New England descent, was certainly one of ascent. Indeed, said the chairman, springing an old joke, "Mr. Twain has become a man of mark." Mark Twain, responding in what a reporter described as "a peculiar, sleepy manner," drawled that he would continue to do his best.

Plymouth Rock and the Pilgrims

First Annual Dinner, New England Society of Philadelphia, December 22, 1881

I rise to protest. I have kept still for years, but really I think there is no sufficient justification for this sort of thing. What do you want to celebrate those people for?—those ancestors of yours, of 1620—the *Mayflower* tribe, I mean. What do you want to celebrate *them* for? Your pardon; the gentleman at my left assures me that you are not celebrating the Pilgrims themselves, but the landing of the Pilgrims at Plymouth Rock on the 22d of December. So you are celebrating their landing. Why, the other pretext was thin enough, but this is thinner than ever; the other was tissue, tinfoil, fish bladder, but this is gold leaf.

Celebrating their landing! What was there remarkable about it, I would like to know? What can you be thinking of ? Why, those Pilgrims had been at sea three or four months. It was the very middle of winter; it was as cold as death off Cape Cod, there. Why shouldn't they come ashore? If they hadn't landed there would be some reason in celebrating the fact. It would have been a case of monumental leatherheadedness which the world would not willingly let die. If it had been *you,* gentlemen, you probably wouldn't have landed, but you have no shadow of right to be celebrating, in your ancestors, gifts which they did not exercise, but only transmitted. Why, to be celebrating the mere landing of the Pilgrims—to be trying to make out that this most natural, and simple, and customary procedure was an extraordinary circumstance—a circumstance to be amazed at and admired, aggrandized and glorified, at orgies like this for two hundred and sixty years—hang it, a horse would have known enough to land; a horse—pardon again; the gentleman on my right assures me that it was not merely the landing of the Pilgrims that we are celebrating, but the Pilgrims themselves. So we have struck an inconsistency here—one says it was the landing, the other says it was the Pilgrims. It is an inconsistency characteristic of your intractable and disputatious tribe, for you never agree about anything but Boston.

Well, then, what do you want to celebrate those Pilgrims for? They were a mighty hard lot—you know it. I grant you, without the slightest unwillingness, that they were a deal more gentle and merciful and just than were the peoples of Europe of that day; I grant you that they were better than their predecessors. But what of that?—that is nothing. People always progress. You are better than your fathers and grandfathers were (this is the first time I have ever aimed a measureless slander at the departed, for I consider such things improper). Yes, those among you who have not been in the penitentiary, if such there be, are better than your fathers and grandfathers were, but is that any sufficient reason for getting up annual dinners and celebrating you? No, by no means—by no means. Well, I repeat, those Pilgrims were a hard lot. They took good care of themselves, but they abolished everybody else's ancestors. I am a border ruffian from the state of Missouri. I am a Connecticut Yankee by adoption. I have the morals of Missouri and the culture of Connecticut, and that's the combination that makes the perfect man.

But where are my ancestors? Whom shall I celebrate? Where shall I find the raw material? My first American ancestor, gentleman, was an Indian—an early Indian. Your ancestors skinned him alive, and I am an orphan. Not one drop of my blood flows in that Indian's veins today. I stand here, lone and forlorn, without an ancestor. They skinned him! I do not object to that, if they needed his fur; but alive, gentlemen—alive! They skinned him alive—and before company! That is what rankles. Think how he must have felt; for he was a sensitive Indian and easily embarrassed. If he had been a bird, it would have been all right, and no violence done to his feelings, because he would have been considered "dressed." But he was not a bird, gentlemen, he was a man, and probably one of the most undressed men that ever was. I ask you to put yourselves in his place. I ask it as a favor; I ask it as a tardy act of justice; I ask it in the interest of fidelity to the traditions of your ancestors; I ask it that the world may contemplate, with vision unobstructed by disguising swallowtails and white cravats, the spectacle which the true New England Society ought to present. Cease to come to these annual orgies in this hollow modern mockery—the surplusage of raiment. Come in character; come in the summer grace, come in the unadorned simplicity, come in the free and joyous costume which your sainted ancestors provided for mine.

Later ancestors of mine were the Quakers, William Robinson, Marmaduke Stephenson, *et al.* Your tribe chased them out of the country for their religion's sake; promised them death if they came back, for your ancestors had forsaken the homes they loved, and braved the perils of the sea, the implacable climate, and the savage wilderness, to acquire that highest and most precious of boons, freedom for every man on this broad continent to worship according to the dictates of his own conscience—and they were not going to allow a lot of pestiferous Quakers to interfere with it. Your ancestors broke forever the chains of political slavery, and gave the vote to every man in this wide land, excluding none!—none except those who did not belong to the orthodox church. Your ancestors—yes, they were a hard lot; but, nevertheless, they gave us religious liberty to worship as they required us to worship, and political liberty to vote as the church required; and so I, the bereft one, I, the forlorn one, am here to do my best to help you celebrate them right.

The Quaker woman, Elizabeth Hooton, was an ancestress of mine. Your people were pretty severe with her—you will confess that. But, poor thing! I believe they changed her opinions before she died, and took her into their fold; and so we have every reason to presume that when she died she went to the same place which your ancestors went to. It is a great pity, for she was a good woman. Roger Williams was an ancestor of mine. I don't really remember what your people did with him. But they banished him to Rhode Island, anyway. And then, I believe, recognizing that this was really carrying harshness to an unjustifiable extreme, they took pity on him and burned him. They were a hard lot! All those Salem witches were ancestors of mine. Your people made it tropical for them. Yes, they did; by pressure and the gallows they made such a clean deal with them that there hasn't been a witch and hardly a halter in our family from that day to this, and that is 189 years. The first slave brought into New England out of Africa by your progenitors was an ancestor of mine—for I am of a mixed breed, an infinitely shaded and exquisite mongrel. I'm not one of your sham meerschaums that you can color in a week. No, my complexion is the patient art of eight generations. Well, in my own time, I had acquired a lot of my kin—by purchase, and swapping around, and one way and another—and was getting along very well. Then, with the inborn perversity of your lineage, you got up a war and took them all away from me. And so, again am I bereft, again am I forlorn; no drop of my blood flows in the veins of any living being who is marketable.

Oh my friends, hear me and reform! I seek your good, not mine. You have heard the speeches. Disband these New England societies—nurseries of a system of steadily augmenting laudation and hosannahing, which, if persisted in uncurbed, may some day in the remote future beguile you into prevaricating and bragging. Oh, stop, stop while you are still temperate in your appreciation of your ancestors! Hear me, I beseech you; get up an auction and sell Plymouth Rock! The Pilgrims were a simple and ignorant race. They had never seen any good rocks before, or at least any that were not watched, and so they were excusable for hopping ashore in frantic delight and clapping an iron fence around this one. But you, gentlemen, are educated; you are enlightened; you know that in the rich land of your nativity, opulent New England, overflowing with rocks, this one isn't worth, at the outside, more than thirty-five cents. Therefore, sell it, before it is injured by exposure, or at least throw it open to the patent medicine advertisements, and let it earn its taxes.

Yes, hear your true friend—your only true friend—list to his voice. Disband these societies, hotbeds of vice, of moral decay—perpetuators of ancestral superstition. Here on this board I see water, I see milk, I see the wild and deadly lemonade. These are but steps upon the downward path. Next we shall see tea, then chocolate, then coffee—hotel coffee. A few more years—all too few, I fear—mark my words, we shall have cider! Gentlemen, pause ere it be too late. You are on the broad road which leads to dissipation, physical ruin, moral decay, gory crime and the gallows! I beseech you, I implore you, in the name of your anxious friends, in the name of your suffering families, in the name of your impending widows and orphans, stop ere it be too late. Disband these New England societies, renounce these soul-blistering saturnalia, cease from varnishing the rusty reputations of your long-vanished ancestors—the super-high-moral old ironclads of Cape Cod, the pious buccaneers of Plymouth Rock—go home, and try to learn to behave!

However, chaff and nonsense aside, I think I honor and appreciate your Pilgrim stock as much as you do yourselves, perhaps; and I endorse and adopt a sentiment uttered by a grandfather of mine once—a man of sturdy opinions, of sincere make of mind, and not given to flattery. He said: "People may talk as they like about that Pilgrim stock, but, after all's said and done, it would be pretty hard to improve on those people; and, as for me, I don't mind coming out flat-footed and saying there ain't any way to improve on them—except having them born in Missouri!"

Text / Composite, based upon: "Mark Twain on the Pilgrims," *Times,* December 26, 1881; "Mark Twain on Pilgrim Affairs," *Courant,* December 27, 1881; "Plymouth Rock and the Pilgrims" in *MTS*(10):17–24; and *MTS*(23):86–92.

William Robinson, Marmaduke Stephenson / Robinson, a young London merchant, and Stephenson, a Yorkshire farmer, came to America in 1657. For preaching the mild doctrine of the Society of Friends, both were hanged on Boston Common in 1659.

Elizabeth Hooton / (d. 1672). In New England as a sixty-year-old missionary, she was imprisoned by John Endicott, whipped through Cambridge, Dedham, and Watertown, then left to starve in a forest. She managed to get to Rhode Island, then to Barbadoes, where her death was probably hastened by the barbarities of the pious New Englanders.

· 47 ·

Louis Honoré Fréchette, the Canadian laureate, was a great admirer of Mark Twain. When the poet came to the United States soon after the two men had met in Montreal in 1881, the latter was an obvious choice for the toast list of the dinner that welcomed the visitor.

At a Dinner for Monsieur Fréchette of Quebec

Hotel Windsor, Holyoke, Massachusetts, January 31, 1882

I have broken a vow in order that I might give myself the pleasure of meeting my friend Fréchette again. But that is nothing to brag about; a person who is rightly constructed will break a vow any time to meet a friend. Before I last met Monsieur Fréchette, he had become the child of good fortune—that is to say, his poems had been crowned by the Academy of France; since I last met him he has become the child of good fortune once more—that is to say, I have translated his poems into English, and written a eulogy of them in the French language to preface the work. He possessed a single-barreled fame before; he will possess a double-barreled fame now; translations always reverse a thing, and bring an entirely new side of it into view, thus doubling the property and making two things out of what was only one thing before. So, in my translation his pathetic poems have naturally become humorous, his humorous poems have become sad. Anybody who knows even the rudiments of arithmetic will know that Monsieur Fréchette's poems are now worth exactly twice as much as they were before. I am glad to help welcome the laureate of Quebec to our soil; and I assure him that we will do our best to leave him no room to regret that he came.

Yes, as I was saying, I broke a vow. If it had been a trim, shiny, brand new one, I should be sorry, of course, for it is always wrong and a pity to mistreat and injure good new property; but this one was different; I don't regret this one, because it was an old ragged ramshackle vow that had seen so much service and been broken so often, and patched and spliced together in so many places, that it was become a disgraceful object, and so rotten that I could never venture to put any strain worth mention upon it. This vow was a vow which I first made eleven years ago, on a New Year's Day, that I would never make another after-dinner speech as long as I lived. It was as good a vow then, as I ever saw; but I have broken it in sixty-four places, since, and mended it up fresh every New Year's.

Seven years ago I reformed in another way; I made a vow that I would lead an upright life—meaning by that that I would never deliver another lecture. I believe I have never broken that one; I think I can be true to it always, and thus disprove the Rev. Petroleum V. Nasby's maxim that "Burglars and lecturers never reform." But this other vow has always been beyond my strength—I mean, I have always been beyond its strength. The reason is simple: it lies in the fact that the average man likes to hear himself talk, when he is not under criticism. The very man who sneers at your after-dinner speech when he reads it in next morning's paper, would have been powerfully moved to make just as poor a one himself if he had been present, with the encouraging champagne in him and the friendly uncritical faces all about him.

But that discourteous man doesn't do all the sneering that is done over your speech; no, he does only about a tenth of it—you do the other nine-tenths yourself. Your little talk, which sounded so fine and warbly and nice when you were delivering it in the mellow light of the lamps and in an enchanted atmosphere of applause and all-pervading good fellowship, looks miserably pale and vapid and lifeless in the cold print of a damp newspaper next morning, with obituaries and cast iron politics all around it and the hard gray light of day shining upon it and mocking at it. You do not recognize the corpse. You wonder if this is really that gay and handsome creature of the evening before. You look him over and find he certainly is those very remains. Then you want to bury him. You wish you could bury him privately.

Text / "At a Dinner to Monsieur Fréchette of Quebec—1880—," MS, MTP; published as "On After-Dinner Speaking," *MTS*(23):83–85. Both texts are misdated.

Nasby / Petroleum Vesuvius Nasby, pen name of David Ross Locke (1833–88). American humorist. Widely known for pro-Union political satire and for humor in the manner of Artemus Ward, he was also a popular and well-paid attraction on the lyceum circuit. Mark Twain called him "Rev." because the "Nasby Letters," begun in 1861, admonished the "Brethren and Sisteren" in the tone of a pastor.

· 48 ·

Of the speech below, time and place of delivery are uncertain. On the manuscript a note in Mark Twain's hand says that it was given "About 1882." His memory for dates was not reliable, but in the absence of conclusive information the talk is conjecturally assigned to the date and occasion specified here, chiefly because the Boston Saturday Morning Club, like its Hartford counterpart, was presumably composed of young people whom he was addressing.

Advice to Youth

Saturday Morning Club, Boston, April 15, 1882

Being told I would be expected to talk here, I inquired what sort of a talk I ought to make. They said it should be something suitable to youth—something didactic, instructive; or something in the nature of good advice. Very well; I have a few things in my mind which I have often longed to say for the instruction of the young; for it is in one's tender early years that such things will best take root and be most enduring and most valuable. First, then, I will say to you, my young friends—and say it beseechingly, urgingly—.

Always obey your parents, when they are present. This is the best policy in the long run; because if you don't, they will make you. Most parents think they know better than you do; and you can generally make more by humoring that superstition than you can by acting on your own better judgment.

Be respectful to your superiors, if you have any; also to strangers, and sometimes to others. If a person offend you, and you are in doubt as to whether it was intentional or not, do not resort to extreme measures; simply watch your chance and hit him with a brick. That will be sufficient. If you shall find that he had not intended any offense, come out frankly and confess yourself in the wrong when you struck him; acknowledge it like a man, and say you didn't mean to. Yes, always avoid violence; in this age of charity and kindliness, the time has gone by for such things. Leave dynamite to the low and unrefined.

Go to bed early, get up early—this is wise. Some authorities say get up with one thing, some with another. But a lark is really the best thing to get up with. It gives you a splendid reputation with everybody to know that you get up with the lark; and if you get the right kind of a lark, and work at him right, you can easily train him to get up at half-past nine, every time—it is no trick at all.

Now as to the matter of lying. You want to be very careful about lying; otherwise you are nearly sure to get caught. Once caught, you can never again be, in the eyes of the good and the pure, what you were before. Many a young person has injured himself permanently through a single clumsy and ill-finished lie, the result of carelessness born of incomplete training. Some authorities hold that the young ought not to lie at all. That, of course, is putting it rather stronger than necessary; still, while I cannot go quite so far as that, I do maintain, and I believe I am right, that the young ought to be temperate in the use of this great art until practice and experience shall give them that confidence, elegance and precision which alone can make the accomplishment graceful and profitable. Patience, diligence, painstaking attention to detail—these are the requirements; these, in time, will make the student perfect; upon these, and upon these only, may he rely as the sure foundation for future eminence. Think what tedious years of study, thought, practice, experience, went to the equipment of that peerless old master who was able to impose upon the whole world the lofty and sounding maxim that "Truth is mighty and will prevail"—the most majestic compound fracture of fact which any of woman born has yet achieved. For the history of our race, and each individual's experience, are sown thick with evidences that a truth is not hard to kill, and that a lie well told is immortal. There in Boston is a monument to the man who discovered anesthesia; many people are aware, in these latter days, that that man didn't discover it at all, but stole the discovery from another man. Is this truth mighty, and will it prevail? Ah, no, my hearers, the monument is made of hardy material, but the lie it tells will outlast it a million years. An awkward, feeble, leaky lie is a thing which you ought to make it your unceasing study to avoid; such a lie as that has no more real permanence than an average truth. Why, you might as well tell the truth at once and be done with it. A feeble, stupid, preposterous lie will not live two years—except it be a slander upon somebody. It is indestructible, then, of course, but that is no merit of yours. A final word: begin your practice of this gracious and beautiful art early—begin now. If I had begun earlier, I could have learned how.

Never handle firearms carelessly. The sorrow and suffering that have been caused through the innocent but heedless handling of firearms by the young! Only four days ago, right in the next farmhouse to the one where I am spending the summer, a mother, old and gray and sweet, one of the loveliest spirits in the land, was sitting at her work, when her young son crept in and got down an old, battered, rusty gun which had not been touched for many years, and was supposed not to be loaded, and pointed it at her, laughing and threatening to shoot. In her fright she ran screaming and pleading toward the door on the other side of the room; but as she passed him he placed the gun almost against her very breast and pulled the trigger! He had supposed it was not loaded. And he was right: it wasn't. So there wasn't any harm done. It is the only case of the kind I ever heard of. Therefore, just the same, don't you meddle with old unloaded firearms; they are the most deadly and unerring things that have ever been created by man. You don't have to take any pains at all, with them; you don't have to have a rest, you don't have to have any sights on the gun, you don't have to take aim, even. No, you just pick out a relative and bang away, and you are sure to get him. A youth who can't hit a cathedral at thirty yards with a Gatling gun in three-quarters of an hour, can take up an old empty musket and bag his mother every time, at a hundred. Think what Waterloo would have been if one of the armies had been boys armed with old rusty muskets supposed not to be loaded, and the other army had been composed of their female relations. The very thought of it makes me shudder.

There are many sorts of books; but good ones are the sort for the young to read. Remember that. They are a great, an inestimable, an unspeakable means of improvement. Therefore be careful in your selection, my young friends; be very careful; confine yourself exclusively to Robertson's *Sermons,* Baxter's *Saint's Rest, The Innocents Abroad,* and works of that kind.

But I have said enough. I hope you will treasure up the instructions which I have given you, and make them a guide to your feet and a light to your understanding. Build your character thoughtfully and painstakingly upon these precepts; and by and by, when you have got it built, you will be surprised and gratified to see how nicely and sharply it resembles everybody else's.

Text / "Advice to Youth—About 1882—," MS, MTP; published as "Advice to Youth," *MTS*(23):104–8.

man who discovered anesthesia / The monument honors Dr. William Thomas Green Morton (1815–68). American surgeon. Others had experimented with anesthetics—Dr. Horace Wells, Dr. Crawford Williamson Long, Dr. Charles Thomas Jackson—but Morton is credited as the discoverer because, having invented an inhalator, he was the first to demonstrate publicly the use of diethyl ether as an anesthetic, administered for a tumor operation at the Harvard Medical School on October 10, 1846. In the Massachusetts General Hospital the date is memorialized as "Ether Day." Biographical data do not suggest, as Mark Twain asserted, that he stole his ideas from anybody.

Gatling gun / Richard Jordan Gatling (1818–1903), an American inventor, devised a revolving battery rapid-fire gun (1862) capable of firing 350 shots per minute. It was adopted by the United States Army (1865).

Robertson's Sermons / Frederick William Robertson (1816–53). British clergyman. His posthumously published *Sermons* (1855, 1857, 1859, 1863) were highly esteemed. There was a complete edition (1870), also *Lectures* (1852, 1858).

Baxter's Saint's Rest / Richard Baxter (1615–91). British nonconformist clergyman. After brief service as chaplain to Charles II, he withdrew from the Church of England. His best known work, *The Saint's Everlasting Rest* (1650), is so charged with sanctity that in strict nineteenth-century households it was considered one of the few books, other than the Bible, a good Christian might read on Sunday without breaking the Sabbath.

· 49 ·

The New England Society of New York conducted its annual dinners with éclat. At the seventy-seventh dinner, the dining room was decorated with American flags and the shields of the thirteen original states. A string band made soft music for 250 gentlemen, among whom were General Grant, General Horace Porter, J. Pierpont Morgan, Noah Brooks, Elihu Root, Joseph H. Choate, Chauncey Depew, Benjamin Silliman, Stewart L. Woodford, three governors, and Mark Twain.

Woman—God Bless Her

Seventy-seventh Annual Dinner, New England Society of New York, Delmonico's, December 22, 1882

The toast includes the sex, universally: it is to Woman, comprehensively, wheresoever she may be found. Let us consider her ways. First comes the matter of dress. This is a most important consideration, in a subject of this nature, and must be disposed of before we can intelligently proceed to examine the profounder depths of the theme. For text, let us take the dress of two antipodal types—the savage woman of Central Africa, and the cultivated daughter of our high modern civilization. Among the Fans, a great Negro tribe, a woman, when dressed for home, or to go to market, or go out calling, does not wear anything at all but just her complexion. That is all; that is her entire outfit. It is the lightest costume in the world, but is made of the darkest material. It has often been mistaken for mourning. It is the trimmest, and neatest, and gracefulest costume that is now in fashion; it wears well, is fast colors, doesn't show dirt; you don't have to send it downtown to wash, and have some of it come back scorched with the flatiron, and some of it with the buttons ironed off, and some of it petrified with starch, and some of it chewed by the calf, and some of it rotted with acids, and some of it exchanged for other customers' things that haven't any virtue but holiness, and ten-twelfths of the pieces overcharged for, and the rest of the dozen "mislaid." And it always fits; it is the perfection of a fit. And it is the handiest dress in the whole realm of fashion. It is always ready, always "done up." When you call on a Fan lady and send up your card, the hired girl never says, "Please take a seat, madam is dressing—she will be down in three-quarters of an hour." No, madam is always dressed, always ready to receive; and before you can get the doormat before your eyes, she is in your midst. Then again, the Fan ladies don't go to church to see what each other has got on; and they don't go back home and describe it and slander it.

Such is the dark child of savagery, as to everyday toilette; and thus, curiously enough, she finds a point of contact with the fair daughter of civilization and high fashion—who often has "nothing to wear"; and thus these widely separated types of the sex meet upon common ground. Yes, such is the Fan woman, as she appears in her simple, unostentatious, everyday toilette. But on state occasions she is more dressy. At a banquet she wears bracelets; at a lecture she wears earrings and a belt; at a ball she wears stockings—and with the true feminine fondness for display, she wears them on her arms; at a funeral she wears a jacket of tar and ashes; at a wedding the bride who can afford it puts on pantaloons. Thus the dark child of savagery and the fair daughter of civilization meet once more upon common ground; and these two touches of nature make their whole world kin.

Now we will consider the dress of our other type. A large part of the daughter of civilization is her dress—as it should be. Some civilized women would lose half their charm without dress; and some would lose all of it. The daughter of modern civilization, dressed at her utmost best, is a marvel of exquisite and beautiful art, and expense. All the lands, all the climes, and all the arts are laid under tribute to furnish her forth. Her linen is from Belfast, her robe is from Paris, her lace is from Venice, or Spain, or France; her feathers are from the remote regions of southern Africa, her furs from the remoter home of the iceberg and the aurora; her fan from Japan, her diamonds from Brazil, her bracelets from California, her pearls from Ceylon, her cameos from Rome; she has gems and trinkets from buried Pompeii; and others that graced comely Egyptian forms that have been dust and ashes, now, for forty centuries; her watch is from Geneva, her card case is from China, her hair is from—from—I don't know where her hair is from; I never could find out. That is, her other hair—her public hair, her Sunday hair; I don't mean the hair she goes to bed with. Why, you ought to know the hair I mean; it's that thing which she calls a switch, and which resembles a switch as much as it resembles a brickbat, or a shotgun, or any other thing which you correct people with. It's that thing which she twists, and then coils round and round her head, beehive fashion, and then tucks the end in under the hive and harpoons it with a hairpin. And that reminds me of a trifle: any time you want to, you can glance around the carpet of a Pullman car and go and pick up a hairpin; but not to save your life can you get any woman in that car to acknowledge that hairpin. Now isn't that strange? But it's true. The woman who has never swerved from cast iron veracity and fidelity in her whole life, will, when confronted with this crucial test, deny her hairpin. She will deny that hairpin before a hundred witnesses. I have stupidly got into more trouble, and more hot water trying to hunt up the owner of a hairpin in a Pullman car than by any other indiscretion of my life.

Well, you see what the daughter of civilization is, when she is dressed; and you have seen what the daughter of savagery is when she isn't. Such is Woman, as to costume. I come, now, to consider her in her higher and nobler aspects—as mother, wife, widow, grass widow, mother-in-law, hired girl, telephone operator, telephone helloer, queen, book agent, wet nurse, stepmother, boss, professional fat woman, professional double-headed woman, professional beauty, and so forth and so on.

We will simply discuss these few—let the rest of the sex tarry in Jericho till we come again. First in the list, of right, and first in our gratitude, comes a woman who—why, dear me, I've been talking three-quarters of an hour! I beg a thousand pardons. But you see, yourselves, that I had a large contract. I have accomplished something, anyway: I have introduced my subject; and if I had till next Forefathers' Day, I am satisfied that I could discuss it as adequately and appreciatively as so gracious and noble a theme deserves. But as the matter stands, now, let us finish as we began—and say, without jesting, but with all sincerity, "Woman—God Bless Her!"

Text / Composite, based upon: "Woman—God Bless Her," MS, Alderman Library, University of Virginia; "Woman," *Courant*, December 25, 1882; "The Dress of Civilized Woman," *MTS*(10):83–84; "Woman, God Bless Her!" in *Eloquence*(R), 1:225–28; and *Eloquence*(T), 1:305–8.

· 50 ·

When George W. Cable gave a program of readings in Hartford, it was a tryout for a newcomer to the platform. Mark Twain, who had a low opinion of unresponsive Hartford audiences, gave the visitor valuable support by assembling the added attraction of a "menagerie" of well-known literary men from New York and Boston.

Introducing George W. Cable

Unity Hall, Hartford, April 4, 1883

A complete stranger myself to Mr. Cable personally, though a great admirer of his books, I appear before you as his sponsor tonight, if he needs one. The original idea was that Mr. William Dean Howells of New York was to introduce Mr. Cable of New Orleans to the Hartford audience, when it occurred to the committee that Mr. Howells was himself a stranger to Hartford and did not know Hartford, nor did Hartford know him. So Mr. Thomas Bailey Aldrich of Boston was brought from Boston to introduce Mr. Howells of New York, who was to introduce Mr. Cable of New Orleans. But someone was necessary to introduce Mr. Aldrich of Boston, so Mr. Gilder of New York was asked to introduce Mr. Aldrich of Boston, who was to introduce Mr. Howells of New York, who was to introduce Mr. Cable of New Orleans. Then the same objection arose. No one knew Mr. Gilder of New York, so Mr. John Boyle O'Reilly of Boston was asked to introduce Mr. Gilder of New York who was to introduce Mr. Aldrich of Boston, who was to introduce Mr. Howells of New York, who was to introduce Mr. Cable of New Orleans.

Once more an awful problem arose in the minds of the committee. Mr. John B. O'Reilly of Boston had never been in Hartford before, and only knew it as a place of five minutes for refreshments on the New Haven Railroad. The question once more arose, who would introduce Mr. O'Reilly of Boston? And for a time no proper person appeared on the horizon. After some deliberation—for the matter was getting serious—we decided to dispense with an introduction altogether, which would occupy another evening at least, and to let

Cable speak for himself. I have, however, here present on the platform all these distinguished gentlemen from our suburban cities, which will account for the menagerie behind me. And this, ladies and gentleman of Hartford, is Mr. Cable of New Orleans.

Text / Laurence Hutton, *Talks in a Library* (1911):416–18.

Mr. Cable / George Washington Cable (1844–1925). American writer. A Confederate cavalryman, then reporter for the New Orleans *Picayune* (1865–79), he made a reputation as local colorist in *Old Creole Days* (1879), *The Grandissimes* (1880), *Madame Delphine* (1881), and others. His strong humanitarianism appears in *The Silent South* (1885) and *The Negro Question* (1890). Taking to the platform in the early 1880s, he made a long speaking tour with Mark Twain (1884–85).

William Dean Howells / (1837–1920). American author, editor and critic. Howells's achievements need not be restated. Suffice to say that he shared with the Reverend Joseph H. Twichell the privilege of being the most intimate friend of Mark Twain.

Thomas Bailey Aldrich / (1836–1907). American writer and editor. In Boston he edited *Every Saturday* (1866–74) and succeeded Howells as editor of the *Atlantic Monthly* (1881–90). He published eight volumes of verse serious and light, and a number of prose works, of which the best known are *The Story of a Bad Boy* (1870), *Marjorie Daw and Other People* (1873), and *Ponkapog Papers* (1903).

Gilder / Richard Watson Gilder (1844–1909). American writer and editor. As an editor for more than forty years—of *Hours at Home, Scribner's Monthly,* and the *Century Magazine*—he was an influential advisor, often censor, of American writers. He published sixteen volumes of verse, also biographies of Lincoln and Cleveland. He was a tireless worker on behalf of civic improvement, civil service reform, and international copyright.

John Boyle O'Reilly / (1844–90). Irish-American poet. His turbulent career was involved with the Fenians, the British Army, and a court-martial that sentenced him to twenty years in Australia, from which he escaped to the United States (1869). He edited the Boston *Pilot* (1874), and organized an expedition to rescue Irish political prisoners from western Australia (1876). He published *Songs From the Southern Seas* (1874), and *Songs, Legends, and Ballads* (1878).

· 51 ·

A note on the manuscript of the speech below says that it was "Delivered about 1880–85. Exact occasion unknown." It was probably given at a dinner of the Royal Literary and Scientific Society, which convened in Ottawa, May 22–26, 1883. Mark Twain was there at the time as a guest of the governor general and his lady, Lord Lorne, and Princess Louise, at Rideau Hall. An obvious assumption is that he was called upon to speak to the society. The conjecture is supported by a passage on Adam in Mark Twain's Notebook 17, May 1883–September 1884, MTP.

On Adam

Royal Literary and Scientific Society Dinner,
Ottawa, May 23, 1883

I never feel wholly at home and equal to the occasion except when I am to respond for the royal family or the President of the United States. But I am full of serenity, courage and confidence then, because I know by experience that I can drink standing and "in silence" just as long as anybody wants me to. Sometimes I have gone on responding to those toasts with mute and diligent enthusiasm until I have become an embarrassment, and people have requested me to sit down and rest myself. But responding by speech is a sore trial to me. The list of toasts being always the same, one is always so apt to forget and say something that has already been said at some other banquet some time or other. For instance, you take the toast to—well, take any toast in the regulation lot, and you won't get far in your speech before you notice that everything you are saying is old; not only old, but stale; and not only stale, but rancid. At any rate, that is my experience. There are gifted men who have the faculty of saying an old thing in a new and happy way—they rub the old Aladdin lamp and bring forth the smoke and thunder, the giants and genii, the pomp and pageantry of all the wide and secret realms of enchantment—and these men are the saviors of the banquet; but for them it must have gone silent, as Carlyle would say, generations ago, and ceased from among the world's occasions and industries. But I cannot borrow their trick; I do not know the mystery of how to rub the old lamp the right way.

And so it has seemed to me that for the behoof of my sort and kind, the toast list ought to be reconstructed. We ought to have some of the old themes knocked out of it and a new one or two inserted in their places. There are plenty of new subjects, if we would only look around. And plenty of old ones, too, that have not been touched. There is Adam, for instance. Who ever talks about Adam at a banquet? All sorts of recent and ephemeral celebrities are held up and glorified on such occasions, but who ever says a good word for Adam? Yet why is he neglected, why is he ignored in this offensive way—can you tell me that? What has he done, that we let banquet after banquet go on, and never give him a lift? Considering what we and the whole world owe him, he ought to be in the list—yes, and he ought to be away up high in the list, too. He ought to take precedence of the Press; yes, and the Army and Navy; and Literature; and the Day we Celebrate; and pretty much everything else. In the United States he ought to be at the very top—he ought to take precedence of the President; and even in the loyalest monarchy he ought at least to come right after the royal family. And be "drunk in silence and standing," too. It is his right; and for one, I propose to stick here and *drink* him in silence and standing till I can't tell a ministering angel from a tax collector. This neglect has been going on too long. You always place Woman at the bottom of the toast list; it is but simple justice to place Adam at the top of it—for if it had not been for the help of these two, where would you and your banquets be?—answer me that. You must excuse me for losing my temper and carrying on in this way; and in truth I would not do it if it were almost anybody but Adam; but I am of a narrow and clannish disposition, and I never can see a relative of mine misused without going into a passion. It is no trick for people with plenty of celebrated kin to keep cool when their folk are misused; but Adam is the only solitary celebrity in our family, and the man that misuses him has got to walk over my dead body—or go around, that is all there is to that. That is the way I feel about Adam. Years ago when I went around trying to collect subscriptions to build a monument to him, there wasn't a man that would give a cent; and generally they lost their temper because I interrupted their business; and they drove me away, and said they didn't care Adam for Adam—and in ninety-nine cases out of a hundred they got the emphasis on the wrong end of the word. Such is the influence of passion on a man's pronunciation. I tried Congress. Congress wouldn't build the monument. They wouldn't sell me the Washington monument, they wouldn't lend it to me temporarily while I could look around for another. I am negotiating for that Bastile yonder by the public square in Montreal, but they say they want to finish it first. Of course that ends the project, because there couldn't be any use of a monument after the man was forgotten. It is a pity, because I thought Adam might have pleasant associations with that building—he must have seen it in his time. But he shall have a monument yet, even if it be only a grateful place in the list of toasts; for to him we owe the two things which are most precious—life, and death. Life, which the young, the hopeful, the undefeated hold above all wealth and all honors; and death, the refuge, the solace, the best and kindliest and most prized friend and benefactor of the erring, the forsaken, the old, and weary, and broken of heart, whose burdens be heavy upon them, and who would lie down and be at rest.

I would like to see the toast list reconstructed, for it seems to me a needed reform; and as a beginning in this direction, if I can meet with a second, I beg to nominate Adam. I am not actuated by family considerations. It is a thing which I would do for any other member of our family, or anybody else's, if I could honestly feel that he deserved it. But I do not. If I seem to be always trying to shove Adam into prominence, I can say sincerely that it is solely because of my admiration of him as a man who was a good citizen at a time when it was difficult to be a good citizen; a good husband at a time when he was not married; a good father at a time when he had to guess his way, having never been young himself; and would have been a good son if he had had the chance. He could have been governor if he had wanted to; he could have been postmaster general, speaker of the House, he could have been anything he chose, if he had been willing to put himself up and stand a canvass. Yet he lived and died a private citizen, without a handle to his name, and he comes down to us as plain simple Adam, and nothing more—a man who could have elected himself Major General Adam or anything else as easy as rolling off a log. I stand up for him on account of his sterling private virtues, as a man and a citizen—as an inventor—inventor of life, and death, and sin, and the fashions—and not because he simply happens to be kin to me.

Text / "On Adam," MS, MTP. Published as "On Adam," *MTS*(23):93–97.

monument / Mark Twain instigated the project of a monument to Adam in 1879 and prepared a petition asking Congress to designate Elmira as the site. Senator Hawley agreed to present the petition but, fearing ridicule, backed out in 1881. See *MTB,* 2:707–9; 4, Appendix P.

that Bastile yonder / The reference to Montreal reinforces the surmise that Mark Twain delivered the speech in Canada.

· 52 ·

The rise of the bicycle craze that began to sweep the country in the early 1880s led to the organization of clubs, one of the most vigorous being the Springfield Bicycle Club, which staged its first tournament in 1883. Another, a year later, attracted an international field of contestants, professional and amateur. Pedaling the old high-wheelers, they competed in a variety of events—ten-mile amateur open, two-mile tricycle, three-mile tandem, three-mile tug of war, and so on. Filling and overflowing the grandstand was an enthusiastic crowd of five thousand, among whom one recent convert to bike riding was Mark Twain. His speech, presumably given at a banquet, is conjecturally assigned to one of the tournament dates.

Dinner Speech

Banquet of Wheelmen, Springfield, Massachusetts,
September 16 or 17, 1884

Mr. Chairman: I am not sure that I have voice enough to make myself heard over such a far-stretching landscape of humanity as this, but I will do what I can. I have been asked to tell, briefly, what bicycling is like, from the novice's point of view. I judge that this is for the instruction of the eight hundred guests, scattered through this vast assemblage, who are not wheelmen; for it is not likely that I could tell the rest of you anything about bicycling which you do not already know. As twelve speakers are to follow me, and as the weather is very warm and close besides, I shall be careful to make quite sure of one thing at least—I will keep well within the ten-minute limit allowed each speaker.

It was on the 10th of May, of the present year, that a brace of curiously contrasted events added themselves to the sum of my experiences; for on that day I confessed to age by mounting spectacles for the first time, and in the same hour I renewed my youth, to outward appearance, by mounting a bicycle for the first time.

The spectacles stayed on.

Text / "Speech at the Banquet of the International Congress of Wheelmen," MS, MTP. Published as "Speech," *MTS*(23):109.

what bicycling is like / Mark Twain wrote an entertaining account of his troubles in learning to ride one of the cumbersome high-wheelers. See "Taming the Bicycle," *What is Man? and Other Essays,* ed. Albert Bigelow Paine (New York, 1917):285–96.

· 53 ·

In the acrimonious presidential campaign of 1884, Mark Twain, hitherto a staunch Republican, defected from the party and its candidate, James G. Blaine, to support the Democratic nominee, Grover Cleveland. Date and occasion of the speech below are not clear, but it was very likely made during the last two weeks before election day. In the files of correspondence, MTP, a postcard dated October 23, 1884, commends Mark Twain for his Hartford speech, which was probably "Turncoats." For his comments on local effects of the acrid campaign, see MTA, *2:13–36.*

Turncoats

Political Meeting, Hartford, Late October 1884

It seems to me that there are things about this campaign which almost amount to inconsistencies. This language may sound violent; if it does, it is traitor to my mood. The Mugwumps are contemptuously called turncoats by the Republican speakers and journals. The charge is true: we have turned our coats; we have no denials to make, as to that. But does a man become of a necessity base because he turns his coat? And are there no Republican turncoats except the Mugwumps? Please look at the facts in the case candidly and fairly before sending us to political perdition without company.

Why are we called turncoats? Because we have changed our opinion. Changed it about what? About the greatness and righteousness of the principles of the Republican party? No, that is not changed. We believe in those principles yet; no one doubts this. What, then, is it that we have changed our opinions about? Why, about Mr. Blaine. That is the whole change. There is no other. Decidedly, we have done that, and do by no means wish to deny it. But when did we change it? Yesterday?—last week?—last summer? No—we changed it years and years ago, as far back as 1876. The vast bulk of the Republican party changed its opinion of him at the same time and in the same way. Will anybody be hardy enough to deny this? Was there more than a handful of really respectable and respectworthy Republicans on the north Atlantic seaboard who did not change their opinion of Mr. Blaine at that time? Was not the Republican atmosphere—both private and journalistic—so charged with this fact that none could fail to perceive it?

Very well. Was this multitude called turncoats at that time? Of course not. That would have been an absurdity. Was any of this multitude held in contempt at that time, and derided and execrated, for turning his Blaine coat? No one thought of such a thing. Now then, we who are called the Mugwumps, turned our coats at that time, and they have remained so turned to this day. If it is shameful to turn one's coat once, what measure of scorn can adequately describe the man who turns it twice? If to turn one's coat once makes one a dude, a Pharisee, a Mugwump and fool, where shall you find language rancid enough to describe a double turncoat? If to turn your coat at a time when no one can impeach either the sincerity of the act or the cleanliness of your motives in doing it, is held to be a pathetic spectacle, what sort of spectacle is it when such a coat-turner turns his coat again, and this time under quite suggestively different circumstances?—that is to say, *after a nomination.* Do these double turncoats exist? And who are they? They are the bulk of the Republican party; and it is hardly venturing too far to say that neither you nor I can put his finger upon a respectable member of that great multitude who can put a denial of it instantly into words and without blush or stammer. Here in Hartford they do not deny; they confess that they are double turncoats. They say they are convinced that when they formerly changed their opinion about Mr. Blaine they were wrong, and so they have changed back again. Which would seem to be an admission that to change one's opinion and turn one's coat is not necessarily a base thing to do, after all. Yet they call my tribe the customary hard names in their next campaign speeches just the same, without seeming to see any inconsistency or impropriety in it. Well, it is all a muddle to me. I cannot make out how it is or why it is that a single turncoat is a reptile and a double turncoat a bird of Paradise.

I easily perceive that the Republican party has deserted us, and deserted itself; but I am not able to see that *we* have deserted anything or anybody. As for me, I have not deserted the Republican code of principles, for I propose to vote its ticket, with the presidential exception; and I have not deserted Mr. Blaine, for as regards him I got my free papers before he bought the property.

Personally I know that two of the best known of the Hartford campaigners for Blaine did six months ago hold as uncomplimentary opinions about him as I did then and as I do today. I am told, upon what I conceive to be good authority, that the two or three other Connecticut campaigners of prominence of that ilk held opinions concerning him of that same uncomplimentary breed up to the day of the nomination. These gentlemen have turned their coats; and they now admire Blaine; and not calmly, temperately, but with a sort of ferocious rapture. In a speech the other night, one of them spoke of the author of the Mulligan letters—those strange Vassar-like exhibitions of eagerness, gushingness, timidity, secretiveness, frankness, naiveté, unsagacity, and almost incredible and impossible indiscretion—as the "first statesman of the age." Another of them spoke of "the three great statesmen of the age, Gladstone, Bismarck and Blaine." Doubtless this profound remark was received with applause. But suppose the gentleman had had the daring to read some of those letters first, appending the names of Bismarck and Gladstone to them; do not you candidly believe that the applause would have been missing, and that in its place there would have been a smile which you could have heard to Springfield? For no one has ever seen a Republican mass meeting that was devoid of the perception of the ludicrous.

Text / "Turncoats," MS, MTP. Published as "Turncoats," *MTS*(23):113–16.

Mugwumps / Independent voters. Derived from "mugquomp," an Algonquin word in John Eliot's Indian Bible (1661), meaning "great captain" or "chief" and equivalent to the more recent term, "egg-head." The name, not new to American politics, was satirically revived in March 1884, by Charles A. Dana, of the New York *Sun*. On the day after the nomination of Blaine, an independent Republican movement originated in Boston; on June 16, 1884, the Mugwumps convened in New York, pledging support to the Democrats if they chose a liberal candidate. Two leaders of the independents were Carl Schurz and George William Curtis.

Mr. Blaine / James Gillespie Blaine (1830–95). American politician. A good party organizer and a persuasive orator who seemed capable of the statesmanship his admirers attributed to him, he was Speaker of the House (1869–75) and secretary of state (1880–81). In 1876 a congressional investigation probed into his allegedly fraudulent dealings with the Little Rock and Fort Smith Railroad and the Northern Pacific Railroad while he was Speaker in 1869. The inquiry was dropped when Blaine suffered a sunstroke, but doubt remained. He never satisfactorily explained how he became wealthy without sufficient visible income, or dissipated suspicion of corruption, which has clouded his reputation to this day.

Mulligan letters / Written by Blaine (1864–76) to Warren Fisher, Jr., a Boston businessman, the letters being acquired by James Mulligan, Fisher's bookkeeper, then retrieved by Blaine, who read portions of them on the floor of the House as an answer to charges against him. Thoroughly aired by the press, the letters reveal the strange mixture of characteristics mentioned by Mark Twain. They also contain much to make the reader skeptical of Blaine's probity: data on bonds he received, the implication that he was being compensated for steering favorable railroad legislation through the House and influencing congressional land grants, and the frequent telltale injunction: "Burn this letter." The Mugwumps were convinced of Blaine's venality. For a summary of their charges against him, see "The Independent Republican State Committee of Connecticut," Boston *Transcript*, October 13, 1884. Two signers of that indictment were Twichell and Mark Twain.

"first statesman of the age" / From a speech by Henry C. Robinson, a prominent citizen of Hartford, who was chairman of a Republican meeting in Allyn Hall on October 17, 1884. He referred to Blaine as "the foremost statesman of the age."

"Gladstone, Bismarck and Blaine" / From a speech by former Governor Long, of Massachusetts. Hyperbole, a commonplace in any political campaign, was up to standard in this one. Blaine adherents acclaimed their leader as "The Plumed Knight," a title invented by Robert Ingersoll. Opposition cartoonists gleefully riddled the exalted image in savage caricatures.

· 54 ·

The Mugwumps were not a third party. They were merely dissident Republicans, some of whom may not have cared much for Cleveland, the Democratic candidate, but who cared even less for the tarnished Blaine. Aided by good speakers like Carl Schurz and George William Curtis, the militant independents were articulate, and they stirred up enough dust to disturb party line Republicans. When a Mugwump rally, Mark Twain presiding, whooped things up in Hartford, the Courant, *organ of the standpatters, did not deign to report the occasion.*

Remarks as Chairman

Mugwump Rally, Allyn Hall, Hartford, October 20, 1884

Ladies and gentlemen: This is an informal meeting. I am asked to preside, and I believe I am the only legally appointed officer. I know it is customary to read a long list of vice-presidents, but I forgot all about it; so all gentlemen present, regardless of their political complexion, will be kind enough to act as vice-presidents.

As far as my own political change of heart is concerned, I have not been convinced by any Democratic means. The opinion I hold of Mr. Blaine is due to the comments of the Republican press before the nomination. Not that they have said bitter or scandalous things, because Republican papers are above that, but the things they said did not seem to be complimentary, and seemed to me to imply editorial disapproval of Mr. Blaine and the belief that he was not qualified to be President of the United States. I had read those papers in the past, and what they said appeared to me to be convincing. The editors seemed to me to consider him unfit to be President of the United States, and, as I had confidence in the integrity of my friends, the editors of the local Republican press, these things reduced my estimate of Mr. Blaine to what it now is. The personality of a man or his character gives immense weight to what he says or does. Take General Hawley's paper, for instance, and what it has said of Blaine in the past. I consider I am a Mugwump constructed by General Hawley.

It is just a little indelicate for me to be here on this occasion before an assemblage of voters, for the reason that the ablest newspaper in Colorado—the ablest newspaper in the world—has recently nominated me for President. It is hardly fit for me to preside at a discussion of the brother candidate; but the best among us will do the most repulsive things the moment we are smitten with a presidential madness. If I had realized that this canvass was to turn on the candidate's private character, I would have started that Colorado paper sooner. I know the crimes that can be imputed and proved against me can be told on the fingers of your hands—not all your hands, but only just simply the most of them. This cannot be said of any other presidential candidate in the field.

Text / Composite, based upon: Boston *Transcript,* October 21, 1884; *MTB,* 2:781. The text is probably incomplete. Mark Twain, scheduled to introduce Carl Schurz, surely added appropriate remarks.

a Mugwump constructed by General Hawley / Like other Republican papers, the *Courant,* managed by Hawley and Charles Dudley Warner, had denounced Blaine after the damning disclosures of 1876. Yet when Blaine was nominated for the presidency in 1884, the *Courant,* again like other Republican papers, swung around to support him. The switch was too much for Warner, who resigned as editor.

· 55 ·

A note on the manuscript of the speech below, MTP, says that it was written "after the election of Grover Cleveland in 1884," but was "probably never delivered in public." On the day after the election Mark Twain and George W. Cable began a long speaking tour; the speech may have been given at a dinner or late supper tendered the speakers at one of the many stops on their route. At any rate, the "Mock Oration," obviously prepared for some function, makes a good companion piece to the "Funeral Oration Over the Grave of the Democratic Party," delivered four years before.

Mock Oration on the Dead Partisan

Early November 1884

Mr. Chairman: That is a noble and beautiful ancient sentiment which admonishes us to speak well of the dead. Therefore let us try to do this for our late friend who is mentioned in the text. How full of life, and strength, and confidence and pride he was, but a few short months ago; and alas, how dead he is today! We that are gathered at these obsequies, we that are here to bury this dust, and sing the parting hymn, and say the comforting word to the widow and the orphan now left destitute and sorrowing by him, their support and stay in the post office, the consulship, the navy yard and the Indian reservation—we knew him, right well and familiarly we knew him; and so it is meet that we, and not strangers, should take upon ourselves these last offices, lest his reputation suffer through explanations of him which might not explain him happily, and justifications of him which might not justify him conclusively. First, it is right and well that we censure him, in those few minor details wherein some slight censure may seem to be demanded; to the end that when we come to speak his praises, the good he did may shine with all the more intolerable a brightness by the contrast.

To begin, then, with the twilight side of his character: he was a slave; not a turbulent and troublesome, but a meek and docile, cringing and fawning, dirt-eating and dirt-preferring slave; and Party was his lord and master. He had no mind of his own, no will of his own, no opinion of his own; body and soul he was the property and chattel of that master, to be bought and sold, bartered, traded, *given* away, at his nod and beck—branded, mutilated, boiled in oil, if need were. And the desire of his heart was to make of a nation of freemen a nation of slaves like to himself; to bring to pass a time when it might be said that "All are for the Party, and none are for the State"; and the labors of his diligent hand and brain did finally compass his desire. For he fooled the people with plausible new readings of familiar old principles, and beguiled them to the degradation of their manhood and the destruction of their liberties. He taught them that the only true freedom of thought is to think as the party thinks; that the only true freedom of speech is to speak as the party dictates; that the only righteous toleration is toleration of what the party approves; that patriotism, duty, citizenship, devotion to country, loyalty to the flag, are all summed up in loyalty to the party. Save the party, uphold the party, make the party victorious, though all things else go to ruin and the grave.

In these few little things, he who lies here cold in death was faulty. Say we no more concerning them, but over them draw the veil of a charitable oblivion; for the good which he did far overpasses this little evil. With grateful hearts we may unite in praises and thanksgivings to him for one majestic fact of his life: that in his zeal for the cause, he finally overdid it. The precious result was that a change came; and that change remains, and will endure; and on its banner is written—

"Not all are for the Party—*now* some are for the State."

Text / "Mock Oration on the Dead Partisan," MS, MTP; "A Tribute," *MTS*(23):117–19.

· 56 ·

The date and occasion of the speech below are conjectural. It is assigned to the Hutton dinner, March 31, 1885, chiefly on the strength of Mark Twain's statement that he kept his New Year's resolution to make no more speeches "from that day to this"—three months, a time that seems reasonable for him.

On Speech-Making Reform

Tile Club Dinner for Laurence Hutton, New York, March 31, 1885

Like many another well-intentioned man, I have made too many speeches. And like other transgressors of this sort, I have from time to time reformed; binding myself, by oath, on New Year's Days, to never make another speech. I found that a new oath holds pretty well; but that when it is become old, and frayed out, and damaged by a dozen annual retyings of its remains, it ceases to be serviceable; any little strain will snap it. So, last New Year's Day I strengthened my reform with a money penalty; and made that penalty so heavy that it has enabled me to remain pure from that day to this. Although I am falling once more now, I think I can behave myself from this out, because the penalty is going to be doubled ten days hence. I see before me and about me the familiar faces of many poor sorrowing fellow sufferers, victims of the passion for speech-making—poor sad-eyed brothers in affliction, who, fast in the grip of this fell, degrading, demoralizing vice, have grown weak with struggling, as the years drifted by, and at last have all but given up hope. To them I say, in this last final obituary of mine, don't give up—don't do it; there is still hope for you. I beseech you, swear one more oath, and back it up with cash. I do not say this to all, of course; for there are some among you who are past reform; some who, being long accustomed to success, and to the delicious intoxication of the applause which follows it, are too wedded to their dissipation to be capable now or hereafter of abandoning it. They have thoroughly learned the deep art of speech-making, and they suffer no longer from those misgivings and embarrassments and apprehension which are really the only things which ever make a speech-maker want to reform. They have learned their art by long observation and slowly compacted experience; so now they know, what they did not know at first, that the best and most telling speech is not the actual impromptu one, but the counterfeit of it; they know that that speech is most worth listening to which has been carefully prepared in private and tried on a plaster cast, or an empty chair, or any other appreciative object that will keep quiet, until the speaker has got his matter and his delivery limbered up so that they will seem impromptu to an audience. The expert knows that. A touch of indifferent grammar flung in here and there, apparently at random, has a good effect—often restores the confidence of a suspicious audience. He arranges these errors in private; for a really random error wouldn't do any good; it would be sure to fall in the wrong place. He also leaves blanks here and there—leaves them where genuine impromptu remarks can be dropped in, of a sort that will add to the natural aspect of the speech without breaking its line of march. At the banquet, he listens to the other speakers, invents happy turns upon remarks of theirs, and sticks these happy turns into his blanks for impromptu use by and by when he shall be called up. When this expert rises to his feet, he looks around over the house with the air of a man who has just been strongly impressed by something. The uninitiated cannot interpret his aspect, but the initiated can.

They know what is coming. When the noise of the clapping and stamping has subsided, this veteran says: "Aware that the hour is late, Mr. Chairman, it was my intention to abide by a purpose which I framed in the beginning of the evening—to simply rise and return my duty and thanks, in case I should be called upon, and then make way for men more able, and who have come with something to say. But, sir, I was so struck by General Smith's remark concerning the proneness of evil to fly upward, that"—etc., etc., etc.; and before you know it he has slidden [*sic*] smoothly along on his compliment to the general, and out of it and into his set speech, and you can't tell, to save you, where it was nor when it was that he made the connection. And that man will soar along, in the most beautiful way, on the wings of a practiced memory; heaving in a little decayed grammar here, and a little wise tautology there, and a little neatly counterfeited embarrassment yonder, and a little finely acted stumbling and stammering for a word—rejecting this word and that, and finally getting the right one, and fetching it out with ripping effect, and with the glad look of a man who has got out of a bad hobble entirely by accident, and wouldn't take a hundred dollars for that accident; and every now and then he will sprinkle you in one of those happy turns on something that has previously been said; and at last, with supreme art, he will catch himself, when in the very act of sitting down, and lean over the table and fire a parting rocket, in the way of an afterthought, which makes everybody stretch his mouth as it goes up, and dims the very stars in heaven when it explodes. And yet that man has been practicing that afterthought and that attitude for about a week.

Well, you can't reform that kind of a man. It's a case of Eli joined to his idols—let him alone. But there is one sort that can be reformed. That is the genuinely impromptu speaker. I mean the man who "didn't expect to be called upon, and isn't prepared"; and yet goes waddling and warbling along, just as if he thought it wasn't any harm to commit a crime so long as it wasn't premeditated. Now and then he says, "but I must not detain you longer"; every little while he says, "Just one word more and I am done"—but at these times he always happens to think of two or three more unnecessary things and so he stops to say them. Now that man has no way of finding out how long his windmill is going. He likes to hear it creak; and so he goes on creaking, and listening to it, and enjoying it, never thinking of the flight of time; and when he comes to sit down at last, and look under his hopper, he is the most surprised person in the house to see what a little bit of a grist he has ground, and how unconscionably long he has been grinding it. As a rule, he finds that he hasn't said anything—a discovery which the unprepared man ought usually to make, and does usually make—and has the added grief of making it at second hand, too.

This is a man who can be reformed. And so can his near relative, who now rises out of my reconstructed past—the man who provisions himself with a single prepared bite, of a sentence or two, and trusts to luck to catch quails and manna as he goes along. This person frequently gets left. You can easily tell when he has finished his prepared bit and begun on the impromptu part. Often the prepared portion has been built during the banquet; it may consist of ten sentences, but it oftener consists of two—oftenest of all, it is but a single sentence; and it has seemed so happy and pat and bright and good that the creator of it, the person that laid it, has been sitting there cackling privately over it and admiring it and petting it and shining it up, and imagining how fine it is going to "go," when, of course, he ought to have been laying another one, and still another one; and maybe a dozen or basketful if it's a fruitful day; yes, and he is thinking that when he comes to hurl that egg at the house there is going to be such an electric explosion of applause that the inspiration of it will fill him instantly with ideas and clothe the ideas in brilliant language, and that an impromptu speech will result which will be infinitely finer than anything he could have deliberately prepared. But there are two damaging things which he is leaving out of the calculation: one is, the historical fact that a man is never called up as soon as he thinks he is going to be called up, and that every speech that is injected into the proceedings ahead of him gives his fires an added chance to cool; and the other thing which he is forgetting is that he can't sit there and keep saying that fine sentence of his over and over to himself, for three-quarters of an hour without by and by getting a trifle tired of it and losing somewhat of confidence in it.

When at last his chance comes and he touches off his pet sentence, it makes him sick to see how shamefacedly and apologetically he has done it; and how compassionate the applause is; and how sorry everybody feels; and then he bitterly thinks what a lie it is to call this a free country where none but the unworthy and the undeserving may swear. And at this point, naked and blind and empty, he wallows off into his *real* impromptu speech; stammers out three or four incredibly flat things, then collapses into his seat, murmuring, "I wish I was in"—he doesn't say where, because he doesn't. The stranger at his left says, "Your opening was very good"; stranger at his right says, "I liked your opening"; man opposite says, "Opening very good indeed —very good"; two or three other people mumble something about his opening. People always feel obliged to pour some healing thing on a crippled man, that way. They mean it for oil; they think it *is* oil; but the sufferer recognizes it for aquafortis.

Text / "On Speech-Making Reform," MS, MTP. Published as "On Speech-Making Reform," *MTS* (23):1–6.

Tile Club / A group of artists who met in an old house on Tenth Street, New York, sometimes in each other's studios, ate oysters and mallards, quaffed hock and burgundy, and amiably wrangled about art and other matters. The name, Tile Club, came from the experiment of painting on tiles and potsherds with vitreous paints. Among members were E. A. Abbey, J. Alden Weir, Winslow Homer, William M. Chase, F. D. Millet, and Augustus St. Gaudens. See *A Book of the Tile Club* (1887); Hamilton Fish Armstrong, *Those Days* (1963).

Laurence Hutton / (1843–1904). American essayist and critic. Literary editor of *Harper's Magazine* (1886–98) and lecturer on English literature at Princeton (1901–04), he published a number of books about the theater: *Plays and Players* (1875), *Curiosities of the American Stage* (1891), *Edwin Booth* (1893), and others. A charter member of the Players Club, he was a veteran banqueter and competent speaker.

Eli joined to his idols / In *Hosea* (4.17), it is Ephraim, not Eli, who is joined to idols. Mark Twain, who was fond of biblical quotations, often misquoted.

· 57 ·

An Actors Fund Fair was a philanthropic project, assisted by the gratis services of actors, musicians, writers, and socialites, who manned bazaars and put on vaudeville acts. Mark Twain, attending the Philadelphia Fair, praised "a superb performance, and of prodigious variety. It began shortly after noon and lasted till 4. There were 4,000 people present, and they sat it through." See letter to Olivia Clemens, April 9, 1885, LLMT.

Remarks

Actors Fund Fair, Academy of Music, Philadelphia, April 9, 1885

Ladies and gentlemen: The—er—this—er—welcome occasion gives me an—er—opportunity to make an—er—explanation that I have long desired to deliver myself of. I rise to the highest honors before a Philadelphia audience. In the course of my checkered career I have, on divers occasions, been charged—er—maliciously with a more or less serious offense. It is in reply to one of the more—er—important of these that I wish to speak. More than once I have been accused of writing obituary poetry in the Philadelphia *Ledger*.

I wish right here to deny that dreadful assertion. I will admit that once, when a compositor in the *Ledger* establishment, I did set up some of that poetry, but for a worse offense than that no indictment can be found against me. I did not write that poetry—at least, not all of it.

Text / "Obituary Poetry," *MTS*(10): 265. The text is misdated.

· 58 ·

An interesting part of Mark Twain's speaking craftsmanship was his practice of reshaping–limbering up, as he put it–his own published narratives to make them more suitable for platform performance. He said that telling a story as it was printed was only relaying at second-hand somebody else's tale, a handicap he sensed even when that somebody was himself. In his copy of volume one of the Tauchnitz edition of Huckleberry Finn, *MTP, revisions in parts of seven chapters show how he reworked them for public recital. The episode here, from chapter sixteen, was a frequent program number, generally identified in his notebooks as "Small-pox" or "Huck Saves Jim." It is given as he revised it, emphasized words and parts of words as he underlined them. The marks were no doubt guides to inflection, although they probably give an over-simplified and inaccurate impression of his shadings of emphasis.*

Huck Saves Jim

From Huckleberry Finn, *a Reading Often Used From 1885 On*

Night after night they kept a sharp lookout for Cairo, where the Ohio River comes in; for there they would land and try to escape far north and east away from the domain of slavery. Jim said if the two big rivers joined together there, that would show. But I said maybe we might think we was passing the foot of an island and coming into the same old river again. That disturbed Jim—and me too. So the question was, what to do? I said, paddle ashore the first time a light showed, and tell them pap was behind, coming along with a trading-scow, and was a green hand at the business, and wanted to know how far it was to Cairo. Jim thought it was a good idea, so we took a smoke on it and waited.

There warn't nothing to do, now, but look out sharp for the *town*, and not pass it without *see*ing it. He said he'd be mighty *sur*e to see it, because he'd be a free *man* the minute he *seen* it; but if he *miss*ed it he'd be in the *slav*e country again and no more show for *freed*om. *Ev*ery little while he jumps up and says:

"*Dah* she is!"

But it *warn*'t. It was only Jack-o-lanterns, or lightning bugs; so he set *down* again, and went to *watch*ing, same as be*fore.* Jim said it made him all over trembly and *fev*erish to be so close to *fre*edom. Well, I can tell you it made *me* all over trembly and feverish, *too,* to *hear* him, because I begun to get it through my head that he *was* most free—and *who was to blame for it?* Why, *me.* The thought struck me cold: I couldn't get that out of my conscience, no how nor no *way.* O, I had committed a *crime!*—I knowed it perfectly *well*—I could *see* it, *now.* It got to troubling me so I couldn't *rest;* I couldn't stay still in one p*lace.* It hadn't ever come h*om*e to me be*fore,* what this thing *was* that I was doing. But *now* it did; and it *staid* with me, and scorched me more and *more.* I tried to make out to myself that *I* warn't to blame, because *I* didn't run Jim off from his rightful owner; but it warn't no *use,* conscience up and *says,* every t*im*e, "But you *knowed* he was running for his freedom, and you could a paddled ashore and *told* somebody." That was *so*—yes, it was *so*—I couldn't get around *that,* no way. That was where it *pinched.* Conscience says to me, "What had poor Miss Watson done to you, that you could see her nigger go off right under your eyes and never say one single *word?* What did that poor old woman do to *you,* that you could treat her so *mean?* Why, she tried to learn you your *book,* she tried to learn you your *mann*ers, she tried to learn you to be a *Chris*tian, she tried to be good to you every way she knowed how. *That's* what she done."

I got to feeling so *mean* and *treach*erous and so *miser*able I most wished I was *dead.* I fidgeted up and down the raft, abusing myself to myself, and *Jim* was fidgeting up and down *past* me. We *neith*er of us could keep *still.* Every time he danced around and says, "*Dah's* Cairo!" it went through me like a *sword,* and I thought if it *was* Cairo I reckoned I would *die* of *miser*ableness.

Jim talked out *loud* all the time while I was talking to *myself.* He was saying how the *first thing* he would do when he got to a free State he would go to *saving up money* and never spend a single *cent,* and when he got enough he would buy his *wife,* which was owned on a farm close to where Miss Watson lived; and then they would *both* work to buy the two *children,* and if their master wouldn't *sell* them, they'd get an Ab'litionist to go and *steal* them. It was *awful* to hear it.

It most *froze* me to hear such talk. He wouldn't ever *dared* to talk such talk in his *life* before. Just *see* what a difference it made in him the minute he judged he was about *free.* It was according to the old saying, "Give a nigger an *inch* and he'll take an *ell*." Thinks I, *this* is what comes of my not *think*ing. Here was this nigger which *I had as good as helped to run away,* coming right out flat-*footed* and saying he would *steal* his children—children that belonged to a man I didn't even *know;* a man that hadn't ever done *me* no *harm.*

I was *sorry* to hear Jim say that, it was such a *lowering* of him. My conscience got to stirring me up hotter than *ever,* until at last I says to it, "Let *up* on me—it ain't too late, *yet*—I'll paddle ashore at the *first light,* and *tell*." O, it was a *blessed* thought! I never can tell how *good* it made me feel—'cuz I *knowed* I was doing *right,* now. I felt easy, and happy, and light as a feather, right *off.* All my troubles was *gone.* I went to looking out sharp for a light, and sort of *singing* to my*self.* By and by one showed. Jim sings out:

"We's *safe,* Huck, we's *safe!* Jump up and crack yo' *heels, dat's* de good ole Cairo at las', I jis *knows* it! We's *safe,* Huck, we's *safe,* shore's you's b*awn*, we *safe!*"

I says:

"I'll take the canoe and go *see,* Jim. It mightn't *be,* you know."

He jumped and got the canoe ready, and put his old coat in the bottom for me to *set* on, and give me the paddle; and as I shoved off, he says:

"Pooty soon I'll be a-shout'n for *joy,* en I'll say, it's *all* on accounts o' *Huck;* I's a *free* man, en I couldn't ever *ben* free ef it hadn' been for *Huck; Huck* done it. Jim won't ever *forgit* you, Huck; you's de bes' fren' Jim's ever *had;* en you's de *only* fren' ole Jim's got *now.* O bless de good old heart o' you, Huck!"

I was paddling off, all in a sweat to *tell* on him; but when he says *this,* it seemed to kind of take the *tuck* all out of me. It kind of all *unsettled* me, and I couldn't seem to *tell* whether I was doing *right* or doing *wrong.* I went along *slow* then, and I warn't right down certain whether I was glad I started or whether I warn't. When I was a hundred and fifty yards off, Jim sings out across the darkness and says:

"*Dah* you goes, de *ole true Huck;* de on'y white genlman dat ever kep' his promise to ole *Jim.*"

Well, I just felt *sick.* But I says, I *got* to do it—I can't get *out* of it. Right then, along comes a skiff with two men in it, with *guns,* and *they* stopped and *I* stopped. One of them says:

"What's *that,* yonder?"

"A piece of a *raft,*" I says.

"Do you belong on it?"

"*Yes,* sir."

"Any *men* on it?"

"Only *one,* sir."

"Well, there's five *niggers* run off to*night,* up yonder above the head of the *bend.* Is your man white or black?"

I didn't answer up *prompt.* I tried to, but the words wouldn't come. I tried, for a second or two, to brace up and out with it, but I warn't *man* enough—hadn't the spunk of a *rabb*it. I see I was weakening. The man says, "*Come,* answer up—is he *white* or black?"—then I hear the voice across the water a-saying, "De good ole Huck, de good ole Huck!" and I just let go and give up and says:

"He's *white.*"

"It took you a good while to get it *out.* I reckon we'll go and see for our*selves.*"

"O! I *wish* you *would,*" says I, "because it's *pap* that's *there,* and maybe you'd help me tow the raft *ashore* where the *light* is. He's *sick*—he's awful sick—and so is mam and Mary Ann, and the baby."

"Oh, the *devil!* we're in a *hurry,* boy. But I s'pose we've *got* to. Come—buckle to your *padd*le, and let's get *along.*"

I buckled to my paddle like Sam *Hill,* and says, "I George! in luck at last!" and they laid to their oars. When we had gone about a hundred yards, I says:

"Pap'll be mighty ob*leeged* to you, *I* can tell you. Everybody goes *away* when I want them to help me tow the raft ashore, and *I* can't do it by my*self.*"

"Well, that's infernal *mean.*" And pretty soon he says: "Looky *here!*—it's *odd,* too. *Say, boy,* what's the *matter* with your father?"

"It's the—a—the—well, it ain't *any*thing much."

They stopped *pulling.* It warn't but a mighty little ways to the raft, now. One says:

"Boy, that's a *lie.* What *is* the matter with your pap? Answer up *square,* now, and it'll be the *better* for you."

[Blubbering.] "I *will,* sir, I will, *honest*—but *don't* leave us, please. It's the—the—gentlemen, if you'll *only pull ahead,* and let me heave you the *head* line, you won't have to come a-*near* the raft—*please* do."

"Set her *back,* John, set her *back!* Keep *away,* boy—keep to *looard.* Con*found* it, I just expect the wind has blowed it to us. *Your pap's got the smallpox,* and you know it precious *well.* Why didn't you come out and *say* so? Do you want to spread it all *over?*"

"Well," says I, "I've told everybody be*fore,* and then and then and then—they just went away and *left* us." [Bellows.]

"Poor devil, there's something *in that.* We are right down *sorry* for you, but we—well, *hang* it, we don't want the *small*pox, you see. Look *here,* I'll *tell* you what to do. Don't you try to land by yourself, or you'll smash everything to *pieces.* You float along down about twenty miles and you'll come to a *town* on the left-hand side of the *river.* It will be *long* after sunup, then, and when you ask for *help,* you tell them your folks are all down with *chills and fever.* Don't be a *fool again,* and let people guess what is *the matter.* I feel *mighty* mean to leave you, but my *kingdom!* it won't do to fool with *small*pox, don't you see?—good-bye, good-bye.

If you see any runaway *niggers,* you get help and nab them, and you can make some *money* by it."

"Good-bye, sir," says I, "I won't let no runaway niggers get by *me* if *I* can help it."

They went *off* and I got aboard the *raft,* feeling bad and *low,* because *I knowed very well I had done wrong,* and I see it warn't no use for me to *try to learn to do right;* a body that don't get *started* right when he's *little,* ain't got no *show*—when the *pinch* comes there ain't nothing to back him up and keep him to his *work,* and so he gets *beat.* Then I *thought* a minute, and says to myself, hold *on*—s'pose you'd a *done right* and give Jim *up;* would you feel *better* than what you do *now?* No, says I, I'd feel *bad*—I'd feel *just the same way* I do *now.* As fur as *I* can see, a conscience is put in you just to *object* to whatever you *do* do, don't make no difference what it *is. Well, then,* says I, what's the use o' learning to do *right,* when it's *troublesome to do right,* and ain't *no trouble to do wrong,* and the wages is just the *same?* I was *stuck.* I couldn't *answer that.* So I reckoned I wouldn't bother no more *about* it, but after this always do *whichever come handiest at the time.*

Text / Part of chapter 16 of *Huckleberry Finn,* as revised by Mark Twain, Tauchnitz edition (1885), MTP.

· 59 ·

Mark Twain, a former jour printer, was in congenial company with members of the Typothetae, an association of master printers who celebrated annually on the birthday of Benjamin Franklin, patron of all printers. On one such occasion, at Keokuk, Iowa, in 1856, young Sam Clemens made his first speech. At the 1886 dinner in New York, the organization honored its distinguished forebear by displaying an oil portrait of Franklin and a model, in sugar, of the Franklin hand press. Of two speeches Mark Twain prepared for the Typothetae, he delivered "The Compositor," but the rejected, untitled version is also given below.

The Compositor

Typothetae Dinner, Delmonico's, New York, January 18, 1886

I am staggered by the compliments which have been lavished and poured out on me by my friend on my right. I am as proud of this compliment as I am staggered. It is uncommon in my experience. It is the first time that anybody in my experience has stood up in the presence of a large and respectable assemblage of gentlemen like this, and confessed that I have told the truth once. If I could return the compliment I would do it.

The chairman's historical reminiscences of Gutenberg have caused me to fall into reminiscences, for I myself am something of an antiquity. All things change in the procession of the years, and it may be that I am among strangers. It may be that the printer of today is not the printer of thirty-five years ago. I was no stranger to him. I knew him well. I built his fire for him in the cold winter mornings; I brought his water from the village pump; I swept out his office; I picked up his type from under his stand; and, if he was there to see, I put the good type in his case and the broken ones among the "hell matter"; and if he wasn't there to see, I dumped it all with the "pi" on the imposing stone—for that was the furtive fashion of the cub, and I was a cub. I wetted down the paper Saturdays, I turned it Sundays—for this was a country weekly; I rolled, I washed the rollers, I washed the forms, I folded the papers, I carried them around at dawn Thursday mornings. The carrier was then an object of interest to all the dogs in town. If I had saved up all the bites I ever received, I could keep M. Pasteur busy for a year. I enveloped the papers that were for the mail—we had a hundred town subscribers and three hundred and fifty country ones; the town subscribers paid in groceries and the country ones in cabbages and cordwood—when they paid at all, which was merely sometimes, and then we always stated the fact in the paper and gave them a puff; and if we forgot it they stopped the paper. Every man on the town list helped edit the thing; that is, he gave orders as to how it was to be edited; dictated its opinions, marked out its course for it, and every time the boss failed to connect, he stopped his paper. We were just infested with critics, and we tried to satisfy them all over. We had one subscriber who paid cash, and he was more trouble to us than all the rest. He bought us, once a year, body and soul, for two dollars. He used to modify our politics every which way, and he made us change our religion four times in five years.

If we ever tried to reason with him, he would threaten to stop his paper, and, of course, that meant bankruptcy and destruction. That man used to write articles a column and a half long, leaded long primer, and sign them "Junius," or "Veritas," or "Vox Populi," or some other high-sounding rot; and then, after it was set up, he would come in and say he had changed his mind—which was a gilded figure of speech because he hadn't any—and order it to be left out. We couldn't stand such a waste as that; we couldn't afford "bogus" in that office; so we always took the leads out, altered the signature, credited the article to the rival paper in the next village, and put it in. Well, we did have one or two kinds of bogus. Whenever there was a barbecue, or a circus, or a baptizing, we knocked off for half a day, and then to make up for short matter we would "turn over ads"—turn over the whole page and duplicate it. The other bogus was deep philosophical stuff, which we judged nobody ever read; so we kept a galley of it standing, and kept on slapping the same old batches of it in, every now and then, till it got dangerous.

Also, in the early days of the telegraph we used to economize on the news. We picked out the items that were pointless and barren of information and stood them on a galley, and changed the dates and localities, and used them over and over again till the public interest in them was worn to the bone. We marked the ads, but we seldom paid attention to the marks afterward; so the life of a "td" and a "tf" ad was equally eternal. I have seen a "td" notice of a sheriff's sale still booming serenely along two years after the sale was over, the sheriff dead, and the whole circumstance become ancient history. Most of the yearly ads were patent medicine stereotypes, and we used to fence with them.

Life was easy with us; if we pied a form we suspended till next week, and we always suspended every now and then when the fishing was good, and explained it by the illness of the editor, a paltry excuse, because that kind of a paper was just as well off with a sick editor as a well one, and better off with a dead one than with either of them. He was full of blessed egotism and placid self-importance, but he didn't know as much as a 3 em quad. He never set any type except in the rush of the last day, and then he would smouch all the poetry, and leave the rest to "jeff" for the solid takes. He wrote with impressive flatulence and soaring confidence upon the vastest subjects; but puffing alms gifts of wedding cake, salty ice cream, abnormal watermelons and sweet potatoes the size of your leg was his best hold. He was always a poet—a kind of poet of the Carter's Address breed—and whenever his intellect suppurated, and he read the result to the printers and asked for their opinion, they were very frank and straightforward about it. They generally scraped their rules on the boxes all the time he was reading, and called it "hogwash" when he got through. All this was thirty-five years ago, when the man who could set 700 an hour could put on just as many airs as he wanted to; and if these New York men, who recently on a wager set 2,000 an hour solid minion for four hours on a stretch had appeared in that office, they would have been received as accomplishers of the supremely impossible, and drenched with hospitable beer till the brewery was bankrupt.

I can see that printing office of prehistoric times yet, with its horse bills on the walls, its "d" boxes clogged with tallow, because we always stood the candle in the "k" box nights, its towel, which was not considered soiled until it could stand alone, and other signs and symbols that marked the establishment of that kind in the Mississippi valley; and I can see, also, the tramping "jour," who flitted by in the summer and tarried a day, with his wallet stuffed with one shirt and a hatful of handbills; for if he couldn't get any type to set he would do a temperance lecture. His way of life was simple, his needs not complex; all he wanted was plate and bed and money enough to get drunk on, and he was satisfied. But it may be, as I have said, that I am among strangers, and sing the glories of a forgotten age to unfamiliar ears, so I will "make even" and stop.

Text / Composite, based upon: "The Typothetae," *Courant,* January 20, 1886; "Mark Twain, Printer," reprinted for the John Leslie Paper Company of Minneapolis, 1937; "The Old-Fashioned Printer" in *MTS*(10):182–85; and *MTS*(23):138–41.

"hell matter" / Matter consigned to the hellbox, which was a receptacle for broken and battered type.

"pi" / Types that are spilled, mixed, or incorrectly distributed.

imposing stone / A stand or table with a smooth flat top, originally of stone, on which to impose—i.e., arrange—type.

Pasteur / Louis Pasteur (1822–95). French chemist. He promulgated the germ theory of fermentation (1857), crusaded for measures to curb the spread of disease by bacilli, and founded the science of immunity. The remark about dog bites is an allusion to Pasteur's study of rabies, begun in 1882, and his development of vaccines to counteract hydrophobia.

leaded long primer / A lead was a thin strip of type metal used to separate lines of type. Long primer is ten-point type.

"bogus" / Print that is, in effect, sham or counterfeit. The word now designates extraneous material set in type, not for use, but to keep linotypists employed. The term is also roughly synonymous with "filler."

"td" and "tf" ad / "td," a symbol apparently unused today, meant an ad that ran for only a short time. Still used, "tf" is an ad that runs "till forbidden" or "till further notice."

pied a form / Pied type is jumbled or confused. A form is a series of pages set up—e.g., a form of eight pages—which, when ready for printing, is locked in a rectangular steel frame called a chase.

3 em quad / An em is the square of the body of any size of type. A quad is a quadrat, which is a piece of type metal lower than the letters and used in spacing between words.

"jeff" for the solid takes / To jeff or "jeffing," a pastime now gone out of fashion, was to gamble with quadrats as with dice, the nick side representing a score of one, the other sides blanks. A take is a sheet of copy as well as each typesetter's contribution to a story that has been distributed to several typesetters simultaneously.

poet of the Carter's Address breed / Probably a reference to William Lorenzo Carter (1813–60). A homespun Vermont poet, known as "The Bensontown Homer," he was the author of "Young [or Fair] Charlotte" and of other verses lachrymose and sentimental.

solid minion / Minion is seven-point type, smaller than long primer and much used in country weeklies in the nineteenth century.

the tramping "jour" / Short for "journeyman," a skilled compositor who wandered from town to town and who could generally be sure of finding a job.

I will "make even" / Equivalent to today's "makeready," the final preparation of a form for printing: making the surfaces of types even by hammering with a mallet, so that the printed page shows no variations of light and dark.

Rejected Version of Typothetae Speech

I began to set type when I was thirteen years old, and have always had a right respect and reverence for that art.

There is not a material marvel of this marvelous age in which we live whose fatherhood cannot be traced distinctly back to a single point, a single remote germ, a single primal source—the movable types of Gutenberg and Faust. That invention, of 538 years ago, was the second supreme event in the globe's creative history; for by an unstrained metaphor one may say that on that day God said again, Let there be light—and there was light. From that faint and far source, divergent threads of light stretch down through the centuries, as from some star-sun, glowing out of dim solitudes of space, to each and every precious and wonderful achievement of man's inventive genius which goes to make up today the sum of what we rightly call the most extraordinary age the world has ever seen. Each of these achievements is the result of the ray that came out from that star-sun; this age is the result of that fan of rays; without that star-sun this age had not been.

What changes have not these movable types witnessed—and wrought—in 538 years! They have seen the implements of war so changed that an army corps of today, with its Gatling guns, and bombs, and rifled cannon and other deadly things would hold a field against the combined armies of Europe of Gutenberg's time, and a single ironclad of today sweep her fleets from the sea. They have seen methods of travel so changed that a citizen of today could give Gutenberg a couple of years start and beat him around the world. They have seen facility of speech so changed by the telephone that even a truth may travel farther in two minutes today than a lie could in a week in his day. They have seen methods of written communication so changed that a New Yorker may send a message to China now quicker than Gutenberg could have carried it upstairs to his wife. They have seen methods of printing so changed that a press of today will turn off a job in a year which a customer of Gutenberg's would have had to wait nearly five centuries for—and then get it, perhaps, when interest in that publication had pretty much died out, and he would wish he hadn't ordered it. They have seen the science of medicine and surgery so immeasurably changed that a doctor of today would save three patients in less time than it would take *his* doctor to kill three hundred. They have seen industrial methods so amazingly accelerated by machinery that today a body of men would manufacture the stuffs and clothe and shoe a whole nation while a like body of Gutenberg's contemporaries were doing the same for its capital city. In a word, those movable types, in these 538 years, have changed, and marvelously accelerated, and advanced and improved every art and every industry known to men; they have utterly changed the face of art and industry in this whole world; so that not one single thing is done today as men saw it done in the day of Gutenberg and Faust.

But no, I am wrong. There is one thing which they have not changed; one thing which remains just what it was in the year 1348, unchanged, unadvanced, unimproved. The movable type has taught the whole world something: it has taught itself nothing. Isn't that a curious thing? Isn't it striking? Isn't it an actually stupefying thought? The type-setting art is the one solitary art in the world which has stood stock still for five hundred years. It is the art creative of arts, yet it can create nothing for itself. Truly it is a sun; it is the source and impulse of all intellectual life, but it stands still. Imagine, if you please, the people of Gutenberg's day suddenly snatched out of their graves and set down in New York, without a cent. What a strange new world it would be to them; what a strange and hopeless place for them. Poor fellows, they would apply here, they would apply there, they would apply yonder; but all to no use, they could get no work; they would find that the trades they learned five hundred years ago were worthless to them now, so sweeping has been the change in methods. Within one week that entire host would be in the poorhouse. With only one exception—old Gutenberg. He would be subbing somewhere. Yes, it is a most curious thing—that which I have been talking about. And the more one thinks it over, the more strange and curious it seems. I confess to you, fellow craftsmen, that I control one of the hundred and one devices and inventions for setting type by machinery, but do not be uneasy, I did not come here to advertise it. I only came to disgorge some grave and thoughtful thoughts, that is all; and you have done me the grace to receive them in a less depreciative spirit than the foreman used to do in an office where I was a reporter twenty years ago. When I brought in that sort of copy, one of them used to say, in printers' parlance, "Here he comes with some more hell matter," and the other said in a parlance of his own, "Here he comes with some more hogwash." Printers are strangely frank in the matter of literary criticism.

Text / Untitled MS, Doheny Memorial Library, St. John's Seminary, Camarillo, California.

Faust / Johann Faust, also known as Fust (d. ca. 1466 or 1467). A German printer, he was a partner of Gutenberg (ca. 1450–55).

the year 1348 / This date for the invention of printing is an error. Mark Twain had evidently not done his homework. The Gutenberg Bible (1456) is generally acknowledged to have been the first book printed with movable types.

I control one of the hundred and one devices, etc. / An allusion to a mechanical typesetter invented by James W. Paige. Mark Twain, putting a great deal of money into this machine, figured on hypothetical profits of millions. But the typesetter was too sensitive to perform consistently, and his dreams of wealth ended in bankruptcy in 1894.

· 60 ·

The struggle of writers and publishers to secure adequate copyright legislation was as dogged as the long battle of feminists for women's rights. When the Authors Copyright League and the Publishers Copyright League joined forces to exert pressure on Congress, Mark Twain, together with members of both Leagues, appeared before a senate committee in 1886. His remarks were rather inconclusive, perhaps because he was unsure of his role or because he did not entirely favor the bill under consideration, drafted by Senator Hawley. At any rate, the Hawley bill became the eleventh copyright measure in forty years that failed to reach the floor, all being killed in committee. An acceptable bill was finally passed, however, in the last hour of the last day of the Fifty-first Congress, March 1891.

Remarks on Copyright

Before the Committee on Patents, United States Senate, Washington, D.C., January 28–29, 1886

January 28

[Robert U. Johnson, secretary of the Authors Copyright League, called upon Mark Twain for a statement.]

Oh, Mr. Chairman, they call upon me! But it really seems to me that this matter has arrived at that point which I thought I foresaw yesterday when I said to these gentlemen, "You are bringing me to Washington without previous instructions. You have not educated me to my part, and I shall not know how to play it. I shall be apt, when the time comes, to play it after the simple honest fashion which was the method of my forefathers, and it may damage this bill, and that I do not want to do." I seem to come here in the interest of the Copyright League, and the Copyright League's interest, as you have heard, is centered upon the first bill mentioned here, called the Hawley bill, and I do not wish to make any speech at all or any remarks, lest I wander from the just path marked out for me by these gentlemen. No doubt it is a just path, but if I am here as a special pleader, I am a special pleader with a weak spot in this cause, and I will not commit myself or this committee further by any remarks. If any gentleman desires to ask me questions, then I do not care whom I commit; I shall come as near telling the truth as the moment's inspiration shall enable me.

[The chairman asked Mark Twain for his opinions on international copyright, regardless of the League.]

I comprehend your position, and you will comprehend mine also. I am in the position of one who would violate a hospitality, rather, if I should speak my mind. I did speak my mind yesterday to the most intelligent member of this committee of the League, besides myself, and it fired him, it grieved him, and I almost promised that I would not divulge what my right feeling was; but I did not promise that I would not take the contrary course.

January 29

[George Walton Green, secretary of the executive committee of the Publishers Copyright League, said: "Now I am going to ask Mr. Clemens to reconsider his decision, if he made a decision, and to speak right out like a little man."]

Well, then, I consider, Mr. Chairman and gentlemen of the committee, that absolves me from all obligation to be dishonest, or furtive, or clandestine, or whatsoever term you may choose to apply to the attitude I have held here before—rather an attitude of silence, in order that I should not commit or in any way jeopard the interests of this bill which the secretary has spoken of, the Hawley bill. As I have understood them in the railway train, or as well as I could understand them—and you yourselves have seen that there is some difficulty in that—they have still been clear upon one point, and that is that they would take a stand upon the Hawley bill in its simplicity and remain there. I disagreed with them yesterday because I had come to exactly the conclusion that General Hawley placed before you a little while ago: that whether it is feasible, whether it is possible to pass the Hawley bill in its rigid simplicity or not, is not to my mind the whole question at all. I do consider that those persons who are called "pirates," and for whom General Hawley has said a kind word, which seemed to me entirely proper, were made pirates by the collusion of the United States Government, which made them pirates and thieves. I do not wish to cast any reflection upon the members of this committee, because you gentlemen were not here at the time that was done. You probably would never have done it. But Congress, if anybody, is to blame for their action. It is not dishonesty. They have that right, and they have been working under that right a long time, publishing what is called "pirated books." They have invested their money in that way, and they did it in the confidence that they would be supported and no injustice done them.

I am afraid that the Hawley bill in its original form, pure and simple, would work a great injustice to men who have vested rights in that direction. And therefore the thing I wanted to say, and which I did not like to say before, occupying the position which I supposed I did, was that I should like to see the printing clause in that bill. I should like to see a copyright bill passed here which shall do no harm to anybody concerned in this matter, and a great many more people are concerned in it than merely the authors. In fact I suppose, if the truth is confessed, the authors are rather less concerned pecuniarly in any copyright measure than many other people—publishers, printers, binders, and so on. The authors have one part in the matter, but theirs is the larger part.

Now I have said just what I wanted to say, and it is not necessary for me to say anything more. I simply consider that there are other rights involved aside from those of the author, and they are vested rights, too, and nobody has a moral right to disturb that relation. And so, as I say, I echo what General Hawley said. I cannot see any objection to the insertion of a clause which shall require that the books of a foreign author when copyrighted here shall be printed on this soil. If there is anything further which the committee desires me to speak upon, I shall be glad to have it indicated.

[The chairman inquired about the status of an American author in England.]

He gets just as perfect a copyright as it is possible for a government to give. No English author is stronger in his copyright than an American author who has copyrighted his book there. Therefore the American author is in the position to say to London publishers, "You must pay my price or I simply will not publish." Then he does not have to publish. If he does not get his price he need not publish his book.

His copyright is good and strong for forty-two years, and it is quite easy to get it; there is no difficulty about that.

[George William Curtis asked about the copyright process.]

I have been through so many processes that I hardly know how to explain it. But the matter has always been simple with regard to England. Whatever complication there has been has occurred with Canada. You merely have to go and remain on British soil, under the British flag, while your book is publishing in England.

[The chairman asked about foreign profits.]

I can speak in my own case, and, I believe, in one other. I have for years received a larger royalty in England than I was receiving in America; I do not mean a proportional profit, but I mean a larger specific royalty in England than here. A similar result would not be shown in the half-yearly statement of account, for the reason that the books here are published at a high price, and there there is only one high-priced edition, and that is limited, so that no matter how large the sale might be, it is a sale of cheap books, and the result is correspondingly small. But I usually expect to receive one-third as much money from England as I receive in the United States on a book; I expect the royalties to result in that way. That, however, does not apply to any other European country. The results from those countries are exceedingly small.

I might also mention that in the case of General Grant's book the royalty paid in England on that book is the largest that ever was paid on a book in any country in any age of the world, and that the royalties paid in Germany and France are exceedingly large, and of course the German and French copyrights on that book result through conventions with England.

Text / *Senate Reports 1st Session 49th Congress. 1885–86.* Vol. 7, Report No. 1188 (Washington, 1886), pp. 8–17.

George William Curtis / (1824–92). American writer and editor. He was editor of the "Easy Chair" of *Harper's Magazine* (1859–92). Familiar to the lecture circuit as an advocate of antislavery and women's rights, he was also a prolific writer whose best known books are *Potiphar Papers* (1853), and *Prue and I* (1857). He was often asked to accept governmental appointments but refused to become involved in politics.

· 61 ·

Melville D. Landon, the "Eli Perkins" of the lecture circuit, who was present on the occasion of the dinner speech below, said of Mark Twain: "He arose slowly and stood, half stooping over the table. Both hands were on the table, palms to the front. There was a look of intense earnestness about his eyes. It seemed that the weight of an empire was upon his shoulders. His sharp eyes looked out from under his shaggy eyebrows, moving from one guest to another, as a lawyer scans his jury in a death trial. Then he commenced, very slowly." See: Kings of the Platform and Pulpit, *ed. Melville D. Landon (1901).*

Our Children

Authors Club Dinner, Gilsey House, New York, April 22, 1886

Our children—yours—and—mine. They seem like little things to talk about—our children, but little things often make up the sum of human life—that's a good sentence. I repeat it, little things often produce great things. Now, to illustrate, take Sir Isaac Newton—I presume some of you have heard of Mr. Newton. Well, once when Sir Isaac Newton—a mere lad—got over into the man's apple orchard—I don't know what he was doing there—I didn't come all the way from Hartford to q-u-e-s-t-i-o-n Mr. Newton's honesty—but when he was there—in the man's orchard—he saw an apple fall and he was a-t-t-racted toward it, and that led to the discovery—not of Mr. Newton—but of the great law of *attraction* and gravitation.

And there was once another great discoverer—I've forgotten his name, and I don't remember what he discovered, but I know it was something very important, and I hope you will all tell your children about it, when you get home. Well, when the great discoverer was once loafin' around down in Virginia, and a-puttin' in his time flirting with Pocahontas—Oh, Captain John Smith, that was the man's name!—and while he and Poca were sitting in Mr. Powhatan's garden, he accidentally put his arm around her and picked something—a simple weed, which proved to be tobacco—and now we find it in every Christian family, shedding its civilizing influence broadcast throughout the whole religious community.

Now there was another great man, I can't think of *his* name either, who used to loaf around, and watch the great chandelier in the cathedral at Pisa, which set him to thinking about the great law of gunpowder, and eventually led to the discovery of the cotton gin.

Now, I don't say this as an inducement for our young men to loaf around like Mr. Newton, and Mr. Galileo, and Captain Smith, but they were once little babies, two days old, and they show what little things have sometimes accomplished.

Text / Composite, based upon: "Our Children," *Kings of the Platform and Pulpit,* ed. Melville D. Landon (Akron, 1901):351–52; "Our Children and Great Discoveries," *MTS*(10):69–70.

· 62 ·

At a monthly meeting of the Military Service Institution, attended by Generals Sherman, Schofield, and James B. Fry, Mark Twain read from the manuscript of A Connecticut Yankee, *which he was desultorily working on at the time. He told his audience that he would explain the first chapter, then follow with selected fragments or, as he put it, "outline the rest of it in bulk, so to speak; do as the dying cowboy admonished his spiritual adviser to do, 'just leave out the details and heave in the bottom facts.'" In the reading the central character, called Hank Morgan in the book, is Sir Robert Smith of Camelot, formerly of Hartford, and there are some differences in diction and phrasing between the spoken version and the published text.*

Yankee Smith of Camelot

Military Service Institution, Governor's Island, New York, November 11, 1886

I am a Yankee of the Yankees, a practical man, nearly barren of sentiment or poetry—in other words, my father was a blacksmith, my uncle was a horse doctor, and I was both. Then I went over to the great arms factory and learned my real trade—learned to make everything, guns, revolvers, cannon, boilers, engines, electric machines, anything, in short, that anybody wanted anywhere in the world. . . . I became head boss and had a thousand men under me. Well, a man like that is full of fight—that goes without saying. With a thousand rough men under one, one has plenty of that sort of amusement.

Well, at last I met my match; I got my dose. It was during a misunderstanding conducted with iron crowbars with a fellow we used to call Hercules. He laid me out with a crusher alongside the head that made everything crack and seemed to make every joint of my skull lap over on its neighbor, and then the world went out in darkness and I felt nothing more, knew nothing more for a while, and when I came to again I was standing under an oak tree and the factory was gone.

Standing under an oak tree on the grass with a beautiful broad country, a landscape spread out before me—all to myself. No, not quite, not entirely to myself. There was a fellow on a horse looking down at me—a fellow fresh out of a picture book. He was in old-time armor from his head to his heel. He had a helmet on like a cheese box with slits on it, and he carried a shield and a sword and a prodigious spear. And his horse had armor on, too, and gorgeous silken trappings, red and green, that hung around him like a bedgown to the ground. And this apparition said to me:

"Fair sir! Will you joust?"

Said I: "Will I which?"

"Will you joust? Will you break a lance for land or lady?"

Said I: "What are you giving me? You go along back to your circus or I'll report you."

Now what does this fellow do but fall back a couple of hundred yards and then come tilting at me, as hard as he could drive, his cheese box down close and his long spear pointed straight at me. I saw he meant business, so I was up the tree when he arrived. Well, he allowed I was his property; the captive of his spear. Well, there was argument on his side and the bulk of the advantage, so I judged it best to humor him, and we fixed up an agreement. I was to go along with him, and he wasn't to hurt me. So I came down, and we started away, I walking by the side of his horse, and we marched comfortably along through glades and over brooks that I could not remember to have seen before. It puzzled me ever so much, and yet we didn't come to any circus, or any sign of a circus, so I gave up the idea of a circus, and concluded he was from an asylum. But we never came to any asylum, so I was up a stump, as you may say.

[When they reach the castle, the Yankee tries to get information from a man he encounters.]

"Now, my friend, if I could see the head keeper just a minute, only just a minute."

He said: "Prithee do not let me."

"Let you what?"

"Do not hinder me, if the word please thee better," and he was an under cook, and had no time to talk, though he would like to another time, for it would just comfort his very liver to know where I got my clothes.

[The Yankee also meets a young page, who casually announces that he was born in the year 513.]

It made the cold chills creep over me. I stopped and said, a little faintly, "Now, maybe I didn't hear you just right. Would you say that again, and say it slow. What year did you say it was?"

"513."

"And, according to your notions, according to your lights and superstitions, what year is it now?"

"Why," he said, "the year 528, the 19th of June." Well, I felt a mournful sinking of the heart, and muttered, "I shall never see my friends again—never see my friends any more; they won't be born for as much as a thousand years."

[Excerpts.]

I made up my mind to two things. If it was still the nineteenth century and I was among lunatics and couldn't get away, I would boss that asylum or know the reason why, and if, on the other hand, it was really the sixth century, all right. I didn't want any better thing; I'd boss the whole country inside of three months, for I judged I'd have the start on the best educated man in the kingdom by 1,300 years. . . . But I'm not a man to waste time, so I said to the boy, "Clarence, if your name should happen to be Clarence, what's the name of that duck, that galoot, who brought me here?"

There didn't seem to be brains enough in the entire nursery to bait a fishhook, but you didn't mind that after a little while, for you saw that brains were not needed in a society like that, and would have marred its symmetry and spoiled it.

Well, of all the d——d contracts, this is boss! I offered to sublet it to Sir Launcelot, to let him have it at ninety days, with no margin, but "No," he had got a better thing. He was going for a menagerie of one-eyed giants and a college of princesses.

Text / "Mark Twain's Story," *Courant*, November 13, 1886.

· 63 ·

Drafted to introduce a speaker, Mark Twain paid him the polite compliments that were expected, sometimes exaggerating to achieve a mildly ironical effect. If well acquainted with the man he was introducing, he was likely to add uncomplimentary lies that were too outrageous to be taken seriously, but were never malicious. Generally he tempered praise with remarks that served as a counterbalance.

Introducing Henry M. Stanley

Tremont Temple, Boston, December 9, 1886

Ladies and gentlemen: If any should ask, Why is it that you are here as introducer of the lecturer? I should answer that I happened to be around and was asked to perform this function. I was quite willing to do so, and, as there was no sort of need of an introduction, anyway, it could be necessary only that some person come forward for a moment and do an unnecessary thing, and this is quite in my line. Now, to introduce so illustrious a name as Henry M. Stanley by any detail of what the man has done is clear aside from my purpose; that would be stretching the unnecessary to an unconscionable degree. When I contrast what I have achieved in my measurably brief life with what he has achieved in his possibly briefer one, the effect is to sweep utterly away the ten-story edifice of my self-appreciation and leave nothing behind but the cellar. When you compare these achievements of his with the achievements of really great men who exist in history, the comparison, I believe, is in his favor. I am not here to disparage Columbus.

No, I won't do that; but when you come to regard the achievements of these two men, Columbus and Stanley, from the standpoint of the difficulties they encountered, the advantage is with Stanley and against Columbus. Now, Columbus started out to discover America. Well, he didn't need to do anything at all but sit in the cabin of his ship and hold his grip and sail straight on, and America would discover itself. Here it was, barring his passage the whole length and breadth of the South American continent, and he couldn't get by it. He'd got to discover it; he couldn't help it. Neither did he have to find any particular part of America, and when he found any portion of it his contract was fulfilled. But Stanley started out to find Dr. Livingstone, who was hidden away somewhere, scattered abroad, as you may say, over the length and breadth of a vast slab of Africa as big as the United States.

It was a blind kind of search. He was the worst scattered man. He was the scarcest commodity there was; he was as scarce as a teetotaler in a prohibition state. Now, it wouldn't do to send me out to hunt for a man. I shouldn't find him; he wouldn't be there when I got there.

But I will throw the weight of this introduction upon one very peculiar feature of Mr. Stanley's character, and that is his indestructible Americanism—an Americanism which he is proud of. And in this day and time, when it is the custom to ape and imitate English methods and fashions, it is like a breath of fresh air to stand in the presence of this untainted American citizen who has been caressed and complimented by half the crowned heads of Europe, who could clothe his body from his head to his heels with the orders and decorations lavished upon him. And yet, when the untitled myriads of his own country put out their hands in welcome to him and greet him, "Well done," through the Congress of the United States, that is the crown that is worth all the rest to him. He is a product of institutions which exist in no other country on earth—institutions that bring out all that is best and most heroic in a man. I introduce Henry M. Stanley.

Text / Composite, based upon: Boston *Transcript,* December 10, 1886; Major J. B. Pond, *Eccentricities of Genius* (1900):265–66; "Henry M. Stanley" in *MTS*(10):157–59; and *MTS*(23):131–32. The *MTS* texts are incorrectly dated.

· 64 ·

The Stationers Board of Trade of New York was an organization of interest to Mark Twain, the long-time writer and emergent publisher. Possibly he considered that, along with his fondness for banquets in general, an appearance at a dinner of the board was good for business. Yet his surprise at being asked to speak, the didn't-expect-to-be-called-on-plea, was undoubtedly assumed. Assuredly he was well prepared and thoroughly rehearsed.

Dinner Speech

Stationers Board of Trade Dinner, Hotel Brunswick, New York, February 10, 1887

Gentlemen, I find this an evening of surprises. I came here through an understanding with the chairman that I, having reformed, was not to break over pledges made and drift into an after-dinner speech unless I saw immoralities or crimes being committed, and lo! I have waited in constant expectation that something would be said or done that would compel me to speak. But concerning what has been said and done here I am bound to say that thus far they have been mere misdemeanors. I have been introduced to you as an example of the author and the publisher. I am one of the latest publishers and I am one of the oldest authors and certainly one of the best. When I came here I expected to remain in some humble capacity outside of the door and never dreamt of being made conspicuous by taking a seat high up among the distinguished guests, but then I am used to being made conspicuous.

As I say I have found nothing really to attack. I expected Mr. Beaman to commit himself—lawyers are always committing themselves—but Mr. Beaman was—was—the fact is his speech can actually be complimented. As to his attacking Ben, that is to say Ben Franklin, an old dead man, that can be explained. Franklin was sober because he lived in Philadelphia. Why, Philadelphia is a sober city today. What must it have been in Franklin's time? Why, it is as good as Sunday to be in Philadelphia now. Franklin was frugal, and as he says himself, with becoming modesty, he had no vices, because, although he little suspected it, he made a vice of frugality. Mr. Beaman wishes that at the last he may be shoved into a barrel of Madeira, but if he had lived here instead of in Philadelphia he would have wanted to get the barrel of Madeira into him.

I am here in the character of author and publisher, but I think I will let that rest. Oh, I can tell you a great deal about publishing, but I don't think I will. I am rather too fresh yet. I am at the honest stage now, but after a while, when I graduate and grow rich, I will tell you all about it.

Education is so common that an education is within the grasp of everyone, and if he does not want to pay for it, why here is the state ready to pay for it for him. But sometimes I want to inquire what an education is. I remember myself, and all of you old fellows probably remember the same of yourselves, that when I went to school I was told that an adjective is an adverb and it must be governed by the third person singular, and all that sort of thing—and when I got out of school I straightway forgot all about it. In my combined character of publisher and author I receive a great many manuscripts from people who say they want a candid opinion whether that is good literature or not. That is all a lie; what they want is a compliment. But as to this matter of education, the first thing that strikes you is how much teaching has really been done and how much is worthless cramming. You have all seen a little book called *English as She is Spoke.* Now, in my capacity of publisher I recently received a manuscript from a teacher which embodied a number of answers given by her pupils to questions propounded. These answers show that the children had nothing but the sound to go by; the sense was perfectly empty. Here are some of their answers to words they were asked to define: auriferous— pertaining to an orifice; ammonia—the food of the gods; equestrian—one who asks questions; parasite—a kind of umbrella; ipecac—a man who likes a good dinner. And here is the definition of an ancient word honored by a great party: Republican—a sinner mentioned in the Bible. And here is an innocent deliverance of a zoological kind: "There are a good many donkeys in the theological gardens." Here also is a definition which really isn't very bad in its way: demagogue—a vessel containing beer and other liquids. Here, too, is a sample of a boy's composition on girls, which, I must say, I rather like:

"Girls are very stuckup and dignified in their maner and behaveyour. They think more of dress than anything and like to play with dowls and rags. They cry if they see a cow in a far distance and are afraid of guns. They stay at home all the time and go to church every Sunday. They are al-ways sick. They are al-ways funy and making fun of boys hands and they say how dirty. They cant play marbles. I pity them poor things. They make fun of boys and then turn round and love them. I don't beleave they ever killed a cat or anything. They look out every nite and say, 'Oh, a'nt the moon lovely!' Thir is one thing I have not told and that is they al-ways now their lessons bettern boys."

Text / Composite, based upon: "Mark Twain in New York," *Courant,* February 14, 1887; "Girls," *MTS*(10):92–93.

I am one of the latest publishers / Mark Twain established his publishing company, under the name of his nephew, Charles L. Webster, in 1884. At the time of his speech the company had just had a tremendous success with General Grant's *Memoirs.*

Mr. Beaman / Charles Cotesworth Beaman (1840–1900). American lawyer. Associated with the law firm of Evarts, Southmayd and Choate, he was a specialist in marine and international law.

English as She is Spoke / By Pedro Carolino, published as *The New Guide of the Conversation in Portuguese and English,* with an introduction by Mark Twain, in 1883. It is a series of lessons in English for Portuguese students, compiled by a foreigner unfamiliar with English idiom, and the results are peculiar: e.g., the expression "in one ear and out the other" becomes "What come in to me for an ear yet out for another." As Mark Twain says, "One cannot open this book anywhere and not find richness." Apparently he invented the title, *English as She is Spoke,* which has been given to an abridged edition published in 1969.

manuscript from a teacher / Published as *English as She is Taught,* with a commentary by Mark Twain, in 1887. It is a collection of juvenile boners historical, literary, and so forth. See Mark Twain's sketch, "English as She is Taught," *What is Man and Other Essays* (1917):240–55.

· 65 ·

Harking back to his brief service as an irregular Confederate soldier, Mark Twain produced a variant for Union Veterans of Maryland. In this version, as in others, fiction no doubt played a prominent role. It is worth noting, however, that at a time when bitterness engendered by the war was still rampant, he could be very much in earnest as he preached the gospel of peace and reconciliation.

An Author's Soldiering

Twenty-second Reunion Banquet, Union Veterans Association of Maryland, Hotel Rennert, Baltimore, April 8, 1887

You Union veterans of Maryland have prepared your feast and offered to me, a rebel veteran of Missouri, the wound-healing bread and salt of a gracious hospitality. Do you realize all the vast significance of the situation? Do you sense the whole magnitude of this conjunction, and perceive with what opulence of blessing for this nation it is freighted? What is it we are doing? Reflect! Upon this stage tonight we play the closing scene of the mightiest drama of modern times, and ring down, for good and all, the curtain raised at Sumter six and twenty years ago. The two grand divisions of the nation, which we name in general terms the North and the South, have shaken hands long ago, and given and taken the kiss of peace. Was anything lacking to make the reconciliation perfect, the fusion of feeling complete? Yes. The great border states attached to those grand divisions, but belonging to neither of them, and independent of both, were silent; had made no forgiving sign to each other across the chasm left by the convulsion of war, and the world grieved that this was so. But tonight the Union veteran of Maryland clasps hands with the rebel veteran of Missouri, and the gap is closed. In this supreme moment the imperfect welding of the broken Union is perfected at last, and from this hour the seam of the joining shall no more be visible. The long tragedy is ended—ring down the curtain!

When your secretary invited me to this reunion of the Union Veterans of Maryland, he requested me to come prepared to clear up a matter which he said had long been a subject of dispute and bad blood in war circles in this country—to wit, the true dimensions of my military services in the Civil War, and the effect which they had upon the general result. I recognize the importance of this thing to history, and I have come prepared. Here are the details. I was *in the Civil War two weeks.*

In that brief time I rose from private to second lieutenant. The monumental feature of my campaign was the one battle which my command fought—it was in the summer of '61. If I do say it, it was the bloodiest battle ever fought in human history; there is nothing approaching it for destruction of human life in the field, if you take in consideration the forces engaged, and the proportion of death to survival. And yet you do not even know the name of that battle. Neither do I. It had a name, but I have forgotten it. It is no use to keep private information which you can't show off. Now look at the way history does. It takes the battle of Boonville, fought nearby, about the date of our slaughter and shouts its teeth loose over it, and yet never even mentions ours; doesn't even call it an "affair"; doesn't call it anything at all; never even heard of it.

Whereas, what are the facts? Why these: In the battle of Boonville there were two thousand men engaged on the Union side, and about as many on the other—supposed to be. The casualties, all told, were two men killed; and not all of these were killed outright, but only half of them, for the other man died in hospital next day. I know that, because his great uncle was second cousin to my grandfather, who spoke three languages, and was perfectly honorable and upright, though he had warts all over him, and used to—but never mind about that, the facts are just as I say, and I can prove it. Two men killed in that battle of Boonville, and that's the whole result. All the others got away—on both sides.

Now then, in our battle there were just fifteen men engaged, on our side—all brigadier generals but me, and I was a second lieutenant. On the other side there was one man. He was a stranger. We killed him. It was night, and we thought he was an army of observation; he looked like an army of observation—in fact, he looked bigger than an army of observation would in the daytime; and some of us believed he was trying to surround us, and some thought he was going to try to turn our position, and so we shot him. Poor fellow, he probably wasn't an army of observation, after all; but that wasn't our fault; as I say, he had all the look of it in that dim light. It was a sorrowful circumstance, but he took the chances of war, and he drew the wrong card; he overestimated his fighting strength, and he suffered the likely result; but he fell as the brave should fall—with his face to the foe and feet to the field—so we buried him with the honors of war, and took his things.

So began and ended the only battle in the history of the world where the opposing force was *utterly exterminated,* swept from the face of the earth—to the last man. And yet, you don't know the name of that battle; you don't even know the name of that man. Now, then, for the argument. Suppose I had continued in the war, and gone on as I began, and exterminated the opposing force every time—every two weeks—where would your war have been? Why, you see yourself, the conflict would have been too one-sided. There was but one honorable course for me to pursue, and I pursued it. I withdrew to private life, and gave the Union cause a chance. There, now, you have the whole thing in a nutshell; it was not my presence in the Civil War that determined that tremendous contest—it was my retirement from it that brought the crash. It left the Confederate side too weak.

And yet, when I stop and think, I cannot regret my course. No, when I look abroad over this happy land, with its wounds healed and its enmities forgotten; this reunited sisterhood of majestic states; this freest of free commonwealths the sun in his course shines upon; this one sole country nameable in history or tradition where a man *is* a man and manhood the only royalty; this people ruled by the justest and wholesomest laws and government yet devised by the wisdom of men; this mightiest of the civilized empires of the earth, in numbers, in prosperity, in progress and in promise; and reflect that there is no North, no South any more, but that as in the old time, it is now and will remain forever, in the hearts and speech of Americans, our land, our country, our giant empire, and the flag floating in its firmament, our flag, I would not wish it otherwise. No, when I look about me and contemplate these sublime results, I feel, deep down in my heart, that I acted for the best when I took my shoulder out from under the Confederacy and let it come down.

Text / "An Author's Soldiering," *Masterpieces of American Eloquence* (1900):438–40.

battle of Boonville / In an engagement at Boonville, Missouri, September 13, 1861, Union forces (First Missouri Infantry and others), under General Nathaniel Lyon, routed about 1,000 Confederates of the Missouri State Guard, commanded by General Sterling Price. Casualties: Union, 1 killed, 4 wounded; Confederate, 12 killed, 30 wounded.

· 66 ·

To celebrate the first successful American run of a Shakespearian comedy, Augustin Daly gave a midnight supper on the stage for the two stars of the cast, John Drew and Ada Rehan. A gay company assembled around a huge circular table twenty-eight feet in diameter: H. H. Furness, Rose Eytinge, General Horace Porter, Elihu Vedder, Bronson Howard, May Irwin, Wilson Barrett, Otis Skinner, Lester Wallack, Laurence Hutton, William Winter, and others. General Sherman, toastmaster, introduced Mark Twain as the chief humorist and philosopher of his time. See Daly, The Life of Augustin Daly: *431–35; also* The Shrew's Centenary, A Reminiscence of the 13th of April by One of the Invited *(New York, 1887).*

Supper Speech

Celebrating the 100th Performance of The Taming of the Shrew,
Daly's Theatre, New York, April 13, 1887

I am glad to be here. This is the hardest theater in New York to get into, even at the front door—I never got in without hard work. Two or three years ago I had an appointment to meet Mr. Daly on the stage of this theater at eight o'clock in the evening. Well, I got on a train at Hartford to come to New York and keep the appointment. All I had to do was to come to the back door of the theater on Sixth Avenue. I didn't believe that—didn't believe it could be on Sixth Avenue—but that's what Daly's note said—come to that door, walk right in, and keep the appointment. It looked very easy. It looked easy enough, but I hadn't much confidence in that Sixth Avenue door.

Well, I was kind of bored on the train, and I bought some newspapers—New Haven newspapers—and there wasn't much news in them, so I read the advertisements. There was one advertisement of a bench show. Now I'd heard of bench shows, and often wondered what there was about them to interest people. I'd seen bench shows—lectured to bench shows, in fact—but I didn't want to advertise them or brag about them. Well, I read on a little, and learned that a bench show was not a bench show—but dogs, not benches at all—only dogs. I began to get interested, and as there was nothing else to do I read every bit of that advertisement. I learned that the biggest thing in this show was a St. Bernard dog that weighed 145 pounds, which is more than dogs usually weigh. Before I got to New York I was so interested in the bench shows that I made up my mind to go to one the first chance I got.

Down on Sixth Avenue, near where that back door might be, I began to take things leisurely. I did not like to be in too much of a hurry. There wasn't anything in sight that looked like a back door. The nearest approach to it was a cigar store, and I went in and bought a cigar—not too expensive, but it cost enough to pay for any information I might get, and leave the dealer a fair profit. Well, I didn't like to be too abrupt, to make the man think me crazy, by asking him if that was the way to Daly's Theatre—so I started in carefully to lead up to the subject—asked him first if that was the way to Castle Garden. When I got to the real question, and he said he'd show me the way, I was astonished.

He sent me through a long hallway, and I found myself in a back yard; then I went through a long passageway and into a little room, and there, before my very eyes, was a big St. Bernard dog lying on a bench. There was another room beyond, and I went there, and was met by a big, fierce man with his fur cap on and his coat off, who remarked,

"Phwat do yez want?"

I told him I wanted to see Mr. Daly.

"Yez can't see Misther Daly this toime of night!" he responded. I urged that I had an appointment with Mr. Daly, and gave him my card, which didn't seem to impress him much.

"Yez can't get in, an' yez can't shmoke here. T'row away that cigar. If yez want to see Misther Daly, yez'll have to be afther goin' to the front door an' buyin' a ticket, and then if yez have good luck, an' he's around that way, yez may see him."

I was getting discouraged, but I had one resource left that had been of service in similar emergencies. Firmly but kindly I told him my other name was Mark Twain, and awaited results. There were none. He was not fazed a bit.

"Phwere's your order to see Misther Daly?" he asked.

I handed him the note, and he examined it intently.

"My friend," I remarked, "you can read that better if you hold it the other side up," but he took no notice of the suggestion, and finally asked, "Where's Misther Daly's name?"

"There it is," I told him, "at the top of the page."

"That's all right," he said, "that's where he always puts it. But I don't see the 'W' in his name." And he eyed me distrustfully. Finally he asked, "Phwat did yez want to see Misther Daly for?"

"Business."

"Business?"

"Yes."

"Show business?"

"Yes." It was my only hope.

"Phwat kind—t'eayters?"

That was too much. I said, "No."

"Phwat kind of shows, then?"

"Bench shows!" It was risky, but I was desperate.

"Bench shows, is it? Where?" The big man's face changed, and he began to look interested.

"New Haven."

"New Haven, is it? Ay, that's goin' to be a foine show. I'm glad to see you. Did yez see a dog in the other room?"

"Yes."

"How much do yez t'ink that dog weighs?"

"One hundred and forty-five pounds."

"Luk at that, now! You're a good judge of dogs, an' no mistake. He weighs all of 138. Set down. Shmoke! Go on, shmoke your cigar. I'll tell Misther Daly you're here."

Well, in a few minutes I was on the stage shaking hands with Mr. Daly, and the big man was standing around, glowing with satisfaction. "Come round in front," said Mr. Daly, "and see the performance. I'll put you in my own box." And as I moved away I heard my honest friend mutter, "Well, he desarves it."

Text / Composite, based upon: Daly, *The Life of Augustin Daly:* 432–34; "Daly Theatre" in *MTS*(10):79–82; and *MTS*(23):157–60.

Daly / John Augustin Daly (1838–99). American playwright and producer. Taking over the Fifth Avenue Theatre (1869), he organized his own company, and in 1873 wrote and produced an extravaganza based on Mark Twain's *Roughing It.* At the theater bearing his name Daly assembled a notable troupe, for whom he adapted about ninety plays. He was a charter member of the Players Club and an enthusiastic banqueter.

Castle Garden / A circular building on the Battery, New York City. Originally a fort built in 1807, it became an opera house. Jenny Lind, the Swedish Nightingale, made her American debut there (1850) under the management of P. T. Barnum. In 1855, commissioners of emigration made the building a clearing house for foreign arrivals, providing information, interpreters, and guides for bewildered immigrants, and attempting to protect them against swindlers.

· 67 ·

An Army and Navy Club banquet, held on the birthday of General Grant, extolled the former commander of the Union armies while charitably dwelling with less fervor upon his abilities as president. Captain V. B. Chamberlain, chairman, cited statistics on Grant's Memoirs, *a best-seller put out in 1886 by Mark Twain's publishing company: 44,350 square yards of cloth in bindings, enough gold in lettering to make $15,446.47 if coined, 276 barrels of binder paste and 302,310 reams of paper used, and 19.5 miles of shelf space needed for the whole edition. Mark Twain's belligerent speech, drubbing the British critic, Matthew Arnold, struck the right note of outraged patriotism. The* Courant *remarked next day: "Mr. Clemens was interrupted with applause after every sentence, and it was sometime after he had finished before order was restored."*

Dinner Speech

Ninth Annual Reunion Banquet, Army and Navy Club of Connecticut, Central Hall, Hartford, April 27, 1887

I will detain you with only just a few words—just a few thousand words; and then give place to a better man—if he has been created. Lately a great and honored author, Matthew Arnold, has been finding fault with General Grant's English. That would be fair enough, maybe, if the examples of imperfect English averaged more instances to the page in General Grant's book than they do in Mr. Arnold's criticism upon the book—but they don't. It would be fair enough, maybe, if such instances were commoner in General Grant's book than they are in the works of the average standard author—but they aren't. In truth, General Grant's derelictions in the matter of grammar and construction are not more frequent than are such derelictions in the works of a majority of the professional authors of our time and of all previous times—authors as exclusively and painstakingly trained to the literary trade as was General Grant to the trade of war. This is not a random statement; it is a fact, and easily demonstrable. I have at home a book called *Modern English Literature: Its Blemishes and Defects,* by Henry H. Breen, F.S.A., a countryman of Mr. Arnold. In it I find examples of bad grammar and slovenly English from the pens of Sydney Smith, Sheridan, Hallam, Whately, Carlyle, both Disraelis, Allison, Junius, Blair, Macaulay, Shakespeare, Milton, Gibbon, Southey, Bulwer, Cobbett, Dr. Samuel Johnson, Trench, Lamb, Landor, Smollett, Walpole, Walker (of the dictionary), Christopher North, Kirke White, Mrs. Sigourney, Benjamin Franklin, Sir Walter Scott, and Mr. Lindley Murray, who made the grammar.

In Mr. Arnold's paper on General Grant's book we find a couple of grammatical crimes and more than several examples of very crude and slovenly English—enough of them to easily entitle him to a *lofty* place in that illustrious list of delinquents just named.

The following passage, all by itself, ought to elect him: "Meade suggested to Grant that he might wish to have immediately under him, Sherman, who had been serving with Grant in the West. *He* begged *him* not to hesitate if *he* thought it for the good of the service. Grant assured *him* that *he* had no thought of moving *him,* and in *his* memoirs, after relating what had passed, *he* adds," etc. To read that passage a couple of times would make a man dizzy; to read it four times would make him drunk. General Grant's grammar is as good as anybody's; but if this were not so, Mr. Breen would brush that inconsequential fact aside and hunt his great book for higher game.

Mr. Breen makes this discriminating remark: "To suppose that because a man is a poet or a historian, he must be correct in his grammar, is to suppose that an architect must be a joiner, or a physician a compounder of medicines." Mr. Breen's point is well taken. If you should climb the mighty Matterhorn to look out over the kingdoms of the earth, it might be a pleasant incident to find strawberries up there. But, great Scott! you don't climb the Matterhorn for strawberries!

I don't think Mr. Arnold was quite wise; for he well knew that that Briton or American was never yet born who could safely assault another man's English; he knew as well as he knows anything, that the man never lived whose English was flawless. Can you believe that Mr. Arnold was immodest enough to imagine himself an exception to this cast iron rule—the sole exception discoverable within the three or four centuries during which the English language proper has been in existence? No, Mr. Arnold did not imagine that; he merely forgot that for a moment he was moving into a glass house, and he had hardly got fairly in before General Fry was shivering the panes over his head.

People may hunt out what microscopic motes they please, but, after all, the fact remains and cannot be dislodged, that General Grant's book is a great, and in its peculiar department unique and unapproachable literary masterpiece. In their line, there is no higher literature than those modest, simple memoirs. Their *style* is at least flawless, and no man can improve upon it; and great books are weighed and measured by their style and matter, not by the trimmings and shadings of their grammar.

There is that about the sun which makes us forget his spots; and when we think of General Grant our pulses quicken and his grammar vanishes; we only remember that this is the simple soldier, who, all untaught of the silken phrase makers, linked words together with an art surpassing the art of the schools, and put into them a something which will still bring to American ears, as long as America shall last, the roll of his vanished drums and the tread of the marching hosts. What do we care for grammar when we think of the man that put together that thunderous phrase: "Unconditional and immediate surrender!" And those others: "I propose to move immediately upon your works!" "I propose to fight it out on this line if it takes all summer!" Mr. Arnold would doubtless claim that that last sentence is not strictly grammatical; and yet it did certainly wake up this nation as a hundred million tons of A No. 1, fourth-proof, hardboiled, hidebound grammar from another mouth couldn't have done. And finally we have that gentler phrase; that one which shows you another true side of the man; shows that in his soldier heart there was room for other than gory war mottoes, and in his tongue the gift to fitly phrase them—"Let us have peace."

Text / Composite, based upon: "Mark Twain's Address," *Courant*, April 28, 1887; "General Grant's Grammar," *MTS*(23):135–37, a misdated text.

Matthew Arnold / (1822–88). British poet, essayist, and critic. An inspector of schools (1851–83), he was professor of poetry at Oxford (1857–67). He published *The Strayed Reveler and Other Poems* (1849), *New Poems* (1867), and other volumes of verse. Among his critical writings are *Essays in Criticism* (1865, 1888), *Culture and Anarchy* (1869), and *Civilisation in the United States* (1888). He made two lecture tours in the United States (1883–84, 1886).

Mr. Arnold's criticism / Arnold reviewed the two volumes of Grant's *Memoirs* in *Murray's Magazine* 1, no. 1 (January 1887):130–44; and 1, no. 2 (February 1887):150–66. He was critical of Grant's failure to distinguish between "shall" and "will," of American expressions like "packed the house" and "badly whipped the enemy," and of a language "without charm." Nevertheless, he commended the appropriateness of the English: "straightforward, nervous, firm, possessing in general the high merit of saying clearly in the fewest possible words what had to be said, and saying it, frequently, with shrewd and unexpected turns of expression." He characterized Grant as an ordinary-looking man, dull and silent, but praised him as a commander who was sensible, resolute, modest, and humane. Let Americans, said Arnold, instead of boasting that they are " 'the greatest nation upon earth,' . . . give us more Lees, Lincolns, Shermans, and Grants." The review is judicious, praise balancing, if not outweighing, censure, yet touchy Americans took offense. For some time Mark Twain carried on a one-man vendetta against Arnold and the British generally. In Notebooks 23 (1), July 1–November 1, 1888, and 23 (2), November 23, 1888–September 24, 1889, are a number of sharp comments on royalty, caste, Mr. Arnold's "moth-eaten" civilization and so forth.

According to Howells, in *My Mark Twain,* Arnold and Mark Twain met at some function in Hartford, where they had a long conversation, and the next night Arnold was a guest at the Clemens home. "I cannot say," Howells remarks, "how they got on, or what they made of each other; if Clemens ever spoke of Arnold, I do not recall what he said, but Arnold had shown a sense of him from which the incredulous sniff of the polite world, now so universally exploded, had already perished."

Sydney Smith / (1771–1845). British clergyman and essayist. Cofounder of the *Edinburgh Review,* he was a lecturer on moral philosophy at the Royal Institute, London (1804–08), and Canon residentiary of St. Paul's (1831). He was a brilliant phrase-maker whose *Wit and Wisdom* was posthumously published in 1856.

Hallam / Henry Hallam (1777–1859). British historian. Contributor to the *Edinburgh Review,* he was the author of *A View of the State of Europe During the Middle Ages* (1818), and *Constitutional History of England* (1827).

Whately / Richard Whately (1787–1863). British theologian and writer. He wrote *Elements of Logic* (1826), and *Rhetoric* (1828).

both Disraelis / The Disraeli other than the prime minister was Isaac (1766–1848). British antiquarian. He is probably best known for *Curiosities of Literature* (1791).

Junius / Pen name of an unknown writer of letters (1768–72) to *The Public Advertiser* supporting John Wilkes, editor of the *North Briton.* Wilkes was opposed to the government of George III, and also opposed to the cause of the American colonies.

Blair / Hugh Blair (1718–1800). Scottish clergyman and rhetorician. He published *Sermons* (1777), and *Lectures on Rhetoric and Belles Lettres* (1783).

Bulwer / William Henry Lytton Earle Bulwer (1801–72). British diplomat and writer. Minister to Spain (1843–48) and ambassador to the United States (1849–50), he instigated the Bulwer-Clayton Treaty (1850) to protect the neutrality of the proposed ship canal across Central America. He wrote *Historical Characters* (1867).

Cobbett / William Cobbett (1762–1835). British journalist and parliamentarian. In 1802 he founded a weekly paper, *Cobbett's Political Register,* which he made influential as editor thereafter. Elected to Parliament in 1832, he was by turns, Tory, radical, and independent. His best known book is *Rural Rides* (1830).

Trench / Richard Chenevix Trench (1807–86). Anglican Archbishop of Dublin. A noted philologist, he published *On the Study of Words* (1851), *English Past and Present* (1855), and conceived the idea that resulted in the Oxford *New English Dictionary.*

Walker / John Walker (1732–1807). British actor, philologist, and lexicographer. He compiled a *Rhyming Dictionary* (1775), and a *Critical Pronouncing Dictionary* (1791) that came out in more than forty editions.

Christopher North / Pen name of John Wilson (1785–1854). Scottish writer. A contributor to *Blackwood's* and other journals, he was embroiled in the literary battles of his time. His *Noctes Ambrosianae* (1843) is a racy commentary on life and letters.

Kirke White / Henry Kirke White (1785–1826). British poet. A hymn writer—"Star of Bethlehem," "Oft in danger, oft in woe"—he was a minor poet and a protégé of Southey, remembered chiefly because of the latter's memoir (1807).

Mrs. Sigourney / Lydia Howard Huntley Sigourney (1791–1865). American writer. Known as "The American Hemans," she was a popular inspirational writer who published *Moral Pieces in Prose and Verse* (1815), *How to be Happy* (1833), *Poems, Religious and Elegiac* (1841), and other homilies.

Lindley Murray / (1745–1826). Expatriate American writer. Emigrating to England in 1784, he published *The Power of Religion on the Mind* (1787), *English Grammar* (1795), and *English Spelling Book* (1804).

General Fry / James Barnet Fry (1827–94). American soldier and writer. A Civil War veteran, he was afterward adjutant general of military divisions of the Pacific, the South, and the Atlantic. He wrote books on military subjects and contributed to *Battles and Leaders of the Civil War* (1884–88). He published an attack on Arnold's review of Grant's *Memoirs,* "Grant and Matthew Arnold. 'An Estimate,' " in the *North American Review* of April 1887. Ignoring favorable comments in the review, Fry based his assault chiefly on ineptitudes in Arnold's own writing. Employing the you're-another tactic, he also accused the Britisher of the kind of bragging for which he had reprehended Americans. Mark Twain apparently did not read Arnold's review, but took his cue from Fry's splenetic outburst; the sentence overloaded with confusing pronouns, which Mark Twain quoted in his dinner speech, was the same passage that Fry had singled out for disparagement.

· 68 ·

For the amusement of 1,200 club members and guests attending a Boston Forefathers Day dinner, Mark Twain delivered what he called his "Patent Adjustable Speech," good for all occasions. He illustrated its possibilities by a manner that varied from gay to lugubrious, even to the simulation of copious tears.

Post-Prandial Oratory

Forefathers Day Dinner, Congregational Club,
Music Hall, Boston, December 20, 1887

In treating of this subject of post-prandial oratory, a subject which I have long been familiar with and may be called an expert in observing it in others, I wish to say that a public dinner is the most delightful thing in the whole world, to a guest. That is one fact. And here is another one: a public dinner is the most unutterable suffering in the whole world, to a guest. These two facts don't seem to jibe—but I will explain. Now at a public dinner when a man knows he is going to be called upon to speak, and is thoroughly well prepared—got it all by heart, and the pauses all marked in his head where the applause is going to come in—a public dinner is just heaven to that man. He won't care to be anywhere else than just where he is. But when at a public dinner it is getting way along toward the end of things, and a man is sitting over his glass of wine, or his glass of milk, according to the kind of banquet it is, in ever-augmenting danger of being called up, and isn't prepared, and knows he can never prepare with the thoughtless gander at his elbow bothering him all the time with exasperating talky-talk about nothing, that man is just as nearly in the other place as ever he wants to be. Why, it is a cruel situation. That man is to be pitied; and the very worst of it is that the minute he gets on his feet he *is* pitied.

Now he could stand the pity of ten people or a dozen, but there is no misery in the world that is comparable to the massed and solidified compassion of five hundred. Why, that wide Sahara of sympathizing faces completely takes the tuck out of him, makes a coward of him. He stands there in his misery, and stammers out the usual rubbish about not being prepared, and not expecting, and all that kind of folly, and he is wandering and stumbling and getting further and further in, and all the time unhappy, and at last he fetches out a poor, miserable, crippled joke, and in his grief and confusion he laughs at it himself and the others look sick; and then he slumps into his chair and wishes he was dead. He knows he is a defeated man, and so do the others.

Now to a humane person that is a heartrending spectacle. It is indeed. That sort of sacrifice ought to be stopped, and there is only one way to accomplish it that I can think of, and that is for a man to go always prepared, always loaded, always ready, whether he is likely to be called upon or not. You can't defeat that man, you can't pity him at all. My scheme is this, that he shall carry in his head a cut-and-dried and thoroughly and glibly memorized speech that will fit every conceivable public occasion in this life, fit it to a dot, and win success and applause every time. Now I have completed a speech of that kind, and I have brought it along to exhibit here as a sample.

Now, then, supposing a man with his cut-and-dried speech, this patent adjustable speech, as you may call it, finds himself at a granger gathering, or a wedding breakfast, or a theological disturbance or a political blowout, an inquest, or funeral anywhere in the world you choose to mention, and be suddenly called up, all he has got to do is to change three or four words in that speech, and make his delivery anguishing and tearful, or chippy and facetious, or luridly and thunderously eloquent just as the occasion happens to call for, and just turn himself loose, and he is all right, but I will illustrate, and instead of explanations I will deliver that speech itself just enough times to make you see the possibilities.

We suppose that it is a granger gathering, and this man is suddenly called on; he comes up with some artful hesitancies and diffidences and repetitions, so as to give the idea that the speech is impromptu. Here, of course, after he has got used to delivering it, he can venture outside and make a genuine impromptu remark to start off with. For instance, if a distinguished person is present, he can make a complimentary reference to him, say to Mr. Depew. He could speak about his great talent or his clothes. Such a thing gives him a sort of opening, and about the time that audience is getting to pity that man, he opens his throttle valve and goes for those grangers. That person wants to be gorgeously eloquent; you want to fire the farmer's heart and start him from his mansard down to his cellar.

Now this man is called up, and he says: "I am called up suddenly, sir, and am indeed not, not prepared to—to—I was not expecting to be called up, sir, but I will, with what effect I may, add my shout to the jubilations of this spirit-stirring occasion. Agriculture, sir, is, after all, the palladium of our economic liberties. By it—approximately speaking—we may be said to live, and move, and have our being. All that we have been, all that we are, all that we hope to be, was, is, and must continue to be, profoundly influenced by that sublimest of the mighty interests of man, thrice glorious agriculture! While we have life, while we have soul, and in that soul the sweet and hallowed sentiment of gratitude, let us with generous accord attune our voices to songs of praise, perennial outpourings of thanksgiving, for that most precious boon, whereby we physically thrive, whereby our otherwise sterile existence is made rich and strong, and grand and aspiring, and is adorned with a mighty and far-reaching and all-embracing grace, and beauty, and purity and loveliness! The least of us knows—the least of us feels—the humblest among us will confess that, whereas—but the hour is late, sir, and I will not detain you."

Now then, supposing it is not a granger gathering at all, but is a wedding breakfast; now, of course, that speech has got to be delivered in an airy, light fashion, but it must terminate seriously. It is a mistake to make it any other way. This person is called up by the minister of the feast and he says: "I am called up suddenly, sir, and am, indeed, not prepared to—to—I was not expecting to be called up, sir, but I will, with what effect I may, add my shout to the jubilations of this spirit-stirring occasion. Matrimony, sir, is, after all, the palladium of our domestic liberties. By it—approximately speaking—we may be said to live, and move, and acquire our being. All that we have been, all that we are, all that we hope to be, was, is, and must continue to be profoundly influenced by that sublimest of the mighty interests of man, thrice glorious matrimony! While we have life, while we have soul, and in that soul the sweet and hallowed sentiment of gratitude, let us with generous accord attune our voices to songs of praise, perennial outpourings of thanksgiving, for that most precious boon whereby we numerically thrive, whereby our otherwise sterile existence is made rich, and strong, and grand, and aspiring, and is adorned with a mighty and far-reaching and all-embracing grace, and beauty, and purity and loveliness! The least of us knows—the least of us feels—the humblest among us will confess, that whereas—but the hour is late, sir, and I will not detain you."

Now, then, supposing that the occasion—I make one more illustration, so that you will always be perfectly safe, here or anywhere—supposing that this is an occasion of an inquest. This is a most elastic speech in a matter of that kind. Where there are grades of men you must observe them. At a private funeral of some friend you want to be just as mournful as you can, but in the case where you don't know the person, grade it accordingly. You want simply to be impressive. That is all. Now take a case halfway between, about No. 4½, somewhere about there, that is, an inquest on a second cousin, a wealthy second cousin. He has remembered you in the will. Of course all these things count. They all raise the grade a little, and—well, perhaps he hasn't remembered you. Perhaps he has left you a horse, an ordinary horse, a good enough horse, one that can go about three minutes, or perhaps a pair of horses. It may have been one pair of horses at hand, not two pair or two pair and a jack. I don't know whether you understand that, but there are people here—. Well, now then, this is a second cousin, and he knows all the circumstances. We will say that he has lost his life trying to save somebody from drowning. Well, he saved the mind-cure physician from drowning, he tried to save him, but he didn't succeed. Of course he wouldn't succeed; of course you wouldn't want him to succeed in that way and plan. A person must have some experience and aplomb and all that before he can save anybody from drowning of the mind-cure. I am just making these explanations here. A person can get so glib in a delivery of this speech, why by the time he has delivered it fifteen or twenty times he could go to any intellectual gathering in Boston even, and he would draw like a prizefight. Well, at the inquest of a second cousin under these circumstances, a man gets up with graded emotion and he says:

"I am called up suddenly, sir, and am, indeed, not prepared to—to—I was not expecting to be called up, sir, but I will, with what effect I may, add my shout—voice to the lamentations of this spirit-crushing occasion. Death, death, sir, is, after all, the palladium of our spiritual liberties. By it—approximately speaking—we may be said to live, and move and have our ending. All that we have been, all that we may be here, all that we hope to be, was, is, and must continue to be profoundly influenced by that sublimest of the mighty interests of man, thrice-sorrowful dissolution. While we have life, while we have soul, and in that soul the sweet and hallowed sentiment of gratitude, let us with generous accord attune our voices to songs of praise, perennial outpourings of thanksgiving, for that most precious boon by which we spiritually thrive, whereby our otherwise sterile existence is made rich, and strong, and grand, and aspiring, and is adorned with a mighty and far-reaching and all-embracing grace, and beauty and purity, and loveliness. The least of us knows—the least of us feels—the humblest among us will confess, that whereas—but the hour is late, sir, and I will not detain you."

The speech as used at a funeral may be used to prop up prohibition, and also anti-prohibition, without change, except to change the terms of sorrow to terms of rejoicing.

The speech as used at a granger meeting may be used in Boston at the sacred feast of baked beans without any alteration except to change agriculture—where it occurs in the second sentence—to "the baked bean," and to "bean culture" where it occurs in the fourth.

The agricultural speech becomes a prohibition speech by putting in that word and changing "economic" to moral, and "physically" to morally. It becomes a Democratic, Republican, Mugwump or other political speech by shoving in the party name and changing "economic" to political, and "physically" to politically.

Any of these forms can be used at a New England Forefathers dinner. *They* don't care what you talk about, so long as it ain't so.

Text / Composite, based upon: "Mark Twain," Boston *Globe,* December 21, 1887; Proof Sheet, Charles Aldrich Autograph Collection, Department of History and Archives, Des Moines, Iowa.

Depew / Chauncey Mitchell Depew (1834–1928). American lawyer and legislator. He was New York secretary of state (1863), minister to Japan (1866), corporation counsel for various railroads (1866–75), president of the New York Central Railroad (1885–98), and senator from New York (1899–1911). Wit and raconteur, he was a popular dinner speaker, often verbally sparring with Mark Twain on the same toast list.

a good enough horse, one that can go about three minutes / A horse that could travel a mile in three minutes—not very speedy. Trotters and pacers of harness racing were faster than that, and so were the horses of spirited drivers who enjoyed impromptu racing on country roads. In winter, snow-covered city boulevards were arenas for brushes between cutters driven by gamesome gentlemen. A three-minute horse would not suit the sporty driver.

but there are people here– / This statement was probably left unfinished because the audience, anticipating the possibilities of "two pair and a jack," began to laugh. Implication was part of Mark Twain's technique. As he once observed of an audience in Paris, Kentucky: "They catch a point before you can get it out—and then, if you are not a muggins, you *don't* get it out; you leave it unsaid." See *LLMT:* 224.

· 69 ·

When Yale conferred an honorary M.A. upon Mark Twain in 1888, Hartford alumni had an additional reason, if they needed one, for calling upon him as dinner speaker. He told the gathering that he had prepared two speeches, but had rejected both. Instead, he talked informally about his first and second meetings with General Grant, and about his recent trip to Washington, where he had appeared in support of another bill on international copyright, this one introduced by Senator Jonathan Chace of Rhode Island. Mark Twain predicted that the bill would fail, and it did fail in 1890, the twelfth such casualty in a forty-five-year series. The speech below is probably one of the discarded texts.

Yale College Speech

Yale Alumni Association Banquet, Foot Guard Hall, Hartford, February 6, 1889

I was sincerely proud and grateful to be made a Master of Arts by this great and venerable university, and I would have come last June to testify this feeling, as I do now testify it, but that the sudden and unexpected notice of the honor done me found me at a distance from home and unable to discharge that duty and enjoy that privilege.

Along at first, say for the first month or so, I did not quite know how to proceed, because of my not knowing just what authorities and privileges belonged to the title which had been granted me, but after that I consulted some students of Trinity, in Hartford, and they made everything clear to me. It was through them that I found out that my title made me head of the governing body of the university, and lodged in me very broad and severely responsible powers. It is through trying to work these powers up to their maximum of efficiency that I have had such a checkered career this year. I was told that it would be necessary for me to report to you at this time, and of course I comply, though I would have preferred to put it off till I could make a better showing: for indeed I have been so pertinaciously hindered and obstructed at every turn by the faculty that it would be difficult to prove that the university is really in any better shape now than it was when I first took charge. In submitting my report, I am sorry to have to begin with the remark that respect for authority seems to be at a quite low ebb in the college. It is true that this has caused me pain, but it has not discouraged me. By advice, I turned my earliest attention to the Greek department. I told the Greek professor I had concluded to drop the use of the Greek written character, because it was so hard to spell with, and so impossible to read after you get it spelled. Let us draw the curtain there. I saw by what followed that nothing but early neglect saved him from being a very profane man.

I ordered the professor of mathematics to simplify the whole system, because the way it was, I couldn't understand it, and I didn't want things going on in the college in what was practically a clandestine fashion. I told him to drop the conundrum system; it was not suited to the dignity of a college, which should deal in facts, not guesses and suppositions; we didn't want any more cases of *if* A and B stand at opposite poles of the earth's surface and C at the equator of Jupiter, at what variations of angle will the left limb of the moon appear to these different parties? I said you just let that thing alone; it's plenty time to get in a sweat about it when it happens; as like as not it ain't going to do any harm anyway. His reception of these instructions bordered on insubordination; insomuch that I felt obliged to take his number, and report him.

I found the astronomer of the university gadding around after comets and other such odds and ends—tramps and derelicts of the skies. I told him pretty plainly that we couldn't have that. I told him it was no economy to go on piling up and piling up raw material in the way of new stars and comets and asteroids that we couldn't ever have any use for till we had worked off the old stock. I said if I caught him strawberrying around after any more asteroids, especially, I should have to fire him out. Privately, prejudice got the best of me there, I ought to confess it. At bottom I don't really mind comets so much, but somehow I have always been down on asteroids. There is nothing mature about them; I wouldn't sit up nights, the way that man does, if I could get a basketful of them. He said it was the best line of goods he had; he said he could trade them to Rochester for comets, and trade the comets to Harvard for nebulae, and trade the nebulae to the Smithsonian for flint hatchets. I felt obliged to stop this thing on the spot; I said we couldn't have the university turned into an astronomical junk shop.

And while I was at it I thought I might as well make the reform complete; the astronomer is extraordinarily mutinous; and so with your approval I will transfer him to the law department and put one of the law students in his place. A boy will be more biddable, more tractable, also cheaper. It is true he cannot be entrusted with important work at first, but he can comb the skies for nebulae till he gets his hand in. I have other changes in mind, but as they are in the nature of surprises, I judge it politic to leave them unspecified at this time.

Text / "Yale College Speech," MS, MTP; published as "Yale College Speech," *MTS*(23):142–44.

Master of Arts / Mark Twain expressed his appreciation in a letter of thanks to President Timothy Dwight (*Courant,* June 29, 1888). He said, in part: "The late Matthew Arnold rather sharply rebuked the guild of American 'funny men' in his latest literary delivery, and therefore your honorable recognition of us is peculiarly forcible and timely. A friendly word was needed in our defense, and you have said it . . . . It could not become us . . . to remind the world that ours is a useful trade, a worthy calling; that with all its lightness and frivolity it has one serious purpose . . . and it is constant to it—the deriding of shams, the exposure of pretentious falsities, the laughing of stupid superstitions out of existence; and that whoso is by instinct engaged in this sort of warfare is the natural enemy of royalties, nobilities, privileges and all kindred swindles, and the natural friend of human rights and human liberties."

Trinity / Trinity College, Hartford, founded in 1823, is a nonsectarian liberal arts college for men. Mark Twain sometimes talked for students and alumni, and drafted Trinity professors for Saturday Morning Club programs.

Rochester / Probably mentioned because the city is the site of Rochester Institute of Technology (1829) and the University of Rochester (1850), and center for the manufacture of scientific precision instruments. A notable optical firm was founded there by John Jacob Bausch and Henry Lomb.

· 70 ·

When James Whitcomb Riley and Bill Nye gave a program of readings in Boston, Major Pond, their manager, induced Mark Twain, on rather short notice, to introduce the pair. His unannounced appearance on the stage provoked a great waving of handkerchiefs and a tumult of applause and cheering, the organist doing his bit by sounding off fortissimo.

Introducing Edgar Wilson "Bill" Nye and James Whitcomb Riley

Tremont Temple, Boston, February 28, 1889

I am very glad indeed to introduce these young people to you, and at the same time get acquainted with them myself. I have seen them more than once, for a moment, but have not had the privilege of knowing them personally as intimately as I wanted to. I saw them first, a great many years ago, when Mr. Barnum had them, and they were just fresh from Siam. The ligature was their best hold then, but literature became their best hold later, when one of them committed an indiscretion, and they had to cut the old bond to accommodate the sheriff.

In that old former time this one was Chang, that one was Eng. The sympathy existing between the two was most extraordinary; it was so fine, so strong, so subtle, that what one ate the other digested; when one slept, the other snored; if one sold a thing, the other scooped the usufruct. This independent and yet dependent action was observable in all the details of their daily life—I mean this quaint and arbitrary distribution of originating cause and resulting effect between the two—between, I may say, this dynamo and this motor. Not that I mean that the one was always dynamo and the other always motor—or, in other words, that the one was always the creating force, the other always the utilizing force; no, no, for while it is true that within certain well-defined zones of activity the one *was* always dynamo and the other always motor, within certain other well-defined zones these positions became exactly reversed.

For instance, in moral matters—in moral matters Mr. Chang Riley was always dynamo, Mr. Eng Nye was always motor; for while Mr. Chang Riley had a high—in fact, an abnormally high and fine—moral sense, this man had high moral sense, you can see the development all over him now—although he had that fine moral sense, he hadn't any machinery to work it with. Whereas, Mr. Eng Nye, who hadn't any moral sense at all, and hasn't yet, as you will observe later, yet had all the necessary plant for the carrying out of a noble deed if he could only get the necessary inspiration on reasonable terms outside.

Now, then, again you see the thing reversed. In intellectual matters Mr. Eng Nye was always the dynamo, and Mr. Chang Riley was always the motor. Mr. Eng Nye had a stately intellect, but couldn't make it go, and at the same time Mr. Chang Riley hadn't, but could. That is to say, that while Mr. Chang Riley couldn't think things himself, he had a marvelous natural grace in setting them down and weaving them together when his pal furnished the raw material.

So they worked together in that way. Thus, working together, they made a strong team; laboring together, they could do miracles; but break the circuit, and both were impotent at once. It has remained so to this day; they must travel together, conspire together, beguile together, hoe, and plant, and plough, and reap, and sell their public together, or there's no result.

I have made this explanation, this analysis, this fire assay, this vivisection, so to speak, in order that you may enjoy these delightful adventurers understandingly. Now while Mr. Eng Nye is drawing a limpid stream of philosophy that flows over and refreshes the region all around with his gracious flood, you remember that it is not his water. It's the other man's. He's only working the pump. And when Mr. Chang Riley enchants your ear and soothes your spirit, and touches your heart with the sweet and tender music of his voice—as sweet and as genuine as any that his friends, the birds and the bees, sang to his other friends, the woods and the flowers—you will remember to place him where justice would put him. It's not his music; it's the other man's—he is only turning the crank.

I beseech for these visitors a fair field, a single-minded, one-eyed umpire, and a score bulletin barren of goose eggs if they earn it—and I judge they will and hope they will. Mr. James Whitcomb Chang Riley will now go to the bat.

Text / Composite, based upon: "Mark Twain, Nye and Riley," *Courant,* March 4, 1889; James B. Pond, *Eccentricities of Genius* (1900):247–49; *Eloquence*(R), 6:910–12; "Introducing Nye and Riley," *MTS*(10):168–70. The *MTS* text is incorrectly dated.

Barnum / Phineas Taylor Barnum (1818–91). American showman. At the American Museum, New York, he exhibited marvels like the midget, General Tom Thumb, and Jumbo, the elephant. He managed the American tour of Jenny Lind (1850–51), assembled "The Greatest Show on Earth" (1871), and toured the lyceum circuit, lecturing on thrift and temperance. The Siamese twins, Eng and Chang (1811–74), were brought to the United States in 1829, became naturalized citizens and married sisters.

Mr. Chang Riley / James Whitcomb Riley (1849–1916). American poet. He is best remembered for his vernacular poems, which made him known as "The Hoosier Poet" in such collections as *The Old Swimmin' Hole* (1883), *Old-Fashioned Roses* (1888), *Home Folks* (1900), and others. He was a skillful storyteller, highly praised by Mark Twain in "How to Tell a Story."

Mr. Eng Nye / Edgar Wilson Nye (1850–96). American humorist. Writer of humorous sketches for western papers and founder of the Laramie, Wyoming, *Boomerang* (1881), he was also a speaker who toured with Riley (1886, 1889). Examples of Nye's humor are *Bill Nye's History of the United States* (1894), and *Bill Nye's History of England* (1896).

fire assay / A method of determining the proportions of gold, silver, and base metals in a mass of ore. See Mark Twain's explanation, chapter 36 of *Roughing It;* also his article, "Silver Bars—How Assayed," written for the Virginia City *Territorial Enterprise,* reprinted in the Stockton, California, *Independent,* February 26, 1863.

· 71 ·

Augustin Daly and Albert M. Palmer were hosts at a midnight supper honoring Edwin Booth for his gift to the Players Club of the property at 16 Gramercy Park, New York. Tables were arranged like a five-pointed star, the arms radiating from a circular mass of roses. Among the eighty guests were Dion Boucicault, Nat Goodwin, John Gilbert, Lawrence Barrett, General Porter, Constant Coquelin, Stephen H. Olin, St. Gaudens, Depew, and General Sherman. Next morning the Times *said that toward the end of the affair, which went on till dawn, "General Porter dropped gracefully into poetry and W. W. Winter fell into it with a dull thud, and afterward shed tears on Edward*

Harrigan's neck." In an autobiographical dictation of December 28, 1906, MTP, Mark Twain says that he was not there because of illness, hence did not speak. Yet the Times *reported him as present, and gave a brief summary of his talk.*

The Long Clam

Supper for Edwin Booth, Delmonico's, New York, March 30, 1889

Although I am debarred from making a speech, by circumstances which I will presently explain, I yet claim the privilege of adding my voice to yours in deep and sincere welcome and homage to Edwin Booth; of adding my admiration of his long and illustrious career and blemishless character; and thereto my gratification in the consciousness that his great sun is not yet westering, but stands in full glory in the zenith.

I wish to ask your attention to a statement, in writing. It is not safe or wise to trust a serious matter to offhand speech—especially when you are trying to explain a thing. Now, to make a clean breast, and expose the whole trouble right at the start, I have been entertaining a stranger; I have been at it two days and two nights, and am worn, and jaded, and in fact defeated. He may be known to some of you. He is classified in natural history as the Long Clam, and in my opinion is the most disastrous fish that swims the sea. If you don't know him personally, let him alone; take him at hearsay, and meddle no further. He is a bivalve. When in his ulster, he is shaped like a weaver's shuttle, but there the resemblance ends; the weaver's shuttle travels, but the Long Clam abides; and you can digest a weaver's shuttle, if you wait, and pray. It is your idea, of course, to entertain yourself with the Long Clam, so you lay him on a bed of coals; he opens his mouth like a carpet sack and smiles; this looks like mutual regard, and you think you are friends, but it is not so; that smile means, "it is your innings now—I'll see you later." You swallow the Long Clam—and history begins. It begins, but it begins so remotely, so clandestinely that you don't know it. You have several hours which you can't tell from repose. Then you go to bed. You close your eyes and think you are gliding off to sleep. It is at this point that the Long Clam rises up and goes to the bat. The window rattles; the Long Clam calls your attention to it. You whirl out of bed and wedge the sash—the wrong sash. You get nearly to sleep;

the sash rattles again. The Long Clam reminds you. You whirl out and pound in some more wedges. You plunge into bed with emphasis; a sort of bogus unconsciousness begins to dull your brain; then some water begins to drip somewhere. Every drop that falls, hurts. You think you will try mind cure on that drip and so neutralize its effects. This causes the Long Clam to smile. You chafe and fret for fifteen minutes, then you earthquake yourself out of bed and explore for that drip with a breaking heart, and language to match. But you never find it. When you go to bed this time, you understand that your faculties are all up for the night, there is business on hand, and you have got to superintend. The procession begins to move. All the crimes you have ever committed, and which you supposed you had forgotten, file past—and every one of them carries a banner. The Long Clam is on hand to comment. All the dead and buried indignities you have ever suffered, follow; they bite like fangs, they burn like fire. The Long Clam is getting in his work, now. He has dug your conscience out and occupied the old stand; and you will find that for real business, one Long Clam is worth thirty consciences. The rest of that night is slow torture at the stake. There are lurid instants at intervals, occupied by dreams; dreams that stay only half a second, but they seem to expose the whole universe, and disembowel it before your eyes; other dreams that sweep away the solar system and leave the shoreless void occupied from one end to the other by just you and the Long Clam. Now you know what it is to sit up with a Long Clam. Now you know what it is to try to entertain a Long Clam. Now you know what it is to keep a Long Clam amused; to try to keep a Long Clam from feeling lonesome; to try to make a Long Clam satisfied and happy. As for me, I would rather go on an orgy with anybody in the world than a Long Clam; I would rather never have any fun at all than try to get it out of a Long Clam. A Long Clam doesn't know when to stop. After you've had all the fun you want the Long Clam is just getting fairly started. In my opinion there is too much company about a Long Clam. A Long Clam is more sociable than necessary. I've got this one along yet. It's two days, now, and this is the third night, as far as I've got. In all that time I haven't had a wink of sleep that didn't have an earthquake in it, or a cyclone, or an instantaneous photograph of Sheol. And so all that is left of me is a dissolving rag or two of former humanity and a fading memory of happier days; the rest is Long Clam. That is the explanation. That is why I don't make a speech. I am perfectly willing to make speeches for myself, but I am not going to make speeches for any Long Clam that ever fluttered. Not after the way I've been treated. Not that I don't respect the Long Clam, for I do. I consider the Long Clam by long odds the capablest creature that swims the salt sea; I consider the

Long Clam the Depew of the watery world, just as I consider Depew the Long Clam of the great world of intellect and oratory. If any of you find life uneventful, lacking variety, not picturesque enough for you, go into partnership with a Long Clam.

Text / Autobiographical dictation of December 28, 1906, MTP.

Booth / Edwin Thomas Booth (1833–93). American actor. After an apprenticeship in his father's company, he leased the Winter Garden, New York, where he staged *Hamlet* for one hundred nights (1864–65). His brother's assassination of Lincoln caused temporary retirement from which he emerged to open Booth's Theatre (1869), where he reached the peak of his fame in Shakespearian roles. Mark Twain characterized Booth as a modest, amiable man so self-effacing that when called upon for a speech he could manage only a few halting sentences.

· 72 ·

A. G. Spalding, president of the Chicago National League Club, financed the first American baseball invasion of the Old World, a globe-circling tour of two teams, the All-Americans and the Chicagos, from October 1888 to April 1889. When they returned to New York, a banquet feted promoter and players for most of a boisterous night. Theodore Roosevelt was there, Charles B. Dillingham, A. C. "Pop" Anson, F. D. Millet, De Wolf Hopper, and several hundred other buoyant gentlemen. "The dinner," said the New York Herald *next day, "was served in nine innings, of course, and the waiters had evidently been trained to make all the champagne bases." Speakers were seated in positions corresponding to those of a baseball team: Chauncey Depew, pitcher; Judge Henry M. Howland, catcher; and so forth. Mark Twain, shortstop, was introduced as a native of the Sandwich Islands.*

The Grand Tour—1. The Sandwich Islands

Baseball Dinner, Delmonico's, New York, April 8, 1889

Though not a native, as intimated by the chairman, I have visited, a great many years ago, the Sandwich Islands—that peaceful land, that beautiful land, that far-off home of profound repose, and soft indolence, and dreamy solitude, where life is one long slumberless Sabbath, the climate one long delicious summer day, and the good that die experience no change, for they but fall asleep in one heaven and wake up in another. And these boys have played baseball *there!*—baseball, which is the very symbol, the outward and visible expression of the drive, and push, and rush and struggle of the raging, tearing, booming nineteenth century! One cannot realize it, the place and the fact are so incongruous; it's like interrupting a funeral with a circus. Why, there's no legitimate point of contact, no possible kinship, between baseball and the Sandwich Islands; baseball is all fact, the Islands all sentiment. In baseball you've got to do everything just right, or you don't get there; in the Islands you've got to do everything just wrong, or you can't stay there. You do it wrong to get it right, for if you do it right you get it wrong; there isn't any way to get it right *but* to do it wrong, and the wronger you do it the righter it is.

The natives illustrate this every day. They never mount a horse from the larboard side, they always mount him from the starboard; on the other hand, they never milk a cow on the starboard side, they always milk her on the larboard; it's why you see so many short people there—they've got their heads kicked off. When they meet on the road, they don't turn out to the right, they turn out to the left. And so, from always doing everything wrong end first, that way, it makes them left-handed—left-handed and cross-eyed; they are all so. When a child is born, the mother goes right along with her ordinary work, without losing half a day—it's the father that knocks off and goes to bed till he gets over the circumstances. And those natives don't trace descent through the male line, but through the female; they say they always know who a child's mother was. Well, that odd system is well enough there, because there a woman often has as many as six or seven husbands, all at the same time—and all properly married to her, and no blemish about the matter anywhere. Yet there is no fussing, no trouble. When a child is born the husbands all meet together in convention, in a perfectly orderly way, and elect the father. And the whole thing is perfectly fair; at least as fair as it would be anywhere. Of course you can't keep politics out—you couldn't do that in any country; and so, if three of the husbands are Republicans and four are Democrats, it don't make any difference how strong a Republican aspect the baby has got, that election is going Democratic every time. And in the matter of that election those poor people stand at the proud altitude of the very highest Christian civilization; for they know, as well as we, that all women are ignorant, and so they don't allow that mother to vote.

In those Islands the cats haven't any tails, and the snakes haven't any teeth; and what is still more irregular, the man that loses a game gets the pot. And as to dress: the native women all wear a single garment—but the men don't. No, the men don't wear anything at all, they hate display; when they even wear a smile they think they are overdressed. Speaking of birds, the only bird there that has ornamental feathers has only two—just barely enough to squeeze through with—and they are under its wings instead of on top of its head, where of course they ought to be to do any good.

The native language is soft, and liquid and flexible, and in every way efficient and satisfactory—till you get mad; then, there you are; there isn't anything in it to swear with. Good judges all say it is the best Sunday language there is; but then all the other six days in the week it just hangs idle on your hands; it isn't any good for business; and you can't work a telephone with it. Many a time the attention of the missionaries has been called to this defect, and they are always promising they are going to fix it; but no, they go fooling along and fooling along, and nothing is done.

Speaking of education, everybody there is educated, from the highest to the lowest; in fact, it is the only country in the world where education is actually universal. And yet every now and then you run across instances of ignorance that are simply revolting—simply degrading to the human race. Think of it—there, the ten takes the ace! But let us not dwell on such things, they make a person ashamed. Well, the missionaries are always going to fix that, but they put it off, and put it off, and put it off, and so that nation is going to keep on going down, and down, and down, till some day you will see a pair of jacks beat a straight flush.

Well, it is refreshment to the jaded, water to the thirsty, to look upon men who have so lately breathed the soft airs of those Isles of the Blest, and had before their eyes the inextinguishable vision of their beauty. No alien land in all the world has any deep, strong charm for me but that one, no other land could so longingly and so beseechingly haunt me, sleeping and waking, through half a lifetime, as that one has done. Other things leave me, but it abides; other things change, but it remains the same. For me its balmy airs are always blowing, its summer seas flashing in the sun, the pulsing of its surfbeat is in my ear; I can see its garlanded crags, its leaping cascades, its plumy palms drowsing by the shore, its remote summits floating like islands above the cloud rack; I can feel the spirit of its woodland solitudes, I can hear the plash of its brooks, in my nostrils still lives the breath of flowers that perished twenty years ago. And these world wanderers who sit before us here, have lately looked upon these things!—and with eyes of flesh, not the unsatisfying vision of the spirit. I envy them that!

Yes, and I would envy them somewhat of the glories they have achieved in their illustrious march about the mighty circumference of the earth, if it were fair; but no, it was an earned run, and envy would be out of place. I will rather applaud—add my hail and welcome to the vast shout now going up, from Maine to the Gulf, from the Florida Keys to frozen Alaska, out of the throats of the other 65,000,000 of their countrymen. They have carried the American name to the uttermost parts of the earth—and covered it with glory every time. That is a service to sentiment; but they did the general world a large practical service, also—a service to the great science of geography. Ah, think of that! We don't talk enough about that—don't give it its full value. Why, when these boys started out you couldn't see the equator at all; you could walk right over it and never know it was there. That is the kind of equator it was. Such an equator as that isn't any use to anybody; as for me, I would rather not have any equator at all than a dim thing like that, that you can't see. But that is all fixed now; you can see it now; you can't run over it now and not know it's there; and so I drink long life to the boys who plowed a new equator round the globe stealing bases on their bellies!

Text / Composite, based upon: "What Mark Twain Said," New York *Sun*, April 9, 1889; "Welcome Home," *MTS*(23):145–49.

· 73 ·

In a dictation of August 28, 1906, MTP, Mark Twain says that at a dinner of the Fellowcraft Club, an organization of magazine writers and illustrators, he induced Major Pond to ask the chairman, Gilder, to recognize an unscheduled speaker who had a foolproof scheme for teaching novices how to make speeches without preparation. Gilder reluctantly consented, and the interloper was announced as Mr. Samuel Langhorne, the audience shouting its disapproval of this gross violation of banqueting etiquette. When Mark Twain arose, he was immediately recognized and cheered, everybody relieved because they thought he was to speak in place of the unknown Langhorne.

Dinner Speech

Fellowcraft Club Dinner, New York, November 15, 1889

I am Langhorne—that is my middle name. I am the inventor of the scheme which has been mentioned, and I think it is a good one and likely to be of great benefit to the world; still this hope may be disappointed, and therefore I can't afford to use my real name, lest in trying to acquire a new and possibly valuable reputation I destroy the valuable one which I already possess, and yet fail to replace it with a new one. I propose to take classes and teach, under this apparently fictitious name. I wish to describe my scheme to you and prove its value by illustration. The scheme is founded upon a certain fact—a fact which long experience has convinced me *is* a fact, and not a fiction of my imagination. That fact is this: those speakers who are called upon at a banquet after the regular toasts have been responded to, are generally merely called upon by name and requested to get up and talk—that is all. No text is furnished them and they are in a difficult situation, apparently—but only apparently. The situation is not difficult at all, in fact, for they are usually men who know that they may be possibly called upon, therefore they go to the banquet prepared—after a certain fashion. The speeches which these volunteers make are all of a pattern. They consist of three first-rate anecdotes—first-water jewels, so to speak, set in the midst of a lot of rambling and incoherent talk, where they flash and sparkle and delight the house. The speech is made solely for the sake of the anecdotes, whereas they shamelessly pretend that the anecdotes are introduced upon sudden inspiration, to illustrate the reasonings advanced in the speech. There *are* no reasonings in the speech. The speech wanders along in a random and purposeless way for a while; then, all of a sudden, the speaker breaks out as with an unforeseen and happy inspiration and says, "How felicitously what I have just been saying is illustrated in the case of the man who"—then he explodes his first anecdote. It's a good one—so good that a storm of delighted laughter sweeps the house and so disturbs its mental balance for the moment that it fails to notice that the anecdote didn't illustrate what the man had been saying—didn't illustrate anything at all, indeed, but was dragged in by the scruff of the neck and had no relation to the subject which the speaker was pretending to talk about. He doesn't allow the laughter to entirely subside before he is off and hammering away at his speech again. He doesn't wait, because that would be dangerous. It would give the house time to reflect; then it would see that the anecdote did not illustrate anything. He goes flitting airily along in his speech in the same random way as before, and presently has another of those inspirations and breaks out again with his "How felicitously what I have just been saying is illustrated in the case of the man who"—then he lets fly his second anecdote, and again the house goes down with a crash. Before it can recover its senses he is away again, and cantering gaily toward the home stretch, filling the air with a stream of empty words that have no connection with anything; and finally he has his third inspiration, introduced with the same set form, "How felicitously what I have just been saying is illustrated in the case of the man who"—then he lets fly his last and best anecdote and sits down under tempests and earthquakes of laughter, and everybody in his neighborhood seizes his hand and shakes it cordially and tells him it was a splendid speech—splendid.

That is my scheme. I hope to get classes. I shall charge a high rate, because the pupil will need but one lesson. By grace of a single lesson I will make it possible for the novice who has never faced an audience in his life to rise to his feet, upon call, without trepidation or embarrassment and make an impromptu speech upon any subject that can be mentioned, without preparation of any kind, and also without even any knowledge of the subject which may be chosen for him. He shall always be ready, for he shall always have his three anecdotes in his pocket, written on a card, and thus equipped he shall never fail. I beg you to give me a text and let me prove what I have been saying—any text, any subject will do—all subjects are alike under my system. Give me a text.

[After noisy discussion, it was proposed that every man write a subject on a slip of paper and drop it in a hat. The hat was passed up to the chairman, who drew out a slip on which the topic was "Portrait Painting."]

It is a good enough text. I want no better. I've already told you that all texts are alike, under this noble system. All that I need to do now is to talk a straight and uninterrupted stream of irrelevancies which shall ostensibly deal learnedly and instructively with the subject of portrait painting. The stream must not break anywhere; I must never hesitate for a word, because under this scheme the orator that hesitates is lost; it can give the house a chance to collect its reasoning faculties, and that is a thing which must not happen.

Portrait painting? That's a good subject for a speech, a very good subject indeed. Portrait painting is an ancient and honorable art, and there are many interesting things to say about it. Yes, it's an ancient and honorable art, although I don't really know how ancient it is. I never heard that Adam ever sat for his portrait, but maybe he did. Maybe he did, but I don't know. And how felicitously what I have just been saying is illustrated in the case of the man who reached home at two o'clock in the morning and his wife said plaintively, "Oh, John when you've had whiskey enough why don't you ask for sarsaparilla?"—and he said, "Why, Maria, when I have had whiskey enough I can't *say* sarsaparilla."

Maybe there never was a portrait of Adam. Even if painting is an ancient and honorable art, it may not be as ancient as all that. And I don't think I ever saw a portrait of any of those old Hebrews, or of the Greeks either. But the Romans did have portraits, carved mostly, not painted. I've never seen a painted portrait of Julius Caesar, but I can recall more than one statue.

And how felicitously what I have just been saying is illustrated in the case of the man who arrived at his home at that unusual unfortunate hour in the super-early morning, and stood there and watched his portico rising and sinking and swaying and reeling, and at last, when it swung around into his neighborhood he made a plunge and scrambled up the steps and got safely on to the portico, stood there watching his dim house rise and fall and swing and sway, until the front door came his way and he made a plunge and got it, and scrambled up the long flight of stairs, but at the topmost step instead of planting his foot upon it he only caught it with his toe, and down he tumbled, and rolled and thundered all the way down the stairs, fetched up in a sitting posture on the bottom step with his arm braced around the friendly newel post and said, "God pity the poor sailors out at sea on such a night as this."

But when we come down a little later, we do find portraits in Rome, portraits of the old Popes, and in Germany we find portraits of their opponents, Calvin and Luther. There's a portrait of Luther in one of those galleries that lingers in my mind as one of the most masterly revelations of character that I ever saw. And speaking of Luther, there was a man in Hartford who had a cat called Luther. [Third anecdote unreported.]

And that's all I know about portrait painting. At least, it's all I have time to tell you this evening. It is an ancient and honorable art; and I'm very glad indeed that you have given me the opportunity of talking to you about it.

Text / Composite, based upon: Autobiographical dictation of August 28, 1906, MTP; Brander Matthews, *The Tocsin of Revolt and Other Essays* (New York, 1922):275–77.

· 74 ·

Mark Twain's humor, his pungent observations and unorthodox opinions made him sought after by newspaper interviewers. Although he believed that a printed version of talk could not catch the nuances implied by tone of voice and shadings of emphasis, he seemed to enjoy chatting with newsmen, and seldom refused to be interviewed. A Times *reporter went up to that remarkable house on Farmington Avenue in Hartford, where Mark Twain discoursed amiably on copyright in his usual lazy drawl. Then he became more animated when he complained heatedly of American reverence for titles and of the insidious influence of European literature on American writers.*

Interview

Hartford, Early December, 1889

[The reporter, commenting on Mark Twain's efforts on behalf of good copyright law, mentioned the bill introduced by Senator Jonathan Chace, of Rhode Island, which had failed to pass in the previous session of Congress.]

Had the same party been in power, I would have gone to Washington with the boys. But I don't know the feeling of the present Congress, and I have not much faith in a Republican Congress anyway. They are more likely to slap on more protection where it isn't needed than to pass a measure which would do some good. Everyone ought to get value for his labor, whether he makes boots or manuscripts.

[The reporter asked: "What do you think of the opinion held by an eminent American author, that American literature is now on its legs, and does not need protection since it has survived and overcome competition with pirated reprints?"]

That is true as far as it goes, but it does not go far enough. Publishers, as it happens, are constructed out of pretty much the same material as other people, and they are not likely to pay a royalty on a book by an unknown American author when they can get works by established authors for nothing. I may as well speak out on this question—a month ago I wouldn't have done it—but now—yes, I will speak out. This, then, understand, is not simply a question of protecting American authors. What becomes of them, whether they live or die, is of no consequence. It is not merely a question of copyright. It is a question of maintaining in America a national literature, of preserving national sentiment, national politics, national thought, and national morals.

What becomes of a dozen chuckleheaded authors, who can go and saw wood if they like, is the merest trifle compared with the great, colossal, national stakes involved. We are fed on a foreign literature, and imbibe foreign ideas. But if I were to go to England and write down what I think of their monarchical shams, pour out my utter contempt for their pitiful Lords and Dukes, and preach my sermon, I would not be able to get my views published. No English publisher would do it. But if a foreigner comes along here, and after looking around for a few minutes goes home and writes a book, abusing our President and reviling our institutions, his views are published and his book is gobbled up by American publishers, and circulated throughout the country for twenty cents a copy.

Foreigners after that tell us that we are thin-skinned. "You Americans are very thin-skinned," they say. Our skin is not so very thin, but it would be tough if it were not lacerated by such things as these. And then, our newspapers are abused. We are told that they are irreverent, coarse, vulgar, ribald. I hope they will remain irreverent. I would like that irreverence to be preserved in America forever and ever—irreverence for all royalties and all those titled creatures born into privilege. Merit alone should constitute the one title to eminence, and we Americans can afford to look down and spit upon miserable titled nonentities.

But I am sorry that some of our newspapers are losing their irreverence. They publish too much about that puppet of an Emperor in Germany. And this dissemination of foreign literature is affecting our women. There are women in America—and perfectly respectable women—who are ready to sell themselves to anything bearing the name of Duke.

[Indignation over sham nobility led to a discussion of Mark Twain's forthcoming book, *A Connecticut Yankee In King Arthur's Court.*]

I want to get at the Englishman, but in order to do that I must deal with the English publisher. And the English publishers are cowards, and so are the English newspapers. I have had to modify and modify my book to suit the English publishers' taste until I really cannot cut it any more. I talked to Mr. Osgood about it, and he said that there was only one publisher in London that would take my book as I wanted to leave it, and that house was not quite reputable. I've got to have a respectable house. And Mr. Osgood said that my London publisher, Mr. Chatto, was one of the bravest of them. Yes; Mr. Chatto will do the best he can, but he will cut my book. All I could do was to appeal to him to cut it as little as possible. I am anxious to know my fate. I see that he has cut my preface. Yes, more than half of my preface is gone, and all because of a little playful remark of mine about the divine right of Kings.

[The reporter asked: "How long were you at work on this book, Mr. Clemens?"]

I projected it four years ago, and it has been in manuscript for three years. I put it in pigeonholes and took it out now and then to see how it was getting on, and replaced it again. I began to think several months ago that it was about ripe, and that the times were about ripe for it. And sure enough it was, for there is Brazil gets rid of her Emperor in twenty-four hours, and there is talk of a republic in Portugal and in Australia. And curiously enough, the proclamation of the Brazilian republicans is very similar—I mean in the idea, not the words—to that which my hero issues abolishing the monarchy.

[There was a discussion of Mark Twain's books and of pirated English editions, during which Mark Twain said of the British pirate, John Camden Hotten: "I should like very much to blow Mr. Hotten's brains out—not that I have any objection to Mr. Hotten, but just to see." Then the reporter changed the subject by asking: "Are you pestered with autograph fiends?"]

Yes, I get my share of them. I write out a few hundred cards now and then and give them to my secretary to mail. When I sent them myself I used to discriminate. I would not send my autograph unless the applicants sent addressed envelopes. No matter whether they sent a thousand cards or a hundred thousand stamps, if they didn't write the address I gobbled their stamps and kept my autograph.

[After an upstairs visit to the billiard room and a great deal of unreported talk by Mark Twain, the reporter asked a final question: "And when may we expect another book?"]

I don't know. I don't write the book. A book writes itself. If there is another book in me, it will come out, and I will put it on paper.

Text / "Mark Twain and His Book / The Humorist on the Copyright Question," *Times,* December 10, 1889.

cut my preface / The part rejected by Chatto, but published in the American edition, is as follows: "The question as to whether there is such a thing as divine right of kings is not settled in this book. It was found too difficult. That the executive head of a nation should be a person of lofty character and extraordinary ability, was manifest and indisputable; that none but the Deity could select that head unerringly, was also manifest and indisputable; that the Deity ought to make that selection, then, was likewise manifest and indisputable; consequently, that He does make it, as claimed, was an unavoidable deduction. I mean, until the author of this book encountered the Pompadour, and Lady Castlemaine, and some other executive heads of that kind; these were found so difficult to work into the scheme, that it was judged better to take the other tack in this book (which must be issued this fall), and then go into training and settle the question in another book. It is, of course, a thing which ought to be settled, and I am not going to have anything particular to do next winter anyway."

· 75 ·

Having heard Bram Stoker tell the christening story in the late 1880s, Mark Twain took it over and often used it for public readings. The setting is a room in a village home, crowded with the family and friends of the infant to be christened. The officiating minister is a rather pompous little man who likes to hear himself talk. He takes the baby in his hands and contemplates it during a short silence while he thinks of high-flown phrases to put into his remarks. Then he speaks. In the text below, comments in brackets are Mark Twain's stage directions.

The Christening Yarn

Often Used From About 1889–90

Ah, my friends, he is but a little fellow. A very little fellow. Yes—a v-e-r-y little fellow. *But!* [With a severe glance around.] What of that! I ask you what of *that!* [From this point, gradually begin to rise—and soar—and be pathetic, and impassioned, and all that.] Is it a crime to be little? Is it a *crime,* that you cast upon him these cold looks of disparagement? Oh, reflect, my friends—reflect! Oh, if you but had the eye of poesy, which is the eye of prophecy, you would fling your gaze afar down the stately march of his possible future, and *then* what might ye not see! *What?* ye disparage him because he is *little?* Oh, consider the mighty ocean! ye may spread upon its shoreless bosom the white-winged fleets of all the nations, and lo they are but as a flock of insects lost in the awful vacancies of interstellar space! Yet the mightiest ocean is made of *little* things; *drops*—tiny little drops—each no bigger than the tear that rests upon the cheek of this poor child! And oh, my friends, consider the mountain ranges, the giant ribs that girdle the great globe and hold its frame together—and what are they? Compacted grains of sand—*little* grains of sand, each no more than a freight for a gnat! And oh, consider the constellations!—the flashing suns, countless for multitude, that swim the stupendous deeps of space, glorifying the midnight skies with their golden splendors—what are *they?* Compacted motes! specks! impalpable atoms of wandering stardust arrested in their vagrant flight and welded into solid worlds! *Little* things; yes, they are made of *little* things. And he—oh, look at him! *Little,* is he?—and ye would disparage him for it! Oh, I beseech you, cast the eye of poesy, which is the eye of prophecy, into his future! Why, he may become a poet!—the grandest the world has ever seen—Homer, Shakespeare, Dante, compacted into one!—and send down the procession of the ages songs that shall contest immortality with human speech itself! Or, he may become a great soldier!—the most illustrious in the annals of his race—Napoleon, Caesar, Alexander compacted into one!—and carry the victorious banner of his country from sea to sea, and from land to land, until it shall float at last unvexed over the final stronghold of a conquered world!—oh, heir of imperishable renown! Or, he may become a—a—he—he—[struggle desperately, here, to think of something else that he may become, but without success—the audience getting more and more distressed and worried about you all the time]—he may become—he—[suddenly] *but what is his name?*

Papa [with impatience and exasperation]. His *name,* is it? Well, his name's *Mary Ann!*

Text / "The Christening Yarn," MS, MTP.

· 76 ·

The Prince and the Pauper *was dramatized by Mrs. Abby Sage Richardson, the production managed by Daniel Frohman and staged by David Belasco. The star was Elsie Leslie, a talented child actress who played the dual roles of Prince Edward and Tom Canty, and whose golden-haired appeal charmed the most acidulous critic. She stood hand in hand with Mark Twain during his curtain speech at the end of the third act. Having walked off with Elsie, he immediately returned with Mrs. Richardson, who took her bows, as the New York* Herald *said next day, "from beneath a pert bonnet of gray silk and from above a gala gown of maroon satin." Thanks to winsome Elsie, the play did fairly well for several weeks in New York and later on the road.*

Curtain Speech

Opening of The Prince and the Pauper, *Broadway Theatre, New York, January 20, 1890*

For fifteen years I have had in my mind's eye such an idyl as we have seen this evening.

Years ago I went to an old friend of mine and told him the story of the prince and the pauper. He didn't know—Stop that hammering back there! [this to some stage hands who were making a dreadful racket behind the drop]—he didn't know anything about dramatic affairs, he was without bias, and he said it would make a rattling play. He used some other phrase that I forget just now, but it was strong and convincing.

So I went home and started to write the play. Somehow I couldn't make it go. I had written books, and knew I could write books as well as anyone. But I couldn't make the play. I found that it required qualities to make a play different from those needed to write a book. To write a book one must have great learning, high moral qualities and—some other little things like that.

But to make a play requires genius. So I spread my story out in a book and waited for the genius to come along to do the dramatizing. And therefore the honor of this curtain call belongs not to me but to

Mrs. Abby Sage Richardson, who, I regret to say, is not in the house tonight or even in the city.

Text / "Rags and Royalty," New York *Herald,* January 21, 1890.

Abby Sage Richardson / (1837–1900). American writer. A quondam actress, then author and lecturer, known as a student of Shakespeare, she published books on literary subjects and adapted plays of Sardou and others for Daniel Frohman's stock company. Her dramatization of *The Prince and the Pauper* precipitated a wrangling lawsuit involving herself, Mark Twain, Daniel Frohman, and Edward H. House. See Paul Fatout, "Mark Twain, Litigant," *American Literature* 31, no. 1 (March 1959):30–45.

Mark Twain's praise of the lady as a genius is at odds with his private grumbling that she had so mangled his story that nothing of his was left in it. He set forth his complaints of her in a strong but apparently unmailed letter to Frohman, February 2, 1890, MTP. It is an explosive example of Mark Twain in eruption.

· 77 ·

Mark Twain, continuing his feud with foreign critics in general and with the ghost of Matthew Arnold in particular, fired another round, conjecturally on the occasion noted below.

On Foreign Critics

Dinner for Max O'Rell, Everett House, Boston, April 27, 1890

If I look harried and worn, it is not from an ill conscience. It is from sitting up nights to worry about the foreign critic. He won't concede that we have a civilization—a "real" civilization. Five years ago, he said we had never contributed anything to the betterment of the world. And now comes Sir Lepel Griffin, whom I had not suspected of being in the world at all, and says "there is no country calling itself civilized where one would not rather live than in America, except Russia." That settles it. That is, it settles it for Europe; but it doesn't make me any more comfortable than I was before.

What is a "real" civilization? Nobody can answer that conundrum. They have all tried. Then suppose we try to get at what it is not; and then subtract the what it is not from the general sum, and call the remainder "real" civilization—so as to have a place to stand on while we throw bricks at these people. Let us say, then, in broad terms, that any system which has in it any one of these things, to wit, human slavery, despotic government, inequality, numerous and brutal punishments for crimes, superstition almost universal, ignorance almost universal, and dirt and poverty almost universal—is not a real civilization, and any system which has none of them, is.

If you grant these terms, one may then consider this conundrum: How old is real civilization? The answer is easy and unassailable. A century ago it had not appeared anywhere in the world during a single instant since the world was made. If you grant these terms—and I don't see why it shouldn't be fair, since civilization must surely mean the humanizing of a people, not a class—there is today but one real civilization in the world, and it is not yet thirty years old. We made the trip and hoisted its flag when we disposed of our slavery.

However, there are some partial civilizations scattered around over Europe—pretty lofty civilizations they are, too—but who begot them? What is the seed from which they sprang? Liberty and intelligence. What planted that seed? There are dates and statistics which suggest that it was the American Revolution that planted it. When that revolution began, monarchy had been on trial some thousands of years, over there, and was a distinct and convicted failure, every time. It had never produced anything but a vast, a nearly universal savagery, with a thin skim of civilization on top, and the main part of that was nickel plate and tinsel. The French, imbruted and impoverished by centuries of oppression and official robbery, were a starving nation clothed in rags, slaves of an aristocracy of smirking dandies clad in unearned silks and velvet. It makes one's cheek burn to read of the laws of the time and realize that they were for human beings; realize that they originated in this world, and not in hell. Germany was unspeakable. In the Scottish lowlands the people lived in styes, and were human swine; in the highlands drunkenness was general, and it hardly smirched a young girl to have a family of her own. In England there was a sham liberty, and not much of that; crime was general; ignorance the same; poverty and misery were widespread; London fed a tenth of her population by charity; the law awarded the death penalty to almost every conceivable offense; what was called medical science by courtesy stood where it had stood for two thousand years; Tom Jones and Squire Western were gentlemen.

The printer's art had been known in Germany and France three and a quarter centuries, and in England three. In all that time there had not been a newspaper in Europe that was worthy the name. Monarchies had no use for that sort of dynamite. When we hoisted the banner of revolution and raised the first genuine shout for human liberty that had ever been heard, this was a newspaperless globe. Eight years later, there were six daily journals in London to proclaim to all the nations the greatest birth this world had ever seen. Who woke that printing press out of its trance of three hundred years? Let us be permitted to consider that we did it. Who summoned the French slaves to rise and set the nation free? We did it. What resulted in England and on the Continent? Crippled liberty took up its bed and walked. From that day to this its march has not halted, and please God it never will. We are called the nation of inventors. And we are. We could still claim that title and wear its loftiest honors, if we had stopped with the first thing we ever invented—which was human liberty. Out of that invention has come the Christian world's great civilization. Without it it was impossible—as the history of all the centuries has proved. Well, then, who invented civilization? Even Sir Lepel Griffin ought to be able to answer that question. It looks easy enough. *We* have contributed nothing! Nothing hurts me like ingratitude.

Yes, the coveted verdict has been persistently withheld from us. Mr. Arnold granted that our whole people—including by especial mention "that immense class, the great bulk of the community," the wage and salary-earners—have liberty, equality, plenty to eat, plenty to wear, comfortable shelter, high pay, abundance of churches, newspapers, libraries, charities, and a good education for everybody's child for nothing. He added, "society seems organized there for their benefit"—benefit of the bulk and mass of the people. Yes, it is conceded that we furnish the greatest good to the greatest number; and so all we lack is a civilization.

Mr. Arnold's indicated civilization would seem to be restricted, by its narrow lines and difficult requirements, to a class—the top class—as in tropical countries snow is restricted to the mountain summits. And from what one may gather from his rather vague and unsure analysis of it, the snow metaphor would seem to fit it in more ways than one. The impression you get of it is, that it is peculiarly hard, and glittering, and bloodless, and unattainable. Now if our bastard were a civilization, it could fairly be figured—by Mr. Arnold's own concessions—by the circulation of the blood, which nourishes and refreshes the whole body alike, delivering its rich streams of life and health impartially to the imperial brain and the meanest extremity.

Text / Composite, based upon: "On Foreign Critics," MS, MTP; "On Foreign Critics," *MTS*(23):150–53.

Max O'Rell / Pen name of Leon Paul Blouet (1848–1903). French humorist. As a newspaperman in England, he published *John Bull and His Island* (1883), which was so popular that he gave up journalism. Lecture tours in the United States (1887, 1890) produced *Jonathan and His Continent* (1889) and *A Frenchman in America* (1891). Mark Twain said that O'Rell was an unoriginal humorist who palmed off as his own the good things of others. See *MTN:*306.

Sir Lepel Griffin / Lepel Henry Griffin (1838–1910). British government official. A veteran of the Bengal Civil Service (1860–89), he was a virulent critic of the United States. The opinion cited by Mark Twain, incorrectly quoted but accurate in substance, is from Griffin's *The Great Republic* (1884):2. Griffin elaborates by calling American life "sordid and mean and ugly." On the same page he also makes the sweeping statement: "America is the country of disillusion and disappointment, in politics, literature, culture, and art; in its scenery, its cities, and its people."

Tom Jones and Squire Western / Characters in Henry Fielding's *The History of Tom Jones, a Foundling* (1749). Neither the irascible, boorish Squire nor the generous but dissipated Tom exemplifies the British conception of a gentleman.

Arnold / In his concluding remarks Mark Twain probably refers to Matthew Arnold's "Civilisation in the United States," *Nineteenth Century* (April 1888). In this essay Arnold commends a flexible political system and charming women, and rejects Griffin's harsh judgment that America is the least fit country, except Russia, to live in. Nevertheless, Arnold gives a substantial list of American shortcomings: exaltation of material wealth, failure in the arts, a society without distinction because of concentration on the average, ugly place names ending in "ville," lying newspapers, and a civilization lacking beauty and elevation. Mark Twain may also have had in mind two other essays by Arnold published in the *Nineteenth Century:* "A Word About America" (May 1882), and "A Word More About America" (February 1885). It is not surprising that the somewhat supercilious manner of Arnold and the sledgehammer tactics of Griffin, not to speak of gratuitous instruction from other foreign visitors, should have irritated Americans.

· 78 ·

Mark Twain went to Washington in September 1890, presumably to induce Senator John P. Jones of Nevada to invest in the Paige typesetter. Mark Twain's persuasive powers won no cash from the senator, but he was a great success at a banquet of the National Druggists Association.

Dinner Speech

National Wholesale Druggists Association Banquet, Washington, D.C., ca. September 1890

About a thousand years ago, approximately, I was apprenticed as a printer's devil to learn the trade, in common with three other boys of about my own age. There came to the village a long-legged individual, of about nineteen, from one of the interior counties; fish-eyed, no expression, and without the suggestion of a smile—couldn't have smiled for a salary. We took him for a fool, and thought we would try to scare him to death. We went to the village druggist and borrowed a skeleton. The skeleton didn't belong to the druggist, but he had imported it for the village doctor, because the doctor thought he would send away for it, having some delicacy about using— The price of a skeleton at that time was fifty dollars. I don't know how high they go now, but probably higher, on account of the tariff.

We borrowed the skeleton about nine o'clock at night, and we got this man—Nicodemus Dodge was his name—we got him down town, out of the way, and then we put the skeleton in his bed. He lived in a little one-storied log cabin in the middle of a vacant lot. We left him to get home by himself. We enjoyed the result in the light of anticipation; but by and by, we began to drop into silence; the possible consequences were preying upon us. Suppose that it frightens him into madness, overturns his reason, and sends him screeching through the streets! We shall spend sleepless nights the rest of our days. Everybody was afraid. By and by, it was forced to the lips of one of us that we had better go at once and see what had happened.

Loaded down with crime, we approached that hut and peeped through the window. That long-legged critter was sitting on his bed with a hunk of gingerbread in his hand, and between the bites he played a tune on a jew's harp. There he sat perfectly happy, and all around him on the bed were toys and gimcracks and striped candy. The darned cuss, he had gone and sold that skeleton for five dollars. The druggist's fifty-dollar skeleton was gone. We went in tears to the druggist and explained the matter. We couldn't have raised that fifty dollars in two hundred and fifty years. We were getting board and clothing for the first year, clothing and board for the second year, and both of them for the third year. The druggist forgave us on the spot, but he said he would like us to let him have our skeletons when we were done with them. There couldn't be anything fairer than that; we spouted our skeletons and went away comfortable.

But from that time the druggist's prosperity ceased. This was one of the most unfortunate speculations he ever went into. After some years one of the boys went and got drowned; that was one skeleton gone, and I tell you the druggist felt pretty badly about it. A few years after another of the boys went up in a balloon. He was to get five dollars an hour for it. When he gets back they will be owing him one million dollars. The druggist's property was decreasing right along. After a few more years, the third boy tried an experiment to see if a dynamite charge would go. It went all right. They found some of him, perhaps a vest pocketful; still, it was enough to show that some more of that estate had gone. The druggist was getting along in years, and he commenced to correspond with me. I have been the best correspondent he has. He is the sweetest-natured man I ever saw—always mild and polite, and never wants to hurry me at all. I get a letter from him every now and then, and he never refers to my form as a skeleton; says: "Well, how is it getting along—is it in good repair?" I got a night-rate message from him recently—said he was getting old and the property was depreciating in value, and if I could let him have a part of it now he would give time on the balance. Think of the graceful way in which he does everything—the generosity of it all. You cannot find a finer character than that. It is the gracious characteristic of all druggists. So, out of my heart, I wish you all prosperity and every happiness.

Text / San Francisco *Argonaut* 28, no. 1 (January 5, 1891):13.

delicacy about using— / Another example of a sentence not completed because the audience anticipated the point and, as often reported, responded with "[Laughter]."

spouted our skeletons / "Spouted" was slang for "pawned."

· 79 ·

At a dinner for Judge Pryor, the host was John Russell Young; among guests were former President Cleveland, Generals Sherman and Sickles, Henry George, Depew, and Joe Jefferson. The Courant *remarked, October 13, 1890: "The only criticism upon the arrangement was that Depew, Mark Twain and Joe Jefferson should not have been placed together. They had too much fun by themselves. The three men most celebrated in the country for entertaining others should have been scattered."*

Dinner Speech

Dinner for Judge Robert A. Pryor, Astor House, New York, October 9, 1890

I have often wondered how after-dinner talkers, such as we have heard tonight, manage to make such clever impromptu speeches. My impromptu speeches are all carefully prepared in advance, but I can't understand how these other fellows manage the thing. Now there is Dougherty; he gets up with all the confidence which is generally inspired by the preparation of a month and he talks just as nicely and smoothly as though he had never thought about the matter before. When he comes to a place to heave in poetry he heaves her in, and when it is time for a story it comes right out. I am not so much surprised about Depew. He once asked me how I managed my impromptu speeches and I told him. I taught him the art and I sometimes wish I hadn't. Henry George appears to have a faucet concealed somewhere about him, and he just turns it on and out the stuff flows.

There has been a good deal of war talk here tonight and I don't appear to have been considered in it. I was in the Confederate Army. I was in it for two weeks. If Pryor had to fight through the whole war to get a position as judge, I suppose that, considering the difference in our abilities, if I had fought four weeks I would have been made President, and if I had fought six weeks the war would have ended.

I am not much of a talker upon this kind of an occasion. You ought to allow me a discount. A few days ago I called at the office of George

Putnam, the publisher. I was met by a very severe-looking clerk, who told me that Mr. Putnam wasn't in. I knew that wasn't true, but I didn't blame the young man, for I don't think he liked the look of my clothes, but I thought as long as I had paid him a visit I would do some business with him, and I said I wanted to buy a book—a book of travel or something of that kind—and he handed me a volume which he said would cost three dollars. I said to him: "I am a publisher myself, and I suppose you allow the usual publisher's discount of 60 percent." The young man looked absent-minded, but said nothing. Then I remarked: "I am also an author, and I suppose you allow the usual author's discount of 30 percent." The young man looked pale. I addressed him further: "I also belong to the human race, and I suppose you allow the usual discount to the human race of 10 percent." The young man said nothing, but he took a pencil from behind his ear and made an arithmetical calculation and remarked: "After adding to that 5 percent discount for natural shyness, I find that the firm owes you fifteen cents." So, gentlemen, if you allow me on my impromptu speech all the discounts which are properly due me, I think you will find that besides this dinner you are indebted to me about fifteen cents, and I hope the hat will be passed around and the amount collected.

Text / "A Notable Dinner," *Courant,* October 13, 1890.

Pryor / Robert Atkinson Pryor (1828–1919). American jurist. A Virginian who had been in Congress (1859–61), he was a veteran of the Third Virginia Infantry and Fitzhugh Lee's cavalry. In New York after the war, Pryor achieved distinction in a legal career, becoming judge of the Court of Common Pleas (1890–94), and a justice of the New York Supreme Court (1894–99).

Dougherty / Daniel Dougherty (1826–92). American lawyer. A successful attorney, he was better known as an orator, acclaimed for speeches nominating Democratic presidential candidates Tilden and Hancock, and for orations on commemorative occasions. On the lyceum circuit he lectured on oratory, the stage, and politics.

Henry George / (1839–97). American political economist. He is remembered for his study of poverty and attempts to improve the lot of the poor, also for his theory of the single tax—i.e., a tax on land. His best known book is *Progress and Poverty* (1879).

Putnam / George Haven Putnam (1844–1912). American publisher and writer. His war experience with the 176th New York Volunteers (1862–65) included a stay in Libby prison. A leader in organizing the

American Copyright League (1887), he was head of the publishing firm of G. P. Putnam's Sons and a director of the Knickerbocker Press. Among his books are *Authors and Publishers* (1883), *George Palmer Putnam* (1912), and *Some Memories of the Civil War* (1924).

· 80 ·

The Lotos Club, founded in 1870, stressed the arts and professions. The original suggestion of the name Melolotos was rejected in favor of Lotos, connoting the peace and harmony of Tennyson's lotos eaters. Mark Twain, in one of his early speeches there, now lost, said that he did not think much of a club that admitted congressmen to membership. In 1893 the club moved into enlarged quarters on Fifth Avenue and honored Mark Twain with the first dinner in the new clubhouse. Among the 300 guests were Howells, Warner, John Hay, Seth Low, Charles A. Dana, Gilder, Stedman, Carnegie, St. Clair McKelway, and General Porter.

Two Dinner Speeches

Lotos Club Dinner for Mark Twain,
New York, November 11, 1893

I have seldom in my lifetime listened to compliments more felicitous, nor praise so well bestowed. I return thanks for them from a full heart and appreciative spirit, and I will say in self-defense that while I am charged with having no reverence for anything, I have a reverence for a man who can say such things as your genial president. And I also have a reverence, deep and sincere, for a club that can confer upon one so confessedly deserving such distinguished tribute of respect. To be the chief guest on an occasion like this is something to be envied, and if I read human nature correctly tonight I am envied.

I am glad to see a club in these palatial quarters. I knew it twenty years ago when it was in a stable, and later when it was in a respectable house, but nothing so fine as this. I am glad to see it is renewing its youth, and I hope it may be continued to the end—and I hope I shall be there.

Now when I was studying for the ministry there were two or three things that struck my attention particularly. One was that unfortunate procedure that was introduced with the first banquet recorded in history, and which has been universally followed down to this present moment; I refer to the annoying custom of making the guest of the evening hop on his feet first. In the first banquet recorded in history, that other Prodigal Son, who had come back from his travels, as I have done, was notified to stand up and say his say. That was unfair. If he had been left alone until his brethren—David, Goliath, and the rest of 'em—had spoken, and if he had had as much experience as I have had, he would have waited until those other people got through talking. We know what happened. He got up and testified to all his failings. He gave himself away. Now if he had waited before telling all about his riotous living until the others had spoken he might not have given himself away as he did, and I am afraid I shall give myself away if I go on. My history is plenty well enough known already. I never wish to add anything to it. Now that you know how I feel about this matter, I will sit down and give the others a chance. If they talk too much, then I will get up and explain, and if I cannot do that, I'll deny it ever happened.

Besides, I don't feel well enough to talk any more. I have been in training with the Democratic party, and the events of last Tuesday have sort of undermined my political health. You can imagine I don't feel very robust. I feel as I do when I see one of those weak-minded young ladies, with an extra charge of poetic soul, towing a pup around the street. When I translate that pup's feelings, I feel that in that pup is concentrated the Democratic party. That ought to be a good excuse.

Now, if I may beg your permission, I would rather sit down and wait until I find out whether I am a prodigal or a fatted calf.

[After talks by Warner, Dana, Seth Low, McKelway and General Porter, some of whom mildly joked the guest of honor, there were loud calls for Mark Twain, who made his second speech of the evening.]

I don't see that I have a great deal to explain away. I have got off very easily indeed, considering the opportunities these gentlemen have had. Neither Mr. Warner nor President Low said anything that I can object to, but I never heard so many—er—lies as Mr. McKelway told you. I consider myself a pretty capable liar, but when he got through I was more than gratified to see how many things he hadn't found out.

I have been on the continent of Europe for two and a half years and I have met many Americans there. I tell you it is very gratifying that wherever you find Americans in Europe they have in almost all cases preserved their Americanism. The American abroad likes to see the flag of his country; he likes to see the Stars and Stripes fluttering proudly in the breeze. In those two and a half years I met only one American lady to be ashamed of. That is a very good record. That woman glorified monarchical institutions and lauded titles of nobility. She was entirely lost in them. She kept on until it was plain to me that she had forgotten such a country as the United States and such a flag as our flag. Finally, when I could stand it no longer, I said: "We have at least one merit—we are not as China is." The lady replied that she would like to know what the difference was. I answered: "China forbids a dissatisfied citizen to leave the country. Thank God, we don't!"

I was born a Mugwump, and I shall probably die a Mugwump. This election merely proves what I have contended abroad. I have said there that when Europe gets a ruler lodged in her gullet, there is no help for it but a bloody revolution; here we go and get a great big, emetical ballot, and heave it up.

Text / Composite, based upon: "'Mark Twain' at Dinner," *Times,* November 12, 1893; *"Lotos Club Dinner in Honor of Mark Twain"* in *MTS*(10):310–13; and *MTS*(23):161–63.

compliments / The chairman introduced Mark Twain as "the bearer of a most distinguished name in the world of letters . . . brimful of wit and eloquence, with no reverence for anything . . . . What name is there in literature that can be likened to his? . . . Himself his only parallel!"

your genial president / Frank Richard Lawrence (1845–1918). American lawyer. He had a long career as a corporation counsel noted for integrity and steadiness. As long-time president of the Lotos Club (1889–1918), he was chairman of all club functions honoring celebrities.

events of last Tuesday / A reference to off-year elections in which Republicans won eight out of eleven state contests. Mark Twain interpreted the result as a victory for Mugwumps. See letter to Olivia Clemens, November 10, 1893, *LLMT*.

Warner / Charles Dudley Warner (1829–1900). American editor and writer. As co-manager, with General Hawley, of the *Courant,* Warner contributed sketches published as *My Summer in a Garden* (1870). He collaborated with Mark Twain on *The Gilded Age* (1873), Warner's *Backlog Studies* coming out that year. Contributing editor of *Harper's Magazine* (1884–98), he published *On Horseback* (1888), *As We Were Saying* (1901), and others. He was a near neighbor of

Mark Twain in the Nook Farm community of Hartford.

Dana / Charles Anderson Dana (1819–97). American journalist. He was city editor of the New York *Tribune* (1847–62), assistant secretary of war (1863–65), and editor of the Chicago *Republican* (1866). In 1868 he became editor of the New York *Sun,* enlivening the paper with brisk headlines and human interest stories.

Seth Low / (1830–1916). American educator and politician. Deserting business for politics, he became mayor of Brooklyn (1881–85). As president of Columbia University (1889–1901), he moved the institution to its uptown location and donated the site of the Low Memorial Library. He was mayor of Greater New York (1901–03) and delegate to the Hague Peace Conference (1907).

McKelway / St. Clair McKelway (1845–1915). American journalist. Reporter for the New York *World* (1866), he was Washington correspondent of the Brooklyn *Eagle* (1868–70), and from 1884 on chief editor of that paper. He was noted for his independent spirit and courageous editorials. As diner-out, he was a brilliant speaker who often traded witty blows with Mark Twain.

General Porter / Horace Porter (1837–1921). American soldier and diplomat. Awarded the Congressional Medal of Honor for gallantry at Chickamauga, he was on the staff of General Grant (1865) and brevet brigadier general (1865). He was assistant secretary of war (1867–68), executive secretary to President Grant (1869–73), ambassador to France (1897–1905), and delegate to the Hague Peace Conference (1907). A good speaker, he was in demand for banquets.

· 81 ·

In the early 1890s Mark Twain's business affairs were in critical condition, mounting liabilities making dreams of great wealth more and more shadowy. Beset by tensions, he was a man much distressed. Yet his public appearances gave no hint of the crisis that was about to force his publishing company into bankruptcy, and cause him to write off the Paige typesetter as a costly failure. The speech below is an example of ostensible good spirits unaffected by financial worries. He was surprised when his ingenious remarks were highly commended, for he thought they did not amount to much. As he wrote to Olivia: "That I should make the only speech that roused prodigious enthusiasm was farthest from my thoughts–I never dreamed of it. But it shows what training can do." See Clara Clemens, My Father, Mark Twain:*134.*

Dinner Speech

Dinner for Brander Matthews, New York, ca. December 1893

You have spoken of him well, and lovingly and heartily and given him the praises which he has earned and which are his right. But you have overlooked what I think is the most notable achievement of his career—namely, that he has reconciled us to the sound of his sombre and awful name—namely—Brander Matthews! his blighting and scathing name—Bran-der Matthews! his lurid and desolating name—BRAND-er MATH-thews! B-r-r-r-an-der Math-thews! makes you think of an imprisoned god of the Underworld muttering imprecations and maledictions. B-r-a-n-d-e-r—it sounds like the mutterings of imprisoned fiends in hell! B-r-ran-der Math-thews! It is full of rumblings and thunderings and rebellions and blasphemies—B-r-ran-der Math-thews! The first time you hear it you shrivel up and shudder and say to yourself that a person has no business using that kind of language when children are present. B-r-a-n-d-e-r—why, it was months after I knew him before I dared to breathe his name on the Sabbath day! It is a searching and soul-stirring sound and makes the most abandoned person resolve to lead a better life. And on the other hand when the veteran profane swearer finds all his ammunition damp and ineffectual from long exposure, how fresh and welcome is the dynamite in that name—B-r-r-RANder M-m-ATHews! You can curse a man's head off with that name if you know how and where to put the emphasis.

To have overcome by the persuasive graces, sincerities and felicities of his literature the disaster of a name like that and reconciled men to the sound of it, is a fine and high achievement; and this, the owner of it has done. To have gone further and made it a welcome sound and changed its discords to music, is a still finer and higher achievement; and this he has also done. And so, let him have full credit. When he got his name it was only good to curse with. Now it is good to conjure with.

Text / Composite, based upon: Letter to Olivia Clemens, December 20, 1893, *My Father, Mark Twain:* 132–34; Matthews, *The Tocsin of Revolt:* 278.

Matthews / James Brander Matthews (1852–1929). American writer and teacher. As a young man he wrote fairly successful comedies about New York life, and in the 1880s took a prominent part in the city's theatrical society. He was a lecturer at Columbia University (1891–92), then professor of literature there (1892–1900). Among his books are *Studies of the Stage* (1894), *The Development of the Drama* (1903), and *A Book About the Theater* (1916).

· 82 ·

Henry H. Rogers, Standard Oil magnate, undertook to disentangle the snarled business affairs of Mark Twain. As a result of this association, which became very friendly, Mark Twain readily agreed to speak at the dedication of the Fairhaven, Massachusetts, Town Hall, which was the gift of Mrs. Rogers. He went up there, along with a governor or two and other notables, in fine style, Rogers providing a private car and plentiful champagne. At the ceremonies he was last on a two-hour program of overture, prayer, chorus, presentation address, presentation of keys, and so forth. He admitted that he became "pretty drowsy" but revived in time. See letter to Olivia Clemens, February 23, 1894, LLMT.

Advice

Dedication of Town Hall, Fairhaven, Massachusetts, February 22, 1894

By a thoughtful and judicious allotment of the privileges of this occasion, each speaker has been appointed to the function best suited to his capacity, his character, and his credit in the community. Chief of all the speakers, and most eloquent, stands the building itself. It is its easy office to declare to you the love of its builder for the town which was her birthplace and the home of her girlhood. It may be trusted to say its say well; and be understood; and be applauded from the heart; and to occupy the platform longer than anybody else, and make the only speech that will be printed right in the papers. Yes, and it is the only speaker of us all, gifted and popular as we try to let on to be, that can dare to stand up here and undertake to hold your unfatigued attention for a hundred years. Why, we couldn't do it for forty.

We all recognize the value of this building as an example and a suggestion—a suggestion to any who are moved by love for their fellow men to make gifts to them of hospitals or town halls or libraries, to build these things while they are alive, not wait till they are dead. If you do it while you are alive, it is really done, and well done; but if you wait till you are dead there is but a barren result and a divided profit; you get credit for the *intention,* and the lawyers get the money. The stomachs of the lawyers of this land are distended to utter discomfort with the eleemosynary architecture that they have swallowed. In all this world there is no joy like to the joy a lawyer feels when he sees a good-hearted inconsiderate person erecting a free library or a town hall or a hospital in his will. He smiles the smile that only he knows how to smile, and goes into training for the anaconda act. Perhaps no one has ever known a dead man to try to do even the least little single thing without making a botch of it. The truth is, a dead man ought to lie still, and keep quiet, and try to behave. But you can't teach him that; you can't teach him any useful thing. Everything about him is perishable but one thing, and that is his inability to accept the fact that circumstances over which he has no control have limited his activities. And first and last and all the time it is impossible to make him understand that there is nothing very large or fine or generous in spending his own money on himself and building hospitals with his children's cash. Why, some people do seem to get duller and duller the deader they get. Oh, well, perhaps it's no matter; it is the way they are made. Probably the mistake was in making them at all. I mean, if it was a mistake; I am no judge of that—but I wouldn't leave it to *them*.

It was a pleasant and patriotic thought to dedicate this building and confirm this grace to Fairhaven on the natal day of Washington—George Washington, first of Americans—George Washington, the Father of his Country—George Washington, the Father of Those Who Cannot Lie. The family has dwindled a good deal. But I am left yet; and when I look back over the waste of years and call up the faces of the others and know that I shall see them no more in this life and that I must remain now solitary and forlornly conspicuous to the last, the sole remnant of that old noble stock, it makes me feel sad, sad, and oh, so lonesome.

What I owe to Washington no words of mine can tell. He was my model from my cradle up. All that I am—morally speaking—I owe to his example. Even in my tenderest youth his spirit was ever near to guide and succor me. The first time I ever stole a watermelon in my life—I think it was the first time—it was the thought of Washington that moved me to make restitution, restored me to the path of rectitude, made me morally whole again. When I found out it was a green watermelon, I was sorry; not superficially, but deeply and honestly sorry. Then came the thought of Washington, and I said to myself, "What would Washington do?" That is what I said to myself. "What would Washington do, if he had stolen a watermelon? Green one. He would make restitution—that is what he would do." And that is what I did. I rose up spiritually refreshed and strong, and carried the watermelon back to the farmer's wagon and restored it to him; and said the merit was not mine, but Washington's. And then I felt that inspiriting something, that electric thrill, that exaltation which rewards duty done, a moral victory won, a moral heroism added to one's stock of dear and precious memories; and I told the farmer he ought to be ashamed of himself going around working off green watermelons on people that had confidence in him; and made him give me a ripe one for it. And he *was* ashamed, and said he wouldn't ever do it again. So I forgave him. For when a person has done wrong and acknowledges it and is ashamed of it, that is enough for me. It was Washington that saved me that time; he has been my guardian angel ever since—and has had an active career. I am glad and proud to have an opportunity at last to help celebrate his memory and do honor to his noble name.

In the distribution of the privileges of this platform I was appointed to temper the gloss of the gay and thoughtless oratory of these others with the wholesome shadow of a few words of sober advice—for there is a time for such things, and it is meet that we recognize this truth and rest our spirits with intervals of seriousness and solemnity. And so, my advice to you—yes, more, my supplication—is, that you live as Washington lived—live as I have lived—and build your gift halls and hospitals while you still live and can build your hearts as well as your money into your gift.

Text / Mark Twain and Fairhaven (Issued by the Millicent Library, Fairhaven, Massachusetts, n.d.):4–7.

· 83 ·

A luncheon given by the International Navigation Company was intended to celebrate the launching of its liner, the St. Paul. *Unfortunately, the ship would not slide into the water. Two hours' work with sledges and with steam hoses to soften the tallow on the ways failed to budge her. The event had to be postponed, but the* Times *reported next day that "Although the launch did not take place the luncheon . . . was served and congratulatory speeches were made."*

Luncheon Speech

Cramp's Shipyard, Philadelphia, March 25, 1895

Day after tomorrow I sail for England in a ship of this line, the *Paris.* It will be my fourteenth crossing in three years and a half. Therefore, my presence here, as you see, is quite natural, quite commercial. I am interested in ships. They interest me more now than hotels do. When a new ship is launched I feel a desire to go and see if she will be good quarters for me to live in, particularly if she belongs to this line, for it is by this line that I have done most of my ferrying.

People wonder why I go so much. Well, I go partly for my health, partly to familiarize myself with the road. I have gone over the same road so many times now that I know all the whales that belong along the route, and latterly it is an embarrassment to me to meet them, for they do not look glad to see me, but annoyed, and they seem to say: "Here is this old derelict again."

Earlier in life this would have pained me and made me ashamed, but I am older now, and when I am behaving myself, and doing right, I do not care for a whale's opinion about me. When we are young we generally estimate an opinion by the size of the person that holds it, but later we find that that is an uncertain rule, for we realize that there are times when a hornet's opinion disturbs us more than an emperor's.

I do not mean that I care nothing at all for a whale's opinion, for that would be going to too great a length. Of course, it is better to have the good opinion of a whale than his disapproval; but my position is that if you cannot have a whale's good opinion, except at some sacrifice of principle or personal dignity, it is better to try to live without it. That is my idea about whales.

Yes, I have gone over that same route so often that I know my way without a compass, just by the waves. I know all the large waves and a good many of the small ones. Also the sunsets. I know every sunset and where it belongs just by its color. Necessarily, then, I do not make the passage now for scenery. That is all gone by.

What I prize most is safety, and in the second place swift transit and handiness. These are best furnished by the American line, whose watertight compartments have no passage through them, no doors to be left open, and consequently no way for water to get from one of them to another in time of collision. If you nullify the peril which collisions threaten you with, you nullify the only very serious peril which attends voyages in the great liners of our day, and makes voyaging safer than staying at home.

When the *Paris* was half torn to pieces some years ago, enough of the Atlantic ebbed and flowed through one end of her, during her long agony, to sink the fleets of the world if distributed among them; but she floated in perfect safety, and no life was lost. In time of collision the rock of Gibraltar is not safer than the *Paris* and other great ships of this line. This seems to be the only great line in the world that takes a passenger from metropolis to metropolis without the intervention of tugs and barges or bridges—takes him through without breaking bulk, so to speak.

On the English side he lands at a dock; on the dock a special train is waiting; in an hour and three-quarters he is in London. Nothing could be handier. If your journey were from a sand pit on our side to a lighthouse on the other, you could make it quicker by other lines, but that is not the case. The journey is from the city of New York to the city of London, and no line can do that journey quicker than this one, nor anywhere near as conveniently and handily. And when the passenger lands on our side he lands on the American side of the river, not in the provinces. As a very learned man said on the last voyage (he is head quartermaster of the New York land garboard strake of the middle watch): "When we land a passenger on the American side there's nothing betwixt him and his hotel but hell and the hackman."

I am glad, with you and the nation, to welcome the new ship. She is another pride, another consolation, for a great country whose mighty fleets have all vanished, and which has almost forgotten what it is to fly its flag at sea. I am not sure as to which St. Paul she is named for. Some think it is the one that is on the upper Mississippi, but the head quartermaster told me it was the one that killed Goliath. But it is not important. No matter which it is, let us give her hearty welcome and godspeed.

Text / Composite, based upon: "An Undelivered Speech" in *MTS*(10):359–62; and *MTS*(23):164–67. As noted by the *Times* report above, the speech was delivered.

· 84 ·

Pudd'nhead Wilson, *dramatized by Frank Mayo, was first performed at Proctor's Opera House, Hartford, on April 8, 1895. Then it moved to New York for the opening on April 15, with Mayo in the title role, Edgar L. Davenport as Chambers, E. J. Henley as Tom Driscoll, and Mary Shaw as Roxy. Mark Twain, attending a performance shortly after his return from England, responded to calls for "Speech! Speech!" at the end of the third act, speaking from his box. Next day the* Times *remarked: "The fact that the humorist was to be present and would probably address the audience was known in advance, and the result was that the auditorium was crowded to its utmost capacity."*

Curtain Speech

Performance of Pudd'nhead Wilson,
Herald Square Theatre, New York, May 22, 1895

I am sure I could say many complimentary things about this play which Mr. Mayo has written and about his portrayal of the chief character in it and keep well within the bounds both of fact and of good taste; but I will limit myself to two or three. I do not know how to utter any higher praise than this—that when Mayo's Pudd'nhead walks this stage here, clothed in the charm of his gentle charities of speech and acts and the sweet simplicities and sincerities of his gracious nature, the thought in my mind is: Why, bless your heart, you couldn't be any dearer or lovelier or sweeter than you are without turning into that man all men love and even Satan is fond of—Joe Jefferson.

I am gratified to see that Mr. Mayo has been able to manage those difficult twins. I tried, but in my hands they failed. Year before last there was an Italian freak on exhibition in Philadelphia who was an exaggeration of the Siamese Twins. This freak had one body, one pair of legs, two heads, and four arms. I thought he would be useful in a book, so I put him in. And then the trouble began. I called these consolidated twins Angelo and Luigi, and I tried to make them nice and agreeable, but it was not possible. They would not do anything my way, but only their own. They were wholly unmanageable, and not a day went by that they didn't develop some new kind of devilishness—particularly Luigi. Angelo was of a religious turn of mind, and was monotonously honest and honorable and upright, and tediously proper; whereas Luigi had no principles, no morals, no religion—a perfect blatherskite, and an inextricable tangle theologically—infidel, atheist, and agnostic, all mixed together. He was of a malicious disposition, and liked to eat things which disagreed with his brother.

They were so strangely organized that what one of them ate or drank had no effect upon himself, but only nourished or damaged the other one. Luigi was hearty and robust, because Angelo ate the best and most wholesome food he could find for him; but Angelo was himself delicate and sickly, because every day Luigi filled him up with mince pies and salt junk, just because he knew he couldn't digest them. Luigi was very dissipated, but it didn't show on him, but only on his brother. His brother was a strict and conscientious teetotaler, but he was drunk most of the time on account of Luigi's habits. Angelo was president of the Prohibition Society, but they had to turn him out, because every time he appeared at the head of the procession on parade, he was a scandalous spectacle to look at.

On the other hand, Angelo was a trouble to Luigi, the infidel, because he was always changing his religion, trying to find the best one, and he always preferred sects that believed in baptism by immersion, and this was a constant peril and discomfort to Luigi, who couldn't stand water outside or in; and so every time Angelo got baptized Luigi got drowned and had to be pumped out and resuscitated. Luigi was irascible, yet was never willing to stand by the consequences of his acts. He was always kicking somebody and then laying it on Angelo. And when the kicked person kicked back, Luigi would say, "What are you kicking me for? I haven't done anything to you." Then the man would be sorry, and say, "Well, I didn't mean any harm. I thought it was you; but, you see, you people have only one body between you, and I can't tell which of you I'm kicking. I don't know how to discriminate. I do not wish to be unfair, and so there is no way for me to do but kick one of you and apologize to the other." They were a troublesome pair in every way. If they did any work for you, they charged for two; but at the boarding house they ate and slept for two and only paid for one.

In the trains they wouldn't pay for two, because they only occupied one seat. The same at the theater. Luigi bought one ticket and deadheaded Angelo in. They couldn't put Angelo out because they couldn't put the deadhead out without putting out the twin that had paid, and scooping in a suit for damages.

Luigi grew steadily more and more wicked, and I saw by and by that the way he was going on he was certain to land in the eternal tropics, and at bottom I was glad of it; but I knew he would necessarily take his righteous brother down there with him, and that would not be fair. I did not object to it, but I didn't want to be responsible for it. I was in such a hobble that there was only one way out. To save the righteous brother I had to pull the consolidated twins apart and make two separate and distinct twins of them. Well, as soon as I did that, they lost all their energy and took no further interest in life. They were wholly futile and useless in the book, they became mere shadows, and so they remain. Mr. Mayo manages them, but if he had taken a chance at them before I pulled them apart and tamed them, he would have found out early that if he put them in his play they would take full possession and there wouldn't be any room in it for Pudd'nhead Wilson or anybody else.

I have taken four days to prepare these statistics, and as far as they go you can depend upon their being strictly true. I have not told all the truth about the twins, but just barely enough of it for business purposes, for my motto is—and Pudd'nhead Wilson can adopt it if he wants to—my motto is, "Truth is the most valuable thing we have; let us economize it."

Text / Composite, based upon: "Mark Twain in the Playhouse," *Times,* May 23, 1895; New York *Herald,* May 23, 1895.

Mayo / Frank Mayo (1839–96). American actor. He began his career in San Francisco (1856), and made his New York debut as Ferdinand in *The Tempest* (1869). In Shakespearian and other roles he built a great reputation as a skillful character actor.

Jefferson / Joseph Jefferson (1829–1905). American actor. In a career of seventy years he became a great favorite as Dr. Pangloss, Bob Acres, Dr. Ollapod, and especially as Rip Van Winkle in the play adapted by himself and revised by Boucicault. Jefferson played this role for 170 nights in 1865. He originated the touring combination system: selecting actors according to their fitness for particular plays and parts, the object being to make the touring performance as good as that on Broadway.

· 85 ·

In July 1895, Mark Twain began a round-the-world speaking tour to pay debts incurred by the failure of his business ventures. At Cleveland, the first of more than twenty stops in the United States and Canada en route to the West Coast, he tried out the method he used throughout the tour. Starting off with a pseudo-serious discussion of a lecture topic, such as morals, he would glide into a ten- or twelve-minute story to illustrate a point, then return, more or less, to the topic, and after a time tell another story, and so on. For each appearance he used several numbers from his extensive repertoire: Mexican Plug, Christening Yarn, Golden Arm, King Sollermun, Jumping Frog, and many other standbys, besides new ones he created out of episodes on his travels. Continually varying the program, rarely using the same choices twice in a row, he made the whole loosely coherent by transitional sentences. At Cleveland he had a bad time, being exasperated by sweltering heat, a forty-minute concert before his entrance, a barking dog, and a crowd of scuffling newsboys sitting behind him on the stage. For details, see Fred W. Lorch, "Mark Twain's 'Morals' Lecture During the American Phase of His World Tour in 1895–96," American Literature *26, no. 1 (March 1954):52–66.*

Morals Lecture

Music Hall, Cleveland, July 15, 1895,
Prototype of Subsequent Tour Performances

I was solicited to go round the world on a lecture tour by a man in Australia. I asked him what they wanted to be lectured on. He wrote back that those people were very coarse and serious and that they would like something solid, something in the way of education, something gigantic, and he proposed that I prepare about three or four lectures at any rate on just morals, any kind of morals, but just morals, and I like that idea. I liked it very much and was perfectly willing to engage in that kind of work, and I should like to teach morals. I have a great enthusiasm in doing that and I shall like to teach morals to those people. I do not like to have them taught to me and I do not know any duller entertainment than that, but I know I can produce a quality of goods that will satisfy those people.

If you teach principles, why, you had better let your illustrations come first, illustrations which shall carry home to every person. I planned my first lecture on morals. I must not stand here and talk all night; get out a watch. I am talking the first time now and I do not know anything about the length of it.

I would start with two or three rules of moral principles which I want to impress upon those people. I will just make the lecture gradual, by and by. The illustrations are the most important so that when that lecture is by and by written and completed it will just be a waveless ocean with this archipelago of smiling green islands of illustrations in the midst of it.

I thought I would state a principle which I was going to teach. I have this theory for doing a great deal of good out there, everywhere in fact, that you should prize as a priceless thing every transgression, every crime that you commit—the lesson of it, I mean.

Make it permanent; impress it so that you may never commit that same crime again as long as you live, then you will see yourself what the logical result of that will be—that you get interested in committing crimes. You will lay up in that way, course by course, the edifice of a personally perfect moral character. You cannot afford to waste any crime, they are not given to you to be thrown away, but for a great purpose. There are 462 crimes possible and you cannot add anything to this, you cannot originate anything. These have been all thought out, all experimented on and have been thought out by the most capable men in the penitentiary.

Now, when you commit a transgression, lay it up in your memory, and without stopping, it will all lead toward moral perfection. When you have committed your 462 you are released of every possibility and have ascended the staircase of faultless creation and you finally stand with your 462 complete with absolute moral perfection, and I am more than two-thirds up there. It is immense inspiration to find yourself climbing that way and have not much further to go. I shall have then that moral perfection and shall then see my edifice of moral character standing far before the world all complete. I know that this should produce it. Why, the first time that I ever stole a watermelon—I think it was the first time, but this is no matter, it was right along there somewhere—I carried that watermelon to a secluded bower. You may call it a bower and I suppose you may not. I carried that watermelon to a secluded bower in the lumber yard, and broke it open, and it was green.

Now, then, I began to reflect; there is the virtual—that is the beginning—of reformation when you reflect. When you do not reflect that transgression is wasted on you. I began to reflect and I said to myself, I have done wrong; it was wrong in me to steal that watermelon—that kind of a watermelon. And I said to myself: now what would a right-minded and right-intentioned boy do, who found that he had done wrong—stolen a watermelon like this. What would he do, what must he do; do right; restitution; make restitution. He must restore that property to its owner, and I resolved to do that and the moment I made that good resolution I felt that electrical moral uplift which becomes a victory over wrong doing. I was spiritually strengthened and refreshed and carried that watermelon back to that wagon and gave it to that farmer—restored it to him, and I told him he ought to be ashamed of himself going around working off green watermelons that way on people who had confidence in him; and I told him in my perfectly frank manner it was wrong. I said that if he did not stop he could not have my custom, and he was ashamed. He was ashamed; he said he would never do it again and I believe that I did that man a good thing, as well as one for myself. He did reform; I was severe with him a little, but that was all. I restored the watermelon and made him give me a ripe one. I morally helped him, and I have no doubt that I helped myself the same time, for that was a lesson which remained with me for my perfection. Ever since that day to this I never stole another one—like that.

Then I have another theory, and that is to teach that when you do a thing do it with all your might; do it with all your heart. I remember a man in California, Jim What-is-his-name, Baker. He was a hearty man of most gentlemanly spirit and had many fine qualities. He lived a good many years in California among the woods and mountains; he had no companionship but that of the wild creatures of the forest. To me he was an observant man. He watched the ways of the different creatures so that he got so that he could understand what the creatures said to each other and translate it accurately. He was the only man I ever knew who could do this. I know he could, because he told me so himself, and he says that some of the animals have very slight education and small vocabulary and that they are not capable of using figures and allegory, but there are other animals that have a large vocabulary. These creatures are very fond of talking. They like to show off, and he placed the bluejay at the head of that list. He said: "Now there is more to the bluejay than any other animal. He has got more different kinds of feeling. Whatever a bluejay feels he can put into language, and not mere commonplace language, but straight out and out book talk, and there is such a command of language. You never saw a bluejay get stuck for a word. He is a vocabularized geyser. Now, you must call a jay a bird, and so he is in a measure, because he wears feathers and don't belong to any church, but otherwise he is just as human nature made him. A bluejay hasn't any more principle than an ex-congressman, and he will steal, deceive and betray four times out of five; and as for the sacredness of an obligation, you cannot scare him in the detail of principle. He talks the best grammar of all the animals. You may say a cat talks good grammar. Well, a cat does; but you let a cat get excited, you let a cat get at pulling fur with another cat on a shed nights and you will hear grammar. A bluejay is human; he has got all a man's faculties and man's weakness. He likes especially scandal; he knows when he is an ass as well as you do." [Baker's bluejay yarn followed, about the jay who tried to fill a cabin with acorns by dropping them through a hole in the roof.]

Now that brings me by a natural and easy transition to Simon Wheeler of California; a pioneer he was, and in a small way a philosopher. Simon Wheeler's creed was that pretty nearly everything that happens to a man can be turned to moral account; every incident in his life, almost, can be made to assist him, to project him forward morally, if he knows how to make use of the lesson which that episode teaches, and he used—well, he was a good deal of a talker. He was an inordinate talker; in fact, he wore out three sets of false teeth, and I told about a friend of his one day—a man that he had known there formerly, and who he had a great admiration for, of one Jim Smiley, and he said it was worth a man's while to know Jim Smiley. Jim Smiley was a man of gift; he was a man of parts; he was a man of learning; he was—well, he was the curiousest man about always betting on anything that turned up that you ever see, if he could get anybody to bet on the other side, and if he couldn't he would change sides. As soon as he got a bet he was satisfied. He prepared himself with all sorts of things—tomcats, rat terriers and all such things, and one day he ketched a frog; said he calculated to educate him. And he took him home and never done nothing but set in his back yard and learn that frog how to jump. Yes, sir, and he did learn him to—he did learn him to. When it came to jumping on a dead level there wasn't no frog that could touch him at all. Come to jump on the dead level, why, he could lay over any frog in the profession, and Smiley broke all the camps around there betting on that frog. By and by he got a misfortune. He used to keep his frog in a little lattice box. The frog's name was Daniel Webster, and he would bring that box down town and lay for a bet. And one day a fellow came along, a stranger in the camp he was, he says, "What might it be that you have got in the box?" "Well," Smiley says, "it ain't anything particular, it's only just a frog." "Well," he says, "what is he good for?" "Well," Smiley says, "I don't know, but I think he is good enough for one thing; he can outjump any frog in Calaveras County." The stranger took that box, turned it around this way and that way, and he examined Daniel Webster all over very critically, and handed it back, and he said, "I don't see any points about that frog that is any better than any other frog." "Oh," Smiley said, "it may be that you understand frogs and may be that you are only an amateur, so to speak; anyway I will risk forty dollars that he can outjump any frog in Calaveras County." Well, that stranger looked mighty sad, mighty sorrowful-grieved, and he said, "I am only a stranger in camp and I ain't got no frog, but if I had a frog I would bet you." Smiley says, "That's all right, just you hold my frog a minute; I will go and get you a frog." So Smiley lit out to the swamp and that stranger took that box and he stood there—well, he stood, and stood, and stood the longest time. At last he got Daniel Webster out of the box and pried his mouth open like that, took a teaspoonful and filled him full of quail shot, filled him full up to the chin and set him down on the floor. Daniel set there.

Smiley he flopped around in the swamp about half an hour. Finally he cotched a frog and fetched him to this fellow. They put up the money, and Smiley says: "Now, let the new frog down on the floor with his front paws just even with Daniel's, and I will give the word." He says, "One, two, three, scoot," and they touched up the frogs from behind to indicate that time was called, and that new frog, he rose like a rocket and came down kerchunk a yard and a half from where he started, a perfectly elegant jump for a non-professional that way. But Smiley's frog gave a heave or two with his shoulders—his ambition was up, but it was no use, he couldn't budge, he was anchored there as solid as an anvil. The fellow took the money, and finally, as he went away, he looked over his shoulder at Daniel, and he said: "Well, I don't see any points about that frog that is any better than any other frog." And Smiley looked down at Daniel Webster, I never see a man so puzzled. And he says: "I do wonder what that frog throwed off for? There must be something the matter with him, looks mighty baggy somehow." He hefted him, and says, "Blame my cats, if he don't weigh five pounds." Turned him upside down and showered out a hatful of shot. And Simon Wheeler said, "That has been a lesson to me." And I say to you, let that be a lesson to you. Don't you put too much faith in the passing stranger. This life is full of uncertainties, and every episode in life, figuratively speaking, is just a frog. You want to watch every exigency as you would a frog, and don't you ever bet a cent on it until you know whether it is loaded or not.

[He led up to another story by transitional sentences, but this portion of the lecture was not reported.]

Now you think from that man's language, which is not very refined, that he was the bravest man that ever was. That man was not afraid of anything. I never was afraid of anything. I have always had nerve, abundance of nerve. I never lost my nerve but once. Once I lost part of my nerve. I will not say all of it. That time it humiliated me so that I always remember it. When a schoolboy it often fell to my lot to come across a rainy day—one of those days which schoolboys all the world over regard as too rainy to go to school, and just rainy enough to go fishing. Forbidden fruit had the same attraction for me as it had for Adam. Some unthinking people criticize Adam—find fault with him because he was weak, and yielded. Oh, that is not fair, that is not right. He hadn't any experience. We have had ages and ages of experience and tuition—we who criticize him and yet see what we are—just see what we are when there is any forbidden fruit around. I have been around a good deal, but I have never been in any place where that apple would have been safe—except Allahabad [or whatever town he was speaking in]. Why, it is the *prohibition* that *makes* anything precious. There is a charm about the forbidden that makes it unspeakably desirable. It was not that Adam ate the apple for the apple's sake, but because it was forbidden. It would have been better for us—oh infinitely better for us—if the serpent had been forbidden.

My father was a magistrate and being a magistrate he was also coroner, sheriff and lord mayor and he had a little bit of an office in what was the sole room in a small house that stood by itself. And that little office had a sofa in it and that used to come handy to me now and then, because often I noticed on my way to school that the weather was not suitable for school and I better go fishing, so I went. But when I came back, when I returned from those excursions, it was not prudent to go home. I always met so many companions and preferences that it was better for me to lodge in that little office, and once while I was off on one of those excursions there was a fight late in the afternoon in that little street and a man was killed and they carried him to that little office and straightened him out there on the floor on his back and got him ready for the inquest in the morning, went away and left him there. I arrived about midnight and I did not know about this circumstance and I slipped in the back way and groped my way through the dark to that sofa and lay there. But just as I was drowsing off to sleep it seemed to me that I could make out a dim outline of a large black mass of some kind stretched on the floor and it made me a little uncomfortable. My first thought was to go and feel of it, but I concluded I would not do that. I sat and watched that thing as it lay in parallelograms and squares of moonlight and I thought I would just wait till that moonlight crept to that thing. It was so slow, that waiting, that finally I got another idea and thought I would turn my face to the wall and I turned over and counted, and counted. I did not get as far as

I intended, but at last I forced myself to count the full hundred and then I turned over and there was a man's hand lying in the square of that moonlight. Why, I never felt so embarrassed in my life. I could not take my eyes away from that object; I watched that moonlight line by line, first revealing an arm, then the white shoulder. By that time it seemed to me that I could stand it no longer; I must pull myself away and I did. Putting my hand on my heart and holding it there a moment, I took one glimpse, only one glimpse, thank God, and there lay that white, white face, snow white face, and the glassy eyes. But something made me think what is the matter with me, as I sat there with my heart beating. I was not scared. I got just that one glimpse and then I went away from there. I did not go in what you might call a hurry, not a great hurry; I went out the window. I took the sash with me; I did not need the sash, but it was handier to take it than to leave it, so I took it.

I shan't have time; the time is too late altogether. I will have to skip that next and come to a matter which illustrates another moral point which I will tell you about presently and that is an episode in the lives of three persons who lived in Missouri a great many years ago. Two boys, Tom Sawyer and Huck Finn, and a very particular old friend of theirs, a middle-aged slave named Jim, and these three were generally disputing about some subject which was rather too large for them. I (Huck Finn) asked him (Tom Sawyer) what was the trouble and he said it was heart-breaking to see the days and the years slip away and him a-getting older and older and no wars breaking out, no way for him to make a name for himself, and he started in to plan out some way to make him celebrated. Pretty soon he struck it and offered to take me and Jim in. We went up in the woods and he told me what, and he said it was a crusade. I asked him what a crusade is, and he said, "Is it possible you don't know what a crusade is?" I told him I didn't and what is more I didn't care. I have lived through to this time without it and I had my health and if you will tell me what it is all right. I'd as soon I didn't know, for I don't care for stacking my head full of information. What is a crusade? I can tell you. Is it a sort of patent right? No, a crusade is war; it is war to rescue the holy land from the heathen cannibals. Which holy land is it? Why there is only one holy land. Do you think there is a million? Well, I said, Tom Sawyer, how did we come to let them get it? We did not come to let them get hold of it. They always had it. If they always had it, it belongs to them. "Why, certainly," he said. "I understand that now. It seems to me that if I had a farm and it was my farm and it belonged to me and another fellow wanted it, would it be right for him to take it? If they own anything at all there is just the mere land: just the land and nothing else. As for the holiness they can take that if they want it." You don't understand it at all. You don't get the hang of it at all. It has nothing to do with farming. It is on a higher plane. It is religious. "What, religious to go and take the land from the people who own it?" Why, of course it is, it has always been considered so.

I shan't attempt to go on with the rest of that program, but I will just close with that which is at the bottom. I have been in bed stretched on my back forty-five days and I am only five days out of that bed and I am, perhaps, not strong enough to stand here and talk. I will just close. It is unbusinesslike to jump at conclusions on too slight evidence and I will close with the case of christening a baby in a Scotch-Irish family. A little clergyman came and when he found that there was a great host of people assembled there he would attempt to exploit his peculiar vanity. He could not resist that temptation. When he took the baby from the father's hands and hefted it, he said: "My friends, he is very little; very little; well, he is a very little fellow, but what of that? I see in your faces disparagement of him because he is little; disparagement for no cause but that he is little. You should reflect that it is from the little things that the great things spring. What is smaller than a grain of granite or sand, and yet it is from grains of granite and sand that this earth is formed. Very little is he. Take the little drop of water and out of little drops of water the great ocean is made. And very little is he and yet he may become like Napoleon, or like Caesar, or like both of them in one. He may conquer empires, he may turn all the world to looking at him. He may be like Hannibal, or like Alexander, or both in one, and become master of the universe. But what is his name? Mary Ann, is it?"

I thank you very cordially for the indulgence with which you have listened to my scheme for revolutionizing the morals of the globe as I go round and I wish to say that I hope to succeed in the work which I have undertaken.

Text / "The Morals Lecture," *Trouble:*321–32. The text is a skillful combination of reports in the Cleveland *Plain Dealer,* July 19, 1895; Calcutta *Englishman,* February 11, 1896; Johannesburg *Standard and Diggers News,* May 29, 1896; and *MTN.* Some of the reporting, as may be noted, is probably inaccurate.

a man in Australia / R. S. Smythe was the Australian manager, but it was Carlyle G. Smythe who accompanied Mark Twain on his travels there. The American part of the tour was managed by Major James B. Pond.

most capable men in the penitentiary / At this point in some performances

Mark Twain digressed to physical ailments, and predicted that medical science would eventually be able to vaccinate an infant against every possible disease. Evidently the implication was to suggest immunization against all forms of immorality.

· 86 ·

The travelers–Mark Twain, Olivia, and daughter Clara–journeyed west by the northern route, pausing for engagements in Duluth, Minneapolis, Butte, Helena, Spokane, Portland, and other towns on the way to Seattle. From there they ferried to Victoria and Vancouver, B.C., then sailed for Australia in late August. Shortly before departure, a Vancouver reporter caught Mark Twain for the interview below.

Interview

Vancouver, B.C., August 19, 1895

[A reporter mentioned the inability of some people to see the point of a joke. Mark Twain took off from there.] When you have a crowded house, some subtle magnetic influence seems to permeate the atmosphere, so that the recognition of the speaker's intention by the audience is unanimous. It often happens that when one is telling a joke to three or four listeners, only one will perceive its meaning, but with a large auditory, it is invariably the large majority. The depressing influence of a small audience is due to several causes. In the first place, the individual members of that audience feel sorry for the lecturer. Mentally they put themselves in his position and sympathize with him—such is the charitable disposition of most people. But should the lecturer become scared and rattled their attitudes change from sympathy to contempt and contempt is fatal. The sympathetic attitude is hard to fight against and the ability to do so comes only with experience.

Personally some of my most enthusiastic audiences have been small ones. Many years ago, I delivered a lecture in St. Louis. The hall was a very large one, with a seating capacity of about a thousand persons I believe, no galleries, but every seat occupying the same level. The night was terribly stormy and there were perhaps eighty people in the hall and with that exception a vast acreage of chair backs confronted me. The feeling of a lecturer at such junctures should not be despondent. Every man's presence should be regarded as an individual compliment. If there are only fifteen people present there are fifteen compliments and it surely is not necessary to multiply a compliment by fifteen in order to appreciate it. I requested everybody to come forward and sit in a solid phalanx. It was like lecturing to the disciples on the edge of the Sahara but I started off, and instead of lecturing for an hour and a half only, I kept it up for more than two hours. Among my auditory, as I afterwards learned, was H. M. Stanley, who took down the lecture in shorthand.

[The subject of hotels came up, particularly changes in lighting systems.] Formerly, when staying at some hotel I would enter my bedroom and find the gas jet turned down, as I thought, and feeling inclined for a read and a smoke I would attempt to turn it up, only to find that the flame was at its maximum. Sometimes I would complain and solicit an amelioration of affairs. Then the hotel people had recourse to a trick, which I soon became aware of and which has never deceived me since. A waiter would put on a pair of overalls and pretend to be an engineer, or a plumber or some such thing. He would tinker with the gas as long as I remained at the hotel, but never improved it as far as I could see. Consequently I found it useful to travel with a wax candle, and when the electric light was introduced into hotels, I was among the first to rejoice.

But commencing at some point, the exact position of which is ambiguous and proceeding westward, the hotels seem to be concerned with the spirit of economy. The electric light is only turned on at a certain hour in the evening and no matter how dark or foggy the day may be—so dark that even those who dwelt in Egyptian darkness would find it impossible to see—unless otherwise provided you cannot obtain artificial light. So even now my wax candle has been of use to me.

Text / Vancouver, B.C., *News Advertiser,* August 20, 1895.

·87·

The story of Jim Blaine and the old ram, one version of which appears in chapter fifty-three of Roughing It, *was a frequent program number on the world tour. Jim is the speaker, moved to tell his story when he is in exactly the right condition: "tranquilly, serenely, symmetrically drunk."*

His Grandfather's Old Ram

Told on the World Tour, 1895–96, and on Other Occasions

Well, as I was a-sayin', he bought that old ram from a feller up in Siskiyou County and fetched him home and turned him loose in the medder, and next morning he went down to have a look at him, and accident'ly dropped a ten-cent piece in the grass and stooped down—so—and was a-fumblin' around in the grass to git it, and the ram he was a-standin' up the slope taking notice; but my grandfather wasn't taking notice, because he had his back to the ram and was int'rested about the dime. Well, there he was, as I was a-sayin', down at the foot of the slope a-bendin' over—so—fumblin' in the grass, and the ram he was up there at the top of the slope, and Smith—Smith was a-standin' there—no, not jest there, a little further away—fifteen foot perhaps—well, my grandfather was a-stoopin' way down—so—and the ram was up there observing, you know, and Smith he . . . (musing) . . . the ram he bent his head down, so . . . Smith of Calaveras . . . no, no it couldn't ben Smith of Calaveras—I remember now that he—b'George it was Smith of Tulare County—course it was, I remember it now perfectly plain.

Well, Smith he just stood there, and my grandfather he stood just here, you know, and he was a-bendin' down just so, fumblin' in the grass, and when the old ram see him in that attitude he took it fur an invitation—and here he come! down the slope thirty mile an hour and his eye full of business. You see my grandfather's back being to him, and him stooping down like that, of course he—why sho! it *warn't* Smith of Tulare at all, it was Smith of Sacramento—my goodness, how did I ever come to get them Smiths mixed like that—why, Smith of Tulare was jest a nobody, but Smith of Sacramento—why the Smiths of Sacramento come of the best Southern blood in the United States; there warn't ever any better blood south of the line than the Sacramento Smiths. Why look here, one of them married a Whitaker! I reckon that gives you an idea of the kind of society the Sacramento Smiths could 'sociate around in; there ain't no better blood than the Whitaker blood; I reckon anybody'll tell you that.

Look at Mariar Whitaker—there was a girl for you! Little? Why yes, she was little, but what of that? Look at the heart of her—had a heart like a bullock—just as good and sweet and lovely and generous as the day is long; if she had a thing and you wanted it, you could have it—have it and welcome; why Mariar Whitaker couldn't have a thing and another person need it and not get it—get it and welcome. She had a glass eye, and she used to lend it to Flora Ann Baxter that hadn't any, to receive company with; well, she was pretty large, and it didn't fit; it was a number 7, and she was excavated for a 14, and so that eye wouldn't lay still; every time she winked it would turn over. It was a beautiful eye and set her off admirable, because it was a lovely pale blue on the front side—the side you look out of—and it was gilded on the back side; didn't match the other eye, which was one of them browny-yellery eyes and tranquil and quiet, you know, the way that kind of eyes are; but that warn't any matter—they worked together all right and plenty picturesque. When Flora Ann winked, that blue and gilt eye would whirl over, and the other one stand still, and as soon as she begun to get excited that handmade eye would give a whirl and then go on a-whirlin' and a-whirlin' faster and faster, and a-flashing first blue and then yaller and then blue and then yaller, and when it got to whizzing and flashing like that, the oldest man in the world couldn't keep up with the expression on that side of her face. Flora Ann Baxter married a Hogadorn. I reckon that lets you understand what kind of blood she was—old Maryland Eastern Shore blood; not a better family in the United States than the Hogadorns.

Sally—that's Sally Hogadorn—Sally married a missionary, and they went off carrying the good news to the cannibals out in one of them way-off islands round the world in the middle of the ocean somers, and they et her; et him too, which was irregular; it warn't the custom to eat the missionary, but only the family, and when they see what they had done they was dreadful sorry about it, and when the relations sent down there to fetch away the things they said so—said so right out—said they was sorry, and 'pologized, and said it shouldn't happen again, said 'twas an accident.

Accident! now that's foolishness; there ain't no such thing as an accident; there ain't nothing happens in the world but what's ordered just so by a wiser Power than us, and it's always fur a good purpose; we don't know what the good purpose was, sometimes—and it was the same with the families that was short a missionary and his wife. But that ain't no matter, and it ain't any of our business; all that concerns us is that it was a special Providence and it had a good intention. No, sir, there ain't no such thing as an accident. Whenever a thing happens that you think is an accident you make up your mind it ain't no accident at all—it's a special Providence.

You look at my Uncle Lem—what do you say to that? That's all I ask you—you just look at my Uncle Lem and talk to me about accidents! It was like this: one day my Uncle Lem and his dog was down town, and he was a-leanin' up against a scaffolding—sick, or drunk, or somethin'—and there was an Irishman with a hod of bricks up the ladder along about the third story, and his foot slipped and down he come, bricks and all, and hit a stranger fair and square and knocked the everlasting aspirations out of him; he was ready for the coroner in two minutes. Now then people said it was an accident.

Accident! there warn't no accident about it; 'twas a special Providence, and had a mysterious, noble intention back of it. The idea was to save that Irishman. If the stranger hadn't been there that Irishman would have been killed. The people said "special Providence—sho! the dog was there—why didn't the Irishman fall on the dog? Why warn't the dog app'inted?" Fer a mighty good reason—the dog would 'a' seen him a-coming; you can't depend on no dog to carry out a special Providence. You couldn't hit a dog with an Irishman because—lemme see, what was that dog's name . . . (musing) . . . oh yes, Jasper—and a mighty good dog too; he wa'n't no common dog, he wa'n't no mongrel; he was a composite. A composite dog is a dog that's made up of all the valuable qualities that's in the dog breed—kind of a syndicate; and a mongrel is made up of the riffraff that's left over. That Jasper was one of the most wonderful dogs you ever see. Uncle Lem got him of the Wheelers. I reckon you've heard of the Wheelers; ain't no better blood south of the line than the Wheelers.

Well, one day Wheeler was a-meditating and dreaming around in the carpet factory and the machinery made a snatch at him and first you know he was a-meandering all over that factory from the garret to the cellar, and everywhere, at such another gait as—why, you couldn't even see him; you could only hear him whiz when he went by. Well, you know a person can't go through an experience like that and arrive back home the way he was when he went. No, Wheeler got wove up into thirty-nine yards of best three-ply carpeting. The widder was sorry, she was uncommon sorry, and loved him and done the best she could fur him in the circumstances, which was unusual. She took the whole piece—thirty-nine yards, and she wanted to give him proper and honorable burial, but she couldn't bear to roll him up; she took and spread him out full length, and said she wouldn't have it any other way. She wanted to buy a tunnel for him but there wasn't any tunnel for sale, so she boxed him in a beautiful box and stood it on the hill on a pedestal twenty-one foot high, and so it was monument and grave together, and economical—sixty foot high—you could see it from everywhere—and she painted on it "To the loving memory of thirty-nine yards best three-ply carpeting containing the mortal remainders of Millington G. Wheeler go thou and do likewise."

Text / Autobiographical dictation of October 10, 1907, *MTE:*217–23.

· 88 ·

On the world tour Mark Twain was often guest of honor at a luncheon, dinner or late supper that generally went on until one or two in the morning. He had been entertained in Minneapolis, twice in Winnipeg, then in Great Falls, Butte, Helena, and Portland, and the wining and dining continued from Vancouver, B.C., to Cape Town, South Africa, Mark Twain speaking on each occasion. Most of these speeches have not survived, but sometimes, as in Melbourne, a reporter managed to acquire a text. At the Yorick Club, an organization of literary and professional men, his reception was so enthusiastic that he spoke at much greater length than usual.

Dinner Speech

Dinner for Mark Twain, Yorick Club,
Melbourne, Australia, October 3, 1895

It is not worth while to try to put into language the delight that you give me when you receive me in this hearty way. Language is for another office. Language is simply to portray the milder emotions of the human heart, but a welcome like this—a welcome that comes out of the heart—deep down—and expressed in a way that one cannot mistake—that is a thing which moves a man all the way through and through. It does seem to me that in order to get such a welcome you've got to come all the way from America to Australia. You Australians seem to deserve the title of "the cordial nation." I have seen so much of your kindness, and have been so moved by it, and so charmed with it, that in thinking things over—I sit and think sometimes, and try to make out the characteristics of this nation and the characteristics of that nation—try to fasten a trademark on them, putting down one as frivolous, another as ox-like and stupid, a third as vivacious, and so on—it seems to me that you should be branded and trademarked as "the cordial nation"—certainly, when you meet me. And that is most pleasant, that is most delightful. Now, I have been to a great many places where there were things to eat, where there was a supper, and where there was a chairman, and the distinctive quality of that chairman was always to make a speech that had nothing in it which you could use as a text afterwards. That was the way with all the chairmen I ever saw—except this one. But he has really so loaded me up with texts that it is an embarrassment of riches. I don't know where to begin. If I used all the texts he has furnished me with there would be nothing left of us when I got through.

There is one fact he brought out happily which stupid people who speak the English language all over this world are prone to overlook or to ignore, and that is—let us chaff and jaw and criticize one another as we please, when all is said and done, the Americans, and the English, and their great outflow in Canada and Australia are all one. You have not stayed at home all your lives, and you know that sentiment which I have felt so many times. I have been around a good deal here and there in the world, and there is one thing that I have always noticed, and which you must have noticed under similar circumstances. Let one of us be far away from his own country—be it Australia, or England, or America, or Canada—and let him see either the English flag or the American flag, and I defy him not to be stirred by it. Oh yes! blood is thicker than water, and we are all related. If we do jaw and bawl at each other now and again, that is no matter at all. We do belong together, and we are parts of a great whole—the greatest whole this world has ever seen—a whole that, some day, will spread over this world, and, I hope, annihilate and abolish all other communities. It will be "the survival of the fittest." The English is the greatest race that ever was, and will prove itself so before it gets done—and I would like to be there to see it. I am getting old. I am getting pretty old—but I don't find it out when I'm around this way. It is when one sits at home, melancholy, perhaps, when nothing is going on. But when I'm around this way with my own kind I don't know that I'm not quite young again—say, fifteen or sixteen—and I feel perfectly comfortable.

My friend on the right and I were talking just now about that very thing. I said I thought that if I had created the human race—oh! I could have done it. I was asked nothing about it, and I didn't suggest anything. But I thought that if I had created the human race, and had discovered that they were a kind of a failure—and had drowned them out—well, I would recognize that that was a good thing. And then, fortified by experience, I would start the thing on a different plan. I would have no more of that 969 years' business. I wouldn't let people grow that old. I would cut them off at thirty. Because a man's youth is the thing he loves to think about, and it is the thing that he regrets. It is the one part of his life that he most thoroughly enjoys. My friend on the right suggests that we should go as far as forty years, as he doesn't want any of his forty years rubbed out. Well, perhaps you really might go up to forty, because then you get a perspective upon youth, and that has its value. That has its charm. But, oh, dear me! I never would have created age. Age has its own value—but that is to other people, not to those who have it.

The chairman, among other things, touched upon my experience as a Mississippi pilot. That is connected with what I am now talking about. That is one of those things that you engage in when you are young and careless—and a man ought always to be young and careless. Then everything that comes is satisfactory. You don't suppose that I should enjoy being a pilot on a Mississippi steamboat now, and be scared to death every time it came a fog. But at that time fogs and dark nights had a charm for me. I didn't own any stock in that steamboat. And that is one of the very advantages of youth. You don't own any stock in anything. You have a good time, and all the grief and trouble is with the other fellows. Youth is a lovely thing, and certainly never was there a diviner time to me in this world. All the rest of my life is one thing—but my life as a pilot on the Mississippi River when I was young—Oh! that was the darling existence. There has been nothing comparable to it in my life since. And, speaking of that, I may tell you a little story.

I had that sort of instinct which anybody would have who had been separated by long years from a life of that kind. He would look back and remember this thing and that thing, and everything that happened to him when he was young; it was all so dear, and so beautiful and so fine—so much finer than anything he had experienced since. Well, I carried out that instinct, and I went out to the Mississippi River about 1880. I had not seen that river for I don't know how long—perhaps for a quarter of a century—and I went there with a sort of longing. One sometimes has a yearning to see again the scenes that were dear to him in his youth, in his prime, in the time when he had the heart to feel, and I thought I would like to see that river and what was left of that steamboat life exactly as I saw it long, long, long ago. And so I went under a fictitious name. I didn't want to be found out. I wanted to be able to go up into the pilot house, and talk to that pilot just as I used to see passengers talk to him, and I wanted to ask him the same idiotic questions. And I wanted to get myself loaded up with the same misinformation just as they used to do. So I went under a fictitious name, and the thing went along very well until, after I had signed my name "John W. Fletcher" on the register of the Southern Hotel in St. Louis, the man behind the counter bowed and said pleasantly—"Show Mr. Clemens to Number 165." Now you can imagine the interest I felt when I really was launched on the steamboat. She was a vile, rusty old steamboat, but she was the only one that was going down the river that day, and I wanted to go. I got on board that boat two hours before she was advertised to sail. I was so anxious to see again that old steamboat life I had been so familiar with. I knew she wouldn't sail at the time she was advertised, but I knew she would go sometime that week. I was loafing about the decks just as happy as a man could be, noticing details in the construction of that boat, which I hadn't seen in any other boat or ship for ever so long.

After a while there came a curious-looking sort of creature slouching up on the hurricane deck. He accosted me and asked where I was from. I said from the state of Connecticut—from the city of Hartford in Connecticut. He said—"You're a good long way from home." I said I recognized that—I felt it. Then he said—"Now I reckon you've no such boat as this there. You never seen a boat like this before?" Well, I intimated that I never had. I wouldn't lie to a man like that. He said—"I was born and raised away in the interior of Wisconsin. I never saw a river or a steamboat till a week ago. Then I came all the way down in a boat like this. If you like, I'll show you round and tell you the names of the different things and what they're for." Well, he seemed kindly disposed, and I went round with him. He showed me this and that, and I soon saw that lots of information had been furnished to him by an expert. He hadn't got a thing right. Some of those people on steamboats can't be depended upon. And they had just loaded him up, giving him false names for things, or, when they gave him the right names, telling him extraordinary uses to which the things were said to be put. So the poor devil didn't know anything about a steamboat at all. Well, he left me, and I didn't see any more of him for some time.

When the boat had sailed I was so impatient that I got up in the morning with the first dawn, to see what I could of that majestic river, which used to be as familiar to me as the joints of my own fingers—a river that I knew foot by foot, detail by detail, night or day, for 1,300 miles. I was impatient to find if that old river was still familiar to me. I did hope that I would recognize some parts of it, but when I came up on that hurricane deck and looked round, I saw that that hope was blighted. I didn't seem to recognize any part of it at all. At length I saw a place on the right-hand side where there were some willows growing that I thought I did recognize, but no, I knew those willows were, so to speak, creatures of a day, and that there must have been hundreds of them since I was there twenty years before. It was a deep disappointment to me. But then I thought—"Never mind, I can cheer up the occasion by getting up into that pilot house, and letting that man load me up with a lot of lies, as they did the historical passenger."

I glanced up three or four times to make sure I had never seen that pilot before. No; he was too young for me to know at all. He must have come into the pilot house after I left the river twenty years before. I crept up in there, and to my joy I was received exactly like the passenger of the old times. The pilot, when he heard the latch of the door, turned round and gave me that sort of indifferent look—a look that was, oh, so indifferent that if you could just get capital enough, and collect enough of it, you wouldn't need any of those refrigerating processes—it would freeze all the sheep in Australia. The old thing exactly. I didn't expect any more notice, and I didn't want any. I sunk down on the bench in the pilot house. There was a little boy about seven years old playing round. I got into conversation with him for a few minutes, and then he went away and we were left alone—I, and that pilot who had no hospitality, no welcome, for me.

And then I began to ask my questions, just as the old-time passenger did. I said, just in the same timid way—"Would you be kind enough to tell me what that thing there is for—that speaking tube?" "Oh," he said, "that speakin' tube; that's to call the chambermaid." Well, I felt so happy. The thing was going beautifully. I asked him another question—about another speaking tube. He said that was to call the boy that scrubbed the deck. "What was that bell for?"—you know, the bell that signals "Go ahead," and so on. That was to call somebody else. Everything was to call somebody. That man could not apparently tell the truth, even by accident. And so I felt perfectly happy. I was getting loaded up just as I wanted, and I would put it in a book. It was jolly good stuff, and I was feeling very comfortable.

All of a sudden he says—"Look here, just hold her a minute, I have to go downstairs and get some coffee." And away he went. Well, instinct made me take the wheel—you mustn't leave a steamer to pilot herself. Then I looked round to see if I could make out where we were; and now I recognized the place at once. I knew it perfectly. It was the only place between St. Louis and a point 200 miles below where there were any dangerous rocks. I recognized it as the very worst place in the whole Mississippi River from Lake Itasca to the ocean—a place called the Grand Chain. Even an apprentice pilot, who had been through it a few times, would never forget it in all his life, because the marks have to be so exactly followed. There is one place where there is a crossing two miles long, and in the very midst of it there are two rocks. Neither of them shows above water, but they make a little break which you can hardly notice. These deadly rocks are only seventy feet apart, and a Mississippi steamboat is twenty-five feet wide, so you must not diverge at all. If you hit one of those rocks you would be in heaven in two minutes. I recognized that I was in the Grand Chain, but didn't know exactly what part of it. I suspected, though, that I was in the part that passes between those two rocks. However, I knew one thing—that that pilot would never have put that wheel into my hands until he had satisfied himself that the boat lay exactly in the right course. He knew that if I had any sense at all I had sense enough to keep between the marks—which I did most diligently. We passed between the rocks, and I saw those breaks, and I didn't do any harm. But I was very glad when he came back. Then he said—"You go and play fictitious names on people and try to get your fun out of them, but I knew your damned drawl the minute you spoke to that boy." Well, of course, we got to be friendly, then. It turned out that just as I was leaving the river he had finished his apprenticeship, but he had struck a pretty bad snag, and he could only get one pilot to sign his application. He was required to have two. He was looking round and he found me, and I signed his papers and saved him—made a pilot of him.

So we had a jolly good time. I was always on his watch—and the other fellow's watch too. I stood all the watches there were. All the day long, no matter which pilot's turn it was, I took the wheel. I couldn't get enough of it. The river was bank full, and from where the Ohio comes in all the way down to New Orleans there was nothing to do but to keep round in this bend and cross into that bend. You could never make any mistake. A jackass could pilot a steamboat in that part of the river if he had just wit enough to follow the shape of the river. So the pilots would leave me there the whole watch, and there in that sunny country I would stand at the wheel, and pilot along down, and ponder, and think, and dream, and dream over all that old vanished time on the river. It was delightful—full of pathos, full of poetry, full of the charm of unconsciousness of anything else in the world but that old past. I heard the latch of the pilot house door raised, but I didn't hear anybody come in. I turned round, and who should be standing there but that Wisconsin hayseed fellow I hadn't seen since he showed me the things on the steamboat at St. Louis. He stood there sort o' petrified, gazing at me, and he said—well, I won't repeat what he said. It was profane, but it was eloquent.

But I mustn't stand here and talk all night of old reminiscences. I was going through all the texts of the chairman, but now I come to think of it—I had forgotten it for the minute—I am entertaining a carbuncle unawares. I have got it on my port hind leg, and it reminds me of its company occasionally. I have greater respect for it than for any other possession I have in the world. I take more care of it than I do of the family. But before I sit down I just want to thank you once again for your kind and cordial reception of me tonight, and to assure you that I do most sincerely appreciate it and value it.

Text / "Mark Twain at the Yorick," Melbourne *Australasian,* October 5, 1895.

· 89 ·

Australian journalists entertained Mark Twain with a lively program of talks, solos vocal and instrumental, lightning sketches, and musical novelties. He was so much pleased with the evening that he made five speeches, four of which were reported.

Four Speeches

Smoke Night, Australian Institute of Journalists, Cathedral Hotel, Melbourne, Australia, October 27, 1895

Mr. Chairman and gentlemen: I thank you very heartily and very sincerely for this testimony of good feeling and comradeship towards me, and also for the additional compliment you have paid me in coupling my wife's name to all you have said. I am glad to perceive at last, after waiting all these many many weary years, which I supposed had been wasted, that in one instance at least my labor has not been in vain. I recognize that in lifting Mr. Dow out of the sheep run I have conferred a benefit upon the human race—and also upon the sheep. It is one more testimony to me that when we sow the seed of our works round the world we never know whether we are sowing upon fruitful ground or scattering the seed upon the rocky land where it will not spring up and bear fruit. Now it was the last thing that I ever thought of, that my experiences as an agricultural newspaper editor were conferring a benefit upon anyone. Why, you see for yourselves the hopelessness of the case. It was the one case perhaps in which I never had hope of any kind, but it is out of my defeat that springs Mr. Dow's success. I performed the functions of that office well and picturesquely—but they were not appreciated—no more than his are by the farmer of today. I was discharged, and all because of my writing about ornamental oyster beds. Just a little thing like that: "ornamental oyster beds" under the heading of "Landscape Gardening." I have no doubt that is a lesser crime than one million he has committed, but it cost me my position.

Now I am very very glad to be here tonight. This is a world of surprises; it is indeed. The longer one lives the more he finds it so. Now I have always contended that shams ought to be banished out of this world. In my small way I have made war upon shams, and yet here I am confronted [pointing to Mr. Dow] with one. I doubt not but that he is a hundred times more valuable than he would be if he were the real article. Now, if there is one thing in this world that I detest more than another it is the peal of a public bell—a bell that rings and chimes and counts the hours for you at night when you want to sleep and when you don't care and don't want to know anything about the hours. But that isn't sufficient. There is a jangle, jangle, jangle that they call chimes. Now, here I come and there at the end of the room is a sham chime. I could sit and listen to that for a week. Now that is a sham, but it is infinitely superior to my ears to the original. And why is that so? I recognize why it is. It is because it is such an absolutely exact imitation of the real thing. When you see a magnificent sunset, or a superb landscape, or the sea in the highest poetry of its motion, you feel in your soul that the very highest compliment you can pay it is to say that it so exactly resembles a scene in a theater. There it is. The scene portrayed in the theater is a sham, not the reality; but you compliment the reality by saying that it is a good imitation of the imitation. And so I shall always remember those chimes, and shall bless them so long as I shall curse the original.

Then there is that music played on the lead pencil. I have been present many a time when an interviewer has played upon a lead pencil—but when I listened to that music from a lead pencil just now I recognized there a superiority of sweetness that I never detected before in a lead pencil at all. I am glad I came here tonight; I would not have missed it for anything. You play a kind of music I understand and like; it is homelike. It suits this uneducated ear of mine. I think that when you delight in the common tunes of a country that that is the highest form of musical education. Possibly it is so; let it be so in my case. The music that we have had here tonight suits me exactly, and I thank the performers, as I thank you, gentlemen, for this very hospitable reception you have given me.

[Alfred L. Deakin, M.L.A., presented a basket of flowers from his own garden as a gift to Mrs. Clemens and Clara.]

I think this is a peculiarly gratifying occurrence, to join my family with me in the hospitalities which you extend to us. We have come a long distance, which at first it was my purpose to traverse alone. But I always have many purposes which fail, for reasons which those who are married among you will understand. I am technically "boss" of the family which I am carrying along but I am grateful to know that it is only technically—that the real authority rests on the other side of the house. It is placed there by a beneficent Providence, who foresaw before I was born, or, if he did not, he has found it out since, that I am not in any way qualified to travel alone. And so it has been my good fortune to be furnished with a wife who is always capable, both by brain and by heart, to make up all shortcomings which exist in me. She has brought me through for twenty-five years successfully, and while I do attribute that to an overruling Providence, my experience with Providence has not been of a nature to give me great confidence in his judgment, and I consider that my wife crept in while his attention was occupied elsewhere. I have a wife and daughter thoroughly well equipped to appreciate these beautiful flowers, and I accept them in their name with very, very sincere thanks.

[By acclamation, the assembly elected Mark Twain an honorary member of the Australian Institute of Journalists.]

I thank you cordially, gentlemen, for the honor you have just done me. I have been a journalist a great many years, and still consider myself a journalist, since I contribute to journalism in America, at least, and it is particularly gratifying to me to be received in this way, and to have this honor conferred upon me. It is not a matter of whether I deserve it or not, and I know that perfectly well; the honor as conferred is out of the heart, and from the heart one receives it. I am very, very glad to receive it indeed. I had already considered before this that this was a peculiarly pleasant evening—a darling evening of my life. I am now on the verge of sixty years; in the month of November, so close at hand, I shall be sixty years of age. I have detested old age from my infancy, and anything that removes from me even for a few moments the consciousness that I am old is gratifying to me. For the two or three hours that I have been here tonight—since nine o'clock struck and I entered this room—I have gone back thirty years, and have rejuvenated. I have been young again; I have renewed my youth, and have felt exactly as I felt thirty years ago, when the boys were having a good time. I have forgotten my grey hairs, and since nine o'clock they have been a sham. I have been utterly happy tonight. And why should I not have been happy? I have eternal Winter [pointing to the chairman] on my right hand, and I have youth and everlasting summer distributed about me. I have been happy before this; but now you have made my happiness perfect.

[After several musical numbers, Mark Twain spoke again.]

May I have the privilege of proposing a toast? I desire to propose the health of the chairman. I do not know the particulars of the chairman's history at all, but on an occasion of this kind it would not be gracious, it would not be pleasant, it would not be in good taste to expose that. Let us overlook his past. Let us consider that whatever he has been before this evening that has all gone by, and from this time out he is a reformed man. So now let us drink his health—not as the health of the man we had known heretofore, but as the man who is going to rise infinitely superior to anything he has been before, and whose character will now shine from this time out with a refulgent light. I don't know what "refulgent light" is, but it is a good expression, and good words make eloquence, whether they mean anything or not. Let us drink with enthusiasm to this "reformed case."

[Mr. Zox, M.L.A., proposed the health of Miss Clara Clemens. Whereupon Mark Twain made his fifth speech of the evening, but it was not reported.]

Text / "Mark Twain Entertained by the Institute of Journalists," Melbourne *Age,* October 28, 1895.

Dow / J. L. Dow, who proposed the toast to "Our Guest," said that he had been a sheep rancher, but had become an agricultural editor after reading Mark Twain's sketch, "How I Edited an Agricultural Paper."

eternal Winter / The chairman was S. V. Winter.

· 90 ·

The Savage Club of Christchurch, New Zealand, assembled a distinguished gathering to honor Mark Twain at a late supper. The menu had a Twainian flavor: Mayonnaise à Mons. Thomas Sawyer, Grenouille sautante a la Smiley, Poudin a la tete de Wilson, Gelee au vin Huckleberry, and other appropriate dishes.

Supper Speech

Savage Club Supper for Mark Twain, Provincial Council Chamber, Christchurch, New Zealand, November 15, 1895

Mr. Chairman and Savages, as you call yourselves, for some reason best known to yourselves, for certainly I should not have taken you for such. I have mixed a good deal with the lower order of savages, and I have seen them in all costumes and in no costumes at all—in all costumes except this one that you wear this evening. With my experience of savages, I know that however picturesque they may be in their dress, and sometimes they are very picturesque, the costume which I see before me is the best one suited to educated and cultured savages. I am glad to meet this kind of savages.

I have been received in such a pleasant way ever since I have been in New Zealand and Australia—and this is another case of the kind—that I should like to return general thanks to all the friends who have given me these pleasant receptions; and I must return special thanks to you, gentlemen, for this great honor in making me an honorary member, and, as you say, the first honorary member of your club. It makes me feel as large as your great moa—and if I go on dissipating like this I shall be as extinct as your great moa.

Have you ever considered how difficult the position of the guest of the evening on an occasion such as this is? For there is only one speech made before he must get on his feet, and that does not generally afford him a very fruitful text to talk upon, for it consists of compliments to him, and if you listened point blank to compliments fired at you at short range, and have had to talk on a text like that, you must know how weak your position is; you must have recognized that however great and fine those compliments are, you do deserve them. If there is a lack anywhere, it is that they fall a little short of your deserts. But even if, for that reason, the text they afford you is not a good one you perceive that it would not be in good taste for you to get up and correct the gentlemen who is speaking. There is that spirit of inborn modesty in an American which forbids him to do a thing of that kind. I think that the prodigal son when he returned was received just like this, and all that was said then must have been compliments, and he could not properly respond to them because he knew they were only compliments.

However, I have not been like him. I have been setting an example to all peoples as I have been going along. I have been doing good. You haven't mentioned any of these things, so I am without a text. The guest of the evening ought always to sit still until all the other people had had their say, and from listening to them he could get a text, and find out how things stand, and be able to talk back. It is much easier to talk back to abuse than to compliments.

We have had a good time these last few days, and I have felt what a good time Christchurch must have been having too. You have never had such opportunities for enlightenment before. You have had the circus. That was spectacular. You have had Mr. Haskett Smith—imagination—and you have had my well beloved friend and shipmate, Michael Davitt—philosophy; and you have had me—cold fact. We are all fading away one by one. Haskett Smith has gone. Michael Davitt has gone. I leave tomorrow, and you have nothing left but the circus. Be grateful for the opportunities you have—hang on to that circus.

I observe in this region a spirit which I do greatly approve. That is the spirit which is leading us gradually and surely along to prohibition. I do not see any signs of it here. It is coming, and let us welcome it. I can tell you one thing, that is if you get it you will find it will put you into most difficult straits. In our country several years ago there was a man came into a prohibition town, a man like you Savages here, and they said to him, "You can't get a drink anywhere except at the apothecary's." So he went to the apothecary, who said, "You can't get a drink here without a prescription from a physician," but the man said, "I'm perishing. I haven't had time to get a prescription." The apothecary replied, "Well, I haven't power to give you a drink except for snake bite." The man said, "Where's the snake?" So the apothecary gave him the snake's address, and he went off. Soon after, however, he came back and said, "For goodness' sake, give me a drink. That snake is engaged for months ahead."

Now I thank you again, particularly for the honorable distinction of membership. I thought it might be that I was a member before, by having membership in the Lotos Club of New York, which is affiliated to the Savage Club of London, but I find that it is not so. However, I am proud to belong to this gang of Savages. I hope to learn that warwhoop of yours; and as I am one of those early birds, and not given to talking except when I do all the talking myself, I will thank you all again and resume my seat.

Text / Unidentified clipping, Scrapbook No. 9, MTP.

Haskett Smith / (1847–1906). British clergyman. He was second master, Lincoln Grammar School (1870–75), and Rector, Brauncewell-cum-Anwick, Lincolnshire (1875–99). Having traveled in eastern countries, he lectured on Egypt, Palestine, and the Orient.

Michael Davitt / (1846–1906). Irish political leader. Sentenced to fifteen years (1870) for sending arms to Ireland, paroled (1877), he lectured in the United States, then founded the Land League (1879) based on principles of Henry George. Elected to Parliament (1892, 1893) but disqualified, Davitt was allowed to take his seat in 1895. He joined William O'Brien to organize the Irish Land League (1898), and resigned from Parliament (1898) as a protest against the Boer War.

prohibition / At Dunedin, New Zealand, a dry town, Mark Twain was pleased to find excellent Scotch whiskey.

that warwhoop / After drinking a toast to the guest of honor, the Savages three times gave the chief's salute in the Maori language: "Ake, ake, ake, kia kaha!"

· 91 ·

A commemoration luncheon celebrated the proclamation of the Province of South Australia on December 28, 1836. Mark Twain spoke for the visitors present. Having apparently recovered from the distemper caused by Matthew Arnold and other British critics, he elaborated upon the theme of international amity.

Speech

Commemoration Luncheon, Glenelg, Australia, December 30, 1895

Necessarily I deplore with Sir Richard Baker any thought or suggestion of war between America and England—for certainly never in the history of mankind would any war or was any war so disastrous as this suggested war would be. We know Lord Macaulay said the effects of the Thirty Years' War were felt in the valley of the Mississippi two hundred years after the event, but the effects of this war may extend over five centuries. It would certainly stand in the way of the progress and intelligence of the whole world for generations. Therefore you will listen to no talk of war between these countries. Blood is thicker than water, and there must be no bloodshed between England and America.

I recognize in the remarks made by the Commissioner of Public Works that feeling, which was also suggested in the speech of His Worship, that feeling of sentiment which exists between England and America, and which is not called into force except under stress like this—this talk of war. I remember reading of some distinguished American traveling through France being suddenly wakened up by a name—the name of that great battle fought by Henry V upon the soil of France—and this American said he felt exalted. He thought, why should that be? Why should it make my heart bound to think that eight thousand Englishmen under Henry V had slaughtered sixty thousand Frenchmen under the French king and the chivalry of France? So he had to stop and reflect of what source the feeling was, and he recognized that it was the English blood flowing in his veins which was answering after five hundred years to his English ancestors. So blood is thicker than water.

I am glad to say I know there is another American present. I did not suspect it until I heard him lift up his voice, and when he lifted it up I knew by certain signs that there was another American here. Those signs are patented. Those signs are these—that his voice was for peace between England and America. Another sign was that in all he said there was no suggestion of anything but cast iron veracity. In all he said there was truth, and by that truth I knew he was an American. There was another sign that there was another American present. I noticed he made more noise than the other seven speakers.

Now, by the voice of the visitors whom I represent, I thank your Worship for the hospitality which you have extended to us. I have the privilege to congratulate you upon certain things—your supreme climate. When it was mentioned by these gentlemen here you did not respond with enthusiasm, but perhaps to you your climate is commonplace, but it is not commonplace to other people at all. I am not used to a climate like this. In these specimens it is altogether perfect, when in midwinter you have summer, and where you have neither mosquitoes nor snow. It is real pleasant to those travelers who are come from the overworked regions of the earth.

What satisfaction it is to find ourselves in this restful South Australia, and where apparently it is always a holiday—and where, when you have no holiday and nothing else to do, it is always a horse race. It has become a blessed land, it seems to me. And then you have a spirit of independence here which cannot be overpraised. You place your holidays, not in accordance with the day, but to suit your own comfort and convenience. I passed through Australia when you were celebrating the Prince of Wales' birthday upon the 8th, upon the 10th, or upon the 11th—skipped the 9th altogether. I suppose there was a horse race.

I consider it a privilege to be present upon this day. No doubt it is your greatest day. There can be no worthier day to celebrate than the day that saw the foundation of this community to join the march of civilization, learning, and liberty. I saw the old gumtree as I came along, and as I approached it it seemed bent down with age, discouragement, and despair, but later I saw it formed a perfect arch, the symbol of strength and perpetuity. May this colony last forever and be always prosperous. It seemed to me that in my responding for the visitors there is a sort of incongruity about it, an infelicity. It seemed impossible for me to stand here in this formal attitude as if a visitor, when I have been in these colonies three and half months, and when from the beginning half of the people seem to recognize me as a member of their family.

[After the luncheon, a select group repaired to a reception in the Mayor's Parlor, where the Premier of the Province proposed the health of Mark Twain. He responded with a humorous speech, which was not reported.]

Text / Adelaide *South Australian Register,* December 31, 1895.

Baker / Richard Chaffey Baker (1842–1911). Australian parliamentarian. He was a member of Parliament from South Australia (1868), attorney general (1870), minister of justice and education (1884), president of the legislative council of South Australia (1893–1901), and president of the first Federal Senate of the Commonwealth (1901–06).

war between America and England / War talk evolved from a dispute over the boundary between Venezuela and British Guiana. On December 18, 1895, President Cleveland, invoking the Monroe Doctrine, sent Congress a message implying that any attempt by the British government to enforce its boundary claim without arbitration would be construed as an act of war by the United States. For a time, on both sides of the Atlantic, the air was clamorous with the brag and bluster of vociferous patriots, Theodore Roosevelt being as pugnacious as any in his eagerness to provoke armed conflict. The crisis passed, however, and the boundary question was arbitrated in 1899.

that great battle fought by Henry V / The Battle of Agincourt (1415) in northern France, where a small body of English bowmen, half-starved and down-at-heel, according to Shakespeare, routed the flower of French chivalry.

· 92 ·

Mark Twain revised a number of short narratives and episodes from his books to make them more congenial to his style of platform delivery: Buck Fanshaw's funeral from Roughing It, *the Grangerford-Shepherdson feud from* Huckleberry Finn, *Baker and the blue jays from* A Tramp Abroad, *"The McWilliamses and the Burglar Alarm," and many others. He tested them by audience response and by his own feelings because he had to enjoy telling a story as much as people enjoyed listening to it. "Punch, Brothers, Punch," below, was a frequent number on his varied programs.*

Punch, Brothers, Punch

Read on World Tour Programs, 1895–96, and on Other Occasions

When the conductor receives a fare, he will punch in the presence of the passenger.

You bought a blue slip or trip slip for the longest distance, eight cents; a buff trip slip, shorter distance, six cents; pink, shortest distance, three cents. These facts were displayed in large print, line after line like a frieze around under the ceiling of the car. It struck some newspaperman that they would make poetry if bunched together. So he bunched them together—and then they read—

Conductor, when you receive a fare,
Punch in the presence of the passenjare
A blue trip slip for an eight-cent fare,
A buff trip slip for a six-cent fare,
A pink trip slip for a three-cent fare,
Punch in the presence of the passenjare!

Chorus

Punch, brothers! punch with care!
Punch in the presence of the passenjare!

I came across these jingling rhymes in the newspaper, and read them a couple of times. They took instant and entire possession of me. All through breakfast they went waltzing through my brain; and when, at last, I was finished, I could not tell whether I had eaten anything or not. I went to my desk and took up my pen, but it was no use. My head kept humming, "A blue trip slip for an eight-cent fare, a buff trip slip for a six-cent fare," a pink etc.—punch in the presence. I suffered all the afternoon; suffered all through an unconscious and unrefreshing dinner; suffered, and cried, and jingled all through the evening; went to bed and rolled, tossed, and jingled right along, the same as ever; got up at midnight frantic, and tried to read; but there was nothing visible upon the whirling page except "Punch! punch in the presence of the passenjare."

Two days later, on Saturday morning, I arose, a tottering wreck, and went forth to fulfill an engagement with a valued friend, the Rev. Mr. ———, to walk to the Talcott Tower, ten miles distant. He stared at me, but asked no questions. We started. Mr. ——— talked, talked, talked—as is his wont. I said nothing; I heard nothing—busy with my jingles. At the ten-mile post, all of a sudden Mr. ——— laid his hand on my shoulder and shouted—

"Oh, wake up! wake up! wake up! Don't sleep all day! Here we are at the Tower, man! I have talked myself deaf and dumb and blind, and never got a response. Just look at this magnificent autumn landscape! Look at it! look at it! Feast your eyes on it! You have traveled; you have seen boasted landscapes elsewhere. Come, now, deliver an honest opinion. What do you say to this?"

I sighed wearily, and murmured—

"A buff trip slip for a six-cent fare, a pink trip slip for a three-cent fare, punch in the presence of the passenjare."

Rev. Mr. ——— stood there, very grave, full of concern, apparently, and looked long at me; then he said—

"Mark, there is something about this that I cannot understand. Those are about the same words you said before; there does not seem to be anything in them, and yet they nearly break my heart when you say them. Punch in the—how is it they go?"

I began at the beginning and repeated all the lines. My friend's face lighted with interest. He said—

"Why, what a captivating jingle it is! It is almost music. It flows along so nicely. I have nearly caught the rhymes myself. Say them over just once more, and then I'll have them, sure."

I said them over. Then Mr. ——— said them. He made one little mistake, which I corrected. The next time and the next he got them right. Now a great burden seemed to tumble from my shoulders. That torturing jingle departed out of my brain, and a grateful sense of rest and peace descended upon me. Then my freed tongue found blessed speech again, and the pent talk of many a weary hour began to gush and flow. It flowed on and on, joyously, jubilantly, until the fountain was empty and dry. As I wrung my friend's hand at parting, I said—

"Haven't we had a royal good time! But now I remember, you haven't said a word for two hours. Come, come, out with something!"

The Rev. Mr. ——— turned a lackluster eye upon me, drew a deep sigh, and said, without animation, without apparent consciousness—

"Punch, brothers, punch with care! Punch in the presence of the passenjare!"

A pang shot through me as I said to myself, "O, poor fellow, *he* has got it now."

I did not see Mr. ——— for two or three days after that. Then, on Tuesday evening, he staggered into my presence and slumped down all in a pile in a chair. He was pale, worn; he was a wreck. He lifted his faded eyes to my face and said—

"Ah, Mark, it was a ruinous investment that I made in those heartless rhymes. They have ridden me like a nightmare, day and night, hour after hour, to this very moment. Since I saw you I have suffered the torments of the lost. Saturday evening I had a sudden call, by telegraph, and took the night train for Boston. The occasion was the death of a valued old friend who had requested that I should preach his funeral sermon. I took my seat in the cars and set myself to framing the discourse. But I never got beyond the opening paragraph; for then the train started and the car wheels began their 'clack, clack—clack-clack-clack!' and right away those odious rhymes fitted themselves to the accompaniment. 'Clack-clack-clack, a blue trip slip, clack-clack-clack, for an eight-cent fare; clack-clack-clack, a buff trip slip, clack-clack-clack, for a six-cent fare, and so on, and so on, and so on—*punch,* in the presence of the passenjare!' Sleep? Not a single wink! I was almost a lunatic when I got to Boston. Don't ask me about the funeral. I did the best I could, but every solemn individual sentence was meshed and tangled and woven in and out with 'Punch, brothers, punch with care, punch in the presence of the passenjare.' And the most distressing thing was that my *delivery* dropped into the undulating rhythm of those pulsing rhymes, and I could actually catch absent-minded people nodding *time* to the swing of it with their stupid heads. And, Mark, before I got through, the entire assemblage were placidly bobbing their heads in solemn unison, mourners, undertaker, and all. Before I had finished, I was in a state bordering on frenzy.

And oh, oh, oh, my closing remark—He is gone from us, my friends and brethren we shall never see him more; haloed he sits with the happy choirs singing—singing—Punch, brothers, punch with care—punch in the presence of the passenjare."

Text / "Punch, Brothers, Punch," as revised by Mark Twain, *The Stolen White Elephant* (1882):129–36, MTP.

Conductor, when you receive a fare, etc. / The original jingle, inspired by a notice in a car of the Fourth Avenue line, New York, was written by Isaac H. Bromley and W. C. Wyckoff of the NY*Trib*, and Noah Brooks of the *Times*. It was published in the NY*Trib*, September 27, 1875. An anonymous composer set it to music. See Winkleried Wolfgang Brown, "The Horse-Car Poetry," *Scribner's Monthly* 11, no. 6 (April 1876):910–12. Mark Twain revised the original jingle slightly.

the Rev. Mr. ——— / Joseph Hopkins Twichell (1838–1918). American clergyman. Civil War chaplain of the Seventy-first New York Volunteers, he was afterward pastor of the Asylum Hill Congregational Church, Hartford (1865–1912). He was an intimate friend of Mark Twain. Although Twichell was a more fluent talker than writer, he published *John Winthrop* (1891), and "Mark Twain," *Harper's Magazine* 92, no. 552 (May 1896):817–27.

· 93 ·

Mark Twain was continually dogged by reporters. Talking to newsmen must have become tiresome, yet, accepting the chore as one of the hazards of fame, he did not avoid them or gruffly turn them away. At times, when exhausted or plagued by illness, he talked aimlessly, as if merely giving the interviewer enough words to fill his column, or told a sort of concocted yarn about himself. Generally, however, as in the Bombay interview below, he had something informative to say.

Interview

Bombay, India, ca. January 22, 1896

[The interviewer asked: "I presume you prepare carefully for your lectures?"]

Yes, I am not for one moment going to pretend I do not. I don't believe that any public man has ever attained success as a lecturer to paid audiences (mark the qualification), who has not carefully prepared, and has not gone over every sentence again and again until the whole thing is fixed upon his memory. I write my lectures, and try to memorize them, but I don't always succeed. If I had a better memory it would be worse in some respects, for when one has to fill up an ellipsis on the spot, there is a spontaneity about the thing which is a considerable relief. I ought really to write the whole thing beforehand, but I don't do it, as I prefer to use material which has appeared in my books. The extracts, however, are seldom exactly the same as they are printed, but are adapted to circumstances. No, I don't localize, because to do that you want to be well posted up, and know exactly what you are about. You must be exactly prepared beforehand. I never pretend that I don't indent on my books for my lectures, for there is no object in doing that. It is all very well to talk about not being prepared and trusting to the spirit of the hour. But a man cannot go from one end of the world to the other, no matter how great his reputation may be, and stand before paid houses in various large cities without finding that his tongue is far less glib than it used to be. He might hold audiences spellbound with unpremeditated oratory in past days when nothing was charged to hear him, but he cannot rely on being able to do so when they have paid for their seats and require something for the money unless he thinks all out beforehand.

You ask me whether my memory has deserted me on the platform sometimes? Yes, it has sometimes entirely. And the worst of it is that, as I prefer to select things from my books, my remarks are often in the narrative form, and if you lose yourself in the narrative it is not very comfortable, because a tale should have an end somewhere. Still I have generally managed to get out of the difficulty in some way or other. It is really very curious to see what a man can do on the platform without the audience suspecting anything to be wrong. A case in point occurred in Paris a year ago. I began some opening remarks at one of my "At Homes" there with an anecdote, as for some reason or another I wanted to fill up the time. I began telling the anecdote, but I found when halfway that my memory regarding it had gone. So I switched on to another line, and was soon leaving the half-told anecdote far behind. My wife and daughter were present, and I afterwards asked them whether they remembered the breakdown. They replied in the negative. I then asked whether they heard the finish of the anecdote with which I had begun my remarks, and they at once replied they had not. As you say, if anyone would be likely to discover a flaw, it would be my wife or my daughter, and when I found that they were unaware of the defect, I was quite satisfied that the audience in general knew nothing about it.

Text / Bombay *Gazette,* January 23, 1896.

· 94 ·

Sailing for Southampton at the end of his globe-circling tour, Mark Twain considered additional platform appearances in England and perhaps one or two seasons in the United States. But tentative plans were cancelled by the death of his daughter, Susy, in August 1896. For a year the Clemens family remained in seclusion in England while he doggedly worked on his travel book, Following the Equator. *Then they were on the continent, in Switzerland and Vienna, where Mark Twain again became an occasional public speaker. He tried out his German on the Concordia, a socialistic club of authors and journalists, who invited him to a* Festkneipe. *A jamboree in a beer hall, it was a noisy affair of boisterous camaraderie, drinking songs, and the banging of steins. Mark Twain's speech in German, both in form and substance, was in keeping with the informal spirit of the occasion.*

Die Schrecken Der Deutschen Sprache

Concordia Festkneipe, Vienna, October 31, 1897

Es hat mich tief gerührt, meine Herren, hier so gastfreundlich empfangen zu werden, von Kollegen aus meinem eigenen Berufe, in diesem von meiner eigenen Heimath so weit entferntem Lande. Mein Herz ist voller Dankbarkeit, aber meine Armuth an deutschen Worten zwingt mich zu groszer Sparzamkeit des Ausdruckes. Entschuldigen Sie, meine Herren, dasz ich verlese, was ich Ihnen sagen will. (Er las aber nicht, Anm. d. Ref.) Die deutsche Sprache spreche ich nicht gut, doch haben mehrere Sächverständige mich versichert, dasz ich sie schreibe wie ein Engel. Mag sein—ich weisz nicht. Habe bis jetzt keine Bekanntschaften mit Engeln gehabt. Das kommt später—wenn's dem lieben Gott gefällt—es hat keine Eile.

Seit lange, meine Herren, habe ich die leidenschaftliche Sehnsucht gehegt, eine Rede auf Deutsch zu halten, aber man hat mir's nie erlauben wollen. Leute, die kein Gefühl für die Kunst hatten, legten mir immer Hindernisse in den Weg und vereitelten meinen Wunsch—zuweilen durch Vorwände, häufig durch Gewalt. Immer sagten diese Leute zu mir: "Schweigen Sie, Ew. Hochwohlgeboren! Ruhe, um Gotteswillen! Suche andere Art und Weise, Dich lästig zu machen."

Im jetzigen Fall, wie gewöhnlich, ist es mir schwierig geworden, mir die Erlaubnisz zu verschaffen. Das Comite bedauerte sehr, aber es konnte mir die Erlaubnisz nich bewilligen wegen eines Gesetzes, das von der Concordia verlangt, sie soll die deutsche Sprache schützen Du liebe Zeit! Wieso hätte man mir das sagen können—mögen—dürfen—sollen? Ich bin ja der treueste Freund der deutschen Sprache—und nicht nur jetzt, sondern von lange her—ja vor swanzig Jahren schon. Und nie habe ich das Verlangen gehabt, der edlen Sprache zu schaden, im Gegentheil, nur gewünscht, sie zu verbessern; ich wollte sie blos reformiren. Es ist der Traum meines Lebens gewesen. Ich habe schon Besuche bei den verschiedenen deutschen Regierungen abgestattet und um Kontrakte gebeten. Ich bin jetzt nach Oesterreich in demselben Auftrag gekommen. Ich wurde nur einige Aenderungen anstreben. Ich wurde blos die Sprachtmethode—die uppige, weitschweifige Konstruktion—zusammenrucken; die ewige Parenthese unterdrücken, abschaffen, vernichten; die Einführung von mehr als dreizehn Subjekten in einen Satz verbieten; das Zeitwort so weit nach vorne rücken, bis man es ohne Fernrohr entdecken kann. Mit einem Wort, meine Herren, ich möchte Ihre geliebte Sprache vereinfachen, auf dasz, meine Herren, wenn Sie sie zum Gebet brauchen, man sie dort oben versteht.

Ich flehe Sie an, von mir sich berathen zu lassen, führen Sie diese erwähnten Reformen aus. Dann werden Sie eine prachtvolle Sprache besitzen und nachher, wenn Sie Etwas sagen wollen, werden Sie wenigstens selber verstehen, was Sie gesagt haben. Aber öfters heutzutage, wenn Sie einen meilenlangen Satz von sich gegeben und Sie etwas angelehnt haben, um auszuruhen, dann müssen Sie eine rührende Neugierde empfinden, selbst herauszubringen, was Sie eigentlich gesprochen haben. Vor mehreren Tagen hat der Korrespondent einer hiesigen Zeitung einen Satz zustande gebracht welcher hundertundzwölf Worte enthielt und darin waren sieben Parenthese eingeschachtelt und es wurde Das Subjekt siebenmal gewechselt. Denken Sie nur, meine Herren, im Laufe der Reise eines einzigen Satzes musz das arme, verfolgte, ermüdete Subjekt siebenmal umsteigen.

Nun, wenn wir die erwähnten Reformen ausführen, wird's nicht mehre so arg sein. Doch noch eins. Ich möchte gern das trennbare Zeitwort auch ein Bischen reformiren. Ich mochte Niemand thun lassen, was Schiller gethan: Der hat die ganze Geschichte des dreizigjährigen Krieges zwischen die zwei Glieder eines trennbaren Zeitwortes eingezwängt. Das hat sogar Deutschland selbst empört; und man hat Schiller die Erlaubnisz verweigert, die Geschichte des hundert jährigen Krieges zu verfassen—Gott sei's gedankt. Nachdem alle diese Reformen festgestellt sein werden, wird die deutsche Sprache die edelste und die schönste auf der Welt sein.

Da Ihnen jetzt, meine Herren, der Charackter meiner Mission bekannt ist, bitte ich Sie, so freundlich zu sein und mir Ihre werthvolle Hilfe zu schenken. Herr Pötzl hat das Publikum glauben machen wollen, dasz ich nach Wien gekommen bin, um die Brüken zu verstopfen und den Verkehr zu hindern, während ich Beobachtungen sammle und aufzeichne. Lassen Sie sich aber nicht von ihm anführen. Meine häufige Anwesenheit auf den Brücken hat einen ganz unschuldigen Grund. Dort giebt's den nöthigen Raum. Dort kann man einen edlen, langen, deutschen Satz ausdehnen, die Brückengeländer entlang, und seinen ganzen Inhalt mit einem Blick übersehen. Auf das eine Ende des Geländers klebe ich das erste Glied eines trennbaren Zeitwortes und das Schluszglied klebe ich an's andere Ende—dann breite ich den Leib des Satzes dazwischen aus. Gewöhnlich sind für meinen Zweck die Brücken der Stadt lang genug: wehn ich aber Pötzl's Schriften studiren will, fahre ich hinaus und benutze die herrliche unendliche Reichsbrücke. Aber das ist eine Verleumdung. Pötzl schreibt das schönste Deutsch. Vielleicht nicht so biegsam wie das meinige, aber in manchen Kleinigkeiten viel besser. Entschuldigen Sie diese Schmeicheleien. Die sind wohl verdient. Nun bringe ich meine Rede um—nein—ich wollte sagen, ich bringe sie zum Schlusz. Ich bin ein Fremder—aber hier, unter Ihnen, habe ich es ganz vergessen. Und so wieder, und noch wieder—biete ich Ihnen meinen herzlichsten Dank!

Text / "Die Schrecken Der Deutschen Sprache," *MTS*(10):42–50.

THE HORRORS OF THE GERMAN LANGUAGE

Mark Twain's Literal Translation of the Concordia Speech

It has me deeply touched, my gentlemen, here so hospitably received to be. From colleagues out of my own profession, in this from my own home so far distant land. My heart is full of gratitude, but my poverty of German words forces me to greater economy of expression.

Excuse you, my gentleman, that I read off, what I you say will. [But he didn't read.]

The German language speak I not good, but have numerous connoisseurs me assured that I her write like an angel. Maybe—maybe—I know not. Have till now no acquaintance with the angels had. That comes later—when it the dear God please—it has no hurry.

Since long, my gentlemen, have I the passionate longing nursed a speech on German to hold, but one has me not permitted. Men, who no feeling for the art had, laid me ever hindrance in the way and made naught my desire—sometimes by excuses, often by force. Always said these men to me: "Keep you still, your Highness! Silence! For God's sake seek another way and means yourself obnoxious to make."

In the present case, as usual it is me difficult become, for me the permission to obtain. The committee sorrowed deeply, but could me the permission not grant on account of a law which from the Concordia demands she shall the German language protect. Du liebe Zeit! How so had one to me this say could—might—dared—should? I am indeed the truest friend of the German language—and not only now, but from long since—yes, before twenty years already. And never have I the desire had the noble language to hurt; to the contrary, only wished she to improve—I would her only reform. It is the dream of my life been. I have already visits by the various German governments paid and for contracts prayed. I am now to Austria in the same task come. I would only some changes effect. I would only the language method—the luxurious, elaborate construction compress, the eternal parenthesis suppress, do away with, annihilate; the introduction of more than thirteen subjects in one sentence forbid; the verb so far to the front pull that one it without a telescope discover can. With one word, my gentlemen, I would your beloved language simplify so that, my gentlemen, when you her for prayer need, One her yonder-up understands.

I beseech you, from me yourself counsel to let, execute these mentioned reforms. Then will you an elegant language possess, and afterward, when you some thing say will, will you at least yourself understand what you said had. But often nowadays, when you a mile-long sentence from you given and you yourself somewhat have rested, then must you have a touching inquisitiveness have yourself to determine what you actually spoken have. Before several days has the correspondent of a local paper a sentence constructed which hundred and twelve words contain, and therein were seven parentheses smuggled in, and the subject seven times changed. Think you only, my gentlemen, in the course of the voyage of a single sentence must the poor, persecuted, fatigued subject seven times change position!

Now, when we the mentioned reforms execute, will it no longer so bad be. Doch noch eins. I might gladly the separable verb also a little bit reform. I might none do let what Schiller did: he has the whole history of the Thirty Years' War between the two members of a separable verb in-pushed. That has even Germany itself aroused, and one has Schiller the permission refused the History of the Hundred Years' War to compose—God be it thanked! After all these reforms established be will, will the German language the noblest and the prettiest on the world be.

Since to you now, my gentlemen, the character of my mission known is, beseech I you so friendly to be and to me your valuable help grant. Mr. Pötzl has the public believed make would that I to Vienna come am in order the bridges to clog up and the traffic to hinder, while I observations gather and note. Allow you yourselves but not from him deceived. My frequent presence on the bridges has an entirely innocent ground. Yonder gives it the necessary space, yonder can one a noble long German sentence elaborate, the bridge-railing along, and his whole contents with one glance overlook. On the one end of the railing pasted I the first member of a separable verb and the final member cleave I to the other end—then spread the body of the sentence between it out! Usually are for my purposes the bridges of the city long enough; when I but Pötzl's writings study will I ride out and use the glorious endless imperial bridge. But this is a calumny; Pötzl writes the prettiest German. Perhaps not so pliable as the mine, but in many details much better. Excuse you these flatteries. These are well deserved.

Now I my speech execute—no, I would say I bring her to the close. I am a foreigner—but here, under you, have I it entirely forgotten. And so again and yet again proffer I you my heartiest thanks.

Text / "The Horrors of the German Language," *MTS*(10):43–51.

· 95 ·

Spending two years in Vienna, Mark Twain became a social lion and a privileged character, known to everybody from the royal family to the man in the street. More than ever before he was the world citizen and United States ambassador at large. But there were not many public appearances: a few readings on behalf of charities sponsored by titled patrons, and once in a while a speech at some function, as at the Press Jubilee, noted below.

Speech

Jubilee of the Emancipation of the Hungarian Press,
Budapest, March 23, 1899

Now that we are all here together, I think it will be a good idea to arrange the Ausgleich. If you will act for Hungary I shall be quite willing to act for Austria, and this is the very time for it. There couldn't be a better, for we are all feeling friendly, fair-minded, and hospitable now, and full of admiration for each other, full of confidence in each other, full of the spirit of welcome, full of the grace of forgiveness, and the disposition to let bygones be bygones.

Let us not waste this golden, this beneficent, this providential opportunity. I am willing to make any concession you want, just so we get it settled. I am not only willing to let grain come in free, I am willing to pay the freight on it, and you may send delegates to the Reichsrath if you like. All I require is that they shall be quiet, peaceable people like your own deputies, and not disturb our proceedings.

If you want the Gegenseitigengeldbeitragendenverhältnismässigkeiten rearranged and readjusted I am ready for that. I will let you off at twenty-eight percent—twenty-seven—even twenty-five if you insist, for there is nothing illiberal about me when I am out on a diplomatic debauch.

Now, in return for these concessions, I am willing to take anything in reason, and I think we may consider the business settled and the Ausgleich ausgegloschen at least for ten solid years, and we will sign the papers in blank, and do it here and now.

Well, I am unspeakably glad to have that Ausgleich off my hands. It has kept me awake nights for anderthalbjahr.

But I never could settle it before, because always when I called at the Foreign Office in Vienna to talk about it, there wasn't anybody at home, and that is not a place where you can go in and see for yourself whether it is a mistake or not, because the person who takes care of the front door there is of a size that discourages liberty of action and the free spirit of investigation. To think the Ausgleich is abgemacht at last! It is a grand and beautiful consummation, and I am glad I came.

The way I feel now I do honestly believe I would rather be just my own humble self at this moment than paragraph 14.

Text / "German for the Hungarians" in *MTS*(10):52–54; and *MTS*(23):176–77. In a letter to Howells, Mark Twain said that he did not give the speech he had prepared, but a very different one based on a remark of the person who introduced him. Whether the text here is the spoken or the rejected version is impossible to say. See *Mark Twain-Howells Letters,* eds. Henry Nash Smith and William M. Gibson (1960), 2:690.

Ausgleich / The agreement that held together the monarchy of Austria-Hungary, it was a schedule for the apportionment of taxes between Austria and Hungary. Renewed every ten years, the Ausgleich was the subject of acrimonious parliamentary debate at the time of Mark Twain's stay in Vienna.

peaceable people like your own deputies / Probably an ironical allusion to rowdy deputies who made parliamentary sessions tumultuous by banging on desks and shouting scurrilous insults at each other. See Mark Twain's "Stirring Times in Austria," *Harper's Magazine* 96, no. 574 (March 1898):532–40.

paragraph 14 / A provision designating the proportion each country should pay to support the imperial army. It aroused great resentment in Hungary.

· 96 ·

When the family returned to London in the early summer of 1899, Mark Twain was immediately sought after, much as he had been on his first visit almost thirty years before. The Savage Club made him its fourth honorary member, the other three being the Prince of Wales, Fridtjof Nansen, and Henry M. Stanley. At a club dinner for the new member, the toastmaster said that the chief guest had no claim to the title of humorist, that his true vocation was statistics, which he loved for their own sake, and that he would have an easy time counting all the real jokes he had ever made. Mark Twain promptly jumped up to make the brief reply given below. Later in the evening he evidently made a full-scale speech, but it has not survived.

Dinner Speech

Savage Club Dinner for Mark Twain, London, June 9, 1899

Perhaps I am not a humorist, but I am a first-class fool—a simpleton; for up to this moment I have believed Chairman MacAlister to be a decent person whom I could allow to mix up with my best friends and relatives. The exhibition he has just made of himself reveals him to be a scoundrel and a knave of the deepest dye. I have been cruelly deceived, and it serves me right for trusting a Scotchman. Yes, I do understand figures, and I can count. I have counted the words in MacAlister's drivel (I certainly cannot call it a speech), and there were exactly three thousand four hundred and thirty-nine. I also carefully counted the lies—there were exactly three thousand four hundred and thirty-nine. Therefore, I leave MacAlister to his fate.

I was sorry to hear my name mentioned as one of the great authors, because they have a sad habit of dying off. Chaucer is dead, Spenser is dead, so is Milton, so is Shakespeare, and I am not feeling very well myself.

Text / "Statistics," *MTS*(10):276–78. *MTB,* 3:1086–87, gives a fragment of his later full-length speech, in which he referred to his first

London visit: "I was 6 feet 4 in those days. Now I am 5 feet 8½ and daily diminishing in altitude, and the shrinkage of my principles goes on. . . . Irving was here then, is here now. Stanley is here, and Joe Hutton, but Charles Reade is gone and Tom Hood and Harry Lee and Canon Kingsley. In those days you could have carried Kipling around in a lunch basket; now he fills the world. I was young and foolish then; now I am old and foolisher."

MacAlister / John Young Walker MacAlister (1856–1926). Scotch journalist and librarian. A journalist in Leeds and Yorkshire, he became librarian of the Gladstone Library (1887), honorary secretary of the Library Association (1887–98), and president (1914–19). He was instrumental in combining medical organizations to form the Royal Society of Medicine.

· 97 ·

As critics have noted, Mark Twain's attitude toward England swung back and forth between opposing views. Generally he was a hearty Anglophile. Then, when displeased by the turn of political events or when ruffled by somebody like Matthew Arnold, he became for a time just as hearty an Anglophobe. In the speech below he is in a friendly mood, preaching the doctrine of good will between the two countries.

Dinner Speech

Authors Club Dinner for Mark Twain,
London, June 12, 1899

It does not embarrass me to hear my books praised so much. It only pleases and delights me. I have not gone beyond the age when embarrassment is possible, but I have reached the age when I know how to conceal it. It is such a satisfaction to me to hear Sir Walter Besant, who is much more capable than I to judge of my work, deliver a judgment which is such a contentment to my spirit.

Well, I have thought well of the books myself, but I think more of them now. It charms me also to hear Sir Spencer Walpole deliver a similar judgment, and I shall treasure his remarks also. I shall not discount the praises in any possible way. When I report them to my family they shall lose nothing. There are, however, certain heredities which come down to us which our writings of the present day may be traced to. I, for instance, read the *Walpole Letters* when I was a boy. I absorbed them, gathered in their grace, wit, and humor, and put them away to be used by and by. One does that so unconsciously with things one really likes. I am reminded now of what use those letters have been to me.

They must not claim credit in America for what was really written in another form so long ago. They must only claim that I trimmed this, that, and the other, and so changed their appearance as to make them seem to be original. You now see what modesty I have in stock. But it has taken long practice to get it there.

But I must not stand here talking. I merely meant to get up and give my thanks for the pleasant things that preceding speakers have said of me. I also wish to extend my thanks to the Authors Club for constituting me a member, at a reasonable price per year, and for giving me the benefit of your legal adviser.

I believe you keep a lawyer. I have always kept a lawyer, too, though I have never made anything out of him. It is service to an author to have a lawyer. There is something so disagreeable in having a personal contact with a publisher. So it is better to work through a lawyer—and lose your case. I understand that the publishers have been meeting together also like us. I don't know what for, but possibly they are devising new and mysterious ways for remunerating authors. I only wish now to thank you for electing me a member of this club—I believe I have paid my dues—and to thank you again for the pleasant things you have said of me.

Last February, when Rudyard Kipling was ill in America, the sympathy which was poured out to him was genuine and sincere, and I believe that which cost Kipling so much will bring England and America closer together. I have been proud and pleased to see this growing affection and respect between the two countries. I hope it will continue to grow, and, please God, it will continue to grow. I trust we authors will leave to posterity, if we have nothing else to leave, a friendship between England and America that will count for much. I will now confess that I have been engaged for the past eight days in compiling a publication. I have brought it here to lay at your feet. I do not ask your indulgence in presenting it, but for your applause.

Here it is: "Since England and America may be joined together in Kipling, may they not be severed in 'Twain.' "

Text / "Authors' Club" in *MTS*(10):215–17; and *MTS*(23):185–86.

Walter Besant / (1836–1901). British novelist. Of his seventeen books, often written in collaboration with James Rice, one of the best known is *All Sorts and Conditions of Men* (1882). He also wrote a biography of Captain Cook, and began a comprehensive history of London, which was unfinished at his death. He had a prominent part in founding the Society of Authors (1884).

Spencer Walpole / (1839–1907). British historian and essayist. He was governor of the Isle of Man (1882–93) and secretary to the post office (1893–99). Among his books are *Life of Lord John Russell* (1889), and *Essays: Political and Historical* (1908).

Walpole Letters / Horace Walpole, fourth earl of Orford (1717–97), was an engaging letter writer. He published *Miscellaneous Letters* (1778); they appeared in a volume of the *Works of Lord Orford* (1798), and in other editions thereafter.

· 98 ·

The Whitefriars Club, one of Mark Twain's favorites, did him proud at an elaborate dinner. Among the 200 diners were the American ambassador, Joseph H. Choate, senator-elect Chauncey Depew, Max O'Rell, Mrs. Frank Leslie, T. P. "Tay Pay" O'Connor, Poultney Bigelow, Mr. and Mrs. Gilbert Parker, and the British suffragist, Beatrice Harraden. Louis Frederic Austin, of the Illustrated London News, *introduced the guest of honor by citing the parallel between Mark Twain and Sir Walter Scott, both of whom had honorably paid debts incurred by business failures.*

Dinner Speech

Whitefriars Club Dinner for Mark Twain,
Hotel Cecil, London, June 16, 1899

Mr. Chairman and Brethren of the Vow—in whatever the vow is; for although I have been a member of this club for five-and-twenty years, I don't know any more about what that vow is than Mr. Austin seems to. But whatever the vow is, I don't care what it is. I have made a thousand vows.

There is no pleasure comparable to making a vow in the presence of one who appreciates that vow, in the presence of men who honor and appreciate you for making the vow, and men who admire you for making the vow.

There is only one pleasure higher than that, and that is to get outside and break the vow. A vow is always a pledge of some kind or other for the protection of your own morals and principles or somebody else's, and generally, by the irony of fate, it is for the protection of your own morals.

Hence we have pledges that make us eschew tobacco or wine, and while you are taking the pledge there is a holy influence about that makes you feel you are reformed, and that you can never be so happy again in this world until—you get outside and take a drink.

I had forgotten that I was a member of this club—it is so long ago. But now I remember that I was here five-and-twenty years ago, and that I was then at a dinner of the Whitefriars Club, and it was in those old days when you had just made two great finds. All London was talking about nothing else than that they had found Livingstone, and that the lost Sir Roger Tichborne had been found—and they were trying him for it.

And at the dinner, Chairman ——— (I do not know who he was)—failed to come to time. The gentlemen who had been appointed to pay me the customary compliments and to introduce me forgot the compliments, and did not know what they were.

And George Augustus Sala came in at the last moment, just when I was about to go without compliments altogether. And that man was a gifted man. They just called on him instantaneously, while he was going to sit down, to introduce the stranger, and Sala made one of those marvelous speeches which he was capable of making. I think no man talked so fast as Sala did. One did not need wine while he was making a speech. The rapidity of his utterance made a man drunk in a minute. An incomparable speech was that, an impromptu speech, and an impromptu speech is a seldom thing, and he did it so well.

He went into the whole history of the United States, and made it entirely new to me. He filled it with episodes and incidents that Washington never heard of, and he did it so convincingly that although I knew none of it happened, from that day to this I do not know any history but Sala's.

I do not know anything so sad as a dinner where you are going to get up and say something by and by, and you do not know what it is. You sit and wonder and wonder what the gentleman is going to say who is going to introduce you. You know that if he says something severe, that if he will deride you, or traduce you, or do anything of that kind, he will furnish you with a text, because anybody can get up and talk against that.

Anybody can get up and straighten out his character. But when a gentleman gets up and merely tells the truth about you, what can you do?

Mr. Austin has done well. He has supplied so many texts that I will have to drop out a lot of them, and that is about as difficult as when you do not have any text at all. Now, he made a beautiful and smooth speech without any difficulty at all, and I could have done that if I had gone on with the schooling with which I began. I see here a gentleman on my left who was my master in the art of oratory more than twenty-five years ago.

When I look upon the inspiring face of Mr. Depew, it carries me a long way back. An old and valued friend of mine is he, and I saw his career as it came along, and it has reached pretty well up to now, when he, by another miscarriage of justice, is a United States Senator. But those were delightful days when I was taking lessons in oratory.

My other master—the Ambassador—is not here yet. Under those two gentlemen I learned to make after-dinner speeches, and it was charming.

You know the New England dinner is the great occasion on the other side of the water. It is held every year to celebrate the landing of the Pilgrims. Those Pilgrims were a lot of people who were not needed in England, and you know they had great rivalry, and they were persuaded to go elsewhere, and they chartered a ship called *Mayflower* and set sail, and I have heard it said that they pumped the Atlantic Ocean through that ship sixteen times.

They fell in over there with the Dutch from Rotterdam, Amsterdam, and a lot of other places with profane names, and it is from that gang that Mr. Depew is descended.

On the other hand, Mr. Choate is descended from those Puritans who landed on a bitter night in December. Every year those people used to meet at a great banquet in New York, and those masters of mind in oratory had to make speeches. It was Doctor Depew's business to get up there and apologize for the Dutch, and Mr. Choate had to get up later and explain the crimes of the Puritans, and grand, beautiful times we used to have.

It is curious that after that long lapse of time I meet the Whitefriars again, some looking as young and fresh as in the old days, others showing a certain amount of wear and tear, and here, after all this time, I find one of the masters of oratory and the others named in the list.

And here we three meet again as exiles on one pretext or another, and you will notice that while we are absent there is a pleasing tranquillity in America—a building up of public confidence. We are doing the best we can for our country. I think we have spent our lives in serving our country, and we never serve it to greater advantage than when we get out of it.

But impromptu speaking—that is what I was trying to learn. That is a difficult thing. I used to do it in this way. I used to begin about a week ahead, and write out my impromptu speech and get it by heart. Then I brought it to the New England dinner printed on a piece of paper in my pocket, so that I could pass it to the reporters all cut and dried, and in order to do an impromptu speech as it should be done you have to indicate the places for pauses and hesitations. I put them all in it. And then you want the applause in the right places.

When I got to the place where it should come in, if it did not come in I did not care, but I had it marked on the paper. And these masters of mind used to wonder why it was my speech came out in the morning in the first person, while theirs went through the butchery of synopsis.

I do that kind of speech (I mean an offhand speech), and do it well, and make no mistake, in such a way to deceive the audience completely and make that audience believe it is an impromptu speech—that is art.

I was frightened out of it at last by an experience of Doctor Hayes. He was a sort of Nansen of that day. He had been to the North Pole, and it made him celebrated. He had even seen the polar bear climb the pole.

He had made one of those magnificent voyages such as Nansen made, and in those days when a man did anything which greatly distinguished him for the moment he had to come on to the lecture platform and tell all about it.

Doctor Hayes was a great, magnificent creature like Nansen, superbly built. He was to appear in Boston. He wrote his lecture out, and it was his purpose to read it from manuscript; but in an evil hour he concluded that it would be a good thing to preface it with something rather handsome, poetical, and beautiful that he could get off by heart and deliver as if it were the thought of the moment.

He had not had my experience, and could not do that. He came on the platform, held his manuscript down, and began with a beautiful piece of oratory. He spoke something like this:

"When a lonely human being, a pigmy in the midst of the architecture of nature, stands solitary on those icy waters and looks abroad to the horizon and sees mighty castles and temples of eternal ice raising up their pinnacles tipped by the pencil of the departing sun—"

Here a man came across the platform and touched him on the shoulder, and said: "One minute." And then to the audience:

"Is Mrs. John Smith in the house? Her husband has slipped on the ice and broken his leg."

And you could see the Mrs. John Smiths get up everywhere and drift out of the house, and it made great gaps everywhere. Then Doctor Hayes began again: "When a lonely man, a pigmy in the architecture—" The janitor came in again and shouted: "It is not Mrs. John Smith! It is Mrs. John Jones!"

Then all the Mrs. Joneses got up and left. Once more the speaker started, and was in the midst of the sentence when he was interrupted again, and the result was that the lecture was not delivered. But the lecturer interviewed the janitor afterward in a private room, and of the fragments of that janitor they took "twelve basketsful."

Now, I don't want to sit down just in this way. I have been talking with so much levity that I have said no serious thing, and you are really no better or wiser, although Robert Buchanan has suggested that I am a person who deals in wisdom. I have said nothing which would make you better than when you came here.

I should be sorry to sit down without having said one serious word which you can carry home and relate to your children and the old people who are not able to get away.

And this is just a little maxim which has saved me from many a difficulty and many a disaster, and in times of tribulation and uncertainty has come to my rescue, as it shall to yours if you observe it as I do day and night.

I always use it in an emergency, and you can take it home as a legacy from me, and it is: "When in doubt, tell the truth."

Text / "To the Whitefriars," in *MTS*(10):375–83; and *MTS* (23):178–84.

the lost Sir Roger Tichborne / Arthur Orton (1834–98) claimed to be Roger Charles Tichborne, heir to the Tichborne baronetcy and supposedly lost at sea in 1854. Orton convinced Lady Tichborne that he was her son, but in 1870, when he brought suit to retrieve title and estates, there was a trial that went on for 102 days (1871–72). Orton's contradictory testimony resulted in his being tried for perjury, convicted and sentenced to fourteen years. Released in 1884, he later made public confession of his imposture. For details of the affair, see Edward H. Smith, "The Lost Heir of

Tichborne," *Mysteries of the Missing* (1927):82–100. Mark Twain, much interested in the Tichborne case, collected a scrapbook of clippings about it, MTP.

Sala / George Augustus Henry Sala (1828–95). British journalist. A contributor to *Household Words,* then Civil War correspondent for the London *Telegraph* (1863), he reported for the *Telegraph* from Spain, Venice and Paris (1866–71), Russia (1876), and Australia (1885). He lectured in the United States (1879, 1885). Among his books are *America in the Midst of War* (1864) and *Life and Adventures* (1895).

Choate / Joseph Hodges Choate (1832–1917). American lawyer and diplomat. In a professional life of forty years, he became known as a great trial lawyer. He was ambassador to Great Britain (1897–1905), Bencher of the Middle Temple (1905), and ambassador to the Hague Peace Conference (1907). An excellent speaker, urbane and witty, he was in demand for banquets and other public occasions.

Hayes / Isaac Israel Hayes (1832–81). American physician and explorer. He went on the second expedition in search of Sir John Franklin (1853), accompanied another expedition that reached latitude 80° 14′ N (1860), served as Union surgeon in the Civil War, and explored Greenland (1869).

Nansen / Fridtjof Nansen (1861–1930). Norwegian explorer and statesman. An Arctic veteran by the age of thirty, he commanded a polar expedition (1893–96) that reached the then record latitude of 86° 14′ N. He was first Norwegian minister to Great Britain (1906–08), headed the first oceanographic expedition to the North Atlantic (1910–14), and after World War I was League of Nations high commissioner for relief of refugees, this service winning for him the Nobel Peace Prize for 1921–22. Among his many publications are *Eskimo Life* (1891), and *Farthest North* (1897).

"twelve basketsful" / An allusion to Christ's miracle of feeding the multitude with five loaves and two fishes. Specifically a reference to *Matthew*(4.20): "And they all did eat and were filled: and they took up of the fragments that remained twelve baskets full."

Robert Buchanan / (1848–1901). Scottish writer. Among his books are *London Poems* (1866); a novel, *A Child of Nature* (1881); and a play, *The Strange Adventures of Miss Brown* (1895). He originated the criticism of the Pre-Raphaelites as "the fleshly school of poetry."

· 99 ·

Among London clubs that honored Mark Twain–and this time Olivia, too–one was the New Vagabonds, who had evolved from the Old Vagabonds. It was a coterie composed largely of writers, actors and painters who attempted to preserve something of the spirit of the Pre-Raphaelites.

Dinner Speech

New Vagabonds Club Dinner for Mr. and Mrs. Clemens,
London, June 29, 1899

It has always been difficult—leave that word difficult—not exceedingly difficult, but just difficult, nothing more than that, not the slightest shade to add to that—just difficult—to respond properly, in the right phraseology, when compliments are paid to me; but it is more than difficult when the compliments are paid to a better than I—my wife.

And while I am not here to testify against myself—I can't be expected to do so, a prisoner in your own country is not admitted to do so—as to which member of the family wrote my books, I could say in general that really I wrote the books myself. My wife puts the facts in, and they make it respectable. My modesty won't suffer while compliments are being paid to literature, and through literature to my family. I can't get enough of them.

I am curiously situated tonight. It so rarely happens that I am introduced by a humorist; I am generally introduced by a person of grave walk and carriage. That makes the proper background of gravity for brightness. I am going to alter to suit, and haply I may say some humorous things.

When you start with a blaze of sunshine and upburst of humor, when you begin with that, the proper office of humor is to reflect, to put you into that pensive mood of deep thought, to make you think of your sins, if you wish half an hour to fly. Humor makes me reflect now tonight, it sets the thinking machinery in motion. Always, when I am thinking, there come suggestions of what I am, and what we all are, and what we are coming to. A sermon comes from my lips always when

I listen to a humorous speech.

I seize the opportunity to throw away frivolities, to say something to plant the seed, and make all better than when I came. In Mr. Grossmith's remarks there was a subtle something suggesting my favorite theory of the difference between theoretical morals and practical morals. I try to instil practical morals in the place of theatrical—I mean theoretical; but as an addendum—an annex—something added to theoretical morals.

When your chairman said it was the first time he had ever taken the chair, he did not mean that he had not taken lots of other things; he attended my first lecture and took notes. This indicated the man's disposition. There was nothing else flying around, so he took notes; he would have taken anything he could get.

I can bring a moral to bear here which shows the difference between theoretical morals and practical morals. Theoretical morals are the sort you get on your mother's knee, in good books, and from the pulpit. You gather them in your head, and not in your heart; they are theory without practice. Without the assistance of practice to perfect them, it is difficult to teach a child to "be honest, don't steal."

I will teach you how it should be done, lead you into temptation, teach you how to steal, so that you may recognize when you have stolen and feel the proper pangs. It is no good going round and bragging that you have never taken the chair.

As by the fires of experience, so by commission of crime, you learn real morals. Commit all the crimes, familiarize yourself with all sins, take them in rotation (there are only two or three thousand of them), stick to it, commit two or three every day, and by and by you will be proof against them. When you are through you will be proof against all sins and morally perfect. You will be vaccinated against every possible commission of them. This is the only way.

I will read you a written statement upon the subject that I wrote three years ago to read to the Sabbath schools. [Here the lecturer turned his pockets out, but without success.] No! I have left it at home. Still, it was a mere statement of fact, illustrating the value of practical morals produced by the commission of crime.

It was in my boyhood—just a statement of fact, reading is only more formal, merely facts, merely pathetic facts, which I can state so as to be understood. It relates to the first time I ever stole a watermelon; that is, I think it was the first time; anyway, it was right along there somewhere.

I stole it out of a farmer's wagon while he was waiting on another customer. "Stole" is a harsh term. I withdrew—I retired that watermelon. I carried it to a secluded corner of a lumber yard. I broke it open. It was green—the greenest watermelon raised in the valley that year.

The minute I saw it was green I was sorry, and began to reflect—reflection is the beginning of reform. If you don't reflect when you commit a crime then that crime is of no use; it might just as well have been committed by someone else. You must reflect or the value is lost; you are not vaccinated against committing it again.

I began to reflect. I said to myself: "What ought a boy to do who has stolen a green watermelon? What would George Washington do, the father of his country, the only American who could not tell a lie? What would he do? There is only one right, high, noble thing for any boy to do who has stolen a watermelon of that class; he must make restitution; he must restore that stolen property to its rightful owner." I said I would do it when I made that good resolution. I felt it to be a noble, uplifting obligation. I rose up spiritually stronger and refreshed. I carried that watermelon back—what was left of it—and restored it to the farmer, and made him give me a ripe one in its place.

Now you see that this constant impact of crime upon crime protects you against further commission of crime. It builds you up. A man can't become morally perfect by stealing one or a thousand green watermelons, but every little helps.

I was at a great school yesterday (St. Paul's), where for four hundred years they have been busy with brains, and building up England by producing Pepys, Miltons, and Marlboroughs. Six hundred boys left to nothing in the world but theoretical morality. I wanted to become the professor of practical morality, but the high master was away, so I suppose I shall have to go on making my living the same old way—by adding practical to theoretical morality.

What are the glory that was Greece, the grandeur that was Rome, compared to the glory and grandeur and majesty of a perfected morality such as you see before you?

The New Vagabonds are old vagabonds (undergoing the old sort of reform). You drank my health; I hope I have not been unuseful. Take this system of morality to your hearts. Take it home to your neighbors and your graves, and I hope it will be a long time before you arrive there.

Text / "Theoretical and Practical Morals" in *MTS*(10):130–35; and *MTS*(23):190–92. Both texts are misdated.

Grossmith / George Grossmith (1847–1912). British comedian. He was a popular singer who had made a name for himself in roles of the light operas of Gilbert and Sullivan.

· 100 ·

Americans in London celebrated the Fourth of July with proper pride, though without much offensive flag-waving or making the eagle scream. The veteran trio of Ambassador Choate, Senator Depew, and Mark Twain were more conciliatory than boastful.

The Day We Celebrate

American Society Dinner, Hotel Cecil, London, July 4, 1899

I noticed in Ambassador Choate's speech that he said: "You may be Americans or Englishmen, but you cannot be both at the same time." You responded by applause.

Consider the effect of a short residence here. I find the Ambassador rises first to speak to a toast, followed by a Senator, and I come third. What a subtle tribute that to monarchical influence of the country when you place rank above respectability!

I was born modest, and if I had not been things like this would force it upon me. I understand it quite well. I am here to see that between them they do justice to the day we celebrate, and in case they do not I must do it myself. But I notice they have considered this day merely from one side—its sentimental, patriotic, poetic side. But it has another side. It has a commercial, a business side that needs reforming. It has a historical side.

I do not say "an" historical side, because I am speaking the American language. I do not see why our cousins should continue to say "an" hospital, "an" historical fact, "an" horse. It seems to me the Congress of Women, now in session, should look to it. I think "an" is having a little too much to do with it. It comes of habit, which accounts for many things.

Yesterday, for example, I was at a luncheon party. At the end of the party a great dignitary of the English Established Church went away half an hour before anybody else and carried off my hat. Now, that was an innocent act on his part. He went out first, and, of course, had the choice of hats. As a rule I try to get out first myself. But I hold that it was an innocent, unconscious act, due, perhaps, to heredity. He was thinking about ecclesiastical matters, and when a man is in that condition of mind he will take anybody's hat. The result was that the whole afternoon I was under the influence of his clerical hat and could not tell a lie. Of course, he was hard at it.

It is a compliment to both of us. His hat fitted me exactly; my hat fitted him exactly. So I judge I was born to rise to high dignity in the Church somehow or other, but I do not know what he was born for. That is an illustration of the influence of habit, and it is perceptible here when they say "an" hospital, "an" European, "an" historical.

The business aspect of the Fourth of July is not perfect as it stands. See what it costs us every year with loss of life, the crippling of thousands with its fireworks, and the burning down of property. It is not only sacred to patriotism and universal freedom, but to the surgeon, the undertaker, the insurance offices—and they are working it for all it is worth.

I am pleased to see that we have a cessation of war for the time. This coming from me, a soldier, you will appreciate. I was a soldier in the Southern war for two weeks, and when gentlemen get up to speak of the great deeds our army and navy have recently done, why, it goes all through me and fires up the old war spirit. I had in my first engagement three horses shot under me. The next shots went over my head, the next hit me in the back. Then I retired to meet an engagement.

I thank you, gentlemen, for making even a slight reference to the war profession, in which I distinguished myself, short as my career was.

Text / Composite, based upon: "The Day We Celebrate" in *MTS*(10): 402–4; and *MTS*(23):187–89.

Congress of Women / An international Council of Women convened in London on June 26, 1899. The Countess of Aberdeen presided; the vice-president was Mrs. Mary Wright Sewall of the United States. Among thousands of women attending were the Duchess of Bedford, Lady Cynthia Vincent, Lady Randolph Churchill, Lady Cavendish, the Austrian Baroness von Suttner, and the American suffragist, Mrs. Stanton Blatch. Principal topics discussed were elementary education, international arbitration, and the enfranchisement of women.

dignitary of the English Established Church / Albert Basil Orme Wilberforce (1841–1916). British Anglican clergyman. Chaplain to the Speaker of the House of Commons, he became archdeacon of Westminster (1900). He was an eloquent advocate of temperance. Notwithstanding that point of view, which was certainly not Mark Twain's, the two became quite friendly.

· 101 ·

Mark Twain had an opportunity to air his views on one of his favorite subjects, copyright, before a House of Lords committee consisting of Lords Monkswell, Avebury, Farrar, Thwing, and Knutsford. In the question-and-answer session, one or two of their lordships became somewhat testy, but Mark Twain preserved his calm and provoked occasional laughter. The London Times *gave a full column to the hearing but merely summarized his remarks in a third-person synopsis. The American press did better, but what he said was probably incompletely reported.*

Remarks on Copyright

Select Committee Hearing, House of Lords, April 3, 1900

I have been taxed by the British government for some years, and on investigation I found that my literature was taxed as gas works. That is literally true and it hurt me.

In my opinion the copyright laws of England and America need only one commercially trifling but morally gigantic amendment to become perfect—the removal of the forty-two year limit and the return to perpetual copyright. I consider that at least one of the reasons advanced in justification of the limited copyright is fallacious—namely, the one which makes a distinction between an author's property and real estate, and pretends that the two are not created, produced, or acquired in the same way, thus warranting a different treatment of the two by law.

The limited copyright makes a distinction between an author's property and real estate, pretending that both are not created, produced and acquired in the same way. The man who purchases a landed estate had to earn the money by the superiority of his intellect; a book is the result of an author's own brain in the same manner—a combination and exploitation of his ideas.

When the copyright dies it does not give the book to the publishers as a free gift; it merely gives the author's profit to the public. Out of every one hundred tons of books sold ninety-nine are light literature; therefore, to benefit the nation substantially, one would need to furnish it with the ninety-nine tons as cheaply as possible—the other ton is of no consequence. My books are light literature—very light.

Many unthinking thinkers think they think that copyright or the absence of it does not affect my books. Here they are sold at two shillings and the destruction of the copyright could not cheapen them much more—certainly not enough to make the empire lose its sleep over the windfall.

The public demand determines the price of a book, not Parliament or the publishers, who will make any honorable sacrifice that has money in it.

The Bible is the only book possessing the fair and honorable grace of perpetual copyright, and that has not deprived the public of marvelously cheap editions.

So few books outlive the forty-two years' limit that the small resulting profit to the state is not worth consideration. A limited copyright does not take enough pennies out of the author's pocket to make the thing worth while. Only three books written by Britons during this century have survived the forty-two year limit, and the authors' royalty on these books would net only about $32,500 a year, the sum the richest country on earth has taken from the pockets of the children of the little handful of illustrious men who had so great a share in building British power and broadening the world's civilization. Is it a matter for pride or congratulation that this ancient and mouldy wrong should be suffered to continue?

I suggest that Parliament fix a period during which the author should produce an edition of his book at one-eighth the original price, and if the book is allowed out of print one year, the copyright should lapse.

Text / Composite, based upon: "Mark Twain a witness on copyright law," *World,* April 4, 1900; "Mr. Clemens Heard," *Courant,* April 4, 1900; *MTB,* 3:1105.

· 102 ·

At the Royal Literary Fund banquet, Mark Twain's audience was not large, but it had distinction. Baron Russell of Killowen, lord chief justice of England, presided, and among guests were Baron Kelvin, Sir E. T. Bewley, Anthony Hope, T. P. O'Connor, and a number of barristers who rated the Q.C.

Literature

One hundred tenth Anniversary Banquet, Royal Literary Fund, Hotel Cecil, London, May 2, 1900

Mr. Hope has been able to deal adequately with this toast without assistance from me. Still, I was born generous. If he had advanced any theories that needed refutation or correction I would have attended to them, and if he had made any statement stronger than those which he is in the habit of making I would have dealt with them.

In fact, I was surprised at the mildness of his statements. I could not have made such statements if I had preferred to, because to exaggerate is the only way I can approximate to the truth. You cannot have a theory without principles. Principles is another name for prejudices. I have no prejudices in politics, religion, literature, or anything else.

I am now on my way to my own country to run for the presidency because there are not yet enough candidates in the field, and those who have entered are too much hampered by their own principles, which are prejudices.

I propose to go there to purify the political atmosphere. I am in favor of everything everybody is in favor of. What you should do is to satisfy the whole nation, not half of it, for then you would only be half a President.

There could not be a broader platform than mine. I am in favor of anything and everything—of temperance and intemperance, morality and qualified immorality, gold standard and free silver.

I have tried all sorts of things, and that is why I want to try the great position of ruler of a country. I have been in turn reporter, editor, publisher, author, lawyer, burglar. I have worked my way up, and wish to continue to do so.

I read today in a magazine article that Christendom issued last year fifty-five thousand new books. Consider what that means! Fifty-five thousand new books meant fifty-four thousand new authors. We are going to have them all on our hands to take care of sooner or later. Therefore, double your subscriptions to the literary fund!

Text / Composite, based upon: "Literature" in *MTS*(10):191–92; and *MTS*(23):207–8.

Hope / Anthony Hope Hawkins (1863–1933). British writer. While practicing law (1887–94), he published five mediocre novels, then had great success with *The Prisoner of Zenda* (1894), and repeated it with *Rupert of Hentzau* (1898). Using modern society themes, he write *Double Harness* (1904), *The Great Miss Driver* (1908), and others. He served in the World War I Ministry of Information and was knighted in 1918.

· 103 ·

A gala affair welcomed Sir Henry Irving on his return from a triumphant American tour. Floral representations of the Union Jack and Stars and Stripes decorated tables at which a distinguished company assembled: among them Ambassador Choate, Sir Lawrence Alma-Tadema, Sir John Tenniel, Anthony Hope, Arthur Wing Pinero, Bret Harte, Edwin A. Abbey, Henry Arthur Jones, and Laurence Irving. Richard D'Oyly Carte presided.

The Drama

Dramatic and Literary Society Dinner for Sir Henry Irving,
Hotel Savoy, London, June 9, 1900

I find my task a very easy one. I have been a dramatist for thirty years. I have had an ambition in all that time to overdo the work of the Spaniard who said he left behind him 400 dramas when he died. I leave behind me 415, and I am not yet dead.

The greatest of all the arts is to write a drama. It is a most difficult thing. It requires the highest talent possible and the rarest gifts. No, there is another talent that ranks with it—for anybody can write a drama—I had 400 of them—but to get one accepted requires real ability. And I never had that felicity yet.

But human nature is so constructed, we are so persistent, that when we know that we are born to a thing we do not care what the world thinks about it. We go on exploiting that talent year after year, as I have done. I shall go on writing dramas, and some day the impossible may happen, but I am not looking for it.

In writing plays the chief thing is novelty. The world grows tired of solid forms in all the arts. I struck a new idea myself years ago. I was not surprised at it. I was always expecting it would happen. A person who has suffered disappointment for many years loses confidence, and I thought I had better make inquiries before I exploited my new idea of doing a drama in the form of a dream, so I wrote to a great authority on knowledge of all kinds, and asked him whether it was new.

I could depend upon him. He lived in my dear home in America—that dear home, dearer to me through taxes. He sent me a list of plays in which that old device had been used, and he said there was also a modern lot. He traveled back to China and to a play dated two thousand six hundred years before the Christian era. He said he would follow it up with a list of the previous plays of the kind, and in his innocence would have carried them back to the Flood.

That is the most discouraging thing that has ever happened to me in my dramatic career. I have done a world of good in a silent and private way, and have furnished Sir Henry Irving with plays and plays and plays. And what has he achieved through that influence? See where he stands now—on the summit of his art in two worlds. His position is unchallenged, and it was I who put him there—that partly put him there.

I need not enlarge upon the influence the drama has exerted upon civilization. It has made even good morals entertaining. I am to be followed by Mr. Pinero. I conceive that we stand at the head of the profession. He has not written as many plays as I have, but he has had that God-given talent, which I lack, of working them off on the manager. I couple his name with this toast, and add the hope that his influence will be supported in exercising his masterly handicraft in that great gift, and that he will long live to continue his fine work.

Text / Composite, based upon: "Two Speeches Made in London by

Mr. Choate and Mark Twain at a Dinner to Sir Henry Irving," *Times, Saturday Review,* July 7, 1900, p. 461; "Twain Has Written Over 400 Dramas," *World,* June 11, 1900; "Henry Irving" in *MTS*(10): 162–64; and *MTS*(23):193–94.

the Spaniard who said he left behind him 400 dramas / Possibly a reference to Lope Felix de Vega Carpio (1562–1635), a Spanish dramatist who wrote 1,800 plays, of which more than 400 have survived.

Henry Irving / Stage name of John Henry Brodribb (1836–1905). British actor. He made his debut in *Richelieu* (1865), had his first success in *The Belle's Strategem* (1866), and gave three hundred performances of *The Two Roses* (1870). In 1878, with Ellen Terry, he leased the Lyceum Theatre, where for twenty years they staged elaborate productions of Shakespearian plays and others. Irving made eight American tours (1883–1904). He was the first British actor to be honored with a knighthood (1895).

Pinero / Arthur Wing Pinero (1855–1914). British dramatist. Although successful with light comedy and farce, he is best known for social dramas that show the influence of Ibsen: *The Second Mrs. Tanqueray* (1893), *The Notorious Mrs. Ebbsmith* (1895), *Iris* (1901), *The Thunderbolt* (1908), and others.

· 104 ·

Shortly before sailing for home, Mark Twain spoke briefly at the opening of a reading room in Kensal Rise. It was the last speech he made in England before departure—or at least the last for which a text has come to light.

Remarks

Reading Room Opening, Kensal Rise,
London, September 27, 1900

I formally declare this reading room open, and I think that the legislature should not compel a community to provide itself with intelligent food, but give it the privilege of providing it if the community so desires.

If the community is anxious to have a reading room it would put its hand in its pocket and bring out the penny tax. I think it a proof of the healthy, moral, financial, and mental condition of the community if it taxes itself for its mental food.

A reading room is the proper introduction to a library, leading up through the newspapers and magazines to other literature. What would we do without newspapers?

Look at the rapid manner in which the news of the Galveston disaster was made known to the entire world. This reminds me of an episode which occurred fifteen years ago when I was at church in Hartford, Connecticut.

The clergyman decided to make a collection for the survivors, if any. He did not include me among the leading citizens who took the plates around for collection. I complained to the governor of his lack of financial trust in me, and he replied: "I would trust you myself—if you had a bell punch."

You have paid me many compliments, and I like to listen to compliments. I endorse all your chairman has said to you about the union of England and America. He also alluded to my name, of which I am rather fond.

A little girl wrote me from New Zealand in a letter I received yesterday, stating that her father said my proper name was not Mark Twain but Samuel Clemens, but that she knew better, because Clemens was the name of the man who sold the patent medicine, and his name was not Mark. She was sure it was Mark Twain, because Mark is in the Bible and Twain is in the Bible.

I was very glad to get that expression of confidence in my origin, and as I now know my name to be a scriptural one, I am not without hopes of making it worthy.

Text / "Reading-Room Opening," *MTS*(10):189–90, incorrectly dated.

Galveston disaster / On September 8–9, 1900, a West Indian hurricane—135-mile winds and heavy seas—devastated Galveston, Texas. The death toll was 5,000, the damage variously estimated at seventeen to forty millions of dollars.

· 105 ·

Home again after a long absence, Mark Twain, disembarking from the liner Minnehaha, *affably withstood a siege of newsmen who bombarded him with questions. Asked what he had been doing all those years, he replied with an impromptu monologue, giving a compact and somewhat inaccurate history of his travels.*

Travelogue

Dockside, New York, October 15, 1900

Now, that's a long story, but I suppose I must give you something, even if it is in a condensed form. I left America June 6, 1891, and went to Aix-les-Bains, France, where I spent the fall and winter. After that I went to Berlin, where I lectured, giving readings from my works. After this my next stop was the Riviera, where I remained for three months, going from there to the baths near Frankfort, where I remained during the cholera season.

Most of 1892 I spent at Florence, where I rented a home. While there I wrote *Joan of Arc* and finished up *Pudd'nhead Wilson.* For the next two years I was in France. I can't speak French yet. In the spring of 1895 I came to the United States for a brief stay, crossing the continent from New York to San Francisco, lecturing every night. In October of that year I sailed from Vancouver for Sydney, where I lectured, or, more properly speaking, gave readings from my works to the English-speaking people. I also visited Tasmania and New Zealand.

This was at the time of the famous Venezuelan message of President Cleveland, and it did my heart good to see that the animosities engendered by that message did not affect the affection of a people in a strange land for me.

I then proceeded to India, lecturing in Ceylon, Bombay, and Calcutta. I then sailed for South Africa, arriving at Delagoa Bay in April, 1896. In South Africa I visited Kimberley, Johannesburg, and finally Cape Town. I met Oom Paul. I had heard and read all about him—hat, beard, frock coat, pipe, and everything else. The picture is a true likeness. At this time the Jameson raiders were in jail, and I visited them and made a little speech trying to console them. I told them of the advantages of being in jail. "This jail is as good as any other," I said, "and, besides, being in jail has its advantages. A lot of great men have been in jail. If Bunyan had not been put in jail, he would never have written *Pilgrim's Progress.* Then the jail is responsible for *Don Quixote,* so you see being in jail is not so bad, after all." Finally I told them that they ought to remember that many great men had been compelled to go through life without ever having been in a jail. Some of the prisoners didn't seem to take much to the joke, while others seemed much amused.

All this time my family was with me, and after a short stay at Cape Town we took a steamer for Southampton. On arriving in England we went to Guilford, where I took a furnished house, remaining two months, after which for ten months our home was in London. All this time I was lecturing, reading, or working hard in other ways, writing magazine stories and doing other literary work.

After London came Vienna, to which city we went in September, 1898, remaining until May of the following year, in order to allow one of my daughters to take music lessons from a man who spelled his name Leschetizky. He had plenty of identification, you see, and with all seemed to be a pretty smart fellow. After Vienna, where, by the way, I had a lot of fun watching the Reichsrath, we returned to London, in which city and Sweden we have been until our departure for home some days ago, and now I am home again, and you have got the history of a considerable part of my life.

Text / "Mark Twain Home Again," *Times,* October 16, 1900.

crossing the continent / One example of Mark Twain's inaccuracy. In 1895 he crossed the continent by the northern route through Minneapolis, Butte, Spokane, and Portland to Seattle. He did not visit San Francisco, and he did not lecture every night. He sailed from Vancouver for Australia in August.

Oom Paul / Familiar name for Stephanus Johannes Paulus Kruger (1825–1904), president of the South African Republic (1883–1900).

Jameson raiders / Sir Leander Starr Jameson (1853–1917), commanding a small force of volunteers and British South Africa Police, invaded the Transvaal, December 29, 1895. On January 2, 1896, surrounded by Boers near Doornkoop, the raiders surrendered and were imprisoned at Pretoria. The British government repudiated Jameson's unauthorized sortie. When he returned to England, he was sentenced to fifteen months in jail, but was released after four months because of illness.

advantages of being in jail / Among those who were not amused by Mark Twain's facetious speech was President Kruger. He ordered more stringent restrictions for the prisoners, but when Mark Twain interceded for them and explained the joke, the severity was eased.

Leschetizky / Theodor Leschetizky (1830–1915). Polish pianist. He was famous as a concert artist and as a teacher in Vienna. Among his pupils was Ignace Jan Paderewski; another was Ossip Gabrilowitsch, who married Mark Twain's daughter, Clara.

· 106 ·

Major Pond had attempted to interest Mark Twain in an American lecture series, offering a very handsome fee, but his proposals were rejected. Mark Twain said that he would never again speak for pay, but that he would continue to give away speeches as long as he lived. He had ample opportunity. Within a few days of his arrival in New York, he was caught up in a whirl of social and speaking engagements. There were dinners, teas, and receptions at which he was guest of honor. Causes, charitable and otherwise, sought his aid. He had become a figure of such world-wide fame that his presence at a function went far to assure its success.

Remarks

Galveston Orphans Bazaar, Hotel Waldorf-Astoria, New York, October 17, 1900

I expected that the Governor of Texas would occupy this place first and would speak to you, and in the course of his remarks would drop a text for me to talk upon, but with the proverbial obstinacy that is proverbial with governors, they go back on their duties, and he has not come here and has not furnished me with a text, and I am here without a text. I have no text except what you furnish me with your handsome faces, and—but I won't continue that, for I could go on forever about attractive faces, beautiful dresses and other things. But, after all, compliments should be in order in a place like this.

I have been in New York two or three days and have been in a condition of strict diligence night and day, the object of this diligence being to regulate the moral and political situation on this planet— put it on a sound basis—and when you are regulating the conditions of a planet it requires a great deal of talk in a great many kinds of ways, and when you have talked a lot the emptier you get, and get also in a position of corking. When I am situated like that, with nothing to say, I feel as though I were a sort of fraud; I seem to be playing a part, and please consider I am playing a part for want of something better, and this is not unfamiliar to me; I have often done this before.

When I was here about eight years ago, I was coming up in a car of the elevated road. Very few people were in that car, and on one end of it there was no one, except on the opposite side, where sat a man about fifty years old, with a most winning face and an elegant eye—a beautiful eye; and I took him from his dress to be a master mechanic, a man who had a vocation. He had with him a very fine little child of about four or five years. I was watching the affection which existed between those two. I judged he was the grandfather, perhaps. It was really a pretty child, and I was admiring her, and as soon as he saw I was admiring her, he began to notice me.

I could see his admiration of me in his eye, and I did what anybody else would do—admired the child four times as much, knowing I would get four times as much of his admiration. Things went on very pleasantly. I was making my way into his heart.

By and by, when he almost reached the station where he was to get off, he got up, crossed over, and he said, "Now, I am going to say something to you which I hope you will regard as a compliment." And then he went on to say, "I have never seen Mark Twain, but I have seen a portrait of him, and any friend of mine will tell you that when I have once seen the portrait of a man I place it in my eye and store it away in my memory, and I can tell you now that you look enough like Mark Twain to be his brother. Now," he said, "I hope you take this as a compliment."

"Certainly," I said, "I take it as more than a compliment. Yes," I said, "this is the proudest moment of my life to be taken for Mark Twain, for most men are always wishing to look like some great man, General Grant, George Washington, or like some Archbishop or other, but all my life I have wanted to look like Mark Twain. Yes," I said, "I have wished to look like that synonym, that symbol of all virtue and purity, whom you have just described. I appreciate it."

He said, "Yes, you are a very good imitation, but when I come to look closer you are probably not that man." I said, "I will be frank with you. In my desire to look like that excellent character I have dressed for the character; I have been playing a part." He said, "That is all right, that is all right; you look very well on the outside, but when it comes to the inside you are probably not in it with the original."

So when I come to a place like this with nothing valuable to say I always play a part, but I will say before I sit down that when it comes to saying anything here I will express myself in this way: I am heartily in sympathy with you in your efforts to help those who were sufferers in this calamity, and in your desire to help those who were rendered homeless, and in saying this I wish to impress on you the fact that I am not playing a part.

Text / Composite, based upon: "The Big Bazaar Closes with a Great Speech by Mark Twain," New York *Journal,* October 18, 1900; "Galveston Orphan Bazaar" in *MTS*(10):279–81; and *MTS* (23):204–6.

· 107 ·

Ladies of the New York Woman's Press Club made much of their chief guest, who relished their flattering attention. Mrs. Ernest Seton-Thompson, his hostess for the afternoon, acted as guide, and also as a protecting bulwark when the girls descended in force upon him. The Reverend Phebe Hanaford presided.

Remarks

Woman's Press Club Tea, Carnegie Hall, New York, October 27, 1900

I was recently asked what I had found striking in this country since my return. I didn't like to say, but what I have really observed is that this is the ungrammatical nation. I am speaking of educated persons. There is no such thing as perfect grammar and I don't always speak good grammar myself. But I have been foregathering for the past few days with professors of American universities and I've heard them all say things like this: "He don't like to do it." Oh, you'll hear that tonight if you listen, or "He would have liked to have done it." You'll catch some educated Americans saying that. When these men take pen in hand they write with as good grammar as any. But the moment they throw the pen aside they throw grammatical morals aside with it.

I quite agree with Mrs. Gaffney, and subscribe to her proposal to boycott all literature which has no right to exist. She must have inspired me out of myself, for to say this means great generosity on my part. I shall not do what I really intended to do, for I was intending to contribute a good deal of this kind of literature myself.

[He said that various pictures had arisen in his mind, suggested by Mrs. Gaffney and several musical numbers.]

I don't know why, I don't see the connection, but there the pictures are. The first of them is at home in the nursery, when my children were little. The second is of a jail where I once was—by request—not for any crime that I had committed—that they had found out, at least—but to see other people who had committed crimes, and the third picture is one that I saw years ago in a house in New York.

Perhaps I am recalled to the first picture by the precosity of your sex in entering the field of literature—you will see it in the family—even in the cradle. On the occasion of which I speak, my daughter, then just out of the cradle, displayed this precosity. Her governess had given her a lesson on the reindeer, which took perhaps an hour. My daughter repeated it to us in a few sentences, possessing decided literary value. This may have come from me. I don't know, but the inaccuracy of the sentences did not come from me. That was original with her.

She said: "The reindeer is a very swift animal. A reindeer once drew a sled 400 miles in two hours." Then, commenting on it, "This was regarded as remarkable. When the reindeer was done drawing that sled 400 miles in two hours it died."

Now, there is the whole process of thought, the putting two and two together and drawing a conclusion.

My next picture is of the prisoners in the Pretoria jail at the time of the Jameson raid. I soothed the feelings of those prisoners. I told them if they were not in that jail they would probably be in another. I pointed out their great opportunity for concentrating their minds. Sir Walter Raleigh would never have written his great history if he had not been imprisoned in the Tower. Another book written in jail was John Bunyan's *Pilgrim's Progress,* a book I could have written myself if I had been in jail. I told those prisoners that instead of trying to get out they should have been paying board in that jail, so great were their opportunites of concentration.

As a final instance of the force of limitatons in the development of concentration, I must mention that beautiful creature, Helen Keller, whom I have known for these many years. I am filled with the wonder of her knowledge, acquired because shut out from all distraction. If I could have been deaf, dumb, and blind I also might have arrived at something. I am only sentimentally blind, morally deaf and sometimes, not always, dumb. No, her grammar isn't "perfect." There's no such thing as "perfect grammar," but she is as near to it as anyone can be.

Text / Composite, based upon: New York *Herald,* October 28, 1900; *World,* October 28, 1900; "Woman's Press Club," *MTS*(10):99–100.

Mrs. Gaffney / Mrs. Fannie Humphreys Gaffney read a paper on "Woman's Attitude and Responsibility Toward Fixing a Standard of Light Literature." She called upon women to boycott unworthy publications.

Helen Keller / Helen Adams Keller (1880–1968). Having lost sight and hearing at the age of nineteen months, she was brought out of isolation by Anna Mansfield Sullivan, of the Perkins Institute for the Blind. In 1890 she was taught to speak by Sarah Fuller, of the Horace Mann School for the Deaf, Boston. In 1904 she graduated, with honors, from Radcliffe. When pressed for money, she lectured, wrote books, and appeared on the Orpheum vaudeville circuit. Mark Twain enlisted the aid of Henry Rogers to provide financial support. Among her books are *The Story of My Life* (1903), *Out of the Dark* (1913), and *Let Us Have Faith* (1940). Helen Keller was one of the world's remarkable citizens.

· 108 ·

The Lotos Club assembled a distinguished gathering to welcome the returned traveler. Among those celebrating the homecoming of "The Dean of American Humor" were Governor-elect Benjamin B. Odell, Jr., former Speaker Thomas B. Reed, Senator Depew, Howells, McKelway, Aldrich, Booker T. Washington, Henry Rogers, George Harvey, Augustus Thomas, John Kendrick Bangs, and Moncure D. Conway. Mark Twain absentmindedly got his dates mixed, failed to appear on time, and had to be summoned from his hotel. His late arrival so delayed the dinner that the speaking did not begin until 10 P.M., but to veteran banqueters the hour was inconsequential.

Dinner Speech

Lotos Club Dinner for Mark Twain, New York, November 10, 1900

I thank you for this greeting; I thank you all out of my heart, for this is a fraternal welcome—a welcome too magnificent for a humble Missourian such as I am, far from his native haunts on the banks of the Mississippi; yet my modesty is in a degree fortified by observing that I am not the only Missourian who has been honored here tonight, for I see at this very table—here is a Missourian, and there is a Missourian, and there is another Missourian—and Hendrix and Clemens; and last but not least, the greatest Missourian of them all—here he sits—Tom Reed, who has always concealed his birth till now. They tell me that since I have been away Reed has deserted politics and is now leading a creditable life. He has reformed, and God prosper him; and I judge, by a remark which he made upstairs a while ago, that he had found a new business that is utterly suited to his make and constitution, and all he is doing now is that he is around raising the average of personal beauty.

But I am grateful to the president for the kind words which he has said of me, and it is not for me to say whether these praises were deserved or not. I prefer to accept them just as they stand, without concerning myself with the statistics upon which they have been built, but only with that large matter, that essential matter, the good fellowship, the kindliness, the magnanimity, and generosity that prompted their utterance. Your president has referred to certain burdens which I was weighted with. I am glad he did, as it gives me an opportunity which I wanted. To speak of those debts, you all know what he meant when he referred to it, and of the poor bankrupt firm of Charles L. Webster & Co. No one has said a word about those creditors. There were ninety-six creditors in all, and not by a finger's weight did ninety-five out of the ninety-six add to the burden of that time. They treated me well; they treated me handsomely. I never knew I owed them anything; not a sign came from them.

"Don't you worry, and don't you hurry," was what they said. How I wish I could have creditors of that kind always! Really, I recognize it as a personal loss to myself to be out of debt. I owe those ninety-five creditors a debt of homage, and I pay it now in such measure as one may pay so fine a debt in mere words. I wasn't personally acquainted with ten of them, you know, and yet they said, "Don't you worry, and don't you hurry." I know that phrase by heart, and if all the other music should perish out of the world it would still sing to me. You are always very kind in saying things about me, but you have forgotten those creditors. They were the handsomest people I ever knew. They were handsomer than I was—handsomer than Tom Reed.

How many things have happened in the seven years I have been away from home! We have fought a righteous war, and a righteous war is a rare thing in history. We have turned aside from our own comfort and seen to it that freedom should exist not only within our own gates, but in our own neighborhood. We have set Cuba free and placed her among the galaxy of free nations of the world. We started out to set those poor Filipinos free, too, and why that most righteous purpose of ours has apparently miscarried I suppose I shall never know.

But we have made a most creditable record in China in these days—our sound and level-headed administration has made a most creditable record over there, and there are some of the Powers that cannot say that by any means. The Yellow Terror is threatening this world today. It is looming vast and ominous on that distant horizon. I do not know what is going to be the result of that Yellow Terror, but our government has had no hand in evoking it, and let's be happy in that and proud of it.

Since I have been away we have been nursing free silver. We have watched by its cradle, we have done our best to raise that child; but every time it seemed to be getting along nicely along came some pestiferous Republican and gave it the measles or something. I fear we shall never raise that child. Well, that's no matter—there's plenty of other things to do, and we must think of something else. Well, we have tried a President four years, criticized him and found fault with him, and here a day or two ago we go and elect him for another four years with votes enough to spare to do it over again. O consistency! consistency! thy name—I don't know what thy name is—Thompson will do—any name will do—but you see there is the fact, there is the consistency. Then we have tried for governor an illustrious Rough Rider, and we liked him so much in that great office that now we have made him Vice-President—not in order that that office shall give him distinction, but that he may confer distinction upon that office. And it's needed, too—it's needed. And now, for a while anyway, we shall not be stammering and embarrassed when a stranger asks us, "What is the name of the Vice-President?" This one is known; this one is pretty well known, pretty widely known, and in some places favorably. I am a little afraid that these fulsome compliments may be misunderstood. I have been away for a long time, and I am not used to this complimentary business; but—well, my old affectionate admiration for Governor Roosevelt has probably betrayed me into the complimentary excess; but I know him, and you know him; and if you give him rope enough—I meant to say—well, it is not necessary for me to say any more; you know him.

And now we have put in his place Mr. Odell, another Rough Rider, I suppose; all the fat things seem to go to that profession now. Why, I would have been a Rough Rider myself if I had known that this political Klondike was going to open up, and I would have been a Rough Rider if I could have gone to war in an automobile—but not on a horse! No, I know the horse too well; I have known the horse in war and in peace, and there is no place where a horse is comfortable. A horse thinks of too many things to do which you do not expect. He is apt to bite you in the leg when you think he is half asleep. The horse has too many caprices, and he is too much given to initiative. He invents too many new ideas. No, I don't want anything to do with a horse.

And then we have taken Chauncey Depew out of a useful and active life and made him a Senator—embalmed him, corked him up. And I am not grieving. That man has said many a true thing about me in his time, and I always said something would happen to him. Look at that gilded mummy! That man has made my life miserable at many a banquet on both sides of the ocean, and palsied be the hand that draws that cork.

All these things have happened, all these things have come to pass, while I have been away, and it just shows how little a Mugwump can be missed in a cold, unfeeling world, even when he is the last one that is left—a Grand Old Party all by himself. And there is another thing that has happened, perhaps the most imposing event of them all: the institution called the Daughters of the Crown—the Daughters of the Royal Crown—has established itself and gone into business. Now, there's an American idea for you; there's an idea born of God knows what kind of specialized insanity, but not softening of the brain—you cannot soften a thing that doesn't exist—the Daughters of the Royal Crown! Nobody eligible but American descendants of Charles II. Dear me, how the fancy product of that old harem still holds out!

Well, I am truly glad to foregather with you again, and partake of the bread and salt of this hospitable house once more. Seven years ago, when I was your guest here, when I was old and worn and down, you gave me the grip and the word that lift a man up and make him glad to be alive; and now I come back from my exile young again, fresh and alive, and ready to begin life once more, and your welcome puts the finishing touch upon my restored youth and makes it real to me, and not a glorious dream that must vanish with the morning. I thank you.

Text / Composite, based upon: "Mark Twain," *Times, Saturday Review,* November 17, 1900, p. 788; "Welcome Home" in *MTS*(10):351–58; and *MTS*(23):197–203.

Hendrix / Joseph Clifford Hendrix (1853–1904). American banker. Postmaster of Brooklyn (1886–90) and congressman (1893–95), he was president of the American Bankers Association (1897–1904).

Reed / Thomas Brackett Reed (1839–1902). American statesman. In Congress (1876–98), he was several times Speaker of the House. Honest and courageous, he supported the tariff, naval rehabilitation, revision of House rules, and liberal spending; opposed filibustering, Cuban intervention, Hawaiian annexation, and professional reformers. He was a vigorous debater whose biting sarcasm made him known as the "Czar" of the House. A scholarly man, he had a knack for aphorism: "A statesman is a successful politician who is dead." At banquets, he and Mark Twain enjoyed joshing each other.

a most creditable record in China / During the Chinese Boxer uprising (1900), the United States sent 5,000 troops to join those of England, Russia, Germany, France, and Japan for the relief of imperiled legations. The United States did not, however, join the punitive expedition under the German commander, Count von Waldersee—a looting foray, according to Mark Twain. At the Peking Conference (1901), the United States opposed the general demand for indemnity. Nevertheless, an indemnity was imposed, and the United

States received $25,000,000. In 1908 President Roosevelt recommended that the surplus of $18,000,000 remaining from the indemnity be returned to China, and Congress returned it.

Odell / Benjamin Barker Odell, Jr. (1854–1926). American politician. Congressman from New York (1894–98), then chairman of the Republican state committee, he played a large part in putting Theodore Roosevelt in office as governor. Odell himself was governor of New York (1900–04). He favored home rule for cities and aided tenement house reform.

· 109 ·

At the New York Press Club reception, Colonel William L. Brown, club president, introduced the guest of honor with such lavish praise that it provoked Mark Twain's first response, in which he turned the tables by dubious compliments paid to Colonel Brown. He sprang up twice again to talk back.

Three Speeches

New York Press Club Reception for Mark Twain, November 12, 1900

And must I always begin with a regret—that I have left my gun behind? I've said so many times that if a gentleman introduced me with compliments and then sat down I'd use a gun. But, as I haven't the gun, I'll just give the chairman a dose of his own medicine. It is my privilege to compliment him in return. I ask you to look at him.

Gentlemen, you behold before you an old, old man. His features would deceive you. Apparently he is hardened—a person dead to all honest impulses. On these features are the marks of unimaginable crimes, and yet the features belie themselves. Instead of having led a life of crime, as his face indicates, he began in a Sunday school—and will end there. He has always led an exemplary life—one of those lives that make you think of all the long words in the vocabulary that suggest virtue, virtue which he appears to have, but has not. His public history has been merely a deception, milestoned every now and then by misdemeanors. But these misdemeanors were only the effervescences of a great nature, the accidents of a great career. He really has all the virtues known, and he practices them secretly. Gentlemen, you know him too well for me to further prolong this introduction.

[Joseph I. C. Clarke, who followed, referred to Mark Twain's map of Paris, which showed that the German army had occupied a depleted brewery. At the conclusion of Clarke's talk, Mark Twain arose for his second speech.]

I rise this time without invitation, in order to defend myself. [Colonel Brown: "You need it, you need it."] Yes, and there are others here older than I who need it more. What I was going to say was this: I don't mind slanders and that sort of thing. The facts are what I object to. I don't want anybody to know my true history, and I appeal to you journalists to keep it from getting abroad. When you live as long as I have you'll find out that the world knows you much more favorably than you know yourself. I tell you, when you wake up in the morning feeling bad and thinking yourself a pretty lowdown kind of a creature it is not on account of what the world thinks or the slanders of other people, but on account of some infamous deed you have committed and which nobody but yourself knows anything about.

Now, the things that those Westerners said about me were all slanders. There was no truth in them. The true things that I did in that region they didn't know, so they couldn't tell them. If they could, they would have put me in a hole.

I have not been an alleged humorist. I have been a wise man, a Solomon. I have kept secret the things I have done. But it is no wonder that those people told slanderous tales about me; I would have done the same thing for another man.

Mr. Clarke is right in saying that the foundation of humor is seriousness, gravity. Contrast is what brings out humor. To show you that this is true, I will tell you how I came to draw that very map of Paris which he spoke about. It was in 1870 or 1871, I think. In my home was a very sick friend of ours. For days and nights my wife and I sat up and worried. What made the strain worse was the fact that we did not know where to locate the family of our sick friend. In vain we made inquiries to discover what was their post office, so that we might reach them by wire. It was no use, and the strain continued for three long weeks. At the end of that time I was completely worn out, exhausted, miserable. Then came the reaction. I sat down and took a big M and made that map of Paris.

But when I went to print the map it was upside down. I had forgotten that the cut of a map had to be made reversely in order to have the map look right on paper. The thing that I printed didn't look any more like Paris than like New York; it was a sight to behold. But it was published, nevertheless, and some people said it was very humorous. Under it I placed a dozen explanatory notes, but they didn't explain. Then I attached some more notes, without improving the value of the map as a map. But folks said it was funny. Some American students in Berlin took it from one beer mill to another and laughed over it; then some native Germans got hold of it and talked excited German about it. These Germans saw nothing funny in it, and there was humor in that very fact. Now, you can see how a very sad experience resulted in arousing my humor, for if it hadn't been for that sick friend of ours, I would never have drawn the map of Paris.

[Mr. Hennessey, who followed, said that he had never read any of Mark Twain's books. The next speaker, John W. Keller, said that he had read them all, and recommended them to newspapermen as a source of inspiration. Whereupon Mark Twain made his third speech.]

I want to say good night. Times have changed, you know. I am old. I am reformed, too. I am just as competent to run all night as I ever was, and more competent to discuss Scotch whiskey when it is good—and I see many before me who can do that. But when one becomes respectable, one must go home early. It is to protect my reputation that I am going. The last time I was with you I was like the rest of you not respectable.

All the slanders that were poured upon me tonight, I know, were pure artificialities. The compliments paid me were the only things that had the imprint of truth. I shall take the compliments home and forget the slanders.

I have one thing to say before I go. Of all these slanders there is only one that rankles, and it is not a slander on me, but on the man that said it. He said he had never read my books. Now that hurts. Really, I can't understand it. He seemed so intelligent, so intelligent. But how could he be so under the circumstances? If he hasn't read those books, his intelligence must be artificial. Mr. Keller has read them, and he simply oozes intelligence; he is brimming over with it.

I bid you good night, and thank you very much.

Text / Composite, based upon: "Reception to Mark Twain," *Times,* November 13, 1900; "Three Other Speeches by Mark Twain," *Times, Saturday Review,* November 17, 1900, pp. 791–92; "The New York Press Club Dinner," *MTS*(10):197–98.

Clarke / Joseph Ignatius Constantine Clarke (1846–1925). American journalist and playwright. On the staff of the New York *Herald,* he wrote *Robert Emmet, a Tragedy* (1888), *Malmora, a Metrical Romance* (1893), and other plays.

took a big M / In printers' language an em, which is the square of the body of any size of type, is represented by M or m. Mark Twain calls his wood block a big M on which he cuts his map, as he says, "wrong end first, except to left-handed people."

map of Paris / See *Tom Sawyer Abroad* (1896):447–50.

Keller / John William Keller (1856–1919). American journalist and politician. He was reporter, dramatic critic, managing editor and editorial writer for six New York papers (1879–1919), New York commissioner of Public Charities (1898–1902), and a sachem of Tammany Hall (1898–1903).

· 110 ·

The Society of American Authors honored the Clemens family with a reception attended by literary and professional New Yorkers and others. Among those present were W. O. Stoddard, Kenyon Cox, Mrs. Theodore Sutro, Edward W. Bok, Count de Lafayette, John Kendrick Bangs, John G. Carlisle, Edgar Saltus, and General Stewart L. Woodford. The chairman, Judge Rastus S. Ransom, introduced the chief guest with the usual extravagant praise that brought remonstrance from Mark Twain.

Speech

Society of American Authors Reception for Mark Twain and Family, Delmonico's, New York, November 15, 1900

It seems a most difficult thing, however well prepared and well posted a chairman is, to say anything about me that is not complimentary. I don't know what charm there is about me that makes it impossible for him to say anything unless it has its flattering side. He spoke of my modesty. One can see that the chairman is envious of it.

But I am not modest. I find my breast heave and lift up when a man says anything creditable to me. Then they tell things about me that never happened. But when you come to sum it up you will find that I enjoy a compliment about as much as any man. But you don't know me. I've got another side unpictured. I've got a wicked side. There are people here who know really what I have done and why I do not repent of it.

These are the facts—this is the truth—all else is fiction, which counts for naught in life. The truth is that I have led a life full of interior sin. That is what makes life so precious to me. It is great trouble for me to get up an exterior life like this you see. I daresay that is the way with most of us. If you could throw an X-ray through your chairman. Oh dear— We are a pair. I have made a life study of trying to appear to be what he seems to think I am. Everybody believes that I am just a monument of all the virtues, but it is nothing of the sort. I am leading two lives, and it keeps me pretty busy.

You see I am not sparing myself. I have made it the business of my life to follow the true, beautiful and good. Some day there will be a chairman who will forget those merits of mine and then he will serve a double purpose—he will tell the truth and take some of this modesty out of me. Yes, I've got modesty, but most of all I have self-esteem and veracity.

At the Press Club the other night there was a speaker who it seemed to me was picturing me sincerely. He was leading up to things, but said nothing to my credit. But when he said that he had never read a book of mine I knew at once that he was a liar, because a man with the intelligence he displayed could never have attained that intelligence without reading one of my books.

I like compliments. I like to go home and tell them all over again to the members of my family. They don't believe them, but I like to tell them in the home circle, all the same. I like to dream of them if I can.

I thank everybody for their compliments, but I don't think that I am praised any more than I am entitled to be.

Text / Composite, based upon: "Authors Honor Mark Twain," *Times,* November 16, 1900; *World,* November 16, 1900; "Society of American Authors," *MTS*(10):186–88.

· 111 ·

At the Nineteenth Century Club dinner the chairman, Dr. Elgin R. L. Gould, said that when he was in Germany he had had to apologize profusely for the liberties a certain American literary man had taken with the German language. The remark, which was the sort of thing Mark Twain called a "text," gave him an opportunity for rebuttal.

The Disappearance of Literature

Nineteenth Century Club Dinner, Sherry's, New York,
November 20, 1900

It wasn't necessary for your chairman to apologize for me in Germany. It wasn't necessary at all. Instead of that he ought to have impressed upon those poor benighted Teutons the service I rendered them. Their language had needed untangling for a good many years. Nobody else seemed to want to take the job, and so I took it, and I flatter myself that I made a pretty good job of it. The Germans have an inhuman way of cutting up their verbs. Now a verb has a hard time enough of it in this world when it's all together. It's downright inhuman to split it up. But that's just what those Germans do. They take part of a verb and put it down here, like a stake, and they take the other part of it and put it away over yonder like another stake, and between these two limits they just shovel in German. I maintain that there is no necessity for apologizing for a man who helped in a small way to stop such mutilation.

We have heard a discussion tonight on the disappearance of literature. That's no new thing. That's what certain kinds of literature have been doing for several years. The fact is, my friends, that the fashion in literature changes, and the literary tailors have to change their cuts or go out of business. Professor Winchester here, if I remember fairly correctly what he said, remarked that few, if any, of the novels produced today would live as long as the novels of Walter Scott. That may be his notion. Maybe he is right; but so far as I am concerned, I don't care if they don't.

Professor Winchester also said something about there being no modern epics like *Paradise Lost.* I guess he's right. He talked as if he was pretty familiar with that piece of literary work, and nobody would suppose that he never had read it. I don't believe any of you have ever read *Paradise Lost,* and you don't want to. That's something that you just want to take on trust. It's a classic, just as Professor Winchester says, and it meets his definition of a classic—something that everybody wants to have read and nobody wants to read.

Professor Trent also had a good deal to say about the disappearance of literature. He said that Scott would outlive all his critics. I guess that's true. The fact of the business is, you've got to be one of two ages to appreciate Scott. When you're eighteen you can read *Ivanhoe,* and you want to wait until you are ninety to read some of the rest. It takes a pretty well-regulated, abstemious critic to live ninety years.

But as much as these two gentlemen have talked about the disappearance of literature, they didn't say anything about my books. Maybe they think they've disappeared. If they do, that just shows their ignorance on the general subject of literature. I am not as young as I was several years ago, and maybe I'm not so fashionable, but I'd be willing to take my chances with Mr. Scott tomorrow morning in selling a piece of literature to the Century Publishing Company. And I haven't got much of a pull here, either. I often think that the highest compliment ever paid to my poor efforts was paid by Darwin through President Eliot, of Harvard College. At least, Eliot said it was a compliment, and I always take the opinion of great men like college presidents on all such subjects as that.

I went out to Cambridge one day a few years ago and called on President Eliot. In the course of the conversation he said that he had just returned from England, and that he was very much touched by what he considered the high compliment Darwin was paying to my books, and he went on to tell me something like this:

"Do you know that there is one room in Darwin's house, his bedroom, where the housemaid is never allowed to touch two things? One is a plant he is growing and studying while it grows" (it was one of those insect-devouring plants which consumed bugs and beetles and things for the delectation of Mr. Darwin) "and the other some books that lie on the night table at the head of his bed. They are your books, Mr. Clemens, and Mr. Darwin reads them every night to lull him to sleep."

My friends, I thoroughly appreciated that compliment, and considered it the highest one that was ever paid to me. To be the means of soothing to sleep a brain teeming with bugs and squirming things like Darwin's was something that I had never hoped for, and now that he is dead I never hope to be able to do it again.

Text / "Disappearance of Literature," in *MTS*(10):193–96; and *MTS*(23):209–10.

Winchester / Caleb Thomas Winchester (1847–1920). American teacher. Librarian of Connecticut Wesleyan University (1869–85), he was Olin Professor of Rhetoric and English Literature there (1873–1920).

Trent / William Peterfield Trent (1862–1939). American teacher. He founded the *Sewanee Review* (1892), and was professor of English literature at Columbia University (1900–29).

Eliot / Charles William Eliot (1834–1926). American educator. As president of Harvard (1869–1909), he established graduate schools in the arts, applied science and business administration, introduced the elective system, and raised standards of medical education. Among his books are *The Happy Life* (1896), *American Contributions to Civilization* (1898), and *The Religion of the Future* (1909).

· 112 ·

The Public Education Association, of which Mrs. Schuyler Van Rensselaer was president, fostered education by free lectures and by concern for school equipment, teaching methods, health, and safety, particularly in the slums of New York's East Side. At the annual meeting of the association, a large audience of several hundred women did not discompose Mark Twain, who startled the ladies by his forthright anti-imperialism.

Remarks

Annual Meeting, Public Education Association, Berkeley Lyceum, New York, November 23, 1900

I don't suppose that I am called here as an expert on education, or, at least, I should hope not, and when I thank the president and members of the society for asking me here at all, I do so with the distinct understanding that I am not expected to furnish information. I am incapable of it.

As I sat here looking around for an idea it struck me that I was called for two reasons. One was to do good to me, a poor unfortunate traveler on the world's wide ocean, by giving me a knowledge of the nature and scope of your society and letting me know that others beside myself have been of some use in the world. The second reason is that I am asked here to operate as a contrast—the contrast of an idle and lazy man in the company of 600 or 700 earnest, energetic women, and, further, to show by this contrast, the possibilities of education. Go on with your good work and you will receive the applause of the idle and lazy as well as the others.

Oh, I have a wild and vague and nebulous idea of the aims and objects of the society, and already I applaud. If I understood fully the grand scope of your organization I might raise my applause to a still higher key. Such as it is, it's genuine and there's plenty of it.

The president has just mentioned the fact that the society has won one great credit mark in the fact that it has been called upon for instruction by the Charter Revision Commission. The commission would not have made this request unless it had felt sure of being able to learn something of its counsels.

Reference has been made to the fact that the pictures of the New York schools have gone here and there throughout Europe for the instruction of foreign governments, and are now in the hands of Russia. Well, that was a compliment that I was not expecting for our educational system, because it has not been an hour since I was reading a cable dispatch in one of the newspapers which began, "Russia proposes to retrench."

When one is not expecting a thunderbolt like that it is exciting. I thought, what a good thing for the whole world! "Russia has 30,000 soldiers in Manchuria," I said to myself, "and this dispatch means that she is going to take them out of there and send them back to their farms to live in peace. If Russia retrenches this way why shouldn't Germany and France follow suit? Why shouldn't all the foreign powers withdraw from China and leave her free to attend to her own business?"

Why should not China be free from the foreigners, who are only making trouble on her soil? If they would only all go home, what a pleasant place China would be for the Chinese!

As far as America is concerned we don't allow the Chinese to come here, and we would be doing the graceful thing to allow China to decide whether she will allow us to go there. China never wanted any foreigners, and when it comes to a settlement of the immigrant question I am with the Boxer every time.

The Boxer is a patriot; he is the only patriot China has. The Boxer believes in driving us out of his country. I wish him success. I am a Boxer myself, because I believed in driving the Chinaman out of this country. The Boxers on this side have won out. Why not give the Boxer on the other side a chance?

It occurred to me to finish that cablegram. The rest said: "Russia, in order to retrench, has resolved to withdraw the appropriation for public schools." Now, I never expected to see any humor in a cable dispatch from Russia. The worst thing about it is that the Russians themselves probably don't see any humor in it. The idea of a country concluding that the best way to save expenses is to cut off the common schools! We, who have been led to believe that out of the schools grows a nation's greatness, can hardly believe this tale.

It is curious to reflect how history repeats itself and how great minds all over the earth are sure at some time to alight on the same great idea. Now, this same Russian plan of retrenchment was brought up once in a township on the Mississippi River when I was a boy. The town was short of money and it was proposed to discontinue the common schools. At a meeting where the scheme was being discussed, an old farmer got up and said:

"I think it's a mistake to try to save money that way. It's not a real saving, for every time you stop a school you will have to build a jail. What you gain at one end you lose at the other. It's like feeding a dog on his own tail. It wouldn't fatten that dog."

This society is much wiser in its day and generation than the Emperor of Russia and all his people. That is not much of a compliment, but it's the best I've got in stock.

Text / Composite, based upon: "Mark Twain to Women," *Times,* November 24, 1900; *World,* November 24, 1900; "Public Education Association" in *MTS*(10):144–46; and *MTS*(23):211–13.

Charter Revision Commission / The Greater New York Charter was being revised at this time. The Public Education Association was one of several civic organizations opposed to some of the new provisions: the constitution of the Municipal Assembly, the six-months' period of the mayor's power of removal, the requirement of a unanimous vote by the Board of Estimate and Apportionment, the bipartisan composition of the Police Board, and the short terms of office of heads of departments.

pictures of the New York schools / Mrs. Van Rensselaer said that pictures of New York's public schools had been exhibited at the Paris Exposition (1900), where they had attracted so much attention that foreign governments had borrowed them.

the Boxer / The Boxers were a Chinese secret society that took a prominent part in the uprising of 1900. The Chinese name, "gee ho chuan," meaning "righteousness, harmony, and fists," implied the athletic training necessary for membership. Mark Twain's defense of the patriotic Boxer, as well as his condemnation of the exploitation of China by foreign powers, expressed attitudes that were far ahead of the temper of the times. His views were not popular with the American public, which was being fed on Chinese atrocity stories.

· 113 ·

Traditional ceremony accompanied the annual banquet of the St. Nicholas Society: the central chandelier festooned with orange streamers, the speakers' table spread with an orange cloth decorated with smilax, waiters dressed as court pages of the House of Orange, silver-lidded Holland beer mugs as souvenirs. Among the 300 banqueters were scions of old Dutch families and other well known men: Netherlands Minister Baron Gevers, Consul General J. Rutgers Planten, Philip Rhinelander, R. B. Roosevelt, A. Cortland Van Rensselaer, John W. Vrooman, Cornelius B. Zabriskie, Frederick A. Juilliard, Barrett Wendell, and William E. Dodge. Frederic de Peyster Foster, garbed in the sash and headgear of his office, presided. Mark Twain was so dilatory about getting there that a posse had to be dispatched in a cab to fetch him.

Our City

Sixty-sixth Annual Banquet, St. Nicholas Society,
Delmonico's, New York, December 6, 1900

These are prosperous days for me. Night before last, in a speech, Bishop Potter complimented me and thanked me for my contributions to theology, and tonight the Rev. Dr. Mackay has elected me to the ministry. I thank both these gentlemen for discovering things in me which I had long before discovered, but which I had begun to fear the world at large would never find out.

Returning to New York after an absence of nine years, I find much improvement in it—a great moral improvement. Some think it is because I have been away, but the more intelligent think that it is because I have come back. But we won't discuss that. Let's get down to the business end of this toast—our city.

We take stock of a city like we take stock of a man. The clothes and appearance are the externals by which we judge. We next take stock of the mind, the intellect. These are the internals. The sum of both is the man or the city. New York has a great many details of the external sort which impress and inform the foreigner. Among these are the skyscrapers, and they are new to him. He hasn't seen their like since the Tower of Babel. The foreigner is shocked by them. I am not.

As seen by daylight these skyscrapers make the city look ugly. They are—well, too chimneyfied—like a mouth full of snags; like a cemetery with all monuments and no gravestones. But at night, seen from the river when the great walls of masonry are all a-sparkle, the city is fairy-like. It is more beautiful than any other city since the days of the Arabian Nights. We can't always have the beautiful aspect of things. Let us make the most of our sights that are beautiful and let the others go. When the disgruntled foreigner has exhausted his objections by day, let us float him down the river by night.

Certainly the skyscraper has its advantages, and we don't need to apologize for it. Then we have elevators in them that elevate—not like the cigar boxes of Europe called "lifts." The European lift is always stopping to reflect between floors. That's well enough in a hearse horse, but not in an elevator. The American elevator acts like the man's patent purge—it worked. As the inventor said, "This purge doesn't waste any time fooling around; it attends strictly to business."

In Europe, when a man starts to the sixth floor on a lift he often photographs his family so he may recognize them when he gets back. Then look at our cable and trolley and elevated cars. They are the cleanest, simplest, most comfortable in the world, and all of them were created and conferred upon us by the New York hackman. He did it, and we ought always to be grateful to him for that service. We have a custom of erecting monuments to our benefactors. We owe him one as much as we owe one to anybody. Let it be a tall one. Not a permanent one, maybe; build it of plaster, say. Then gaze at it and realize how grateful we are—for the time being—and then pull it down and throw it on the ash heap. That's the way to honor your public heroes.

As to our streets, I find them cleaner than they used to be. I miss those dear old landmarks, the symmetrical mountain ranges of dust and dirt that used to pile up along the streets for the wind and rain to tear down at their pleasure. Yes, New York is cleaner than Bombay. But I'm not here to flatter Bombay.

Compared with the wretched attempts of London to light that city, New York may fairly be said to be a well-lighted city. Why, London's attempt at good lighting is almost as bad as London's attempt at rapid transit. You can get no one to believe that you rode on a London underground road unless you have a cinder in your eye, and, as for the buses, some find it cheaper to ride on a London bus than to pay board. There is just one good system of rapid transit in London—the "Tube," and that, of course, had been put in by Americans. Perhaps, after a while, those Americans will come back and give New York also a good underground system. Perhaps they have already begun. I have been so busy since I came back that I haven't had time as yet to go down cellar.

But it is by the laws of the city, it is by the manners of the city, it is by the ideals of the city, it is by the customs of the city and by the municipal government which all these elements correct, support, and foster, by which the foreigner judges the city. It is by these that he realizes that New York may, indeed, hold her head high among the cities of the world. It is by these standards that he knows whether to class the city higher or lower than the other municipalities of the world.

Gentlemen, you have the best municipal government in the world—the purest and most fragrant. The very angels in heaven envy you, and wish they could establish a government like it in heaven. You got it by a noble fidelity to civic duty. You got it by stern and ever-watchful exertion of the great powers with which you are charged by the rights which were handed down to you by your forefathers, by your manly refusal to let base men invade the high places of your government, and by instant retaliation when any public officer has insulted you in the city's name by swerving in the slightest from the upright and full performance of his duty. It is you who have made this city the envy of the cities of the world. God will bless you for it—God will bless you for it. Why, when you enter the gates of heaven the angels will say,

"Here they come! The citizens who saw their civic duty and did it. Show them to the archangel's box, and turn the limelight on them!"

Text / Composite, based upon: "Twain's View of New York," *Times*, December 7, 1900; "Municipal Government" in *MTS*(10):123–27; and *MTS*(23):214–17.

Bishop Potter / Henry Codman Potter (1835–1908). American Episcopal clergyman. Rector of eastern churches (1858–84), he became Bishop of New York (1887). An enlightened cleric, he advocated social and civic reform, and flouted convention. To make the saloon a respectable poor man's club, he officiated at the opening of the Subway Tavern, Bleecker and Mulberry Streets (1904): blessing the premises, making a speech, and closing with the Doxology. The place did a booming business thereafter. Mark Twain greatly admired Bishop Potter.

Dr. Mackay / Donald Sage Mackay (1863–1908). Scotch Congregational clergyman. After pastorates in Vermont and New Jersey, he was minister of the Collegiate Church of St. Nicholas, New York (1899–1908). He too, like Bishop Potter, was not an ivory tower sort of clergyman.

elected me to the ministry / Dr. Mackay, first on the speakers' list and responding to the toast, "St. Nicholas," praised the saint as a symbol of genial religion, and remarked: "There is gospel in a smile, and in my opinion a man like Mark Twain is as much a preacher of righteousness in this world today as any consecrated bishop, priest, or minister."

erecting monuments to our benefactors / Mark Twain's mention of a memorial to New York hackmen was an ironical allusion to the temporary arch of lath and plaster that had been erected on lower Fifth Avenue in honor of Admiral George Dewey. It was there for several years, gradually succumbing to scabrous dilapidation.

the best municipal government / Mark Twain's closing remarks were an ironical reference to corrupt New York City politics in the grip of Richard Croker's Tammany machine.

· 114 ·

The twenty-six-year-old Winston Churchill, London Morning Post *correspondent in the Boer War, had been taken prisoner at Natal but had escaped and reached Durban, where he was made a lieutenant of the South African Light Horse. His story of these adventures,* From London to Ladysmith via Pretoria, *had recently been published. When he came to the United States for a speaking tour, there was resentment among Americans opposed to British policy in South Africa. Howells, Henry Van Dyke, J. Kennedy Tod, Edward Van Ness, and others refused to serve on the official reception committee. Churchill was annoyed by the controversy, but it caused enough stir to pack the grand ballroom of the Waldorf with what was called "a fashionable audience" of about 1,200. Mark Twain, who presided, ruffled the jingoes by his blunt remarks. The* Times *editorially reproved him for unpatriotic opposition to the American adventure in the Far East.*

Introducing Winston S. Churchill

Grand Ballroom, Hotel Waldorf-Astoria, New York,
December 12, 1900

Mr. Churchill and I do not agree on the righteousness of the South African war, but that is of no consequence. There is no place where people all think alike—well, there is heaven; there they do, but let us hope it won't be so always.

For years I have been a self-appointed missionary, and have wrought zealously for my cause—the joining together of America and the motherland in bonds of friendship, esteem and affection—an alliance of the heart which should permanently and beneficently influence the political relations of the two countries. Wherever I have stood before a gathering of Americans or Englishmen, in England, India, Australia or elsewhere, I have urged my mission, and warmed it up with compliments to both countries and pointed out how nearly alike the two peoples are in character and spirit. They ought to be united.

Behold America, the refuge of the homeless, the hunted, the oppressed from everywhere (who can pay ten dollars admission)—

anyone except a Chinaman—standing up for human rights everywhere, even helping to make China admit the foreigner when she didn't want him, and to let him in free when she wanted to charge him fifty dollars if he was a harmless Christian or kill him if he was a missionary. And how England, mother of human liberty, uttered that great word, "the slave that sets his foot upon English soil is free" and with her strong hand made that gospel good in every acre of that vast Empire whose dominions girdle the globe; and how unselfishly England has wrought for the open door for all.

And how nobly and piously America also has stood for that same door in all cases where it wasn't her own; and how generous we have been, and how generous England has been in not requiring fancy rates for extinguishing missionaries, the way Germany does, but willing to take produce for them—firecrackers and tea—while Germany has to have territory and cash, and monuments and any other loot that's in reach—and memorial churches, and has thus made true changes of heart and regeneration, and the other details of German trinity so expensive that China won't be able to afford German missionaries any more till she gets in better shape financially; and how self-respectingly England and America have refrained from imitating German bluster, German rapacity, the mailed fist with a burglar's jimmy in it, and the investing mouth above it which alternately chortles bargain counter piety and "no quarter" according to the state of the market; and how nobly (and shamefacedly) we both stood timorously by at Port Arthur and wept sweetly and sympathizingly and shone while France and Germany helped Russia to rob the Japanese; and how gallantly we went to the rescue of poor Cuba, friendless, despairing, borne down by centuries of bitter slavery, and broke off her chains and set her free—with approving England at our back in an attitude toward European powers which did us good service in those days, and we confess it now.

Yes, as a missionary I have sung this song of praise and still sing it; and yet I think that England sinned in getting into a war in South Africa which she could have avoided without loss of credit or dignity—just as I think we have sinned in crowding ourselves into a war in the Philippines on the same terms.

Mr. Churchill will tell you about the war in South Africa, and he is competent—he fought and wrote through it himself. And he made a record there which would be a proud one for a man twice his age. By his father he is English, by his mother he is American—to my mind the blend which makes the perfect man. We are now on the friendliest terms with England. Mainly through my missionary efforts I suppose; and I am glad. We have always been kin: kin in blood, kin in religion, kin in representative government, kin in ideals, kin in just and lofty purposes; and now we are kin in sin, the harmony is complete, the blend is perfect, like Mr. Churchill himself, whom I now have the honor to present to you.

Text / Composite, based upon: "Speech introducing Winston Churchill," TS, MTP; "Mark Twain as a Missionary," Boston *Transcript,* December 14, 1900; "China and the Philippines," *MTS*(10):128–29.

"the slave that sets his foot upon English soil is free" / In a case involving James Somerset, a Negro, Lord Mansfield ruled, June 22, 1772, that when a slave set foot upon English soil he became free. See Francis Hargrave, "An Argument in the case of James Somersett, a Negro, wherein it is attempted to demonstrate the present unlawfulness of Domestic Slavery in England" (1772).

fancy rates for extinguishing missionaries / A reference to massacres of missionaries during the Chinese Boxer uprising (1900), and to retributive payment, measured by large sums and quantities of goods collected or stolen by foreign powers. According to news stories, the most rapacious invaders were the Germans and Russians, who were said to have looted and burned villages, and to have slaughtered Chinese with indiscriminate ferocity. Some critics blamed the missionaries for the Boxer uprising, and various sects exchanged acrimonious recriminations. In late 1900, New York papers published many stories about the missionaries and the Chinese.

Port Arthur / A strongly fortified town in Manchuria, it was captured by the Japanese (1894), but in 1898 a Russian-German-French coalition forced the Chinese government to lease it to Russia for twenty-five years. At the outbreak of the Russo-Japanese War, Port Arthur was the scene of disasters for the Russian navy and surrendered, after a siege, to the Japanese (1905).

kin in sin / According to an anonymous listener, Mark Twain began thus: "Fellow thieves and robbers! I take it that this audience consists of English people and Americans, so I commence my remarks, fellow thieves and robbers—the Americans in the Philippines and the English in South Africa. But never mind, we're *kith* and *kin* in *war* and *sin*." See *Mark Twain's Jest Book,* ed. Cyril Clemens (1963):15. This passage does not appear in any other report of the occasion. Yet if he did not say those precise words, they represent his angry indignation over British and American imperialism.

· 115 ·

At a dinner of the City Club, the talk was mostly about the scandalous state of New York politics. Mark Twain, Bishop Potter, St. Clair McKelway, Charles Sprague Smith, and others proposed correctives.

The Causes of Our Present Municipal Corruption

City Club Dinner, New York, January 4, 1901

The Bishop has just spoken of a condition of things which none of us can deny, and which ought not to exist; that is, the lust of gain—a lust which does not stop short of the penitentiary or the jail to accomplish its ends. But we may be sure of one thing, and that is that this sort of thing is not universal. If it were, this country would not be. You may put this down as a fact: that out of every fifty men, forty-nine are clean. Then why is it, you may ask, that the forty-nine don't have things the way they want them? I'll tell you why it is. A good deal has been said here tonight about what is to be accomplished by organization. That's just the thing. It's because the fiftieth fellow and his pals are organized and the other forty-nine are not that the dirty one rubs it into the clean fellows every time.

You may say organize, organize, organize; but there may be so much organization that it will interfere with the work to be done. The Bishop here had an experience of that sort, and told all about it downtown the other night. He was painting a barn—it was his own barn—and yet he was informed that his work must stop; he was a nonunion painter, and couldn't continue at that sort of job.

Now, all these conditions of which you complain should be remedied, and I am here with the utmost seriousness of manner to tell you what's to be done, and how to do it. I've been a statesman without salary for many years, and I have accomplished great and widespread good. I don't know that it has benefited anybody very much, even if it was good; but I do know that it hasn't harmed me very much, and it hasn't made me any richer. I am a statesman not for reward, but for the peace of mind it brings me. I am too old to learn, but I am not too old to teach.

We hold the balance of power. Put up your best men for office, and we shall support the better one. With the election of the best man for Mayor would follow the selection of the best man for Police Commissioner and Chief of Police.

Now, to set this whole thing right is very simple. I know all about it. It has been said by somebody, and if it hasn't it will be now, that we must learn wisdom out of the mouths of babes and sucklings or something of that sort. The whole solution of the question rests just there. My first lesson in the craft of statesmanship was taken at an early age. Fifty-one years ago I was fourteen years old, and we had a society in the town I lived in, patterned after the Freemasons, or the Ancient Order of United Farmers, or some such thing—just what it was patterned after doesn't matter. It had an inside guard and an outside guard, and a past grand warden, and a lot of other things, so as to give dignity to the organization and offices to the members. The party was called the Cadets of Temperance. Its members wore red merino scarfs and walked in church parades and picnics. On entering it a boy had to promise not to smoke, never to drink or gamble, to keep the Sabbath, and not to steal watermelons. In fact, you promised to leave behind all the liberties that were of any value, and pursue a career of virtue that was irksome to yourself and a reproach to all other people.

There were thirty-four members of the party, and they were divided into two factions, the reds and the blues. Five of the members were purchasable, and they had to be purchased every month, when there was an election. They got to be an infernal nuisance. Every time we had an election the candidates had to go around and see the purchasable members. The price per vote was paid in doughnuts, and it depended somewhat on the appetites of the individuals as to the price of the votes. There were two boys—the most incapable of the lot, but the most enterprising, who were always to the fore. There was Croker Brown on one side and Platt Higgins on the other, and one or the other managed to get himself elected every time. The good boys stood no show at all. They couldn't get elected.

When we had stood this thing a long time, we got an idea. We good boys stepped out when we saw the balance of power with the purchasables, and formed another party. We called ourselves the incorruptibles, but we were not always known by that name. We had obloquy heaped on us, and we got the name of the "Anti-Doughnut Party" because we couldn't be approached on the usual terms. Well, we started wrong by putting up one of our members for office, and of course he got licked.

But we stuck together, we twelve, and enunciated new principles. They were that none of us would ever accept office of any kind. We are here, we said, to put some virtue into the gang, and we're going to do it. We won't take office, but we warn you—meaning the other two parties—that you've got to put up your best men for office or you won't get our support. We were strong enough to make those terms, and that was the end of the Crokers and the Platts. The good boys were put up, and then we picked the best one and voted for him and he was elected.

There's the problem, gentlemen, solved. What we want today is an Anti-Doughnut party that won't take office, but will keep the other parties safe. I am sure that it can be done. An Anti-Doughnut party of 60,000 or 80,000 can do the trick. It would spread from the city to the country, and in time it would dictate the nomination of every office holder from constable to President. All it would ask for was the best possible man, and its support would mean the best man's election. I was an Anti-Doughnut in my boyhood, and I'm an Anti-Doughnut still. The modern designation is Mugwump. There used to be quite a number of us Mugwumps, but I think I'm the only one left. I had a vote this fall, and I began to make some inquiries as to what I had better do with it.

Not long ago we had two men running for President. There was Mr. McKinley on the one hand and Mr. Bryan on the other. If we'd had an Anti-Doughnut party neither would have been elected. I didn't know much about finance, but some friend told me that Bryan was all wrong on the money question, so I didn't vote for him. I know enough about the Philippines to have a strong aversion to sending our bright boys out there to fight with a disgraced musket under a polluted flag, so I didn't vote for the other fellow. I've got that vote, and it's clean yet, ready to be used when you form your Anti-Doughnut party that will want only the best men for the offices, no matter what party they belong to, and which will solve all your political problems.

Text / Composite, based upon: "Bishop Potter Says He Was Approached / The Anti-Doughnut Party," *Times,* January 5, 1901; "Municipal Corruption" in *MTS*(10):118–22; and *MTS*(23): 218–21.

Croker Brown / A reference to Richard Croker (1841–1922). American political boss. An Irish immigrant, he was a prizefighter in New York slums, joined Tammany Hall (1865), opposed Boss Tweed and rose to leadership in 1886. Discredited (1894), he returned to England but came back (1897) to put Robert C. Van Wyck in office as mayor of Greater New York. In 1901 the Fusion party temporarily wrecked Croker's machine, and he retired to Ireland, where he had a stable of racehorses.

Platt Higgins / A reference to Thomas Collier Platt (1833–1910). American politician. As powerful state Republican boss of New York, he arranged legislative programs and dispensed favors to adherents who made large contributions to party funds. His power began to decline when Governor Roosevelt opposed him.

Anti-Doughnut party / Mark Twain's suggestion was, in effect, adopted by the formation in 1901 of a New York City Fusion party composed of independent Republicans and Democrats.

Bryan / William Jennings Bryan (1860–1925). American political leader. As Democratic presidential candidate (1896, 1900, 1904), he was the champion of the agrarians. A popular Chautauqua lecturer for thirty years, he was editor of the weekly *Commoner* (1901–13) and secretary of state under Woodrow Wilson (1913–15). Bryan supported direct election of senators, graduated income tax, woman's suffrage, and prohibition. At the Scopes trial (1925) he defended fundamentalism against Darwinism, making a poor showing against his formidable opponent, Clarence Darrow.

· 116 ·

The Hebrew Technical School for Girls, a philanthropic institution incorporated in 1884, was the only one in the city offering vocational training to Jewish girls. At the annual meeting of the society, President Nathaniel Meyers reviewed the work of the school on Henry Street, and urged that people of means remember it in their wills. Mark Twain, as was to be expected, spoke to a packed house.

Speech

Annual Meeting, Hebrew Technical School for Girls,
Temple Emanu-El, New York, January 20, 1901

Mr. Meyers has conducted this matter with distinguished ability, but at the end of this report I noticed a defect. He made such a strong appeal to those people who are going to make their wills. Some of you are here, you know. Such an appeal loosens your purse strings and you want to give. Well, when he was talking I thought, "Now he's going to do it." Why, I'm twice as old as he, and I've had so much experience that I would say to him, when he makes his appeal for help: "Don't make it for today or tomorrow, but collect the money on the spot." It's a great mistake to get everybody ready to give money and then not pass the hat.

We are all creatures of sudden impulse. We must be worked up by steam, as it were. Get them to write their wills now, or it may be too late by-and-by. Some years ago in Hartford we all went to the church on a hot, sweltering night, to hear the annual report of Mr. Hawley, a city missionary, who went around finding the people who needed help and didn't want to ask for it. He told of the life in the cellars where poverty resided, he gave instances of the heroism and devotion of the poor. The poor are always good to each other. When a man with millions gives a hundred thousand dollars it makes a great noise in the world, but he does not miss it. It's noise in the wrong place; it's the widow's mite that makes no noise but does the best work.

Well, Hawley worked me up to a great state. I couldn't wait for him to get through. I had four hundred dollars in my pocket, and I wanted to give that and borrow more to give. You could see greenbacks in every eye. But he didn't pass the plate, and it grew hotter and we grew sleepier. My enthusiasm went down, down, down—one hundred dollars at a time, till finally when the plate came round I stole ten cents out of it. So you see a neglect like that may lead to crime. Oh, many a time have I thought of that and regretted it, and I adjure you all to give while the fever is on you.

Referring to woman's sphere in life, I'll say that woman is always right. Man has made woman what she is. He has kept her down in her proper place. Your president sits here in that self-satisfied conceit of his, and assumes that I don't know anything about women. Why, I've been in favor of women's rights for years. I see in this school a hope for the realization of a project I have always dreamed of. Why, do you know, when I looked at my gray-haired old mother, with her fine head and noble thoughts, I really almost suspected, toward the last, that she was quite as capable of voting as I was. He's got the wrong notion if he thinks I don't know anything about women.

I know that since the women started out on their crusade they have scored in every project they undertook against unjust laws. I would like to see them help make the laws and those who are to enforce them. I would like to see the whiplash in women's hands. The suffrage in the hands of the men degenerates into a couple of petrified parties. The man votes for his party and gets the city in the condition this one is in now—a disgrace to civilization. If I live seventy-five years more—well, I won't—fifty years, then, or twenty-five, I think I'll see women use the ballot. It's the possession of the ballot that counts. If women had it you could tell how they would use it.

Bring before them such a state of affairs as existed in New York City today and they would rise in their strength at the next election, elect a mayor, and sweep away corruption.

True, they might sit ten years and never use it, but on such occasions they would cast it. Or in the case of an unjust war. Why, war might even pass away and arbitration take its place. It never will so long as men have the votes.

How many of our 600,000 women are vicious? Not enough to amount to anything. If women could vote, each party would feel compelled to put up the best candidate it could or take the risk of being voted down by the women. States are built on morals—not intellects. And men would never get any morals at all if the women didn't put it into them when they were boys. If women could vote the good women would all vote one way. Men won't do that. It's a choice of evils with them.

[He referred to President Meyer's remark that a year earlier the school's board of managers had all been women, but that at present it was all men.]

And now he says they have twenty-one typewriters, whereas before they had only four. Oh, I like that modesty. We men are all like that. Well, at any rate I hope a lot of us will die and leave something in our wills.

Text / Composite, based upon: "Mark Twain Says Women Should Vote," *Times,* January 21, 1901; "Votes for Women" in *MTS*(10):101–3; and *MTS*(23):222–24.

Hawley / D. Hawley, brother of General Hawley, was self-appointed missionary and good samaritan of Hartford, devoted to aiding the poor and helpless. Mark Twain several times gave benefit lectures to aid Father Hawley's "clients," as he called them.

twenty-one typewriters / Mark Twain surely meant, not machines, but women typists, highlighting the irony that whereas there were no women on the board of managers, the number had increased in subordinate jobs.

· 117 ·

The chief object of the University Settlement Society was to combat the poverty of New York slums. Its Settlement House at Rivington and Eldridge Streets, modeled after Toynbee Hall, London, had a library of 1,800 volumes and a Penny Provident Bank, which had a thousand depositors. Called "the organization from uptown," it had the support of such philanthropic citizens as Abram S. Hewitt, Stephen J. Olin, J. G. Phelps Stokes, Mrs. Nicholas Murray Butler, and Carl Schurz. Mrs. Schuyler Van Rensselaer was in the charge of the Women's Auxiliary. Seth Low was chairman of the annual meeting; among speakers were Columbia sociologist Franklin R. Giddings, Mrs. Edward R. Hewitt, Mrs. Bond Thomas, and Richard Watson Gilder. The chairman remarked that Mark Twain said the meeting should have adjourned when he was due to speak. As he began his speech, Mark Twain explained.

Speech

Annual Meeting, University Settlement Society,
New York, February 2, 1901

It was because I had nothing to do and you had. I was thinking of you, for I myself would like to talk for two or three hours, as usual. I was reared to think of others always—never of myself; and I have ever tried to spread that doctrine—by proxy.

The older we grow the greater becomes our wonder at how much ignorance one can contain without bursting one's clothes. Ten days ago I did not know anything about the University Settlement except what I'd read in the pamphlets sent me. Now, after being here and hearing Mrs. Hewitt and Mrs. Thomas, it seems to me I know of nothing like it at all. It's a charity that carries no humiliation with it.

The speakers before me have told how you have to drive pupils away from your schools instead of into them. It was not that way in my young days. When I came down here this afternoon I saw in the building a dancing class. You must pay a cent for a lesson. You can't get it for nothing. It is well to make people pay for what they get. That is why your charity does not humiliate. By the way, the reason I never learned to dance was because these schools for that art charged money.

But it was the pawnbroker's shop you have here that interested me mightily. I have known something about pawnbrokers' shops in my time, but here you have a wonderful plan. The ordinary pawnbroker is allowed to collect from his patrons an enormous percentage; he fleeces the straggling stranger. I have paid much to them. Just now I saw a man pledge a watch in your shop for two dollars. He wanted the money only for a fortnight, and the price charged for the loan for that time was only a penny. I wish I could have gotten such terms when I was young. The reason I speak so feelingly on the subject of pawnshops is that I once had a romance which was closely connected with an establishment of the kind. The other day I was looking through that autobiography, which I am building for the instruction of the world, when I came across an incident that I had written several years before. It was something that happened in San Francisco a long time ago.

At that time I was a newspaperman. I was out of a job. There was a friend of mine, a poet, but, as he could not sell his poems, he also had nothing to do for a living, and he was having a hard time of it, too. There was a love passage in it, too, but I will spare you that and leave you to read it in my book. Well, my friend, the poet, said to me that his life was a failure, and I told him I thought it was, and then he said he thought he ought to commit suicide, and I said, "All right," which was disinterested advice to a friend in trouble. My advice was positive. It was somewhat disinterested, but there were a few selfish motives behind it. As a reporter, I knew that a good "scoop" would get me employment, and so I wanted him to kill himself without letting anybody but me know about the deed. Then I could sell the news and get a new start in life. The poet could be spared, and so, largely for his own good and partly for mine, I urged him not to delay in doing the thing. I kept the idea in his mind. You know, there is no dependence in a suicide—he may change his mind.

He had a preference for a pistol, which was an extravagance, for we hadn't enough between us to hire a pistol. A fork would have been easier. I told him that, as we were financially crippled, we could not buy a revolver. Then he wanted a knife. To that I objected, too, on the same grounds. At last he mentioned drowning, and asked me what I thought of it. I said that it was a very good way, except that he was a fine swimmer, and I did not know whether it would turn out well on this account. But I consented to the plan, seeing no better one in sight.

So we went down to the beach. I went with him because I wanted to see that the thing was done right. You know the curiosity some people have. When we reached the shore of the sea a wonderful thing happened.

He was all ready to take the fatal leap. I was ready to see him do it. Providence interposed. From out the ocean, borne, perhaps, from the other side of the Pacific, there was washed up on the sand at our feet a gift—a gift that the sea had been tossing around for weeks, maybe, waiting for us to come down to the coast and receive it. What was it? It was a life preserver.

Now, you can imagine the complications that arose. The plan to do the suicide act by the drowning method fell through with a crash. With that life preserver, you see, he might have stayed in the water for weeks. I couldn't afford to wait that long. Suddenly I had an idea. That was no trouble for me, for I have the habit of having them often. He never had any, especially when he was going to write poetry. I suggested that he pawn the life preserver and get a revolver. The preserver was a good one. To be sure, the ocean had kept it for us a long time, and it had a few holes in it, but yet it was good enough to pawn somewhere. We sought the pawnbroker. He wanted ten percent a month on the loan from the life preserver. I didn't object, for I never expected to try to get it out again. All I wanted was a revolver—quick.

The pawnbroker gave us an old derringer, which is a kind of pistol that has but one barrel and shoots a bullet as big as a hickory nut. It was the only firearm he would let us have. Then he grew suspicious, wanted to know what we were going to do with the derringer. I drew him aside. "My friend is a poet," I said, "and he wants to kill himself with it." Upon which he replied, "Oh, well, if he is only a poet, it is well. God speed him."

We went out and loaded the pistol. Just then I had some qualms about staying to see the act of my friend. I hadn't objected to witnessing a drowning, but this shooting was different; the drowning might have been looked upon as accidental, but not so with this. But I calmed myself, for when I suggested that I might go away he grew uneasy and acted as though he would not carry out his purpose if I did not stay beside him. So I stayed. He placed the barrel at his temple. He hesitated. In spite of all I could do I waxed impatient. "Pull the trigger!" I cried. He pulled it. The ball went clean through his head. I held my breath. Then I found that the bullet had cleaned out all the gray matter. It had made a new man of him. Before he shot that shot he was nothing but a poet. Now he is a useful citizen. The ball just carried the poetic faculty out of the back door. Ever since then, although I am aware that I assisted him in the crime for selfish ends, I have been wishing that I might again help some other poet, or many of them, in the same way.

Now, therefore, I realize that there's no more beneficent institution than this penny fund of yours, and I want all the poets to know this. I am going to tell all the poets I know where your shop is located. Of course, you have lots of other good things in your establishment besides the pawnshop, and I have been thinking of sending you my check to help along your work. But I have decided, instead, to send to your library a lot of those books of mine that I hear one of your small boys has dubbed "Strawberry Finn."

Text / Composite, based upon: "Mark Twain Tells About Pawnbrokers," *Times,* February 3, 1901; "Mark Twain," New York *Journal,* February 3, 1901; "University Settlement Society" in *MTS*(10):140–43; and *MTS*(23):225–27.

Mrs. Hewitt / Mrs. Edward R. Hewitt was in charge of the kindergarten work of the auxiliary.

I never learned to dance / Perhaps he meant that he had had no formal instruction. Nevertheless, he was such a lively dancer that during his Washoe days San Francisco ladies gave a ball in his honor at the Lick House (1863). Thirty years afterward, at late parties, he was still kicking up his heels like a young man. See Louis J. Budd, "Twain Could Mark the Beat," *Journal of the Midcontinent American Studies Association,* 4, no. 1 (Spring 1963):39–44.

· 118 ·

The celebration of Lincoln's birthday jammed Carnegie Hall. Among those present were Carnegie, Dr. Lyman Abbott, J. Pierpont Morgan, Robert C. Ogden, Frederick A. Stokes, Oscar Straus, F. W. Vanderbilt, Whitelaw Reid, Daniel S. Lamont, Kilaen Van Rensselaer, and a bevy of generals Union and Confederate: Miles, Dodge, Wheeler, Howard, Greene, Sickles, McCook, and others. Veterans of the blue and the gray filled the stage. Five hundred singers of the People's Choral Union, directed by Frank Damrosch, sang the old war songs, and the Fifth United States Artillery band rendered stirring marches. Mark Twain, chairman, announced the songs to be sung by the chorus, escorted Miss Tracey, soprano, front and center for several solos, read a letter of regret from President McKinley, and introduced the principal speaker.

Remarks as Chairman

Lincoln Celebration, Benefit of Lincoln Memorial University, Carnegie Hall, New York, February 11, 1901

There remains of my duties as presiding officer on this occasion two things to do—only two—one easy, the other difficult. It is easy to introduce to you the orator of the evening, and then to keep still and give him a chance is the difficult task.

To tell an American audience who Henry Watterson is is not at all necessary. Just to mention his name is enough. A name like his mentioned to an audience would be like one of those blazing sentiments on the Madison Square tower. Just the mention of his name touches the chords of your memory tenderly and lovingly. Distinguished soldier, journalist, orator, statesman, lecturer, politician, rebel. What is better, he is a reconstructed rebel. Always honest, always noble, always loyal to his confessions, right or wrong, he is not afraid to speak them out. And, last of all, whether on the wrong side or on the right side, he has stood firm and brave, because his heart has always been true.

It is a curious circumstance, a peculiar circumstance—and it is odd that it should come about—that in the millions of inhabitants of this great city two Confederates, one-time rebels, should be chosen for the honorable privilege of coming here and bowing our heads in reverence and love to that honorable soul whom, forty years ago, we tried with all our hearts and all our strength to defeat and suppress—Abraham Lincoln. But are not the blue and the gray one today? By these signs we may answer here, "Yes." There was a rebellion, and we understand it is now closed.

I was born and reared in a slave state. My father was a slave owner before the Civil War, and I was a second lieutenant in the Confederate service—for a while.

Oh, I could have stayed longer. There was plenty of time. The trouble was with the weather. I never saw such weather. I was there, and I have no apologies to offer. But I will say that if this second cousin of mine, Henry Watterson, the orator of the evening, who was born and reared in a slave state and was a colonel in the Confederate service, had rendered me such assistance as he could and had taken my advice the Union armies would never have been victorious. I laid out the whole plan with remarkable foresight, and if Colonel Watterson had carried out my orders I should have succeeded in my vast enterprise.

It was my intention to drive General Grant into the Pacific Ocean—if I could get transportation. If I could have had the proper assistance from Colonel Watterson it would have been accomplished. I told Watterson to surround the eastern armies and wait until I came up. But he was insubordinate and stood upon the punctilio of military etiquette and refused to take orders from a second lieutenant of the Confederate army, and so the Union was saved. Now, this is the first time that this secret has ever been revealed. No one outside of the family has known these facts, but they're the truth of how Watterson saved the Union, and to think that up to this very hour that man gets no pension! That's the way we treat people who save Unions for us. There ought to be some blush on the cheek of those present this evening, but, to tell the truth, we are out of practice.

The hearts of this whole nation, North and South, were in the war. We of the South were not ashamed of the part we took. We believed in those days we were fighting for the right—and it was a noble fight, for we were fighting for our sweethearts, our homes, and our lives. Today we no longer regret the result, today we are glad that it came out as it did, but we of the South are not ashamed that we made an endeavor; we did our bravest best, against despairing odds, for the cause which was precious to us and which our consciences approved; and we are proud—and you are proud—the kindred blood in your veins answers when I say it—you are proud of the record we made in those mighty collisions in the fields.

When the great conflict began the soldiers from the North and South swung into line to the tune of that same old melody, "We are coming, Father Abraham, three hundred thousand strong." The choicest of the young and brave rose up from Maine to the Gulf, went forth to fight and shed their blood under the flag and for what they thought was right. They endured hardships equivalent to circumnavigating the globe four or five times in the olden days. They suffered untold hardships and fought battles night and day.

North and South we put our hearts into that colossal struggle, and out of it came the blessed fulfilment of the prophecy of the immortal Gettysburg speech which said: "We here highly resolve that these dead shall not have died in vain; that this nation, under God, shall have a new birth of freedom; and that a government of the people, by the people, for the people, shall not perish from the earth."

We are here to honor the birthday of the greatest citizen, and the noblest and the best, after Washington, that this land or any other land has yet produced. The old wounds are healed, and you of the North and we of the South are brothers again. We consider it an honor to be of the soldiers who fought for the Lost Cause, and now we consider it a high privilege to be here tonight and assist in laying our humble homage at the feet of Abraham Lincoln, and in forgetting that you of the North and we of the South were ever enemies, and remembering only that we are now indistinguishably fused together and nameable by one common great name—Americans!

Text / Composite, based upon: "Blue and Gray Pay Tribute to Lincoln," *Times,* February 12, 1901; untitled fragment, *MTB,* 4:1123–24; "Watterson and Twain as Rebels," *MTS*(10):295–97; "On Lincoln's Birthday," *MTS*(23):228–31.

Henry Watterson / (1840–1920). American editor. Staff officer under Generals Forrest, Polk, and Hood, he was chief of scouts in the Atlanta campaign. Cofounder of the Louisville *Courier-Journal* (1896), he was editor thereafter, making the paper influential in the South and well known elsewhere. Advocating Southern home rule, he helped to nominate Tilden for the presidency (1876) and was a Democratic congressman (1876–77). He published *"Marse Henry," an Autobiography* (1919); Arthur Krock compiled *Editorials of Henry Watterson* (1923).

"We are coming, Father Abraham" / From a popular war song, "Three Hundred Thousand More," by James Sloane Gibbons, first published in the New York *Evening Post,* July 16, 1862.

· 119 ·

In Albany, a legislative committee hearing on the Seymour bill to license osteopaths in the state of New York was talkative and acrid. Five physicians from the New York County Medical Society opposed the measure and berated Mark Twain for speaking in support of it. Dr. Frank Van Fleet caustically dismissed him as merely a funny man whose condemnation of American policy in the Philippines would have got him mobbed if anybody had taken him seriously. Dr. Robert T. Morris maintained that a humorist had no place in a sober discussion of a matter involving life and death. Dr. Henry T. Didema said that Mark Twain's common sense should not permit him to endorse such a bad piece of legislation as the Seymour bill. Mark Twain, apparently unruffled by these assaults, held the floor for almost an hour. His approval of osteopathy brought a reprimand from the Times, *February 28, 1901, which called him "a defender of quacks," deplored his "capacity for making grave mistakes in serious matters," and said that in advocating the cause of "this band of ignorant pretenders. . . . Mr. Clemens is engaged in a very bad business. He is setting himself up in exact opposition to all decent authority, and, however unintentionally, he is assuming the role of a public enemy."*

Remarks on Osteopathy

Committee on Public Health, New York General Assembly,
Albany, February 27, 1901

Dr. Van Fleet is the gentleman who gave me the character. I have heard my character discussed a thousand times before you were born, sir, and shown the iniquities in it, and you did not get more than half of them.

Now, gentlemen of the committee, when I came here, I came with a purpose of some kind, but it is difficult for me to find out now just what it was. These debaters have knocked it all out of my head. They have put my mind in a sort of maze with their scientific terms. I must say that I was both touched and distressed when they brought out that part of a child. I suppose the object of it was to prove that you cannot take a child apart in that way, and I suppose we must concede that they have proved that.

Why, sir, when I listened to all those remarkable names of diseases which our learned medical friends have thrown out to us here this afternoon it made me envious of the man who had them all. I don't suppose I shall ever enjoy the felicity of having them all in the span of life allotted to me, but I am truly thankful for those I have had. I am an experimenter. I have had a number of diseases, but am willing to take more, but I want to distribute them among not only doctors but the mountebanks.

I am so constituted that I want to give everybody a chance. I want to give the mountebank a chance, if you please. And I do not want to have any restrictions put upon my free will when I have that disposition. I could not stand here and advocate osteopathy without knowing much more about it than I do. One of the gentlemen who spoke referred to my having acquired such knowledge of osteopathy as I had in Sweden. That is true. About a year and a half ago in London I met Mr. Kellgren, who I believe is the most noted practitioner of this kind abroad. He calls himself Mr. because he has not acquired the privilege of giving a certificate when a patient dies on his hands. He has been practicing in London for twenty-seven years.

My meeting with him was quite by chance. I heard of him through a friend of mine whom he had cured of dysentery after eminent physicians had failed to give any relief, and after my friend had been brought close to the point of death. The friend I speak of is Poultney Bigelow. Now, of course, there may have been some flaw in Mr. Bigelow's cure, but he seemed to me to have been restored to full strength and health, and he himself insisted that he was. I thought he ought to know, though doubtless our medical friends will not agree with me on that point.

Now I am always wanting to try everything that comes along. It doesn't matter much what it is, I want to try it. And so I went to Mr. Kellgren, was treated by him in London, and later on in Switzerland, and he did me a lot of good, as I thought, although I must admit that my education doesn't qualify me to say just when I am in good health.

I see in the Bell Anti-Christian Science bill that you permit the grandmother to continue to dose the babe. Well, you couldn't stop her. It is well that you put in that provision. As a matter of fact, we all know that our population is really divided in allegiance between two schools of medicine, the regular physicians and the grandmothers. Now all I ask is the same liberty you give to the grandmother. The grandmother has been practicing without a license as far as the memory of any one of us goes back, and, on the whole, her success has been such that the medical profession is willing to have her continue in practice.

I like full liberty, full liberty to do with my body as I like, to my own peril or to the peril of anyone else. It doesn't matter; I'm not particular as to that. The state stands for liberty and it doesn't seem likely to change its position and will not interfere with your soul in the matter of health. When my soul is sick, unlimited spiritual liberty is given me by the state. Now then, it doesn't seem logical that the state shall depart from this great policy, the health of the soul, and change about and take the other position in the matter of smaller consequence—the health of the body.

Now the Bell bill will drive all the osteopaths out of the state. I suppose if you do drive them out, they will go up to Vermont, which has been characterized as the "garbage ground of the profession," and which, since it became that, has also become one of the healthiest states in the Union, and I suppose I can go up there without much trouble. Then you create the same condition as existed in the Garden of Eden. You want something and it is forbidden. Adam probably didn't want the apple until he found he couldn't have it, just as he would want an osteopath. He was different from the Clemens flock, especially this one. I wouldn't have taken one apple, but the whole crop.

I believe we ought to retain all of our liberties. We can't afford to throw any of them away. They didn't come to us in a night, like Jonah's gourd, if Jonah was the man who had a gourd. The moment you start to drive anybody out of the state, then you have the same situation which existed in the Garden of Eden. I don't know as I cared much about these osteopaths until I heard you were going to drive them out of the state, but since I heard that I haven't been able to sleep.

Now what I contend is that my body is my own, at least, I have always so regarded it. If I do it harm through my experimenting it is I who suffer, not the state. And if I indulge in dangerous experiments the state don't die. I attend to that. I hold my mother responsible for my desire for experiment. She bought any patent medicine that came along, whether she would need it or not, and would try any new disease that happened to be around. She experimented on me. I didn't enjoy it then, but I do now. When my mother heard of a new cure, she didn't select one from the flock haphazardly. No, she chose judiciously, and chose the one she could spare, which was myself.

I can remember well when the cold water cure was first talked about. I was then about nine years old, and I remember how my mother used to stand me up naked in the back yard every morning and throw buckets of cold water on me, just to see what effect it would have. Personally, I had no curiosity upon the subject. And then, when the dousing was over, she would wrap me up in a sheet wet with ice water and then wrap blankets around that and put me into bed. I never realized that the treatment was doing me any particular good physically. But it purified me spiritually. For pretty soon after I was put into bed I would get up a perspiration that was something worth seeing. Mother generally put a life preserver in bed with me. And when finally she let me out and unwound the sheet, I remember that it was all covered with yellow color, but that was only the outpourings of my conscience, just spiritual outpourings, and, fortunately, it removed all that, so that I am not troubled with it now.

But I am willing to say that sometimes my mother's experiments had such an effect upon me that she was obliged to call in "that ministering angel with the pills" to bring me around. And remembering that, I do not bar allopathy in my experiments now. No, I am willing to take a chance at that just for old times' sake. My mother three times tried new remedies on me, and they left me so low that they had to pull me out by means of the family doctor. I like osteopathy. It is quicker and you don't have to take any medicine. So I want liberty to do as I choose with my physical body and experiment as much as possible.

The physicians think they are moved by regard for the best interests of the public. Isn't there a little touch of self-interest back of it all? It seems to me there is, and I don't claim to have all the virtues—only nine or ten of them.

I was born in the "Banner State," and by "Banner State" I mean Missouri. I was born there and so was osteopathy, and both of us are getting along reasonably well, I trust. But in my state then the word "dispute" meant quarreling and quarreling in anger. Neither did we know of any other kind of a doctor than the one who went around carrying his pills in his saddlebag. Well, one day my father took me to my uncle's house and he had a picture on the wall of a room showing Christ disputing with the doctors. Now, although I was the model Sunday school boy of our section, I couldn't quite understand that. For to my mind to dispute meant to quarrel. There was an old slave in the house, Uncle Ben by name, who came into the room when I was revolving the problem of the picture in my mind. I thought perhaps Uncle Ben might be able to enlighten me, for he was a sort of doctor himself, a herb doctor, unlicensed, of course.

"Uncle Ben," I asked him, "what does that picture mean? Christ surely didn't begin the dispute, did He?"

"Naw, the doctors, they begin it," he said.

"And what did they want to quarrel with Christ for?"

" 'Cause he ain't got no license, dat's why dey say He bust dem up in business."

That is it. The objection is, people are curing people without a license and you are afraid it will bust up business. You ought to compromise so you can all get a chance at these people around here.

Text / Composite, based upon: "Mark Twain, Osteopath," *Times,* February 28, 1901; "Mark Twain's Humor," *Courant,* February 28, 1901; "Mark Twain Favors Osteopathy," unidentified clipping, n.d., MTP; "Osteopathy" in *MTS*(10):252–55; and *MTS*(23):232–34.

that part of a child / Dr. Morris displayed the vertebrae of a child to prove that osteopaths could not, as they claimed, "adjust" the immovable bones.

Kellgren / Heinrick Kellgren practiced osteopathy in Sanna, Sweden. Mark Twain and family had gone there in 1899 in the hope that "the Swedish movements," as the treatment was called, would cure or check the epilepsy of Jean Clemens.

Bigelow / Poultney Bigelow (1855–1924). American traveler and writer. Wrecked off Japan on a sailing voyage at age twenty, he became interested in colonial governments, and thereafter traveled widely: to China, Borneo, Java, the Philippines, Australia, Africa, and the West Indies. Among his books are *History of the German Struggle for Liberty* (1896–1905), *The Children of the Nations* (1901), and the autobiographical *Seventy Summers* (1925). He was a social being and popular banqueter.

Bell Anti-Christian Science bill / This bill, to prohibit Christian Science healers from practicing in the state of New York, had been written by the New York County Medical Society. The committee hearing on it was more tumultuous than that on osteopathy. The same doctors, reinforced by others, spoke in favor of the bill; opposing it were prominent Scientists, several lawyers, and even some physicians, including Dr. Mary Walker, the lady who wore pants and founded a female colony called "Adamless Eden." Opticians, as well as vendors of patent medicines and artificial limbs, claimed that the Bell bill would ruin their business. Invoking the Bible, opponents said that the bill was an attack on religious liberty. There was so much wrangling disagreement that the Bell bill did not reach the floor.

my experimenting / In a letter to the *Times,* March 1, 1901, Annie Nathan Meyer reproved Mark Twain for his casual attitude on health. Describing him as "humorist, author, lecturer, critic of the Government, maligner of the flag, osteopath," she said that he, Mrs. Eddy, and Mrs. Emma Stetson, a well-known Christian Scientist of New York City, should be permitted to try on themselves any treatment they wished, preferably the more severe the better, provided their ailments were not contagious.

· 120 ·

The New York Senate, not to be outdone by the House, invited Mark Twain to address the assembled senators. Not lobbying for any legislation this time, he spoke briefly and facetiously.

Remarks

Floor of the Senate, New York General Assembly, Albany, February 28, 1901

Mr. President and gentlemen: I do not know how to thank you sufficiently for this high honor which you are conferring upon me. I have for the second time now enjoyed this kind of prodigal hospitality—in the other House yesterday, today in this one. I am a modest man, and diffident about appearing before legislative bodies, and yet utterly and entirely appreciative of a courtesy like this when it is extended to me, and I thank you very much for it.

If I had the privilege, which unfortunately I have not got, of suggesting things to the legislators in my individual capacity, I would so enjoy the opportunity that I would not charge anything for it at all. I would do that without a salary. I would give them the benefit of my wisdom and experience in legislative bodies, and if I could have had the privilege for a few minutes of giving advice to the other House I should have liked to, but of course I could not undertake it, as they did not ask me to do it—but if they had only asked me!

Now that the House is considering a measure which is to furnish a water supply to the city of New York, why, permit me to say I live in New York myself. I know all about its ways, its desires, and its residents, and—if I had the privilege—I should have urged them not to weary themselves over a measure like that to furnish water to the city of New York, for we never drink it.

But I will not venture to advise this body, as I only venture to advise bodies who are not present.

Text / "Water-Supply," *MTS*(10):256–57.

· 121 ·

At a monthly meeting of the New York City Male Teachers Association, Mark Twain took his text from the remarks of Superintendent Charles Skinner, who spoke on "Patriotism for the Young." As reported by the Times, *March 17, 1901, he said in part: "Our schools must make our citizens, and our richest assets are our children. In these times . . . citizenship means . . . a very great responsibility to put on our boys. Our Republic has changed its place from a doubtful position in the line to the first place among the nations of the earth. . . . Today we do not care to own Cuba, Porto Rico, or the Philippines, but we do want to keep them from the dark rule of a barbarian people."*

Training That Pays

Monthly Supper, Male Teachers Association,
Hotel Albert, New York, March 16, 1901

We cannot all agree. That is most fortunate. If we could all agree life would be too dull. I believe if we did all agree I would take my departure before my appointed time, that is if I had the courage to do so. I do agree in part with what Mr. Skinner has said. In fact, more than I usually agree with other people. I believe that there are no private citizens in a republic. Every man is an official: above all, he is a policeman. He does not need to wear a helmet and brass buttons, but his duty is to look after the enforcement of the laws.

If patriotism had been taught in the schools years ago the country would not be in the position it is in today. Mr. Skinner is better satisfied with the present conditions than I am. I would teach patriotism in the schools, and teach it this way: I would throw out the old maxim, "My country, right or wrong," and instead I would say, "My country when she is right."

I would not take my patriotism from my neighbor or from Congress. I should teach the children in the schools that there are certain ideals, and one of them is that all men are created free and equal. Another that the proper government is that which exists by the consent of the governed. If Mr. Skinner and I had to take care of the public schools I would raise up a lot of patriots who would get into trouble with him.

I should also teach the rising patriot that if he ever became the government of the United States and made a promise that he should keep it. I will not go any further into politics as I would get excited, and I don't like to get excited. I prefer to remain calm. I have been a teacher all my life, and never got a cent for teaching.

[*Times:* "The speaker then cited some incidents from his boyhood life which, he said, he had later incorporated in his books. The fence whitewashing incident in 'Tom Sawyer,' he said, brought him in $4,000 in the end, when he never expected to get anything for teaching the other boys how to whitewash way back in 1849."]

I have a benevolent faculty. It does not always show, but it is there. We have had some millionaires who gave money to colleges. Now we have Mr. Carnegie building sixty-five new libraries. There is an educator for you on a large scale. I was going to do it myself, but when I found out it would cost over five millions I changed my mind, as I was afraid it would bankrupt me.

When I found out Mr. Carnegie was going to do it, I told him he could have my ideas gratis. I said to him, "Are the books that are going to be put into the new libraries on a high moral plane?" If they are not, I told him he had better build the libraries and I would write the books. With the wealth I would get out of writing the books, I could build libraries and then he could write books.

I am glad that Mr. Carnegie has done this magnificent thing, and as the newspapers have suggested, I hope that other rich men will follow his example and continue to do so until it becomes a habit they cannot break.

Text / "Mark Twain on Training That Pays," *Times,* March 17, 1901.

Skinner / Charles Rufus Skinner (1844–1928). American educator. As deputy state superintendent of public instruction (1895–1904), he compiled a *Manual of Patriotism for the Schools of New York* (1900), and put in force a regulation requiring a display of the American flag over or near every public school in the state.

"My country, right or wrong" / At a dinner in Norfolk, Virginia, in 1816, Stephen Decatur proposed the toast: "Our country! in her intercourse with foreign nations may she always be in the right; but our country, right or wrong!"

Carnegie / Andrew Carnegie (1835–1919). Scottish-born American industrialist and philanthropist. A multimillionaire steel man, he gave up business (1901) to foster social and economic development. He founded the Carnegie Institute of Technology (1900), the

Carnegie Foundation for the Advancement of Teaching (1905), and the Carnegie Corporation for the Advancement of Civilization (1911). He is probably best remembered for establishing Carnegie libraries in many small American towns, the community providing site and maintenance, Carnegie constructing and equipping the building. Mark Twain, who looked upon Carnegie as an entertaining human specimen, was both amused and irritated by his misplaced pride in trivial matters, and by his repetitious stories of meeting prominent people. For Mark Twain's comments, see *MTE*:35–60.

· 122 ·

A Lotos Club dinner for the governor of New York was accompanied by the proper ceremony and good humor for which the club and Frank Lawrence, its president and dinner chairman, were noted. On the toast list were Republican party stalwarts, Vice-President Roosevelt and Chauncey Depew; the independent editor, St. Clair McKelway; and the mugwump, Mark Twain. The latter arrived late in the evening but in time to be the final speaker.

Dinner Speech

Lotos Club Dinner for Governor Benjamin B. Odell, Jr., New York, March 23, 1901

I lately had the pleasure and the honor of visiting Governor Odell on matters of public business in his political home in the State House, in the bosom of his political family, the legislature, a family made up in the proportion of three Republicans for business to one Democrat for ornament and social elevation. I went up there without salary to plead against the reduction, the proposed reduction, of the citizen's liberties, and to vote against the Ramapo bill in the Senate, if I could get a chance to enter upon the floor of the House, and to introduce a police bill. Not because they were running short of police bills. And if the governor would promise to sign it, my bill would pass. I am privileged on the floor of the House anywhere in all the legislative bodies in the world, a thing that happened by accident rather than merit.

I wanted to introduce that police bill. It seemed to me that it was a very good idea. Now it was not like any other police bill that has ever been introduced anywhere. There was a little self-interest in it, here and there, and my scheme was to have none but authors on the police. Let us abolish policemen who carry clubs and revolvers, and put in a squad of poets armed to the teeth with poems on spring and love. Well, for myself, I wanted to be the chief of police, not because I thought I was really qualified for the place, but because I was tired and wanted a rest. I wanted Mr. Howells for first deputy, not because Mr. Howells knows anything about those things, but because he was tired too. A lot of us authors are tired. And now that Mr. Depew has published speeches and other books, and has become an author, I wanted him for second deputy. Not because he is tired, because he isn't, but because he is one of those men who do all things well, and he could run the police business and I could take the salary! And, besides, more than that, he and I have a tie. Indeed, we are members of the celebrated class of '53 of Yale, only he was there before I was. And another thing, he is a Missourian, like me. And in the Missourians there is no guile. And there is a nearer tie still. When I was born I was a member of a firm of twins. And one of them disappeared, and it has been borne in upon me of late that the personal resemblance between Depew and me, and the general handsome style and grace of form and figure and things of that sort, and activity of speech, and—well, it proves to me that that long lost twin is here!

Well, I wanted—I wanted Stedman, and Aldrich, and Brander Matthews, and Crawford, and Cable for the Broadway squad, and others for the red light district, and others still to take care of the pretty manicurists, and to modify the activities of the cadets. Now, Depew could do that.

If my bill passed I'd just fill up the red light district with poets—the best people we've got—armed not with barbaric clubs, but with their own poems, and I would make them corral those poor unkempt people of that locality and I would have my poetic policemen read their poems to them until that region was so elevated and uplifted and reformed that the inhabitants over there themselves wouldn't know it. I would assign the most soulful poets to that district, all heavily armed with their poems. I would station them on the corners after they had rounded up all the depraved people of the district so they could not escape, and then have them read from their poems to the poor unfortunates. The plan would be very effective in causing an emigration of the depraved element.

Now, that bill I drew myself. That was my dream; it was my hope; my ambition; but it failed like so many bright dreams in this disappointing world. Governor Odell wouldn't favor it. He said that authors were well enough in their place, but he said, "It wouldn't do for me to leave the city unprotected." Now, that remark was irrelevant. It wasn't discreet. The very thing I was trying to do was to protect the city. He said the authors as police—that it would be worse than Ramapo, but I can't agree with him. Ramapo is authorized to bring on a water famine—authors never do that.

Well, I shall never forget to be grateful to the legislature up there for the hospitalities extended to me and for the chance that I had to hear a reverend gentleman speak from his impromptu speech which he read from typewritten manuscript, and in which he did for me again what has been done so often before—blasted my character—what was left of it. He said that if I had my just deserts I would not be a guest there, I should be a guest somewhere else maybe, or be dangling from a lamp post somewhere. He was telling about the last time that I broke jail—and said that I carried off several pairs of boots belonging to other folks. This statement was a lie, only that; and he knew that perfectly well. He was there a guest in that place, and so was I; and he was so interested in drawing my character in the past—although he came there to absolutely obliterate me before the people. He hadn't anything personal against me, except that I was opposed to the political war, and he said I was a traitor and didn't go to fight in the Philippines. That doesn't prove anything. That doesn't prove a man is a traitor. Where's the evidence? There are seventy-five millions of us working our patriotism. He did the same thing himself. It would be an entirely different question if the country's life was in danger, its existence at stake; then—that is one kind of patriotism—we would all come forward and stand by the flag, and stop thinking about whether the nation was right or wrong; but when there is no question that the nation is in any way in danger, but only some little war away off, then it may be that on the question of politics the nation is divided, half patriots and half traitors, and no man can tell which from which.

Text / Composite, based upon: "Lotos Club's Welcome to the Governor," *Times,* March 24, 1901; "Poets as Policemen," *MTS*(10):77, a misdated text; "Samuel L. Clemens at the Dinner to Benjamin B. Odell, Jr., March 23, 1901," *Lotos:* 12–15.

Ramapo bill / A bill to annul the charter of the Ramapo Water Company of Brooklyn. It provoked a long wrangle in the New York legislature (1900–01) and extensive press coverage, in which the company was denounced as the "Ramapo water monster" and "Ramapo monopoly." The charter was revoked by an almost unanimous vote, March 12, 1901.

Stedman / Edmund Clarence Stedman (1833–1908). American poet. Washington correspondent of the New York *World* (1861–63) and member of the New York Stock Exchange (1864–1900), he was a rare combination of businessman and poet. Among his books are *Poems, Lyric and Idyllic* (1860), and *Lyrics and Idyls* (1879).

Crawford / Francis Marion Crawford (1854–1909). American novelist. Travel in India produced his first book, *Mr. Isaacs* (1882). Moving to a villa near Naples, where he lived thereafter, he wrote fifteen novels of Roman life, and thirty other volumes. *The Novel: What It Is* (1893) advances the theory that the only purpose of art is to entertain.

cadets / A cadet was a man who lived on the earnings of a prostitute; also a panderer, a procurer.

· 123 ·

The Eastman Club was an organization of alumni of the Eastman Business College of Poughkeepsie, New York. At the second annual banquet, Mark Twain was introduced as a friend of that rising young businessman, Tom Sawyer. He took his text from the remarks of James G. Cannon, vice-president of the Fourth National Bank of New York, who discussed principles essential to the success of young men.

Dinner Speech

Second Annual Banquet, Poughkeepsie Eastman Club, Twenty-third Street Y.M.C.A. Hall, New York, March 30, 1901

Mr. Cannon has furnished me with texts enough to last as slow a speaker as myself all the rest of the night. I took exception to the introducing of Mr. Cannon as a great financier. As if he was the only great financier present! I am a financier. But my methods are not the same as Mr. Cannon's.

I cannot say that I have turned out the great businessman that I thought I was when I began life. But I am comparatively young yet, and may learn. I am rather inclined to believe that what troubled me was that I got the big head early in the game. I want to explain to you a few points of difference between the principles of business as I see them and those that Mr. Cannon believes in.

He says that the primary rule of business success is loyalty to your employer. That's all right—as a theory. What is the matter with loyalty to yourself? As nearly as I can understand Mr. Cannon's methods, there is one great drawback to them. He wants you to work a great deal. Diligence is a good thing, but taking things easy is much more—restful. My idea is that the employer should be the busy man and the employee the idle one. The employer should be the worried man and the employee the happy one. And why not? He gets the salary. My plan is to get another man to do the work for me. There's more repose in that. What I want is repose first, last, and all the time.

Mr. Cannon says that there are three cardinal rules of business success; they are diligence, honesty, and truthfulness. Well, diligence is all right. Let it go as a theory. Honesty is the best policy—when there is money in it. But truthfulness is one of the most dangerous—why, this man is misleading you.

I had an experience today with my wife which illustrates this. I was acknowledging a belated invitation to another dinner for this evening, which seemed to have been sent about ten days ago. It only reached me this morning. I was mortified at the discourtesy into which I had been brought by this delay, and wondered what was being thought of me by my hosts. As I had accepted your invitation, of course I had to send regrets to my other friends.

When I started to write this note my wife came up and stood looking over my shoulder. Women always want to know what is going on. Said she: "Should not that read in the third person?" I conceded that it should, put aside what I was writing, and commenced over again. That seemed to satisfy her, and so she sat down and let me proceed. I then—finished my first note—and so sent what I intended, I never could have done that if I had let my wife know the truth about it. Here is what I wrote:

To the Ohio Society—I have at this moment received a most kind invitation (eleven days old) from Mr. Southard, president; and a like one (ten days old) from Mr. Bryant, president of the Press Club. I thank the society cordially for the compliment of these invitations, although I am booked elsewhere and cannot come.

But, oh, I should like to know the name of the Lightning Express by which they were forwarded; for I owe a friend a dozen chickens, and I believe it will be cheaper to send eggs instead, and let them develop on the road.

Sincerely yours, Mark Twain

I want to tell you of some of my experiences in business, and then I will be in a position to lay down one general rule for the guidance of those who want to succeed in business. My first effort was about twenty-five years ago. I took hold of an invention—I don't know now what it was all about—but someone came to me and told me that there was lots of money in it. He persuaded me to invest $15,000, and I lived up to my beliefs by engaging a man to develop it. To make a long story short, I sunk $40,000 in it.

Then I took up the publication of a book. I called in a publisher and said to him: "I want you to publish this book along lines which I shall lay down. I am the employer, and you are the employee. I am going to show them some new kinks in the publishing business. And I want you to draw on me for money as you go along," which he did. He drew on me for $56,000. Then I asked him to take the book and call it off. But he refused to do that.

My next venture was with a machine for doing something or other. I knew less about that than I did about the invention. But I sunk $170,000 in the business, and I can't for the life of me recollect what it was the machine was to do.

I was still undismayed. You see, one of the strong points about my business life was that I never gave up. I undertook to publish General Grant's book, and made $140,000 in six months—and lost it all in the next six months. My axiom is—to succeed in business, avoid my example.

Text / Composite, based upon: "Mark Twain Tells of His Business Ventures," *Times,* March 31, 1901; "Business" in *MTS*(10):341–44; and *MTS*(23):235–38.

my experiences in business / If not strictly factual, the recital is true to the spirit of speculation that was firmly imbedded in Mark Twain. As critics have pointed out, he was an easy mark for salesmen of gold bricks. Furthermore, his account is refreshingly different from the actuality, in which he was often inclined to blame scapegoats for his failures, generally convinced that he had been swindled by somebody or that the enterprise had been wrecked by the bungling of others. Here he puts the blame on himself, which is undoubtedly where it belonged, or most of it at least.

· 124 ·

A distinguished gathering honored Hamilton W. Mabie, editor of the Outlook. *Henry Van Dyke was dinner chairman, and among those present were Howells, Gilder, Carnegie, Brander Matthews, Walter H. Page, Horace White, Arthur H. Scribner, James Lane Allen, F. Hopkinson Smith, David Graham Phillips, and, of course, Mark Twain. Whatever disfavor the latter may have incurred by unorthodox opinions on controversial subjects, it did not affect his standing as a popular dinner speaker.*

Dinner Speech

University Club Dinner for Hamilton W. Mabie, New York, April 29, 1901

Mr. Chairman and gentlemen: This man knows now how it feels to be the chief guest, and if he has enjoyed it he is the first man I have ever seen in that position that did enjoy it. And I know by side remarks which he made to me before his ordeal came upon him, that he was feeling as some of the rest of us have felt under the same circumstances. He was afraid that he would not do himself justice; but he did—to my surprise. It is a most serious thing to be a chief guest on an occasion like this, and it is admirable, it is fine. It is a great compliment to a man that he shall come out of it so gloriously as Mr. Mabie came out of it tonight—to my surprise. He did it well.

He appears to be editor of *The Outlook,* and notwithstanding that, I have every admiration, because when everything is said concerning *The Outlook,* after all one must admit that it is frank in its delinquencies, that it is outspoken in its departures from fact, that it is vigorous in its mistaken criticisms of men like me. I have lived in this world a long, long time, and I know you must not judge a man by the editorials that he puts in his paper. A man is always better than his printed opinions. A man always reserves to himself on the inside a purity and an honesty and a justice that are a credit to him, whereas the things that he prints are just the reverse.

Oh yes, you must not judge a man by what he writes in his paper. Even in an ordinary secular paper a man must observe some care about it; he must be better than the principles which he puts in print. And that is the case with Mr. Mabie. Why, to see what he writes about me and the missionaries you would think he did not have any principles. But that is Mr. Mabie in his public capacity. Mr. Mabie in his private capacity is just as clean a man as I am.

In this very room, a month or two ago, some people admired that portrait; some admired this, but the great majority fastened on that, and said, "There is a portrait that is a beautiful piece of art." When that portrait is a hundred years old it will suggest what were the manners and customs in our time. Just as they talk about Mr. Mabie tonight, in that enthusiastic way, pointing out the various virtues of the man and the grace of his spirit, and all that, so was that portrait talked about. They were enthusiastic, just as we men have been over the character and work of Mr. Mabie. And when they were through they said that portrait, fine as it is, that work, beautiful as it is, that piece of humanity on that canvas, gracious and fine as it is, does not rise to those perfections that exist in the man himself. Come up, Mr. Alexander. Now, I should come up and show myself. But he cannot do it, he cannot do it. He was born that way, he was reared that way. Let his modesty be an example, and I wish some of you had it, too. But that is just what I have been saying—that portrait, fine as it is, is not as fine as the man it represents, and all the things that have been said about Mr. Mabie, and certainly they have been very nobly worded and beautiful, still fall short of the real Mabie.

Text / Composite, based upon: "The Speech of Mark Twain," *Times, Saturday Review,* May 4, 1901, p. 317; "Dinner to Hamilton W. Mabie" in *MTS*(10):165–67; and *MTS*(23):239–41.

Mabie / Hamilton Wright Mabie (1845–1916). American editor. A Columbia graduate (1869), he practiced law, then became associate editor of the *Christian Union* (1884), where he remained, the *Union* becoming the *Outlook* (1893). Writer and lecturer, he stressed broad general culture.

me and the missionaries / As a sardonic protest against reported extortions by missionaries after the Boxer uprising, and against unedifying machinations of the great powers, Mark Twain published "To the Person Sitting in Darkness," *North American Review* 172, no. 581 (February 1901):161–76. This article was particularly hard on an American missionary, William S. Ament, who was said to have collected 300 taels for each of three hundred Christians killed, in addition to payment for all property destroyed, and to have assessed fines thirteen times greater than the amount of the idemnity—all these extortions to be used for propagation of the gospel. The article stirred up a hubbub, partly approving but mostly condemnatory. Ament's defenders indignantly denied that he was vindictive or greedy, and asserted that he had assessed a lower fine than thirteen times the indemnity. In the *Outlook,* February 16, 1901, the editor, maintaining that Mark Twain had not investigated all the facts, said that the article "will amuse the general reader, and confirm in opinions already formed those who believe that the course of America in the Philippines and in China has been indefensible." The *Outlook* also reported, March 30, 1901, that the Missionary Association at Peking had resolved to forward to the *North American Review* a demand that Mark Twain retract his libelous attacks on Ament. Mark Twain's reply was a second article, "To My Missionary Critics," *North American Review* 172, no. 583 (April 1901):520–34. In this one he reaffirmed his previous statements, and emphasized his conviction that there was no moral difference between a small theft and a large one.

that portrait / A portrait of John Alexander (see following note) hanging on the wall behind his chair at the dinner table.

Alexander / John White Alexander (1856–1915). American painter. After working in the art department of Harper and Brothers, he traveled abroad, lived in Munich and Paris, and became a member of the Societé Nationale des Beaux Arts. He painted six lunettes for the Library of Congress, also portraits of writers and actors—Mark Twain, Howells, Gilder and others—one of the best being that of Walt Whitman, Metropolitan Museum, New York.

· 125 ·

At the first banquet of the Missouri Society of New York, speakers talked about Missouri, and about the Louisiana Purchase Exposition that was due to open in St. Louis in 1903. Augustus Thomas, chairman, facetiously remarked upon Missouri as a great producer of zinc and mules. C. H. Spencer, vice-president of the Exposition, confidently stated that St. Louis would soon have $25,000,000 to promote the World's Fair. He also gave figures on Missouri production of zinc and lead. Mark Twain, an unannounced addition to the program, received a rousing welcome.

Dinner Speech

First Banquet, Missouri Society of New York,
Hotel Waldorf-Astoria, May 28, 1901

I have been as much impressed as has the chairman by Mr. Spencer's speech, and confused also. Statistics always have that effect. As they rise higher and higher to the sky, they become in the same proportion more and more inexplicable. I was glad when I heard it stated that Missouri had turned out 25,000,000 mules. It's from Missouri, and it is expected to be believed. When I was young and in Missouri, I could believe such things. It was a habit, but now that I have come to this grave part of the country, where the people rely largely upon truth, it is not to be expected.

I don't know what this Louisiana Purchase is, but if they have appropriated in some questionable manner twenty-five millions, I suppose they propose to use it for the purchase of Louisiana. They ought to know that they can't have Louisiana for this money. This glorifying of St. Louis is likely to have a bad effect upon you, because it is likely to raise your pride in your state. But there is room for it between here and the zenith. You must keep these things in bounds.

George Washington was a Missourian. He was that, not by accident of birth, but by his primacy in the achievement of liberty and the other great things he did for his country. That made him a Missourian. Caesar was a Missourian. They are all Missourians by right. Abraham

Lincoln, Robert E. Lee, General Grant—they are all Missourians by right of their achievements. We have soldiers in plenty by that right. John Hay has by that right become a half Missourian. He lived in that state for a short time. I, in my quality as lay preacher, say live your lives in virtue, that when you come to lay your life down you shall not descend, but ascend—to Missouri.

Text / "A Missouri Society Now / Representative Missourians, According to Mark Twain," *Times,* May 29, 1901.

John Hay / John Milton Hay (1838–1905). American writer and diplomat. Secretary to Lincoln (1861–65), he was attaché of legations in Paris, Vienna, and Madrid (1865–70), and ambassador to Great Britain (1897–98). As secretary of state (1898–1904), he advocated the open door policy and aided in negotiations for the Panama Canal. He was one of the first government officials to use the press conference. Among his books are *Pike County Ballads* (1871), *The Bread-Winners,* a novel (1884), and, with John Nicolay, the ten-volume *Abraham Lincoln* (1890).

· 126 ·

At Bar Harbor, Mark Twain demonstrated speech-making technique to a group of young people. When he asked for a text, they gave him "Marriage Engagements." He said he had noticed that few girls knew how to blush properly, and that he hoped to have a class to whom he might teach the art of the Graduated Blush. A well-trained girl, he said, would not furnish a pale No. 1 blush when the occasion called for a vivid No. 6 or a crimson No. 14. He illustrated by concentrating on one of the girls present—to get back at her for suggesting the topic—but says that he let her off before producing the No. 31 Conflagration.

Speech-Making Experiment

Bar Harbor, Maine, August 14, 1901

Now here at my side sits a young lady to whom I have given nineteen lessons, and I will prove to you that she is an expert. When I call for a No. 1 she'll not make the mistake of furnishing a No. 4, which would be overdoing it. When I call for No. 10, No. 14, and so on, you will see the exactly proper and requisite sunset flush rise in these beautiful cheeks—there, just that casual little remark, you see, brings a No. 2. Now if you will look into her lovely blue eyes, if you will examine her charming features, her satin skin, her tawny hair, the fine intelligence which beams in her face—there now, look at that! Here where I touch her cheek with my finger an inch in front of her dainty ear, is the meridian which marks the degrees reaching from 1 to 5. See the color steal toward 5. Now it crosses it. Keep your eye on it. I move my finger forward toward her delicate nostril—see the rich blood follow it! When I tell you that here is the loveliest form, the loveliest spirit that perhaps exists in the world today, that she is a darling of the darlings—but I need go no further. The blush has reached her nostril and her collar, and is a No. 16—the most engaging blush, the most charming blush, the most beautiful blush that can adorn the face of any earthly angel, save and except No. 31, which is the last and final possibility, and it is called the "San Francisco, or the Combined Earthquake and Conflagration." I will now produce that blush.

Text / Dictation of August 28, 1906, MTP.

· 127 ·

A New York municipal election coming up in the fall of 1901, independent voters of the city, outraged by Croker's Tammany regime, formed a Citizens Union, known as the Fusion party. An active group was the Order of Acorns, chiefly composed of newspapermen, whom Croker contemptuously referred to as "The Popcorns." Mark Twain, a confirmed Mugwump, enthusiastically supported the Fusionists. At an Acorns dinner he read a long indictment of Tammany, mainly devoid of his usual humor, although he interpolated a few typically Twainian remarks.

Edmund Burke on Croker and Tammany

The Acorns Dinner, Hotel Waldorf-Astoria, New York, October 17, 1901

Great Britain had a Tammany and a Croker a good while ago. This Tammany was in India, and it began its career with the spread of the English dominion after the battle of Plassey. Its first boss was Clive, a sufficiently crooked person sometimes, but straight as a yardstick when compared with the corkscrew crookedness of the second boss, Warren Hastings. That old-time Tammany was the India Company's government, and had its headquarters at Calcutta. Ostensibly it consisted of a Great Council of four persons, of whom one was the Governor General, Warren Hastings; really it consisted of one person—Warren Hastings—for by usurpation he concentrated all authority in himself, and governed the country like an autocrat.

Ostensibly the Court of Directors, sitting in London and representing the vast interests of the stockholders, was supreme in authority over the Calcutta Great Council, whose membership it appointed and removed at pleasure, whose policies it dictated, and to whom it conveyed its will in the form of sovereign commands; but whenever it suited Hastings, he ignored even that august body's authority and conducted the mighty affairs of the British empire in India to suit his own notions.

At his mercy was the daily bread of every official, every trader, every clerk, every civil servant, big and little, in the whole huge India Company's machine; and the man who hazarded his bread by any failure of subserviency to the Boss, lost it.

Now then, let the supreme masters of British India, the giant corporation of the India Company in London, stand for the voters of the City of New York; let the Great Council of Calcutta stand for Tammany; let the corrupt and money-grubbing great hive of serfs which served under the Indian Tammany's rod stand for the New York Tammany's serfs; let Warren Hastings stand for Richard Croker, and it seems to me that the parallel is exact and complete. And so, let us be properly pious and thank God and our good luck that we didn't invent Tammany!

No, it is English. We are always imitating England; sometimes to our advantage, oftenest the other way. And if we can't find something recent to imitate, we are willing to go back a hundred years to hunt for a chance.

The Calcutta Tammany—like our own Tammany—had but one principle, one policy, one moving spirit of action—avarice, money-lust. So that it got money it cared not a rap about the means and the methods. It was always ready to lie, forge, betray, steal, swindle, cheat, rob; and no promise, no engagement, no contract, no treaty made by its boss was worth the paper it was written on or the polluted breath that uttered it. Is the parallel still exact? It seems to me to be twins.

But there the parallel stops. Further it cannot go. Beyond that line our Boss and Warren Hastings are no longer kin. Beyond that line Warren Hastings stands alone in the history of modern Christendom. He stands alone, in a desolate and awful isolation; in a black solitude of perjury, treachery, heartlessness, shamelessness, and an indifference to guiltless suffering, pain and misery properly describable as fiendish. Beyond the stated line we will not insult Mr. Croker by bracketing his name with the unspeakable name of Warren Hastings.

The most of us know no Hastings but Macaulay's, and there is good reason for that: when we try to read the impeachment charges against him we find we cannot endure the pain of the details. They burn, they blister, they wrench the heart; they drive us out of ourselves, they make us curse and swear; and we wonder why it took a dozen years to try that demon, when the mere reading of the first charge in the interminable list ought to have sent him to the scaffold before dark.

II

However, that is a side issue. We are dealing with the parallel, now, and that reaches down only to the stated line drawn above.

Edmund Burke, regarded by many as the greatest orator of all times, conducted the case against Warren Hastings in that renowned trial which lasted years and which promises to keep its renown for centuries to come. I wish to quote some of the things he said. I wish to imagine him arraigning Mr. Croker and Tammany before the voters of New York City and pleading for the overthrow of that combined iniquity on the 5th of November. In the following passage, for "My Lords," read "Fellow Citizens." For "Kingdom" read "city." For "Parliamentary process" read "political campaign." For "two Houses" read "two parties":

My Lords, I must look upon it as an auspicious circumstance to this cause, in which the honor of the Kingdom is involved, that from the first commencement of our Parliamentary process to this the hour of solemn trial, not the smallest difference of opinion has arisen between the two Houses.

In the following, let "persons" stand for "Tammany." For "India" read "Tammany." For "Parliament" read "parties." For "nation" read "city." For "India" read "New York":

My Lords, there are persons who, looking rather upon what was to be found in our records and histories than what was to be expected from the public justice, had formed hopes consolatory to themselves and dishonorable to us. They flattered themselves that the corruptions of India would escape amidst the dissensions of Parliament. They are disappointed. They will be disappointed in all the rest of their expectations. . . . What the greatest inquest of the nation has begun its highest tribunal will accomplish. At length justice will be done to India.

In the following, for "Commons do" read "we who represent the Fusion ticket do." In the closing sentence of the paragraph, infer that Mr. Croker is more or less casually referred to:

My Lords, I must confess that amidst these encouraging prospects the Commons do not approach your bar without awe and anxiety. The magnitude of the interests which we have in charge will reconcile some degree of solicitude for the event with the undoubting confidence with which we repose ourselves upon your Lordships' justice. For we are men, my Lord, and men are so made, that it is not only the greatness of danger, but the value of the adventure, which measures the degree of our concern in every undertaking. I solemnly assure your Lordships that no standard is sufficient to estimate the value which the Commons set upon the event of the cause they now bring before you. My Lords, the business of this day is not the business of *this man,* it is not solely whether the prisoner at the bar be found innocent or guilty, but whether millions of mankind shall be made miserable or happy.

For "India" in the following, read "New York City." For "distant empire" read "city":

Your Lordships will see, in the progress of this cause, that there is not only a long, connected, systematic series of misdemeanors, but an equally connected system of maxims and principles invented to justify them. Upon both of these you must judge. According to the judgment that you shall give upon the past transactions in India, inseparably connected as they are with the principles which support them, the whole character of your future government in that distant empire is to be unalterably decided. It will take its perpetual tenor, it will receive its final impression from the stamp of this very hour.

In the following, for "India" read "New York City." For "part of the British" read "city of the American." For "decided" read "affected." For "national" read "municipal." For "nation" read "city." For "Kingdom" read "community":

It is not only the interest of India, now the most considerable part of the British empire, which is concerned, but the credit and honor of the British nation itself will be decided by this decision. We are to decide by this judgment whether the crimes of individuals are to be turned into the public guilt and national ignominy, or whether this nation will convert the very offenses which have thrown a transient shade upon its government into something that will reflect a permanent lustre upon the honor, justice, and humanity of this Kingdom.

In the following paragraph we will suppose that Mr. Croker's famous confession is referred to—his frank and blunt confession, under judicial examination, that his interest in the city government began and ended with the money to be gotten out of it. His words were, *"I am working for my pocket every time":*

In an early stage of the proceeding the criminal desired to be heard. He was heard; and he produced before the bar of the House that insolent and unbecoming paper which lies upon our table. It was deliberately given in his own hand, and signed with his own name.

In the following, for "Mr. Hastings" read "Mr. Croker":

We urge no crimes that were not crimes of forethought. We charge him with nothing that he did not commit upon deliberation—that he did not commit against advice, supplication, and remonstrance—that he did not commit against the direct command of lawful authority—that he did not commit after reproof and reprimand, the reproof and reprimand of those who were authorized by the laws to reprove and reprimand him. The crimes of Mr. Hastings are not only crimes in themselves, but aggravated by being crimes of contumacy. They were crimes, not against forms, but against those eternal laws of justice which are our rule and our birthright. His offences are, not in formal, technical language, but in reality, in substance and effect, *high* crimes and high misdemeanors.

Here is something further that fits Mr. Croker's case:

When you consider the late enormous power of the prisoner—when you consider his criminal, indefatigable assiduity in the destruction of all recorded evidence—when you consider the influence he has over almost all living testimony—I believe your Lordships, and I believe the world, will be astonished that so much, so clear, so solid, and so conclusive evidence of all kinds has been obtained against him.

Here is some more about the two Tammanies, in the following strikingly faithful description of the New York situation of today. For "magistrates," in the second sentence, read "placemen." For "Mr. Hastings," in the closing sentence of the extract, read "Mr. Croker":

There is nothing to be in propriety called people to *watch,* to inspect, to balance against the power of office. The power of office . . . is the sole power in the country: the consequence of which is, that, being a Kingdom of magistrates, what is commonly called the *esprit du corps* is strong in it. This spirit of the body predominates equally in all its parts; by which the members must consider themselves as having a common interest. . . . No control upon them exists. . . . Therefore, in a body so constituted, confederacy is easy, and has been general. Your Lordships are not to expect that that should happen in such a body which has never happened in any body or corporation—that is, that they should, in any instance, be *a proper check and control upon themselves.* It is not in the nature of things. . . . By means of this peculiar circumstance it has not been difficult for Mr. Hastings to embody abuse and to put himself at the head of a regular system of corruption.

We all realize that Tammany's fundamental principle is monopoly—monopoly of office; monopoly of the public feed trough; monopoly of the blackmail derivable from protected gambling hells, protected prostitution houses, protected professional seducers of country girls for the New York prostitution market, and all that: monopoly all around, "in some sense or other." I know what I'm talking about, for I run a good deal with the police—and the clergy. It's the safest thing to do both here and for the hereafter. Here's a letter received by me yesterday, written by an Irish policeman, who signs his full name. Now here's what he says: "Sir: I'm a policeman and I saw an interview with you the other day. I must tell you the men are with Seth most to a man."

Now, that's good. He speaks out. It don't always do, however, for a man to speak out what he thinks. We can't all be independent. Wives and children take a good deal of independence from us. I've lost nearly all of mine. The letter continues: "I wish you success in your support of the Hon. Seth Low." That's even better. See, at the end he becomes respectful. That letter sounds good.

One of Burke's compact sentences indicates that the Indian Tammany's base rock is the same one that ours roosts upon:

> The fundamental principle of the whole of the East India Company's system is monopoly, in some sense or other.

Here is another accurate piece of portraiture of Mr. Hastings-Croker:

> He was fourteen years at the head of that service; and there is not an instance, no, not one single instance, in which he endeavored to detect corruption, or that he ever, in any one single instance, attempted to punish it; but the whole service, with that whole mass of enormity which he attributes to it, slept, as it were, at once under his terror and his protection: under the protection, if they did not dare to move against him; under terror, from his power to pluck out individuals and make a public example of them, when he thought fit. And therefore that service, under his guidance and influence, was, beyond even what its own nature disposed it to, a service of confederacy, a service of connivance, a service composed of various systems of guilt, of which Mr. Hastings was *the head and the protector.*

And now, at last, we find—and not without pain—that the prophetic eye of Edmund Burke has cast a sorrowing glance down the long procession of unborn years, and it falls with a dull thud upon Mr. Shepard. For "Englishmen" read "Tammany":

But now it is true, that after seeing the power and profits of these men—that there is neither power, profession, nor occupation to be had which a reputable person can exercise, except through that channel—men of higher castes, and born to better things, have thrown themselves into that disgraceful servitude, and have become menial servants to Englishmen, that they might . . . .

I have not quoted the whole of the passage; for its final clause contains a reproach which Mr. Shepard has not earned. It would do him an injustice; and that is a thing which Edmund Burke never wittingly did to any man. If he were here now he would know Mr. Shepard better than he was able to forecast him a century ago, and he would leave it out; therefore for the honor I bear the unsmirched great name of Edmund Burke I do him the justice to leave it out for him.

Now we come to the marvel of marvels—the immortal Irish orator's portrait of Richard Croker, as placed before us thinly disguised as Warren Hastings. He does not spring it upon you out of an atmosphereless vacancy, but leads you up to his great work with these notable words of introduction and preparation:

. . . So far as to the crimes. As to the criminal, we have chosen him on the same principle on which we selected the crimes. We have not chosen to bring before you a poor, puny, trembling delinquent, misled, perhaps, by those who ought to have taught him better, but who have afterwards oppressed him by their power, as they had first corrupted him by their example. Instances there have been many, wherein the punishment of minor offences, in inferior persons, has been made the means of screening crimes of a high order, and in men of high description. Our course is different. We have not brought before you an obscure offender, who, when his insignificance and weakness are weighed against the power of the prosecution, gives even to public justice something of the appearance of oppression. . . .

Then he flings Richard Croker upon the canvas. (For the first "India" read "Tammany"; for the second "India" read "New York City.") Consider this astonishing photograph—consider the amazing perfection of it: Richard Croker, detail by detail, in his moral personality, from topknot down to heeltap—and remember that the man who made it has been in his grave a hundred years! Croker is Tammany; Tammany is Croker: and experts of our own who know the combination to the marrow have not been able to depict it with an exacter brush:

What Burke Said

No, my Lords, we have brought before you the first man of India, in rank, authority and station. We have brought before you the *chief of the tribe,* the head of the whole body of Eastern offenders, *a captain-general of iniquity,* under whom *all the fraud, all the peculation, all the tyranny in India is embodied, disciplined, arrayed, and paid.* This is the person, my Lords, that we bring before you. We have brought before you such a person, that, if you strike at him with the firm and decided arm of justice, you will not have need of a great many more examples. *You strike at the whole corps if you strike at the head.*

What our Experts Say
Letter to Croker from President of Anti-Croker League

In the meantime, we desire to emphasize the fact that it is entirely due to your political venality that corruption is rampant in our municipal government, and that the agencies of our civilization are controlled by the depraved elements of society. Under your guidance and inspiration, Tammany Hall has been turned into a machine for stock jobbing purposes, and for furthering schemes in which you and your cronies are financially interested. Its energies are largely devoted to blackmailing corporations for the benefit of your private pockets. A gamblers' syndicate, made up of your intimate political coadjutors, is running the Police Department, through its accredited agent, Chief Devery. It issues licenses to lawbreakers, and collects revenues from vice and crime. The income from moral degradation is regulated by certain Tammany leaders on a cash register basis. You are the chief beneficiary of this vile system, and with your share of the filthy spoils you manage to maintain a lordly estate in England.

The issue before the Lords was *Hastings and Hastingsism*; the only issue before New York in the imminent election is *Croker and Crokerism.* The two issues are the same, under differing names. If Edmund Burke were here he could change the names and make his speech again, and it would fit our circumstances exactly. Would he make it? We know by the heart of that great Irishman, and by his history, and by the noble hatred that was in him of all forms of wrong, dishonesty, chicane and oppression, that he would; and that he would beseech New York, with all the powers of his tongue and brain, and all the persuasions of his eloquence, to vote into obliteration and vacancy Mr. Croker and the infamies which he represents. And so we are privileged to imagine him here present and uttering again the righteous indignation which fell from his lips so long ago. And we know how he would close. We know that he would paraphrase his majestic impeachment of Warren Hastings, and say to the voters of New York:

"We know that we can commit safely the interests of this great metropolis into your hands. Therefore it is with confidence that, ordered by the people—

"I impeach Richard Croker of high crimes and misdemeanors.

"I impeach him in the name of the people, whose trust he has betrayed.

"I impeach him in the name of all the people of America, whose national character he has dishonored.

"I impeach him in the name and by virtue of those eternal laws of justice which he has violated.

"I impeach him in the name of human nature itself, which he has cruelly outraged, injured, and oppressed, *in both sexes, in every age, rank, situation, and condition of life.*"

Text / Composite, based upon: "Edmund Burke on Croker and Tammany," MS, Berg Collection, New York Public Library; "Mark Twain Makes a Speech," *Times,* October 18, 1901; "Edmund Burke on Croker and Tammany," *Harper's Weekly,* Supplement, 45, no. 2339 (October 19, 1901):1602.

battle of Plassey / Plassey is in Bengal, northeastern India. In a battle there (1757) Clive, with an army of about 3,000 Englishmen and natives, defeated Surajah Dowlah's force of some 60,000. Before the battle Clive had plotted with Mir Jaffier, one of the nawab's generals, promising to reward his treachery with the throne of Bengal. The victory gave the British control of a large part of northern India.

Clive / Robert, Baron Clive of Plassey (1725–74). British soldier and empire builder. A clerk in the East India Company, he developed a natural gift for military service, and became a commander who succeeded by boldness and by machination, his usual tactic being to play off one claimant of a throne against another. His victory at Wandewash in southern India (1760) assured British dominion of the country. Clive's methods were subjected to parliamentary inquiry (1773), but he was exonerated. The next year he committed suicide.

Warren Hastings / (1732–1818). British politician. As a top level administrator in the East India Company, he was high-handed and often unscrupulous. In 1788 he was impeached, charged with corruption and oppression of native princes. The case, prosecuted by Burke and Richard Brinsley Sheridan, was in effect an arraignment of the entire East India system, as well as of its chief representative, Hastings. After a long trial he was acquitted (1795), but it was said that the airing of testimony resulted in some improvement of behavior in India.

no Hastings but Macaulay's / Macaulay published a long essay on Hastings in the *Edinburgh Review* (October 1841). It deals gently with shortcomings, lauds virtues. Macaulay, admitting that the principles of Hastings were "somewhat lax" and that "His heart was somewhat hard," praises "his rare talents for command, for administration . . . his dauntless courage, his honorable poverty, his fervent zeal for the interests of the state."

Edmund Burke / (1729–97). Irish-born British statesman. He was a brilliant parliamentary orator, friendly to the American colonies, but opposed to the French Revolution. A cultured man, he was one of Dr. Johnson's circle and a member of the famous Literary Club. Among his books are *A Philosophical Inquiry Into the Origin of Our Ideas of the Sublime and Beautiful* (1756), *On Conciliation With the American Colonies* (1775), and *Letters on a Regicide Peace* (1795–97).

Fusion ticket / The Fusion party nominated Seth Low for mayor, William Travers Jerome for district attorney, Edward M. Grout for comptroller, Samuel Seabury for judge of the City Court.

Shepard / Edward Morse Shepard (1850–1911). American politician. As Democratic candidate for mayor of New York (1901), he was considered the one honorable man on the Tammany ticket. The New York press commended his integrity but deplored his alliance with Croker's gang.

· 128 ·

Mark Twain threw himself into the municipal campaign with great enthusiasm. Presiding at a noonday mass meeting in a vacant storeroom on lower Broadway, he introduced Seth Low to a cheering crowd that jammed the makeshift hall, while hundreds gathered outside. Tammany roughs tried to break up the meeting, but they were unceremoniously ejected.

Two Political Speeches

Noonday Meeting, Order of Acorns, 350 Broadway, New York, October 29, 1901

I have been ill. It was indiscriminate eating. I ate a banana, thinking that by doing so I might conciliate the Italian party of our population and prevail upon them to vote the Fusion ticket. Gentlemen, it was a Tammany banana. Now a Tammany banana is a strange thing. The first nibble of it is white and pure, but all the rest of it is rotten and will contaminate. We all have respect for Mr. Shepard. He is the pure part of the banana, but all the rest of the Tammany ticket is rotten, and the best we can do is to get rid of the whole Tammany banana, Shepard and all.

I have eaten only one banana, but still I feel as if I had swallowed a whole bunch of Tammany tigers, and they were wrestling for the spoils in my interior. New York has eaten the Tammany banana, and needs a doctor. I think I can introduce to you a competent one in Dr. Seth Low.

[After Low's brief speech, shouts of "Twain! Twain!" brought Mark Twain up again to say a few words about the Order of Acorns. Then he concluded with the remarks below.]

You have heard in a vague way of the "red light" cadets. They are Croker's knights, who went out into the New England states and lured young, innocent girls into houses of ill fame in this city. Things are going on in this city which would disgrace any community in the civilized or uncivilized world. New York has far exceeded Sodom and Gomorrah. If you do not know about the wickedness of those cities, it only goes to show your lack of Biblical knowledge. Sodom and Gomorrah were well enough in their time, but Tammany could have given them points.

Text / Composite, based upon: "Mark Twain Presides at a Low Meeting," *Courant,* October 30, 1901; "Twain on the Tiger Banana," NY*Trib,* October 30, 1901.

· 129 ·

When the Fusionists won the election, the Acorns staged a jubilee. At their headquarters, decorated with brooms symbolic of a clean sweep, Mark Twain, who had got out of a sick bed to join the celebration, delivered a mock eulogy of Tammany. Then he and Acorns officers, in a carriage, led a parade of five thousand uptown, the marchers detouring to pass Tammany Hall while the Old Guard band played "Go Waaa-y Back and Sit Down." At Forty-second Street Mark Twain reviewed the long line of paraders, who then headed downtown. At the Metropolitan Opera House they paused to burn Croker in effigy, the band playing "The Battle Cry of Freedom," the crowd singing lustily. When the police moved in, a riot seemed imminent, but somebody created a diversion by proposing three cheers for Mark Twain. After the cheering had subsided, the effigy was in ashes, and no riot occurred.

Mock Eulogy of Tammany

Acorns Election Jubilee, New York, November 6, 1901

It is a victory as was suggested in the letter you have read, a success in part prophetic. The old gang has been defeated all along the line, and I prophesy, because I was born a prophet, that the next time we go to the polls we go there 100,000 strong. I am not surprised at the superb majority we had. What surprises me is that Tammany got a single vote, with the entire pulpit and almost the entire press against it. But while a thirty-thousand majority was not nearly large enough, we will not quarrel with Tammany about the result. Tammany is dead, and it is no use to quarrel with a corpse.

We are not here to attend the funeral of Tammany. Tammany is dead, and there is wailing in the land. We shall miss so many familiar faces. Van Wyck, the gentle peddler of lifesaving ice at sixty cents per hundred, is gone. Ike Fromme—we shall never see Fromme again. He is gone. His name isn't German, but I suppose he took it from the Germans. We shall never see his gentle face again.

And Unger. Yes, he is also gone. Unger is a German name also. In the original it had an H in it. Yes, Unger is gone, with his great appetite unsatisfied.

And Murphy, that shadow of a shadow: that political spectre. Farewell to Murphy. He is gone to the unsolidified space of which he has been so long a part.

And Devery! That indescribable! He has gone to the realms of darkness. His character is so black that even Egyptian darkness would make white spots on it.

And there is Asa Bird Gardiner, who said, "To hell with reform." Well, his reform has been started in the way indicated, and we do not care how soon he goes the same way.

And last, but not least, there is Croker. Croker. He can now go back to England. We can spare him here. Yes, farewell to Croker forever, the Baron of Wantage, the last, and I daresay the least desirable, addition to English nobility.

Text / Composite, based upon: " 'The Acorns' Hold an Election Jubilee," *Times,* November 7, 1901; "Croker Burned in Effigy," NY*Trib,* November 7, 1901.

I prophesy . . . that the next time, etc. / Mark Twain's prophecy was unfortunately not fulfilled. The reform movement lost its steam, Seth Low failed of reelection in 1903, and some of the old gang were back in business again.

Van Wyck / Robert Anderson Van Wyck (1851–1918). American politician. A Columbia graduate (1872), he practiced law, then became judge of the City Court of New York (1889–97). As mayor of Greater New York (1897–1901), he was sharply criticized for the corruption of municipal affairs, especially of the police, who were accused of being hand in glove with criminals.

Unger / Henry W. Unger was assistant district attorney of New York County in Van Wyck's administration, and Democratic nominee for district attorney (1901). The *Times* said that his nomination had been dictated by Frank Farrell, head of the city gambling combine, which ruled the entire Tammany organization. The Fusionists charged Unger with dismissing grand jury indictments, interfering with the district attorney, and other irregularities.

Murphy / Charles Francis Murphy (1858–1924). American political boss, known as "Silent Charley." Organizer of the Sylvian Club, forerunner of Tammany, and the owner of saloons, he was influential with bibulous voters. As commissioner of docks and ferries, he was charged with graft and extortion, but he was a hard man to dislodge. Upon the retirement of Croker, Murphy became the leader of Tammany (1902–24).

Devery / William S. Devery, deputy police commissioner under Van Wyck, was a major target of the Fusionists' attack. They charged him with condoning vice, crime, brutal police tactics, and widespread bribery of policemen, from patrolmen to captains. New York papers (1900–01) published many news stories and editorials on police corruption. Yet Devery was another who was not easily disposed of. When Seth Low did not win reelection in 1903, Devery returned to the political scene and remained for several years.

Asa Bird Gardiner / (1838–1919). American lawyer. Awarded the Congressional Medal of Honor (1872) for gallantry at Gettysburg, he was judge advocate of military divisions of the South (1871–73) and Atlantic (1878–87), and acting secretary of war (1887–88). As district attorney of New York County (1897–1900), he was charged with misconduct and malfeasance. Governor Roosevelt sustained the charges and removed Gardiner from office.

"To hell with reform" / The *Times,* October 14, 1897, reporting Gardiner's speech at a Democratic meeting in Harlem, printed this passage: "In all the history of municipal government, there was never a party that made such a showing as the Democratic party and Tammany Hall. Now, don't you forget that, and when any of these people talk to you about reform—(excuse me, for I have been in the army), tell them, as I do, 'To hell with reform.' "

· 130 ·

At a dinner of the Good Citizenship Association, Clarence Gordon, chairman, said that he had had trouble persuading Mark Twain to appear. As the Times *reported, November 8, 1901: "Mr. Clemens did not want to come. It was not the first time I had tried to capture Mr. Clemens, whom I have known for many years. Not long ago I found him in a barber's chair next to mine. . . . and I hailed Mr. Clemens. He did not seem to recognize me. He said, 'You are a bunco steerer; by-by.' But I caught him at Riverside by showing him the membership of this club, and when I told him that our motto was 'Our neighbor is ourselves in another body,' he agreed to come."*

Speech

Good Citizenship Association, East Side Settlement House,
New York, November 7, 1901

I may have taken Mr. Gordon for a bunco steerer. He had the light in his eyes which told me that he wanted something out of me. I am, however, very glad to be here with you, "captured." I have been too busy to prepare an address, and will read from a recent magazine article of mine telling how a chimney sweep got the ear of the Emperor. It explains how watermelon is a cure for dysentery. There are many remedies most people know little about. Incidentally the impossible may happen.

You go to the drug store to get something to keep the hair from falling out. Beware of drug stores. My hair was rapidly leaving me, and I spoke to a friend of mine, a very old and wise man like myself. He told me that if I would just plow my hair twice a day with a stiff brush it would be all right. I have not lost a hair in eleven years, and there is quite some of it.

I told the remedy to our pastor in Hartford. One Saturday night he was through with the preparation of his sermon and saw a bottle on the dressing table. He took it for a hair restorer and forgot about plowing the hair with a brush. In the morning his hair was green. He had used a very good hair dye. He had to preach the sermon, but the congregation wondered about his hair and forgot about the sermon.

For eight years I was troubled with indigestion, which took the form of an insurrection in my stomach, after I went to bed. The various things I thought were good things began quarreling among themselves, and trying to agree upon a fusion ticket that would win out. Four years ago I was in a foreign land where there were no drug stores, so I had to resort to the Swedish cure, which does not allow one to take medicine. Therefore, I used carbonate of soda every night. When the heartburn came on I took a handful of it. One night when I had no soda I said to myself, "I would rather stand the pain." Purely by accident I stretched myself on my left side, and, curiously enough, the pain passed away. I made the same experiment several times with the same result.

When I went to London I spoke to my friend, who is the secretary of the Royal Medical Society, and asked him why the heartburn passed away when I lay on my left side. He said he didn't know. Well, that was in a place where doctors were passing through each day by the hundred, and I asked him to see if any of them could tell me. None of them could. One doctor, a very famous one, no less than Sir William Thompson, said he remembered hearing of it fifty years ago when his own heartburn was cured that way by an old man in Germany, but he had never thought of it since. There was a case where a simple and certain cure was in his hands and yet he had forgotten it and emptied drug stores into his patients without result.

[He concluded by reading his story, "How the Chimney-Sweep Got the Ear of the Emperor," published in the *Century Magazine,* November, 1901. Jimmy, a chimney sweep, tells his friend Tommy that a ripe watermelon is a sure cure for the Emperor's ailment, which has baffled the royal physicians. The boys get word to the palace by telling the butcher, who tells the old chestnut-seller, who tells a rich aunt, who tells a friend, who tells a sergeant of police, who tells the captain, and so the word is passed via magistrate, mayor, master of hounds, head groom and others until it reaches the page who fans flies off the Emperor and who tells His Highness. The watermelon treatment succeeds.]

Text / Composite, based upon: "Twain's Rival Story Teller," *Times,* November 8, 1901; "Mark Twain on Medicine," NY*Trib,* November 8, 1901.

Sir William Thompson / (d. 1918). British physician. He was demonstrator of anatomy, Trinity College, Dublin (1887–91), Dunville Professor of Physiology, Queen's College, Belfast (1893–1902), and King's Professor of the Institute of Medicine, Trinity College (1902–18). A distinguished professional man, he published many papers on medical subjects.

· 131 ·

With characteristic fanfare the Lotos Club welcomed Ambassador Choate on his return from England. Among guests were Carnegie, Reed, W. E. Dodge, Depew, and Judge Howland. Mark Twain arrived late; beginning to feel the strain of steady banqueting, he had taken to sauntering in only when the speech-making was about to get under way.

Dinner Speech

Lotos Club Dinner for Joseph H. Choate, New York, November 16, 1901

Mr. Carnegie has told you that on the other side of the water they consider it necessary to train men for the diplomatic service, and he also suggested that on this side we did not find it necessary to do that, but had been able to produce ready-made diplomats when occasion required; and I have waited, and I have listened, and I have expected to hear somebody tell an anecdote which has not been told, and it becomes necessary for me to tell it. You have heard that anecdote many times, and you will hear it many more times, but you have never known, perhaps, its historic significance. You have never known how much was bound up in that anecdote.

The greatness of this country rests upon two anecdotes. The first was of the time when young George Washington told his father about the little hatchet, when he was eight years of age, long ago in 1740; and that anecdote produced one of the foundations upon which the greatness of America rests, the foundation of true speaking, which is a characteristic of the nation.

And then the other one. The other anecdote, which, as I shall show you, produced the other great feature of this country, that is, the prosperity, the material prosperity of this country, which dates from so short a time back—the largest portion of it underlies that anecdote. I refer to a time when his Excellency, the guest of the evening, was engaged in a lawsuit, and he had as his pal a Hebrew lawyer of great ability, and in the process of skinning the client, or, rather, when it was over, when they had won the suit or lost it, they didn't know which, they were not particular, the main thing was to come yet, and that was to collect a bill for their services in skinning the man—services is the term used by that craft to signify the kind of function which they perform, a diplomatic expression for things diplomatic in their nature—and the Hebrew lawyer, Mr. Choate's co-respondent, proposed to make out the bill, and he did. He made out a bill for $500 for these services, so-called, and submitted it to his confederate for his criticism; and Mr. Choate said: "Perhaps I had better attend to that myself." And the next day Mr. Choate made out a bill and collected it, and handed to this friend of his $5,000, and said: "That is your half of the loot." And this simple little Hebrew was profoundly touched and he said, looking up with deep reverence: "Almost thou persuadest me to be a Christian." Now, many laughed, which was right; but the deep thinkers didn't merely laugh; they stopped to think, and they said: "There, that is a rising man. That man has in him qualities which deserve high place; that man must be rescued from the law and consecrated to diplomacy." For they said, "When a man has the capacity to take care of his private advantage like that, when he has this quality in such generous measure, then he only needs spreading it, and in this case there seems to be enough to spread out, and it can cover and take care of the advantages of the world; the commercial advantages of a great nation will not suffer in that man's keeping." They kept their eyes upon that rising man, and the time came when they said, "We require a man, now that America has grown so great, with perhaps seventy or eighty millions of people, we require a man now not to take care of the moral character of America before the world, for Washington and his anecdote have done that; we require a man to take care of her commercial well-being." They saw with their prophetic eyes the significance of that anecdote; they foresaw that out of that would grow commercial prosperity for this country by that quality so ripe and complete, which would last down, down, down the centuries, until this country's prosperity has attained its summit, and has been so firmly established upon eternal foundations, and so it has proved. Mr. Choate has carried that quality with him to England. And as Mr. Carnegie says, he has worked like a mole, underground. We say that the mole has been doing great and good service. He tried himself to tell you what he did there. He started to, three or four times, but didn't reveal anything except the reason that brought him to this country. As to his services over there, that they have been more than merely suggestive, we know, for he has been there only three years, and now you see the results. Why, American railroad iron is so cheap in England, that the poorest families can have it for breakfast.

He has so tickled those ministers, that cabinet of England, when he has seemed to be spending these weekends, as they call it over there, referred to here tonight; when he has been simply socially conversing, perhaps, he has been really pushing canal schemes and working the Monroe Doctrine, successfully spreading the commerce of this country for these three years, and now you know the result. Foreign commerce with the United States has augmented by tenfold, twenty and thirtyfold even; and he has depressed English commerce in the same ratio. Brethren, the principle underlying the anecdote of the lawyer and the principle of the man, was the principle which guided his course, and that principle was the principle of give and take; that is diplomacy—give one and take ten.

As a result, we have in the one anecdote the character of this nation for truth, for veracity, for absolute trustworthiness when a man speaks, established upon everlasting foundations; that is the moral character of the country—no man can budge it while that anecdote of Washington and his hatchet lasts. And Mr. Choate has placed the country upon the same perpetual foundation or substratum by the principle involved in that other anecdote.

And as long as this club shall swing amongst the other stars and constellations and whatnot that make night beautiful, so long as they shall last, this country's moral character is safe on the one foundation, and its commercial prosperity is safe on the other. We owe to Mr. Choate a vast debt of gratitude for what he has done in England. This whole nation owes him a vast debt of gratitude. Let us with all our hearts strengthen his hands, and in all sincerity thank him, do our share in thanking him, and paying our share of the great debt, right here and now.

Text / Composite, based upon: "Samuel L. Clemens at the Dinner to Joseph H. Choate, November 16, 1901," *Lotos:*35–38; "Mark Twain's Anecdote," *Times,* November 17, 1901; "The Dinner to Mr. Choate" in *MTS*(10):152–53; and *MTS*(23):242–43. *MTS* texts are misdated.

· 132 ·

Five hundred Scotsmen and guests gathered for the 145th annual dinner of the St. Andrew's Society. Andrew Carnegie presided at the speakers' table, on which reposed the traditional symbol of St. Andrew's, a large fleece-covered snuff box. Among guests were Seth Low, British Consul General Sir Percy Sanderson, George C. Lorimer, Carl Schurz, Frederic J. de Peyster, W. E. Dodge, Horace White, Judge Henry Howland, and representatives of other societies: Holland, New England, St. George's, St. Patrick's, St. Nicholas's, St. David's. Pipe Major James MacDonald of the Black Watch skirled "Cock o' the North" and a special number he had composed, "Carnegie of Skibo." A band played "Annie Laurie," "Robin Adair," "Little Annie Rooney." The main dish, a haggis, was borne in by a dozen waiters escorted by MacDonald piping "Bannocks o' Barley." The entire company stood up and cheered, and kept on cheering when another squad marched in laden with Scotch whiskey. After each of the nine toasts the assembly sang heartily: "Scots Wha Hae," "Muirland Willie," "Gae Bring to me a Pint o' Wine," and so on down to the finale, "Auld Lang Syne."

Scotch Humor

One hundred forty-fifth Annual Dinner, St. Andrew's Society, Delmonico's, New York, November 30, 1901

The President of St. Andrew's, the Lord Rector of Dublin, no, Glasgow, isn't it? No. Well, he is higher up than I thought he was—told me that Scotch humor is non-existent. How is he a Lord Rector, anyway? What does he know about ecclesiastics? I suppose he don't care so long as the salary is satisfactory.

I have never examined the subject of humor until now. I am surprised to find how much ground it covers. I have got its divisions and frontiers down on a piece of paper. I find it defined as a production of the brain, as the power of the brain to produce something humorous, and the capacity of perceiving humor. The third subdivision is possessed by all English-speaking people, even the Scotch. Even the Lord Rector is humorous. He has offered of his own motion to send me a fine lot of whiskey. That is certainly humor.

Goldsmith said that he had found some of the Scotch possessed wit, which is next door to humor. He didn't overurge the compliment.

Josh Billings defined the difference between humor and wit as that between the lightning bug and the lightning. There is a conscious and unconscious humor. That whiskey offer of the Lord Rector's was one of unconscious humor. A peculiarity of that sort is a man is apt to forget it.

I have here a few anecdotes to illustrate these definitions. I hope you will recognize them. I like anecdotes which have had the benefit of experience and travel, those which have stood the test of time, those which have laid claim to immortality. Here is one passed around a year ago, and twelve years old in its Scotch form.

A man receives a telegram telling him that his mother-in-law is dead and asking, "Shall we embalm, bury, or cremate her?" He wired back, "If these fail, try dissection." Now, the unconscious humor of this was that he thought they'd try all of the three means suggested, anyway.

An old Scotch woman wrote to a friend, "First the child died, then the callant"—for the benefit of those not Scotchmen here, I will say that a callant is a kind of shepherd dog. That is, this is the definition of the Lord Rector, who spends six months in his native land every year to preserve his knowledge of its tongue.

Another instance of unconscious humor was of the Sunday school boy who defined a lie as "An abomination before the Lord and an ever present help in time of trouble." That may have been unconscious humor, but it looked more like hard, cold experience and knowledge of facts.

Then you have the story of the two fashionable ladies talking before a sturdy old Irish washerwoman. One said to the other, "Where did you spend the summer?" "Oh, at Long Branch," was the reply. "But the Irish there; oh, the Irish! Where were you?" she asked her companion in turn. "At Saratoga; but the Irish there; oh, the Irish!" Then spoke up the old Irish woman, and asked, "Why didn't you go to Hades? You wouldn't have found any Irish there."

Let me tell you now of a case of conscious humor. It was of William Cary, late of the *Century,* who died a few weeks ago, a man of the finest spirit and thought. One day a distinguished American called at the *Century* office. There was a new boy on duty as sentry. He gruffly gave the gentleman a seat and bade him wait. A short time after, Mr. Cary came along and said, "Why, what are you doing here?" After explanations Mr. Cary brought out three pictures, one of Washington, one of Lincoln, and one of Grant. "Now, young man," he said to the boy, "didn't you know that gentleman? Now, look at these pictures carefully, and if any of these gentlemen call show them right in."

I am grateful for this double recognition. I find that, like St. Andrew, my birthday comes on the 30th of November. In fact, I was sixty-six years old about thirty-four minutes ago. It was cold weather when I was born. What a chance there was of my catching cold! My friends never explained their carelessness, except on the plea of custom, but what does a child of that age care for custom?

Text / "Sons of Scotland Feast and Make Merry," *Times,* December 1, 1901.

Lord Rector of Dublin / Carnegie, who had established a trust fund to assist education in Scottish universities, had been made lord rector of St. Andrew's University.

Josh Billings / Pen name of Henry Wheeler Shaw (1818–85). American humorist. He was a popular writer and lecturer in the manner of Artemus Ward. For many years he published annual editions of *Josh Billings' Farmers' Allminax,* then collected his sketches in *Josh Billings, His Works Complete* (1876).

· 133 ·

Mark Twain made an unscheduled appearance at a Yale alumni dinner in Hartford. The Courant *reported next day that when he casually strolled in, accompanied by his old friend Twichell, "The familiar features and flowing hair of the gifted humorist were quickly recognized and the entire party rose, cheered, clapped and yelled with a waving of napkins and other demonstrations of delight."*

Dinner Speech

Yale Alumni Association Dinner, Allyn Hall, Hartford, January 31, 1902

I didn't want to be invited and the reason was I wanted to come and I couldn't come if invited as I pledged myself last summer that I wouldn't accept any invitation outside of New York, except to funerals. I have no toast, no text and therefore it is fortunate that I was so long a resident of Hartford and a member of the Monday Evening Club, and if you don't know what the peculiarities of that club are, I will tell you. It was to take men who were not born to speak and never could be made to speak, so that they could get up at any time and speak. No member of the club could speak for more than ten minutes. It has also taught Colonel Greene who could always talk on emptiness and veracity. We took "Charley" Clark when he didn't know anything and couldn't tell it. And now he can.

President Smith is a graduate of the club. There is a man for whom we all have great regard and who can get up here and talk for all the 479 colleges in the country. He has tried to make us believe that he knows all about them and has even suggested that President Hadley be made an admiral. He could never have done it without the training he received in the Monday Evening Club. He also tries to make you believe that he believes what he says he does.

I knew all these people for about thirty years and remember that Colonel Greene there learned the use of sentences. There were other able men, Dunham and Colonel Cheney. Greene used to talk the ten minutes and wind up his graceful sentences with an explosion grand

and effective. Twichell also is a graduate of the club who learned the spirit of self-sacrifice and when he got on a subject he couldn't understand, used to talk on it and pass it along to the next. Then we had Judge Hamersley (who I hope is not here). He was trained in the club and his utterances were learned there. He would talk and when he got to the end there would be a great explosion. Greene would go voyaging around after a German verb and when he had found that German verb would come back and let us have it. Burton, the great-hearted Dr. Nathaniel Burton, was also a member of the club. He had the most wonderful vocabulary and would sit with his great head bowed and when one of us finished, would arouse and say, "There she blows." Greene would make you believe that he knew what he was talking about and you would believe him, but he didn't.

I was in the club thirty years ago and was then the greatest man in it. I never came across so great a man. Then there was Dr. Bushnell, that great mind. He resigned from the club before I joined it and when I afterwards saw him he was feeble in body but his great mind and great heart were as big and full of loving kindness as ever.

[The text above is incomplete. In additional remarks he thanked Yale for the honorary degree of Litt. D. conferred upon him—along with Aldrich, Cable, Howells, and Gilder—at the university's bicentennial celebration in October, 1901. He also said that Yale needed only a Monday Evening Club to become famous.]

Text / "Yale Alumni / Mark Twain and the Monday Evening Club," *Courant,* February 1, 1902.

Monday Evening Club / Founded in Hartford in 1869, it had no officers or dues. Among members were Trinity College professors, local lawyers, businessmen, journalists, and clergymen. They met every two weeks in each other's homes, the chairman being the host of the evening, the program a paper read by one member, followed by discussion. Mark Twain was elected in 1873. See *The List of Members of the Monday Evening Club Together with the Record of Papers Read at Their Meetings 1869–1954* (Hartford: privately printed, 1954).

Greene / Jacob L. Greene (1835–1905). Hartford businessman. He was president of the Connecticut Mutual Life Insurance Company, and a member of the Monday Evening Club, elected in 1883.

Clark / Charles Hopkins Clark (1848–1916). American journalist. A native of Hartford, he joined the staff of the *Courant* (1871), became assistant editor (1890), and chief editor (1900). He was elected to the Monday Evening Club in 1879.

Smith / George Williamson Smith (1836–1925). American educator. He was chaplain and teacher of mathematics at the Naval Academy (1865–68), rector of Long Island and Brooklyn churches, then president of Trinity College (1883–1904). He was a member of the Monday Evening Club (1883–1925).

Hadley / Arthur Twining Hadley (1856–1930). American educator. He was professor of political science at Yale (1886–91), of political economy (1891–99), and president (1899–1921).

Dunham / Austin C. Dunham (18[?]–1917). Hartford businessman. He was president of the Hartford Electric Light Company, and Monday Evening Club member, elected in 1870.

Hamersley / William Hamersley (1838–1920). American jurist. City attorney of Hartford (1865–68), he was a law lecturer at Trinity College (1875–1900), judge of the Superior Court (1887), and associate justice of the Supreme Court of Errors (1898–1909). He was a charter member of the Monday Evening Club.

Burton / Nathaniel Judson Burton (1824–89). American clergyman. Yale Divinity School graduate (1854), he was pastor of the Second Congregational Church of Fairhaven, Connecticut, then moved to the Hartford Fourth Congregational Church (1857), and Park Church (1870). A charter member of the Monday Evening Club, he was esteemed for broad culture and original thought.

Bushnell / Horace Bushnell (1802–76). American clergyman. For more than thirty years he was pastor of North Church, Hartford. In California (1856), he helped to organize the College of California, Oakland, which became the University of California, Berkeley. He declined the presidency of this institution because of failing health, which forced retirement from the ministry (1861). He was politically antislavery but not abolitionist, and his enlightened theology had a liberalizing effect on Protestant doctrine. He was one of the founders of the Monday Evening Club.

· 134 ·

As a man who had become a universal spokesman, whose opinion on any subject was likely to be publicized, Mark Twain was not disconcerted when appearing before specialized groups, cultural, scientific, technical or legal. He could be interesting to engineers, chemists, painters and, as in the speech below, to medical jurists who gathered to celebrate the 20th anniversary of the founding of their society.

Dinner Speech

Twentieth Anniversary Dinner, Society of Medical Jurisprudence, Hotel Savoy, New York, March 8, 1902

It is a pleasure to watch a company of gentlemen in that condition which is peculiar to gentlemen who have had their dinners. That was a time when the real nature of man came out. As a rule, we go about with masks, we go about looking honest, and we are able to conceal ourselves all through the day. But when the time comes that man has had his dinner, then the true man comes to the surface. I could see it here this evening. I noticed the burst of applause when Judge O'Brien got up to speak, and I knew that he was either an exceedingly able man or else that a lot of you practice in his court. You have been giving yourselves away all evening. One speaker got up here and urged you to be honest, and there was no response.

Now, I want you to remember that medicine has made all its progress during the past fifty years. One member of this society sent me a typewritten judicial decision of the year 1809 in a medical case, with the suggestion that this was the kind of medicine to have, and that the science of medicine had not progressed, but gone back. This decision went on and described a sort of medicine I used to take myself fifty years ago, and which was in use also in the time of the Pharaohs, and all the knowledge up to fifty years ago you got from five thousand years before that.

I now hold in my hand Jaynes's Medical Dictionary, published in 1745. In that book there is a suggestion as to what medicine was like a long time ago. How many operations that are in use now were known fifty years ago?—they were not operations, they were executions.

I read in this book the case of a man who "died from a severe headache." Why "severe?" The man was dead. Didn't that cover the ground? This book goes on to say: "A certain merchant about fifty years of age, of a melancholy habit, and deeply involved in affairs of the world, was, during the dog days"—with a capital D—"seized with a violent pain of his head, which some time after kept him in bed. I being called"—remember this man was a regular—"ordered vennisection in the arms, bleeding; I also ordered the application of leeches to the vessels of his nostrils; I also ordered the application of leeches to his forehead and temples, and also behind his ears."

Now you see, he has got him fringed all over with leeches. But that was not enough, for he goes on to say: "I likewise ordered the application of cup glasses, with scarification on his back." Now, he has township maps carved all over him, and all this is for a headache. But notwithstanding these precautions the man dies, or rather, perhaps, I might have said, because of these precautions the man dies. Now this physician goes on to say: "If any surgeon skilled in arterial anatomy had been present, I should also have ordered an operation." He was not satisfied with what he had done, with the precautions he had already taken, but he wanted apparently to put a pump into that man and pump out what was left.

Now all that has passed away, and modern medicine and surgery have come in. Medicine was like astronomy, which did not move for centuries. When a comet appeared in the heavens it was a sign that a Prince was going to die! It was also a sign of earthquakes and of pestilence and other dreadful things. But they began to drop one thing after another. They finally got down to earthquakes and the death of a Prince as the result of the appearance of a comet, until in 1818 a writer in *The Gentlemen's Magazine* found at least one thing that a comet was sent for, because it was of record that when the comet appeared in 1818 all the flies in London went blind and died. Now they had got down to flies.

In 1829 a clergyman found still one thing that a comet was sent for, because while it was in the heavens all the cats in Westphalia got sick. But in 1868 that whole scheme was swept away and the comet was recognized to be only a pleasant summer visitor, and as for the cats and flies they never were so healthy as they were then. From that time dates the great step forward that your profession has taken.

Text / "Mark Twain on Medicine," *Times,* March 9, 1902.

O'Brien / Morgan Joseph O'Brien (1852–1937). American jurist. He was a justice of the New York Supreme Court (1887–1930) and presiding justice of the Appellate Court (1905). The *Times* reported that, responding to the toast "The Law," he "related some incidents of judicial life that excited much amusement, and concluded with a definition of constitutional law and its place in human society that was loudly cheered."

· 135 ·

When the University of Missouri honored Mark Twain with an LL.D., he made a sentimental journey to the banks of the Mississippi. Four days in Hannibal were crowded with meeting old friends, much talking, rambling around town, and being at all times the center of affectionate attention. He presided at the Decoration Day ceremonies in the Presbyterian Church on the afternoon of May 30, and in the evening spoke at the high school graduation exercises, then distributed diplomas. After he had left town on June 3, the Hannibal Morning Journal *said next day: "Mark Twain has gone. He has perhaps made his last visit to the town in which he spent his boyhood and early manhood. . . . Yes, Mark Twain has gone, but he has left his impress upon the citizens of Hannibal. There is not a man or woman in Hannibal who saw him while here but that feels better by his coming."*

Remarks

Hannibal High School Graduation Exercises,
Park Theatre, May 30, 1902

It should have been my privilege to have been here a year ago. I received an invitation then from the high school, and I want to thank you now for that invitation. I appreciated it and I would have accepted it, had it not been that infirmity—that infirmity which has pursued me all my life and will pursue me to the end—an infirmity that is called by many names, and that is—well—in plain English, laziness. It was not born with me; I acquired it in Hannibal; I acquired many things here; and among others, laziness, which is now complicated with old age. I should have been here, but long ago I took a distaste to traveling on land. I don't mind a sea voyage, and if I could have come by water, I should have come. This may not seem to you a sufficient excuse, but it is—it is sufficient to me. My weakness came upon me, and I yielded.

I have come now. I am older now. Besides I have been invited to come to Columbia, to have a degree conferred upon me by the University of my native state—to be made a Doctor of Laws. I seem peculiarly fitted for that avocation. I say I received an invitation from Columbia. In form it was an invitation, but in spirit it was a command for me to come and receive a degree which I have not earned. I appreciate the compliment however and obey the command of the University. All the learning that I acquired to fit me for that degree, I received at a little schoolhouse here in Hannibal presided over by Mrs. Horr, Mrs. Torrey, Mr. Dawson and Mr. Cross. They qualified me—and it was no Sunday job. There were difficulties in the way of the process.

In going around over Hannibal today, I notice great differences between the Hannibal of today and that of two generations ago. Among other things, I notice a difference in matters of intellectual taste. I noticed at the Presbyterian Church this afternoon that the style of oratory has changed. In my day the speakers made more noise. Their oratory was bombastic, full of gesticulation, pounding the pulpit, and all sorts of exterior suggestions of sense, combined with the utter absence of that quality. Today I discovered, as I discover here tonight, that the speakers had the modern grace of expression, the felicity of phrasing, every sentence charged with an idea. This was true of every speech—and I don't even include my own. I don't make addresses on fifteen minutes' notice but I think if I had three or four weeks' preparation, I could have done just as well as they did—I think I could.

I was glad and proud to be in a Presbyterian pulpit in Hannibal. Many and many a time in my boyhood days here, I went to the Presbyterian Church—by request. And often and often in those days I desired earnestly to stand in that Presbyterian pulpit, and give instructions—but I was never asked until today. My ambition of two generations ago has been satisfied at last!

In those old days at Cross's school we had exhibitions once or twice a year. And here, too, I notice a difference. These young ladies tonight had grace in their delivery and originality in their productions.

I say young ladies, for I wonder why the superior sex is in such a limited sort of minority. It is not so in life.

It may be this is all you have—but get more. However, I must compliment these young gentlemen too, for arriving at this—in the face of so much opposition. But as I was saying, in those old days, whenever there was an exhibition, all ages and both sexes took part. If there had been a dozen sexes they would all have taken part, but there was never any instance where any speech had the least atom of originality. And a pupil that studied Latin! There was one boy, George RoBards, who attained that great solitary eminence—that Alpine summit! George RoBards studied Latin! Perhaps as many as twenty-five of you have reached that height.

Yes, there was a difference in what we did. Instead of original work, such as you have for the most part presented here tonight, in what we did there was not a line of original thought or any originality of expression. It would have been thought there was something the matter with a boy or girl who would attempt such a thing. We had recitations—not culled out of literature, but a certain number, and these same ones were all recited every time. They were all poetry—but one—and they were not tame poetry either. They were poems full of fire and action. That one prose selection was recited every time. It was "Give me LIBERTY or give me DEATH!" I never tried that one, but I believe I could repeat it now, word for word, from having heard it so often then by the other boys.

We had three pieces of poetry. One was:

> The Assyrian came down like a wolf on the fold,
> And his cohorts were gleaming with purple and gold.

Another was:

> Lochiel, Lochiel, beware of the day
> When the lowlands shall meet you in battle array,
> For a field of the dead rushes red on my sight,
> And the clans of Culloden were scattered in flight.

But the one poem that was never omitted—the one poem that saved the intellectual life of Hannibal at that time—the standby that was never, never absent from any program was:

> The boy stood on the burning deck.

Today it has been so pathetic to shake the hand and look into the eye of old gray-headed boys and imagine—for I could imagine them saying, "The boy stood on the burning deck." I must have met a half dozen of these boys today who used to recite it—and always in the same way. They never departed from their model. Why, I have stood on that burning deck with that Ancient Mariner that introduced me this evening as many as a hundred times—and without any fire insurance either.

Now, this seems a strange way to identify a boy; but a couple of years ago when I was away off on the other side of the world, on a British-India steamer, sailing on the Bay of Bengal from Ceylon to Bombay—no that isn't right, but you must not hold me responsible for my geography. I acquired it in Hannibal—a fellow on an outgoing steamer shouted, "Hello, Mark." I answered, "Hello yourself and see how you like it; who are you?" He said, "Don't you remember Cross's school in Hannibal? I used to recite 'The boy stood on the burning deck.' " Now, how should I know who he was. There was not a boy in Hannibal who did not recite it—it was a cold day when there was not a half dozen boys to recite it.

I have been told that I am to distribute diplomas. Now, I never distributed any diplomas before, therefore I can do it with greater confidence. There is nothing that saps one's confidence as the knowing how to do a thing. I am going to distribute these as they come, and you may toss up for them afterwards. You see I am frank and open about it. Always be frank and open—as Miss Fisher said, "Punch in the presence of the passenjare."

I would suggest that while I am delivering these diplomas that the Ancient Mariner recite for you "The boy stood on the burning deck." I am helping him. If I had not consented to do this, he would have had to do it himself.

[Mark Twain accompanied his haphazard distribution of diplomas with such remarks as "That's a nice one; take that one" and "We want these to go round." Then prolonged cheering brought him to the front for a brief conclusion.]

I thank you very much indeed for this just appreciation of what my friend, the Ancient Mariner, and I have tried to do for you. We wanted you to be pleased and it seems to meet with your appreciation. I thank you for him and for myself.

Text / "Address of Mark Twain," *Hannibal Morning Journal,* June 4, 1902.

The Assyrian came down, etc. / A slight misquotation of the opening lines of Byron's "The Destruction of Sennacherib."

Lochiel, Lochiel, etc. / From "Lochiel's Warning," by Thomas Campbell (1777–1844).

The boy stood on the burning deck / From "Casabianca," by Felicia

Dorothea Hemans (1793–1835).

that Ancient Mariner / W. H. C. Nash, a boyhood schoolfellow. In 1902, as president of the school board, he conducted the graduation exercises and introduced Mark Twain.

· 136 ·

At the University of Missouri Commencement, honorary degrees were conferred upon James Wilson, secretary of agriculture; Ethan Allen Hitchcock, secretary of the interior; B. T. Galloway, chief of the Bureau of Plant Industry; Robert S. Brookings; and the chief attraction of the occasion, Mark Twain. Wearing his Yale academic gown, he was the last candidate to be presented. After the brief ceremony, he seemed uncertain whether to say something or to sit down. When the audience rose to chant "M-i-s-s-o-u-r-i," then to burst into a storm of cheers and applause, he stepped to the front for a speech.

Speech

University of Missouri Commencement, Columbia, June 4, 1902

I have been in Missouri for about a week and it seems very like it did a long time ago. It has been so pleasant to me, notwithstanding the fact that it has been an intensely emotional week.

I have come back after so long an absence—and have spent that week in a town which was a small village when I left there as a small boy and you can conceive of what it must be to meet face to face old men and old women whom you have not seen for sixty years.

I looked in the faces of women—faces clothed in wrinkles and whose heads were as gray as mine—faces which when I last saw them were beautiful with the peach bloom of early youth—now on their heads the frosts of age, and in their faces wrinkles and the weatherbeaten look, not that which comes from exposure to bad weather. I experienced emotions that I had never expected, and did not know were in me. I was profoundly moved and saddened to think that this was the last time, perhaps, that I would ever behold those kind old faces and dear old scenes of childhood.

I have been through all of that in the last week and while it has been to me a blessed thing, while it has charged me with feelings which I would have been glad to have felt, yet it has been intensely emotional. I am glad to be back here and I should like to feel that my visit has not been in vain with the University of Missouri. It is not in vain on my part in view of the honor that I am to receive. It is as if all the world has risen up rejoicing that I will be out of the way soon—the jealous part of the world. The jealous part of it—they began to confer honors upon me several years ago, only they were in a little too much of a hurry. I was not ready to start that soon. When Yale conferred upon me the degree of Master of Arts there were a great many people who were ready to inquire what kind of arts I was acquainted with, what kind of business I proposed to run.

Then when the degree of Doctor of Literature was conferred upon me there were people who were unkind enough to question what I was going to doctor and say, "He don't know anything about art, what can he do about anything along that line," or "Yes, he will have plenty of practice in doctoring his own literature."

Now that I am Doctor of Laws there will be more queries of that kind. People will be saying now, "What does he know about doctoring laws?" But that's all right. We won't borrow trouble. It is perfectly right that I be made Doctor of Laws. People who doctor the laws and the people who make the laws do not have to obey them. Their share of the duties is in making them.

I think it was intended for me when the Swiss Bell Ringers played "The Last Rose of Summer." I am that rose, the last rose of my summer, I suppose. I shall not be here any more, I imagine. I am not an expert in music. I am not trained. I do not know the first principles of music and I should say that there are no standards of music, none at all, except for those people who have climbed through years of exertion until they stand upon the cold Alpine heights, where the air is so rarefied that they can detect a false note, and they lose much by that. I do not detect the false note, and it took me some time to get myself educated up to the point where I could enjoy Wagner. I am satisfied if I get it in the proper doses but I do feel about it a good deal as Bill Nye said. He said he had heard that Wagner's music was better than it sounds.

[He jocularly referred to the compliments that had been paid to Mr. Hitchcock.] I could, however, have paid him a few compliments myself and added one or two that he forgot to tell the gentleman. I have known him a long time. I did not know there was so much to his credit. I did not know the same of the other Cabinet doctor. I am really so glad—I did not know that Mr. Wilson was a Scotchman. I have known him for a long time but he has concealed that fact from an ulterior motive, no doubt. I do not know how a man could have known him for so long a time and not discovered it—all Scotchmen are named either David Wilson or James McDonald.

He was trying to interest me in the music. He loved those Scotch airs so. But really I did not know that it was a Scotch air. But it is pleasant. I found out things about him that I never expected.

In Mr. Galloway's case, he and I stand together—we stand together—we do not need any biography at all. I did notice a biographical sketch of me and pretty soon I—I—I won't say anything about it. I wish it was the disposition of these jealous men here to let your biography alone—there are naturally things in it that you would not confess to everybody.

This Mr. Galloway returned to Missouri when I did; he returned after a very few years' absence—I after sixty years' absence—and if he had waited as long as I did, he would not be as respectable as I am.

I should be sorry to go away from this place, go away from Missouri, feeling that I had left it as needy as it was and you understand that if I should forget to properly state my thanks for the honors that have been conferred upon me it is only an oversight. I will present them as soon as I can get them raised in my head. Since I have been in Missouri, I have distributed more wisdom than ever before, and I am sure that much good will result from my visit. I have had many honors conferred upon me, but I deserved them all. I sometimes suspect when you confer these honors you mean it as a sort of hint that I have been with you long enough. Some of the eastern colleges seemed to be rather in a hurry about getting me out of the way, and began conferring honors upon me years ago, but as I stated before, I deserve them all, and am always willing to accept anything in the way of honors that you have to offer.

In the course of the several days I have been here in Missouri, I have noticed some most remarkable changes. What I notice particularly is the change in moral elevation. The elevation of morals which has come about since I was here, not that I had anything to do with it, but it is so and I know, now that I recognize what the standards for the changes are and gone higher, that things which were then considered of minor importance are now considered to be serious things.

A newspaper said the other day that I, while a boy up in Hannibal, used to steal watermelons and peaches. And I knew from the tone of voice it was said in that it was meant as a reproach. Although in my time we should not have regarded little things like that. While we did do these things when I was a boy I do not think it is quite proper to say that we stole peaches. We took them. We would not want to apply such an epithet—everybody took peaches. I think the grown people as well as the younger ones took peaches. I believe that I can honestly say that I have never stolen as much as a ton of peaches. We did take watermelons; I do not know that there was any harm in it. The first time I ever stole a watermelon, I think it was the first time, I stole that watermelon—I removed the watermelon from a farmer's wagon while he was attending to another customer, and I took it down into the seclusion of a lumber yard. I took that watermelon there and broke it open and—it was green. The greenest watermelon ever raised in the Mississippi Valley. Well! How we are affected by little things. The minute I saw that that watermelon was green I was sorry. Sorry. And I began to reflect. Now reflection is the beginning of reform. When you have committed a sin if you do not reflect upon it and upon the probable consequences upon your character and career that sin has been wasted upon you. It is just as well that it had been committed by someone else. But I began to reflect and thence came the reform. This is it—the result which you now see before you. I began to reflect and I said that I had done wrong—to steal a green watermelon.

Now, then, when you have done wrong, what should you do next? What would George Washington do in such a case? Why, there is only one thing for him to do. There is only one right and righteous thing for any high-principled boy to do, and that is to restore it. Restore it to its rightful owner. That is what George Washington would do. And I said that is what I will do. Not many boys would have done that. And the moment that I made that good resolution I felt that moral upliftment which comes when you have been doing the wrong thing and have then conquered the evil one. I felt that uplifting and I took that watermelon back and restored it to the owner, that is, what was left of it—and I made him give me a ripe one. Even at that early age my teaching proclivities had developed to some extent and I began to teach him that he had done wrong. I went to him and told him that he ought to be ashamed of himself—working off green watermelons on people that had confidence in him, and I did not spare him. I told him if he did not break off that habit he could not have any more of my custom. And he was ashamed and promised to do better. And he showed that his reform had begun and was sincere and he showed that he wanted to make reparation. He went right down into the wagon and brought out another one.

It is so much better to sacrifice yourself that way for others. Why should you be going around selfishly remoulding your own morals and neglecting your neighbor's? It is much better to look after his morals than your own and very much easier. He just took his knife and plugged down deep into that watermelon—took a piece out of its heart about six inches deep—a great big red melon. I told the man I would forgive him and he has long since gone to the great beyond.

[He thanked the University for the great honor it had conferred upon him.] And I have taken it upon myself to believe that if it is not deserved—which is a matter of no sort of consequence to the University of Missouri, I consider it all the more a compliment.

Text / Composite, based upon: "Mark Twain's Speech," *Columbia Missouri Herald,* June 6, 1902; "Degree for Mark Twain," *Times,* June 5, 1902; "Missouri University Speech," *MTS*(10):338–40.

"The Last Rose of Summer" / A popular sentimental song of the nineteenth century, by Thomas Moore (1780–1852), an Irish poet: " 'Tis the last rose of summer. / Left blooming alone."

Hitchcock / Ethan Allen Hitchcock (1835–1909). American public official. He was the first American ambassador to Russia (1898). As secretary of the interior (1898–1907), he was instrumental in putting an end to public land frauds.

Wilson / James Wilson (1836–1920). American agriculturalist. Republican congressman (1873–77, 1883–85), he was professor of agriculture, Iowa State College (1891–97), and secretary of agriculture (1897–1913).

Galloway / Beverly Thomas Galloway (1863–1938). American botanist. Horticulturist and plant pathologist, University of Missouri (1884–88), he was chief of the Federal Bureau of Plant Industry (1901–12), assistant secretary of agriculture (1913–14), and dean of the College of Agriculture, Cornell University (1914–16).

· 137 ·

Heading back toward New York, Mark Twain paused in St. Louis for four days of dinners, luncheons, and receptions. He was the central figure at the christening of his waterborne namesake, the harbor boat Mark Twain. *For half an hour he took the wheel of the craft, her deck and pilot house crowded with spectators. A leadsman sang out the depth in traditional river fashion, the pilot impassively repeating the call: "Mark t-h-r-e-e," "Q-u-a-r-t-e-r t-w-a-i-n," then "M-a-r-k t-w-a-i-n," which brought a rousing cheer from the passengers. When he relinquished the wheel, he said, "That is the last time I will ever play the pilot." After luncheon and a speech by Mayor Wells, the countess de Rochambeau, handed a bottle of champagne by former Governor Francis, crashed it down on the deck as she said, "I christen thee, good boat,* Mark Twain."

Remarks

Christening of Harbor Boat Mark Twain, *St. Louis, June 6, 1902*

First of all, no—second of all—I wish to offer my thanks for the honor done me by naming this last rose of summer of the Mississippi Valley for me, this boat which represents a perished interest, which I fortified long ago, but whose life I did not save. And, in the first place, I wish to thank the Countess de Rochambeau for the honor she has done me in presiding at this christening.

I believe that it is peculiarly appropriate that I should be allowed the privilege of joining my voice with the general voice of St. Louis and Missouri in welcoming to the Mississippi Valley and this part of the continent these illustrious visitors from France.

I consider it just and right that I should be allotted this from the fact that for many years I have represented the people of the United States without special request, and without salary, as Special Ambassador to the World.

We owe much to the French, and I am sure that we will always remember and shall never forget it. We are glad to welcome these visitors here, to show them the results of what was done long ago by their ancestors, and we are glad to point out the fact that St. Louis is a French city. When La Salle came down this river a century and a quarter ago there was nothing on its banks but savages. He opened up this great river and by his simple act was gathered in this great Louisiana territory. I would have done it myself for half the money.

The name of La Salle will last as long as the river itself—will last until commerce is dead. We have allowed the commerce of the river to die, but it was to accommodate the railroads, and we are grateful. We have here with us a man who tells me he knew this river in the early ages, Pierre Chouteau, who says that he can remember when he could jump over it, and I believe that statement because he made it. Under no other circumstances would I.

I have come across a quality of veracity here in St. Louis which is new to me. It is the development of these later ages. I must call your attention to the fact that on this boat you are quite safe. I am here with a knowledge acquired long ago with the peculiarities of these waters, which is so pleasant to the strangers, from the color it bears and from its taste, but you will have to take the testimony of others for that.

Now the governor and the mayor have utilized their opportunities to advertise the World's Fair and I have taken the occasion to advertise myself, so there is nothing remaining but to again extend that welcome to our illustrious guests and to assure them that that welcome is heartfelt and sincere, and I am sure that we will spread open to them wide the doors of the whole continent.

Text / Composite, based upon: "Mark Twain's Farewell," *Times,* June 7, 1902; "The St. Louis Harbor-Boat 'Mark Twain,'" *MTS*(10):423–24.

these illustrious visitors / A French delegation had come over for the dedication of the grounds of the Louisiana Purchase Exposition, which would open in St. Louis in 1904, a year later than expected. In the group were the marquis de Lafayette and the count and countess de Rochambeau.

Pierre Chouteau / (1789–1865). He was an American fur trader who was born in St. Louis.

· 138 ·

Most of the harbor boat christening party moved on to the unveiling of a bronze tablet marking the birthplace of Eugene Field. Before releasing the flag that draped the plaque, Mark Twain spoke briefly. When Roswell Field, a brother, later said that the house was not within a mile of the birthplace, Mark Twain observed: "Never mind. It is of no real consequence. A rose in any other garden will bloom as sweet." See MTB, *3:1175.*

Remarks

Unveiling of a Tablet Commemorating Eugene Field,
St. Louis, June 6, 1902

My friends: We are here with reverence and respect to commemorate and enshrine in memory the house where was born a man who by his life made bright the lives of all who knew him, and by his literary efforts cheered the thoughts of thousands who never knew him. I take pleasure in unveiling this tablet to Eugene Field.

Text / "Mark Twain Unveils a Tablet to Eugene Field," *Harper's Weekly* 46, no. 2376 (July 5, 1902):851.

Eugene Field / (1850–95). American writer. His column, "Odds and Ends," in the Denver *Tribune,* led to his first book, *A Tribune Primer* (1882). On the Chicago *Morning Record* (1883–95), his "Sharps and Flats" often satirized the pretensions of the meat-packing aristocracy. Poems like "Little Boy Blue" and "Wynken, Blynken, and Nod" made him known as "the poet of childhood." He also wrote *Culture's Garland* (1887), and *The Love Affairs of a Bibliomaniac* (1896).

· 139 ·

At the St. Louis art students' luncheon for Mark Twain, Professor Halsey C. Ives, director of the Museum of Fine Arts, conferred upon the chief guest the degree of "Master Doctor of Arts." Mark Twain enjoyed himself, although he was chagrined by a scheduling mixup that forced him to leave the luncheon party before the end.

Speech on Art

Art Students Association Luncheon for Mark Twain, Museum of Fine Arts, St. Louis, June 7, 1902

Ladies and gentlemen, and the Art Students Association: I am sorry myself that that mistake was made, and I do not know how it was made. I was promising myself a long sojourn here with you, and through that misfortune I am to lose that. I am to go straightway to some other place and do some other thing—I don't know what it is, something for the furthering of the public good or the advancement of civilization; but if I could only stay here a little longer, I should like to go into a disquisition of some sort concerning art, now that I feel reenforced for work like that by this degree which has just been conferred upon me.

I have always had the impression that I was intended for an instructor in art, but I never have felt full confidence, because that sort of recognition which is the sort of thing that gives confidence, had not arrived. Just as soon as you become a master doctor of arts, you know all about it, for you have a better opportunity to know, and from that moment you are competent to teach in these high matters of art. I feel now entirely competent to teach. Before, I should have considered that what I might offer in the matter of instruction would properly be considered a matter of opinion, but now I consider it is a matter of law. I consider that now I know how to talk to you on art.

A long time ago, when I used to examine the old masters on the other side of the water, I did not consider myself competent to teach other people, but I did consider myself competent to teach myself. But I found as I went along that I had overestimated my ability in that line, too, for I was not able to appreciate. I was not able to find in the old masters the joys which other people found there. I could not find beauty or anything to enthuse me in a Saint Sebastian stuck full of arrows. Moreover, I objected to every Saint Sebastian that I ever saw, because they all seemed to be enjoying it. And I said, "That old master that considers that saint or sinner can be a pincushion of arrows, and smile, does not know human nature, and his art is all wrong." Many things in art I was not able to see. I did not know what I wanted to see. I went into the Pitti Palace, where they have those treasures of art, as they call them, and there was a Titian Venus five or six feet long on a bed sixteen or seventeen feet long, with a dog close by that you could put in a snuffbox. The drawing and perspective were all wrong. The drawing was atrocious—to me—and I finally said to a man who was away up in art, "What do you find in that picture?" He said, "It is not worth while for me to tell you. Because certain qualities are required in order that you shall see the marvels in that picture, and you are not qualified to see them. You are born with a lack that cannot be supplied by education. You cannot learn, and you may as well give it up."

And he told me about a lady who said to Turner, once, "Why, Mr. Turner, I have spent many years in Venice, at one time and another, but I have never seen the colors in the Grand Canal that are in this picture of yours." And he said, "Don't you wish you could?"—meaning that she had not an educated eye. There are two things concerned there: in the first place, natural ability that can be educated, a vision that can be educated, so that by and by you can see everything that is in a great picture; but without that original equipment, reenforced by education, you cannot expect to see those things in the great masters. That thought struck me, and I began to see that there was a reason why so many went as I did through the galleries of Europe and came away disappointed at finding there nothing that was entitled to the vast encomiums that they had heard pronounced, and I saw that there must be something I could not understand. Finally, someone taught me what I have been intimating, that if you have no natural gift for art, then it is not worth while to meddle with art. If you have a natural gift, it is not going to be valuable until you have the right teaching.

A man in Hartford came of a race of painters—they were good painters in the view of all New England. One of them was this young man, who had been painting pictures quite satisfactorily for several years and was making a handsome reputation. One day that greatest clergyman that the last century produced, Rev. Dr. Bushnell, a man regarded as authority in every possible way in that region, came into Mr. Flagg's studio, and Flagg recognized that it was a great honor, indeed, and he welcomed him with deference and enthusiasm. He was proud to know that Dr. Bushnell would now see what sort of an artist he was. Dr. Bushnell went to the easel and looked at a picture, evidently with an absorbed interest, and the pride and satisfaction was growing, growing in Flagg's soul. He probably intended to tell his parents about it when he got home. Finally, Dr. Bushnell said, "You must learn to draw!" That was a thunderbolt out of the blue. Flagg thought he knew how to draw. But Bushnell said, "No, no, you must learn to draw!" Then he said, "Where is your library?" Flagg said, "There it is." It was a shelf full of French novels. Bushnell shook his head, and said, "Do you know mathematics?" And Flagg said, "No." "Then you must learn mathematics." This struck Flagg as odd; mathematics was a thing he did not know he must know. But Bushnell said, "You must learn!" And then he said, "Have you ever dissected a human body?" And Flagg said, "No." "You must learn to dissect a human body." Then he looked the picture over again and said, "All these things are necessary in order to educate your eye. You must learn to see." Flagg said he thought he knew how to see. "No," Bushnell said, "I mean no offense when I say it, but really, in this picture, I see that you have only the vision of a cow. By that I mean that you see only the outside of things. In your daisies, your trees, your weeds, you see only the outside. Your spiritual vision has not been educated. You have the vision of a cow. A cow admires and knows a daisy as much as you do, and if she could paint, that is the kind of daisy she would put on canvas. You must not remain with the vision of a cow. You must get the finer and higher vision that comes through teaching under competent masters." Flagg said, "What shall I do?" Dr. Bushnell said, "Go to Paris. Go to the Beaux Arts. Don't waste your young manhood here in this uneducated work. Go to headquarters. Learn to do it right. Good-bye."

He went away, and Flagg sailed for France the next day. He was convinced. He sailed with his brother, and he convinced him without trouble. His brother was an artist of repute, and had a fine opinion of his abilities. When they arrived, they found they had an afternoon to spare, and they went straight to the Louvre and wandered along through, looking at this old master and that old master, until they had examined an acre or two of old masters, and yet they expressed no opinion in words; and finally they came to the Mona Lisa. "You say it." And the other said, "No, you say it." And so it was my Flagg who said, "Well, this is the Mona Lisa! This is the picture that we have heard so much about and have worshiped from a distance, because other people did in books. It is just an old smoked herring!" Then, when they came before the teachers in the Beaux Arts, one of the teachers said, "What is your grade? How far have you reached?" They said,

"We paint in oils," and the teacher said, "From what?" And they said, "From nature," and he said, "Let me see you draw something." So they drew something, and he said, "Well, it is not time yet for you to begin colors, not time for you to begin to paint from nature: first let us learn to draw."

He put those boys at plaster busts, and taught them how to draw a drygoods box, and kept them at it three months. He made them buy a corpse and dissect it. He taught them mathematics. He gave them the whole course, just as Bushnell had advised. In six months they had not had a holiday, and were worked nearly to death. One day they looked into the Louvre galleries again, and looked at those same masters, all along those acres of old masters, and finally arrived again in front of the Mona Lisa. They looked at it a long time in silence, and one said, "You say it," and the other said, "You say it." "Well," he said, "I will. It is true—we had the vision of a cow." It was the very verdict that Bushnell had rendered so long before. "Now," they said, "we recognize that we did not know how to draw or paint in colors. We did not know how to paint nature, and we might have learned it earlier if we had had somebody to advise us."

That is my lesson for you to convey to the incoming class. You do not need it yourselves, and, as I have not time to wait for the incoming class, you will have to teach it secondhand, from one whom you know to be a master doctor of arts, and competent.

Text / "The St. Louis Speech on Art," Cyril Clemens, *Mark Twain The Letter Writer* (1932):111–16.

Turner / James Mallord William Turner (1775–1851). British painter. A professional by the age of ten, famous at twenty-five, he gained his knowledge of landscape painting by observation on walking tours of more than twenty miles a day in the British Isles and western Europe. A man of tremendous industry, he produced a great many finished pictures, besides thousands of drawings, sketches and watercolors. Well known paintings are *Calais Pier* (1803), *The Fighting Temeraire* (1819), and *The Slave Ship* (1840).

Flagg / Charles Noel Flagg (1848–1916). American painter. He studied in Paris (1872–82), then returned to teach in New York, St. Paul and Minneapolis, before settling in Hartford, where he founded a free art school for workingmen, which became the Connecticut League of Art Students. Of his many portraits of Hartford citizens, perhaps the best known is that of Mark Twain, Metropolitan Museum, New York.

· 140 ·

Back in New York after a tumultuous stay in Missouri, Mark Twain soon returned to the banqueting circuit. Although he was not a typical clubman who loitered in the easy chairs of the clubhouse, he enjoyed club dinners. The visit of General Porter, ambassador to France, on a briefing mission, was enough to unroll the red carpet at the Lotos Club, and to induce Mark Twain to speak at some length.

Dinner Speech

Lotos Club Dinner for General Horace Porter,
New York, June 17, 1902

The chairman has told the truth. He hasn't had much practice, but he did it this time. I did say that I should be very glad indeed to say something in case anybody preceding me should furnish me a text. That anybody preceding me should furnish you statistics that need to be corrected, or facts of any kind that seemed feasible things, did not occur to me. It is my line to correct them. I have stood for truth all my life. I have been a sort of symbol of veracity, and it has not always been recognized. But there have been things said tonight which furnish me here and there a text, and they are pleasing texts. I don't see that I have any real fault to find with anything that I have heard.

I didn't quite like to hear men whose heads are still brown, like the chairman's, and black, like the guest's, talk too much of people who have been in this club longer than they have, meaning me. And to hear them calling your distinct attention to the stuff which I wear upon my head and which has been tanned to its present tone by hard work in the interest of civilization! I have first to correct an opinion of the guest of the evening, as everybody can have an opinion. Compliments are paid to him in a gracious way, and in a truthful and righteous way, the way in which Mr. Lawrence has turned these compliments, when he speaks of this brilliant bird of passage from the coal hole of the Lotos Club. I like to hear him pay these compliments. I like to see the chairman show off what he can do with language. And I like to see him throw out his culture and his knowledge in this mysterious way, and talk about the date of the battle of Bunker Hill just as if he was there and knew all about it. He throws out this historical information with a scandalous air of having it always on tap. He has been studying a cyclopedia today. There was a man here who knew the date of the battle of Bunker Hill. I don't take these random historians at par. I shall look myself when I get home, and see if they're right.

Why, General Porter stands up here, and he also throws out very nice things, and sometimes they suggest Wagner's music from the pen and point of view of Bill Nye. Bill Nye said that he had heard that Wagner's music was better than it sounded. You can take what General Porter says in the same way. Now he has been abroad over five years, and has been working in my interest and Mr. Armour's interest, trying to get our literature introduced, our pork from the pen. Well, that is a good thing to do, and he has been and is working very hard, and has done admirably well. He has sold more than forty copies of my works in France every year, and it was only half that when he went away. He has done exceedingly well. We have never had a representative there who has done his work more to my satisfaction than General Porter.

And he has been learning French. I wish he had made his speech in French. Not because anyone would have understood it, I could not have understood my share, perhaps. But I should like to hear him. I think General Porter did know French before he went away. He has complimented me on my study of the German language; I think I did yeoman service in trying to tame that language. I had not the same success with it that he had with the French. I have great reverence for the German language. I did the best I could with it. I stood by it many years. I worked it hard and it worked me hard. There were many pleasant incidents connected with the struggle. We had a very dear old lady, a sweet old soul, who took a great fancy to a young lady who was traveling with us. She took so strong a fancy to that young American woman, that she poured out her practical German affection upon her, and she couldn't say too much, or find too much to praise in that young person and everything connected with her. And this dear old lady was always trying to find similarities between the Germans and the Americans, and was always delighted when she could show a sort of relationship in methods of expression and feelings. And she said one day, "Why, you talk the same as we talk. We say, 'Ach Gott,' and you say, 'God damn.' "

But the remarks of Admiral Barker carry me back to the time when I was in Austria. That was the time when the war broke out. It was threatening daily, that Spanish war, and the admiral says that Americans are more comfortable there on the other side, and are now treated with higher regard than they were at any earlier time. It is no doubt true. At the time I speak of, 1898, Americans who were sojourning in Vienna had a sufficiently uncomfortable time, for it was said, it came from America, that we were going to fight Spain for Cuba's sake, and that our sole reason for that was the humanitarian one that we were going to put forth our strength to achieve the freedom of the downtrodden Cubans, and that we should not charge anything for that, but would do it simply from our American principle of standing by weak nations who were struggling for their freedom, and ask nothing for that but the consciousness of doing this thing. They thought we were too selfish to pour out blood and treasure for that cause. I had to stand hearing people say in all kinds of German, with languages mixed, that that was all nonsense, folly, romance, humbug, that we had an ulterior motive for that war, and that our humanitarian purpose was a mere pretense. I had to stand all that. Everybody in that country had to stand that, and put up with that. It was hard enough, because I believed thoroughly that we had no object in view but the high and noble one of setting that people free. And I said it; and I instructed the young American people, younger than I was, and we were in trouble, and met with scoffs on all hands, and jeers. And I strengthened them, and I said to them, "Don't you be afraid. It is all true, absolutely true. Speak out and say so. These people don't understand fighting for any purpose such as this, but we understand it, and we do it. Stand by your flag and don't be afraid."

We went all through that and we have waited to see the result, and now I should like to stand in Vienna and say, "See what we have done. We have done everything. We have kept our word. We set those Cubans free. We said we should do it and we did it." If there is anything in this world we have to be proud of for a long time, it is that fact. I am glad I have lived long enough to be able to say to those Viennese that I was right and they were wrong.

General Porter has done a great many things to be proud of; and a great many things for which we have reason to be proud of him. More than one of you have understood in one way or another what General Porter has accomplished in that short life which has resulted in that black head of his. Men get older some time or another. All of you know how brilliant he is. He should have a school. He has done some meritorious things, but you haven't heard of the greatest victory he ever won, on the battlefields or in the diplomacy of Paris over wise men. I saw him put to a test one night that would have taxed any other man severely. He saw it through, and I should tell you about that for his everlasting credit.

Fifteen or twenty-five years ago the Fellowcraft Club was formed. They had sixty-five members, and they held one meeting very successfully that I remember. At this meeting Mr. Gilder was chairman, and just for fun I made a proposition. I got Major Pond to say to Mr. Gilder that there was a young man here from down South who had a plan by which he proposed to teach young men how to make after-dinner speeches without any preparation. He would teach them how to choose any subject, take any text, and speak to that text without embarrassment of any kind. Mr. Gilder didn't want to introduce this young person, but he was persuaded to do so. Major Pond said that this man's name was Samuel Langhorne—Langhorne is part of my name—and when he stated what the man's name was, he said he hoped the club would call for Mr. Langhorne. And then Mr. Gilder called it out. I stepped forward.

I said: "There is no swindle about this, Langhorne is part of my name." I wanted to try this project, and I wanted a class to teach people after-dinner speaking. I wanted to try it on the dog, as the actors say, and I wanted to make the experiment there. My scheme was this, and it is based on this, that, as a rule, after-dinner speeches seem to me to consist of anecdotes, and remarks attached. From observation it seemed to me that the anecdotes are made for the speaker, and just this. A man gets up on his feet to make a speech, and he talks along and talks very handsomely. Presently he approaches an anecdote. You can see it in the air. You can smell it. And presently he says, "Now, how felicitously what I have just been saying is illustrated in the case of the man who," and then he tells the anecdote, and those people are caught, and they laugh, and the thing goes off, and it doesn't occur to them that that anecdote didn't illustrate a thing. But that doesn't matter, he talks along, and presently he brings out another anecdote, and they still don't notice that it doesn't illustrate, and the man goes on and takes out these anecdotes, and the people go home. And after all, his anecdotes never illustrated anything he had to say. And then I got those people to give me a text, to show them what I could do with it. And I asked them to send around a hat, and have everybody propose a text. I said it would make no difference what the text was, one was just as good as another on this plan. And after that they sent a hat around and somebody reached in and got one out.

The text I got was portrait painting. Well, it wasn't much of a text, considering what I knew about that subject. But I said that would do, one was just as good as another. And then I began to deliver the facts and the history about it, starting back to the primeval man who sketched the mammoth, and so on, and every now and then I dropped in an anecdote. I always said, you can see how felicitously what I have just said is illustrated in the case of the man who, and I went right along.

Now you see the whole scheme. Everybody here ought to be able to act on this line. He must have his anecdote ready, and he must always remember to say, "You see how felicitously this is illustrated in the case of the man who."

There wasn't a man there who got through his speech, because he never got to an anecdote without all those people jumping in to help him out, until it got to General Porter. And General Porter stood up there, and told nineteen anecdotes. They tried to shut him off, to shout him down, but they couldn't do it. He introduced each one by saying, "You see how felicitously what I have just been saying is illustrated in the case of the man who." There never was so much courage exhibited. He took a text himself, that "Truth is stranger than fiction." He didn't illustrate it in a single instance. He always said he did, and it always carried, and he finished most happily. Now all the anecdotes had been told before, taken from here and there. And General Porter said it was true from his own personal experience. He said he made a voyage across the Atlantic, a very stormy voyage. You see how he handled the thing, and he had the people's hair standing on end about the dangers, and he got up on that, that the ship was leaking and they had to keep at the pumps all the time, day and night, all the way. And then he wound up, "Why, we pumped the Atlantic Ocean through her sixteen times." That was his idea of truth being stranger than fiction. Everybody could see that it was. I have immense admiration for General Porter. I have more admiration for him than for the tax assessor of Tarrytown.

The tax assessors of Tarrytown understand their business better than anybody else. There are Tarrytown people here tonight. The way those tax assessors work is that in order to verify their figures they find out what the fellow is worth, and multiply it by fifty-seven. They would tax Porter on his personal appearance if he lived there. Oh, I am going to have a time up there. I am up there, and I have got to put an addition on that place. I have got to get a chicken coop, and you can't have a chicken coop in Tarrytown without risking something. I am going to build that one of chilled iron. I am going to save the coop itself when the assessor comes. I don't propose to get taken up. It is a great place. I am enjoying the prospect of going there. I haven't got there yet. It's a great place. It has a lower death rate and a higher tax rate than any place on the civilized globe.

But I welcome General Porter back to his native shore. I welcome him with all my heart. I have a reverent affection for him, and this feeling has grown with the years during which I have observed him. He grows in my estimation all the time. I have a great opinion of his abilities, and a great opinion of his career as he has made it, and great hope that he will make it greater in the future. And if next time I don't have an opportunity to vote for Theodore Roosevelt for President, I hope to vote for Porter.

Text / Composite, based upon: "Samuel L. Clemens at the Dinner to Horace Porter, June 17, 1902," *Lotos:* 99–107; "Gen. Porter Honored at Lotos Club," *Times,* June 18, 1902.

Armour / Jonathan Ogden Armour (1863–1927) assumed control of the meat-packing business upon the death of his father, Philip Danforth Armour (1832–1901).

our pork from the pen / General Porter said that many Frenchmen did not know that America was the home of the works of Mark Twain, Chicago pork, and other products of the pen.

Barker / Albert Smith Barker (1845–1916). American naval officer. An Annapolis graduate (1861), he served in the Union Navy during the Civil War. Commanding U.S.S. *Enterprise,* he ran a line of deep sea soundings around the world (1883–86), commanded the *Newark* and *Oregon* in the Spanish-American War, became rear admiral (1899) and commandant of the New York Navy Yard (1900–03).

· 141 ·

Colonel George Harvey, host at the sixty-seventh birthday dinner for Mark Twain, assembled an eminent coterie: Howells, Charles Frohman, John Hay, Wayne MacVeagh, Adolph S. Ochs, Booth Tarkington, Howard Pyle, Hamlin Garland, August Belmont, McKelway, F. Hopkinson Smith, Cable, Alden, Mabie, Gilder, Richard Le Gallienne, Henry Van Dyke, Matthews, Henry Rogers, and some forty others. Harvey slyly varied the usual banquet routine by introducing eight speakers before the guest of honor. Some of them, with mock seriousness, discussed the shortcomings of "Mr. Twain." Tom Reed elaborated upon his habitual inaccuracy of statement. John Kendrick Bangs read a rhymed "Post-Prandial Obituary." Depew said that when he and Mark Twain were in Homburg while the Prince of Wales was there, "Mark was walking with me, and his trousers were too short, because they had been worn too long; the sleeves of his coat had the same general expression." The prince "wanted to know who this apparition was." Several times Mark Twain, on the verge of jumping up to reply, had to be gently restrained by the chairman. Finally the chief guest got the floor and held it for some time, delivering what one listener called "a blasting coruscation of wit and wisdom, of humor and pathos–Mark Twain at his inimitable best." See J. Henry Harper, I Remember *(1934):105.*

Dinner Speech

Sixty-seventh Birthday Dinner for Mark Twain, Metropolitan Club, New York, November 28, 1902

I think I ought to be allowed to talk as long as I want to, for the reason that I have cancelled all my winter's engagements of every kind, for good and sufficient reasons, and am making no new engagements for this winter, and therefore this is the only time, the only chance I shall have to disembowel my skull for a year—close the mouth in that portrait for a year. I want to offer thanks and homage to the chairman for this innovation which he has introduced here, which is an improvement, as I consider it, on the old-fashioned style of conducting occasions like this. That was bad—that was a bad, bad, bad arrangement. Under that old custom the chairman got up and made a speech; he introduced the prisoner at the bar, and covered him all over with compliments—nothing but compliments, not a thing but compliments—never a slur, and sat down and left that man to get up and talk without a text. You cannot talk on compliments; that is not a text. No modest person, and I was born like that, can talk on compliments. A man gets up and is filled to the eyes with happy emotions, but his tongue is tied; he has nothing to say, he is in the condition of Dr. Rice's friend who came home drunk and explained it to his wife, and his wife said to him, "John, when you have drunk all the whiskey you want, you ought to ask for sarsaparilla." He said, "Yes, but when I have drunk all the whiskey I want I can't say sarsaparilla." And so I think it is much better to leave a man unmolested until the testimony and pleadings are all in. Otherwise he is dumb—he is at the sarsaparilla stage.

Before I get to the higgledy-piggledy point, as Mr. Howells suggested I do, I want to thank you, gentlemen, for this very high honor you are doing me, and I am quite competent to estimate it at its value. I see here around me the captains of industry in all the great illustrious industries, most distinguished men; there are more than fifty here, I believe, and I believe that out of those fifty I know thirty-nine of them well. I could probably borrow money from—well—from the others, anyway. It is a proud thing to me, indeed, to see such a distinguished gathering come here on such an occasion as this, when there is no foreign prince to be feted—when you have come here, as I take it you do, not to do honor to hereditary privilege and ancient lineage, but to do reverence to mere moral excellence and elemental veracity—and, dear me, how old it seems to make me! Sixty-seven. I look around me and I see three or four persons I have known so many, many years. I have known John Hay and Tom Reed and the Rev. Mr. Twichell close upon thirty-six years. Close upon thirty-six years I have known those venerable men. I have known Mr. Howells nearly thirty-four years, and I knew Chauncey Depew before he could walk straight, and before he learned to tell the truth. Twenty-seven years ago I heard him make the most noble and eloquent and beautiful speech that has ever fallen from even his capable lips. Tom Reed said that my principal defect was inaccuracy of statement. Well, suppose that that is true. What's the use of telling the truth all the time? I never tell the truth about Tom Reed—but that is his defect, truth; he speaks the truth always.

Tom Reed has got a good heart and he has got a good intellect, but he hasn't got any judgment. Why, when Tom Reed was invited to lecture to the Ladies' Society for the Procreation or Procrastination, or something, of morals, I don't know what it was—advancement, I suppose, of pure morals—he had the immortal indiscretion to begin by saying that some of us can't be optimists, but by judiciously utilizing the opportunities that Providence puts in our way, we can all be bigamists. You perceive his limitations. Anything he has got to state, he states, if he thinks it is true. Well, that was true, but that was no place to say that—so they fired him out. Well, he has had a good deal to say about that yachting cruise last spring down in the West Indies in Mr. Rogers's yacht, and so has Colonel Harvey said some things about that. But, dear me, that was not a poker-playing trip at all. There was poker, but not much poker. There was perhaps what a crowd like this would call a great deal of poker—but a crowd like that! We didn't go down there to play poker anyway; we went down there to hunt up Martinique and start up that volcano; and that was a remarkable voyage in various ways.

We had a storm, so I got out of my berth at two o'clock in the morning, and went up to the poker chapel to see if I could find something to hang on to, and presently I heard Tom Reed lumbering up that companionway and grunting and blaspheming, and butting the bulkhead, carrying on—good land! I thought something was the matter with his appendicitis. Then he appeared up there in his pajamas, and he was going it. Well, he said: "I couldn't stay in my berth at all; it's wet." "Why," I said, "you old thing, you ought to be ashamed of yourself—scared to that extent."

A lot of accounts have been settled here tonight for me; I have held grudges against some of these people, but they have all been wiped out by the very handsome compliments that have been paid me. Even Wayne MacVeagh—I have had a grudge against him many years. The first time I saw Wayne MacVeagh was at a private dinner party at Charles A. Dana's, and when I got there he was going on, and I tried to get a word in here and there—but you know what Wayne MacVeagh is when he is started, and I could not get in five words to his one—or one word to his five. I struggled along, and struggled along, and—well, I wanted to tell, and I was trying to tell a dream I had had the night before, and it was a remarkable dream, a dream it was worth people's while to listen to, and it was a dream such as the revivalists describe—some general reception in heaven. I was on a train and had stopped at the celestial way station—I had a through ticket—and I noticed a man sitting alongside of me that was asleep and had his ticket in his hat. He was the remains of the Archbishop of Canterbury; I recognized him by his photograph. I had nothing against him, so I took his ticket and let him have mine. He didn't object—he wasn't in a condition to object—and presently when the train stopped at the heavenly station—well, I got off and he went on by request. There they all were, the angels, you know—millions of them—every one with a torch; they had arranged for a torchlight procession; they were expecting the Archbishop, and when I got off they started to raise a shout, but it didn't materialize. I don't know whether they were disappointed. I suppose they had a lot of superstitious ideas about the Archbishop and what he looked like, and I didn't fill the bill, and I was trying to explain to St. Peter, and I was doing it in the German tongue, because I didn't want to be too explicit.

Well, I found it was no use trying to tell that story. I couldn't get along, for Wayne MacVeagh was occupying the whole place, and I said to Mr. Dana, "What is the matter with that man? Who is that man with the long tongue? What's the trouble with him, getting up a conflagration like this, without giving a man a chance—that other incendiary, that long, lank cadaver, that old oil derrick out of a job—who is that?" "Well, now," Mr. Dana says, "you don't want to meddle with him; you had better keep quiet; just keep quiet, because that's a bad man. Talk! He was born to talk. Don't let him get out with you; he'll skin you." I said, "I have been skinned, skinned, and skinned right along; there's nothing left." He says, "Oh, you'll find there is; that man is the very seed and inspiration of that proverb which says, 'It's no matter how close you skin an onion, a clever man can always peel it again.' " Well, I reflected and I quieted down. That would never occur to Tom Reed. He's got no discretion. Well, MacVeagh is just the same man; he hasn't changed a bit in all those years; he has been peeling Mr. Mitchell lately. That's the kind of man he is.

Mr. Howells—that poem of his is admirable; that's the way to treat a person. Howells has a peculiar gift for seeing the merits of people, and he has always exhibited them in my favor. Howells has never written anything about me that I couldn't read six or seven times a day; he is always just and always fair; he has written more appreciatively of me than anyone in this world, and published it in the *North American Review*. He did me the justice to say that my intentions—he italicized that—that my intentions were always good, that I wounded people's conventions rather than their convictions. Now, I wouldn't want anything handsomer than that said of me. I would rather wait, with anything harsh I might have to say, till the convictions become conventions. Bangs has traced me all the way down. He can't find that honest man, but I will look for him in the looking glass when I get home.

I heard it intimated by the Colonel that it is New England that makes New York and builds up this country and makes it great, overlooking the fact that there's a lot of people here who came from elsewhere, like John Hay from away out West, and Wayne MacVeagh from away out in my state, and Howells from Ohio, and St. Clair McKelway and me from Missouri, and we are doing what we can to build up New York a little—elevate it. Why, when I was living in that village of Hannibal, Missouri, on the banks of the Mississippi, and Hay up in the town of Warsaw, also on the banks of the Mississippi River—well it was an emotional bit of the Mississippi, and if it is low water you have to climb up to the town on a ladder, and when it floods you have to hunt for it with a deep sea lead. It was a simple, simple life, cheap but comfortable, and full of sweetness, and there was nothing of this rage of modern civilization there at all. It was a delectable land.

I went out there last June, and I met in that town of Hannibal a schoolmate of mine, John Briggs, whom I had not seen for more than fifty years. I tell you, that was a meeting! That pal whom I had known as a little boy long ago, and knew now as a stately man three or four inches over six feet and browned by exposure to many climes, he was back there to see that old place again. We spent a whole afternoon going about here and there and yonder, and hunting up the scenes and talking of the crimes which we had committed so long ago. It was a heartbreaking delight, full of pathos, laughter, and tears, all mixed together; and we called the roll of the boys and girls that we picnicked and sweethearted with so many years ago, and there were hardly half a dozen of them left; the rest were in their graves; and we went up there on the summit of that hill, a treasured place in my memory, the summit of Holliday's Hill, and looked out again over that magnificent panorama of the Mississippi River, sweeping along league after league, a level green paradise on one side, and retreating capes and promontories as far as you could see on the other, fading away in the soft, rich lights of the remote distance. I recognized then that I was seeing now the most enchanting river view the planet could furnish. I never knew it when I was a boy; it took an educated eye that had traveled over the globe to know and appreciate it; and John said, "Can you point out the place where Bear Creek used to be before the railroad came?" I said, "Yes, it ran along yonder." "And can you point out the swimming hole?" "Yes, out there." And he said, "Can you point out the place where we stole the skiff?" Well, I didn't know which one he meant. Such a wilderness of events had intervened since that day, more than fifty years ago, it took me more than five minutes to call back that little incident, and then I did call it back; it was a white skiff, and we painted it red to allay suspicion. And the saddest, saddest man came along—a stranger he was—and he looked that red skiff over so pathetically, and he said, "Well, if it weren't for the complexion I'd know whose skiff that was." He said it in that pleading way, you know, that appeals for sympathy and suggestion; we were full of sympathy for him, but we weren't in any condition to offer suggestions. I can see him yet as he turned away with that same sad look on his face and vanished out of history forever. I wonder what became of that man. I know what became of the skiff. Well, it was a beautiful life, a lovely life. There was no crime. Merely little things like pillaging orchards and watermelon patches and breaking the Sabbath—we didn't break the Sabbath often enough to signify—once a week perhaps. But we were good boys, good Presbyterian boys, all Presbyterian boys, and loyal and all that; anyway, we were good Presbyterian boys when the weather was doubtful; when it was fair, we did wander a little from the fold.

Look at John Hay and me. There we were in obscurity, and look where we are now. Consider the ladder which he has climbed, the illustrious vocations he has served—and vocations is the right word; he has in all those vocations acquitted himself with high credit and honor to his country and to the mother that bore him. Scholar, soldier, diplomat, poet, historian—now, see where we are. He is Secretary of State and I am a gentleman. It could not happen in any other country. Our institutions give men the positions that of right belong to them through merit; all you men have won your places not by heredities, and not by family influence or extraneous help, but only by the natural gifts God gave you at your birth, made effective by your own energies; this is the country to live in.

Now, there is one invisible guest here. A part of me is present; the larger part, the better part, is yonder at her home; that is my wife, and she has a good many personal friends here, and I think it won't distress any one of them to know that, although she is going to be confined to that bed for many months to come from that nervous prostration, there is not any danger and she is coming along very well—and I think it quite appropriate that I should speak of her. I knew her for the first time just in the same year that I first knew John Hay and Tom Reed and Mr. Twichell—thirty-six years ago—and she has been the best friend I have ever had, and that is saying a good deal; she has reared me—she and Twichell together—and what I am I owe to them. Twichell—why, it is such a pleasure to look upon Twichell's face! For five-and-twenty years I was under the Rev. Mr. Twichell's tuition, I was in his pastorate, occupying a pew in his church, and held him in due reverence. That man is full of all the graces that go to make a person companionable and beloved; and wherever Twichell goes to start a church the people flock there to buy the land. They find the real estate goes up all around the spot, and they always try to get Twichell to start a church somewhere else after a while, and wherever you see him go you can go and buy land there with confidence, feeling sure that there will be a double price for you before long. I am not saying this to flatter Mr. Twichell; it is the fact. Many and many a time I have attended the annual sale in his church, and bought up all the pews on a margin—and it would have been better for me spiritually and financially if I had stayed under his wing.

I have tried to do good in this world, and it is marvelous in how many different ways I have done good, and it is comfortable to reflect—now, there's Mr. Rogers—just out of the affection I bear that man many a time I have given him points in finance that he had never thought of—and if he could lay aside envy, prejudice, and superstition, and utilize those ideas in his business, it would make a difference in his bank account.

Well, I like the poetry. I like all the speeches and the poetry, too. I liked Dr. Van Dyke's poem. I wish I could return thanks in proper measure to you, gentlemen, who have spoken and violated your feelings to pay me compliments—some were merited and some you overlooked, it is true—and Colonel Harvey did slander every one of you, and put things into my mouth that I never said, and never thought at all.

And now I say there is your double guest, my wife and me, and we together, out of our single heart, return you our deepest and most grateful thanks—and—yesterday was her birthday.

Text / Composite, based upon: "When Twain Got His Say," *Times,* November 29, 1902; "They Let Mark Twain Talk," New York *Sun,* November 30, 1902; "Sixty-Seventh Birthday" in *MTS*(10):363–74; and *MTS*(23):244–53.

close the mouth in that portrait / As a memento of the occasion, each dinner guest received a sketch of Mark Twain, "done entirely by myself," he said, "in pen and ink without previous instruction. The ink warranted to be the kind used by the very best artists." The face has no mouth because, he said, "I cannot make a good mouth, therefore leave it out. There is enough without it anyway." See "Amended Obituaries," *Harper's Weekly,* November 15, 1902.

the higgledy-piggledy point / Howells described Mark Twain's literary method as "inspired higgledy-piggledy." Similar to that comment is another remark by Howells, who once wrote: "So far as I know, Mr. Clemens is the first writer to use in extended writing the fashion we all use in thinking, and to set down the thing that comes into his mind without fear or favor of the thing that went before or the thing that may be about to follow."

Rogers / Henry Huttleston Rogers (1840–1909). American capitalist. One of the organizers of the Standard Oil Company, and with financial interests in railroads, mines, banking and the steel business, he was reputedly worth $100,000,000. Along with other multimillionaires, Rogers was heavily attacked during muckraking days. Ida Tarbell called him a gentlemanly pirate who flew a black flag in Wall Street. Yet he had a generous side, aiding Helen Keller and Twichell when they were pressed for money, and bringing order out of the chaos of Mark Twain's affairs.

Colonel Harvey / George Brinton McClellan Harvey (1864–1928). American publisher. After experience on the staff of the New York *World* (1883–92), he made a fortune with William C. Whitney, bought the *North American Review* (1899), and assumed the management of Harper and Brothers (1900). Well known to politicos of both parties, he was ambassador to Great Britain (1921–23). He was an enthusiastic banqueter and skillful toastmaster.

that volcano / Mt. Pelee, on the island of Martinique, West Indies. An eruption of May 8, 1902, destroyed the town of San Pierre and killed 30,000 people.

MacVeagh / Isaac Wayne MacVeagh (1833–1917). American public man. District attorney of Chester County, Pennsylvania (1859–64), he was a leader of state Republicans opposed to boss Simon Cameron. MacVeagh was minister to Turkey (1870–71), head of the commission (1877) that ended reconstruction in Louisiana, and ambassador to Italy (1893–97). Advocating government reform and opposing machine politics, he was confidential advisor to presidents and a useful adjustor in troublesome situations.

Mitchell / John Mitchell (1870–1919). American labor leader. He directed the anthracite strike (1900) and in 1902 led a strike for union recognition, an eight-hour day, and a 20 percent increase in wages. When mine owners refused to negotiate, President Roosevelt intervened: the miners got a nine-hour day and a 10 percent increase. Mitchell was president of the United Mine Workers (1898–1908), and vice-president of the American Federation of Labor (1899–1914).

peeling Mr. Mitchell / MacVeagh acted as arbitrator in the anthracite strike, which had gone on for more than six months at great cost to workers, mine owners, and industry generally. Mark Twain was apparently implying that MacVeagh had laid down the law to Mitchell, but it was not so. In his summary of negotiations, MacVeagh said that conferences with Mitchell had been amicable and reasonable, no intransigence on either side. See MacVeagh's statement, *Times,* November 24, 1902.

Howells—that poem of his / Howells read "A Double-barrelled Sonnet to Mark Twain," which mentioned in its "First Barrel" feuds with missionaries, imperialists, and cabmen. The "Second Barrel" said that the dinner had been scheduled for Friday, November 28, because the birthday, November 30, fell on Sunday. To Mark Twain's objection that on Friday he was only sixty-six, the Muse replies: "I must insist upon the Colonel's date. / Besides, what matter whether soon or late / Your birthday comes whose fame all dates defies? / Still, to have everything beyond cavil right, / We will dine with you here till Sunday night."

Bangs / John Kendrick Bangs (1862–1922). American humorist. While on the editorial staffs of *Life, Puck, Harper's Weekly,* and other New York periodicals, he published many volumes of humor in prose and verse. Among them are *Coffee and Repartee* (1893), *The Idiot* (1895), and *The Houseboat on the Styx* (1896). He was a popular lecturer whose favorite platform number was "Salubrities I Have Met."

that honest man / Bangs's long "Post-Prandial Obituary" touched upon episodes in Mark Twain's career, and hailed him as "Diogenes, the Cynic Sage": "By day and night each passer-by he'd scan, / In hopes sometime to find an honest man, / With a success that seemingly was ill, / For, far as I can learn, he's at it still, / Although he's on the verge, for as you see, / He's got that eagle eye on me."

Van Dyke / Henry Van Dyke (1852–1933). American clergyman and writer. A Presbyterian pastor in New York City (1883–1900), he was professor of English literature at Princeton (1900–13), then minister to the Netherlands (1913–16). Briefly serving as chaplain in the United States Navy, he returned to Princeton (1919). He wrote homilies in prose and verse, inspirational essays and cheerful fiction: *The Story of the Other Wise Man* (1896), *Fisherman's Luck* (1899), *The Unknown Quantity* (1912), and others.

Dr. Van Dyke's poem / Van Dyke read "A Toast to Mark Twain," which commented upon his exuberance, wisdom and humor: "No parrot is this bird, though he / Can talk beside the best; / He's no repeater: every tone / And every word is all his own: / . . . He's gay as any buck can be, / He's wise as any owl. / And, like the Phoenix, he survives / The fires that wreck less noble lives."

· 142 ·

For his seventieth birthday dinner, Mark Twain emerged from retirement caused by the last illness of Olivia Clemens and her death in Italy in June 1904. George Harvey, host and chairman, assembled a blue-ribbon list of guests, including a galaxy of American writers from George Ade to Jesse Lynch Williams. Delmonico's famous red room was the setting, a forty-piece orchestra from the Metropolitan Opera House played background music, and each guest received a foot-high plaster bust of Mark Twain. A departure from banqueting custom was the presence of more than sixty women, writers, and others: among them, Alice Brown, Frances Hodgson Burnett, Josephine Daskam Bacon, Dorothy Canfield, Willa Cather, Mary Wilkins Freeman, Alice Duer Miller, Emily Post, Ruth McEnery Stuart, May Sinclair, and Princess Troubetskoy. The toast list also flouted convention by including three feminine speakers: Kate Douglas Riggs, Agnes Repplier, and Carolyn Wells. Howells, toastmaster, introduced the guest of honor by reading another twenty-eight-line "sonnet" that defined the American joke: "I jolly the whole earth, / But most I love to jolly my own kind, / Joke of a people great, gay, bold, and free, / I type their master-mood. Mark Twain made me." Howells concluded his introduction with the words: "I will not say, 'Oh King, live forever,' but 'Oh King, live as long as you like!' "

Dinner Speech

Mark Twain's Seventieth Birthday Dinner, Delmonico's,
New York, December 5, 1905

Well, if I made that joke, it is the best one I ever made, and it is in the prettiest language, too. I never can get quite to that height. But I appreciate that joke, and I shall remember it—and I shall use it when occasion requires.

I have had a great many birthdays in my time. I remember the first one very well, and I always think of it with indignation; everything was so crude, unesthetic, primeval. Nothing like this at all. No proper appreciative preparation made; nothing really ready. Now, for a person born with high and delicate instincts—why, even the cradle wasn't whitewashed—nothing ready at all. I hadn't any hair, I hadn't any teeth, I hadn't any clothes, I had to go to my first banquet just like that. Well, everybody came swarming in. It was the merest little bit of a village—hardly that, just a little hamlet, in the backwoods of Missouri, where nothing ever happened, and the people were all interested, and they all came; they looked me over to see if there was anything fresh in my line. Why, nothing ever happened in that village—I—why, I was the only thing that had really happened there for months and months and months; and although I say it myself that shouldn't, I came the nearest to being a real event that had happened in that village in more than two years. Well, those people came, they came with that curiosity which is so provincial, with that frankness which also is so provincial, and they examined me all around and gave their opinion. Nobody asked them, and I shouldn't have minded if anybody had paid me a compliment, but nobody did. Their opinions were all just green with prejudice, and I feel those opinions to this day. Well, I stood that as long as—well, you know I was born courteous, and I stood it to the limit. I stood it an hour, and then the worm turned. I was the worm; it was my turn to turn, and I turned. I knew very well the strength of my position; I knew that I was the only spotlessly pure and innocent person in that whole town, and I came out and said so. And they could not say a word. It was so true. They blushed; they were embarrassed. Well, that was the first after-dinner speech I ever made. I think it was after dinner.

It's a long stretch between that first birthday speech and this one. That was my cradle song, and this is my swan song, I suppose. I am used to swan songs; I have sung them several times.

This is my seventieth birthday, and I wonder if you all rise to the size of that proposition, realizing all the significance of that phrase, seventieth birthday.

The seventieth birthday! It is the time of life when you arrive at a new and awful dignity; when you may throw aside the decent reserves which have oppressed you for a generation and stand unafraid and unabashed upon your seven-terraced summit and look down and teach—unrebuked. You can tell the world how you got there. It is what they all do. You shall never get tired of telling by what delicate arts and deep moralities you climbed up to that great place. You will explain the process and dwell on the particulars with senile rapture. I have been anxious to explain my own system this long time, and now at last I have the right.

I have achieved my seventy years in the usual way: by sticking strictly to a scheme of life which would kill anybody else. It sounds like an exaggeration, but that is really the common rule for attaining to old age. When we examine the program of any of these garrulous old people we always find that the habits which have preserved them would have decayed us; that the way of life which enabled them to live upon the property of their heirs so long, as Mr. Choate says, would have put us out of commission ahead of time. I will offer here, as a sound maxim, this: That we can't reach old age by another man's road.

I will now teach, offering my way of life to whomsoever desires to commit suicide by the scheme which has enabled me to beat the doctor and the hangman for seventy years. Some of the details may sound untrue, but they are not. I am not here to deceive; I am here to teach.

We have no permanent habits until we are forty. Then they begin to harden, presently they petrify, then business begins. Since forty I have been regular about going to bed and getting up—and that is one of the main things. I have made it a rule to go to bed when there wasn't anybody left to sit up with; and I have made it a rule to get up when I had to. This has resulted in an unswerving regularity of irregularity. It has saved me sound, but it would injure another person.

In the matter of diet—which is another main thing—I have been persistently strict in sticking to the things which didn't agree with me until one or the other of us got the best of it. Until lately I got the best of it myself. But last spring I stopped frolicking with mince pie after midnight; up to then I had always believed it wasn't loaded. For thirty years I have taken coffee and bread at eight in the morning, and no bite nor sup until seven-thirty in the evening. Eleven hours. That is all right for me, and is wholesome, because I have never had a headache in my life, but headachy people would not reach seventy comfortably by that road, and they would be foolish to try it. And I wish to urge upon you this—which I think is wisdom—that if you find you can't make seventy by any but an uncomfortable road, don't you go. When they take off the Pullman and retire you to the rancid smoker, put on your things, count your checks, and get out at the first way station where there's a cemetery.

I have made it a rule never to smoke more than one cigar at a time. I have no other restriction as regards smoking. I do not know just when I began to smoke, I only know that it was in my father's lifetime, and that I was discreet. He passed from this life early in 1847, when I was a shade past eleven; ever since then I have smoked publicly. As an example to others, and not that I care for moderation myself, it has always been my rule never to smoke when asleep, and never to refrain when awake. It is a good rule. I mean, for me; but some of you know quite well that it wouldn't answer for everybody that's trying to get to be seventy.

I smoke in bed until I have to go to sleep; I wake up in the night, sometimes once, sometimes twice, sometimes three times, and I never waste any of these opportunities to smoke. This habit is so old and dear and precious to me that I would feel as you, sir, would feel if you should lose the only moral you've got—meaning the chairman—if you've got one; I am making no charges. I will grant, here, that I have stopped smoking now and then, for a few months at a time, but it was not on principle, it was only to show off; it was to pulverize those critics who said I was a slave to my habits and couldn't break my bonds.

Today it is all of sixty years since I began to smoke the limit. I have never bought cigars with life belts around them. I early found that those were too expensive for me. I have always bought cheap cigars—reasonably cheap, at any rate. Sixty years ago they cost me four dollars a barrel, but my taste has improved, latterly, and I pay seven now. Six or seven. Seven, I think. Yes, it's seven. But that includes the barrel. I often have smoking parties at my house; but the people that come have always just taken the pledge. I wonder why that is?

As for drinking, I have no rule about that. When the others drink I like to help; otherwise I remain dry, by habit and preference. This dryness does not hurt me, but it could easily hurt you, because you are different. You let it alone.

Since I was seven years old I have seldom taken a dose of medicine, and have still seldomer needed one. But up to seven I lived exclusively on allopathic medicines. Not that I needed them, for I don't think I did; it was for economy; my father took a drug store for a debt, and it made cod liver oil cheaper than other breakfast foods. We had nine barrels of it, and it lasted me seven years. Then I was weaned. The rest of the family had to get along with rhubarb and ipecac and such things, because I was the pet. I was the first Standard Oil Trust. I had it all. By the time the drug store was exhausted my health was established and there has never been much the matter with me since. But you know very well it would be foolish for the average child to start for seventy on that basis. It happened to be just the thing for me, but that was merely an accident; it couldn't happen again in a century.

I have never taken any exercise, except sleeping and resting, and I never intend to take any. Exercise is loathsome. And it cannot be any benefit when you are tired; and I was always tired. But let another person try my way, and see where he will come out.

I desire now to repeat and emphasize that maxim: We can't reach old age by another man's road. My habits protect my life but they would assassinate you.

I have lived a severely moral life. But it would be a mistake for other people to try that, or for me to recommend it. Very few would succeed: you have to have a perfectly colossal stock of morals; and you can't get them on a margin; you have to have the whole thing, and put them in your box. Morals are an acquirement—like music, like a foreign language, like piety, poker, paralysis—no man is born with them. I wasn't myself, I started poor. I hadn't a single moral. There is hardly a man in this house that is poorer than I was then. Yes, I started like that—the world before me, not a moral in the slot. Not even an insurance moral. I can remember the first one I ever got. I can remember the landscape, the weather, the—I can remember how everything looked. It was an old moral, an old secondhand moral, all out of repair, and didn't fit, anyway. But if you are careful with a thing like that, and keep it in a dry place, and save it for processions, and chautauquas, and World's Fairs, and so on, and disinfect it now and then, and give it a fresh coat of whitewash once in a while, you will be surprised to see how well she will last and how long she will keep sweet, or at least inoffensive. When I got that mouldy old moral, she had stopped growing, because she hadn't any exercise; but I worked her hard, I worked her Sundays and all. Under this cultivation she waxed in might and stature beyond belief, and served me well and was my pride and joy for sixty-three years; then she got to associating with insurance presidents, and lost flesh and character, and was a sorrow to look at and no longer competent for business. She was a great loss to me. Yet not all loss. I sold her—ah, pathetic skeleton, as she was—I sold her to Leopold, the pirate King of Belgium; he sold her to our Metropolitan Museum, and it was very glad to get her, for, without a rag on, she stands fifty-seven feet long and sixteen feet high, and they think she's a brontosaur. Well, she looks it. They believe it will take nineteen geological periods to breed her match.

Morals are of inestimable value, for every man is born crammed with sin microbes, and the only thing that can extirpate these sin microbes is morals. Now you take a sterilized Christian—I mean, you take *the* sterilized Christian, for there's only one. Dear sir, I wish you wouldn't look at me like that.

Threescore years and ten!

It is the Scriptural statute of limitations. After that, you owe no active duties; for you the strenuous life is over. You are a time-expired man, to use Kipling's military phrase. You have served your term, well or less well, and you are mustered out. You are become an honorary member of the republic, you are emancipated, compulsions are not for you, nor any bugle call but "lights out." You pay the timeworn duty bills if you choose, or decline if you prefer—and without prejudice—for they are not legally collectible.

The previous engagement plea, which in forty years has cost you so many twinges, you can lay aside forever; on this side of the grave you will never need it again. If you shrink at thought of night, and winter, and the late homecoming from the banquet and the lights and the laughter through the deserted streets—a desolation which would not remind you now, as for a generation it did, that your friends are sleeping, and you must creep in a-tiptoe and not disturb them, but would only remind you that you need not tiptoe, you can never disturb them more—if you shrink at thought of these things, you need only reply, "Your invitation honors me, and pleases me because you still keep me in your remembrance, but I am seventy; seventy, and would nestle in the chimney corner, and smoke my pipe, and read my book, and take my rest, wishing you well in all affection, and that when you in your turn shall arrive at pier No. 70 you may step aboard your waiting ship with a reconciled spirit, and lay your course toward the sinking sun with a contented heart."

Text / Composite, based upon: "Mark Twain's 70th Birthday," *Harper's Weekly, Supplement* (December 23, 1905):1885–86; "Celebrate Mark Twain's Seventieth Birthday," *Times,* December 6, 1905; "Seventieth Birthday" in *MTS*(10):425–34; and *MTS*(23):254–62.

associating with insurance presidents / For forty years insurance companies had been using large surpluses to engage in speculation and other financial operations not their function. The result was a loss of public confidence, and evidence of shady practice by company officers and wealthy financiers. Insurance presidents were in bad odor. An investigation conducted by Charles Evans Hughes, who held fifty-seven public hearings (1905), led to the enactment of New York laws that forbade speculative investment of insurance company funds, and prohibited insurance companies from holding stock in banks or trust companies, also from engaging in underwriting syndicates. Similar measures were adopted elsewhere in the United States.

Leopold / (1835–1909). Leopold II, king of Belgium (1865–1909), founded the Congo Free State (1884–85), where he amassed a huge fortune by ruthless exploitation of native labor. His barbarity became a public scandal that forced the Belgian government to take over the Congo (1908). Leopold's private life was as outrageous as his public conduct. See Mark Twain's *King Leopold's Soliloquy* (1905); also interview, *World,* December 3, 1905, under the headline, "Twain Calls Leopold Slayer of 15,000,000."

· 143 ·

The remark in the birthday speech about nestling in the chimney corner was one of Mark Twain's stretchers. Ready as always to sally forth, he was part of a distinguished audience at a benefit matinee in aid of Jewish victims of the abortive Russian revolution of 1905. Among box holders were Mr. and Mrs. Isaac Guggenheim, Mr. and Mrs. Henry Lehman, Mr. and Mrs. Jacob Adler, and Mr. and Mrs. Jacob Schiff. Margaret Anglin, Ilka Palmay, Kitty Cheatham, Kate Condon, Henry Miller, Chauncey Olcott, and other Broadway performers put on a program of songs, skits, and dances. The main attractions were Sarah Bernhardt and Mark Twain. The Divine Sarah presented a one-act play, L'Escarpolette, *written by an American, Miss G. Constant Lounsbury. Mark Twain talked.*

Remarks

Benefit Matinee for Russian Jewish Sufferers,
Casino, New York, December 18, 1905

Ladies and gentlemen: It seems a sort of cruelty to inflict upon an audience like this our rude English tongue, after we have heard that divine speech flowing in that lucid Gallic tongue. It has always been a marvel to me—that French language; it has always been a puzzle to me. How beautiful that language is. How expressive it seems to be. How full of grace it is. And when it comes from lips like those, how eloquent and how liquid it is. And, oh, I am always deceived—I always think I am going to understand it.

Oh, it is such a delight to me, such a delight to me, to meet Madame Bernhardt, and laugh hand to hand and heart to heart with her. I have seen her play, as we all have, and, oh, that is divine; but I have always wanted to know Madame Bernhardt herself—her fiery self. I have wanted to know that beautiful character.

Madame Bernhardt is so marvelously young. Why, she is the youngest person I ever saw, except myself—for I always feel young when I come in the presence of young people. She and I are two of the youngest people alive.

I have a pleasant recollection of an incident so many years

ago—when Madame Bernhardt came to Hartford, where I lived, and she was going to play and the tickets were three dollars, and there were two lovely women—a widow and her daughter—neighbors of ours, highly cultivated ladies they were; their tastes were fine and elevated, but they were very poor, and they said, "Well, we must not spend six dollars on a pleasure of the mind, a pleasure of intellect; we must spend it, if it must go at all, to furnish to somebody bread to eat."

And so they sorrowed over the fact that they had to give up that great pleasure of seeing Madame Bernhardt, but there were two neighbors equally highly cultivated and who could not afford bread, and those good-hearted Joneses sent that six dollars—deprived themselves of it—and sent it to those poor Smiths to buy bread with. And those Smiths took it and bought tickets with it to see Madame Bernhardt. Oh yes, some people have tastes and intelligence also.

Now, I was going to make a speech—I supposed I was, but I am not. It is late, late; and so I am going to tell a story; and there is this advantage about a story, anyway, that whatever moral or valuable thing you put into a speech, why, it gets diffused among those involuted sentences and possibly your audience goes away without finding out what that valuable thing was that you were trying to confer upon it; but, dear me, you put the same jewel into a story and it becomes the keystone of that story, and you are bound to get it—it flashes, it flames, it is the jewel in the toad's head—you don't overlook that.

Now, if I am going to talk on such a subject as, for instance, the lost opportunity—oh, the lost opportunity. Anybody in this house who has reached the turn of life—sixty, or seventy, or even fifty, or along there—when he goes back along his history, there he finds it milestoned all the way with the lost opportunity, and you know how pathetic that is. You younger ones cannot know the full pathos that lies in those words—the lost opportunity; but anybody who is old, who has really lived and felt this life, he knows the pathos of the lost opportunity.

Now, I will tell you a story whose moral is that, whose lesson is that, whose lament is that. I was in a village which is a suburb of New Bedford several years ago—well, New Bedford is a suburb of Fairhaven, or perhaps it is the other way; in any case, it took both of those towns to make a great center of the great whaling industry of the first half of the nineteenth century, and I was up there at Fairhaven some years ago with a friend of mine.

There was a dedication of a great town hall, a public building, and we were there in the afternoon. This great building was filled, like this great theater, with rejoicing villagers, and my friend and I started down the center aisle. He saw a man standing in that aisle, and he said, "Now, look at that bronzed veteran—at that mahogany-faced man. Now, tell me, do you see anything about that man's face that is emotional? Do you see anything about it that suggests that inside that man anywhere there are fires that can be started? Would you ever imagine that that is a human volcano?"

"Why, no," I said, "I would not. He looks like a wooden Indian in front of a cigar store."

"Very well," said my friend. "I will show you that there is emotion even in that unpromising place. I will just go to that man and I will just mention in the most casual way an incident in his life. That man is getting along toward ninety years old. He is past eighty. I will mention an incident of fifty or sixty years ago. Now, just watch the effect, and it will be so casual that if you don't watch you won't know when I do say that thing—but you just watch the effect."

He went on down there and accosted this antiquity, and made a remark or two. I could not catch up. They were so casual I could not recognize which one it was that touched that bottom, for in an instant that old man was literally in eruption and was filling the whole place with profanity of the most exquisite kind. You never heard such accomplished profanity. I never heard it also delivered with such eloquence. I never enjoyed profanity as I enjoyed it then—more than if I had been uttering it myself. There is nothing like listening to an artist—all his passions passing away in lava, smoke, thunder, lightning, and earthquake.

Then this friend said to me, "Now, I will tell you about that. About sixty years ago that man was a young fellow of twenty-three, and had just come home from a three years' whaling voyage. He came into that village of his, happy and proud because now, instead of being chief mate, he was going to be master of a whale ship, and he was proud and happy about it.

"Then he found that there had been a kind of a cold frost come upon that town and the whole region roundabout; for while he had been away the Father Mathew temperance excitement had come upon the whole region. Therefore, everybody had taken the pledge; there wasn't anybody for miles and miles around that had not taken the pledge.

"So you can see what a solitude it was to this young man, who was fond of his grog. And he was just an outcast, because when they found he would not join Father Mathew's Society they ostracized him, and he went about that town three weeks, day and night, in utter loneliness—the only human being in the whole place who ever took grog, and he had to take it privately.

"If you don't know what it is to be ostracized, to be shunned by your fellow man, may you never know it. Then he recognized that there was something more valuable in this life than grog, and that is the fellowship of your fellow man. And at last he gave it up, and at nine o'clock one night he went down to the Father Mathew Temperance Society, and with a broken heart he said, 'Put my name down for membership in this society.'

"And then he went away crying, and at earliest dawn the next morning they came for him and routed him out, and they said that new ship of his was ready to sail on a three years' voyage. In a minute he was on board that ship and gone.

"And he said—well, he was not out of sight of that town till he began to repent, but he had made up his mind that he would not take a drink, and so that whole voyage of three years was a three years' agony to that man because he saw all the time the mistake he had made.

"He felt it all through; he had constant reminders of it, because the crew would pass him with their grog, come out on the deck and take it, and there was the torturous smell of it.

"He went through the whole three years of suffering, and at last coming into port it was snowy, it was cold, he was stamping through the snow two feet deep on the deck and longing to get home, and there was his crew torturing him to the last minute with hot grog, but at last he had his reward. He really did get to shore at last, and jumped and ran and bought a jug and rushed to the society's office and said to the secretary,

" 'Take my name off your membership books and do it right away! I have got a three years' thirst on.'

"And the secretary said, 'It is not necessary. You were black-balled!' "

Text / Composite, based upon: "Benefit Matinee for Jewish Sufferers," *Times,* December 19, 1905; "Russian Sufferers" in *MTS*(10):288–94; and *MTS*(23):263–68.

Madame Bernhardt / Sarah Bernhardt, stage name of Henriette Rosine Bernard (1844–1923). French actress. Her debut at the Theatre Francaise (1862) launched a career of more than fifty years, during which she became internationally famous, touring England and Europe, and making nine visits to the United States. An emotional actress with a golden voice, she was the Divine Sarah, lauded and indulged even in the role of Hamlet. After a leg amputation in 1914, she was still good for top billing and $7,000 a week at New York's Palace Theatre. She had talent as painter, writer, and sculptor, but these skills were hidden from a public that knew her only as a magnetic stage personality.

the jewel in the toad's head / *As You Like It* (2.2): "Sweet are the uses of adversity; / Which, like the toad, ugly and venomous, / Wears yet a precious jewel in his head; / And this our life, exempt from public haunt, / Finds tongues in trees, books in the running brooks, / Sermons in stones, and good in everything."

Father Mathew temperance excitement / Theobald Mathew (1790–1856). Irish priest. Taking a pledge of total abstinence in 1838, he barnstormed through Ireland on an anti-rum campaign that made him known as "The Apostle of Temperance." On a similar crusade in the United States (1849–51), he was said to have traveled 37,000 miles and to have persuaded 500,000 topers to take the pledge.

· 144 ·

Among guests at the Society of Illustrators dinner were Carnegie, Sir Purdon Clarke, Arthur Scribner, Frederick Remington, Norman Hapgood, and Daniel Beard. As Mark Twain rose to speak, a winsome young woman appeared as Joan of Arc in armor, accompanied by a page boy carrying a banner. Gravely she presented to the speaker a wreath of bay leaves on a satin pillow. He was so moved by this tribute that he could only stammer, "I thank you," then pause a moment or two to pull himself together. The Times *remarked next day that his speech was "all tinged with the melancholy that has come to Mark Twain these days."*

Dinner Speech

Society of Illustrators Dinner, Aldine Association Club, New York, December 21, 1905

Now there is an illustration [pointing to the retreating Joan of Arc]. That is exactly what I wanted—precisely what I wanted—when I was describing to myself Joan of Arc, after studying her history and her character for twelve years diligently. That was the product—not the conventional Joan of Arc. Wherever you find the conventional Joan of Arc in history, she is an offense to anybody who knows the story of that wonderful girl.

Why, she was—she was almost supreme in several details. She had a marvelous intellect; she had a great heart, had a noble spirit, was absolutely pure in her character, her feeling, her language, her words, her everything—she was only eighteen years old.

Now put that heart into such a breast—eighteen years old—and give it that masterly intellect which showed in the face, and furnish it with that almost godlike spirit, and what are you going to have? The conventional Joan of Arc? Not by any means. That is impossible. I cannot comprehend any such thing as that.

You must have a creature like that young and fair and beautiful girl we just saw. And her spirit must look out of the eyes. The figure should be—the figure should be in harmony with all that, but, oh, what we get in the conventional picture, and it is always the conventional picture!

I hope you will allow me to say that your guild, when you take the conventional, you have got it at second hand. Certainly, if you had studied and studied, then you might have something else as a result, but when you have the common convention you stick to that.

You cannot prevail upon the artist to do it; he always gives you a Joan of Arc—the lovely creature that started a great career at thirteen, but whose greatness arrived when she was eighteen; and merely because she was a girl he cannot see the divinity in her, and so he paints a peasant, a coarse and lubberly figure—the figure of a cotton bale, and he clothes that in the coarsest raiment of the peasant region—just like a fish woman, her hair cropped like that of a Russian peasant, and that face of hers, which should be beautiful and which should radiate all the glories which are in the spirit and in her heart—that expression in that face is always just the fixed expression of a ham.

But now Mr. Beard has intimated a moment ago, and so has Sir Purdon Clarke also, that the artist, the illustrator, does not often get the idea of the man whose book he is illustrating. Here is a very remarkable instance of the other thing in Mr. Beard, who illustrated a book of mine. You may never have heard of it. I will tell you about it now—*A Yankee in King Arthur's Court.*

Now, Beard got everything that I put into that book and a little more besides. Those pictures of Beard's in that book—oh, from the first page to the last is one vast sardonic laugh at the trivialities, the servilities of our poor human race, and also at the professions and the insolence of priestcraft and kingcraft—those creatures that make slaves of themselves and have not the manliness to shake it off. Beard put it all in that book. I meant it to be there. I put a lot of it there and Beard put the rest.

That publisher of mine in Hartford had an eye for the pennies, and he saved them. He did not waste any on the illustrations. He had a very good artist—Williams—who had never taken a lesson in drawing. Everything he did was original. The publisher hired the cheapest wood engraver he could find, and in my early books you can see a trace of that. You can see that if Williams had had a chance he would have made some very good pictures. He had a good heart and good intentions.

I had a character in the first book he illustrated—*The Innocents Abroad.* That was a boy seventeen or eighteen years old—Jack Van Nostrand—a New York boy, who, to my mind, was a very remarkable creature. I tried to get Williams to understand that boy, and make a picture of Jack that would be worthy of Jack.

Jack was a most singular combination. He was born and reared in New York here. He was as delicate in his feelings, as clean and pure and refined in his feelings as any lovely girl that ever was, but whenever he expressed a feeling he did it in Bowery slang, and it was a most curious combination—that delicacy of his and that apparent coarseness. There was no coarseness inside of Jack at all, and Jack, in the course of seventeen or eighteen years, had acquired a capital of ignorance that was marvelous—ignorance of various things, not of all things. For instance, he did not know anything about the Bible. He had never been in Sunday school. Jack got more out of the Holy Land than anybody else, because the others knew what they were expecting, but it was a land of surprises to him.

I said in the book that we found him watching a turtle on a log, stoning that turtle, and he was stoning that turtle because he had read that "The song of the turtle was heard in the land," and this turtle wouldn't sing. It sounded absurd, but it was charged on Jack as a fact, and as he went along through that country he had a proper foil in an old rebel colonel who was superintendent and head engineer in a large Sunday school in Wheeling, West Virginia. That man was full of enthusiasm wherever he went, and would stand and deliver himself of speeches, and Jack would listen to those speeches of the colonel and wonder.

Jack had made a trip as a child almost across this continent in the first overland stagecoach. That man's name who ran that line of stages—well, I declare, that name is gone. Well, names will go.

Holladay—ah, that's the name—Ben Holladay, your uncle [turning to Carnegie]. That was the fellow—Ben Holladay—and Jack was full of admiration at the prodigious speed that that line of stages made—and it was good speed—one hundred and twenty-five miles a day, going day and night, and it was the event of Jack's life, and there at the Fords of the Jordan the colonel was inspired to a speech (he was always making a speech), so he called us up to him. He called up five sinners and three saints. It has been only lately that Mr. Carnegie beatified me. And he said, "Here are the Fords of the Jordan—a monumental place. At this very point, when Moses brought the children of Israel through—he brought the children of Israel from Egypt through the desert you see there—he guarded them through that desert patiently, patiently during forty years, and brought them to this spot safe and sound. There you see—there is the scene of what Moses did."

And Jack said, "Moses who?"

"Oh," he said, "Jack, you ought not to ask that! Moses, the great lawgiver! Moses, the great patriot! Moses, the great warrior! Moses, the great guide, who, as I tell you, brought these people through these three hundred miles of sand in forty years, and landed them safe and sound."

Jack said, "There's nothin' in that! Three hundred miles in forty years! Ben Holladay would have snaked 'em through in thirty-six hours."

Well, I was speaking of Jack's innocence, and it was beautiful. Jack was not ignorant on all subjects. That boy was a deep student in the history of Anglo-Saxon liberty, and he was a patriot all the way through to the marrow. There was a subject that interested him all the time. Other subjects were of no concern to Jack, but that quaint, inscrutable innocence of his I could not get Williams to put into the picture.

Yes, Williams wanted to do it. He said, "I will make him as innocent as a virgin." He thought a moment, and then said, "I will make him as innocent as an unborn virgin," which covered the ground.

I was reminded of Jack because I came across a letter today which is over thirty years old that Jack wrote. Jack was doomed to consumption. He was very long and slim, poor creature, and in a year or two after he got back from that excursion to the Holy Land he went on a ride on horseback through Colorado, and he did not last but a year or two.

He wrote this letter, not to me, but to a friend of mine, and he said, "I have ridden horseback"—this was three years after—"I have ridden horseback four hundred miles through a desert country where you never see anything but cattle now and then, and now and then a cattle station—ten miles apart, twenty miles apart. Now you tell Clemens that in all that stretch of four hundred miles I have seen only two books—the Bible and *Innocents Abroad*—the Bible in good repair."

I say that he had studied, and he had, the real Saxon liberty, the acquirement of our liberty, and Jack used to repeat some verses—I don't know where they came from, but I thought of them today when I saw this letter—that that boy could have been talking of himself in these quoted lines from that unknown poet:

> For he had sat at Sidney's feet
> And walked with him in plain apart,
> And through the centuries heard the beat
> Of Freedom's march through Cromwell's heart.

And he was that kind of a boy. He should have lived, and yet he should not have lived, because he died at that early age—he couldn't have been more than twenty—he had seen all there was to see in the world that was worth the trouble of living in it; he had seen all of this world that is valuable; he had seen all of this world that was illusion, and illusion is the only valuable thing in it. He had arrived at the point where presently the illusions would cease and he would have entered upon the realities of life, and God help the man that has arrived at that point.

Text / Composite, based upon: "Joan of Arc" in *MTS*(10):241–48; and *MTS*(23):269–75.

a creature like that young and fair and beautiful girl / Mark Twain would surely have approved of the attractive young actresses who have played the role of Joan of Arc in plays by Shaw and others during the past fifty years: Winifred Lenihan, Ingrid Bergman, Katharine Cornell, Uta Hagen, and Siobhan McKenna.

Beard / Daniel Carter Beard (1850–1941). American illustrator and Boy Scout leader. President of the Society of Illustrators and of the Camp Fire Club of America, he founded the Boy Pioneers (1905), then the Boy Scouts of America (1910). Until his death he was a national scout commissioner, affectionately known as "Uncle Dan." Among his books are *American Boys' Book of Wild Animals* (1921), and the autobiographical *Hardly a Man is Now Alive* (1939).

Clarke / Caspar Purdon Clarke (1846–1911). British art authority and architect. He made art collections for the South Kensington Museum and the government, and designed churches and other buildings. Knighted (1902), he was royal commissioner to the Louisiana Purchase Exposition and a director of the Metropolitan Museum, New York (1905–11).

Those pictures of Beard's / In illustrating *A Connecticut Yankee,* Beard made Arthurian characters look like famous and notorious people of the nineteenth century: a slave-driver has the face of Jay Gould, Merlin that of Tennyson. Also recognizable are Queen Victoria, Kaiser Wilhelm, and Edward, Prince of Wales. See Louis J. Budd, *Mark Twain: Social Philosopher* (1962), illustrations, chapter 6.

Ben Holladay / (1818–87). American entrepreneur. He organized the Holladay Overland Stage Company (1862), which operated on 2,700 miles of western roads. Hundreds of employees, 6,000 horses and mules, 260 coaches, and many wagons made him known as "The Napoleon of the Plains." After selling out to Wells Fargo (1866), he was equally successful with railroads and ship lines. He had a palatial home in Washington, D.C., another, called "Ophir Place," on the Hudson, and his two daughters married titles. His prosperity ebbed, however, about 1876.

· 145 ·

A meeting to stimulate contributions to an endowment fund of $1,800,000 for Tuskegee Institute crowded Carnegie Hall. White ties were in evidence, evening gowns and resplendent jewels. In the boxes were Mrs. John D. Rockefeller, Mrs. Clarence H. Mackay, Mrs. Henry H. Rogers, Mrs. Collis P. Huntington, Mrs. Felix Warburg, Mrs. Jacob H. Schiff, J. G. Phelps Stokes, Nicholas Murray Butler, George Foster Peabody, Carl Schurz, and other representatives of finance and philanthropy. Booker T. Washington, presiding, had the support of first-rate speakers: Robert C. Ogden, Joseph H. Choate, and Mark Twain. Between speeches a Negro octet sang spirituals. Choate, who preceded Mark Twain, referred to the indolent habits the latter had talked about in his seventieth birthday speech.

Speech

Meeting on Behalf of Tuskegee Institute, Carnegie Hall, New York, January 22, 1906

These habits, of which Mr. Choate has told you, are the very habits which have kept me young until I am seventy years old. I have lain in bed all day today, expect to lie in bed all day tomorrow, and will continue to lie in bed all day throughout the year. There is nothing so refreshing, nothing so comfortable, and nothing fits one so well for the kind of work which he calls pleasure. Mr. Choate has been careful not to pay me any compliments. It wasn't because he didn't want to—he just couldn't think of any.

I came here in the responsible capacity of policeman—to watch Mr. Choate. This is an occasion of grave and serious importance, and it seemed necessary for me to be present so that if he tried to work off any statements that required correction, reduction, refutation or exposure, there would be a tried friend of the public here to protect the house. But I can say in all frankness and gratitude that nothing of the kind has happened. He has not made one statement whose veracity fails to tally exactly with my own standard. I have never seen a person improve so. This does not make me jealous, it only makes me thankful. Thankful and proud; proud of a country that can produce such men—two such men. And all in the same century. We can't be with you always; we are passing away—passing away; soon we shall be gone, and then—well, everything will have to stop, I reckon. It is a sad thought. But in spirit I shall still be with you. Choate, too—if he can.

There being nothing to explain, nothing to refute, nothing to excuse, there is nothing left for me to do, now, but resume my natural trade—which is, teaching. At Tuskegee they thoroughly ground the student in the Christian code of morals; they instil into him the indisputable truth that this is the highest and best of all systems of morals; that the nation's greatness, its strength, and its repute among the other nations, is the product of that system; that it is the foundation upon which rests the American character; that whatever is commendable, whatever is valuable in the individual American's character is the flower and fruit of that seed. They teach him that this is true in every case, whether the man be a professing Christian or an unbeliever; for we have none but the Christian code of morals, and every individual is under its character-building powerful influence and dominion from the cradle to the grave; he breathes it in with his breath, it is in his blood and bone, it is the web and woof and fibre of his mental and spiritual heredities and ineradicable. And so, every born American among the eighty millions, let his creed or destitution of creed be what it may, is indisputably a Christian to this degree—that his moral constitution is Christian.

All this is true, and no student will leave Tuskegee ignorant of it. Then what will he lack, under this head? What is there for me to teach him, under this head, that he may possibly not acquire there, or may acquire in a not sufficiently emphasized form? Why, *this* large fact, this important fact—that there are two separate and distinct kinds of Christian morals; so separate, so distinct, so unrelated, that they are no more kin to each other than are archangels and politicians. The one kind is Christian private morals, the other is Christian public morals. The loyal observance of Christian private morals has made this nation what it is—a clean and upright people in its private domestic life, an honest and honorable people in its private commercial life; no alien nation can claim superiority over it in these regards, no critic, foreign or domestic, can challenge the validity of this truth. During 363 days in the year the American citizen is true to his Christian private morals, and keeps undefiled the nation's character at its best and highest; then in the other two days of the year he leaves his Christian private morals at home, and carries his Christian public morals to the tax office and the polls, and does the best he can to damage and undo his whole year's faithful and righteous work. Without a blush he will vote for an unclean boss if that boss is his party's Moses, without compunction he will vote against the best man in the whole land if he is on the other ticket. Every year, in a number of cities and states, he helps to put corrupt men in office, every year he helps to extend the corruption wider and wider; year after year he goes on gradually rotting the country's political life; whereas if he would but throw away his Christian public morals, and carry his Christian private morals to the polls, he could promptly purify the public service and make the possession of office a high and honorable distinction and one to be coveted by the very best men the country could furnish. But now—well, now he contemplates his unpatriotic work and sighs, and grieves, and blames every man but the right one—which is himself.

Once a year he lays aside his Christian private morals and hires a ferry boat and piles up his bonds in a warehouse in New Jersey for three days, and gets out his Christian public morals and goes to the tax office and holds up his hand and swears he wishes he may never-never if he's got a cent in the world, so help him! The next day the list appears in the papers—a column and a quarter of names, in fine print, and every man in the list a billionaire and a member of a couple of churches. I know all those people. I have friendly, social, and criminal relations with the whole lot of them. They never miss a sermon when they are so's to be around, and they never miss swearing-off day, whether they are so's to be around or not. The innocent man can not remain innocent in the disintegrating atmosphere of this thing. I used to be an honest man. I am crumbling. No—I have crumbled. When they assessed me at $75,000 a fortnight ago, I went out and tried to borrow the money, and couldn't; then when I found they were letting a whole crop of millionaires live in New York at a third of the price they were charging me, I was hurt, I was indignant, and said, "This is the last feather! I am not going to run this town all by myself." In that moment—in that memorable moment—I began to crumble. In fifteen minutes the disintegration was complete. In fifteen minutes I was become just a mere moral sand pile; and I lifted up my hand along with those seasoned and experienced deacons, and swore off every rag of personal property I've got in the world, clear down to cork leg, glass eye, and what is left of my wig. Those tax officers were moved; they were profoundly moved. They had long been accustomed to seeing hardened old grafters act like that, and they could endure the spectacle; but they were expecting better things of me, a chartered professional moralist, and they were saddened. I fell visibly in their respect and esteem, and I should have fallen in my own, except that I had already struck bottom, and there wasn't any place to fall to.

At Tuskegee they will jump to misleading conclusions from insufficient evidence, along with Dr. Parkhurst, and they will deceive the student with the superstition that no gentleman ever swears. Look at those good millionaires; aren't they gentlemen? Well, they swear. Only once a year, maybe, but there's enough bulk in it to make up for the lost time. And do they lose anything by it? No, they don't; they save enough in three minutes to support the family seven years. When they swear, do we shudder? No—unless they say "damn!" Then we do. It shrivels us all up. Yet we ought not to feel so about it, because we all swear—everybody. Including the ladies. Including Dr. Parkhurst, that strong and brave and excellent citizen, but superficially educated. For it is not the *word* that is the sin, it is the spirit back of the word. When an irritated lady says "Oh!" the spirit back of it is "damn!" and that is the way it is going to be recorded against her. But if she says "damn," and says it in an amiable, nice way, it isn't going to be recorded at all. The idea that no gentleman ever swears is all wrong; he can swear and still be a gentleman if he does it in a nice and benevolent and affectionate way. The historian, John Fiske, whom I knew well and loved, was a spotless and most noble and upright Christian gentleman, and yet he swore once. Not exactly that, maybe; still he—but I will tell you about it. One day when he was deeply immersed in his work, his wife came in, much moved and profoundly distressed, and said, "I am sorry to disturb you, John, but I must, for this is a serious matter, and needs to be attended to at once." Then, lamenting, she brought a grave accusation against their little son. She said, "He has been saying his Aunt Mary is a fool and his Aunt Martha is a *damned* fool." Mr. Fiske reflected upon the matter a minute, then said, "Oh, well, it's about the distinction I should make between them myself."

Mr. Washington, I beg you to convey these teachings to your great and prosperous and most beneficent educational institution, and add them to the prodigal mental and moral riches wherewith you equip your fortunate protégés for the struggle of life.

Text / Composite, based upon: "Choate and Twain Plead for Tuskegee," *Times,* January 23, 1906; "Mark Twain at Carnegie Hall, January 22," galley proof, MTP; "Taxes and Morals" in *MTS*(10): 108–13; and *MTS*(23):276–80.

Parkhurst / Charles Henry Parkhurst (1842–1933). American reformer. He was pastor of Congregational churches in Massachusetts and New York City (1880–1918). As president of the Society for the Prevention of Crime (1891), he exposed police corruption that led to the defeat of Tammany (1894), and was active in civic reform thereafter. Among his books are *Our Fight With Tammany* (1895), and *My Forty Years in New York* (1923).

John Fiske / (1842–1901). American philosopher and historian. Lecturer on philosophy at Harvard (1869–71), and assistant college librarian (1872–79), he wrote voluminously on history and philosophy. An interpreter rather than an original thinker, he was a valuable expositor and popularizer. His most important philosophical work is *Outlines of Cosmic Philosophy* (1874). On American history he published, among others, *The Critical Period of American History, 1783–1789* (1888), and *The American Revolution* (1891).

Washington / Booker Taliafero Washington (1856–1915). American educator. Born in a slave cabin, growing up determined to get an education, he entered Hampton Normal and Agricultural Institute (1872), where he paid his way by working as a janitor. A teacher by 1875, he was on the Hampton staff (1879), then became head of a new Negro school at Tuskegee, Alabama. It had neither money nor equipment. He built up the institution by enlisting the aid of well-wishers and millionaires: Peabody, Ogden, Rockefeller, Mackay, Carnegie, and others. Washington told his remarkable story in *Up From Slavery* (1901).

· 146 ·

A dinner of the American branch of the Dickens Fellowship celebrated the ninety-fourth anniversary of the birth of Charles Dickens. Mark Twain was there, but not necessarily as an admirer of Dickens. Indeed, his most frequently cited remark about the novelist is that he could never find anything humorous in Pickwick Papers. *In his dinner speech, however, he did not bring up the subject of Dickens.*

Dinner Speech

Manhattan Dickens Fellowship Dinner, Press Club,
New York, February 7, 1906

I always had taken an interest in young people who wanted to become poets. I remember I was particularly interested in one budding poet when I was a reporter. His name was Butter.

One day he came to me and said, disconsolately, that he was going to commit suicide—he was tired of life, not being able to express his thoughts in poetic form. Butter asked me what I thought of the idea. I said I would; that it was good idea. "You can do me a friendly turn. You go off in a private place and do it there, and I'll get it all. You do it, and I'll do as much for you some time."

At first he determined to drown himself. Drowning is so nice and clean, and writes up so well in a newspaper. But things ne'er do go smoothly in weddings, suicides, or courtships. Only there at the edge of the water, where Butter was to end himself, lay a life preserver—a big round canvas one, which would float after the scrap iron was soaked out of it.

Butter wouldn't kill himself with the life preserver in sight, and so I had an idea. I took it to a pawnshop, and soaked it for a revolver. The pawnbroker didn't think much of the exchange, but when I explained the situation he acquiesced. We went up on top of a high building, and this is what happened to the poet:

He put the revolver to his forehead and blew a tunnel straight through his head. The tunnel was about the size of your finger. You could look right through it. The job was complete; there was nothing in it.

Well, after that that man could never write prose, but he could write poetry. He could write it after he had blown his brains out. There is lots of that talent all over the country, but the trouble is they don't develop it.

I am suffering now from the fact that I, who have told the truth a good many times in my life, have lately received more letters than anybody else urging me to lead a righteous life. I have more friends who want to see me develop on a high level than anybody else.

Young John D. Rockefeller, two weeks ago, taught his Bible class all about veracity, and why it was better that everybody should always keep a plentiful supply on hand. Some of the letters I have received suggest that I ought to attend his class and learn, too. Why, I know Mr. Rockefeller, and he is a good fellow. He is competent in many ways to teach a Bible class, but when it comes to veracity he is only thirty-five years old. I'm seventy years old. I have been familiar with veracity twice as long as he.

And the story about George Washington and his little hatchet has also been suggested to me in these letters—in a fugitive way, as if I needed some of George Washington and his hatchet in my constitution. Why, dear me, they overlook the real point in that story. The point is not the one that is usually suggested, and you can readily see that.

The point is not that George said to his father, "Yes, father, I cut down the cherry tree; I can't tell a lie," but that the little boy—only seven years old—should have his sagacity developed under such circumstances. He was a boy wise beyond his years. His conduct then was a prophecy of later years. Yes, I think he was the most remarkable man the country ever produced—up to my time, anyway.

Now then, little George realized that circumstantial evidence was against him. He knew that his father would know from the size of the chips that no full-grown hatchet cut that tree down, and that no man would have haggled it so. He knew that his father would send around the plantation and inquire for a small boy with a hatchet, and he had the wisdom to come out and confess it. Now, the idea that his father was overjoyed when he told little George that he would rather have him cut down a thousand cherry trees than tell a lie is all nonsense. What did he really mean? Why, that he was absolutely astonished that he had a son who had the chance to tell a lie and didn't.

I admire old George—if that was his name—for his discernment. He knew when he said that his son couldn't tell a lie that he was stretching it a good deal. He wouldn't have to go to John D. Rockefeller's Bible class to find that out. The way the old George Washington story goes down it doesn't do anybody any good. It only discourages people who can tell a lie.

Text / "On Poetry, Veracity, and Suicide," *MTS*(10):347–50.

Rockefeller / John Davison Rockefeller, Jr. (1874–1960). American philanthropist. He was trustee and chairman of the General Education Board (1902–39), and chairman of the Rockefeller Foundation (1917–40). Among numerous philanthropic and other projects, he conceived and built Rockefeller Center, New York, and gave the land for the United Nations headquarters (1947). For Mark Twain's comments on John D., Jr., see *MTE*:83–91.

· 147 ·

The Ends of the Earth Club had no quarters, no constitution, no dues. Mark Twain was honorary head; Rudyard Kipling and Admiral Dewey were on the honorary council. Once a year members gathered from the ends of the earth, swapped stories of their experiences, listened to fictitious reports from a pseudo secretary and treasurer, and discussed so-called items of business–such as supplanting the orchestra with a Japanese band and Geisha girls. At the February dinner, noted below, when Mark Twain strolled in at 10 P.M., he was greeted with a chorus, "For he's a jolly good fellow." His evening was not entirely pleasant. In a dictation of September 7, 1906 (MTP), he was still indignant over the arrogance of the dinner chairman, General James L. Wilson, who had loudly proclaimed that they were all of the Anglo-Saxon race, "and when the Anglo-Saxon wants a thing he just takes it." *Mark Twain said it meant that Americans and Englishmen were thieves, highwaymen, and pirates, and proud of it.*

Reminiscences

The Ends of the Earth Club Dinner, Hotel Savoy, New York, February 16, 1906

I don't quite get the hang of this club. You don't know what the Treasurer's report furnishes except that it doesn't furnish anything. I might just as well be in the S.P.C.A. I don't know whether you adopted that method or whether the Society for the Propagation of Cruelty to Animals adopted it. Only you do come out better than they do.

[He talked about writing *The Gilded Age.*] When I was writing the book, I had great trouble with Mulberry Sellers. I had the man's name written originally as Mulberry Sellers. A friend told me I ought to change it.

"Make it Eschol Sellers," he advised.

"But I'm afraid," I replied. "An Eschol Sellers may be living and we may get into trouble." However, I made it Eschol Sellers and one day a man from Philadelphia, a stately and cultivated gentleman, approached me.

"Sir," he said, "my name is Eschol Sellers. I'll give you fifteen minutes to take my name out of that book."

We did it, but that didn't end the trouble, for a Mulberry Sellers turned up in Wisconsin, one on the Wabash, and others from various parts of the country.

I met a man on the streets of New York a few weeks ago. He was my old friend Fuller, ninety years gone and gray-headed. I was glad to see him, and the moment I laid eyes upon him I was brought back to my first lecture in New York, at Cooper Institute. Fuller was the man who proposed it. I demurred.

"Nobody knows me here, Fuller," I said, "and the thing will be a failure."

"No such thing," he argued. "We will fill the house at a dollar a head."

I was young enough to be deceived by his flamboyant talk and immediately had dreams of filling the house at a dollar a head. He suggested Cooper Institute. I've been there once, and don't want to go again.

They advertised me as the "Eloquent and Celebrated Mark Twain." They hung up in the city buses great bunches of flimsy cards advertising my coming lecture. The cards were to be pulled down and read by anybody interested. I saw them and got to haunting those buses. I rode up and down, up and down through this town of New York watching with beating heart and hoping that someone would pull one of those sheets.

I never saw anybody do it. I finally advised Fuller to flood the city with paper, and we did so. We sent out barrels of complimentary tickets. When the eventful night came, the streets were blocked with struggling men and women. The house was jammed with people. I felt flattered, for it was my first lecture in the East. It was a magnificent triumph. We had a superb time, and we took in $35. I remarked about this to Fuller the other day.

"No," he said, "it was $350."

I didn't hold that against him and ask him for the money, because it happened too long ago.

Text / "Ends of the Earthers Foregather Here Again," *Times,* February 17, 1906. The text is incomplete. Parts of the speech were summarized, not reported verbatim.

Fuller / Frank Fuller (1827–1915). American lawyer. Lincoln sent him to Utah to take charge during the Civil War when the regular appointee, Alfred Cumming, wavered in the face of Mormon opposition. Fuller's meeting with Mark Twain at the home of

Governor Nye in Carson City, Nevada, began a friendly relationship that endured thereafter. Fuller was an active promotor of Mark Twain's first New York lecture at Cooper Union, May 6, 1867, providing most, if not all, of the money to stage the event. See "Utah's War Governor Talks of Many Famous Men," *Times,* October 1, 1911; also *MTB,* 1:312–17.

· 148 ·

The date of the introduction below is conjectural, and the occasion is unknown to the editor of this volume. The time was probably shortly before March 4, because of some similarity between the speech of that date and the introduction of Dr. Van Dyke.

Introducing Dr. Henry Van Dyke

Late February or Early March 1906

I am here—ostensibly—to introduce to you the lecturer of the occasion, the Rev. Dr. Van Dyke, of Princeton University: not to tell you who he is, you know that already: not to praise his delicious books, they praise themselves better than any words of mine could do it for them. Then is there any real use or advantage in my being here at all? Yes; I am here to talk and put in the time while Dr. Van Dyke reflects upon what he is going to say, and whether he had better say it or not.

Chance has furnished me a text—a text which offers me an opportunity to teach, an opportunity to be instructive; and if I have a passion for anything, it is for teaching. It is noble to teach oneself; it is still nobler to teach others—and less trouble. My text is a telegram from the *Daily Review,* an Illinois newspaper which says, "In what book of yours will we find a definition of a gentleman?" This question has been asked me a number of times by mail in the past month or two, and I have not replied; but if it is now going to be taken up by telegraph, it is time for me to say something, and I think that this is the right time and place for it.

The source of these inquiries was an Associated Press telegram of a month or so ago, which said, in substance, that a citizen of Joplin, Missouri, who had just died, had left $10,000 to be devoted to the dissemination, among young men, of Mark Twain's idea of the true gentleman. This was a puzzle to me, for I had never in my life uttered in print a definition of that word—a word which once had a concrete meaning, but has no clear and definite meaning now, either in America or elsewhere. In England, long ago, and in America in early times the term was compact and definite, and was restricted to a certain grade of birth, and it had nothing to do with character; a gentleman could commit all the crimes and bestialities known to the Newgate Calendar, and be shunned and despised by everybody, great and small, yet he would still be unquestionably a gentleman just the same, and no one could dispute it. But in our day how would you define that loose and shackly and shadowy and colorless word?—in case you had thirty-five years to do it in. None but a very self-complacent and elaborately incompetent person would ever try to define it; and then the result wouldn't be worth the violent mental strain it had cost.

The weeks drifted along, and I remained puzzled; but at last when this telegram came, I suddenly remembered! Remembered that I had once defined the word? Not at all. What I remembered was this: In the first fortnight of March, four years ago, a New York lady defined the word in a published interview. The main feature of her definition was, that no man is a gentleman who hasn't had a college education. Oh, dear me—Adam, for instance! And Arkwright—and Watt—and Stephenson—and Whitney—and Franklin—and Fulton—and Morse—and Elias Howe—and Edison—and Graham Bell—and Lincoln—and Washington—and—and me. What a project! to select and set apart a majestic and monumental class for the people's reverence and homage, then degrade it, belittle it, make it trivial, make it comical, make it grotesque, by leaving out of it the makers of history, the uplifters of man, the creators and preservers of civilization! The idea of leaving *us* out! It was my privilege to laugh, if I did it privately. Very well, I did it privately. Considering the fact that the person who proposes to define that word must be equipped with almost limitless knowledge and daring and placid self-confidence, it seemed to me that the late Simon Hanks, of Cape Cod, had surely changed his sex and was come again. The poet says:

> The Lord knows all things, great and small,
> With doubt He's never vexed;
> Ah yes, the good Lord knows it all—
> But Simon Hanks comes next.

The matter seemed settled. But the New York papers have long known that no large question is ever really settled until I have been consulted; it is the way they feel about it, and they show it by always sending to me when they get uneasy; so the interviewers came up to Riverdale to get the verdict. I was in bed, trying to amuse the bronchitis, therefore I got myself excused. I said not a word upon the subject to anyone. Yet there was a long and fictitious interview, pretending to come from me, in one of the papers the next morning—the only instance in which a paper on either side of the Atlantic had treated me uncourteously and unfairly for many years. I was made to speak in the first person, and to furnish my idea of what a gentleman is.

You will perceive that there is a sort of grotesque and degraded humor about that situation. All definers of the modern gentleman are agreed that among his qualities must be honesty, courtesy, and truthfulness. Very well, here is a journalist who sends to me a forger to represent him, then prints the forger's product and filches money with it from his deceived readers—yet if I should assert that he is not a gentleman his friends could quite properly require me to prove it, and I couldn't do it; for I don't know what a gentleman is—a gentleman on the indefinite modern plan. It's the fourth dimension to me, with the unsquared circle and the nebular theory added.

There is also another humorous detail or two about the situation. The forged interview deceived and beguiled that trusting and well-meaning citizen of Joplin before he died, and pillaged his heirs after he was in his grave. They can't get the bequested money, for it has to go to the dissemination of my definition of what a gentleman is. The proposed class in gentlemanliness can't get it, for my definition doesn't exist and has never existed. The money is tied up, for good and all. I believe it is the most dismally and pathetically and sardonically humorous incident I have ever come across.

Now then, can't we define the American gentleman at all? As a whole—no. We can define the best part of him, the valuable part, it is as far as we can get. The rest of him is hazy, diffused, uncertain; it is this, that and the other thing, it is everything and nothing, according to Tom, Dick and Harry's undigested notion; and when you've got the jumble all jumbled together to suit you, if it still seems to lack something, whitewash it with a college education and call game.

What shall we say is the best part, the accepted part, the essential part, of the American gentleman? Let us say it is courtesy and a blemishless character. What is courtesy? Consideration for others. Is there a good deal of it in the American character? So far as I have observed—no. Is it an American characteristic? So far as I have observed, the most striking, the most prominent, the most American of all American characteristics is the poverty of it in the American character. Even the foreigner loses his kindly politeness as soon as we get him Americanized. When we have been abroad among either the naked savages or the clothed civilized, for even so brief a time as a year, the first thing we notice when we get back home is the wanton and unprovoked discourtesies that assail us at every turn. They begin at the customs pier, and they follow us everywhere. Such of you as have been abroad will feel with remembered pangs and cheek-burnings, that I am speaking the truth; the rest of you will confess it some day when you come home from abroad. You will step into the trolley with your heart so full of thankfulness to be at home again that you can't speak; you are so glad, so happy, so grateful, that the tears blur everything, and you say to yourself, "Oh, *am* I really at home once more!" Then the conductor bawls out, "Come, step lively, will you!" and you realize that you are. It is a shameful phrase which is preserved and perpetuated for him and for us by the president and directors of the company—by their indifference, and by their contempt for the public. They and they alone are responsible for it, not he. They could stop it forever with a single command. He utters their voice and their feeling. They are gentlemen—on the modern plan. Yes, you are at home again—unquestionably. You realize that in no country on the planet, savage or civilized, but your own could you hear your unoffending old father and mother and your gentle young sister assailed with that brutal insult; also, that no people on the planet but ours is meek enough to stand it. We allow our commonest rights to be trampled under foot every day and everywhere; among us citizenship is an unknown virtue. We have never claimed to be the Meek Nation, the Timid Nation, I don't know why, there being no competition. We have never claimed to be the Uncourteous Nation, the Unpolite Nation, I don't know why, there being no competition. Is it because we are also the Too-Modest Nation? Probably. Is that why we still keep that old, quiet, courtly, uninsolent, uncharacteristic *E pluribus Unum* for our national motto, instead of replacing it with an up-to-date one, full of national character: "Come, *step* lively!"

I am working hard, day and night, without salary or hope of applause, upon my high and self-appointed task of reforming our national manners, and I ask for your help. Am I polite, do you ask? Well—no, I'm an American myself. Why don't I begin by reforming my own manners? I have already explained that, in the beginning. I said, it is noble to teach others—and less trouble.

Having now finished this extraneous and unofficial lecture, I invite the real lecturer to approach and deliver to you his message: but I do it courteously; you will never hear me say to Rev. Dr. Van Dyke, whom I and the nation revere, "Come, *step* lively!"

Text / Composite, based upon: "Introducing Dr. Henry Van Dyke," MS, MTP; "Introducing Doctor Van Dyke," *MTS*(23):296–301.

Newgate Calendar / A biographical record, beginning in 1773, of the most notorious criminals in Newgate Prison, London. The prison was pulled down in 1902.

Arkwright / Richard Arkwright (1732–92). British inventor. He established at Nottingham the first cotton mill in England (1768), and invented a mechanical cotton-spinning frame (patented 1769) operated by water power, later by steam. He was a pioneer in the use of machinery on a large scale in textile manufacture.

Watt / James Watt (1736–1819). British civil engineer. He experimented with the steam engine about 1760, with the condensing engine (1765), and began to manufacture steam engines in 1775. He also designed aqueducts for the British canal system. The watt, a unit of electrical energy, is named for him.

Stephenson / George Stephenson (1781–1848). British engineer. He developed the locomotive, making the first successful trial in 1814. He was engineer of the Stockton and Darlington Railway (1825), and of the Liverpool and Manchester line (1830).

Whitney / Eli Whitney (1765–1825). American inventor. He invented the cotton gin (1792), but the machine was stolen before he could patent it. Then he made a fortune manufacturing firearms at Whitneyville, Connecticut. He was the first to suggest interchangeable parts for machinery.

Howe / Elias Howe (1819–67). American inventor. He invented the sewing machine (1845), then developed several improved models. He founded the successful Howe Machine Company, Bridgeport, Connecticut.

· 149 ·

The announcement that Mark Twain would speak at a Y.M.C.A. meeting in the Majestic Theatre attracted several thousand people, who milled around in front of the building waiting for the doors to open. The crowd spread over the street, stalled traffic, and brought out police reserves, who aggravated confusion by harrying, bullying, and club-brandishing. There were no arrests or casualties, however, and the chief results were ruffled tempers, torn coats, a shattered front door, and some five hundred citizens who could not get inside. Mark Twain had a painful time. In a dictation of April 3, 1906 (MTP), he says that he suffered through a succession of speakers who could not speak, a singer who could not sing, a string band that made strange noises—then mistook audience reaction for approval and did the noises again for an encore—and a Bible reader who could not read. The Reverend Charles P. Fagnani, who introduced the chief guest, reprehended police brutality, but said that Mark Twain was a man "well worth being clubbed to hear."

Remarks

West Side Branch Y.M.C.A. Meeting, Majestic Theatre, New York, March 4, 1906

I thank you for this signal recognition of merit. I have been listening to what has been said here about citizenship. You complain of the police. You created the police, and you are responsible for the police. They must reflect you, their masters. Consider that before you blame them. They are citizens, just as we are.

A little of citizenship ought to be taught at the mother's knee and in the nursery. Citizenship is what makes a republic; monarchies can get along without it. What keeps a republic on its legs is good citizenship. Citizenship is of the first importance in a land where a body of citizens can change the whole atmosphere of politics, as has been done in Philadelphia. I was going to move to Philadelphia, but it is no place for enterprise now.

Dr. Russell spoke of organization. Organization is necessary in all things. It is even necessary in reform. I was an organization myself once—for twelve hours, and accomplished things I could never have done otherwise. I was traveling from Chicago with my publisher and stenographer—I always travel with a bodyguard—and engaged a stateroom on a certain train. For above all its other conveniences, the stateroom gives the privilege of smoking. When we arrived at the station the conductor told us he was sorry the car with our stateroom was left off. I said, "You are under contract to furnish a stateroom on this train. I am in no hurry. I can stay here a week at the road's expense. It'll have to pay my expenses and a little over."

Then the conductor called a grandee, and, after some argument, he went and bundled some meek people out of the stateroom, told them something not strictly true, and gave it to me. About eleven o'clock the conductor looked in on me, and was very kind and winning. He told me he knew my father-in-law—it was much more respectable to know my father-in-law than me in those days. Then he developed his game. He was very sorry the car was only going to Harrisburg. They had telegraphed to Harrisburg, Pittsburgh, San Francisco, and couldn't get another car. He threw himself on my mercy. But to him I only replied: "Then you had better buy the car."

I went into the dining car the next morning for breakfast. Ordinarily I care only for coffee and rolls, but this particular morning I espied an important-looking man on the other side of the car eating broiled chicken. I asked for broiled chicken, and I was told by the waiter and later by the dining car conductor that there was no broiled chicken. There must have been an argument, for the Pullman conductor came in and remarked: "If he wants broiled chicken, give it to him. If you haven't got it on the train, stop somewhere. It will be better for all concerned!" I got the chicken.

I had forgotten all about this, when some time after Mr. Thomson of the Pennsylvania heard I was going to Chicago again, and wired:

"I am sending my private car. Clemens cannot ride on an ordinary car. He costs too much."

It is from experiences such as these that you get your education of life, and you string them into jewels or tinware, as you may choose. I have received recently several letters asking my counsel or advice. The principal request is for some incident that may prove helpful to the young. There were a lot of incidents in my career to help me along—sometimes they helped me along faster than I wanted to go.

Here is such a request. It is a telegram from Joplin, Missouri, and it reads: "In what book of your works can we find the definition of a gentleman?"

I have not answered that telegram, either; I couldn't. It seems to me that if any man has just merciful and kindly instincts he would be a gentleman, for he would need nothing else in the world.

I received the other day a letter from my old friend, William Dean Howells—Howells, the head of American literature. No one is able to stand with him. He is an old, old friend of mine, and he writes me, "Tomorrow I shall be sixty-nine years old." Why, I am surprised at Howells writing that! I have known him longer than that. I'm sorry to see a man trying to appear so young. "I was born to be afraid of dying, not of getting old," he says. Well, I'm the other way. It's terrible getting old. You gradually lose things, and become troublesome. People try to make you think you are not. But I know I'm troublesome.

Then he says no part of life is so enjoyable as the eighth decade. That's true. I've just turned into it, and I enjoy it very much. If old men were not so ridiculous, why didn't he speak for himself? "But," he goes on, "they are ridiculous, and they are ugly." I never saw a letter with so many errors in it. Ugly! I was never ugly in my life! Forty years ago I was not so good-looking. A looking glass then lasted me three months. Now I can wear it out in two days.

Let's see. Howells says now, "You've been up in Hartford burying poor old Patrick. I suppose he was old, too." No, he was never old. Patrick came to us thirty-six years ago—a brisk, lithe young Irishman. He was as beautiful in his graces as he was in his spirit, and he was as honest a man as ever lived. For twenty-five years he was our coachman, and if I were going to describe a gentleman in detail I would describe Patrick.

At my own request I was his pall bearer with our old gardener. He drove me and my bride so long ago. As the little children came along he drove them, too. He was all the world to them, and for all in my house he had the same feelings of honor, honesty, and affection.

He was sixty years old, ten years younger than I. Howells suggests he was old. He was not so old. He had the same gracious and winning ways to the end. Patrick was a gentleman, and to him I would apply the lines:

> So may I be courteous to men, faithful to friends,
> True to my God, a fragrance to the path I trod.

He was with us in New Hampshire, with us last summer, and his hair was just as black, his eyes were just as blue, his form just as straight, and his heart just as good as on the day we first met. In all the long years Patrick never made a mistake. He never needed an order, he never received a command. He knew. I have been asked for my idea of an ideal gentleman, and I give it to you—Patrick McAleer.

Text / Composite, based upon: "Police Hustle Crowd Awaiting Mark

Twain," *Times,* March 5, 1906; "Layman's Sermon" in *MTS*(10): 136–39; and *MTS*(23):281–83.

Philadelphia / Remarks on the changed political atmosphere of Philadelphia probably referred to the City party, organized there in 1905 to combat graft and bossism: such blatant frauds, for example, as recording votes of citizens long dead, and votes of parrots, cats, and dogs.

Russell / James Earl Russell (1864–1945). American educator. Professor of education at Teachers College, New York (1897–1913), and dean until 1927, he was influential in making Teachers College part of Columbia University.

· 150 ·

At a Barnard College reception, the girls swarmed around Mark Twain with a gratifying display of flattering attention. He enjoyed the society of young women. In MTA*(2:172), he says: "Girls are charming creatures. I shall have to be twice seventy years old before I change my mind about that. I am to talk to a crowd of them this afternoon, students of Barnard College . . . and I think I shall have just as pleasant a time as I had with the Vassar girls twenty-one years ago." He did have a pleasant time, recording in a dictation next day his great satisfaction in being fussed over. Escorted to the platform by Miss Russell, president of Barnard, and Miss Hill, dean, he stood before a painted backdrop depicting a woodsy setting, and faced a house crowded with admiring femininity. Introduced as one whom all the girls loved, he spoke for an hour, and afterward shook hands with everybody, his youthful listeners assuring him that his words would undoubtedly make them lead better lives.*

Speech

Barnard College Union Reception for Mark Twain, Columbia University, New York, March 7, 1906

If anyone here loves me, she has my sincere thanks. Nay, if anyone here is so good as to love me—why, I'll be a brother to her. She shall have my sincere, warm, unsullied affection. When I was coming up in the car with the very kind young lady who was delegated to show me the way, she asked me what I was going to talk about. And I said I wasn't sure. I said I had some illustrations, and I was going to bring them in. I said I was certain to give those illustrations, but that I hadn't the faintest notion what they were going to illustrate.

Now, I've been thinking it over in this forest glade [indicating the woods of Arcady on the scene setting], and I've decided to work them in with something about morals and the caprices of memory. That seems to me to be a pretty good subject. You see, everybody has a memory and it's pretty sure to have caprices. And, of course, everybody has morals.

It's my opinion that everyone I know has morals, though I wouldn't like to ask. I know I have. But I'd rather teach them than practice them any day. "Give them to others"—that's my motto. Then you never have any use for them when you're left without. Now, speaking of the caprices of memory in general, and of mine in particular, it's strange to think of all the tricks this little mental process plays on us. Here we're endowed with a faculty of mind that ought to be more supremely serviceable to us than them all. And what happens? this memory of ours stores up a perfect record of the most useless facts and anecdotes and experiences. And all the things that we ought to know—that we need to know—that we'd profit by knowing—it casts aside with the careless indifference of a girl refusing her true lover. It's terrible to think of this phenomenon. I tremble in all my members when I consider all the really valuable things that I've forgotten in seventy years—when I meditate upon the caprices of memory.

There's a bird out in California that is one perfect symbol of the human memory. I've forgotten the bird's name (just because it would be valuable for me to know it—to recall it to your own minds, perhaps).

But this fool of a creature goes around collecting the most ridiculous things you can imagine and storing them up. He never selects a thing that could ever prove of the slightest help to him; but he goes about gathering iron forks, and spoons, and tin cans, and broken mousetraps—all sorts of rubbish that is difficult for him to carry and yet be any use when he gets it. Why, that bird will go by a gold watch to bring back one of those patent cake pans.

Now, my mind is just like that, and my mind isn't very different from yours—and so our minds are just like that bird. We pass by what would be of inestimable value to us, and pack our memories with the most trivial odds and ends that never by any chance, under any circumstances whatsoever, could be of the slightest use to anyone.

Now, things that I have remembered are constantly popping into my head. And I am repeatedly startled by the vividness with which they recur to me after the lapse of years and their utter uselessness in being remembered at all.

I was thinking over some on my way up here. They were illustrations I spoke about to the young lady on the way up. And I've come to the conclusion, curious though it is, that I can use every one of these freaks of memory to teach you all a lesson. I'm convinced that each one has its moral. And I think it's my duty to hand the moral on to you.

Now, I recall that when I was a boy I was a good boy—I was a very good boy. Why, I was the best boy in my school. I was the best boy in that little Mississippi town where I lived. The population was only about twenty million. You may not believe it, but I was the best boy in that state—and in the United States, for that matter.

But I don't know why I never heard anyone say that but myself. I always recognized it. But even those nearest and dearest to me couldn't seem to see it. My mother, especially, seemed to think there was something wrong with that estimate. And she never got over that prejudice.

Now, when my mother got to be eighty-five years old her memory failed her. She forgot little threads that hold life's patches of meaning together. She was living out West then, and I went on to visit her.

I hadn't seen my mother in a year or so. And when I got there she knew my face; knew I was married; knew I had a family, and that I was living with them. But she couldn't, for the life of her, tell my name or who I was. So I told her I was her boy.

"But you don't live with me," she said.

"No," said I, "I'm living in Hartford."

"What are you doing there?"

"Going to school."

"Large school?"

"Very large."

"All boys?"

"All boys."

"And how do you stand?" said my mother.

"I'm the best boy in that school," I answered.

"Well," said my mother, with a return of her old fire, "I'd like to know what the other boys are like."

Now, one point in this story is the fact that my mother's mind went back to my school days, and remembered my little youthful self-prejudice when she'd forgotten everything else about me.

The other point is the moral. There's one there that you will find if you search for it.

Now, here's something else I remember. It's about the first time I ever stole a watermelon. "Stole" is a strong word. Stole? Stole? No, I don't mean that. It was the first time I ever withdrew a watermelon, retired it from circulation—the first time I ever *extracted* a watermelon. That is exactly the word I want—"extracted." It is definite. It is precise. It perfectly conveys my idea. Its use in dentistry connotes the delicate shade of meaning I am looking for. You know we never extract our own teeth.

And it was not my watermelon that I extracted. I extracted that watermelon from a farmer's wagon while he was inside negotiating with another customer. I carried that watermelon to one of the secluded recesses of the lumber yard, and there I broke it open.

It was a green watermelon.

Well, do you know when I saw that I began to feel sorry—sorry-sorry. It seemed to me that I had done wrong. I reflected deeply. I reflected that I was young—I think I was just eleven. But I knew that though immature I did not lack moral advancement. I knew what a boy ought to do who had extracted a watermelon—like that.

I considered George Washington, and what action he would have taken under similar circumstances. Then I knew there was just one thing to make me feel right inside, and that was—Restitution.

So I said to myself: "I will do that. I will take that green watermelon back where I got it from." And the minute I had said it I felt that great moral uplift that comes to you when you've made a noble resolution.

So I gathered up the biggest fragments, and I carried them back to the farmer's wagon, and I restored the watermelon—what was left of it. And I made him give me a good one in place of it, too.

And I told him he ought to be ashamed of himself going around working off his worthless, old, green watermelons on trusting purchasers who had to rely on him. How could they tell from the outside whether the melons were good or not? That was his business. And if he didn't reform, I told him I'd see that he didn't get any more of my trade—nor anybody else's I knew, if I could help it.

You know that man was as contrite as a revivalist's last convert. He said he was all broken up to think I'd gotten a green watermelon. He promised me he would never carry another green watermelon if he starved for it. And he drove off—a better man.

Now, do you see what I did for that man? He was on a downward path, and I rescued him. But all I got out of it was a watermelon.

Yet I'd rather have that memory—just that memory of the good I did for that depraved farmer—than all the material gain you can think of. Look at the lesson he got! I never got anything like that from it. But I ought to be satisfied. I was only eleven years old, but I secured everlasting benefit to other people.

The moral in this is perfectly clear, and I think there's one in the next memory I'm going to tell you about.

To go back to my childhood, there's another little incident that comes to me from which you can draw even another moral. It's about one of the times I went fishing. You see, in our house there was a sort of family prejudice against going fishing if you hadn't permission. But it would frequently be bad judgment to ask. So I went fishing secretly, as it were—way up the Mississippi. It was an exquisitely happy trip, I recall, with a very pleasant sensation.

Well, while I was away there was a tragedy in our town. A stranger, stopping over on his way east from California, was stabbed to death in an unseemly brawl.

Now, my father was justice of the peace, and because he was justice of the peace he was coroner; and since he was coroner he was also constable; and being constable he was sheriff; and out of consideration for his holding the office of sheriff he was likewise county clerk and a dozen other officials I don't think of just this minute.

I thought he had power of life or death, only he didn't use it over other boys. He was sort of an austere man. Somehow I didn't like being round him when I'd done anything he disapproved of. So that's the reason I wasn't often around.

Well, when this gentleman got knifed they communicated with the proper authority, the coroner, and they laid the corpse out in the coroner's office—our front sitting room—in preparation for the inquest the next morning.

About nine or ten o'clock I got back from fishing. It was a little too late for me to be received by my folks, so I took my shoes off and slipped noiselessly up the back way to the sitting room. I was very tired, and I didn't wish to disturb my people. So I groped my way to the sofa and lay down.

Now, I didn't know anything of what had happened during my absence. But I was sort of nervous on my own account—afraid of being caught, and rather dubious about the morning affair. And I had been lying there a few moments when my eyes gradually got used to the darkness, and I became aware of something on the other side of the room.

It was something foreign to the apartment. It had an uncanny appearance. And I sat up looking very hard, and wondering what in heaven this long, formless, vicious-looking thing might be.

First I thought I'd go and see. Then I thought, "Never mind that."

Mind you, I had no cowardly sensations whatever, but it didn't seem exactly prudent to investigate. But I somehow couldn't keep my eyes off the thing. And the more I looked at it the more disgreeably it grew on me. But I was resolved to play the man. So I decided to turn over and count a hundred, and let the patch of moonlight creep up and show me what the dickens it was.

Well, I turned over and tried to count, but I couldn't keep my mind on it. I kept thinking of that gruesome mass. I was losing count all the time, and going back and beginning over again. Oh no; I wasn't frightened—just annoyed. But by the time I'd gotten to the century mark I turned cautiously over and opened my eyes with great fortitude.

The moonlight revealed to me a marble-white human hand. Well, maybe I wasn't embarrassed! But then that changed to a creepy feeling again, and I thought I'd try the counting again. I don't know how many hours or weeks it was that I lay there counting hard. But the moonlight crept up that white arm, and it showed me a lead face and a terrible wound over the heart.

I could scarcely say that I was terror-stricken or anything like that. But somehow his eyes interested me so that I went right out of the window. I didn't need the sash. But it seemed easier to take it than to leave it behind.

Now, let that teach you a lesson—I don't know just what it is. But at seventy years old I find that memory of peculiar value to me. I have been unconsciously guided by it all these years. Things that seemed pigeonholed and remote are a perpetual influence. Yes, you're taught in so many ways. And you're so felicitously taught when you don't know it.

Here's something else that taught me a good deal.

When I was seventeen I was very bashful, and a sixteen-year-old girl came to stay a week with us. She was a peach, and I was seized with a happiness not of this world.

One evening my mother suggested that, to entertain her, I take her to the theater. I didn't really like to, because I was seventeen and sensitive about appearing in the streets with a girl. I couldn't see my way to enjoying my delight in public. But we went.

I didn't feel very happy. I couldn't seem to keep my mind on the play. I became conscious, after a while, that that was due less to my lovely company than my boots. They were sweet to look upon, as smooth as skin, but fitted ten times as close. I got oblivious to the play and the girl and the other people and everything but my boots until—I hitched one partly off. The sensation was sensuously perfect. I couldn't help it. I had to get the other off, partly. Then I was obliged to get them off altogether, except that I kept my feet in the legs so they couldn't get away.

From that time I enjoyed the play. But the first thing I knew the curtain came down, like that, without my notice, and I hadn't any boots on. What's more, they wouldn't go on. I tugged strenuously. And the people in our row got up and fussed and said things until the peach and I simply had to move on.

We moved—the girl on one arm and the boots under the other.

We walked home that way, sixteen blocks, with a retinue a mile long. Every time we passed a lamp post death gripped me at the throat. But we got home—and I had on white socks.

If I live to be nine hundred and ninety-nine years old I don't suppose I could ever forget that walk. I remember it about as keenly as the chagrin I suffered on another occasion.

At one time in our domestic history we had a colored butler who had a failing. He could never remember to ask people who came to the door to state their business. So I used to suffer a good many calls unnecessarily.

One morning when I was especially busy he brought me a card engraved with a name I did not know. So I said, "What does he wish to see me for?" and Sylvester said, "Ah couldn't ask him, sah; he wuz a genlmun." "Return instantly," I thundered, "and inquire his mission. Ask him what's his game." Well, Sylvester returned with the announcement that he had lightning rods to sell. "Indeed," said I, "things are coming to a fine pass when lightning rod agents send up engraved cards." "He has pictures," added Sylvester. "Pictures indeed! He may be peddling etchings. Has he a Russia leather case?" But Sylvester was too frightened to remember. I said, "I am going down to make it hot for that upstart!"

I went down the stairs, working up my temper all the way. When I got to the parlor I was in a fine frenzy concealed beneath a veneer of frigid courtesy. And when I looked in the door, sure enough he had a Russia leather case in his hand. But I didn't happen to notice that it was our Russia leather case.

And if you'd believe me that man was sitting with a whole gallery of etchings spread out before him. But I didn't happen to notice that they were our etchings, spread out by some member of my family for some unguessed purpose.

Very curtly I asked the gentleman his business. With a surprised, timid manner he faltered that he had met my wife and daughter at Onteora, and they had asked him to call. Fine lie, I thought, and I froze him.

He seemed to be kind of nonplussed, and sat there fingering the etchings in the case until I told him he needn't bother, because we had those. That pleased him so much that he leaned over, in an embarrassed way, to pick up another from the floor. But I stopped him. I said, "We've got that, too." He seemed pitifully amazed, but I was congratulating myself on my great success.

Finally the gentleman asked where Mr. Winton lived; he'd met him in the mountains, too. So I said I'd show him gladly. And I did on the spot. And when he was gone I felt queer, because there were all his etchings spread out on the floor.

Well, my wife came in and asked me who had been in. I showed her the card, and told her all exultantly. To my dismay she nearly fainted. She told me had been a most kind friend to them in the country, and had forgotten to tell me that he was expected our way. And she pushed me out of the door, and commanded me to get over to the Wintons in a hurry and get him back.

I came into the drawing room, where Mrs. Winton was sitting up very stiff in a chair, beating me at my own game. Well, I began to put another light on things. Before many seconds Mrs. Winton saw it was time to change her temperature. In five minutes I had asked the man to luncheon, and she to dinner, and so on.

We made that fellow change his trip and stay a week, and we gave him the time of his life. Why, I don't believe we let him get sober the whole time.

I trust that you will carry away some good thought from these lessons I have given you, and that the memory of them will inspire you to higher things, and elevate you to plans far above the old—and—and—

And I tell you one thing, young ladies: I've had a better time with you today than with that peach fifty-three years ago.

Text / Composite, based upon: "Morals and Memory" in *MTS*(10): 224–37; and *MTS*(23):284–91.

watermelon / If Mark Twain, like other speakers, repeated his stories, he varied details, wording and emphasis. Here, placing the onus of moral failure on the farmer makes a new story out of an old one.

colored butler / George Griffin, one of several long-time servants in the Clemens household in Hartford; others were Patrick McAleer, John Lewis, and Katy Leary. For an illuminating portrait of Griffin and a detailed discussion of his duties in the Hartford household, see Arthur G. Pettit, *Mark Twain & The South* (Lexington, 1974).

Onteora / A summer resort in the Catskills, where the Clemens family spent the summer of 1890.

· 151 ·

A Freundschaft Society dinner honored Charles Putzel, former president of the society, who had been appointed tax commissioner. Chairman Julius J. Frank, introducing Mark Twain, referred to the maxim of Pudd'nhead Wilson: "When in doubt, tell the truth." The New York American *reported next day that "the gray-haired humorist never was in better voice."*

Dinner Speech

Freundschaft Society Dinner for Charles Putzel,
New York, March 8, 1906

Mr. Chairman, Mr. Putzel and gentlemen of the Freundschaft: That maxim I did invent, but never expected it to be applied to me. I did say, "When you are in doubt," but when I am in doubt myself I use more sagacity.

Mr. Grout suggested that if I have anything to say against Mr. Putzel, or any criticism of his career or his character, I am the last person to come out on account of that maxim and tell the truth. That is altogether a mistake.

I do think that it is right for other people to be virtuous so that they can be happy hereafter, but if I knew every impropriety that even Mr. Putzel has committed in his life, I would not mention one of them. My judgment has been maturing for seventy years, and I have got to the point where I know better than that.

Mr. Putzel stands related to me in a very tender way—through the tax office—and it does not behoove me to say anything which could by any possibility militate against that condition of things.

Now, that word, taxes, taxes, taxes! I have heard it tonight. I have heard it all night. I wish somebody would change that subject, that is a very sore subject to me.

I was so relieved when Judge Leventritt did find something that was not taxable—when he said that the commissioner could not tax your patience. And that comforted me. We've got so much taxation. I don't know of a single foreign product that enters this country untaxed except the answer to prayer.

On an occasion like this the proprieties require that you merely pay compliments to the guest of the occasion, and I am merely here to pay compliments to the guest of the occasion, not to criticize him in any way, and I can say only complimentary things to him.

When I went down to the tax office some time ago, for the first time in New York, I saw Mr. Putzel sitting in the "Seat of Perjury." I recognized him right away. I warmed to him on the spot. I didn't know that I had ever seen him before, but just as soon as I saw him I recognized him. I had met him twenty-five years before, and at that time had achieved a knowledge of his abilities and something more than that.

I thought: "Now, this is the same man whom I saw twenty-five years ago." On that occasion I not only went free at his hands, but carried off something more than that. I hoped it would happen again.

It was twenty-five years ago when I saw a young clerk in Putnam's book store. I went in there and asked for George Haven Putnam and handed him my card, and then the young man said Mr. Putnam was busy and I couldn't see him. Well, I had merely called in a social way, and so it didn't matter.

I was going out when I saw a great big, fat, interesting-looking book lying there and I took it up. It was an account of the invasion of England in the fourteenth century by the Preaching Friar, and it interested me.

I asked him the price of it and he said four dollars.

"Well," I said, "what discount do you allow to publishers?" He said, "Forty percent off." I said, "All right, I am a publisher."

He put down the figure, forty percent off, on a card.

Then I said, "What discount do you allow to authors?" and he said, "Forty percent off." "Well," I said, "set me down as an author."

"Now," said I, "what discount do you allow to the clergy?" He said, "Forty percent off." Well, I said, I was only on my way there, kind of studying for the ministry. I asked him wouldn't he knock off twenty percent for that. He set down the figure, and he never smiled once.

I was working off these humorous brilliancies on him and getting no return—not a scintillation in his eye, not a spark of recognition of what I was doing there. I was almost in despair.

I thought I might try him once more, so I said, "Now, I am also a member of the human race—will you let me have ten percent off for that?" He set it down and never smiled.

Well, I gave it up. I said, "There is my card with my address on it, but I have not any money with me. Will you please send the bill to Hartford?" I took up the book and was going away.

He said, "Wait a minute. There is forty cents coming to you."

When I met him in the tax office, I thought maybe I could make something again, but I did not. But I had not any idea I could when I came, and as it turned out I did not get off entirely free.

I put up my hand and made a statement. It gave me a good deal of pain to do that. I was not used to it. I was born and reared in the higher circles of Missouri, and there we don't do such things—didn't in my time, but we have got that little matter settled—got a sort of a tax levied on me.

Then he touched me. Yes, he touched me this time, because he cried—cried! He was moved to tears to see that I, a virtuous person only a year before, after immersion for one year—during one year in the New York morals—had no more conscience than a millionaire. I would like to compliment him, anyway, for I may get relief next year.

Attorney General Mayer suggested that I might be a Supreme Court judge. I can't be that, for I know nothing of the administration of justice. But I understand from his speech he is the propagator of crime for the whole state, and, as I am reasonably familiar with crime, I might have his job.

Text / Composite, based upon: " 'N.Y. Left My Conscience as Bad as a Millionaire's'—Mark Twain," New York *American,* March 9, 1906; "Twain's Waning Conscience," *Times,* March 9, 1906; "When in Doubt, Tell the Truth" in *MTS*(10):397–401; and *MTS*(23): 292–95.

Grout / Edward Marshall Grout (1861–1931). American lawyer. He prosecuted cases of street railway graft in Brooklyn (1892–95), was first president of the Borough of Brooklyn (1897–1901), and comptroller of Greater New York (1901–05).

Leventritt / David Leventritt (1845–1926). American jurist. A New York City lawyer (1872–98), he was a justice of the New York Supreme Court (1898–1908).

Mayer / Julius M. Mayer (1865–1925). American jurist. Counsel for the Excise Board of New York (1895–96), justice of the Court of Special Sessions (1902–04), and attorney general for the State of New York (1905–07), he was appointed judge of the United States Circuit Court of Appeals (1921). He was a tough courtroom fighter and a rigorous judge.

· 152 ·

Mark Twain presided at a public fund-raising meeting of the New York State Association for Promoting the Interests of the Blind, an organization sponsored by such humanitarian New Yorkers as Lyman Abbott, John Shaw Billings, Felix Adler, Nicholas Murray Butler, Archibishop Farley, Robert W. De Forest, and Joseph H. Choate. Its most effective pleader was Helen Keller, for whom Mark Twain–indeed, everybody–had great admiration. Unable to be present because of illness, she sent a letter in which she praised "the eloquence of our newest Ambassador to the blind. We have not had such advocates before." The meeting filled the grand ballroom of the Waldorf-Astoria with a capacity audience, many of whom were blind.

Speech as Presiding Officer

Public Meeting of the New York State Association for Promoting the Interests of the Blind, Hotel Waldorf-Astoria, March 29, 1906

If you detect any awkwardness in my movements and infelicities in my conduct I will offer the explanation that I never presided at a meeting of any kind before in my life, and that I do find it out of my line. I supposed I could do anything anybody else could, but I recognize that experience helps, and I do feel the lack of that experience. I don't feel as graceful and easy as I ought to be in order to impress an audience. I shall not pretend that I know how to umpire a meeting like this, and I shall just take the humble place of the Essex band.

Some twenty-five years ago there was a great gathering in a New England town. There were orators and singers and all sorts of things. It was really an extraordinary occasion. The little local paper went into ecstasies in trying to do justice to it and in praising the speakers, the militia companies, the bands and everything else. Toward the end the writer ran out of adjectives and phrases of glorification, and then found that he had one band left over. He had to say something about it, so he simply added: "The Essex band done the best it could."

I am the Essex band of this occasion, but I'll do the best I can, with good intentions. I've got all the documents of the objects of this association and this meeting and a lot of statistics, but I never could do anything with figures. The multiplication table is the only mathematics I know, and as soon as I get up to nine times seven I don't know that—84, I think it is. I can't even figure on the name of the society, it is so long. I would write it out for you to take home with you, but I can't spell it, and Andrew Carnegie is somewhere down in Virginia.

This association, which is in the hands of very energetic and capable persons, who will surely push it to success, has for its purpose to search out all the blind and find work for them to do so that they can earn their own bread. Now it is dismal enough to be blind—it is dreary, dreary life at best, but it is a life that can be largely ameliorated if we can find something for them to do with their hands and to relieve them of the sense that they subsist on charity, and often reluctant charity. It is the only way we can turn their night into day and give them happy hearts.

Most of these sufferers have seen the light and know how to miss it, and it is for us to relieve their dreary lives by teaching them the many profitable industries they can pursue. That association from which this draws its birth in Cambridge, Massachusetts, has taught its blind to make many things. They make them better than most people, and more honest than people who have the use of their eyes. The goods they make are readily salable. People like them. And so they are supporting themselves, and it is a matter of cheer, cheer. They pass their time now not too irksomely as they formerly did.

What this association needs and wants is $15,000. The figures are set down, and what the money is for, and there is no graft in it or I wouldn't be here. And they hope to beguile that out of your pockets, and you will find affixed to the program an opportunity, that little blank which you will fill out and promise so much money now or tomorrow or sometime. Then, there is another opportunity which is still better, and that is that you shall subscribe an annual sum.

I have invented a good many useful things in my time, but never anything better than that of getting money out of people who don't want to part with it. It is always for good objects, of course. This is the plan: When you call upon a person to contribute to a great and good object, and you think he should furnish about $1,000, he disappoints you as like as not. Much the best way to work him to supply that thousand dollars is to split it into parts and contribute, say a hundred dollars a year, or fifty, or whatever the sum may be. Let him contribute ten or twenty a year. He doesn't feel that, but he does feel it when you call upon him to contribute a large amount. When you get used to it you would rather contribute than borrow money.

I tried it in Helen Keller's case. Mr. Hutton wrote me in 1896 or

1897 when I was in London and said: "The gentleman who has been so liberal in taking care of Helen Keller has died without making provision for her in his will, and now they don't know what to do." They were proposing to raise a fund, and he thought $50,000 enough to furnish an income of $2,400 or $2,500 a year for the support of that wonderful girl and her wonderful teacher, Miss Sullivan, now Mrs. Macy. I wrote to Mr. Hutton and said: "Go on, get up your fund. It will be slow, but if you want quick work, I propose this system," the system I speak of, of asking people to contribute such and such a sum from year to year and drop out whenever they please, and he would find there wouldn't be any difficulty, people wouldn't feel the burden of it. And he wrote back saying that he had raised the $2,400 a year indefinitely by that system in a single afternoon. We would like to do something just like that tonight. We will take as many checks as you care to give. You can leave your donations in the big room outside.

Now, I want you who have sight to know what it means, what a calamity it is, to be blind, to be in the dark. I know what it is to be blind. I was blind once. I shall never forget that experience. I have been as blind as anybody ever was for three or four hours, and the sufferings that I endured and the mishaps and the accidents that are burning in my memory make my sympathy rise when I feel for the blind and always shall feel. It occurred after an excursion from Heidelberg to a medieval town about twenty miles away. I took a clergyman along with me, the Rev. Joseph Twichell, of Hartford, who is still among the living despite that fact. I always like a minister with me on an excursion. He makes a fine lightning rod for such excursions as the one we made. The Reverend Twichell is one of those people filled with patience and endurance, two good ingredients for a man traveling with me, so we got along very well together. We went up by rail, and circumstances were such as to bring us back on a raft.

In that old town they have not altered a house nor built one in fifteen hundred years. We went to the inn and they placed Twichell and me in a most colossal bedroom, the largest I ever saw or heard of. It was as big as this room. I didn't take much notice of the place. I didn't really get my bearings. I noticed Twichell got a German bed about two feet wide, the kind in which you've got to lie on your edge, because there isn't room to lie on your back, and he was way down south in that big room, and I was way up north at the other end of it, with a regular Sahara in between.

We went to bed. Twichell went to sleep, but then he had his conscience loaded and it was easy for him to get to sleep. I couldn't sleep. It was one of those torturing kinds of lovely summer nights when you hear various kinds of noises now and then. Off in the southwest of that room a mouse got busy, and I threw something at it. It pleased the mouse, and it kept on making a noise. But I couldn't stand it, and about two o'clock I got up and thought I would give it up and go out in the square where there was one of those tinkling fountains, and sit on its brink and dream, full of romance.

I got out of bed, and I ought to have lit a candle, but I didn't think of it until it was too late. It was the darkest place that ever was. There has never been darkness any thicker than that. It just lay in cakes.

I thought that before dressing I would accumulate my clothes. I pawed around in the dark and found everything packed together on the floor except one sock. I couldn't get on the track of that sock. It might have occurred to me that maybe it was in the wash. But I didn't think of that. I went excursioning on my hands and knees. Presently I thought, "I am never going to find it; I'll go back to bed again." That is what I tried to do during the next three hours. I had lost the bearings of that bed. I was going in the wrong direction all the time. By and by I came in collision with a chair and that encouraged me.

It seemed to me, as far as I could recollect, there was only a chair here and there and yonder, five or six of them scattered over this territory, and I thought maybe after I found that chair I might find the next one. Well, I did. And I found another and another and another. I kept going around on my hands and knees, having those sudden collisions, and finally when I banged into another chair I almost lost my temper. And I raised up, garbed as I was, not for public exhibition, right in front of a mirror fifteen or sixteen feet high.

I hadn't noticed the mirror; didn't know it was there. And when I saw myself in the mirror I was frightened out of my wits. I don't allow any ghosts to bite me, and I took up a chair and smashed at it. A million pieces. Then I reflected. That's the way I always do, and it's unprofitable unless a man has had much experience that way and has clear judgment. And I had judgment, and I would have had to pay for that mirror if I hadn't recollected to say it was Twichell who broke it.

Then I got down on my hands and knees and went on another exploring expedition. As far as I could remember there were six chairs in that Oklahoma, and one table, a great big heavy table, not a good table to hit with your head when rushing madly along. In the course of time I butted thirty-six chairs and enough tables to fill the dining room of the Waldorf. It was a hospital for decayed furniture, and it was in a worse condition when I got through with it. I went on and on, and at last got to a place where I could feel my way up, and there was a shelf. I was delighted. I knew that wasn't in the middle of the room. I was then certain that I had not passed the city limits.

I was very careful and pawed along that shelf, and there was a pitcher of water about a foot high, and it was at the head of Twichell's bed, but I didn't know it. I felt that pitcher going and I grabbed at it, but it didn't help any and came right down in Twichell's face and nearly drowned him. But it woke him up. I was grateful to have company on any terms. He lit a match, and there I was, way down south when I ought to have been back up yonder. My bed was out of sight it was so far away. You needed a telescope to find it. Twichell comforted me and I scrubbed him off and we got sociable.

I have never found the sock, but the hours of darkness I experienced in the exploration in that room were not empty hours. They served their purpose. The Rev. Joe Twichell had longer legs than I, and we both wore pedometers on that trip. As I walk in my sleep, I always wore mine to bed with me. When I got up in the morning I found that I had gained sixteen miles on Twichell. Again, my reflecting after the mirror incident made me remember to tell the landlord that Twichell had broken it. But that adventure taught me what it is to be blind. That was one of the most serious occasions of my whole life, yet I never can speak of it without somebody thinking it isn't serious. You try it and see how serious it is to be as the blind are and I was that night.

[After reading letters of regret from former President Cleveland and Helen Keller, Mark Twain introduced Joseph H. Choate.]

It is now my privilege to present to you Mr. Choate. I don't have to really introduce him. I don't have to praise him, or to flatter him. I could say truly that in the forty-seven years I have been familiarly acquainted with him he has always been the handsomest man America has ever produced. And I hope and believe he will hold the belt forty-five years more. He has served his country ably, faithfully, and brilliantly. He stands at the summit, at the very top in the esteem and regard of his countrymen, and if I could say one word which would lift him any higher in his countrymen's esteem and affection, I would say that word whether it was true or not.

Text / Composite, based upon: "Mark Twain Asks Money for Blind," New York *Herald,* March 30, 1906; "Twain and Choate Talk at Meeting for Blind," *Times,* March 30, 1906; "In Aid of the Blind" in *MTS*(10):322–32; and *MTS*(23):306–14.

I never presided at a meeting / Mark Twain had presided a number of times at meetings charitable and political. His remark here is one of those errors perhaps attributable to absent-mindedness, though it is often not clear whether his misstatements were the result of forgetfulness or of deliberate intention, to achieve some effect.

I can't spell it, and Mr. Carnegie is, etc. / A reference to Carnegie's attempt to simplify English spelling. He started the movement about 1904, established a fund to carry it on, and appointed Brander Matthews chairman of a committee to further spelling reform. We shall hear more about it from Mark Twain.

· 153 ·

When the Women's University Club gave a reception for Mark Twain, the World *headed its next day's story: "Mark Twain Was Wreathed in Girls." Five hundred gratified the guest of honor by rapturously fluttering around, shaking hands, exchanging a few words, and sometimes lining up to shake hands again: "girls in Easter bonnets and charming frocks; girls all blushes and delight in the presence of their universal sweetheart." When they brought a low platform for him to stand on, he asked for something higher because, he said, "I can't tell what people are thinking unless I can see their faces." They put a chair on the platform, and he stood on the chair. For his comments on the occasion, see* MTA, *2:315.*

Remarks

Women's University Club Reception for Mark Twain, New York, April 3, 1906

I am not here, young ladies, to make a speech, but what may look like one in the distance. I don't dare to make a speech, for I haven't made any preparation, and if I tried it on an empty stomach—I mean an empty mind—I don't know what iniquities I might commit.

I am going to tell you a practical story about how once upon a time I was blind—a story I should have been using all these months, but I never thought about telling it until the other night, and now it is too late, for on the 19th of this month, at Carnegie Hall, I am going to take formal leave of the platform forever and ever, as far as appearing for pay is concerned and before people who have to pay to get in, but I have not given up for other occasions.

I shall now proceed to infest the platform all the time under conditions that I like—when I am not paid to appear and when no one has to pay to get in, and I shall only talk to audiences of college girls. I have labored for the public good for many years, and now I am going to talk for my own contentment.

[He then told the sock-hunting story, and concluded]: And now let this be a lesson to you—I don't know what kind of a lesson; I'll let you think it out.

Text / Composite, based upon: "Mark Twain Talks to College Women," *Times,* April 4, 1906; "Mark Twain Was Wreathed in Girls," *World,* April 4, 1906; "College Girls," *MTS*(10):90–91.

· 154 ·

The cause of Russian freedom met sympathetic response in the United States, and its apostle, Maxim Gorky, was warmly received. On a committee to raise money for revolutionary purposes were Howells, Mark Twain, Robert Collyer, Finley Peter Dunne, and Jane Addams. At a testimonial dinner for Gorky, Mark Twain and others affirmed their endorsement of aid to the oppressed. A few days later, however, enthusiasm cooled abruptly when Gorky was discovered to be living, not with Mme. Gorky as had been supposed, but with a Russian actress, Mme. Andreieva. The American revolutionary spirit was not revolutionary enough for goings-on like that. In a spasm of moral indignation the couple was ejected from the Hotel Belleclaire, then from the Lafayette-Brevoort and the Rhinelander Apartments. A proposed dinner of literary men to honor Gorky was abandoned, and in Boston erstwhile good will withered in the frigid air of disapproval. Nevertheless, Barnard College girls, who organized a clandestine reception for Mme. Andreieva, concluded that the lady was "too sweet for anything." Mark Twain was not so much scandalized as he was disgusted by the complication that upset their plans. For his comments, see "The Gorky Incident," Letters From the Earth: *155–56.*

Dinner Speech

Club A Dinner for Maxim Gorky, New York, April 11, 1906

If we can build a Russian republic to give to the persecuted people of the Czar's domain the same measure of freedom that we enjoy, let us go ahead and do it. We need not discuss the methods by which that purpose is to be attained. Let us hope that fighting will be postponed or averted for a while, but if it must come—

I am most emphatically in sympathy with the movement, now on foot in Russia, to make that country free. I am certain that it will be successful, as it deserves to be. Any such movement should have and deserves our earnest and unanimous cooperation, and such a petition for funds as has been explained by Mr. Hunter, with its just and powerful meaning, should have the utmost support of each and every one of us. Anybody whose ancestors were in this country when we were trying to free ourselves from oppression, must sympathize with those who now are trying to do the same thing in Russia.

The parallel I have just drawn only goes to show that it makes no difference whether the oppression is bitter or not; men with red, warm blood in their veins will not endure it, but will seek to cast it off. If we keep our hearts in this matter Russia will be free.

Text / "Russian Republic," *MTS*(10):286–87.

Maxim Gorky / (1868–1936). Russian writer. After his first story (1892), he was both writer and revolutionary. Arrested at Riga (1905), then released, he came to the United States (1906) to raise money for the cause. After living in Italy, he returned to the homeland (1914) as the foremost living Russian writer. Among his books are *Twenty-six Men and a Girl* (1899), *Foma Gordeyev* (1902), and *Decadence* (1927). His play, *The Lower Depths* (1902), is a notable example of naturalism. At the Club A dinner Gorky remarked upon the many Russian editions of the books of Mark Twain.

Hunter / Wiles Robert Hunter (1874–1922). American social worker. He was on the Chicago Board of Charities (1896–1902), head worker, University Settlement, New York (1902–03), and chairman, New York Child Labor Commission (1902–06). He wrote *Poverty* (1904) and *The Crisis* (1909). At the Club A dinner he read a manifesto inaugurating the American auxiliary movement to aid the cause of Russian freedom.

Russia will be free / There was much adverse criticism of the appointment of an American committee to aid revolution in Russia. Critics maintained that peace-loving Americans should not abet violence. In an interview, *Times,* April 15, 1906, Mark Twain answered these critics. He said, in part: "we were quite willing to accept France's assistance when we were in the throes of our Revolution, and we have always been grateful . . . . It is our turn now to pay that debt of gratitude by helping another oppressed people . . . and we must either do it or confess that our gratitude to France was only eloquent words, with no sincerity back of them. . . . Inasmuch as we conducted our own Revolution with guns and the sword, our mouths are closed against preaching gentler methods to other oppressed nations. Revolutions are achieved by blood and courage alone. So far as I know there has been but one revolution which was carried to a successful issue without bloodshed." In the light of subsequent Russian developments, Mark Twain's hope of freeing a people from oppression is tinged with colossal irony—which he would surely be quick to savor.

· 155 ·

Mark Twain was first vice-president of the Fulton Monument Association, of which Cornelius Vanderbilt was president. The purpose of the organization was to erect a monument to Robert Fulton in New York City. At a benefit staged by the association in Carnegie Hall, General Frederick D. Grant presided in full-dress uniform, the Old Guard band played, and a capacity house enjoyed the foolery of Mark Twain.

Speech

Robert Fulton Monument Association Benefit, Carnegie Hall, New York, April 19, 1906

I wish to deliver a historical address. I've been studying the history of—er—a—let me see—a [pretending to be confused, he walked across the stage to consult General Grant in a stage whisper, then resumed]. Oh, yes! I've been studying Robert Fulton. I've been studying a biographical sketch of Robert Fulton, the inventor of—er—a—let's see—oh, yes, the inventor of the electric telegraph and the Morse sewing machine. Also, I understand he invented the air—diria—pshaw! I have it at last—the dirigible balloon. Yes, the dirigible—but it is a difficult word, and I don't see why anybody should marry a couple of words like that when they don't want to be married at all and are likely to quarrel with each other all the time. I should put that couple of words under the ban of the United States Supreme Court, under its decision of a few days ago, and then take 'em out and drown 'em.

I used to know Fulton. It used to do me good to see him dashing through the town on a wild broncho.

And Fulton was born in—er—a—well, it doesn't make much difference where he was born, does it? I remember a man who came to interview me once, to get a sketch of my life. I consulted with a friend—a practical man—before he came, to know how I should treat him.

"Whenever you give the interviewer a fact," he said, "give him another fact that will contradict it. Then he'll go away with a jumble that he can't use at all. Be gentle, be sweet, smile like an idiot—just be natural." That's what my friend told me to do, and I did it.

"Where were you born?" asked the interviewer.

"Well—er—a," I began, "I was born in Alabama, or Alaska, or the Sandwich Islands; I don't know where, but right around there somewhere. And you had better put it down before you forget it."

"But you weren't born in all those places," he said.

"Well, I've offered you three places. Take your choice. They're all at the same price."

"How old are you?" he asked.

"I shall be nineteen in June," I said.

"Why, there's such a discrepancy between your age and your looks," he said.

"Oh, that's nothing," I said, "I was born discrepantly."

Then we got to talking about my brother Samuel, and he told me my explanations were confusing.

"I suppose he is dead," I said. "Some said that he was dead and some said that he wasn't."

"Did you bury him without knowing whether he was dead or not?" asked the reporter.

"There was a mystery," said I. "We were twins, and one day when we were two weeks old—that is, he was one week old and I was one week old—we got mixed up in the bathtub, and one of us drowned. We never could tell which. One of us had a strawberry birthmark on the back of his hand. There it is on my hand. This is the one that was drowned. There's no doubt about it."

"Where's the mystery?" he said.

"Why, don't you see how stupid it was to bury the wrong twin?" I answered. I didn't explain it any more because he said the explanation confused him. To me it is perfectly plain.

But, to get back to Fulton. I'm going along like an old man I used to know, who used to start to tell a story about his grandfather. He had an awfully retentive memory, and he never finished the story, because he switched off into something else. He used to tell about how his grandfather one day went into a pasture, where there was a ram. The old man dropped a silver dime in the grass, and stooped over to pick it up. The ram was observing him, and took the old man's action as an invitation.

Just as he was going to finish about the ram this friend of mine would recall that his grandfather had a niece who had a glass eye. She used to loan that glass eye to another lady friend, who used it when she received company. The eye didn't fit the friend's face, and it was loose. And whenever she winked it would turn over.

Then he got on the subject of accidents, and he would tell a story about how he believed accidents never happened.

"There was an Irishman coming down a ladder with a hod of bricks," he said, "and a Dutchman was standing on the ground below. The Irishman fell on the Dutchman and killed him. Accident? Never! If the Dutchman hadn't been there the Irishman would have been killed. Why didn't the Irishman fall on a dog which was next to the Dutchman? Because the dog would have seen him coming."

Then he'd get off from the Dutchman to an uncle named Reginald Wilson. Reginald went into a carpet factory one day, and got twisted into the machinery's belt. He went excursioning around the factory until he was properly distributed and was woven into sixty-nine yards of the best three-ply carpet. His wife bought the carpet, and then she erected a monument to his memory. It read:

Sacred to the memory
of
Sixty-nine yards of the best three-ply carpet
containing the mortal remainders of
REGINALD WILSON
Go thou and do likewise

And so on he would ramble about telling the story of his grandfather until we never were told whether he found the ten-cent piece or whether something else happened.

[At the close of the meeting Mark Twain said farewell, and appealed for aid to stricken San Francisco, which had been shaken by the earthquake of April 18, and was still being ravaged by fire.]

This is my last appearance on the paid platform. I shall not retire from the gratis platform until I am buried, and courtesy will compel me to keep still and not disturb the others. Now, since I must, I shall say good-bye. I see many faces in this audience well known to me. They are all my friends, and I feel that those I don't know are my friends, too. I wish to consider that you represent the nation, and that in saying good-bye to you I am saying good-bye to the nation.

In the great name of humanity, let me say this final word: I offer an appeal in behalf of that vast, pathetic multitide of fathers, mothers, and helpless little children. They were sheltered and happy two days ago. Now they are wandering, forlorn, hopeless, and homeless, the victims of a great disaster. So I beg of you, I beg of you to open your hearts and open your purses and remember San Francisco, the smitten city.

[Talking to newsmen afterward, Mark Twain delivered a short

impromptu on San Francisco and earthquakes.]

I haven't been there since 1868, and that great city of San Francisco has grown up since my day. When I was there she had 118,000 people, and of this number 18,000 were Chinese. I was a reporter on the Virginia City *Enterprise* in Nevada in 1862, and stayed there, I think, about two years, when I went to San Francisco and got a job as a reporter on the *Call.* I was there three or four years.

I remember one day I was walking down Third Street in San Francisco. It was a sleepy, dull Sunday afternoon and no one was stirring. Suddenly as I looked up the street about three hundred yards the whole side of a house fell out. The street was full of bricks and mortar. At the same time I was knocked against the side of a house and stood there stunned for a moment.

I thought it was an earthquake. Nobody else had heard anything about it and no one said earthquake to me afterward, but I saw it and I wrote it. Nobody else wrote it, and the house I saw go into the street was the only house in the city that felt it. I've always wondered if it wasn't a little performance gotten up for my especial entertainment by the nether regions.

Text / Composite, based upon: "Mark Twain Appeals for the Smitten City / A Unique Talk on Fulton," *Times,* April 20, 1906; "Robert Fulton Fund," *MTS*(10):298–303; Interview, *Times,* April 20, 1906; "San Francisco Earthquake," *MTS*(10):282–83.

Grant / Frederick Dent Grant (1850–1912). American soldier. A West Pointer (1871) who resigned from the army (1881), he was minister to Austria-Hungary (1889–93), and police commissioner of New York City (1895–97). Returning to the army (1898) as colonel of volunteers, then brigadier general, he campaigned in Cuba and the Philippines. He became a major general (1906).

decision of a few days ago / On April 16, 1906, the United States Supreme Court handed down a five to four decision that a divorce valid in all states cannot be granted by the courts of any state in which only one party to the marriage resides. Justices Holmes, Brown, Brewer, and Harlan dissented.

paid platform / Mark Twain's farewell to the platform as a paid performer was only a technicality, for he had long since ceased to accept pay for speaking. Tendered $1,000 for the Fulton speech, he donated the fee to the Monument Association.

· 156 ·

Marshaling forces for the relief of devastated San Francisco, women of New York swung into action at once. Two leaders were Mrs. W. K. Vanderbilt and Mrs. Herman Oelrichs, and for spokesman a natural choice was Mark Twain.

Remarks as Presiding Officer

San Francisco Relief Meeting, Casino, New York, April 21, 1906

We must not let our minds dwell upon the dead. After life's fitful fever they rest well.

Our sorrows and our sympathies are for the living, suffering thousands. The last time I saw San Francisco was thirty-eight years ago. It was then my home. It is your home, too, and every sentiment endears it to us. Forty-eight hours ago I pledged myself not to speak to any audience that paid to get in. However, you didn't pay to get in here; you're going to pay to get out. This earthquake and fire transcends anything in human history, ancient or modern, but the same energy that built San Francisco in fifty years to be destroyed in a day, will build it again. Everybody is in a mood to contribute, from the hands of poverty up to those of the millionaire. But it is the poor man that gives most.

The Salvation Army is the best means I know of to do this work. They are of the poor, and they know how to reach the poor. I have seen their work all over the world—always good.

Food can and will be carried to the sufferers at once. What they need is covering. We want a committee of women to go to the mayor and say:

"Give us some of this money that has been subscribed, and we will buy clothes and bedding for the people who have none, and do it now."

[After the audience had cheered the reading of a telegram to be sent to San Francisco, Mark Twain spoke again briefly.]

Before you give your cheers for the Californians, I hope you'll include the doctors who have done such noble service in the afflicted district. I don't like doctors on general principles, but those men out there have done some great work. Put the firemen and the soldiers in, too.

Text / "California's Women Here are Going to Aid / Twain Presides at Meeting," *Times,* April 22, 1906.

After life's fitful fever / A slight misquotation from *Macbeth* (3.2) of Macbeth's somber reflections on his murder of the King: "Duncan is in his grave; / After life's fitful fever he sleeps well! / Treason has done his worst; nor steel nor poison, / Malice domestic, foreign levy, nothing / Can touch him further."

· 157 ·

An international billiards tournament in New York attracted the world's best players: the French champion, Louis Cure, and American experts Ora Morningstar, Jacob Schaeffer, George F. Slosson, George Sutton, and William F. "Willie" Hoppe, the Boy Wonder. Mark Twain, a tireless billiards addict, was there with Henry Rogers on the opening night, April 9. Later, when the billiardists gave an exhibition of trick shots and fancy cue work for the benefit of San Francisco, he came again, and this time told a story.

Story

Billiards Exhibition
Concert Hall, Madison Square Garden, New York, April 24, 1906

The game of billiards has destroyed my naturally sweet disposition. Once, when I was an underpaid reporter in Virginia City, whenever I wished to play billiards I went out to look for an easy mark. One day a stranger came to town and opened a billiard parlor. I looked him over casually. When he proposed a game, I answered, "All right."

"Just knock the balls around a little so that I can get your gait," he said; and when I had done so, he remarked, "I will be perfectly fair with you. I'll play you left-handed." I felt hurt, for he was cross-eyed, freckled, and had red hair, and I determined to teach him a lesson. He won first shot, ran out, took my half dollar, and all I got was the opportunity to chalk my cue.

"If you can play like that with your left hand," I said, "I'd like to see you play with your right."

"I can't," he said. "I'm left-handed."

Text / "Billiards" in *MTS*(10):269; and *MTS*(23):302.

· 158 ·

An Associated Press dinner, attended by 150 journalists, was a lively and protracted affair. The menu was a booklet in which the typography was that of mid-nineteenth century newspapers, the whole illustrated by cartoons of the speakers and verses for each. Mark Twain was shown with a Pegasus-like hobbyhorse: "With wings of driven snow, / And everywhere that Sammy went / His hobby too would go." The program moved at a leisurely pace. By 9 P.M. the banqueters had worked down to Mousse de volatile a la Montargis and St. Estephe, while Clifford Wiley, baritone, rendered the toreador song from Carmen, *then "The Song That Reached My Heart." To accompany another course, Frank Lincoln spoke in English, French, German, and politico-American without saying an intelligible word in any language. Off and on an orchestra played–"In the Good Old Summer Time," "Waltz Me Around Again, Willie"–and between numbers Mr. and Mrs. Alfred Pearson presented* Aux Italiens, *a romantic playlet. Melville Stone, head of the Associated Press, presided.*

Dinner Speech

Associated Press Banquet, Hotel Waldorf-Astoria,
New York, September 19, 1906

I am here to make an appeal to the nations in behalf of the simplified spelling. I have come here because they cannot all be reached except through you. There are only two forces that can carry light to all the corners of the globe—only two—the sun in the heavens and the Associated Press down here. I may seem to be flattering the sun, but I do not mean it so; I am meaning only to be just and fair all around. You speak with a million voices; no one can reach so many races, so many hearts and intellects, as you—except Rudyard Kipling, and he cannot do it without your help. If the Associated Press will adopt and use our simplified forms, and thus spread them to the ends of the earth, covering the whole spacious planet with them as with a garden of flowers, our difficulties are at an end.

Every day of the three hundred and sixty-five the only pages of the world's countless newspapers that are read by all the human beings and angels and devils that can read, are those pages that are built out of Associated Press dispatches. And so I beg you, I beseech you—oh, I implore you to spell them in our simplified forms. Do this daily, constantly, persistently, for three months—only three months—it is all I ask. The infallible result?—victory, victory, all down the line. For by that time all eyes here and above and below will have become adjusted to the change and in love with it, and the present clumsy and ragged forms will be grotesque to the eye and revolting to the soul. And we shall be rid of phthisis and phthisic and pneumonia, and pneumatics, and diphtheria and pterodactyl, and all those other insane words which no man addicted to the simple Christian life can try to spell and not lose some of the bloom of his piety in the demoralizing attempt. Do not doubt it. We are chameleons, and our partialities and prejudices change places with an easy and blessed facility, and we are soon wonted to the change and happy in it. We do not regret our old, yellow fangs and tushes after we have worn nice fresh uniform store teeth a while.

Do I seem to be seeking the good of the world? That is the idea. It is my public attitude; privately I am merely seeking my own profit.We all do it, but it is sound and it is virtuous, for no public interest is anything other or nobler than a massed accumulation of private interests. In 1883, when the simplified spelling movement first tried to make a noise, I was indifferent to it; more—I even irreverently scoffed at it. What I needed was an object lesson, you see. It is the only way to teach some people. Very well, I got it. At that time I was scrambling along, earning the family's bread on magazine work at seven cents a word, compound words at single rates, just as it is in the dark present. I was the property of a magazine, a seven-cent slave under a boiler iron contract. One day there came a note from the editor requiring me to write ten pages on this revolting text: "Considerations concerning the alleged subterranean holophotal extemporaneousness of the conchyliaceous superimbrication of the ornithorhyncus, as foreshadowed by the unintelligibility of its plesiosaurian anisodactylous aspects."

Ten pages of that. Each and every word a seventeen-jointed vestibuled railroad train. Seven cents a word. I saw starvation staring the family in the face. I went to the editor, and I took a stenographer along so as to have the interview down in black and white, for no magazine editor can ever remember any part of a business talk except the part that's got graft in it for him and the magazine. I said, "Read that text, Jackson, and let it go on the record; read it out loud." He read it: "Considerations concerning the alleged subterranean holophotal extemporaneousness of the conchyliaceous superimbrication of the ornithorhyncus, as foreshadowed by the unintelligibility of its plesiosaurian anisodactylous aspects."

I said, "You want ten pages of those rumbling, great long summer thunder peals, and you expect to get them at seven cents a word?"

He said, "A word's a word, and seven cents is the contract; what are you going to do about it?"

I said, "Jackson, this is cold-blooded oppression. What's an average English word?"

He said, "Six letters."

I said, "Nothing of the kind; that's French, and includes the spaces between the words; an average English word is four letters and a half. By hard honest labor I've dug all the large words out of my vocabulary and shaved it down until the average is three letters and a half. I can put 1,200 words on your page, and there's not another man alive that can come within two hundred of it. My page is worth $84 to me. It takes exactly as long to fill your magazine pages with long words as it does with short ones—four hours. Now then, look at the criminal injustice of this requirement of yours. I am careful, I am economical of my time and labor. For the family's sake I've got to be so. So I never write 'metropolis' for seven cents, because I can get the same money for 'city.' I never write 'policeman,' because I can get the same price for 'cop'." And so on and so on. I never write 'valetudinarian' at all, for not even hunger and wretchedness can humble me to the point where I will do a word like that for seven cents; I wouldn't do it for fifteen. Examine your shameful text, please; count the words."

He counted and said it was 24. I asked him to count the letters. He made it 203.

I said, "Now, I hope you will see the whole size of your contemplated crime. With my vocabulary I would make 60 words out of those 203 letters, and get $4.20 for it; whereas for your inhuman 24 I would get only $1.68. Ten pages of these skyscrapers of yours would pay me only about $300; in my simplified vocabulary the same space and labor would pay me $840. I do not wish to work upon this scandalous job by the piece. I want to be hired by the year." He coldly refused.

I said, "Then for the sake of the family, if you have no feeling for me, you ought at least to allow me overtime on that word 'extemporaneousness.' " Again he coldly refused. I seldom say a harsh word to anyone, but I was not master of myself then, and I spoke right out and called him an anisodactylous plesiosaurian conchyliaceous ornithorhyncus, and rotten to the heart with holophotal subterranean extemporaneousness. God forgive me for that wanton crime; he lived only two hours!

From that day to this I have been a devoted and hard-working member of that heaven-born institution, the International Association for the Prevention of Cruelty to Authors, and now I am laboring with Carnegie's Simplified Committee, and with my heart in the work.

Now then, let us look at this mighty question reasonably, rationally, sanely—yes, and calmly, not excitedly. What is the real function, the essential function, the supreme function, of language? Isn't it merely to convey ideas and emotions? Certainly. Then if we can do it with words of phonetic brevity and compactness, why keep the present cumbersome forms? But can we? Yes. I hold in my hand the proof of it. Here is a letter written by a woman, right out of her heart of hearts. I think she never saw a spelling book in her life. The spelling is her own. There isn't a waste letter in it anywhere. It reduces the phonetics to the last gasp—it squeezes the surplusage out of every word—there's no spelling that can begin with it on this planet outside of the White House. And as for the punctuation, there isn't any. It is all one sentence, eagerly and breathlessly uttered, without break or pause in it anywhere. The letter is absolutely genuine—I have the proofs of that in my possession. I can't stop to spell the words for you, but you can take the letter presently and comfort your eyes with it. I will read the letter:

"Miss ——— dear freind i took some Close into the armerry and give them to you to Send too the suffrers out to California and i Hate to truble you but i got to have one of them Back it was a black oll woole Shevyott With a jacket to Mach trimed Kind of Fancy no 38 Burst measure and passy menterry acrost the front And the color i woodent Trubble you but it belonged to my brothers wife and she is Mad about It i thoght she was willin but she want she says she want done with it and she was going to Wear it a Spell longer she ant so free harted as what i am and she Has got more to do with Than i have having a Husband to Work and slave For her i gess you remember Me i am shot and stout and light complected i torked with you quite a spell about the suffrars and said it was orful about that erth quake i shoodent wondar if they had another one rite off seeine general Condision of the country is Kind of Explossive i hate to take that Black dress away from the suffrars but i will hunt round And see if i can get another One if i can i will call to the armerry for it if you will jest lay it asside so no more at present from your True freind i liked your appearance very Much."

Now you see what simplified spelling can do. It can convey any fact you need to convey; and it can pour out emotions like a spellbinder. I beg you, I beseech you, to adopt our spelling, and print all your dispatches in it.

Now, I wish to say just one entirely serious word:

I have reached a time of life, seventy years and a half, where none of the concerns of this world have much interest for me personally. I think I can speak dispassionately upon this matter, because, in the little while that I have got to remain here I can get along very well with these old-fashioned forms, and I don't propose to make any trouble about it at all. I shall soon be where they won't care how I spell so long as I keep the Sabbath.

There are 82,000,000 of us people that use this orthography, and it ought to be simplified in our behalf, but it is kept in its present condition to satisfy 1,000,000 people who like to have their literature in the old form. That looks to me to be rather selfish, and we keep the forms as they are while we have got 100,000 people coming in here from foreign countries every month and they have got to struggle with this orthography of ours, and it keeps them back and damages their citizenship for years until they learn to spell the language, if they ever do learn. There is really no argument against reform except merely sentimental argument.

People say it is the spelling of Chaucer and Spenser and Shakespeare and a lot of other people who did not know how to spell anyway, and it has been transmitted to us and we preserved it and wish to continue to preserve it because of its ancient and hallowed associations.

Now, I don't see that there is any real argument about that. If that argument is good, then it would be a good argument not to banish the flies and the cockroaches from hospitals because they have been there so long that the patients have got used to them and they feel a tenderness for them on account of the associations. Why, it is like preserving a cancer in a family because it is a family cancer, and we are bound to it by the test of affection and reverence and old mouldy antiquity.

I think that this declaration to improve this orthography of ours is our family cancer, and I wish we could reconcile ourselves to have it cut out and let the family cancer go.

Now, you see before you the wreck and ruin of what was once a young person like yourselves. I am exhausted by the heat of the day. I must take what is left of the wreck and ruin out of your presence and carry it away to my home and spread it out there and sleep the sleep of the righteous. There is nothing much left of me but my age and my righteousness, but I leave with you my love and my blessing, and may you always keep your youth.

Text / Composite, based upon: "Spelling and Pictures and Twain at Dinner," *Times,* September 20, 1906; "Mark Twain on Simplified

Spelling," Simplified Spelling Board, Circular No. 9, November 10, 1906; "Spelling and Pictures" in *MTS*(10):204–12; and *MTS*(23):315–22.

simplified spelling / Mark Twain's defense of reformed spelling reflected current agitation over a movement initiated by Carnegie and endorsed by President Roosevelt. Yet it was surprising how much controversy such an apparently inoffensive topic stirred up. The British objected to proposed spelling reforms, and the clergy, as well as others, took issue. Perhaps that was why Mark Twain, implying in a dictation of November 19, 1906, that he had no strong feelings about the matter, said that he got into the spelling debate because he liked to have a hand in whatever was going on.

Carnegie's Simplified Committee / Carnegie had appointed a Simplified Spelling Board of twenty-eight members from all parts of the country: Brander Matthews, chairman, Mark Twain, William James, David Starr Jordan, O. C. Blackmer, Lyman J. Gage, Nicholas Murray Butler, Thomas R. Lounsbury, Gilder, Thomas Wentworth Higginson, and others. The Board had an office on Madison Avenue, from which it distributed circulars, such as Mark Twain's AP speech, and other propaganda. Proposed reforms were phonetic, or as they put it, "fonetic": "lite" for "light," "wisht" for "wished," "thru" for "through," and so on. Most of the simplifications have not been adopted, although a few, like "sulfate" for "sulphate" and "gage" for "gauge," are accepted as reputable usage today. For Mark Twain's comments on the reform argument, see: "The Carnegie Spelling Reform," *Harper's Weekly* (April 7, 1906):488; dictation of November 19, 1906, MTP; "Simplified Spelling," *Letters From the Earth:* 159–63.

"Miss ——— dear freind," etc. / The badly-written letter was not genuine, as Mark Twain supposed, but, as he learned later, the work of a writer named Grace Donworth. She adopted his suggestion that she continue the letters and make a book of them. It is *The Letters of Jennie Allen to Her Friend, Miss Musgrove* (Boston, 1908).

· 159 ·

When Clara Clemens made her American concert debut as a contralto, news stories referred to her as "Mark Twain's daughter." The identification annoyed her but delighted her father. Under strict orders not to usurp the limelight, he attended the concert, sat quietly in the third row, and applauded the singing, as well as the solos of Isadore Luckstone, accompanist, and Marie Nichols, a Boston violinist. Then, when he took a bow with Clara at the end of the program, neither was surprised that the audience clamored for a speech.

Remarks

American Concert Debut of Clara Clemens, Eldridge Gymnasium, Norfolk, Connecticut, September 22, 1906

My heart goes out in sympathy to anyone who is making his first appearance before an audience of human beings. By a direct process of memory I go back forty years, less one month—for I'm older than I look.

I recall the occasion of my first appearance. San Francisco knew me then only as a reporter, and I was to make my bow to San Francisco as a lecturer. I knew that nothing short of compulsion would get me to the theater. So I bound myself by a hard-and-fast contract so that I could not escape. I got to the theater forty-five minutes before the hour set for the lecture. My knees were shaking so that I didn't know whether I could stand up. If there is an awful, horrible malady in the world, it is stage fright—and seasickness. They are a pair. I had stage fright then for the first and last time. I was only seasick once, too. It was on a little ship on which there were two hundred other passengers. I—was—sick. I was so sick there wasn't any left for those other two hundred passengers.

It was dark and lonely behind the scenes in that theater, and I peeked through the little peek holes they have in theater curtains and looked into the big auditorium. That was dark and empty, too. By and by it lighted up, and the audience began to arrive.

I had got a number of friends of mine, stalwart men, to sprinkle themselves through the audience armed with big clubs. Every time I said anything they could possibly guess I intended to be funny they were to pound those clubs on the floor. Then there was a kind lady in a box up there, also a good friend of mine, the wife of the governor. She was to watch me intently, and whenever I glanced toward her she was going to deliver a gubernatorial laugh that would lead the whole audience into applause.

At last I began. I had the manuscript tucked under a United States flag in front of me where I could get at it in case of need. But I managed to get started without it. I walked up and down—I was young in those days and needed the exercise—and talked and talked.

Right in the middle of the speech I had placed a gem. I had put in a moving, pathetic part which was to get at the hearts and souls of my hearers. When I delivered it they did just what I hoped and expected. They sat silent and awed. I had touched them. Then I happened to glance up at the box where the governor's wife was—you know what happened.

Well, after the first agonizing five minutes, my stage fright left me, never to return. I know if I was going to be hanged I could get up and make a good showing, and I intend to. But I shall never forget my feelings before the agony left me, and I got up here to thank you for her for helping my daughter, by your kindness, to live through her first appearance. And I want to thank you for your appreciation of her singing, which is, by the way, hereditary.

Text / "Mark Twain's First Appearance" in *MTS*(10):221–23; and *MTS*(23):303–5.

my first appearance / This story, similar to the version in chapter 78 of *Roughing It,* may be only a fanciful recollection of what happened at Mark Twain's first San Francisco lecture on October 2, 1866. See Paul Fatout, "Mark Twain's First Lecture: a Parallel," *Pacific Historical Review* 25, no. 4 (November 1956):347–54.

· 160 ·

Mark Twain went to Washington to deliver opinions once again to a congressional committee on the perennial subject of copyright. In early winter, the city shivering in blustery December weather, he startled the natives by wearing a suit of immaculate white flannel. Before being called by the committee, he was briefly a conspicuous figure in the House gallery, then a center of attraction in the Speaker's room, congressmen deserting the floor in numbers to be entertained by his drawling remarks. He was naturally pursued by reporters, who scarcely needed to ask a question to get him started.

Interview

Washington, D.C., December 7, 1906

I suppose everyone is wondering why I am wearing such apparently unseasonable clothes. I'll tell you. This is a uniform. It is the uniform of the American Association of Purity and Perfection, of which I am president, secretary and treasurer, and the only man in the United States eligible to membership.

I was seventy-one years old last Saturday, and when a man reaches that age he has a right to arrogate to himself many privileges to which younger men cannot aspire. When you are over seventy-one you are privileged to dress in the fashion that conforms most to your comfort and enjoyment. I have reached the age where dark clothes have a depressing effect on me. Light-colored clothing is more pleasant to the eye and enlivens the spirit. Now, of course, I cannot compel everyone to wear such clothing just for my especial benefit, so I do the next best thing and wear it myself.

Of course, before a man reaches my years, the fear of criticism might prevent him from indulging his fancy. I am not afraid of that. I prefer light clothing, colors, like those worn by the ladies at the opera. Whenever I go to the opera and see the men sitting around with those beautifully gowned ladies they are no more cheering than a lot of old crows. If nobody else will wear colors that cheer me up I shall wear them myself. Men's clothing is bad in color and generally uncomfortable.

After all, what is the purpose of clothing? Are not clothes intended primarily to preserve dignity and also to afford comfort to the wearer? The finest clothing made is a person's own skin, but, of course, society demands something more than that. The best-dressed man I have ever seen, however, was a native of the Sandwich Islands, who attracted my attention forty years ago. Now, when that man wanted to don especial dress to honor a public occasion or holiday, why he occasionally put on a pair of spectacles. Otherwise the clothing with which God had provided him sufficed.

Clothes, in our modern civilization, are to preserve decency, and for us to get as much comfort out of as possible. But how any man can get comfort out of the clothing made for men today I cannot see. Nothing is more absurd, ungraceful and uncomfortable than modern man's clothing, day or night, and at night man wears the most ridiculous of all garbs—evening clothes. What can be more depressing than the somber black which custom requires me to wear on state occasions.

Of course, I have ideas of dress reform. For one thing, why not adopt some of the women's styles? Goodness knows, they adopt enough of ours. Why should we not learn from them? They always have beautiful fabrics, splendid colors, and, moreover, women's clothes are always pretty. Take the peek-a-boo waist, for instance. It has the obvious advantages of being cool and comfortable, and in addition it is almost always made up in pleasing colors, which cheer and do not depress.

I would go back to the Middle Ages for the gorgeous, glorious, gaudy costumes of that time. Then we could wear colors. Back to the days before buttons were invented, when they laced their clothing up, and it took a little time to do it; back to the days of tights and helmet! Yes, I admit that it might be uncomfortable for a bald-headed man wearing a tightly screwed-on helmet, with a bee or fly imprisoned therein.

It is true that I dressed the Connecticut Yankee at King Arthur's court in a plug hat, but, let's see, that was twenty-five years ago. Then no man was considered fully dressed until he donned a plug hat. Nowadays I think that no man is dressed until he leaves it home in the tightly-tied box in which it came from the hatter's. Why, when I left home yesterday they trotted out a plug hat for me to wear.

"You must wear it," they told me; "why, just think of going to Washington without a plug hat!" But I said no; I would wear a derby or nothing. Why, I believe I could walk along the streets of New York—I never do—but still I think I could—and I should never see a well-dressed man wearing a plug hat. If I did I should suspect him of something, I don't know what, but I would suspect him.

Why, when I got up on the second story of that Pennsylvania ferryboat coming down here yesterday, I saw Howells coming along. He was the only man on the boat with a plug hat, and I tell you he felt ashamed of himself. He said he had been persuaded to wear it against his better sense, but just think of a man nearly seventy years old who hasn't a mind of his own on such matters.

But I am not here to talk fashions, but copyright law. If you had ten authors and an equal number of publishers in Congress more would be known of copyright laws. With 25,000 bills a Congress coming in, I don't see how members have an opportunity to even read the titles.

Congress is made up of lawyers, agriculturists and all sorts of persons with all sorts of opinions, gained by experience, but men will not study the copyright laws unless they have been both author and publisher. I have been both author and publisher and have been smashed.

There are women who write, idiots and well-meaning persons who write, who know nothing about copyrights, but I profess to have some knowledge on this subject. There are between 5,000 and 7,000 books issued every year. Ten may live twenty-eight years, the first period of the present copyright, and two to be renewed to bring them up to the forty-two-year limit. Then the author dies and his children starve.

I shall hardly get into heaven before my children will have no book on which to live. Out of all the 150,000 books published during the last half century, but two have been extended to the forty-two-year term period. One of them is *Science and Health,* by Mrs. Mary Baker Eddy, and the other is my own *Innocents Abroad.*

Text / Composite, based upon: "Mark Twain in White Amuses Congressmen," *Times,* December 8, 1906; "Mark Twain in Cream-Colored Summer Flannel," *World,* December 8, 1906; "Dress Reform and Copyright," *MTS*(10):85–89.

dress reform / The reforms Mark Twain proposed for men have come about during the past generation. Male attire has achieved a gorgeousness of which he surely would have approved.

· 161 ·

At the hearing before the Committee on Patents, Richard R. Bowker and Robert Underwood Johnson appeared for the American Copyright League; F. D. Millet represented painters, John Philip Sousa musicians. Writers were there in force: Howells, Edward Everett Hale, Thomas Nelson Page, and Mark Twain, who was last to be heard and who made a long speech. The proposed law protected not only authors, but also musical composers, painters, and illustrators.

Remarks on Copyright

Hearing, Congressional Committee on Patents,
Washington, D.C., December 7, 1906

I have read this bill. At least I have read such portions as I could understand. Nobody but a practiced legislator can read this bill and thoroughly understand it, and I am not a practiced legislator. I have had no practice at all in unraveling confused bills. Not that this is more confused than any other bill. I suppose they are all confused.

Necessarily I am interested particularly and especially in the part of the bill which concerns my trade. I like the bill, and I like that proposed extension from the present limit of copyright life of forty-two years to the author's life and fifty years after. I think that will satisfy any reasonable author, because it will take care of his children. Let the grandchildren take care of themselves. "Sufficient unto the day." That would satisfy me very well. That would take care of my daughters, and after that I am not particular. I shall then long have been out of this struggle and independent of it. Like *all* the trades and occupations of the United States, ours is represented and protected in that bill. I like it. I want them to be represented and protected and encouraged. They are all worthy, all important, and if we can take them under our wing by copyright, I would like to see it done. I should like to have you encourage oyster culture in it, and anything else that comes into your minds. I have no illiberal feeling toward the bill. I think it is just, I think it is righteous, and I hope it will pass without reduction or amendment of any kind.

I am aware that copyright must have a limit, because that is required by the Constitution of the United States, which sets aside the earlier Constitution, which we call the Decalogue. The Decalogue says you shall not take away from any man his property. I don't like to use the harsh term. What the Decalogue really says is, "Thou shalt not steal," but I am trying to use more polite language.

But the laws of England and America do take property away from the owner. They select out the people who create the literature of the land. They always talk handsomely about the literature of the land; they always say what a fine, great, monumental thing a great literature is, and in the midst of their enthusiasm they turn around and do what they can to crush it, discourage it, and put it out of existence.

I know we must have that limit, but forty-two years is too much of a limit. I am quite unable to guess why there should be a limit at all to the possession of the product of a man's labor. There is no limit to real estate. As Dr. Hale has just suggested, you might just as well, after you had discovered a coal mine and worked it forty-two years, have the government step in and take it away.

The excuse for a limited copyright in the United States is that an author who has produced a book and has had the benefit of it for that term has had the profit of it long enough, and therefore the government takes the property, which does not belong to it, and generously gives it to the 88,000,000 of people. That is the idea. If it did that, that would be one thing. But it doesn't do anything of the kind. It merely takes the author's property, merely takes from his children the bread and profit of that book, and gives the publisher *double* profit. He goes on publishing the book and as many of his confederates as choose to go into the conspiracy do so, and they rear families in affluence. And they continue the enjoyment of these illgotten gains generation after generation, for they never die. They live forever, publishers do.

As I say, this proposed limit is quite satisfactory to me—for the author's life, and fifty years after. In a few weeks, or months, or years I shall be out of it. I hope to get a monument. I hope I shall not be entirely forgotten, and I shall subscribe to the monument myself. But I shall not be caring what happens if there is fifty years' added life of my copyright. My copyrights produce annually a good deal more money than I have any use for, but my children can use it. I can take care of myself as long as I live. I know half a dozen trades, and I can invent half a dozen more. I can get along. But I like the fifty years' extension because that benefits my two daughters, who can't get along as well as I can, because I have carefully raised them as young ladies, who don't know anything and can't do anything. So I hope Congress will extend to them that charity which they have failed to get from me.

Why, if a man who is not even mad, but only strenuous—strenuous about race suicide—should come to me and try to get me to use my large political and ecclesiastical influence to get a bill passed by Congress limiting families to twenty-two children by one mother, I should try to calm him down. I should reason with him. I should say to him, "That is the very parallel to the copyright limitation by statute. Leave it alone. Leave it alone and it will take care of itself. There are only one or two couples at one time in the United States that can reach that limit. Now, if they reach that limit let them go on. Let them have all the liberty they want. You are not going to hurt anybody that way. Don't cripple that family and restrict it to twenty-two children. In doing so you are merely conferring discomfort and unhappiness on one family per year in a nation of 88,000,000, which is not worth while."

It is the very same with copyright. One author per year produces a book which can outlive the forty-two-year limit; that's all. This nation can't produce three authors a year that can do it; the thing is demonstrably impossible. All that a limited copyright can do is to take the bread out of the mouths of the children of that one author per year, century in and century out. That is all you get out of limiting copyright.

I made an estimate once when I was to be called before the copyright committee of the House of Lords, as to the output of books, and by my estimate we had issued and published in this country since the Declaration of Independence 220,000 books. What was the idea of protecting those books by copyright? They are all gone. They had all perished before they were ten years old. There is only about one book in a thousand that can outlive forty-two years of copyright. Therefore why put a limit at all? You might just as well limit a family to twenty-two children. It will take care of itself.

If you try to recall to your minds the number of men in the nineteenth century who wrote books in America whose books lived forty-two years you will begin with Fenimore Cooper, follow that with Washington Irving, Harriet Beecher Stowe, and Edgar A. Poe, and you will not go far until you begin to find that the list is sharply limited. You come to Whittier and Holmes and Emerson, and you find Howells and Thomas Bailey Aldrich, and then the list gets pretty thin and you question if you can find twenty persons in the United States in a whole century who produced books that could outlive or did outlive the forty-two-year limit. Why, you can take all the authors in the United States whose books have outlived the forty-two-year limit and you can seat them on one of those benches there. Allow three children to each of them, and you can certainly put the result down at one hundred persons and seat them on three more benches.

One hundred persons—that is the little, insignificant crowd whose bread and butter is to be taken away for what purpose, for what profit to anybody? Nobody can tell what that profit is. It is only those books that will outlast the forty-two-year limit that have any value after ten or fifteen years. The rest are all dead. Then you turn those few books into the hands of the pirate and of the legitimate publisher, too, and they get the profit that should have gone to the wife and children. I do not think that this is quite right.

The English idea of copyright, as I found, was different, when I was before the committee of the House of Lords. The chairman was a very able man, Lord Thwing, a man of great reputation, but he didn't know anything about copyright and publishing. Naturally he didn't, because he hadn't been brought up to this trade. It is only people who have had intimate personal experience with the triumphs and griefs of an occupation who know how to treat it and get what is justly due.

Now that gentleman had no purpose or desire in the world to rob anybody of anything, but this was the proposition—fifty years' extension—and he asked me what I thought the limit of copyright ought to be.

"Well," I said, "perpetuity." I thought it ought to last forever.

Well, he didn't like that idea much. I could see some resentment in his manner, and he went on to say that the idea of perpetual copyright was illogical, and so forth, and so on. And here was his reason: *that it has long ago been decided that ideas are not property,* that there can be no such thing as *property in ideas.*

I said there was property in ideas before Queen Anne's time; it was recognized that books had perpetual copyright up to her day. Dr. Hale has explained, a moment ago, why they reduced it to fourteen years in Queen Anne's time. That is a very charitable explanation of that event. I never heard it before. I thought a lot of publishers had got together and got it reduced. But I accept Dr. Hale's more charitable view, for he is older than I, but not much older, and knows more than I do, but not much more.

That there could be no such thing as property in an intangible idea, was his position. He said, "What is a book? A book is just built from base to roof of ideas, and there can be no property in them."

I said I wished he could mention any kind of property existing on this planet, that had a pecuniary value, which value was not derived from an idea or ideas—solely.

"Well," he said, "landed estate—real estate."

"Why," I said, "take an assumed case, of a dozen Englishmen traveling through South Africa—they camp out; eleven of them see nothing at all; they are mentally blind. But there is one on the party who knows what that nearby harbor means, what this lay of the land means; to him it means that some day—you cannot tell when—a railway will come through here, and there on that harbor a great city will spring up. *That is his idea.* And he has *another* idea, and so, perhaps, he trades his last bottle of Scotch whiskey and a horse blanket to the principal chief of that region for a piece of land the size of Pennsylvania. There is the value of an idea *applied to real estate.* That day will come, as it was to come when the Cape-to-Cairo Railway should pierce Africa and cities should be built; there was some smart person who bought the land from the chief and received his everlasting gratitude, just as was the case with William Penn, who bought for forty dollars' worth of stuff the giant area of Pennsylvania. He did a righteous thing. We have to be enthusiastic over it, because that was a thing that had never happened before probably. There again was the *application of an idea to real estate.* Every *improvement* that is put upon real estate is the result of an *idea* in somebody's head. A skyscraper is another idea. The railway was another idea.The telephone and all those things are merely *symbols* which *represent ideas.* The washtub was the result of an idea. The thing hadn't existed before. There is no penny's worth of property on this earth that does not derive its pecuniary value from *ideas* and association of ideas applied and applied and applied again and again and again, as in the case of the steam engine. You have several hundred people contributing their ideas to the improvement and the final perfection of the great thing, whatever it is—telephone, telegraph, and all."

A book *does* consist solely of ideas, from the base to the summit, *like any other property,* and should not be put under the ban of any restriction, but should be the property of the author and his heirs forever and ever, just as a butcher shop is, or—*anything,* I don't care what it is. It all has the same basis. The law should recognize the right of perpetuity in this and every other kind of property. Yet for this property I do not ask that at all. Fifty years from now I shall not be here. I am sorry, but I shall not be here. Still, I should like to see the limit extended.

Of course we have to move by slow stages. When an event happens in this world, like that of 1714, under Queen Anne, it is a disaster, yet all the world imagines there was an element of justice in it. They do not know why they imagine it, but it is because somebody else has said so. The slow process of recovery has continued until our day, and will keep constantly progressing. First, fourteen years was added, and then a renewal for fourteen years; then you encountered Lord Macaulay, who made a speech on copyright when it was about to achieve a life of sixty years, which kept it at forty-two—a speech that was read and praised all over the world by everybody who did not know that Lord Macaulay did not know what he was talking about. So he inflicted this disaster upon his successors in the authorship of books. The recovery of our lost ground has to undergo regular and slow development—evolution.

Here is this bill, one instance of it. Make the limit the author's life and fifty years after, and, fifty years from now, Congress will see that that has not convulsed the world; has not destroyed any San Francisco. No earthquakes concealed in it anywhere. It has merely fed some starving author's children. Mrs. Stowe's two daughters were close neighbors of mine, and—well, they had their living very much limited.

That is about all I was to say, I believe. I have some notes—I don't know in which pocket I put them—and probably I can't read them when I find them.

There was another thing that came up in that committee meeting. Lord Thwing asked me on what ground I could bring forth such a monstrosity as that—the idea of a perpetual copyright on literature.

He said, "England does not do that." That was good argument. If England doesn't do a thing, that is all right. Why should anybody else? England doesn't do it. England stands for limited copyright, and will stand for limited copyright, and not give unlimited copyright to anybody's books.

I said, "You are excepting one book."

He said, "No; there is no book in England that has perpetual copyright."

I said, "Yes; there is one book in England that has perpetual copyright, and that is the Bible."

He said, "There is no such copyright on the Bible in England."

But I had the documents with me, and I was able to convince him that not only does England confer perpetual copyright upon the Old and New Testaments, but also on the Revised Scriptures, and also on four or five other theological books, and confers those perpetual copyrights and the profits that may accrue not upon some poor author and his children, but upon the well-to-do Oxford University Press, which can take care of itself without perpetual copyright. There was that one instance of injustice, the discrimination between the author of the present day and the author of thousands of years ago, whose copyright had really expired by the statute of limitations.

I say again, as I said in the beginning, I have no enmities, no animosities toward this bill. This bill is plenty righteous enough for me. I like to see all these industries and arts propagated and encouraged by this bill. This bill will do that, and I do hope that it will pass and have no deleterious effect. I do seem to have an extraordinary interest in a whole lot of arts and things. The bill is full of those that I have nothing to do with. But that is in line with my generous, liberal nature. I can't help it. I feel toward those same people the same wide charity felt by the man who arrived at home at two o'clock in the morning from the club and was feeling so perfectly satisfied with life, so happy, and so comfortable, and there was his house weaving and weaving and weaving around. So he watched his chance, and by and by when the steps got in his neighborhood he made a jump and climbed up on the portico.

And the house went on weaving and weaving and weaving, but he watched the door, and when it came around his way he plunged through it. He got to the stairs, and when he went up on all fours the house was so unsteady that he could hardly reach the top step; his toe hitched on that step, and of course he crumpled all down and rolled all the way down the stairs and fetched up at the bottom with his arm around the newel post, and he said, "God pity the poor sailors out at sea on a night like this!"

Text / Composite, based upon: *Statement before the Committee on Patents of the Senate and House of Representatives, conjointly, on the Bills S. 5330 and H.R. 19853,* Washington, 1906; "Mark Twain in White Amuses Congressmen," *Times,* December 8, 1906; "Copyright" in *MTS*(10):314–21; and *MTS*(23):323–29.

Hale / Edward Everett Hale (1822–1909). American clergyman, writer and editor. Pastor of New England churches from 1846 on, he was editor of the *Christian Examiner,* associate editor of *The Lookout,* and chaplain of the United States Senate (1903–09). He was a popular lecturer and a prolific writer who published more than sixty volumes of essays, stories, and sermons. His best known story is "The Man Without a Country" (1863).

perpetual copyright up to her day / Before the eighteenth century, the only form of copyright in England was that secured by entry in the Stationers' Register. This procedure ignored the author. The Stationers' Company was powerful in the sixteenth century and, aided by the Licensing Act (1662), well along into the seventeenth century. Its authority waned, however, and the lapse of the Licensing Act (1694) opened the door to unrestrained publishing and widespread piracy. In all this time booksellers, who were the publishers of the day, were more important than authors, who received little consideration.

they reduced it to fourteen years in Queen Anne's time / The first British copyright law was passed in 1709. Said to have been drafted by Jonathan Swift and called "An Act for the Encouragement of Learning," it provided that the owner of an old book, whether author or bookseller, had the exclusive right to print it for twenty-one years from April 10, 1710. The author of a new book was granted the monopoly of publishing for fourteen years and, if living at the end of that time, for a further fourteen years. Authors were slow to realize the advantages of this law. They continued to sell their work outright, and booksellers continued to believe that they owned copyright in perpetuity.

When an event happens . . . like that of 1714 . . . it is a disaster / The disastrous event of 1714 is not clear. The copyright act of 1709 remained in force until 1814, when a new law allowed copyright for twenty-eight years from date of first publication and, if the author were still living at the end of that time, copyright for the rest of his life.

Macaulay, who made a speech on copyright / Macaulay spoke in the House of Commons, February 5, 1841, when the House was considering a bill to extend copyright for sixty years after the death of the author. He proposed either copyright for life or for forty-two years, whichever was longer. The bill failed. When Viscount Mahon (Philip Henry, fifth earl of Stanhope) brought in a subsequent bill to extend copyright for twenty-five years after the author's death, Macaulay, before a committee of the Commons, April 6, 1842, proposed copyright for forty-two years from the date of first publication. Lord Mahon's bill passed.

· 162 ·

To entertain about twenty guests at a New Year's Eve dinner party in honor of Clara Clemens, Mark Twain put on a performance with the aid of a young man dressed in white, like the host. The pair had their arms around each other, and they were tied together by a pink sash that symbolized the ligature of the Siamese twins. Mark Twain harked back to upright Angelo and dissipated Luigi, whose vagaries he had described in a curtain speech at a performance of Pudd'nhead Wilson *in 1895. Convincingly acting his role by staggering around as the twin kept nipping from a flask, he brought down the house so noisily that he could not continue the "lecture." The report of the party on the front page of the* Times *gives a rare glimpse of Mark Twain, the actor, when not on public display. Yet he was so insistent upon keeping details of private occasions out of the papers that the bold guest who gave the story to the* Times *may have incurred strong displeasure.*

Burlesque Temperance Lecture

Dinner Party for Clara Clemens, 21 Fifth Avenue, New York, December 31, 1906

We come from afar. We come from very far; very far, indeed—as far as New Jersey. We are the Siamese twins, but we have been in this country long enough to know something of your customs, and we have learned as much of your language as it is written and spoken as—well—as the newspapers.

We are so much to each other, my brother and I, that what I eat nourishes him and what he drinks—ahem!—nourishes me. I often eat when I don't really want to because he is hungry, and, of course, I need hardly tell you that he often drinks when I am not thirsty.

I am sorry to say that he is a confirmed consumer of liquor—liquor, that awful, awful curse—while I, from principle, and also from the fact that I don't like the taste, never touch a drop.

[*Times:* "Mark then went on to say that he had been asked to take up the temperance cause and had done so with great success, taking his brother along as a horrible example."]

It has often been a source of considerable annoyance to me, when going about the country lecturing on temperance, to find myself at the head of a procession of white-ribbon people so drunk I couldn't see. But I am thankful to say that my brother has reformed.

[*Times:* "At this point the Siamese brother surreptitiously took a drink out of a flask."]

He hasn't touched a drop in three years.

[Twin: "Another drink."]

He never will touch a drop.

[Twin: "Another drink."]

Thank God for that.

[The twin took several drinks.]

And if, by exhibiting my brother to you, I can save any of you people here from the horrible curse of the demon rum, I shall be satisfied.

[*Times:* "Mark hiccoughed several times."]

Zish is wonderful reform—

[Another drink.]

Wonder'l 'form we are 'gaged in. Glorious work—we doin' glorious work—glori-o-u-s work. Best work ever done, my brother and work of reform, reform work, glorious work. I don' feel jus' right.

[When uproarious laughter stopped the show, Mark Twain was lurching tipsily about the improvised stage, and the twin was still putting down drinks. Then telharmonium music, transmitted from upper Broadway, ushered in the New Year with "Auld Lang Syne." Afterward, said the *Times,* "Mr. Clemens had something to say about politics," but his remarks were not reported.]

Text / "Mark Twain and Twin Cheer New Year's Party," *Times,* January 1, 1907.

telharmonium / Invented in 1906 by Thaddeus Cahill, an American who had been working on it since 1895, the telharmonium was the earliest musical device to generate sound electrically. Before the advent of loud speakers, rotating electromagnetic generators produced electrical impulses that were converted into sound by telephone receivers. Thus the telharmonium was the ancestor of present-day music synthesizers. The *Times* reported that "the first thing [Mark Twain] did in 1907 was to glory in the fact that he would be able to rejoice over other dead people when he died in having been the first man to have telharmonium music turned on in his house—'like gas.' "

· 163 ·

The Times *memorialized the centenary of the birth of Longfellow by publishing tributes and reminiscent comments from Mark Twain, Howells, Van Dyke, Thomas Wentworth Higginson, and John Bigelow. Mark Twain's acquaintance with the poet had been slight, but he remembered vividly his burlesque of Longfellow, Emerson, and Holmes at the Whittier dinner in 1877.*

Reminiscences of Longfellow and Others

Interview, February 23, 1907

I first lectured in New York in '67. The next year I lectured in Boston—I was always lecturing in those days. But on that first Boston occasion there was no Longfellow present, so far as I can remember. On that visit I called on Holmes. Again, another time, soon after that, my wife and I called on Emerson. Nothing happened. But—yes, yes, we went once, Mrs. Clemens and I, just about that time, and took luncheon with Longfellow at Craigie House. And then there was another time, during the same visit, when I was present at a little dinner given in Boston to Wilkie Collins. Longfellow was there, and Emerson, Whittier, Holmes, Whipple, J. T. Fields, and J. T. Trowbridge. Trowbridge survives. I also survive—ostensibly. The others are dead. I used to meet all those men with some little frequency—before they had passed away, of course—in those early days at Fields's house, both before and after Fields's death. Unhappily for the purposes of this Longfellow reminiscence, there was no striking incident, so far as I can recall, connected with my contact with Mr. Longfellow: whereas with those others it was different. In my various contacts with them things happened to happen that have left little landmarks in my memory and which might be edifying to relate if we were not on the subject of Longfellow.

In my mind's eye, however, I only see Mr. Longfellow. I see his silky white hair, his benignant face, as he appeared to me surrounded by his friends. But I don't hear his voice. It may be that things happened in his case, also, that left an impression in my memory. But at the present moment I can't recall them.

I remember that there were dinners in those days, just as there are now. One dinner that I especially recall took place just thirty years ago. This dinner was given in honor of Whittier's seventieth birthday. I was invited to attend. I thought I was going to do one of the gayest things in my whole career. But things happened differently, and before I left I had turned that dinner into a funeral. What did I do? The time has not yet come for a recital of those painful events. I will publish a full account of it, however, in my "Autobiography," which is running along indefinitely in *The North American Review*. The feeling of remorse for the part I took on that festive occasion has gone away now. But I confess that for two years after that dinner I used to kick myself regularly every morning for half an hour on account of what I had done.

Speaking of affairs of this kind, I have one most poignant recollection connected with Mr. Longfellow. This was not a dinner. It was a thing that happened not long after his death, when there was a Longfellow Memorial Authors' Reading in the Globe Theatre, in Boston. This reading was to begin at two o'clock in the afternoon. I was number three on the list of readers. The piece I was to read would ordinarily take twelve minutes to finish; but by art and hard work I reduced its length to ten and a half minutes before I carried it to Boston. My train was to leave Boston for New York at four o'clock. I vacated the stage of that theater the moment I had finished my brief stunt, and I had only barely time left in which to catch that train. When I left, third in the list, as I have said, that orgy had already endured two hours. Six other readers were still to be heard from, and not a man in the list experienced enough in the business to know that when a person has been reading twelve minutes the audience feel that he ought to be gagged, and that when he has been reading fifteen minutes they know he ought to be shot. I learned afterward—at least I was told by a person with an average reputation for trustworthiness, that at six o'clock half the audience had been carried out on stretchers, and that the rest were dead—with a lot of readers still to hear from.

Text / "Mark Twain Tells of His Visits," *Times*, Picture Section, February 24, 1907.

Collins / William Wilkie Collins (1824–89). British novelist. Called "Father of the English detective novel," he was a master of the involved plot, and an adept contriver of mystery and suspense. Among his many books are *The Dead Secret* (1857), *The Woman in*

White (1860), and *The Moonstone* (1868).

Whipple / Edwin Percy Whipple (1819–86). American essayist. He was a well-known lyceum lecturer, generally speaking on subjects literary and inspirational. Among his books are *Character and Characteristic Men* (1886), and *Recollections of Eminent Men* (1887).

Fields / James Thomas Fields (1817–81). American writer and editor. Senior partner of Fields and Osgood, publishers, he succeeded Lowell as editor of the *Atlantic Monthly* (1861–70), and was a popular lecturer whose Boston office was a speakers' exchange. Mark Twain and Howells met there in 1869. Fields wrote *Yesterdays With Authors* (1872), *In and Out of Doors With Charles Dickens* (1876), and other prose and verse. He was a convivial companion and good storyteller.

Trowbridge / John Townsend Trowbridge (1827–1916). American editor and writer. Contributing and managing editor of *Our Young Folks* (1865–73), which merged with *St. Nicholas,* he wrote children's books: *Cudjo's Cave* (1864) and others; verse, *The Book of Gold* (1877) and others; a postwar survey, *The South: a Tour of Its Battlefields and Ruined Cities* (1866); and autobiography, *My Own Story* (1903).

Authors' Reading / An authors' reading was a program given on behalf of a charitable or other cause by a group of writers who generally read from their own works. In *MTA*, 2:147–51, Mark Twain says that these "traveling afflictions" began about 1885 and that most of the readers ran far overtime because they had not rehearsed orally, with the aid of a watch. Howells, he complains, could never learn that useful method. Mark Twain was scrupulous about timing; if allotted ten minutes, he spoke for ten minutes. He usually asked for third place on the program so that he could leave when the readings dragged on.

· 164 ·

The Educational Alliance was founded by public-spirited citizens concerned with giving aid to immigrants. Among sponsors were Isador Straus, Felix M. Warburg, Benjamin Altman, and Albert Friedlander. The Children's Theatre was a project of the Alliance in which Mark Twain took great interest. At a matinee performance of The Prince and the Pauper, *which he attended with his daughter, Howells, and Daniel Frohman, he was delighted by a cast of juvenile actors, and by the audience of 800, mostly children. He made a curtain speech at the end of the second act.*

Curtain Speech

Performance of The Prince and the Pauper, *Educational Alliance, Children's Theatre, New York, April 14, 1907*

I have not enjoyed a play so much, so heartily, and so thoroughly since I played Miles Hendon twenty-two years ago. I used to play in this piece with my children, who, twenty-two years ago, were little youngsters. One of my daughters was the Prince, and a neighbor's daughter was the Pauper, and the children of other neighbors played other parts. But we never gave such a performance as we have seen here today. It would have been beyond us.

My late wife was the dramatist and stage manager. Our coachman was the stage manager, second in command. We used to play it in this simple way, and the one who used to bring in the crown on a cushion—he was a little fellow then—is now a clergyman way up high—six or seven feet high—and growing higher all the time. We played it well, but not as well as you see it here, for you see it done by practically trained professionals.

I was especially interested in the scene which we have just had, for Miles Hendon was my part. I did it as well as a person could who never remembered his part. The children all knew their parts. They did not mind if I did not know mine. I could thread a needle nearly as well as the player did whom you saw today. The words of my part I could supply on the spot. The words of the song that Miles Hendon sang here I did not catch. But I was great in that song. [Singing]:

There was a woman in her town,
She loved her husband well,
But another man just twice as well.

How is that?

It was so fresh and enjoyable to make up a new set of words each time that I played the part.

If I had a thousand citizens in front of me, I would like to give them information, but you children already know all that I have found out about the Educational Alliance. It's like a man living within thirty miles of Vesuvius and never knowing about a volcano. It's like living for a lifetime in Buffalo, eighteen miles from Niagara, and never going to see the Falls. So I had lived in New York and knew nothing about the Educational Alliance.

This theater is a part of the work, and furnishes pure and clean plays. This theater is an influence. Everything in the world is accomplished by influences which train and educate. When you get to be seventy-one and a half, as I am, you may think that your education is over, but it isn't.

If we had forty theaters of this kind in this city of four millions, how they would educate and elevate! We should have a body of educated theater-goers.

It would make better citizens, honest citizens. One of the best gifts a millionaire could make would be a theater here and a theater there. It would make of you a real Republic, and bring about an educational level.

[Interrupted by a young actress, he said]: I must apologize. I only want to tell this story and then I'll stop. [He told the story of a Negro who paid two dollars for a marriage license that had the wrong woman's name on it. But he concluded to marry that one rather than pay for another license because "there wasn't two dollars' difference between the two women."]

Text / Composite, based upon: "Mark Twain tells of Being an Actor," *Times,* April 15, 1907; "Educating Theatre-Goers" in *MTS* (10):71–73; and *MTS*(23):330–31.

There was a woman in her town, etc. / From a long ballad popular with rivermen in the nineteenth century. In *Life on the Mississippi,* chapter 3, a raftsman sings fourteen stanzas of this song.

· 165 ·

The 1907 Actors Fund Fair went on for ten days, sponsored by theater people, the press, and social leaders like Mrs. Stuyvesant Fish, Mrs. Herman Oelrichs, and Mrs. Arthur Iselin. There were bazaars, vaudeville staged by Robert Mantell, James J. Corbett, Vesta Victoria, and others, Green Room sideshows–albino girl, human skeleton, wild man from Harlem–a polling booth to vote for most popular actress at ten cents a vote, and a miniature race track where horse players could lose money as easily as at Saratoga. A soap booth was in charge of Douglas Fairbanks, who was said to be leaving the stage to go into the soap business. Mark Twain, scheduled to assist at the Century Theatre Club booth, unwittingly provoked a minor tempest. Mrs. Sidney Rosenfeld, president of the club and a follower of Mary Baker Eddy, said she would not have him because of his hostility to Christian Science. After indignation meetings and a flurry of correspondence, Daniel Frohman diplomatically eased the tension by transferring Mark Twain to the Players Club booth. On May 6 President Roosevelt, in Washington, pressed a button that lighted up the Metropolitan for the opening of the Fair. Daniel Frohman, president of the Actors Fund of America, made the first speech, Mark Twain followed, and afterward busily sold autographs.

Remarks

Actors Fund Fair, Metropolitan Opera House, New York, May 6, 1907

As Mr. Frohman has said, charity reveals a multitude of virtues. This is true, and it is to be proved here before the week is over. Mr. Frohman has told you something of the object and something of the character of the work. He told me he would do this—and he has kept his word! I had expected to hear of it through the newspapers. I wouldn't trust anything between Frohman and the newspapers—except when it's a case of charity!

You should all remember that the actor has been your benefactor many and many a year. When you have been weary and downcast he has lifted your heart out of gloom and given you a fresh impulse. You are all under obligation to him. This is your opportunity to be his benefactor—to help provide for him in his old age and when he suffers from infirmities.

At this fair no one is to be persecuted to buy. If you offer a twenty-dollar bill in payment for a purchase of one dollar, you will receive nineteen dollars in change. There is to be no robbery here. There is to be no creed here—no religion except charity. We want to raise $250,000—and that is a great task to attempt.

The President has set the fair in motion by pressing the button in Washington. Now your good wishes are to be transmuted into cash.

By virtue of the authority in me vested I declare the fair open. I call the ball game. Let the transmuting begin.

Text / Composite, based upon: "Actors' Fund Fair Opens With Vim," *Times,* May 7, 1907; "Charity and Actors" in *MTS*(10):284–85; and *MTS*(23):357–58.

Frohman / Daniel Frohman (1851–1940). American theatrical manager. Starting as office boy for the New York *Tribune* (1866), he spent five years in journalism, then managed touring companies and several New York theaters. Organizing the Lyceum Stock Company (1880), he attracted such stars as E. H. Sothern, James K. Hackett, Henry Miller, Henrietta Crossman, and May Robson. Among Frohman's reminiscences are *Memoirs of a Manager* (1911), *Daniel Frohman Presents* (1935), and *Encore* (1937).

the actor has been your benefactor / Mark Twain, as a quasi-actor himself, defended the profession, and sought to overcome prejudice against the theater that existed in the nineteenth and early twentieth centuries. One of his strongest statements is a denunciation of the Reverend Mr. Sabine, a New York clergyman who had refused to read the burial service for George Holland, an actor, and had contemptuously suggested that a little church around the corner would probably perform the service. Mark Twain condemned the insult to "honored and honorable old George Holland" inflicted by "this crawling, slimy, sanctimonious, self-righteous reptile!" See "The Indignity Put Upon the Remains of George Holland by the Rev. Mr. Sabine," *Galaxy,* February 1871.

We want to raise $250,000 / Receipts fell short of that sum, but they were respectable—something over $75,000. Mark Twain did his bit by returning to the fair to auction flowers on the afternoon of May 8. When people said they would be glad to take a chance on him, he replied, "I've been sold a good many times, but not in that way." He strolled in again during the evening of the eighth while Ethel Barrymore was auctioning dolls. The *Times* said next day: "The greeting they exchanged made all the men wish that they also were the authors of funny books."

The title of most popular actress went to Pauline Frederick, who won by 15,000 votes.

· 166 ·

In Annapolis to deliver a benefit lecture, probably a series of anecdotes, Mark Twain spent part of his leisure time rambling around the Naval Academy and getting caught smoking in a sector where, as sailors put it, the smoking lamp was out. Then he was fêted at dinner by the governor, assorted politicos and other important people at the official residence. Called upon to speak, naturally, the guest of honor responded in good form.

Dinner Speech

Government House, Annapolis, Maryland, May 10, 1907

Yes, I have been arrested. I was arrested twice, so that there could be no doubt about it. I have lived many years in the sight of my country an apparently uncaught and blameless life, a model for the young, an inspiring example for the hoary-headed. But at last the law has laid its hand upon me.

Mine was no ordinary offense. When I affront the law I choose to do so in no obscure, insignificant, trivial manner. Mine was a crime against nothing less than the federal government. The officers who arrested me were no common, or garden, policemen; they were clothed with the authority of the federal Constitution. I was charged with smoking a cigar within a government reservation. In fact, I was caught red-handed. I came near setting a stone pile on fire.

It is true that the arrest was not made effective. One of the party whispered to the marines what Governor Warfield was going to say, and did say, in introducing me to the audience at my lecture—that I was one of the greatest men in the world. I don't know who proposed to tell that to the marines, but it worked like a charm. The minions of the law faltered, hesitated, quailed, and today I am a free man. Twice they laid hands upon me; twice were overcome by my deserved reputation.

Perhaps I ought not to say myself that it is deserved. But who am I, to contradict the governor of Maryland? Worm that I am, by what right should I reverse the declared opinion of that man of wisdom and judgment whom I have learned to admire and trust?

I never admired him more than I did when he told my audience that they had with them the greatest man in the world. I believe that was his expression. I don't wish to undertake his sentiments, but I will go no further than that—at present. Why, it fairly warmed my heart. It almost made me glad to be there myself. I like good company.

Speaking of greatness, it is curious how many grounds there are for great reputations—how many different phases, that is to say, greatness may take on. There was Bishop Potter. He was arrested a few months ago for a crime similar to mine, though he lacked the imagination to select United States government property as the scene of his guilty deed. Now, Bishop Potter is a great man. I am sure he is, because a streetcar motorman told me so. A motorman is not a governor of Maryland, but then Bishop Potter is not a humorist. He could hardly expect a certificate like mine.

I rode with the motorman one day on the front seat of his car. There was a blockade before we got very far, and the motorman, having nothing to do, became talkative. "Oh, yes," he said, "I have a good many distinguished men on this trip. Bishop Potter often rides with me. He likes the front seat. Now there's a great man for you—Bishop Potter."

"It is true," I responded. "Dr. Potter is indeed a mighty man of God, an erudite theologian, a wise administrator of his diocese, an exegete of—"

"Yes," broke in the motorman, his face beaming with pleasure as he recognized the justice of my tribute and hastened to add one of his own. "Yes, and he's the only man who rides with me who can spit in the slot every time."

That's a good story, isn't it? I like a good story well told. That is the reason I am sometimes forced to tell them myself. Here is one, of which I was reminded yesterday as I was investigating the Naval Academy. I was much impressed with the Naval Academy. I was all over it, and now it is all over me. I am full of the navy. I wanted to march with them on parole, but they didn't think to ask me: curious inattention on their part, and I just ashore after a celebrated cruise.

While I was observing the navy on land, I thought of the navy at sea and of this story, so pathetic, so sweet, so really touching. This is one of my pet stories. Something in its delicacy, refinement, and the elusiveness of its humor fits my own quiet tastes.

The time is two A.M. after a lively night at the club. The scene is in front of his house. The house is swaying and lurching to and fro. He has succeeded in navigating from the club, but how is he going to get aboard this rolling, tossing thing? He watches the steps go back and forth, up and down. Then he makes a desperate resolve, braces himself, and as the steps come around he jumps, clutches the handrail, gets aboard, and pulls himself safely up on the piazza. With a like maneuver he gets through the door. Watching his chance, he gains the lowest step of the inside staircase, and painfully makes his way up the swaying and uncertain structure. He has almost reached the top when in a sudden lurch he catches his toe and falls back, rolling to the bottom. At this moment his wife, rushing out into the upper hall, hears coming up from the darkness below, from the discomfited figure sprawled on the floor with his arms around the newel post, this fervent, appropriate, and pious ejaculation, "God help the poor sailors out at sea."

I trust this matter of my arrest will not cause my friends to turn from me. It is true that, no matter what may be said of American public morals, the private morals of Americans as a whole are exceptionally good. I do not mean to say that in their private lives all Americans are faultless. I hardly like to go that far, being a man of carefully weighed words and under a peculiarly vivid sense of the necessity of moderation in statement. I should like to say that we are a faultless people, but I am restrained by recollection. I know several persons who have erred and transgressed—to put it plainly, they have done wrong. I have heard of still others—of a number of persons, in fact, who are not perfect. I am not perfect myself. I confess it. I would have confessed it before the lamentable event of yesterday. For that was not the first time I ever did wrong. No; I have done several things which fill my soul now with regret and contrition.

I remember, I remember it so well. I remember it as if it were yesterday, the first time I ever stole a watermelon. Yes, the first time. At least I think it was the first time, or along about there. It was, it was, must have been, about 1848, when I was thirteen or fourteen years old. I remember that watermelon well. I can almost taste it now.

Yes, I stole it. Yet why use so harsh a word? It was the biggest of the load on a farmer's wagon standing in the gutter in the old town of Hannibal, Missouri. While the farmer was busy with another—another—customer, I withdrew this melon. Yes, "I stole" is too strong. I extracted it. I retired it from circulation. And I myself retired with it.

The place to which the watermelon and I retired was a lumber yard. I knew a nice, quiet alley between the sweet-smelling planks and to that sequestered spot I carried the melon. Indulging a few moments' contemplation of its freckled rind, I broke it open with a stone, a rock, a dornick, in boy's language.

It was green—impossibly, hopelessly green. I do not know why this circumstance should have affected me, but it did. It affected me deeply. It altered for me the moral values of the universe. It wrought in me a moral revolution. I began to reflect. Now, reflection is the beginning of reform. There can be no reform without reflection.

I asked myself what course of conduct I should pursue. What would conscience dictate? What should a high-minded young man do after retiring a green watermelon? What would George Washington do? Now was the time for all the lessons inculcated at Sunday school to act.

And they did act. The word that came to me was "restitution." Obviously, there lay the path of duty. I reasoned with myself. I labored. At last I was fully resolved. "I'll do it," said I. "I'll take him back his old melon." Not many boys would have been heroic, would so clearly have seen the right and so sternly have resolved to do it. The moment I reached that resolution I felt a strange uplift. One always feels an uplift when he turns from wrong to righteousness. I arose, spiritually strengthened, renewed and refreshed, and in the strength of that refreshment carried back the watermelon—that is, I carried back what was left of it—and made him give me a ripe one.

But I had a duty toward that farmer, as well as to myself. I was as severe on him as the circumstances deserved. I did not spare him. I told him he ought to be ashamed of himself giving his—his customers green melons. And he was ashamed. He said he was. He said he felt as badly about it as I did. In this he was mistaken. He hadn't eaten any of the melon. I told him that the one instance was bad enough, but asked him to consider what would become of him if this should become a habit with him. I pictured his future. And I saved him. He thanked me and promised to do better.

We should always labor thus with those who have taken the wrong road. Very likely this was the farmer's first false step. He had not gone far, but he had put his foot on the downward incline. Happily, at this moment a friend appeared—a friend who stretched out a helping hand and held him back. Others might have hesitated, have shrunk from speaking to him of his error. I did not hesitate nor shrink. And it is one of the gratifications of my life that I can look back on what I did for that man in his hour of need.

The blessing came. He went home with a bright face to his rejoicing wife and I—I got a ripe melon. I trust it was with him as it was with me. Reform with me was no transient emotion, no passing episode, no Philadelphia uprising. It was permanent. Since that day I have never stolen a water—never stolen a green watermelon.

Text / "Mighty Mark Twain Overawes Marines," *Times,* May 12, 1907.

Warfield / Edwin Warfield (1848–1920). American politician. He was president of the Maryland Senate (1886), surveyor of the Port of Baltimore (1886–90), and governor of Maryland (1904–08).

slot / On a cable car the slot was a continuous opening at the top of a conduit through which the shank of the grip passed and along which it moved. On an electric trolley car there was evidently a comparable opening to test the passenger's accuracy.

· 167 ·

Early in May 1907, Mark Twain was informed that Oxford had conferred upon him an honorary Litt.D. He was delighted. In a dictation of May 23, 1907, he says that he was as happy with a new degree as an Indian with a fresh scalp. But he was also human enough to grumble privately about American universities that, year after year, had overlooked him when bestowing honors upon hundreds of men, many of them nonentities, few of them internationally known. He had a point. We may wonder at the academic obtuseness that failed to recognize the most famous American of his time. To receive the Oxford degree in person, he embarked for England aboard the S.S. Minneapolis *on June 8, chatting with reporters before sailing.*

Interview

Aboard S.S. Minneapolis, *New York, June 8, 1907*

I may never go to London again until I come back to this sphere after I am dead, and then I would like to live in London. I spent seven years there, and I am going back to see the boys.

Work? I retired from work on my seventieth birthday. Since then I have been putting in merely twenty-six hours a day dictating my autobiography, which, as John Phoenix said in regard to his autograph, may be relied upon as authentic, as it is written exclusively by me, but I don't want it published until after I am dead. And I want to be thoroughly dead when it is published. No rumors, but really dead. I have made it as caustic, fiendish, and as devilish as I possibly can. I might be what you call a sensation, for I have spared no one. It will fill many volumes, and I will go right on writing until I am called to the angels and receive a harp.

The story of my life will make certain people sit up and take notice, but I will use my influence not to have it published until the persons mentioned in it and their children and grandchildren are dead. I tell you it will be something awful. It will be what you might call good reading.

[He was asked what notable people had come down to see him off.] I don't know. I am so shy. My shyness takes a peculiar phase. I never look a person in the face. The reason is that I am afraid they may know me and that I may not know them, which makes it very embarrassing for both of us. I always wait for the other person to speak. I know lots of people, but I don't know who they are. It is all a matter of ability to observe things. I never observe anything now. I gave up the habit years ago. You should keep a habit up if you want to become proficient in it. For instance, I was a pilot once, but I gave it up, and I do not believe the captain of the *Minneapolis* would let me navigate his ship to London. Still, if I think that he is not on the job I may go up on the bridge and offer him a few suggestions.

Text / Composite, based upon: "Mark Twain Sails for Oxford Honors," *Times,* June 9, 1907; a fragment erroneously included in "Dress Reform and Copyright," *MTS*(10):88–89.

John Phoenix / Pen name of George Horatio Derby (1823–61), also known as "Squibob." American soldier and humorist. A West Point graduate and Mexican War veteran, he was in the United States Topographical Bureau (1847–48), explored Minnesota Territory (1848–49), then conducted explorations in California (1849–56), where he turned to humor as a relief from the exactions of engineering. Examples are *Phoenixiana* (1855), and *The Squibob Papers* (1859).

· 168 ·

Mark Twain's stay in England was a continual round of engagements and of being greeted by everybody, from longshoremen who hailed him as he disembarked, to King Edward at the royal garden party. At this event a great crush of celebrities British and foreign swirled about the grounds of Windsor Castle. Mark Twain went up from London with Henniker Heaton, Sir Henry Campbell-Bannerman, Sir Mortimer Durand, Fridtjof Nansen, and Ellen Terry. From the Windsor railroad station to the castle they drove through streets lined by cheering crowds, Mark Twain bowing repeatedly right and left like a visiting potentate. He chatted with the king and queen, and naturally told reporters about it.

Monologue on the Royal Garden Party

Windsor Castle, England, June 22, 1907

His Majesty was very courteous. In the course of the conversation I reminded him of an episode of sixteen years ago, when I had the honor to walk a mile with him at the time he was taking the waters at Homburg in Germany. I said that I had often told about that episode, and that whenever I was the historian I made good history of it, and it was worth listening to, but that it had found its way into print once or twice in an unauthentic way and was badly damaged thereby. I said I should like to go on repeating this history, but that I should be quite fair and reasonably honest, and while I should probably never tell it twice in the same way, I should at least never allow it to deteriorate in my hands.

His Majesty intimated his willingness that I should continue to disseminate that piece of history, and he added a compliment, saying that he knew good and sound history would not suffer at my hands, and that if the good and sound history needed any improvement beyond the facts he would trust me to furnish these embellishments.

I think it is not an exaggeration to say that the Queen looks as young and beautiful as she did thirty-five years ago, when I saw her first. I didn't say this to her, because I learned long ago never to say the obvious thing, but leave the obvious thing to commonplace and inexperienced people to say.

That she still looks to me as young and beautiful as she looked thirty-five years ago is good evidence that ten thousand people have already noticed this, and have mentioned it to her. I could have said it and spoken the truth, but I have been too wise for that. I have kept the remark unuttered, and saved her Majesty the vexation of hearing it the ten thousandth-and-oneth time.

All that report about my proposal to buy Windsor Castle and its grounds is a false rumor—I started it myself.

One newspaper said I patted his Majesty on the shoulder—an impertinence of which I was not guilty; I was reared in the most exclusive circles of Missouri and I know how to behave. The King rested his hand upon my arm a moment or two while we were chatting, but he did it of his own accord. The newspaper which said I talked with her Majesty with my hat on spoke the truth, but my reasons for doing it were good and sufficient—in fact unassailable. Rain was threatening, the temperature had cooled, and the Queen said, "Please put your hat on, Mr. Clemens." I begged her pardon and excused myself from doing it. After a moment or two she said, "Mr. Clemens, put your hat on"—with a slight emphasis on the word "on"—"I can't allow you to catch cold here." When a beautiful queen commands it is a pleasure to obey, and this time I obeyed—but I had already disobeyed once, which is more than a subject would have felt justified in doing; and so it is true, as charged; I did talk with the Queen of England with my hat on, but it wasn't fair in the newspaper man to charge it upon me as an impoliteness, since there were reasons for it which he could not know of.

Text / Composite, based upon: "Twain Amuses King and Queen," *Times,* June 23, 1907; Sydney Brooks, "England's Ovation to Mark Twain," *Harper's Weekly* 51, no. 2640 (July 27, 1907):1086; *MTB,* 4:1385–86.

· 169 ·

Among the 250 guests at the Society of the Pilgrims luncheon were H. Rider Haggard, Anthony Hope Hawkins, Sir Gilbert Parker, Chauncey Depew, T. P. O'Connor, Sir Thomas Lipton, H. Beerbohm Tree, Sir Douglas Straight, Henry Rogers, Norman Hapgood, and T. Fisher Unwin. On the speakers' table was a statuette of Mark Twain garbed in a pilgrim's robe, carrying a long pen in lieu of a staff, and leading a huge frog. On the menu were Saumon du Mississippi Froid, Asperges Sauce Hannibal, Savoury Calaveras, Tokay Extra Dry, Braunelberger, and Chandon Dry Imperial. The Right Honorable Augustine Birrell, chief secretary for Ireland, presided. Introducing the guest of honor, he called Mark Twain "a true consolidator of nations," a man whose "delightful humor . . . dissipates and destroys national prejudices," whose "love of truth . . . and love of honor overflow all boundaries. . . . Long may he live to reap the plentiful harvest of hearty honest human affection."

Our Guest

Society of the Pilgrims Luncheon for Mark Twain,
Hotel Savoy, London, June 25, 1907

Pilgrims, I desire first to thank those undergraduates of Oxford. When a man has grown so old as I am, when he has reached the verge of seventy-two years, there is nothing that carries him back to the dreamland of his life, to his boyhood, like the recognition of those young hearts up yonder. And so I thank them out of my heart. I desire, too, to thank the Pilgrims of New York also for their kind notice and message which they have cabled over here. Mr. Birrell says he does not know how he got here. But he will be able to get away all right—he has not drunk anything since he came here. I am glad to know about those friends of his—Otway and Chatterton—fresh, new names to me. I am glad of the disposition he has shown to rescue them from the evils of poverty, and if they are still in London, I hope to have a talk with them. For a while I thought he was going to tell us the effect which my books had upon his growing manhood. I thought he was going to tell us how much that effect amounted to, and whether it really made him what he now is, but with the discretion born of

Parliamentary experience he dodged that, and we do not know whether he read the books or not. He did that very neatly. I could not do it any better myself.

My books have had effects, and very good ones, too, here and there, and some others not so good. There is no doubt about that. But I remember one monumental instance of it years and years ago. Professor Norton, of Harvard, was over here, and when he came back to Boston I went out with Howells to call on him. Norton was allied in some way by marriage with Darwin. Mr. Norton was very gentle in what he had to say, and almost delicate, and he said: "Mr. Clemens, I have been spending some time with Mr. Darwin in England, and I should like to tell you something connected with that visit. You were the object of it, and I myself would have been very proud of it, but you may not be proud of it. At any rate, I am going to tell you what it was, and to leave you to regard it as you please. Mr. Darwin took me up to his bedroom and pointed out certain things there—pitcher plants, and so on, that he was measuring and watching from day to day—and he said, 'The chambermaid is permitted to do what she pleases in this room, but she must never touch those plants and never touch those books on that table by that candle. With those books I read myself to sleep every night.' Those were your own books." I said, "There is no question to my mind as to whether I should regard that as a compliment or not. I do regard it as a very great compliment, and a very high honor, that that great mind, laboring for the whole human race, should rest itself on my books. I am proud that he should read himself to sleep with them."

Now, I could not keep that to myself—I was so proud of it. As soon as I got home to Hartford I called up my oldest friend—and dearest enemy on occasion—the Rev. Joseph Twichell, my pastor, and I told him about that, and, of course, he was full of interest and venom. Those people who get no compliments like that feel like that. He went off. He did not issue any applause of any kind, and I did not hear of that subject for some time. But when Mr. Darwin passed away from this life, and some time after Darwin's *Life and Letters* came out, the Rev. Mr. Twichell procured an early copy of that work and found something in it which he considered applied to me. He came over to my house—it was snowing, raining, sleeting, but that did not make any difference to Twichell. He produced the book, and turned over and over, until he came to a certain place, when he said, "Here, look at this letter from Mr. Darwin to Sir Joseph Hooker." What Mr. Darwin said—I give you the idea and not the very words—was this: I do not know whether I ought to have devoted my whole life to these drudgeries in natural history and the other sciences or not, for while I may have gained in one way I have lost in another. Once I had a fine perception and appreciation of high literature, but in me that quality is atrophied. "That was the reason," said Mr. Twichell, "he was reading your books."

Mr. Birrell has touched lightly—very lightly, but in not an uncomplimentary way—on my position in this world as a moralist. I am glad to have that recognition, too, because I have suffered since I have been in this town; in the first place, right away, when I came here, from a newsman going around with a great red, highly displayed placard in the place of an apron. He was selling newspapers, and there were two sentences on that placard which would have been all right if they had been punctuated; but they ran those two sentences together without a comma or anything, and that would naturally create a wrong impression, because it said, "Mark Twain arrives Ascot Cup stolen." No doubt many a person was misled by those sentences joined together in that unkind way. I have no doubt my character has suffered from it. I suppose I ought to defend my character, but how can I defend it? I can say here and now—and anybody can see by my face that I am sincere, that I speak the truth—that I have never seen that Cup. I have not got the Cup—I did not have a chance to get it. I have always had a good character in that way. I have hardly ever stolen anything, and if I did steal anything I had discretion enough to know about the value of it first. I do not steal things that are likely to get myself into trouble. I do not think any of us do that. I know we all take things—that is to be expected—but really, I have never taken anything, certainly in England, that amounts to any great thing. I do confess that when I was here seven years ago I stole a hat, but that did not amount to anything. It was not a good hat, and was only a clergyman's hat, anyway.

I was at a luncheon party, and Archdeacon Wilberforce was there also. I daresay he is an Archdeacon now—he was a Canon then—and he was serving in the Westminster Battery, if that is the proper term—I do not know, as you mix military and ecclesiastical things together so much. He left the luncheon table before I did. He began this, I did steal his hat, but he began by taking mine. I make that interjection because I would not accuse Archdeacon Wilberforce of stealing my hat—I should not think of it. I confine that phrase to myself. He merely took my hat. And with good judgment, too—it was a better hat than his. He came out before the luncheon was over, and sorted the hats in the hall, and selected one which suited. It happened to be mine. He went off with it. When I came out by and by there was no hat there which would go on my head except his, which was left behind. My head was not the customary size just at that time. I had been receiving a good many very nice and complimentary attentions, and my head was a couple of sizes larger than usual, and his hat just suited me. The bumps and corners were all right intellectually. There were results pleasing to me—possibly so to him. He found out whose hat it was, and wrote me saying it was pleasant that all the way home, whenever he met anybody his gravities, his solemnities, his deep thoughts, his eloquent remarks were all snatched up by the people he met, and mistaken for brilliant humorisms.

I had another experience. It was not unpleasing. I was received with a deference which was entirely foreign to my experience by everybody whom I met, so that before I got home I had a much higher opinion of myself than I have ever had before or since. And there is in that very connection an incident which I remember at that old date which is rather melancholy to me, because it shows how a person can deteriorate in a mere seven years. It is seven years ago. I have not that hat now. I was going down Pall Mall, or some other of your big streets, and I recognized that that hat needed ironing. I went into a big shop and passed in my hat, and asked that it might be ironed. They were courteous, very courteous, even courtly. They brought that hat back to me presently very sleek and nice, and I asked how much there was to pay. They replied that they did not charge the clergy anything. I have cherished the delight of that moment from that day to this. It was the first thing I did the other day to go and hunt up that shop and hand in my hat to have it ironed. I said when it came back, "How much to pay?" They said, "Ninepence." In seven years I have acquired all that worldliness, and I am sorry to be back where I was seven years ago.

But now I am chaffing and chaffing and chaffing here, and I hope you will forgive me for that; but when a man stands on the verge of seventy-two you know perfectly well that he never reached that place without knowing what this life is—heartbreaking bereavement. And so our reverence is for our dead. We do not forget them; but our duty is toward the living; and if we can be cheerful, cheerful in spirit, cheerful in speech and in hope, that is a benefit to those who are around us.

My own history includes an incident which will always connect me with England in a pathetic way, for when I arrived here seven years ago with my wife and daughter—we had gone around the globe lecturing to raise money to clear off a debt—my wife and one of my daughters started across the ocean to bring to England our eldest daughter. She was twenty-four years of age and in the bloom of young womanhood, and we were unsuspecting. When my wife and daughter—and my wife has passed from this life since—when they had reached mid-Atlantic, a cablegram—one of those heartbreaking cablegrams which we all in our days have to experience—was put into my hand. It stated that that daughter of ours had gone to her long sleep. And so, as I say, I cannot always be cheerful, and I cannot always be chaffing; I must sometimes lay the cap and bells aside, and recognize that I am of the human race like the rest, and must have my cares and griefs. And, therefore, I noticed what Mr. Birrell said—I was so glad to hear him say it—something that was in the nature of these verses here at the top of this menu.

> He lit our life with shafts of sun
>   And vanquished pain.
> Thus two great nations stand as one
>   In honoring Twain.

I am very glad to have those verses. I am very glad and grateful for what Mr. Birrell said in that connection. I have received since I have been here, in this one week, hundreds of letters from all conditions of people in England—men, women, and children—and there is in them compliment, praise, and, above all and better than all, there is in them a note of affection. Praise is well, compliment is well, but affection—that is the last and final and most precious reward that any man can win, whether by character or achievement, and I am very grateful to have that reward. All these letters make me feel that here in England—as in America—when I stand under the English flag, I am not a stranger. I am not an alien, but at home.

Text / Composite, based upon: Sydney Brooks, "England's Ovation to Mark Twain," *Harper's Weekly* 51, no. 2640 (July 27, 1907):1088; "Books, Authors, and Hats" in *MTS*(10):31–40; and *MTS* (23):335–43.

Birrell / Augustine Birrell (1850–1923). British statesman and writer. Member of Parliament from Fifeshire West and Bristol North (1889–1900, 1906–18), he was professor of law at the University of London (1896–99), president of the Board of Education (1905–07), and chief secretary for Ireland (1907–16). He collected his critical essays as *Obiter Dicta* (1884), and *More Obiter Dicta* (1924), edited Boswell's life of Johnson (1897), and wrote biographies of Charlotte Bronte, Andrew Marvell, and William Hazlitt.

Otway / Thomas Otway (1753–85). British dramatist. After Dryden, Otway was the principal dramatist of the Restoration. Of the classical school, he wrote tragedies in blank verse; the best known are *The Orphan* (1680), and *Venice Preserved* (1682).

Chatterton / Thomas Chatterton (1752–70). British poet. At the age of twelve he began writing poems in a pseudo-medieval style purporting to be the lost literary remains of a fifteenth-century monk named Thomas Rowley. Some critics maintain that Chatterton, a suicide at the age of eighteen, could have become one of the great English poets.

Norton / Charles Eliot Norton (1827–1908). American scholar. He was editor, with Lowell, of the *North American Review* (1864–68), and professor of art history at Harvard (1874–98). He translated Dante's *Divina Commedia* (1892), and edited the letters of Lowell (1893).

Hooker / Joseph Dalton Hooker (1817–1911). British botanist. Surgeon and naturalist of the Ross antarctic expedition (1839–43), he accompanied parties exploring the Himalayas and eastern Bengal (1847–51), Syria and Palestine (1860), and the Rocky Mountains and California (1877). Hooker, a friend of Darwin, was influential in persuading him to publish *Origin of Species.*

my position as a moralist / In his introduction Birrell, alluding to "the wild humorist of the Pacific slope" and "the moralist of the Main," said, "Here he is, still the humorist, still the moralist. His humor enlivens and enlightens his morality, and his morality is all the better for his humor. That is one of the reasons why we love him."

these verses here / On the menu was a short poem, "To Mark Twain," by Owen Seaman, editor of *Punch:* "Still where the countless ripples laugh above / The blue of halcyon seas long may you keep / Your course unbroken, buoyed upon a love / Ten thousand fathoms deep!" See *MTB,* 4:1389.

· 170 ·

Mark Twain was chief guest at the lord mayor's dinner for his fellow members of the Savage Club. In a dictation of August 16, 1907, he says that on the way down from Oxford on the afternoon of June 29 he had been talked into stopping at Stratford to call on Marie Corelli. The visit so fatigued him, he says, and the lady so annoyed him that by the time he got to the lord mayor's dinner he made a botch of his speech. The audience did not think so. For his comments on Miss Corelli, see MTE:*323–28.*

Dinner Speech

Lord Mayor's Dinner for the Savage Club,
Mansion House, London, June 29, 1907

I don't make speeches—as I have no time to prepare them. I have been so busy since I landed in England trying to rehabilitate my character about that Ascot Cup that I have had no time to prepare a speech. I do assure you that I am not so dishonest as I look.

I began years and years ago to frame for myself a moral constitution that would impress the world. I was not so honest then as I am now—but I was reasonably honest. Since that time I have done nothing that has called my honesty into question. Well, you know how a man is influenced by his surroundings. I had once an experience which I have ever used as a warning to myself, and the result is I have climbed step by step to where I am now—or to where I was before the Ascot Cup was stolen. You don't know the difference between the true claim to honesty—which did not exist—at the time of the experience to which I refer, and the claim of today which does exist.

It all came about by an indiscretion on my part, when they were passing round the hat for a collection. In the city where I lived at that time—it is twenty-five or thirty years ago—there was a man of most noble and self-sacrificing nature, Father Hawley. He used to go into the poorer parts of the town, and so got to know the people and their needs, and he would raise collections for them. Every year when the time came round Father Hawley would assemble the congregation and would tell us what he had done. The place was always crowded, for the man had a great fascination.

I was there once. The place was thronged and suffocatingly hot. Well, they made a mistake that ought never to have been made. You know that there are moments when you are so moved by what you hear that you want to put your hand in your pocket and give all you have. If they had passed the hat round at the right moment they would have got a collection worth having. You should not let the emotional feeling fall off. If you want a good collection have one speaker, not a hundred.

After Father Hawley had spoken for twenty minutes the house was so thrown into tears that it was the dampest place I have ever known on shore. The speaker had the power of putting those vivid pictures before one. We were all affected. That was the moment for the hat. I would have put two hundred dollars in it. Before he had finished I could have put in four hundred dollars. I felt I could have filled out a blank check—with somebody else's name—and dropped it in. I was full of generosity.

But they didn't pass the hat round then. They got another man to stand up and talk for another fifteen minutes. Well, he had none of the experience of Father Hawley, and could not move the house. He cast a chill over us. I felt that chill, and reduced my subscription to two hundred dollars. Then another man got up and swept the rest of it away, so I had all the four hundred dollars left, and I was not in a hurry at all for them to bring round the hat. The inspiration was gone. I knew human nature, and my desire to contribute had dribbled away. When at last the hat got to me I put in ten cents—and took out twenty-five.

Now it is not right to put in ten cents and take out twenty-five. I knew that, but my moral character was building and it was a lesson to me always after that to avoid temptation. And from that day to this I have preserved that lesson and have never gone into a place where they were going to lift a collection.

Seeing Mr. Bram Stoker reminds me of the first time he brought Sir Henry Irving to America. At a dinner given to celebrate the occasion Mr. Stoker told an anecdote that has remained in my mind ever since. It was a christening by a minister. Mr. Stoker described him as a Scotch Presbyterian, but I don't know what that is. The house was full of the baby's kinsfolk, and the minister was betrayed into oratory—oratory of the spread-eagle kind, which is very dangerous, as it gets you into the clouds, and without a parachute you cannot get down. He took the child from the father. The little one was about the size of a sweet potato. He held it in his hands until the silence should work, and then "Ah," he said, "I see in your faces disparagement. And why? Because he is little. Because he is little you disparage him. If there was more of him you would look into his future. But the great are framed out of the little. The vast oak tree grows from the little acorn. He may be the greatest general; he may be Napoleon and Alexander compacted into one. He may be a poet, the greatest poet the world has ever seen; a Shakespeare, a Homer, a Shelley, a Keats, a Byron compacted into one. He may sing songs that may live as long as the land. He may become—What's his name?"—this to the father. "Mary Ann," replied the parent.

I am going from here in a week or two. I came to get the honorary degree from Oxford, and I would have encompassed the seven seas for an honor like that—the greatest honor that has ever fallen to my share. I cannot feel too grateful to the University and to the Lord Curzon for conferring it upon me, and I am sure my country must appreciate it, because first and foremost it is an honor to my country.

And now I am going home again across the sea. I am in spirit young but in the flesh old, so that it is unlikely that when I go away I shall ever see England again. But I shall ever retain the recollection of what I have experienced here in the way of generous, most kindly welcomes. I took in the welcome you gave me when I entered the room, and I am duly grateful for it. I suppose I must say good-by, and in saying good-by, I do so not with my lips, but with my whole heart.

Text / Composite, based upon: "Lord Mayor's Greeting to the Savages," London *Telegraph,* July 1, 1907; "The Ascot Gold Cup," *MTS*(10):384–85.

Stoker / Bram Abraham Stoker (1847–1912). British writer and theatrical manager. He was an Irish civil servant for ten years, then for thirty years the manager of Henry Irving. Stoker is best known for his horror novel, *Dracula* (1897), which is still published in paperback editions.

Lord Curzon / George Nathaniel, first baron of Kedleston and first marquis Curzon of Kedleston (1859–1925). British statesman. He was undersecretary of state for India (1891–92), undersecretary for foreign affairs (1895–96), and viceroy of India (1898–1905). Chancellor of Oxford at the time of Mark Twain's visit, he was afterward in the World War I cabinet, Lord Chancellor (1916–24), and secretary of state for foreign affairs (1919–24). Among his many books are *Russia and Central Asia* (1889), *Problems of the Far East*(1894), and *Frontiers* (1908).

· 171 ·

When the American Society gave its Fourth of July dinner in the largest banqueting hall in London, every seat was taken, and the gallery was filled with ladies. Ambassador Whitelaw Reid was there, Nicholas Murray Butler, Sir Norman Lockyer, Justice Oliver Wendell Holmes, Sir William Ramsay, Major General R. S. S. Baden-Powell, Augustine Birrell, Field Marshal Sir Evelyn Wood, T. P. O'Connor, Ridgeley Carter, and some five hundred other gentlemen. Newton Crane presided, and former Ambassador Choate called upon Mark Twain to respond to the toast, "The Day We Celebrate."

The Day We Celebrate

American Society Dinner, Hotel Cecil, London, July 4, 1907

Mr. Chairman, my Lord, and gentlemen: Once more it happens, as it has happened so often since I arrived in England a week or two ago, that instead of celebrating the Fourth of July properly as has been indicated, I have to first take care of my personal character.

Sir Mortimer Durand still remains unconvinced. Well, I tried to convince these people from the beginning that I did not take the Ascot Cup; and as I have failed to convince anybody that I did not take the Cup, I might as well confess I did take it and be done with it. I don't see why this uncharitable feeling should follow me everywhere, and why I should have that crime thrown up to me on all occasions. The tears I have wept over it ought to have created a different feeling than this—and, besides, I don't think it is very right or fair that, considering England has been trying to take a cup of ours for forty years—I don't see why they should make so much trouble when I tried to go into the business myself.

Sir Mortimer Durand, too, has had trouble from going to a dinner here, and he has told you what he suffered in consequence. But what did he suffer? He only missed his train and one night of discomfort, and he remembers it to this day. Oh! if you could only think what I have suffered from a similar circumstance. Two or three years ago, in New York, with that Society there which is made up of people from all British Colonies, and from Great Britain generally, who were educated in British colleges and British schools, I was there to respond to a toast of some kind or other, and I did then what I have been in the habit of doing, from a selfish motive, for a long time, and that is, I got myself placed No. 3 in the list of speakers—then you get home early.

I had to go five miles upriver, and had to catch a particular train or not get there. But see the magnanimity which is born in me, which I have cultivated all my life. A very famous and very great British clergyman came to me presently, and he said: "I am away down in the list; I have got to catch a certain train this Saturday night; if I don't catch that train I shall be carried beyond midnight and break the Sabbath. Won't you change places with me?" I said: "Certainly I will." I did it at once. Now, see what happened. Talk about Sir Mortimer Durand's sufferings for a single night! I have suffered ever since because I saved that gentleman from breaking the Sabbath—yes, saved him. I took his place, but I lost my train, and it was I who broke the Sabbath. Up to that time I had never broken the Sabbath in my life, and from that day to this I never have kept it.

Oh! I am learning much here tonight. I find I didn't know anything about the American Society—that is, I didn't know its chief virtue. I didn't know its chief virtue until his Excellency our Ambassador revealed it—I may say, exposed it. I was intending to go home on the 13th of this month, but I look upon that in a different light now. I am going to stay here until the American Society pays my passage.

Our Ambassador has spoken of our Fourth of July, and the noise it makes. We have got a double Fourth of July—a daylight Fourth and a midnight Fourth. During the day in America, as our Ambassador has indicated, we keep the Fourth of July properly in a reverent spirit. We devote it to teaching our children patriotic things—reverence for the Declaration of Independence. We honor the day all through the daylight hours, and when night comes we dishonor it. Presently—before long—they are getting nearly ready to begin now—on the Atlantic coast, when night shuts down, that pandemonium will begin, and there will be noise, and noise, and noise—all night long—and there will be more than noise—there will be people crippled, there will be people killed, there will be people who will lose their eyes, and all through that permission which we give to irresponsible boys to play with firearms and firecrackers, and all sorts of dangerous things. We turn that Fourth of July, alas! over to rowdies to drink and get drunk and make the night hideous, and we cripple and kill more people than you would imagine.

We probably began to celebrate our Fourth of July night in that way one hundred and twenty-five years ago, and on every Fourth of July night since these horrors have grown and grown, until now, in our five thousand towns of America, somebody gets killed or crippled on every Fourth of July night, besides those cases of sick persons whom we never hear of, who die as the result of the noise or the shock. They cripple and kill more people on the Fourth of July in America than they kill and cripple in our wars nowadays, and there are no pensions for these folk. And, too, we burn houses. Really we destroy more property on every Fourth of July night than the whole of the United States was worth one hundred and twenty-five years ago. Really our Fourth of July is our day of mourning, our day of sorrow. Fifty thousand people who have lost friends, or who have had friends crippled, receive that Fourth of July, when it comes, as a day of mourning for the losses they have sustained in their families.

I have suffered in that way myself. I have had relatives killed in that way. One was in Chicago years ago—an uncle of mine, just as good an uncle as I have ever had, and I had lots of them—yes, uncles to burn, uncles to spare. This poor uncle, full of patriotism, opened his mouth to hurrah, and a rocket went down his throat. Before that man could ask for a drink of water to quench that thing, it blew up and scattered him all over the forty-five states, and—really, now, this is true—I know about it myself—twenty four hours after that it was raining buttons, recognizable as his, on the Atlantic seaboard. A person cannot have a disaster like that and be entirely cheerful the rest of his life. I had another uncle, on an entirely different Fourth of July, who was blown up that way, and really it trimmed him as it would a tree. He had hardly a limb left on him anywhere. All we have left now is an expurgated edition of that uncle. But never mind about these things; they are merely passing matters. Don't let me make you sad.

Sir Mortimer Durand said that you, the English people, gave up your colonies over there—got tired of them—and did it with reluctance. Now I wish you just to consider that he was right about that, and that he had his reasons for saying that England did not look upon our Revolution as a foreign war, but as a civil war fought by Englishmen.

Our Fourth of July which we honor so much, and which we love so much, and which we take so much pride in, is an English institution, not an American one, and it comes of a great ancestry. The first Fourth of July in that noble genealogy dates back seven centuries lacking eight years. That is the day of the Great Charter—the Magna Charta—which was born at Runnymede in the next to the last year of King John, and portions of the liberties secured thus by those hardy Barons from that reluctant King John are a part of our Declaration of Independence, of our Fourth of July, of our American liberties. And the second of those Fourths of July was not born until four centuries later, in Charles the First's time, in the Bill of Rights, and that is ours, that is part of our liberties. The next one was still English, in New England, where they established that principle which remains with us to this day, and will continue to remain with us—no taxation without representation. That is always going to stand, and that the English Colonies in New England gave us.

The Fourth of July, and the one which you are celebrating now, born in Philadelphia on the 4th of July, 1776—that is English, too. It is not American. Those were English colonists, subjects of King George III, Englishmen at heart, who protested against the oppressions of the home government. Though they proposed to cure those oppressions and remove them, still remaining under the Crown, they were not intending a revolution. The revolution was brought about by circumstances which they could not control. The Declaration of Independence was written by a British subject, every name signed to it was the name of a British subject. There was not the name of a single American attached to the Declaration of Independence—in fact, there was not an American in the country in that day except the Indians out on the plains. They were Englishmen, all Englishmen—Americans did not begin until seven years later, when that Fourth of July had become seven years old, and then the American Republic was established. Since then there have been Americans. So you see what we owe to England in the matter of liberties.

We have, however, one Fourth of July which is absolutely our own, and that is that great proclamation issued forty years ago by that great American to whom Sir Mortimer Durand paid that just and beautiful tribute—Abraham Lincoln. Lincoln's proclamation, which not only set the black slaves free, but set the white man free also. The owner was set free from the burden and offense, that sad condition of things where he was in so many instances a master and owner of slaves when he did not want to be. That proclamation set them all free. But even in this matter England suggested it, for England had set her slaves free thirty years before, and we followed her example. We always followed her example, whether it was good or bad.

And it was an English judge that issued that other great proclamation, and established that great principle that, when a slave, let him belong to whom he may, and let him come whence he may, sets his foot upon English soil, his fetters by that act fall away and he is a free man before the world. We followed the example of 1833, and we freed our slaves as I have said.

It is true, then, that all our Fourths of July, and we have five of them, England gave to us, except that one that I have mentioned—the

Emancipation Proclamation, and, lest we forget, let us all remember that we owe these things to England. Let us be able to say to Old England, this great-hearted, venerable old mother of the race, you gave us our Fourths of July that we love and that we honor and revere, you gave us the Declaration of Independence, which is the Charter of our rights, you, the venerable Mother of Liberties, the Protector of Anglo-Saxon Freedom—you gave us these things, and we do most honestly thank you for them.

Text / "Independence Day" in *MTS*(10):405–12; and *MTS*(23): 344–50.

trying to take a cup of ours / The *America's* Cup, won off the Isle of Wight in 1851. Up to 1903 the British had made twelve unsuccessful attempts to lift the cup. The most persistent challenger was Sir Thomas Lipton, of the Royal Ulster Yacht Club, who failed five times between 1899 and 1930 with his yachts *Shamrock I, II, III, IV,* and *V.* An Australian challenge was turned back in 1970, and in 1974 another Australian challenger, *Southern Cross,* was defeated by the American defender, *Courageous.*

Mortimer Durand / (1850–1924). British statesman. He was foreign secretary in India (1884–94), minister at Teheran (1894–1900), ambassador and consul general at Madrid (1900–03), and ambassador to the United States (1903–06). An industrious writer, he published *Nadir Shah* (1908), *A Holiday in South Africa* (1911), and others.

the example of 1833 / In a wave of legislation inspired by the Reform Bill of 1832, a law of 1833 freed all slaves owned by British subjects or in British dominions, prohibited future slavery, and provided £20,000,000 to pay slave owners for the loss of their property. The measure aroused great resentment among West Indian planters and South African Boers. In the United States, Lincoln worked out a plan for gradual abolishment of slavery by federal payment to slave owners, pointing out that such a procedure would cost much less than war, but his ideas got nowhere.

· 172 ·

The Savage Club dinner introduced something new in entertainment. Louis Brennan, an inventor, demonstrated his monorail car, sending a six-foot model on wire cables swooping around the room, in and out among diners and wine bottles, to the great delight of Mark Twain. Always fascinated by mechanical devices, he enjoyed the show immensely. He was further pleased to be presented with a portrait of himself signed by all the members of the Savage Club. To climax the evening, he was handed a note from one of his "confederates" involved in the theft of the Ascot Cup, together with a package containing a facsimile of the trophy, on the top of which was a small wooden likeness of Mark Twain. The confederate said: "I changed the acorn atop for another nut with my knife." See MTB, *4:1400.*

Dinner Speech

Savage Club Dinner for Mark Twain, London, July 6, 1907

Mr. Chairman and fellow Savages: I am very glad indeed to have that portrait. I think it is the best one that I have ever had, and there have been opportunities before to get a good photograph. I have sat to photographers twenty-two times today. Those sittings added to those that have preceded them since I have been in England—if we average at that rate—must have numbered one hundred to two hundred sittings. Out of all those there ought to be some good photographs. This is the best I have had, and I am glad to have your honored names on it.

I did not know Harold Frederic personally, but I have heard a great deal about him, and nothing that was not pleasant, and nothing except such things as lead a man to honor another man and to love him. I consider that it is a misfortune of mine that I have never had the luck to meet him, and if any book of mine read to him in his last hours made those hours easier for him and more comfortable, I am very glad and proud of that. I call to mind such a case, many years ago, of an English authoress, well known in her day, who wrote beautiful child tales, touching and lovely in every way. In a little biographical sketch of her I found that her last hours were spent partly in reading a book of mine, until she was no longer able to read. That has always remained in my mind, and I have always cherished it as one of the good things of my life. I had read what she had written, and had loved her for what she had done.

Stanley, apparently, carried a book of mine feloniously away to Africa, and I have not a doubt that it had a noble and uplifting influence there in the wilds of Africa—because on his previous journeys he never carried anything to read except Shakespeare and the Bible. I did not know of that circumstance. I did not know that he had carried a book of mine. I only noticed that when he came back he was a reformed man. I knew Stanley very well in those old days. Stanley was the first man who ever reported a lecture of mine, and that was in St. Louis for one of the papers there. When I was down there the next time to give the same lecture I was told to give them something fresh, as they had read that before in the papers. I met Stanley here when he came back from that first expedition of his which closed with the finding of Livingstone. You remember how he would break out at the meetings of the British Association, and find fault with what people said, because Stanley had notions of his own, and could not contain them. They had to come out, or break him up—and so he would go round and address geographical societies, and he was always on the warpath in those days, and people always had to have Stanley contradicting their geography for them and improving it. But he always came back and sat drinking beer with me in the hotel up to two in the morning, and he was one of the most civilized human beings that ever was.

I saw in the *Westminster Gazette* this evening a reference to an interview which appeared in one of the papers the other day, in which the interviewer said that I characterized Mr. Birrell's speech the other day at the Pilgrims Club as "bully." Now, if you will excuse me, I never use slang to an interviewer or anybody else. That distresses me. Whatever I said about Mr. Birrell's speech was said in English, as good English as anybody uses. If I could not describe Mr. Birrell's delightful speech without using slang I would not describe it at all. I would close my mouth and keep it closed, much as it would discomfort me.

Now, that comes of interviewing a man in the first person, which is an altogether wrong way to interview him. It is entirely wrong because none of you—I, or anybody else—could interview a man, could listen to a man, talking any length of time, and then go off and reproduce that talk in the first person. It can't be done. What results is merely that the interviewer gives the substance of what is said, puts it in his own language, and puts it in your mouth. It will always be either better language than you use, or worse, and in my case it is always worse. I have a great respect for the English language. I am one of its supporters, its promotors, its elevators. I don't degrade it. A slip of the tongue would be the most you would get from me. I have always tried hard and faithfully to improve my English, and never to degrade it. I always try to use the best English to describe what I think and what I feel or what I don't feel and what I don't think.

I am not one of those who in expressing opinions confine themselves to facts. I don't know anything that mars good literature so completely as too much truth. Facts contain a great deal of poetry, but you can't use too many of them without damaging your literature. I love all literature, and as long as I am a doctor of literature—I have suggested to you for twenty years I have been diligently trying to improve my own literature, and now, by virtue of the University of Oxford, I mean to doctor everybody else's.

Now, here in your own Parliament you report everybody, except the Prime Minister, perhaps, in the third person. He is the only man who gets justice done him, as far as I can see. When you read a speech in the third person you have to turn it back into the first to understand it. Nobody can understand it until that is done. The Duke of Brighton gets up and quotes from Tennyson:

> The splendor falls on castle walls and snowy scenes,
> old in story;
> The long light shakes across the lakes, and the wild
> cataract leaps in glory.

He is reported like this: "The noble lord said that in the course of events the splendor fell on the castle walls and snowy scenes. He added, and proceeded to say, that the long light shook on the lakes and all that sort of thing, and the wild cataract, he further observed, leaped in glory." He has not altered the thing, not a word, except to put in that rubbish to help him through; but he has taken all the dignity out of those verses by that degrading fashion of reporting it. Why could he not put it as it was said? Nothing is saved in space, but speech has been made silly and stupid.

Now I think I ought to apologize for my clothes. At home I venture things that I am not permitted by my family to venture in foreign parts. I was instructed before I left home, and ordered to refrain from white clothes in England. I meant to keep that command fair and clean, and I would have done it if I had been in the habit of obeying instructions, but I can't invent a new process in life right away. I have not had white clothes on since I crossed the ocean until now.

In these three or four weeks I have grown so tired of grey and black that you have earned my gratitude in permitting me to come as I have. I wear white clothes in the depth of winter in my home, but I don't go out in the streets in them. I don't go out to attract too much attention. I like to attract some, and always I would like to be dressed so that I may be more conspicuous than anybody else.

If I had been in ancient Briton, I would not have contented myself with blue paint, but I would have bankrupted the rainbow. I so enjoy gay clothes in which women clothe themselves that it always grieves me when I go to the opera to see that, while women look like a flower bed, the men are a few grey stumps among them in their black evening dress. There are two or three reasons why I wish to wear white clothes. When I find myself in assemblies like this, with everybody in black clothes, I know I possess something that is superior to everybody else's. Clothes are never clean. You do not know whether they are clean or not, because you can't see.

Here or anywhere, you must scour your head every two or three days or it is full of grit. Your clothes must collect just as much dirt as your hair. If you wear white clothes you are clean, and your cleaning bill gets so heavy that you have to take care. I am proud to say that I can wear a white suit of clothes for three days without a blemish. If you need any further instruction in the matter of clothes I shall be glad to give it to you. I hope I have convinced some of you that it is just as well to wear white clothes as any other kind. I do not want to boast. I only want to make you understand that you are not clean.

As to age, the fact that I am nearly seventy-two years old does not clearly indicate how old I am, because part of every day—it is with me as with you—you try to describe your age, and you cannot do it. Sometimes you are only fifteen; sometimes you are twenty-five. It is very seldom in a day that I am seventy-two years old. I am older now sometimes than I was when I used to rob orchards—a thing which I would not do today—if the orchards were watched. I am so glad to be here tonight. I am so glad to renew with the Savages that now ancient time when I first sat with a company of this club in London in 1872. That is a long time ago. But I did stay with the Savages a night in London long ago, and, as I had come into a very strange land, and was with friends, as I could see, that has always remained in my mind as a peculiarly blessed evening, since it brought me into contact with men of my own kind and my own feelings.

I am glad to be here, and to see you all again, because it is very likely that I shall not see you again. It is easier than I thought to come across the Atlantic. I have been received, as you know, in the most delightfully generous way in England since I came here. It keeps me choked up all the time. Everybody is so generous, and they do seem to give you such a hearty welcome. Nobody in the world can appreciate it higher than I do. It did not wait till I got to London, but when I came ashore at Tilbury the stevedores on the dock raised the first welcome—a good and hearty welcome from the men who do the heavy labor in the world, and save you and me from having to do it. They are the men, who, with their hands, build empires and make them prosper. It is because of them that the others are wealthy and can live in luxury. They received me with a "Hurrah!" that went to my heart. They are the men that build civilization, and without them no civilization can be built. So I came first to the authors and creators of civilization, and I blessedly end in this happy meeting with the Savages who destroy it.

Text / Composite, based upon: "Mark Twain at the Savage Club," London *Western Press,* July 8, 1907; "The Savage Club Dinner" in *MTS*(10):386–92; and *MTS*(23):351–56.

Harold Frederic / (1856–98). American writer. He was London correspondent of the New York *Times* (1884–98). Among his books are *The Damnation of Theron Ware,* a novel (1896), and story collections: *The Copperhead and Other Stories* (1893), *In the 'Sixties* (1897), and *The Deserter and other Stories* (1898).

any book of mine read to him / In proposing the health of their guest, J. Scott Stokes said that he had read from the books of Mark Twain to Harold Frederic during his last illness.

an English authoress / Possibly Anna Sewell (1820–78). Crippled in childhood, she was an invalid most of her life. A vigorous crusader against cruelty to animals, she wrote children's books in verse and prose; the best known is *Black Beauty* (1877).

· 173 ·

To attend the lord mayor's dinner in Liverpool, Mark Twain, accompanied by T. P. O'Connor, went up in great style aboard a private car usually reserved for the Prince of Wales. Met by the lord mayor's carriage manned by liveried attendants, the travelers were transported in state to the Town Hall, but arrived too late for dining. Several hundred banqueters, including a number of lady mayoresses, had finished an elaborate menu: twelve courses, along with Amontillado, Liebfraumilch 1893, Rauzan Gaussies Margaux 1895, Heidsick Dry, Monopole 1898, and Cockburn 1887, besides liqueurs. There were three toasts: "The King" and "The President of the United States," proposed by John Japp, the lord mayor; and "Our Guest," proposed by Sir Edward Russell, seconded by T. P. O'Connor.

Our Guest

Lord Mayor's Banquet for Mark Twain, Town Hall, Liverpool, July 10, 1907

My Lord Mayor, my Lord Bishop, and gentlemen: I want to thank you, my Lord Mayor, for the welcome you have given me tonight, and I thank these gentlemen for their hearty response in which they have received the toast; and I will thank—any other name? I only know him by "Tay Pay." I have another name—Langhorne—but it really doesn't belong to me.

Then you have a telegram from Professor Boyce, who says he still has a watch. That comes of having a fleeting reputation. I came to this country distinguished for honesty—and then somebody took that Ascot Cup just as I arrived, which has thrown a gloom over my whole stay here, and will provide sorrow and lamentations for my friends on the other side. And now I am held responsible for the regalia which has been stolen from Dublin Castle. What will become of my reputation if I do not get out of the country very soon? People say it is a curious coincidence that the Ascot Cup and the regalia from Dublin Castle should have been stolen during my stay, and so it is. I was going to Dublin. Fortunately for the rags of my reputation I could not get there.

And you say, what is this?—it is rumor. Nobody comes out and charges me with carrying away that robbery. It is mere human testimony, and it does not amount to testimony, it is merely rumor, circumstantial evidence, mere human speech, assertion, rumor and suspicion. But circumstantial evidence is the best evidence in the world. Once a month for five hundred years certain officers whose function it is go down the cellars in Dublin Castle, and there they find the safe in which the precious jewels are kept, and take them out one by one daily just to see that they are all right, and put them back in the safe. They have been doing this for five hundred years, and they have got so used to it that they did not shut up the safe. I should like to know whether that is a good safe and a valuable safe. That is an important feature for me, because, with the reputation which I have got now, all the circumstantial evidence would point to the fact that if I took anything at all I would not merely have carried off the regalia, but the safe along with it. All this is testimony in my favor, and yet Professor Boyce is afraid to bring along his watch, which is probably only a Waterbury, and an old one at that.

Mr. O'Connor has furnished you information that enabled you to understand that I have been a jack-of-all-trades. That is quite true. He said a word about my father. He was a lawyer, but my father was entitled to more words than that. He was another of my kind. He was not just merely a lawyer, but in that little village on the banks of the Mississippi, when I was a boy, he was mayor of the town, the chief of police, the postmaster, the one policeman, and the sheriff who had to hang all the malefactors. In fact, he was the entire government—concentrated. Now, you can't pass by a man like that with just a word.

Mr. O'Connor spoke of my mother, too. Well, my brother and I were twins. He was born ten years before I was—a little discrepancy that never could be accounted for. It was the intention that that brother of mine should be a lazy person. I know that perfectly well, but somehow or other it missed fire, and I was born that way instead. I have been lazy ever since, and indolent; while that brother, the twin—he was full of energy and the spirit of labor. Whatever he put his hand to he worked at it hard and faithfully, and the result was—the result was he could never make a living anyhow.

I can't help being frivolous tonight, because I have followed out my instructive and natural custom this afternoon by having a sleep and resting myself. Whenever I am rested and feeling good I can't help being frivolous. It is only when I am weary and worn-out and discouraged that the time comes for me to take a hold on great national questions and handle them. I wanted to talk real instructive wisdom tonight; but this rest has intervened, and put it all out of my mind.

I have been two or three weeks discussing cheap penny international postage with Mr. Henniker Heaton, and I have told him all I know about it. And now he knows nothing about it himself. I said I was born lazy, but I was born wise also; and the only time I ever lost a situation—the only time I was ever discharged from a post—was in San Francisco, more than forty years ago, when I was a reporter on the *Morning Call.* I was discharged just that once in my life, and the only thing they could bring against me was that I was incompetent, and incandescent, and inharmonious, and everything they could think of in three syllables; but mainly, I was lazy and inefficient. That was the only time anybody ever found fault with me for a thing like that. It was occurring all the time; in fact, it was monotonous, and it was no use picking out a thing like that.

According to Tay Pay, I have been a little of everything. This time I am an Ambassador. I like that position very well. I don't mind it as it has not a salary attached to it, because a salary limits your energy. It does mine, always. I would rather be free to do my ambassadorial work after my own fashion, and I intend to keep up this ambassadorial business right along. Whenever I find a chance of encouraging the good feeling between this old mother country and her eldest child over there, I intend to put in my word and keep up the ambassadorial work.

The University of Oxford, in making me a doctor, has added one more function to my numerous functions, and somebody asked me a rather pointed question—"Was it not rather a delicate thing to make you a Doctor of Literature? Are you competent to doctor your own a little?" That is all wrong. I have been doctoring my own literature. It is only now by the authority of Oxford that I propose to doctor other people's, and I hope you will see results. Why, I have always had an interest in literature outside my own concern. I have always been ready to give a helping hand to a rising young author.

I saved one poet in San Francisco forty years ago, and I don't forget it. I did a good turn to that poet. I was ready to doctor him or anybody else. Well, he wasn't much of a poet—a kind of poet good enough for the early days of the Pacific. He was not prosperous, and he was named Eddystone. We called him Eddystone Lighthouse. That was sarcasm. He was not a lighthouse. He was in trouble and I came to the young man's help. I was a reporter, but I was likely to lose the employment at any time, and I knew it would be such a good thing for me if I could do something rather extraordinary to keep ahead of the other papers.

Well, the young poet got discouraged. His poetry began to be a drug, he could not sell it, and by and by, when he could not give it away, his circumstances were desperate, and he came to me as a friend and wise adviser, and he proposed to commit suicide. I told him it was a good idea. It was a good idea in various ways. It would relieve him from writing poetry, and it would relieve the community from reading it, and it would give me a chance with my newspaper, I being the only other person present at the suicide—I would take care of that. He was a little sorry to see me so enthusiastic. I could not help that; my heart was in it.

We discussed methods, and I told him the most picturesque was the revolver to blow his brains out with. He did not like that idea very much, but I reconciled him to it. But we did not have any money to buy a revolver, and we went round to the place with the three balls. There was a revolver there, just the right thing, but we could not borrow that revolver without furnishing some money. I told the gentleman that this was the only chance the young man had, but he was that kind of man that you could not persuade at all—a man who has no human sympathy, although it does not cost anything.

Then I suggested drowning to my friend. That would be a neat thing. It could not be as fine for me as the other, but drowning was good enough when you could not get anything better. So we went out to the seashore, and he did not like the looks of the water, and wanted me to try how it would go; but no, I was not in that line at all. Then a most curious thing—one of the strangest things, a thing you would never imagine at all—happened. From some ship, that had foundered perhaps a thousand miles away, there came an object of some interest at that moment. There were, in fact, two events gradually coming together. While this young man was brooding and contemplating suicide there was a life preserver floating in from that ship. A life preserver for a man who was about to commit suicide!

It looked ridiculous at first, but we took the life preserver to the pawnbroker and traded with him for the revolver. And then we made all the arrangements. But he didn't like to put the firearm to his forehead. I said, "It will be over in a minute," and this seemed to reassure him, for he bucked up and blew his brains out. People said it wasn't brains; but it was. There was not much of it; but it was real grey matter, which is supposed to constitute intelligence so far as it can. Well, that was the making of that boy. Why, when he got well, all obstructions were gone! And I have thought many times since that if poets when they get discouraged would blow their brains out, they could write very much better when they got well.

I landed in this town of Liverpool thirty years ago—the first time I ever put my foot on English soil—and I had an adventure. As a matter of fact, Liverpool is connected with one or two adventures of a very pleasant sort. I went to the outside edge of town, and I saw the scenery—the blocked-up windows to escape the window tax, and various other exciting things—and finally, I took a cab and drove around. The man was a very good-natured, pleasant, middle-aged Scotchman, and he asked where he should drive me to. I said anywhere just around for an hour or two hours. He drove me a little way, and then stopped and asked me again. Well, I wanted to think—I was full of some great project—and finally, when this had occurred several more times, in desperation I said, "Oh, take me to Balmoral."

I did not say a word, and I did not pay any attention to where he was going. I wanted to think. I did not know where I was. I was away somewhere in the country, and I hailed him and asked him where he was going, and he said, "On the way to Balmoral." So he was. I got him to turn round and get back to Liverpool if he could, to catch a train for London, if possible. When we got back I asked him what I had to pay, and he said—well, it was equivalent to four hundred dollars. I asked him if he was in earnest, and he said he was, as outside the city he could charge any reasonable price. He said that Balmoral was four hundred miles away, and it would be four hundred dollars.

It seemed a sorry and embarrassing situation. I proposed to go before the rulers of the city or his Majesty or something of that sort to lay the case and he did. I said he had made a mistake, and the authorities said he had a right to charge anything reasonable. It seemed a large sum he had charged, and they said it was not the cabman's fault—it was four hundred miles to Balmoral and four shillings a mile was not unreasonable, especially as he would have to come back at his own expense. Well, the man acted very handsomely; he compromised for twelve dollars. Though stupid tradition says that Scotchmen did not profess a sense of humor, I say that that man has a sense of humor.

What was Tay Pay's early statement that requires refutation? [Mr. O'Connor: "I said that you had been a financier."] I was, but I am not now; I didn't succeed in it. He also mentioned another matter, and he paid me the compliment to mention that at the time when I was bankrupt, heavily in debt, I paid every dollar. This is often mentioned—very pleasing to me to hear—and I feel that I ought to get on my feet and tell you all about it—how my business man, my longheaded commercial friend said, "In this bankruptcy business you pay thirty cents to the dollar and you go free." Now, a man can easily be persuaded to go outside the strict moral line, but it is not so with a woman and a wife. My wife said, "No, you shall pay a hundred cents to the dollar and I will go with you all the way." And she kept her word. Let us give credit where credit is due, and it is more due to her than to me.

I don't think I will say anything about the relations of amity existing between our two countries. It is not necessary, it seems to me. The ties between the two nations are so strong that I do not think we need trouble ourselves about them being broken. Anyhow, I am quite sure that in my time, and in yours, my Lord Mayor, those ties will hold good, and please God, they always will. English blood is in our veins, we have a common language, a common religion, a common system of morals, and great commercial interests to hold us together.

Home is dear to us all, and I am now departing for mine on the other side of the ocean. Oxford has conferred upon me the loftiest honor that has ever fallen to my fortune, the one I should have chosen as outranking any and all others and more precious to me than any and all others within the gift of men and states to bestow upon me. And I have had, in the four weeks that I have been here, another lofty honor, a continuous honor, an honor which has known no interruption in all these twenty-six days, and a most moving and pulse-stirring honor: the hearty hand grip and the cordial welcome which does not descend from the pale grey matter of the brain, but comes up with the red blood out of the heart! It makes me proud, and it makes me humble. Many and many a year ago I read an anecdote in Dana's book, *Two Years Before the Mast.* A frivolous little self-important captain of a coasting sloop in the dried apple and kitchen furniture trade was always hailing every vessel that came in sight, just to hear himself talk, and air his small grandeurs. One day a majestic Indiaman came plowing by, with course on course of canvas towering into the sky, her decks and yards swarming with sailors; with macaws and monkeys and all manner of strange and romantic creatures populating her rigging; and thereto her freightage of precious spices lading the breeze with gracious and mysterious odors of the Orient. Of course, the little coaster captain hopped into the shrouds and squeaked out a hail: "Ship ahoy! what ship is that, and whence and whither?" In a deep and thunderous bass came the answer back through a speaking trumpet: "The *Begum of Bengal,* a hundred and twenty-three days out from Canton—homeward bound! What ship is that?" The little captain's vanity was all crushed out of him, and most humbly he squeaked back: "Only the *Mary Ann*—fourteen hours out from Boston, bound for Kittery Point with—with nothing to speak of!" The eloquent word "only" expressed the deeps of his stricken humbleness.

And what is my own case? During perhaps one hour in the twenty-four—not more than that—I stop and reflect. Then I am humble, then I am properly meek, and for that little time I am "only the *Mary Ann,*" fourteen hours out, and cargoed with vegetables and tinware; but all the other twenty-three my vain self-satisfaction rides high and I am the stately Indiaman, plowing the great seas under a cloud of sail, and laden with a rich freightage of the kindest words that were ever spoken to a wandering alien, I think; my twenty-six crowded and fortunate days seem multiplied by five, and I am the *Begum of Bengal,* a hundred and twenty-three days out from Canton—homeward bound!

Text / Composite, based upon: "Speech at Liverpool," MS, MTP; Liverpool *Post,* July 11, 1907; *MTB,* 4:1401–2.

"Tay Pay" / Thomas Power O'Connor (1848–1929). Irish journalist and parliamentarian. Entering Parliament (1880), he became president of the Irish National League of Great Britian (1883), and from 1887 on founded several papers, the most successful being *T. P.'s Weekly.* A strong supporter of the Parnell party, he lectured in the United States on the Irish cause (1881, 1906, 1917). He was a prolific writer who published, among other things, *Gladstone's House of Commons* (1885), *The Parnell Movement* (1886), and *Memoirs of an Old Parliamentarian* (1929).

Boyce / Rubert William Boyce (1863–1911). British pathologist. Specialist on jungle diseases, he was professor of pathology, University of Liverpool, member of the Royal Commission on Tuberculosis, and dean of the Liverpool School of Tropical Medicine. He published *A Textbook of Morbid Histology* (1892), *Papers on Tropical Sanitation* (1894–95), and other contributions to medical science.

only a Waterbury / The Waterbury watch, an American product, price one dollar, was the cheapest timepiece on the market.

Henniker Heaton / John Henniker Heaton (1848–1914). British parliamentarian. Known as the "Father of Imperial Penny Postage," he was also a leader in promoting Anglo-American penny postage, and other postal improvements.

an anecdote . . . Two Years Before the Mast / The story is in chapter 35. Mark Twain varied the details of Dana's narrative and elaborated upon them, as he always did when he took over somebody else's story and put his own stamp upon it. The "homeward bound" conclusion of the Liverpool speech had a tremendous effect upon the audience—deservedly so, for it is one of Mark Twain's finest efforts. See comments of T. P. O'Connor, *T. P.'s Weekly,* July 19, 1907; also Charles Vaile, "Mark Twain as an Orator," *The Forum* 44 (July 1910):1–13.

twenty-six crowded days / Very much so. Besides the affairs at which he made the speeches given in this volume, there were public and private breakfasts, luncheons, teas, and dinners of groups ranging from an intimate half dozen to several hundred. Among hosts and guests were Bernard Shaw, Max Beerbohm, Archibald Henderson, Whitelaw Reid, Henry W. Lucy, Lord Curzon, Lord Avebury, Robert Porter, T. Fisher Unwin, Henniker Heaton, T. P. O'Connor, Sir James Knowles, members of the House of Commons, Sidney Lee, Canon Wilberforce, Harvey Brittain, J. W. MacAlister, Moberly Bell, Sir Norman and Lady Lockyer, the earl and countess of Portsmouth, Lady Stanley, Sir Gilbert and Lady Parker, Lord Kelvin, Sir Charles Lyell, Oxford students of All Souls and Christ Church Colleges, Rhodes scholars, and the staff of *Punch.* He was invited to many morning and afternoon functions, but it is not clear whether he attended: e.g., the Society of Women Journalists, the Legion of Frontiersmen, the Master and Wardens of the Worshipful Company of Gardeners, the celebration of the king's birthday at the Foreign Office, and a river jaunt of the Whitefriars Club. Mark Twain plunged through the tumult with the vigor of a youth, letting his secretary, Ralph Ashcroft, act as buffer between him and the public, and taking short naps when he could elude reporters, photographers, portrait painters, autograph-hunters, and insistent well-wishers.

· 174 ·

Mark Twain sailed for home on the Minnetonka *on July 13. Two days out the ship collided with the bark* Sterling, *but neither was seriously damaged. The* Times *reported, July 23, that Mark Twain, aroused by the collision, "grabbed his bath robe, and rushed to the deck to see what the trouble was. Some of the passengers say that he thought he had grabbed his bath robe, but that in reality he had put on his Oxford gown in the darkness." Arriving in New York on the twenty-second, he was met by a crowd of newsmen who fired a barrage of questions.*

Interview

Dockside, New York, July 22, 1907

Doctor Twain, if you please. That is the only title I am using now. Just how my old friends are going to get away from calling me "Mark" is something they will have to work out for themselves, and when they see me in my new cap and gown they will be bound to fall.

My dinner with the King? Did he enjoy it? How do I like America? What do I think of the English women? Did I get away with the Ascot Cup? The Dublin jewels, too? What's the best story I heard in England? Who—one minute, boys. Give me a chance to think. I haven't had any practice for nine days, and you remind me of work.

Well, the King enjoyed the dinner and that is enough. I like America very much. I was prepared for that question and nearly all the others, but being a good Christian I do not dread the worst. As to English women, I will not commit myself just now. This is so sudden. I must have time to consider these great questions. As to the Ascot Cup, I don't mind taking you all into my confidence. Sh! It's on board this ship, and I expect to go ashore with it if I have any luck and use diplomacy. Oh, yes, I have the cup on board, and I hope some of you reporters are slick enough to help me smuggle it in through the Custom House. It would be too bad to give it up after getting so close to home with it.

But I didn't get the Dublin jewels. The idea is absurd. Wasn't the safe left? With the character they gave me over on the other side I should certainly not have left the safe. I would have taken both.

The best story I heard in England is not one that I am going to tell now. I get thirty cents a word for stories.

My rate is the same for jokes—no rebate. Did the King crack a joke at the dinner? Yes; but I'm keeping that, too. I've got a place in the country, you know, that I have to pay rent for. No, I wasn't interviewed much in London, but my secretary was. Someone has asked me if anybody else ever succeeded in getting a joke through the English hide. Now, that does not suggest a broad view of the situation. Humor isn't a thing of race or nationality. So much depends upon the environment of a joke. To be good it must absorb its setting. The American joke does this, so does the English. Believe it or not, I have met English jokes that were funny. I had not the slightest trouble in getting mine through their heads.

[He was asked if he objected to telling his age.] Not in the least. I shall be seventy-two in November. I do not mind it. Every year that I gain furnishes a new privilege, and all I want to dodge is second childhood.

At two o'clock in the morning I feel as old as any man. At that time you must know that life in every person is at its lowest. At that hour I feel as sinful, too, as possible. But the rest of the time I feel as though I were not over twenty-five years old. You know one gets back both youth and courage by six o'clock in the morning.

Text / Composite, based upon: "Mark Twain Home in Good Humor," *Times,* July 23, 1907; "Mark Twain Home, Captive of Little Girl," *World,* July 23, 1907.

My dinner with the King / It is not clear whether a dinner with King Edward, and perhaps others members of the royal family, was fact or fiction. The London papers did not mention this event, and Mark Twain gave no details.

· 175 ·

Mark Twain was soon involved in the familiar routine of dinners and ceremonials, his presence having become a greater attraction because of the Oxford honor. Elaborate plans were made to celebrate Fulton Day at the Jamestown Exposition. Henry Rogers's yacht, Kanawha, *was to transport Mark Twain and Grover Cleveland, orator of the day. Arrived off Jamestown, they were to steam in between lines of battleships and yachts while salutes boomed and a marine parade formed. These plans collapsed. Mr. Cleveland could not make the trip because of illness, no battleships appeared, no marine parade occurred, and high seas delayed the shore program until 4* P.M. *But the shore part went better. Mark Twain, introduced by Lieutenant Governor Ellyson, was greeted by a storm of applause and cheers. When he held up his hand for silence, too moved to speak, the audience burst forth louder than before.*

Speech

Fulton Day, Jamestown Exposition, Jamestown, Virginia, September 23, 1907

Ladies and gentlemen: I am but human, and when you give me a reception like that I am obliged to wait a little while I get my voice. When you appeal to my head, I don't feel it; but when you appeal to my heart, I do feel it.

We are here to celebrate one of the greatest events of American history, and not only in American history, but in the world's history. Indeed it was—the application of steam by Robert Fulton.

It was a world event—there are not many of them. It is peculiarly an American event, that is true, but the influence was very broad in effect. We should regard this day as a very great American holiday. We have not had many that are exclusively American holidays. We have the Fourth of July, which we regard as an American holiday, but it is nothing of the kind. I am waiting for a dissenting voice. All great efforts that led to the Fourth of July were made, not by Americans, but by English residents of America, subjects of the King of England.

They fought all the fighting that was done, they shed and spilt all the blood that was spilt, in securing to us the invaluable liberties which are incorporated in the Declaration of Independence; but they were not Americans. They signed the Declaration of Independence; no American's name is signed to that document at all. There never was an American such as you and I are until the Revolution, when it had all been fought out and liberty secured, after the adoption of the Constitution, and the recognition of the independence of America by all powers.

While we revere the Fourth of July—and let us always revere it, and the liberties it conferred upon us—yet it was not an American event, a great American day.

It was an American who applied that steam successfully. There are not a great many world events, and we have our full share. The telegraph, telephone, and the application of steam to navigation—these are great American events.

Today I have been requested, or I have requested myself, not to confine myself to furnishing you with information, but to remind you of things, and to introduce one of the nation's celebrants.

Admiral Harrington here is going to tell you all that I have left untold. I am going to tell you all that I know, and then he will follow up with such rags and remnants as he can find, and tell you what he knows.

No doubt you have heard a great deal about Robert Fulton and the influences that have grown from his invention, but the little steamboat is suffering neglect.

You probably do not know a great deal about that boat. It was the most important steamboat in the world. I was there and saw it. Admiral Harrington was there at the time. It need not surprise you, for he is not as old as he looks. That little boat was interesting in every way. The size of it. The boat was one [whispering to Admiral Harrington], he said ten feet long. The breadth of that boat [consulting the admiral], two hundred feet. You see, the first and most important detail is the length, then the breadth, and then the depth; the depth of that boat was [another consultation]—the admiral says it was a flatboat. Then her tonnage—you know nothing about a boat until you know two more things: her speed and her tonnage. We know the speed she made. She made four miles—and sometimes five miles. It was on her initial trip, on August 11, 1807, that she made her initial trip, when she went from [consulting the admiral] Jersey City—to Chicago. That's right. She went by way of Albany. Now comes the tonnage of the boat. Tonnage of a boat means the amount of displacement; displacement means the amount of water a vessel can shove in a day. The tonnage of man is estimated by the amount of whiskey he can displace in a day.

Robert Fulton named the *Clermont* in honor of his bride, that is, Clermont was the name of the county seat.

I feel that it surprises you that I know so much. In my remarks of welcome to Admiral Harrington I am not going to give him compliments. Compliments always embarrass a man. You do not know anything to say. It does not inspire you with words. There is nothing you can say in answer to a compliment. I have been complimented myself a great many times, and they always embarrass me—I always feel that they have not said enough.

The admiral and myself have held public office, and were associated together a great deal in a friendly way in the time of Pocahontas. That incident where Pocahontas saves the life of Smith from her father, Powhatan's club, was gotten up by the admiral and myself to advertise Jamestown. At that time the admiral and myself did not have the facilities of advertising that you have.

I have known Admiral Harrington in all kinds of situations—in public service, on the platform, and in the chain gang now and then—but it was a mistake. A case of mistaken identity. I do not think it is at all necessary to tell you Admiral Harrington's public history. You know that it is in the histories. I am not here to tell you anything about his public life, but to expose his private life.

I am something of a poet. When the great poet laureate, Tennyson, died, and I found that the place was open, I tried to get it—but I did not get it. Anybody can write the first line of a poem, but it is a very difficult task to make the second line rhyme with the first. When I was down in Australia there were two towns named Johnswood and Par-am. I made this rhyme:

The people of Johnswood are pious and good;
The people of Par-am they don't care a ———.

I do not want to compliment Admiral Harrington, but as long as such men as he devote their lives to the public service the credit of the country will never cease. I will say that the same high qualities, the same moral and intellectual attainments, the same graciousness of manner, of conduct, of observation, and expression have caused Admiral Harrington to be mistaken for me—and I have been mistaken for him. A mutual compliment can go no further, and I now have the honor and privilege of introducing to you Admiral Harrington.

Text / Composite, based upon: *New York at the Jamestown Exposition,* prepared by Cuyler Reynolds (1909), pp. 414–19; "Fulton Day,

Jamestown" in *MTS*(10):304–9; and *MTS*(23):359–63.

Harrington / Purnell Frederick Harrington (1844–1937). American naval officer. After Civil War service in the North Atlantic and Gulf of Mexico blockading squadrons (1863–65), he was a Naval Academy instructor (1868–70, 1880–83), commanded many ships, served in the Spanish-American War, and was commandant of navy yards at Portsmouth (1898–1901), and Norfolk (1903–06). He ended forty-seven years' service as a rear admiral (1906). He was chairman of the Naval Board of the Jamestown Exposition.

· 176 ·

The speech below may not have been delivered. If it was, the circumstances are obscure. It was written for an occasion in honor of the visit of the Right Reverend Winnington-Ingram, lord bishop of London. He had come over to present the King's Bible to Bruton Parish Church of Williamsburg, Virginia, the oldest church of Anglican communion in continuous use in the United States. On October 15, 1907, the Pilgrims gave a dinner for the lord bishop at the Plaza, New York, but Mark Twain was not reported to have been among the notables present. Perhaps he had been kept away for reasons unknown, for it is unthinkable that he should not have been invited to such a large public function. At any rate, having prepared a fairly long manuscript, he obviously expected to deliver the speech somewhere.

Bishop Speech

Between October 5 and 17, 1907

Now Eliot you have delivered the King's Bible, sir. The rest of your sojourn among us—which I hope will be long and pleasant—will naturally be devoted to acquiring information about our great country—the greatest on earth, as you will already have learned, from the reporters as you came up the Bay, and from other shy and blushing sources. I am glad of this opportunity to add to your accumulation of American fact, and will help you all I can. And where

I cannot add a fact I shall hope to be useful in explaining facts drawn by you from other authorities.

Our form of government, sir, is the best that can be devised by human wisdom, it being a monarchy, a great and free and progressive and enlightened monarchy like your own at home. There is a difference, but it is only slight and not readily perceptible. Yours is hereditary monarchy under a permanent family, ours is hereditary monarchy under a permanent political party. Sometimes you call your system a monarchical republic; ours is a republican monarchy. There is no real difference. And I can tell you this—both have come to stay! You couldn't dislodge ours with dynamite. Is it good? Well, not as good for the nation as it would be if the two great parties held the power turn about and kept each other from abusing it.

You will read and hear much of the President of the United States. Dear sir, do not be deceived—there is no such person. And no such office. There is a President of the Republican party, but there has been only one President of the United States since the country lost Mr. Lincoln forty-two years ago. The highest duty of the President of the Republican party is to watch diligently over his party's interest, urgently promoting all measures, good or bad, which may procure votes for it, and as urgently obstructing all, good or bad, which might bring its rule into disfavor. The party, only, is hereditary, now, but the headship of it will be hereditary by and by, in a single family.

Pray do not overlook our patriotism, sir. There is more of it here than exists in any other country. It is all lodged in the Republican party. The party will tell you so. All others are traitors, and are long ago used to the name. We impose no penalty upon them except the half of the taxes, but Russia would send them to Siberia.

Publicly, sir, we are intensely democratic, and much given to mocking at royalties and aristocracies, but privately we have that hankering after them and worship of them which has never been absent from any section of the human race. We love to look at photographs of princes and princelings and dukes and duchesses, greatly preferring them to any other kind of pictures. Our illustrated papers and magazines know this, and they keep this appetite liberally fed. The source of this adulation of ours is the same that it is all over the world—envy; envy of the conspicuous. While a President is in office we have pictures of them daily; and the telegrams record every wonderful thing they say, just as your newspapers do with the profound remarks of august children on your side of the water. An American girl would rather marry a title than an angel. We are nearly ripe for a throne here; in fact all we lack is the name.

We are a stirring, and energetic and enterprising people, sir, and we do things on a large scale. Look at our statistics. There is nothing elsewhere on the planet like them. In Europe you think it a proud thing if you kill one or two people a week with automobiles, whereas our weekly output amounts to a Bartholomew Massacre.

Your British railways carry more passengers than do ours, yet when it comes to killing and crippling, where are you? Out of sight. If you kill and cripple a few dozen people in a year you think it a great thing. Dear sir, it is nothing. Our railways kill 10,000 passengers every year and injure 60,000. If you would do away with your obstructive block system and protected crossings, you could do as well.

In England you attach an almost sentimental importance to human death and mutilation; you are too fastidious about it.

We used to be like that, but we have gotten over it. Our streets are the property of the transit cars, and all that in them is. In our great city the cars kill a human being every fifteen hours the year round. That is the crop of the suddenly killed: 700 a month, 8,500 a year; ten or 12,000 a year if you count those that by and by succumb to their injuries and get no mention. By car accidents we kill and injure, together, 5,600 a month, without counting Sundays—70,000 a year, just the duplicate of what our 209,000 miles of American railways do, you see. Aggregate—140,000 per annum. Can you beat that? Can you even approach it? No, sir; no country can approach it; at least no foreign country, except perhaps Sheol. If that is a foreign country. I don't know. When I think of some of our shipments to it I realize that I should feel more or less at home there. It wouldn't surprise me there to recognize our American twang here and there—and now and then the pleasant accent of your own great country, sir.

When you have a trial which is particularly salacious and rotten with indecencies, your courts shut out the public and the reporters. Our way is better and more popular. Although we do not allow obscene books and pictures to be placed on sale either publicly or privately, or sent through the mails, we exploit our Thaw trials in open court and place the lust-breeding details, per newspaper and mail, under the eyes of 60,000,000 persons, per day, young and old, and do not perceive the curious incongruity of it. A "wave of crime" quite naturally and of necessity follows, throughout the land, resulting in hundreds and hundreds of atrocities that come to light, and those of thousands that are concealed, out of shame, by the victims and their friends, and do not reach the light—say one revealed case to 200 that are never heard of by the public. Then we clamor for an increased police force to stop the wave. That is to say, we build a fire in a powder magazine, then double the fire department to put it out. We inflame wild beasts with the smell of blood, and then innocently wonder at the wave of brutal appetite that sweeps the land as a consequence. There is going to be another wave, sir; if you will wait for the new Thaw trial I offer to bet you 500 to one that you will see that wave—I mean if you are accustomed to that time-honored British way of arriving at facts that are in doubt. If you prefer, I will keep it perfectly private.

You have been hearing about the international yacht race. Do not let that pretty phrase deceive you, sir. It is not international, not in exchange of benefits; all of the really valuable results go to Great Britain—we get none of them. The races steadily improve the science of seamanship and the art of ship building; but as our monarchy forbids us to have either seamen or ships, we get not a single valuable thing out of them, unless you may call by that name our never-failing showy but spectral and empty victories. Great Britain gets all the champagne, we get the bottle. Great Britain gets the oyster, we get the shell. But if we could abolish that expensive and unprofitable sarcasm, the "international" yacht race, and substitute an international horse race, we could equalize the benefits, for we could meet you and often beat you on equable terms and improve our great Blue Grass stock in the operation—for a while: then Congress would interfere and require our native horses to sail under a foreign register and a foreign flag, like our ships.

I beg you, sir, to observe our street pavements. They are our own invention. This is the only place in the world where the pavements consist exclusively of holes with asphalt around them. And they are the most economical in the world, because holes never get out of repair.

But I must not weary you with adulations of our merits, lest I give you the impression that we have no defects—which is not the case. We have them, but we have the art of concealing them. It comes from long practice.

I hope, my Lord Bishop, that my native country is treating you as well as that old mother land of ours whence you came has lately treated me—as cordially, as hospitably, as kindly. And how kindly it was! I hope I may without too much presumption use a still warmer word and say affection—for it looked like that, and I prize that above all the rest. At the pier the assembled brawny longshoremen received me with a welcome that touched me deeply, and when I had finished my four weeks' sojourn there was no rank nor grade that had not said the pleasant word to me, from the Stevedore to the Throne. If I could express my thanks for this, I would do it; but there are thanks which cannot be put into words, words are not adequate.

That proud honor which was conferred upon me by the most illustrious of all universities, and which carried with it the added honor of being proferred, not on the spot but from over sea, carried with it yet another and still higher distinction, since in conferring it upon me, subordinately, Lord Curzon was conferring it first of all upon my "great country," as he said in his letter, using just that phrase. And so, as I stood in his stately presence and listened in innocent and ignorant contentment to his melodious Latin compliments, I could not help holding my head a little high, for I realized that I had surpassed my life's loftiest ambition, since, whether I deserved the great place or not, I was nevertheless representing in my person, and properly gowned in imposing scarlet, one of the giant nations of the earth.

You yourself, my Lord Bishop, are representing in your person tonight another giant nation; and we offer you honor, and good will, and affection; and through you we offer them to England—whom God preserve!

Text / "Bishop Speech," MS, MTP.

Eliot / The Very Reverend Philip Frank Eliot (1835–1917), dean of Windsor and domestic chaplain to His Majesty, King Edward VII. Mark Twain was confused. As noted above, the lord bishop of London delivered the King's Bible.

Bartholomew Massacre / A slaughter of French Huguenots that began on St. Bartholomew's Day, August 24, 1572, instigated by the duke of Guise, the queen mother (Catherine de Médicis), and Charles IX. The number of victims is variously given as 20,000 to 30,000.

Thaw trials / On June 25, 1906, Harry Kendall Thaw, millionaire playboy, shot and killed the architect, Stanford White, during a performance of *Ma'mzelle Champagne,* on the Madison Square Garden Roof. The motive was jealousy over White's alleged seduction of Thaw's beautiful wife, the former chorus girl and member of the Floradora Sextette, Evelyn Nesbit. When the case came to trial on January 27, 1907, it was the *cause célebre* of the new century. Prosecutor William Travers Jerome was opposed by seven defense lawyers, besides other transient attorneys who wandered in and out of the case. Among a large corps of reporters were top newsmen like Irvin S. Cobb, Samuel Hopkins Adams, and Roy Howard, together with sob sisters—all of them providing tremendous press coverage ranging from the factual to the lachrymose. Evidence was graphic. On the supposed seduction, Evelyn Thaw's testimony—perjured, some thought—shocked the clergy, shocked Congress, shocked President Roosevelt, and the public generally, but they kept on reading it just the same. New York papers, except for the impartial *Times,* defamed White, yet Thaw emerged as anything but a savory character. Testimony revealed him as a problem child given to tantrums, as a rakehell lighting cigarettes with five-dollar bills, as a reckless spender who once gave a dinner for a hundred actresses and chorus girls at $400 per girl, and as a sadist fond of abnormal sex pastimes. Calm at first, he became erratic and paranoid as the trial proceeded, quarreling with his family and lawyers, and being obsessed with the limelight and sensationalism. The man seemed deranged, but alienists called by both sides gave conflicting testimony that resulted in a hung jury.

new Thaw trial / The second Thaw trial began on January 6, 1908, Jerome again prosecuting. This time the verdict was not guilty because of insanity, and Thaw was committed to Matteawan Hospital for the Criminally Insane. He escaped in August 1913, and fled to Canada, where immigration officials apprehended him after a lively scrimmage. Seventeen Thaw lawyers tried to prevent extradition, but he was brought back across the border with the aid of Jerome, who had gone to Canada as special deputy attorney general. They got as far as Concord, New Hampshire, where twelve more lawyers fought to prevent Thaw's being sent back to Matteawan, but he was returned there in December 1914. Judged sane in 1915, he was released and divorced from Evelyn, only to be arrested two years later for kidnapping a boy, then recommitted to an insane hospital, where he spent seven years. After that he was involved in breach of promise proceedings, a brawl in an Atlantic City nightclub, and beating up a speakeasy hostess, but in 1934 he sent flowers for the funeral of Jerome. Thaw died in Florida in 1947. For more detailed accounts of this notorious case, see: F. A. Mackenzie, *The Trial of Harry Thaw* (1928); Richard O'Connor, *Courtroom Warrior* (1963), chapters 7, 8, 11.

international yacht race / Sir Thomas Lipton, the perennial challenger, issued another challenge in 1907, but no race occurred.

· 177 ·

To stimulate interest in the Children's Theatre, Mark Twain invited a remarkable audience to a special performance. Among several hundred guests were Governor Charles Evans Hughes, District Attorney Jerome, President Eliot of Harvard, Carnegie, Dan Beard, Mr. and Mrs. Samuel Guggenheim, Mrs. John Drew, Richard Harding Davis, Mr. and Mrs. Depew, John Burroughs, Walter Damrosch, Hamilton W. Mabie, Poultney Bigelow, Frederick A. Stokes, George Harvey, Brander Matthews, and other well-known citizens. The gathering was a tribute to the eminence of Mark Twain. Probably few other people, if any, could have brought together such a diverse and distinguished assembly.

Curtain Speech

Invitational Performance of The Prince and the Pauper,
Children's Theatre, New York, November 19, 1907

Just a word or two to let you know how deeply I appreciate the honor which the children who are the actors and frequenters of this cozy playhouse have conferred upon me. They have asked me to be their ambassador to invite the hearts and brains of New York to come down here and see the work they are doing. I consider it a grand distinction to be chosen as their intermediary. Between the children and myself there is an indissoluble bond of friendship.

I am proud of this theater and this performance—proud, because I am naturally vain—vain of myself and proud of the children.

I wish I could reach more children at one time. I am glad to see that the children of the East Side have turned their backs on the Bowery theaters to come to see the pure entertainments presented here.

This Children's Theatre is a great educational institution. I hope the time will come when it will be part of every public school in the land. I may be pardoned in being vain. I was born vain, I guess. [Offstage whistle.] That settles it; there's my cue to stop. I was to talk until the whistle blew, but it blew before I got started. It takes me longer to get started than most people. I guess I was born at slow speed. My time is up, and if you'll keep quiet for two minutes I'll tell you something about Miss Herts, the woman who conceived this splendid idea. She is the originator and the creator of this theater. Educationally, this institution coins the gold of young hearts into external good.

Text / Composite, based upon: "Whistle Cuts Mark Twain's Speech Short," *World*, November 20, 1907; "The Educational Theatre" in *MTS*(10):74–75; and *MTS*(23):332–33.

Miss Herts / Alice M. Herts was chiefly responsible for the development of the Children's Theatre. She interested children in the plays of Shakespeare and others, and directed the plays the young actors put on. The price of admission to a performance was ten cents.

· 178 ·

The Associated Societies of Engineers gave a dinner honoring Carnegie for his gift to the Engineers Club of a million-dollar clubhouse on Fortieth Street, New York. T. C. Martin, president of the club, who introduced Mark Twain, referred to a passage in the latter's autobiography in which he wrote of arriving in New York as a young man with three dollars in his pocket and a ten-dollar bill sewed into his coat. Several speakers had praised Carnegie so lavishly that Mark Twain evened the balance somewhat by poking fun at him and at simplified spelling.

Dinner Speech

Associated Societies of Engineers Dinner for Andrew Carnegie, Engineers Club, New York, December 9, 1907

It seems to me that I was around here in the neighborhood of the Public Library about fifty or sixty years ago. I don't deny the circumstance, although I don't see how you got it out of my autobiography, which was not to be printed until I am dead, unless I'm dead now. I had that three dollars in change, and I remember well the ten dollars which was sewed in my coat. I have prospered since. Now I have plenty of money and a disposition to squander it, but I can't. One of those trust companies is taking care of it.

Now, as this is probably the last time that I shall be out after nightfall this winter, I must say that I have come here with a mission, and I would make my errand of value.

Many compliments have been paid to Mr. Carnegie tonight. I was expecting them. They are very gratifying to me.

I have been a guest of honor myself, and I know what Mr. Carnegie is experiencing now. It is embarrassing to get compliments and compliments and only compliments, particularly when he knows as well as the rest of us that on the other side of him there are all sorts of things worthy of our condemnation.

Just look at Mr. Carnegie's face. It is fairly scintillating with fictitious innocence. You would think, looking at him, that he had never committed a crime in his life. But no—look at his pestiferous simplified spelling. You can't any of you imagine what a crime that has been. Torquemada was nothing to Mr. Carnegie. That old fellow shed some blood in the Inquisition, but Mr. Carnegie has brought destruction to the entire race. I know he didn't mean it to be a crime, but it was, just the same. He's got us all so we can't spell anything.

The trouble with him is that he attacked orthography at the wrong end. He meant well, but he attacked the symptoms and not the cause of the disease. He ought to have gone to work on the alphabet. There's not a vowel in it with a definite value, and not a consonant that you can hitch anything to. Look at the "h's" distributed all around. There's "gherkin." What are you going to do with the "h" in that? What the devil's the use of "h" in gherkin, I'd like to know. It's one thing I admire the English for: they just don't mind anything about them at all.

But look at the "pneumatics" and the "pneumonias" and the rest of them. A real reform would settle them once and for all, and wind up by giving us an alphabet that we wouldn't have to spell with at all, instead of this present silly alphabet, which I fancy was invented by a drunken thief. Why, there isn't a man who doesn't have to throw out about fifteen hundred words a day when he writes his letters because he can't spell them! It's like trying to do a St. Vitus's dance with wooden legs.

Now I'll bet there isn't a man here who can spell "pterodactyl." No, not one. Except perhaps the prisoner at the bar. God only knows how he would simplify it. I'd like to hear him try once—but not in public, for it's too near Sunday, when all extravagant histrionic entertainments are barred. I'd like to hear him try in private, and when he got through trying to spell "pterodactyl" you wouldn't know whether it was a fish or a beast or a bird, and whether it flew on its legs or walked with its wings. The chances are that he would give it tusks and a trunk and make it lay eggs.

Let's get Mr. Carnegie to reform the alphabet, and we'll pray for him—if he'll take the risk. If we had adequate, competent vowels, with a system of accents, giving to each vowel its own soul and value, so every shade of that vowel would be shown in its accent, there is not a word in any tongue that we could not spell accurately. That would be competent, adequate, simplified spelling, in contrast to the clipping, the hair punching, the carbuncles, and the cancers which go by the name of simplified spelling—leaving the old thing substantially what it was before, only bald-headed and unsightly.

If I ask you what *b-o-w* spells you can't answer till you know which bow I am referring to; the same with *r-o-w;* the same with *sore,* and *bore,* and *tear,* and *lead,* and *read*—and all the rest of that asinine family of bastard words born out of wedlock and don't know their own origin and nobody else does.

I ask you to pronounce *s-o-w,* and you ask me what kind of a one. If we had a sane, determinate alphabet, instead of a hospital of compound comminuted cripples and eunuchs, you would not have to waste time asking me which sow I mean, the one that is poetic, and recalls to you the furrowed field and the farmer scattering seed, or the one that recalls the lady hog and the future ham.

It's a rotten alphabet! I appoint Mr. Carnegie to get after it, and leave simplified spelling alone. Simplified spelling brought about sun spots, the San Francisco earthquake; it has brought the vast industries of this country to a standstill and spread a blight of commercial stagnation and undeserved poverty, hunger, nakedness and suffering from Florida to Alaska and from the Great Lakes to the Gulf.

O Carnegie, O prisoner at the bar, reform, reform! There's never been a noble, upright, right-feeling prophet in this world, from David and Goliath down to Sodom and Gomorrah who wouldn't censure you for what you've done! And yet you have meant well; you have not been purposely criminal, and your simplied spelling is not destitute of merit—but I must be just, I must be sternly just, and I say to you this: your simplified spelling is well enough, but like chastity—it can be carried too far!

Text / Composite, based upon: Dictation of December 10, 1907, *MTE*:57–60; "Mark Twain Jeers at Simple Spelling," *Times,* December 10, 1907; "The Alphabet and Simplified Spelling" in *MTS*(10):199–203; and *MTS*(23):364–67.

Torquemada / Tomas de Torquemada (ca. 1420–98). Spanish priest. He was a Dominican friar appointed by Ferdinand and Isabella as first Inquisitor General for Castile (1483). Organizing the Inquisition, be became infamous for severity, his victims estimated at 2,000 to 9,000.

commercial stagnation / A reference to the recession, called "panic" at the time, that occurred in 1907.

· 179 ·

At the Pleiades Club dinner for Mark Twain, menus were decorated with illustrated quotations from his books. Carter S. Cole, chairman, introduced the guest of honor by paying tribute to his eminence in American literature, praising so lavishly that Mark Twain began his speech with a mild protest.

Dinner Speech

Pleiades Club Dinner for Mark Twain, Hotel Brevoort, New York, December 22, 1907

It is hard work to make a speech when you have listened to compliments from the powers in authority. A compliment is a hard text to preach to. When the chairman introduces me as a person of merit, and when he says pleasant things about me, I always feel like answering simply that what he says is true, that it is all right, that, as far as I am concerned, the things he said can stand as they are. But you always have to say something, and that is what frightens me.

I remember out in Sydney once having to respond to some complimentary toast, and my one desire was to turn in my tracks like any other worm—and run for it. I was remembering that occasion at a later date when I had to introduce a speaker. Hoping, then, to spur his speech by putting him, in joke, on the defensive, I accused him in my introduction of everything I thought it impossible for him to have committed. When I finished there was an awful calm. I had been telling his life history by mistake.

One must keep one's character. Earn a character first if you can, and if you can't, then assume one. From the code of morals I have been following and revising and revising for seventy-two years I remember one detail. All my life I have been honest—comparatively honest. I could never use money I had not made honestly—I could only lend it.

Last spring I met General Miles again, and he commented on the fact that we had known each other thirty years. He said it was strange that we had not met years before, when we had both been in Washington. At that point I changed the subject, and I changed it with art. But the facts are these:

I was then under contract for my *Innocents Abroad,* but did not have a cent to live on while I wrote it. So I went to Washington to do a little journalism. There I met an equally poor friend, William Davidson, who had not a single vice, unless you call it a vice in a Scot to love Scotch. Together we devised the first and original newspaper syndicate, selling two letters a week to twelve newspapers and getting one dollar a letter. That $24 a week would have been enough for us—if we had not had to support the jug.

But there was a day when we felt that we must have three dollars right away—three dollars at once. That was how I met the general. It doesn't matter now what we wanted so much money at one time for, but that Scot and I did occasionally want it. The Scot sent me out one day to get it. He had a great belief in Providence, that Scottish friend of mine. He said: "The Lord will provide."

I had given up trying to find the money lying about, and was in a hotel lobby in despair, when I saw a beautiful unfriended dog. The dog saw me, too, and at once we became acquainted. Then General Miles came in, admired the dog, and asked me to price it. I priced it at three dollars. He offered me an opportunity to reconsider the value of the beautiful animal, but I refused to take more than Providence knew I needed. The general carried the dog to his room.

Then came in a sweet little middle-aged man, who at once began looking around the lobby.

"Did you lose a dog?" I asked. He said he had.

"I think I could find it," I volunteered, "for a small sum."

"How much?" he asked. And I told him three dollars.

He urged me to accept more, but I did not wish to outdo Providence. Then I went to the general's room and asked for the dog back. He was very angry, and wanted to know why I had sold him a dog that did not belong to me.

"That's a singular question to ask me, sir," I replied. "Didn't you ask me to sell him? You started it." And he let me have him. I gave him back his three dollars and returned the dog, collect, to its owner. That second three dollars I carried home to the Scot, and we enjoyed it, but the first three dollars, the money I got from the general, I would have had to lend.

The general seemed not to remember my part in that adventure, and I never had the heart to tell him about it.

Text / Composite, based upon: "How Mark Twain 'Worked' Gen. Miles," *Times,* December 23, 1907; "General Miles and the Dog," *MTS*(10):393–96.

Miles / Nelson Appleton Miles (1839–1925). American soldier. He was under fire in many battles of the Army of the Potomac. As colonel of the Fortieth Infantry, regular army, he was famous for Indian campaigns in the West (1874–86). Brigadier general (1880), he was commander of the army (1895), and campaigned in Puerto Rico (1898). An outspoken man, he filed a report on military abuses in the Philippines (1902) that caused a furor in Washington. He retired (1903) after more than forty years of service.

· 180 ·

At the Lotos Club dinner for Mark Twain, the menu was rolled like a diploma, on which was a picture of the chief guest in his Oxford gown, the margins decorated with drawings of characters from his books. Guests dined and wined on Innocent Oysters Abroad, Roughing It Soup, Fish Huckleberry Finn, Joan of Arc Filet of Beef, Punch Brothers Punch, Hadleyburg Salad, Pudd'nhead Cheese, White Elephant Coffee, Chateau Yquem Royale, and Pommery Brut. About the time Jumping Frog Terrapin came on, Mark Twain had to retire for a nap. He reappeared, however, when the banquet had arrived at Henkow Cognac, and resumed his armchair at the speakers' table. Frank R. Lawrence, club president, remarked upon Lotos dinners for Mark Twain fourteen and seven years before, and repeated the jocular proposal that the club continue to honor him every seven years.

Dinner Speech

Lotos Club Dinner for Mark Twain, 558 Fifth Avenue, New York, January 11, 1908

I wish to begin this time at the beginning, lest I forget it again. And that is to say, I wish to thank you now for this welcome that you are giving me, and to thank you also for the welcome which you gave me seven years ago, and which I forgot to thank you for at that time. And I also wish to thank you for the welcome which you gave me fourteen years ago, and which I forgot to thank you for at that time.

You know how it is when you are in a parlor with ladies and you have been at dinner in somebody's house, and when you are going away, why, common decency or your own conscience should suggest to you that it was a customary thing to say to the lady of the house that you have had an excellent and handsome time. Everybody can remember to say that except myself, and therefore I always detest myself when I come away having forgotten the common courtesy due to the lady. And I am now paying back these honors by thanking you this time. I say that now because if I tried to say that when I get through I should not think of it again until next week, and therefore I had better say it now.

I hope that you will continue this excellent custom of giving me a dinner every seven years. I have enjoyed it so much on these three occasions that although I have had the purpose in my mind some time of joining the hosts in the other world, I don't know which one of the worlds, I am willing to postpone it for another seven years.

When you are the guest of honor at a banquet you are always in a sort of embarrassed position, because the topics you are to talk to are compliments. Mr. Lawrence has paid me many compliments. Mr. Porter has paid me many compliments, and that is what always happens. It is very difficult to talk to compliments. I don't care whether you deserve the compliments or not, it is just as difficult to talk to them.

The other night, at the Engineers dinner, I sat there and enjoyed the squirms of Mr. Carnegie here, because they were complimenting him. He was trying to think of something to say when they got through; and when they got through, of course he couldn't. They were all compliments and they were not deserved, and I tried to help him out by a few criticisms and references to times which he and I know about and nobody else does.

They say that one cannot live on bread alone, but I could live on compliments. I can manage to digest them; those things give me no trouble at all. I have often thought that I missed so much in this life that I didn't make a collection of compliments and put them away where I could take them out now and then and look them over and enjoy them. And last autumn, when I came back from England—I had been through a good deal of complimenting there—I began to think that I missed it again.

Now I am beginning to collect compliments, and store them away, as other people collect pipes, and autographs, dogs and cats and books, and such things; I am collecting compliments. I have brought some of these compliments along, and you can see what they are. I wrote them down to preserve them, and I think they are very good, extraordinarily just.

Here is Hamilton Mabie; he wrote an article in the *Outlook* a short time ago, and he put this in. I think it is one of the handsomest. He says: "La Salle was the first man to make the voyage of the great stream of the Mississippi, to which hordes of smaller streams are tributary; but Mark Twain was the first man to chart, light, and indicate it for the whole world." If that could have been published at the time of the issue of my book on the Mississippi, it would have been money in my pocket.

You can see how difficult it is to frame a compliment gracefully and make it ring true. It is a talent itself. I never possessed it. I wish I did.

But a man who can pay a compliment of the nature of that compliment in public need not make one ashamed of one's self.

Here is the compliment of Albert Bigelow Paine, my biographer. He has written four octavo volumes about me. He has been right at my elbow for two years and a half, making notes, and under these circumstances if he doesn't know me, who does know me? This is his testimony. He says: "Mark Twain is not merely a great writer, but a great philosopher and a great man. He is the supreme expression of the human being, with his strength and his weakness."

What a talent for compression! It takes a genius in compression to compact as many facts as that. And now then, I come to Mr. Howells's compliment. Howells, writing in the December *Atlantic,* last month, going over his reminiscences of ancient days when he was editor of the *Atlantic Monthly* about thirty-five years ago, or a little before that; and in this December *Atlantic,* when he had reached seventy years of his life, he was passing in procession before him Emerson, and Lowell, and Holmes, and Whittier, and other men that were in those days writing for the *Atlantic,* that is, thirty-five years ago; and then he came round to the younger men, the men that were just coming along, and he reached out to me, and he said of me, then and now: "Later, 1871, came Mark Twain, originally of Missouri, but then of Hartford, and now ultimately of the solar system, not to say the universe."

It seems to me that that is a satisfying kind of compliment. I know that if we can prove that my fame has reached to Neptune and Uranus, and possibly to some systems a little beyond there, why, that would satisfy me. Howells knows how to say those things; that courteous man, you know Howells, how sweet and gentle he is, how painfully modest and retiring he is; but you know, deep down, that man is as full of vanity as I am, and just as ready to show off as I am. You know Howells, they called him over there, and made him an Oxford LL.D.; and he came back with his red gown, and you'd always think that Howells wouldn't dare put that fiery gown on his back, with all his ostensible modesty. Now that is a mistake. He told me himself ten days ago that when he was going to a public function up here of some kind at Columbia University, he sent and asked what kind of a gown he had got to wear, the American black gown or the Oxford red gown, and they sent him word that it was not customary to appear in anything but the ordinary black university gown of America. And Howells said he went there, and in the great crowd of black gowns there were three of those red Oxford badges. Howells was so ashamed of himself and vexed with himself, because he could have been one of those angels of light in that red, instead of being unnoticed with the general crowd of black men.

And this is Mr. Edison's compliment. Edison was at that Engineers dinner the other night, where you, Mr. Carnegie, believed a lot of pleasant things that were not so. And this I took from a newspaper that said that when I had finished speaking and went home, Mr. Edison wrote on his dinner card and passed it to his neighbor. What he wrote was: "An American loves his family. If he has any love left over for some other person, he generally selects Mark Twain." I think the world of that great compliment; that suits me best, it is what I like to see.

And finally, here is the compliment of a little Montana girl, at some little town in Montana. She didn't send it to me; some person in that town or some visitor sent it to Chicago, and it was sent out to me. This little girl was in a neighbor's house, and she was noticed gazing musingly at a large photograph of me on the mantelpiece, and presently she said reverently, "We have got a John the Baptist like that at home, only ours has more trimmings." I suppose she meant the halo, and mine hasn't arrived yet.

Now, here is a gold miner's compliment, and this one is forty-two years old. I remember the circumstances perfectly well. It was the introduction of Mark Twain, lecturer, to an audience of gold miners at Red Dog, California, in 1866, by one of themselves. It was in a log house, a large schoolhouse, and the audience occupied benches without any back, and there were no ladies present, they didn't know me then; but all just miners with their breeches tucked into their boot tops and with clay all over them. And they wanted somebody to introduce me to them, and they pitched upon this miner, and he objected. He said he had never appeared in public, and had never done any work of this kind; but they said it didn't matter, and so he came on the stage with me and introduced me in this way. He said:

"I don't know anything about this man, anyway. I only know two things about him. One is, he has never been in jail; and the other is, I don't know why."

Well, gentlemen, I shall value that collection when I get in finished. I don't care where a compliment falls, nor from whose lips it comes, it is always a blessed, blessed thing to receive. Mr. Lawrence has spoken of certain compliments and attentions to me in England, and I remember them so pleasantly. They were compliments from great personages, and notice taken of me by great personages; and it pleases me to think that that notice was taken of me all the way down, all the way down to where what Robert Louis Stevenson and I, sitting in Union Square and Washington Square a great many years ago, tried to find a name for, the submerged fame, that fame that permeates the great crowd of people you never see and never mingle with; people with whom you have no speech, but who read your books and become admirers of your work and have an affection for you. You may never find it out in the world, but there it is, and it is the faithfulness of the friendship, of the homage of those men, never criticizing, that began when they were children. They have nothing but compliments, they never see the criticisms, they never hear any disparagement of you, and you will remain in the home of their hearts' affection forever and ever. And Louis Stevenson and I decided that of all fame, that was the best, the very best.

I knew His Majesty the King of England long ago, years and years ago. I didn't meet him for the first time this time at all, but the first time since he has been king, and now there was one thing there that I regretted. I regret that very much. It distressed me. That was that some newspaper said that I talked to the Queen of England with my hat on. Very well, that could have been explained. I didn't approach the Queen of England with my hat on, but with it in my hand, where it belonged. I would not wear a hat; I trust I have better sense than that, and better manners than that; I know we have here. I didn't put my hat on when first she asked me to put it on; and I neglected that, and then Her Majesty told me to put it on. There is a command; and, in fact, the first invitation was a command. It seemed to me that I had made my reputation for democracy, that I had gone far enough when I disobeyed twice, and I drew the line there. It was to please her. I hadn't any use for a hat, and never did have.

There were some other things there that have never been in print, but they did rejoice my soul. The very first thing they gave me, when I stepped ashore from that ship on English soil, a great body of the bone and sinew of England, the stevedores, gathered together and received me with a hearty English cheer. And I liked that so much. And in Mr. Porter's house, I was his guest in Oxford, the butler from some neighbor of his came over and proposed to, and did, superintend all the arrangements for a large luncheon party so that he could look at me. He said he had read every book of mine, and he just wanted to see me. And that was an immense compliment. He could quote from those books; he remembered what was in them. I don't. That was a compliment most valuable of all.

And then, who was that talked about the police? Why, it was proper that the police should know me over there. Why, the police know me everywhere. And I tell you that the knowledge of the London police, their knowledge of me, was a very high compliment indeed. It has always pleased me. There never was a time when I went up to London that one of those men, those splendid policemen, didn't salute me, and that salute was a compliment; and he then would put up that all-powerful hand of his and arrest the commerce of the world, to let me cross that street uncrippled. And he would treat me just as he would a duchess. I appreciated that ever so much.

And, finally, there was that distinction that I had to take back from England, one that I take particular and peculiar pride in, and that is, that old *Punch*—*Punch,* which never in all its long history allowed any foreigner the privilege of entering that great dining room in the *Punch* building where those men sit once a week, and have for fifty years—Leech, and Burnand, and Russell, and du Maurier, and all the men that have made *Punch* great in England—and *Punch* is great in England, is the greatest periodical in the world on its own soil. I say on its own soil for the reason that you know you can't understand an Englishman's joke, and the Englishman can't understand our jokes. The cause is very simple, it is for the reason that we are not familiar with the conditions that make the point of the English joke. But *Punch* is a great periodical.

As I say, *Punch* never had granted that grace to any foreigner before, to sit down at that great board; but it extended that great privilege to me. I went there and sat with the editors of *Punch* and the cartoonists; that is where they meet once a week and lay out the next week's *Punch;* and when everything was ready and everybody seated at the table, the editor said, "Just a minute; there is to be a little ceremony," and then out of a little bit of a closet, where she had been shut up, a little bit of a creature, eight years old probably, a little girl all pink and white and blue, pretty as a picture, danced out of that closet and made a curtsey to me. She had in her hand the original of the *Punch* cartoon of the previous week, in which *Punch* is drinking my health. And that pretty little creature, that little fairy, probably eight years old, just innocence itself, broke me all up. The child expected to go back in the closet, but they gave her a greeting, and she came and sat in her father's lap, the chief editor, until half the dinner was over. And the prettiest decoration of that wonderful table was that beautiful child. When she was sent away she came and said, "Good night," to me. I said, "Oh, my dear, you are not going to leave me. Why, we have hardly got acquainted; you ought to stay." And she replied, "No, they never let me come here before; and now they will never let me come again." And that is one of the beautiful instances that I cherish of those days there.

And lest you should imagine that I didn't heartily appreciate the English hospitality, and lest you should think that I didn't do what little I could to confess what I felt about them, I will conclude with a few sentences with which I closed the last speech that I made in England, the night before I sailed. It was at the banquet given to me by the Lord

Mayor of Liverpool, and I said:

"I am now to say good-bye. Home is dear to all of us, and I am now departing to my home beyond the ocean. Oxford has conferred upon me the highest honor that has ever fallen to my share in this life's prizes, and which was the very one I would have chosen; it is the very one I would have chosen as being more gracious than any other honor that could be conferred upon me by men or state. And during my four weeks' stay here in England I have had another lofty honor, a continuous honor, an honor which has flowed willingly along without hold or cessation during all these twenty-six days, a most gratifying, most delightful honor in this, this treatment, the heartfelt grip of the hand, and the compliment that doesn't descend from the blue-grey matter of the brain, but rushes by red blood out of the heart, and, so voiced, is manifestly freighted with affection, that dearest reward that any man can earn by character or achievements in this world. And, my Lord, it makes me proud, and sometimes, sometimes it makes me humble. Many, many years ago I gathered an incident from Mr. Dana's *Two Years Before the Mast.* It was like this: There was a poor little ignorant, self-satisfied skipper of a coasting sloop of New England engaged in the dried apples and kitchen furniture trade, and he was always hailing every vessel that passed, and he only did it just to hear himself talk, and air his small greatness, just as I am always doing myself, always showing off, always trying to attract attention and notice. And that poor little man couldn't help that. He was born that way, and so was I.

"And one day a majestic Indiaman came floating by, with course on course of canvas towering into the sky, and with its decks and yards swarming with sailors, and full burdened to the Plimsoll line with spices, aromatic spices and gums, lading all the breezes with the gracious and mysterious odors of the Orient, a noble spectacle, a sublime spectacle, that great ship. Of course that little skipper hopped into the shrouds and squeaked out the hail, 'Ship ahoy! What ship is that, and whence, and whither?' And then—a deep and thunderous voice came back booming across the tops of the waves, 'The *Begum of Bengal;* one hundred and forty-eight days out from Canton; homeward bound. What ship is that?'

"And, you know, that just crushed that poor little creature flat, and he squawked back this: 'Only the *Mary Ann;* fourteen hours out from Boston; bound for Kittery Point.' Oh, the eloquence of that word, 'Only'; the eloquence of that phrase, 'Only the *Mary Ann,*' to express the depths of his humbleness.

"And that is just my case, my Lord, just my case. During one short hour in the twenty-four I pause and reflect; during one short hour in the silent watches of the night, with the music of your English welcomes still ringing in my ears, and I am humble; then I recognize, and then I confess to myself that I am 'Only the *Mary Ann,*' fourteen hours out, cargoed with vegetables, and bound—where? But during all the other twenty-three hours my satisfied vanity rides high on the white crests of your approval, and then I am the stately Indiaman, flying across the seas under a cloud of canvas, and laden to the Plimsoll mark with the most redolent spices that were ever passed to a wanderer alone in this world; and then my twenty-six days on this old mother soil seem ample for themselves, and I am the '*Begum of Bengal;* one hundred and forty-eight days out from Canton; and homeward bound.' "

[At the conclusion of the speech, Colonel Porter brought forward the red gown of Oxford, which Mark Twain donned as the company cheered.]

Oh, this is all right! I should have brought them myself if I had thought of it. I like the giddy costume. I was born for a savage. There isn't any color that is too bright and too strong for me, and the red—isn't that red? There is no such red as that outside the arteries of an archangel that could compare with this. I should just like to wear it all the time, and to go up and down Fifth Avenue and hear the people envy me and wish they dared to wear a costume like that. I am going to have luncheon shortly with ladies—just ladies. I will be the only lady there of my sex, and I shall put on this gown and make those ladies look dim.

Text / Composite, based upon: "Samuel L. Clemens at the Dinner in His Honor, January 11, 1908," *Lotos:*344–55; "Mark Twain Now After Compliments," *Times,* January 12, 1908; "Compliments and Degrees," *MTS*(10):25–30; "The Last Lotos Club Speech," *MTS*(23):368–74.

Porter / Robert Percival Porter (1854–1917). British-American journalist. A reporter for the Chicago *Inter-Ocean* (1872), and the New York *Tribune* (1889), he founded the New York *Press* (1889), and was on the staff of the London *Times* (1904–17). Among his books, chiefly on economic subjects, are *Breadwinners Abroad* (1885), and *Other People's Money* (1900).

Leech / John Leech (1817–64). British humorous artist. He began sending sketches to *Punch* (1841), of which he was thereafter chief cartoonist until his death. He also made illustrations for the *New Monthly Magazine* (1840–42), *Christmas Stories of Charles Dickens* (1843–48), *Shilling Magazine* (1845–48), and others.

Burnand / Francis Cowley Burnand (1836–1917). British editor and writer. On the staff of *Punch* (1862–1906), he was chief editor (1880–1906). He wrote many burlesques, farces and comedies, and adapted a number of plays for the American company of Augustin Daly.

du Maurier / George Louis Palmella Busson du Maurier (1834–96). French-born British writer and painter. He was a *Punch* cartoonist, who also illustrated the novels of Mrs. Gaskell, Thackeray, Meredith, and others. Du Maurier is probably best known, however, for his own popular novels: *Peter Ibbetson* (1891), and *Trilby* (1894).

little girl all pink and white and blue / Joy Agnew, daughter of the chief editor, presented to Mark Twain the original of the cartoon that had been published in *Punch* on June 26. See *MTB,* 4, facing 1400.

luncheon . . . with ladies / To answer feminine complaints of exclusion from stag parties, Mark Twain instigated a "Doe luncheon," for women only, on January 14, 1908, and another on February 11. At these luncheons Clara Clemens acted as hostess, and her father did all the talking. Among guests at one or other of these affairs were Kate Douglas Riggs, Mrs. Robert Collyer, Mrs. Frank Doubleday, Geraldine Farrar, and Ethel Barrymore. Mme. Marcella Sembrich sent regrets. Kate Riggs may have been present at both luncheons. She said (*MTB,* 4:1435): "A lady who is invited to and attends a *doe luncheon* is, of course, a doe. The question is, if she attends *two* doe luncheons in succession is she a doe-doe? If so she is extinct and can never attend a third."

· 181 ·

Like other functions of the Pilgrims of New York, the dinner for Whitelaw Reid stressed the motif of hands-across-the-sea: the dining hall decorated with the Stars and Stripes and the Union Jack, the audience singing British and American national anthems, and drinking toasts to the president and the king. J. P. Morgan was there, Ogden Mills, Seth Low, Carnegie, Bishop Potter, General Frederick D. Grant, and some three hundred others. Joseph H. Choate presided.

Dinner Speech

Pilgrims Club Dinner for Whitelaw Reid,
New York, February 19, 1908

I am very proud to respond to this toast, as it recalls the proudest day of my life. The delightful hospitality shown me at the time of my visit to Oxford I shall cherish until I die. In that long and distinguished career of mine I value that degree above all other honors. When the ship landed even the stevedores gathered on the shore and gave an English cheer. Nothing could surpass in my life the pleasure of those four weeks. There didn't seem to be anyone above taking me by the hand. Even the police would do so. I think I have been in every capital in Christendom, and I have always been an object of interest to the police; but London surpassed them all.

The London police always saluted me—sometimes with a suspicious eye, but not always. And the policeman there would lift his hand and paralyze the commerce of the world to let me pass. I liked that.

I approve heartily of the message which Bishop Lawrence, of New England, has conveyed. But he has overlooked one thing, and I ask permission to add it.

It is important. I read in a telegram from Washington today that Congress will immediately pass a bill restoring to our gold coinage the words "In God We Trust." I'm glad of that; I'm glad of that. I was troubled when that motto was removed. I thought we would get into difficulties if we left it off, and straightway they came.

The prosperity of the whole nation went down in a pile when we ceased to trust in God in that conspicuous and well advertised way. I knew it would come. And if Pierpont Morgan hadn't stepped in just then, and—well, if the Bishop will add in his message to the old country that we have resumed our trust in God, we will discharge Mr. Morgan from his high office with honor.

Mr. Reid said an hour or so ago something about my ruining my health by my activities last summer. They were not ruined, they were renewed. I am stronger now—much stronger. I suppose that the spiritual uplift I received increased my physical power more than anything I ever had before. I was dancing last night at 12:30 o'clock.

Mr. Choate is full of history—and some of it is true, too. He mentioned the long line of ministers we sent to England—people I never heard of before, and he elected five to the presidency by his own vote. I'm glad and proud to find Mr. Reid in that high position, because he didn't look like it when I first saw him forty years ago. Raking among his old relics in his house the other day, he told me that he had found an old autograph of mine written in those days. I didn't know I had an autograph then; nobody ever asked for it.

I remember the first time I came from the Pacific coast a stranger to New York and had my first New York dinner—that is, the first I didn't pay for; Whitelaw Reid paid for it. There were present Whitelaw Reid, John Hay and myself. And I have lived all this long stretch of time and have seen Whitelaw Reid rise and rise, and enjoyed his hospitality in London, at the embassy that Choate blackguards so. I'd like to live there. I visited him, too, at No. 123 Victoria Street. The position suited him.

Some people say they couldn't live on the salary, but I could live on the salary and the nation together. Some of us don't appreciate what this country can do. There's John Hay, Reid, Choate and me. This is the only country in the world where such characters could do these things. It shows what we can do without means, and what people can do with talent and energy when they find it in people like us.

When I first came to New York they were all struggling young men, and I am glad to see that they have got on in the world. I knew John Hay when I had no white hairs in my head and more hair than Reid has now. Those were days of joy and hope. Reid and Hay were on the staff of the *Tribune*. I went there once in that old building, and I looked all around, and I finally found a door ajar and looked in. It wasn't Reid or Hay there, but it was Horace Greeley. Those were the days when Horace Greeley was a king. I remember it was the first time I ever saw him—also the last.

I was admiring him when he stopped and seemed to realize that there was a fine presence there somewhere. He tried to smile, but he was out of smiles. He looked at me a moment, and said, "What in H—— do you want?"

He began with that word "H." That's a long word and a profane word. I don't remember what the word was now, but I recognized the power of it. I had never used that language myself, but at that moment I was converted. It has been a great refuge for me in time of trouble. If a man doesn't know that language he can't express himself on strenuous occasions. When you have that word at your command let trouble come.

But later Hay rose, and you know what summit Whitelaw Reid has reached, and you see me. Those two men have regulated troubles of nations and conferred peace upon mankind. And in my humble way, of which I am quite vain, I was the principal moral force in all those great international movements. These great men illustrated what I say. Look at us great people—we all come from the dregs of society. That's what can be done in this country. That's what this country does for you.

Choate here—he hasn't got anything to say, but he says it just the same, and he can do it so felicitously, too. I said long ago he was the handsomest man America ever produced. May the progress of civilization always rest on such distinguished men as it has in the past!

Text / Composite, based upon: "Morgan, Reid and Carnegie Sang 'The Bowery,' " *World,* February 20, 1908; "Dinner to Whitelaw Reid" in *MTS*(10):171–74; and *MTS*(23):382–85.

Lawrence / William Lawrence (1850–1941). American Protestant Episcopal clergyman. He was bishop of Massachusetts (1893–1926). Among his books are *Visions of Service* (1896), and *Life of Phillips Brooks* (1930).

"In God We Trust" / In 1907 President Roosevelt, correctly maintaining that "In God We Trust" had no legal sanction, proposed that it be removed from coins, and commissioned St. Gaudens to design coins without the motto. Roosevelt said: "to put such a motto on coins, or to use it in any kindred manner, not only does no good but does positive harm, and is in effect irreverence which comes dangerously close to sacrilege." See *The Letters of Theodore Roosevelt,* ed. Elting E. Morison (Cambridge, 1951–54), 5:842–43. The proposal blew up such a storm of protest from clergymen and other pious citizens that the president abandoned the idea. The next session of Congress made "In God We Trust" mandatory on coins.

Morgan / John Pierpont Morgan (1837–1919). American financier.

His firm was a leader in government financing and international banking. Many business interests and great wealth made him the symbol of Wall Street control and the target of attacks by opponents of centralized money power. Yet as Mark Twain ironically implied, Morgan eased the panic of 1907 by rallying bankers, and he gave generously to museums, churches, and hospitals. He had a magnificent library and a great art collection, now housed in the Metropolitan Museum, New York.

Reid / Whitelaw Reid (1837–1912). American editor and diplomat. As editor of the New York *Tribune* (1872–1905), he improved foreign coverage, attracted contributors like Mark Twain, R. H. Stoddard, and Bret Harte, and made the *Tribune* the foremost Republican paper in America. Reid was minister to France (1889–92), on the commission to negotiate peace with Spain (1898), and ambassador to Great Britain (1905–12). Mark Twain's public praise of him was at variance with his private opinion, which was less favorable.

dancing last night at 12:30 / He may have been referring to a musicale on February 13, given by Clara Clemens and assistants for an invited audience at 21 Fifth Avenue. The concert was followed by a supper and ball at Sherry's. Mark Twain was undoubtedly one of the dancers.

Horace Greeley / (1811–72). American editor. Founding the New York *Tribune* (1841), he was editor thereafter. Engaging writers like Charles A. Dana, Margaret Fuller, George Ripley, Bayard Taylor, and other newsworthy contributors, Greeley was one of the great American editors. A strong Unionist, he advocated the Free Soil movement, Fourierism, antislavery, temperance, universal suffrage, and post-Civil War amnesty. A liberal Republican presidential candidate (1872), he met a crushing defeat that probably hastened his death. He wrote *The American Conflict* (1864–66), *Recollections of a Busy Life* (1868), and others.

· 182 ·

On February 22, 1908, Mark Twain sailed on the Bermudian *for Bermuda, where he remained about six weeks. A mild climate and a life more leisurely than the relentless pace of New York were attractions something like the lure of the Sandwich Islands. Still the professional speaker, however, he was drafted for benefit affairs in Hamilton on behalf of the Bermuda Cottage Hospital and the Aquarium, giving each time a program of stories. He also talked briefly to children of the garrison there.*

Story

Told to Garrison Children, Hamilton, Bermuda, April 6, 1908

As I was on my way up the hill, I saw a cat jump over a wall, and that reminded me of a little incident of my childhood that may interest you. I was a little boy once on a time, and before that I was a little girl, perhaps, though I don't remember it.

There was a good deal of cholera around the Mississippi Valley in those days, and my mother used to dose us children with a medicine called Patterson's Patent Pain Killer. She had an idea that the cholera was worse than the medicine, but then she had never taken the stuff. It went down our insides like liquid fire and fairly doubled us up. I suppose we took fifty bottles of that pain killer in our family. I used to feed mine to a crack in the floor of our room when no one was looking.

One day when I was doing this our cat, whose name was Peter, came into the room, and I looked at him and wondered if he might not like some of that pain killer. He looked hungry, and it seemed to me that a little of it might do him good. So I just poured out the bottle and put it before him. He did not seem to get the real effect of it at first, but pretty soon I saw him turn and look at me with a queer expression in his eyes, and the next minute he jumped to the window and went through it like a cyclone, taking all the flower pots with him, and seeing that cat on the wall just now reminded me of the little incident of my childhood after many years.

Text / "Mark Twain Tells About the Cat," *Times,* April 19, 1908, part six.

· 183 ·

Mark Twain returned to New York aboard the Bermuda *in mid-April. Smoking a long black cheroot and accompanied by Henry Rogers, he met reporters under a shipboard sign warning that smoking annoyed seasick passengers.*

Interview

New York, April 13, 1908

Birds of a feather. You know the rest of it. It's a terrible strain, this being a financier. It is also a strain traveling with one. I offered to loan Rogers two dollars, though I knew I was taking an awful risk. Rogers thought it was simply a courtesy and so did not take me up. Now I am two dollars ahead.

I have returned from my trip a reformer. I have joined the ranks of the anti-noise society. I have retired both from the making of after-dinner speeches and the lecture platform. No one can tolerate noise, you know, unless they are the noisemakers. I am through making a noise, and so I now insist on quiet. Mrs. Rice started her crusade at the right time for me.

[He was asked what he thought of the scheme to improve interior waterways by dredging a fourteen-foot channel down the Mississippi River.] I have no sentimental interest in such a project, and I have too many realities to deal with to be chasing a will-o'-the-wisp. When the Almighty built this earth He knew very well that a fourteen-foot channel from Chicago to the Gulf would have been a very excellent and much-needed thing, but He also knew that it would tax even His resources. If there were fourteen Banks of England behind the scheme, and fourteen more behind them, there would not be enough available money to finance the scheme.

I know the Mississippi Valley and its oozy soil too well. The digging of the channel would be but the beginning. A thousand dredges could not keep it clear.

[He talked of high seas en route. On Sunday, he said, when he was wearing his white suit and standing at the stern rail with Dorothy Sturgis, of Boston, a great wave washed aboard and drenched them both.]

Text / "Twain and Rogers Back From Bermuda," *Times,* April 14, 1908.

anti-noise society / Mark Twain became a member of the Advisory Board of the Society for the Prevention of Unnecessary Noise. Probably his duties, if any, were nominal, as very likely they were for other posts he theoretically occupied: e.g., member of the Advisory Board of the Hispanic Society of America, trustee of the Lincoln Farm Association, member of the General Committee of the People's Institute, and member of the Board of Governors of the Hudson River Day Line.

· 184 ·

Senator Patrick H. McCarren, Henry Rogers, and Mark Twain were the chief guests at a rowdy dinner of cartoonists and newsmen. Mam'selle Fay Douglas, in a fetching bathing costume, entertained the disorderly crowd with songs, and cartoonists amused themselves by drawing caricatures on the large menus, on which were printed, in scarehead type, only "Steak" and "Beer." The pace became so boisterous that the Times *said next day: "At 11 o'clock it appeared that the proper name of the organization would be the Mutual Protective Bail Bond Association." Mark Twain was reluctant to talk across a long room, but he was finally persuaded to say something.*

Remarks

Humorists and Cartoonists Beefsteak Dinner,
Reisenweber's, New York, April 18, 1908

In the matter of courage we all have our limits. There never was a hero who did not have his bounds. I suppose it may be said of Nelson and all the others whose courage has been advertised that there came times in their lives when their bravery knew it had come to its limit.

I have found mine a good many times. Sometimes this was expected—often it was unexpected. I know a man who is not afraid to sleep with a rattlesnake, but you could not get him to sleep with a safety razor.

I never had the courage to talk across a long, narrow room. I should be at the end of the room facing all the audience. If I attempt to talk across a room I find myself turning this way and that, and thus at alternate periods I have part of the audience behind me. You ought never to have any part of the audience behind you; you can never tell what they are going to do.

I'll sit down.

Text / Composite, based upon: "Twain and McCarren Mix Wit With Art," *Times,* April 19, 1908; "Courage," in *MTS*(10):151; *MTS*(23):386.

· 185 ·

Mark Twain returned once again to his favorite Children's Theatre, where he spoke briefly between performances of Editha's Burglar *and* Op-o'-Me-Thumb. *Both productions were put on by juvenile actors and juvenile stagehands, all of whom, in a great flutter of excitement, gathered in the wings and peeked through the curtain while he was talking.*

Curtain Speech

Children's Theatre of the Educational Alliance, New York, April 23, 1908

The work will be reorganized under a new board of directors. The honorary president will be Mr. Samuel L. Clemens—I am that.

I will be strictly honest with you; I am only fit to be honorary president. It is not to be expected that I should be useful as a real president. But when it comes to things ornamental I, of course, have no objection. There is, of course, no competition. I take it as a very real compliment because there are thousands of children who have had a part in this request. It is promotion in truth.

It is a thing worth doing that is done here. You have seen the children play. You saw how little Sally reformed her burglar. She could reform any burglar. She could reform me. This is the only school in which can be taught the highest and most difficult lessons—morals. In other schools the way of teaching morals is revolting. Here the children who come in thousands live through each part.

They are terribly anxious for the villain to get his bullet, and that I take to be a humane and proper sentiment. They spend freely the ten cents that is not saved without a struggle. It comes out of the candy money, and the money that goes for chewing gum and other necessaries of life. They make the sacrifice freely. This is the only school which they are sorry to leave.

Text / Composite, based upon: *World,* April 24, 1908; "The Educational Theatre" in *MTS*(10):75–76; and *MTS*(23):333–34.

new board of directors / On the board were Robert Collyer, the Reverend Percey Stickney Grant, and Stanley Hall, president of Clark University.

reformed her burglar / "Editha's Burglar" (1888), a story by Frances Eliza Hodgson Burnett (1849–1924), was dramatized by Augustus Thomas. In a Broadway production (1888) Elsie Leslie played the role of Editha, and E. H. Sothern that of the burglar.

· 186 ·

Dedication ceremonies at the City College of New York attracted dignitaries academic and political. At the exercises in the main hall, Mayor McClelland spoke, British Ambassador James Bryce, Joseph H. Choate, and Mark Twain. The latter, a vivid splash of color in the red gown of Oxford, told reporters that he was not at all embarrassed by such a conspicuous garb. Undergraduates swarmed around him with so much noisy attention that the Times *observed the day after: "It was the City College's day and Mark Twain's."*

Speech

Dedication of the College of the City of New York,
May 14, 1908

How difficult, indeed, is the higher education. Mr. Choate evidently needs a little of it. He is not only short as a statistician of New York, but he is off, way off, in his mathematics. The four thousand citizens of Greater New York, indeed!

But I don't think it was wise or judicious on the part of Mr. Choate to show this higher education he has obtained. He has said that seventy years ago he sat in the lap of that great educator, Horace Mann. I was there at the time—and see the result, the lamentable result. Maybe if he had had a sandwich here to sustain him the result would not have been so serious.

For seventy-two years I have been striving to acquire that higher education which stands for modesty and diffidence—and it doesn't work.

And then look at Ambassador Bryce, who referred to his alma mater, Oxford. He might just as well have included me. Well, I am a later production.

If I am the latest graduate, I really and sincerely hope I am not the final flower of its seven centuries; I hope it may go on for seven ages longer.

Text / Composite, based upon: "Jubilee Dedication For City College," *Times,* May 15, 1908; "Dedication Speech," *MTS*(10):41.

Horace Mann / (1796–1859). American educator. As secretary of the Massachusetts Board of Education (1837–48), he reorganized the state's school system, popularized the cause of common schools, lengthened the school year to six months, increased teachers' salaries, and got larger educational appropriations. In Congress (1848–52), he was an antislavery Whig opposed to sectarian control of schools. As president of Antioch College (1852–59), he advocated coeducation and higher academic standards.

Bryce / James Bryce (1838–1922). British historian and statesman. Liberal member of Parliament (1880–1907), he was chancellor for the Duchy of Lancaster (1892), chief secretary for Ireland (1895), and ambassador to the United States (1907–13). He was a delegate to the Hague tribunal (1913) and one of the founders of the League of Nations. Among his many books, the best known is *The American Commonwealth* (1888).

· 187 ·

After the dedication ceremony, alumni of the City College of New York assembled for a dinner. Four hundred drank toasts to their alma mater, and when Mark Twain made a late appearance, they hailed him as "First in war, first in peace, and first in the hearts of his countrymen." Previous speakers having been interrupted by cries of "Louder!" he said, according to the Times *next day: "If you have a voice loud enough to state what you have to state you don't have to have anything in what you say." When he departed at 11:45 P.M., his last word was: "I have an important engagement at a quarter of eleven."*

Dinner Speech

Associated Alumni of City College of New York,
Hotel Waldorf-Astoria, New York, May 14, 1908

I agreed when the mayor said that there was not a man within hearing who did not agree that citizenship should be placed above everything else, even learning. And then I thought—is there in any college of the land a chair of citizenship where good citizenship and all that it implies is taught? There is not one—that is, not one where sane citizenship is taught. There are some which teach insane citizenship, bastard citizenship, but that is all. Patriotism! Yes; but patriotism is usually the refuge of the scoundrel. He is the man who talks the loudest.

You can begin that chair of citizenship in the College of the City of New York. You can place it above mathematics and literature, and that is where it belongs.

Some years ago on the gold coins we used to trust in God. I think it was in 1863 that some genius suggested that it be put on the gold and silver coins which circulated among the rich. They didn't put it on the nickels and coppers because they didn't think the poor folks had any trust in God.

Good citizenship would teach accuracy of thinking and accuracy of statement. That statement on the gold coins, "In God We Trust," was an overstatement. Those congressmen had no right to commit this whole country to a theological doctrine. But since they did, Congress ought to state what our creed should be.

There is not a nation in the world which ever put its faith in God. It is a statement made on insufficient evidence. In the unimportant cases of life, perhaps, we do trust in God—that is, if we rule out the gamblers and burglars, and plumbers, for of course they do not believe in God.

If the cholera or black plague should ever come to these shores, perhaps the bulk of the nation would pray to be delivered from it, but the rest of the population would put their trust in the Health Board of the City of New York. If I remember rightly, the President required or ordered the removal of that sentence from the coins. Well, I didn't see that the statement ought to remain there. It wasn't true. But I think it would better read, "Within certain judicious limitations we trust in God," and if there isn't enough room on the coin for this, why, enlarge the coin.

I read in the papers within the last day or two of a poor young girl who they said was a leper. Did the people in that populous section of the country where she was—did they put their trust in God? The girl was afflicted with the leprosy, a disease which cannot be communicated from one person to another.

Yet, instead of putting their trust in God, they harried that poor creature, shelterless and friendless, from place to place, exactly as they did in the Middle Ages, when they made lepers wear bells, so that people could be warned of their approach and avoid them. Perhaps those people in the Middle Ages thought they were putting their trust in God.

[He told of the forty-two Biblical children devoured by bears, despite the prophets' injunction to trust in God.] But I have a great respect for the bald-headed prophets. I expect to be one myself sometime. I don't know Mr. Bryan, but he's got that sort of a head. If Congress puts that motto back on the coins I hope they will modify it.

Now I want to tell a story about jumping at conclusions. It was told to me by Bram Stoker, and it concerns a christening. There was a little clergyman who was prone to jump at conclusions sometimes. One day he was invited to officiate at a christening. He went. There sat the relatives—intelligent-looking relatives they were. The little clergyman's instinct came to him to make a great speech. He was given to flights of oratory that way—a very dangerous thing, for often the wings which take one into clouds of oratorical enthusiasm are wax and melt up there, and down you come.

But the little clergyman couldn't resist. He took the child in his arms, and, holding it, looked at it a moment. It wasn't much of a child. It was little, like a sweet potato. Then the little clergyman waited impressively, and then: "I see in your countenances," he said, "disappointment of him. I see you are disappointed with this baby. Why? Because he is so little. My friends, if you had but the power of looking into the future you might see that great things may come of little things. There is the great ocean, holding the navies of the world, which comes from little drops of water no larger than a woman's tears. There are the great constellations in the sky, made up of little bits of stars. Oh, if you could consider his future you might see that he might become the greatest poet of the universe, the greatest warrior the world has ever known, greater than Caesar, than Hannibal, than—er—er" (turning to the father)—"what's his name?"

The father hesitated, then whispered back: "His name? Well, his name is Mary Ann."

Text / Composite, based upon: "400 Alumni at the Waldorf," *Times,* May 15, 1908; "Education and Citizenship" in *MTS*(10):147–50; and *MTS*(23):378–81.

patriotism is usually the refuge of the scoundrel / A slight modification of a remark made by Dr. Johnson on April 7, 1775, when he dined, according to Boswell, "At a Tavern, with a numerous company," which was the famous Literary Club. "Patriotism," roared Johnson, "is the last refuge of a scoundrel."

it was in 1863 / "In God We Trust" began to appear on coins about 1864. Heightened religious sentiment during the Civil War induced clergymen and others to broach the motto idea to Lincoln. He passed it on to Salmon P. Chase, secretary of the treasury, who asked the director of the Philadelphia Mint to select a suitable motto. Among rejected suggestions were "God Our Trust" and "God and Our Country."

· 188 ·

When the American Booksellers Association convened in New York, all the speakers at the annual dinner were writers: Burgess Johnson, Will Irwin, Holman Day, and Mark Twain. The latter's speech is incomplete. According to next day's Times, *he also talked about using his royalties to build a farmhouse where he expected to take a vacation of thirty or forty years before finishing the five books he was working on.*

Dinner Speech

American Booksellers Association Dinner,
Aldine Rooms, New York, May 20, 1908

This annual gathering of booksellers from all over America comes together ostensibly to eat and drink, but really to discuss business; therefore I am required to talk shop. I am required to furnish a statement of the indebtedness under which I lie to you gentlemen for your help in enabling me to earn my living. For something over forty years I have acquired my bread by print, beginning with *The Innocents Abroad,* followed at intervals of a year or so by *Roughing It, Tom Sawyer, Gilded Age,* and so on. For thirty-six years my books were sold by subscription. You are not interested in those years, but only in the four which have since followed. The books passed into the hands of my present publishers at the beginning of 1904, and you then became the providers of my diet. I think I may say, without flattering you, that you have done exceedingly well by me. Exceedingly well is not too strong a phrase, since the official statistics show that in four years you have sold twice as many volumes of my venerable books as my contract with my publishers bound you and them to sell in five years. To your sorrow you are aware that frequently, much too frequently, when a book gets to be five or ten years old its annual sale shrinks to two or three hundred copies, and after an added ten or twenty years ceases to sell. But you sell thousands of my mossbacked old books every year—the youngest of them being books that range from fifteen to twenty-seven years old, and the oldest reaching back to thirty-five and forty.

By the terms of my contract my publishers had to account to me for

50,000 volumes per year for five years, and pay me for them whether they sold them or not. It is at this point that you gentlemen come in, for it was your business to unload 250,000 volumes upon the public in five years if you possibly could. Have you succeeded? Yes, you have—and more. For in four years, with a year still to spare, you have sold the 250,000 volumes, and 240,000 besides.

Your sales have increased each year. In the first year you sold 90,328; in the second year, 104,851; in the third, 133,975; in the fourth year—which was last year—you sold 160,000. The aggregate for the four years is 500,000 volumes, lacking 11,000.

Of the oldest book, *The Innocents Abroad*—now forty years old—you sold upward of 46,000 copies in the four years; of *Roughing It*—now thirty-eight years old, I think—you sold 40,334; of *Tom Sawyer*, 41,000. And so on.

And there is one thing that is peculiarly gratifying to me: the *Personal Recollections of Joan of Arc* is a serious book; I wrote it for love, and never expected it to sell, but you have pleasantly disappointed me in that matter. In your hands its sale has increased each year. In 1904 you sold 1,726 copies; in 1905, 2,445; in 1906, 5,381; and last year, 6,574.

Text / Composite, based upon: "Mark Twain Gives Thanks," *Times*, May 21, 1908; "Booksellers" in *MTS*(10):218–20; and *MTS*(23): 375–77.

· 189 ·

A note accompanying texts in both editions of MTS *says that Mark Twain, at the British Schools and Universities Club dinner, began his eulogy of Queen Victoria by telling the story of the abortive Nevada duel in 1864. On the following day the* Times *reported: "He prefaced his remarks by reciting one or two of his humorous experiences, including an imaginary interview . . . between Livingstone and Stanley, when the latter found Livingstone in Central South Africa. . . . Mark Twain overheard Stanley tell how the rulers of most of the countries had been changed, finally concluding, 'and Horace Greeley has changed his political faith.'" Perhaps he also told the duel story, and others as well.*

Queen Victoria—An American Tribute

British Schools and Universities Club Dinner, Delmonico's, New York, May 25, 1908

It also happened that I was the means of stopping dueling in Nevada, for a law was passed sending all duelists to jail for two years, and the governor, hearing of my marksmanship, said that if he got me I should go to prison for the full term. That's why I left Nevada, and I have not been there since.

You do me a high honor, indeed, in selecting me to speak of my country in this commemoration of the birthday of that noble lady whose life was consecrated to the virtues and the humanities and to the promotion of lofty ideals, and was a model upon which many a humbler life was formed and made beautiful while she lived, and upon which many such lives will still be formed in the generations that are to come—a life which finds its just image in the star which falls out of its place in the sky and out of existence, but whose light still streams with unfaded luster across the abysses of space long after its fires have been extinguished at their source.

As a woman the Queen was all that the most exacting standards could require. As a far-reaching and effective beneficent moral force she had no peer in her time among either monarchs or commoners. As a monarch she was without reproach in her great office. We may not venture, perhaps, to say so sweeping a thing as this in cold blood about any monarch that preceded her upon either her own throne or upon any other. It is a colossal eulogy, but it is justified.

In those qualities of the heart which beget affection in all sorts and conditions of men she was rich, surprisingly rich, and for this she will still be remembered and revered in the far-off ages when the political glories of her reign shall have faded from vital history and fallen to a place in that scrap heap of unverifiable odds and ends which we call tradition. Which is to say, in briefer phrase, that her name will live always. And with it her character—a fame rare in the history of thrones, dominions, principalities, and powers, since it will not rest upon harvested selfish and sordid ambitions, but upon love, earned and freely vouchsafed. She mended broken hearts where she could, but she broke none.

What she did for us in America in our time of storm and stress we shall not forget, and whenever we call it to mind we shall always remember the wise and righteous mind that guided her in it and sustained and supported her—Prince Albert's. We need not talk any idle talk here tonight about either possible or impossible war between the two countries; there will be no war while we remain sane and the son of Victoria and Albert sits upon the throne. In conclusion, I believe I may justly claim to utter the voice of my country in saying that we hold him in deep honor, and also in cordially wishing him a long life and a happy reign.

Text / Composite, based upon: "Twain Eulogizes Queen Victoria," *Times,* May 26, 1908; "Queen Victoria" in *MTS*(10):238–40; and *MTS*(23):387–88.

the means of stopping dueling / The opening paragraph is a good example of differences that often show up between Mark Twain's recollections and what actually happened. The dueling law was already in effect when he become involved, and because of the law he departed hurriedly for San Francisco. The skillful marksmanship, which appears in the *Roughing It* version of the duel story, is entirely fiction. As to never returning to Nevada, he did return briefly on lecture tours in 1866 and 1868. As he himself admitted, what he remembered best were things that were not so, and he evidently repeated romantic versions of past history until they solidified as facts.

· 190 ·

After Mark Twain had moved into his new home, Stormfield, one of the first events was an invasion by burglars. Another event, in which he played a prominent role, was the establishment of a library at Redding. He donated books, and, as a prime mover, became first president of the Library Association, of which Dr. Ernest H. Smith was vice-president, and William E. Grumman was librarian. On the afternoon of the opening, Mark Twain spoke briefly.

Remarks

Opening of the Mark Twain Library, Redding, Connecticut, October 28, 1908

I am here to speak a few instructive words to my fellow farmers. I suppose you are all farmers. I am going to put in a crop next year, when I have been here long enough and know how. I couldn't make a turnip stay on a tree now after I had grown it. I like to talk. It would take more than the Redding air to make me keep still, and I like to instruct people. It's noble to be good, and it's nobler to teach others to be good, and less trouble. I am glad to help this library. We get our morals from books. I didn't get mine from books, but I know that morals do come from books—theoretically at least. Mr. Beard or Mr. Adams will give some land, and by and by we are going to have a building of our own.

I am going to help build that library with contributions—from my visitors. Every male guest who comes to my house will have to contribute a dollar or go away without his baggage. If those burglars that broke into my house recently had done that they would have been happier now, or if they'd have broken into this library they would have read a few books and led a better life. Now they are in jail, and if they keep on they will go to Congress. When a person starts downhill you can never tell where he's going to stop. I am sorry for those burglars. They got nothing that they wanted and scared away most of my servants. Now we are putting in a burglar alarm instead of a dog. Some advised the dog, but it costs even more to entertain a dog than a burglar. I am having the ground electrified, so that for a mile around anyone who puts his foot across the line sets off an alarm that will be heard in Europe. The burglar who steps within this danger zone will set loose a bedlam of sounds, and spring into readiness for action our elaborate system of defenses. As for the fate of the trespasser, do not seek to know that. He will never be heard of more. Now I will introduce the real president to you, a man whom you know already—Dr. Smith.

Text / Composite, based upon: *MTB,* 4:1472–73; "Books and Burglars," *MTS*(10):213–14.

Beard or Adams will give some land / Dan Beard and Theodore Adams were residents of the region. According to Paine, neither had been consulted before Mark Twain made his spur-of-the-moment suggestion about giving land. Adams responded by donating a site for the library.

· 191 ·

At a dinner of the directors and faculty of the New York Postgraduate Medical School and Hospital, Mark Twain, resplendent in white, was appropriately introduced as "Dr. Samuel L. Clemens." The chairman mentioned the Stormfield burglary.

Dinner Speech

New York Postgraduate Medical School and Hospital Dinner, Delmonico's, New York, January 20, 1909

Gentlemen and doctors: This is the first opportunity I have had to thank the Post Graduate for the honorary membership conferred upon me two years ago; a distinction which is a real distinction, and which I prize as highly as anyone could. I am glad to be among my own kind tonight. I was once a sharpshooter, but now I practice a much higher and equally as deadly a profession. It wasn't so very long ago that I became a member of your cult, and for the time I've been in the business my record is one that can't be scoffed at.

As to the burglars, I am perfectly familiar with these people. I have always had a good deal to do with burglars—not officially, but through their attentions to me. I never suffered anything at the hands of a burglar. They have invaded my house time and time again. They never got anything. Then those people who burglarized our house in September—we got back the plated ware they took off, we jailed them, and I have been sorry ever since. They did us a great service—they scared off all the servants in the place.

I consider the Children's Theatre, of which I am president, and the Post Graduate Medical School as the two greatest institutions in the country. This school in bringing its twenty thousand physicians from all parts of the country, bringing them up to date, and sending them back with renewed confidence, has surely saved hundreds of thousands of lives which otherwise would have been lost.

When the distinction of an honorary membership in the Post Graduate College was conferred upon me, I felt it my duty to put aside other matters for a time and qualify myself for the position before beginning to practice. I have been practicing now for seven months. When I settled on my farm in Connecticut in June I found the community very thinly settled—and since I have been engaged in practice it has become more thinly settled still. This gratifies me, as indicating that I am making an impression on my community. I suppose it is the same with all of you.

I beg you to allow me to read a paper which I have prepared for your instruction—a very short one. I am only a country doctor, out on a farm in Connecticut, but I suppose you are similarly situated, around over the United States, out in the back settlements. The paper which I am now to read to you is entitled "On the Three Great Laws to be Observed in the Treatment of Bright's Disease of the Kidneys."

First: The first great law to be observed when professionally approaching the patient whom an all-wise Providence has deemed it necessary to inflict with that always serious and often fatal—

You know you can't carry on a great work competently without organization. So as soon as I had taken up my residence last June in the house I had built on the high hill overlooking the distant farms and the deep solitudes, I started a branch of the Post Graduate, and paid my alma mater the deserved compliment of naming it for her—"The Redding, Connecticut, Branch of the New York Post Graduate College of Medicine."

Of course, the practice of medicine and surgery in a remote country district has its disadvantages, but in my case I am happy in a division of responsibility. I practice in conjunction with a horse doctor, a sexton, and an undertaker. The combination is airtight, and once a man is stricken in our district escape is impossible for him.

These four of us—three in the regular profession and the fourth an undertaker—are all good men. There is Bill Ferguson, the Redding undertaker. Bill is there in every respect. He is self-made and self-educated. He intends to go on with his education by and by, but at present he still signs his name with a rubber stamp. Like my old southern friend, he is one of the finest planters anywhere.

Then there is Jim Ruggles, the horse doctor. Ruggles is one of the best men I have got. He is not well up in medicine as yet, but he is an elegant horse doctor—one of the very best, I think. Ferguson doesn't make any money off him.

You see, the combination started this way. When I got up to Redding and had become a doctor, I looked around to see what my chances were for aiding in the great work. The first thing I did was to determine what manner of doctor I was to be. Being a Connecticut farmer, I naturally consulted my farmacopia, and at once decided to become a farmeopath.

Then I got circulating about, and got in touch with Ferguson and Ruggles. Ferguson joined readily in my ideas, but Ruggles kept saying that, while it was all right for an undertaker to get aboard, he couldn't see where it helped horses.

Well, we started to find out what was the trouble with the community, and it didn't take long to find out that there was just one disease, and that was race suicide. And driving about the countryside I was told by my fellow farmers that it was the only rational human and valuable disease. But it is cutting into our profits so that we'll either have to stop it or we'll have to move.

Where was I?

Oh, yes. Well, as I was saying, the first great law to be observed when professionally approaching a patient whom an all-wise President—no, Providence, I mean—

We've had some funny experiences up there in Redding. Not long ago a fellow came along with a rolling gait and a distressed face. We asked him what was the matter. We always hold consultations on every case, as there isn't business enough for four. He said he didn't know, but that he was a sailor, and perhaps that might help to give a diagnosis. We treated him for that, and I never saw a man die more peacefully.

Danbury has the farm next to mine, and is a man of a jealous and sarcastic spirit, and ridicules our College and does everything he can to break up our practice. When we tried to raise money to build a hospital he said we didn't need a hospital, what we wanted was a cemetery. Everybody else is respectful, and calls our institution the Post Graduate, but he calls it the Postmortem. When we've been holding a consultation in a sick room, he doesn't call it that, he calls it Preliminary Inquest. Well, anyway, his Connecticut farm is a pretty poor one compared to mine, and he is bitterly jealous because he can't raise as many rocks on it as I can. Oh, well, let him talk, if it does him good: I know one thing—we've improved things ever so much up there; when we started in, seven months ago, there were lots and lots of sick people. There aren't any now.

We are admired and looked up to, and I may even say revered, by everybody but that man—that Danbury. They scatter flowers before us, but he never does. And they call us the Big Four, but he calls us the Four Flush. Often I have wanted to say, damn such a man, but I never would. It would distress my parents if I had some.

The first great law to be observed when professionally approaching—

Of course we make mistakes in diagnosis: everybody does, especially beginners. I remember the time the horse doctor—no, it was the Rubber Stamp—came and said he had found a case the other side of the hill, of a colored lady from New York suffering from nervous prostitution on account of overwork, and we went there and held consultation, and it wasn't *so*—nothing nervous about it, just the ordinary thing, and we took hold of her and in a week she was all right, and ready to resume her activities same as ever.

Yes, a mistake now and then in diagnosis is unavoidable, no matter how careful you are. Now there was the instance where the horse doctor came and said he had hunted down a case of vermifuge appendix. He had a good dog, and we have to use dogs now, because the inhabitants have become diffident and shy, and when a person gets sick they conceal it and hush it up. So we went there to hold a consultation—and went through the usual flummery, you know, same as you do when you are at home. No occasion for it, nothing in it, but it impresses the family and the patient:

"Hold out your tongue. M-m—good deal coated; fetch me some sandpaper. Lemme feel your pulse. M-m—94 above normal; indications of approaching fever; stick this thing under your tongue. M-m-m—temperature hundred and seventeen in the shade; fever liable to supervene at any moment." And so on, and so on—the same old usual thing, you know, that you are so familiar with in your own practice.

We all did that, and then thumped the patient on back and front, and mashed our ears against his breast and listened to his works, then we consulted. I voted with the horse doctor for appendicitis and dead against the obstetrician, who said, with decision, and urgently, "Gents, this ain't no appendicitis, there's something the matter with this feller's umbilical cord." He used to be before the mast before he came with us, and he wanted to get it out and take a reef in it and tauten it up. The undertaker wouldn't give an opinion. I reckon you've all noticed, yourselves, that in consultations you never can get the undertaker to show his hand when there's a disagreement. So there was a majority for the appendix, for the employment of the Caesarian operation to get it out. Well, after considerable rummaging around we got it out, but it turned out to be a lung. This wouldn't have made so much difference, ordinarily, but it did this time, because this was the only one he had. His appendix was dangling in a bottle in the parlor, but we didn't know it. A fine man. He was a great loss. Just an ideal patient. Always ailing—thought he was, anyway—always paid up promptly, never looked at the bill; often he would pay the same old bill four times and never say a word—same as if it was a gas bill and he couldn't help himself. Yes, a fine man and a great loss. But he is gone; gone from us never to return, and we shall have to live within our means now.

The three great laws to be observed, especially and particularly in the first stage of Bright's Disease of the kidneys—

In our practice we mainly adhere to the ancient and time-proven systems of those princes of the medical arts, Galen, and Hippocrates, and Euripides, and Cantharides, and Deuteronomy and those others. We believe in bleeding a patient as long as he—Danbury—that rotten Danbury, says—but never mind that. In my opinion Danbury is a man whose statements are based solely on malignity and jealousy, and a wanton desire to injure, and even destroy the Redding Branch of this great and noble institution, the Post Graduate College of New York, and I for one am above repeating anything he says or in any other way taking notice of him. Why, once he said—and it was only a week ago—he was talking about our branch to another infidel, and he said,

"Oh yes, the Postmortem's all right. Now that it's prosperous and has got a move on"—got a move on—that's just in his line, slang is—"now that it's prosperous and got a move on, they've set up a coat of arms: device, Hunyadi label; motto, 'Constipation is the thief of time.' "

Now, that is just a plain, straight out *lie.* That's all it is. It is true that we've got a coat of arms, but it's not a Hunyadi label; it is a facsimile of the seal of our great original here, and the motto on it sheds luster upon both our great original and its Redding Branch: to wit, "We are sternly opposed to adulterated drugs; we are sternly opposed to *all* forms of adultery, except those which custom has addicted us to."

The first great law to be observed when professionally approaching the patient whom an all-wise Providence has deemed it necessary to afflict with that always serious and often fatal malady, Brights Disease of the kidneys—

But it is too late to read it now. I will take it to your homes and read it to you there.

Text / Composite, based upon: "On the Three Great Laws to be Observed in the Treatment of Bright's Disease of the Kidneys," TS, MTP; "Dr. Mark Twain, Farmeopath," *MTS*(10):333–37.

Hippocrates / (ca. 460 B.C.–ca. 377). Greek physician. Known as the Father of Medicine, he was a widely traveled man who wrote seventy or eighty works on medical subjects. Substituting observation for ancient superstition, he believed that every effect had a cause, which was not of supernatural origin. The Hippocratic Oath, sworn by modern physicians, was not written by Hippocrates, but it is consistent with his practice.

Hunyadi label / Janos Hunyadi or Hunyady (ca. 1387–1456) was a Hungarian soldier, statesman, and hero. His son László or Ladislaus (1432–57) was also a soldier and statesman. The picture of a national hero on a patent medicine label gave authority to the contents, like the pictures of Lydia Pinkham on a bottle of vegetable compound, of the bearded Smith brothers on a box of cough drops, and of King Edward on a box of cigars. New York papers advertised "Hunyadi Janos, Best Natural Laxative Water for Constipation. Try it *now.*"

· 192 ·

The Lotos Club honored Carnegie for having come to the rescue of the club when it was about to go under in the financial panic of 1907. Among speakers were former Ambassador Tower, Gilder, McKelway, John H. Finley, president of City College, and Mark Twain. Chairman Lawrence introduced the latter as "St. Mark."

Dinner Speech

Lotos Club Dinner for Andrew Carnegie, New York, March 17, 1909

I am glad that at last a man has been found with justice enough in his heart to pay me the compliment which I have so long deserved, and which has been denied me by so many generations of supposedly intelligent beings. Ranking me with the saints! There is nothing which pleases me more than that, because there is nothing left which I have deserved more than just that. I have ranked myself with St. Andrew for several years, and I really think that this should have been a dinner to the two of us, as St. Andrew was born on the same day in the same year as I was. If St. Andrew had not been born as early as he was on the 30th of November, I should stand now about where he stands. He got in a little ahead of me.

St. Clair there is a saint, but a minor sort of saint. He is a Missourian. So am I. Look at St. Clair McKelway! You wouldn't think he came from a state like that, he looks so proud and respectable. The state of Missouri has for its coat of arms a barrel head, and two Missourians are on each side of it, leaning there together, with the motto, a misleading motto altogether, which says, "United we stand, divided we fall."

Now it is an interesting thing, St. Andrew here is here as a special guest, and he has heard himself complimented, and complimented, and complimented. You know, it is anybody's experience who has had any large experience in being the chief guest at a banquet, and you must know how entirely undeserved that entire proceeding is, for the reason that the chairman begins by filling him up with compliments, and while they are well done, they are not quite high enough to meet the demand.

Now, this man has suffered this evening from hearing compliments poured out on him, apparently with lavishness, but he knows deep down in his heart that if he could overcome his diffidence he could improve those compliments. But he tries to dissemble, as our chief guest always does—look at the expression he has got on now! And the man always thinks he is doing well! Anybody who knows, knows that it is a pretty awkward performance, that diffidence that he is working on his countenance doesn't deceive anybody; but it is always interesting to see what people will find to say about a man. It is not a matter of what Carnegie has done, for I would have done it myself, if I had had to.

I don't know just what Mr. Lawrence told you about how Mr. Carnegie came to the rescue of this club when it was likely to get into trouble, for I came in late; but I judge from remarks that followed that he did tell you about that, and that it was a fine thing to do. And they tell me that it was at a banquet given by the Lotos Club to me; it was at that banquet that Mr. Carnegie had that inspiration. But, of course, he gets the entire credit! It never occurs to anybody that perhaps I furnished that inspiration. I don't say I did. I live a modest life, and people can see that by my features; I don't want to advertise the way others do.

Why, the first thing that Mr. Carnegie starts out to tell you is what Scotland has contributed to this world. It has contributed everybody that has been of any value to the United States. I am not denying it. I am saying that it is momentous, that's all. I don't know that Andrew Carnegie and Mr. Tower told it, but they all came from Dunfermline. What would have happened if all Scotland had turned out?

I understand that Mr. Carnegie claims that Columbus was born in Dunfermline, and he discovered the country, and two or three other men established religion, where they didn't have any; and from this fact they go on distributing Dunfermline people all over this country, and acquiring advantages thereby. Mr. Tower moved back and called his hand one or two points better. Well, I don't know how far Tower did go, but he furnished us a saint out of Scotland that I always thought was from Ireland. That is not the right thing to do on St. Patrick's Day. St. Patrick was well enough, not St. Andrew's equal, but well enough. I don't think Mr. Tower ought to back him up at this time and go on distributing Scotchmen out of Dunfermline.

St. Clair McKelway followed up the compliment with a veritable compliment of compliments, away on top of anything that these men have been able to pay Mr. Carnegie when they were trying as largely as they could. Mr. McKelway makes a compliment away beyond all others, beyond which nobody can go, when he says that "there is a man who wants to pay more taxes than are charged to him." I have never listened to such extravagance of compliment, and I have never seen a case when it was so well deserved. Well, McKelway had to come in and pay his compliment, and McKelway did it very well, and so did Gilder—very well for a poet. And he took the opportunity to advertise his magazine, and that it has the distinction of having Mr. Carnegie as a contributor; but, worse than that, he said that it pays Mr. Carnegie, otherwise you might feel that his magazine was getting that literature for nothing. Now, he gets that into the Associated Press in the morning, and his magazine will fly pretty high and mighty, and the people will hear of Mr. Carnegie; and, the next thing, Gilder will be trying to hire me!

I have gone on through this world now nearly seventy-four years, and all through it I have preserved—all that I have preserved is my diffidence, my chief virtue, a moderate modesty and diffidence. I am getting pretty old now, likely to run out, and can't work; but I am going to sit down, and before I sit down I do want to wish for Mr. Carnegie long life and continued prosperity, and eventually a measure of respectability.

Text / Composite, based upon: "Carnegie Honored by Club He Financed," *Times*, March 18, 1909; "St. Andrew and St. Mark," *Eloquence*(T), 1:286–88; "Carnegie the Benefactor," *MTS*(10):345–46.

Tower / Charlemagne Tower (1848–1923). American diplomat. He was a Philadelphia lawyer (1878–82), then concerned with mining and railroads in Minnesota (1882–87). He was minister to Austria-Hungary (1897–99), ambassador to Russia (1899–1902), and ambassador to Germany (1902–08).

· 193 ·

Businessmen of Norfolk, Virginia, honored Henry H. Rogers at a dinner celebrating the completion of the 442-mile Virginian Railway, a road Rogers controlled and for which he had provided most of the $40,000,000 it had cost to build. The chairman introduced Mark Twain as "one who has made millions laugh—not the loud laughter that bespeaks the vacant mind, but the laugh of mirth, intelligent mirth, the mirth that helps the human heart and the human mind."

Dinner Speech

Businessmen's Dinner for Henry H. Rogers, Monticello Hotel, Norfolk, Virginia, April 3, 1909

I thank you, Mr. Toastmaster, for the compliment which you have paid me, and I am sure I would rather have made people laugh than cry, yet in my time I have made some of them cry; and before I stop entirely I hope to make some more of them cry. I like compliments. I deal in them myself. I have listened with the greatest pleasure to the compliments which the chairman has paid to Mr. Rogers and that road of his tonight, and I hope some of them are deserved.

It is no small distinction to a man like that to sit here before an intelligent crowd like this and to be classed with Napoleon and Caesar. Why didn't he say that this was the proudest day of his life? Napoleon and Caesar are dead, and they can't be here to defend themselves. But I'm here!

The chairman said, and very truly, that the most lasting thing in the hands of man are the roads which Caesar built, and it is true that he built a lot of them; and they are there yet.

Yes, Caesar built a lot of roads in England, and you can find them. But Rogers has only built one road, and he hasn't finished that yet. I like to hear my old friend complimented, but I don't like to hear it overdone.

I didn't go around today with the others to see what he is doing. I will do that in a quiet time, when there is not anything going on, and when I shall not be called upon to deliver intemperate compliments on a railroad in which I own no stock.

They proposed that I go along with the committee and help inspect that dump down yonder. I didn't go. I saw that dump. I saw that thing when I was coming in on the steamer, and I didn't go because I was diffident, sentimentally diffident, about going and looking at that thing again—that great, long, bony thing; it looked just like Mr. Rogers's foot.

The chairman says Mr. Rogers is full of practical wisdom, and he is. It is intimated here that he is a very ingenious man, and he is a very competent financier. Maybe he is now, but it was not always so. I know lots of private things in his life which people don't know, and I know how he started, and it was not a very good start. I could have done better myself. The first time he crossed the Atlantic he had just made the first little strike in oil, and he was so young he did not like to ask questions. He did not like to appear ignorant. To this day he don't like to appear ignorant, but he can look as ignorant as anybody. On board the ship they were betting on the run of the ship, and they proposed that this youth from the oil regions should bet on the run of the ship. He did not like to ask what a half crown was, and he didn't know; but rather than be ashamed of himself he did bet half a crown on the run of the ship, and in bed he could not sleep. He wondered if he could afford that outlay in case he lost. He kept wondering over it, and said to himself, "A king's crown must be worth $20,000, so half a crown would cost $10,000." He could not afford to bet away $10,000 on the run of the ship, so he went up to the stakeholder and gave him $150 to let him off.

I like to hear Mr. Rogers complimented. I am not stingy in compliments to him myself. Why, I did it today when I sent his wife a telegram to comfort her. That is the kind of person I am. I knew she would be uneasy about him. I knew she would be solicitous about what he might do down here, so I did it to quiet her and to comfort her. I said he was doing real well for a person out of practice. There is nothing like it. He is like I used to be. There were times when I was careless—careless in my dress when I got older. You know how uncomfortable your wife can get when you are going away without her superintendence. Once when my wife could not go with me (she always went with me when she could—I always did meet that kind of luck), I was going to Washington a long time ago, in Mr. Cleveland's first administration, and she could not go; but, in her anxiety that I should not desecrate the house, she made preparation. She knew that there was to be a reception of those authors at the White House at seven o'clock in the evening. She said, "If I should tell you now what I want to ask of you, you would forget it before you got to Washington, and, therefore, I have written it on a card, and you will find it in your dress vest pocket when you are dressing at the Arlington—when you are dressing to see the President." I never thought of it again until I was dressing, and I felt in that pocket and took it out, and it said, in a kind of imploring way, "Don't wear your arctics in the White House."

You complimented Mr. Rogers on his energy, his foresightedness, complimented him in various ways, and he has deserved those compliments, although I say it myself; and I enjoy them all. There is one side of Mr. Rogers that has not been mentioned. If you will leave that to me I will touch upon that. There was a note in an editorial in one of the Norfolk papers this morning that touched upon that very thing, that hidden side of Mr. Rogers, where it spoke of Helen Keller and her affection for Mr. Rogers, to whom she dedicated her life book. And she has a right to feel that way, because, without the public knowing anything about it, he rescued, if I may use that term, that marvelous girl, that wonderful southern girl, that girl who was stone deaf, blind, and dumb from scarlet fever when she was a baby eighteen months old; and who now is as well and thoroughly educated as any woman on this planet at twenty-nine years of age. She is the most marvelous person of her sex that has existed on this earth since Joan of Arc.

That is not all Mr. Rogers has done; but you never see that side of his character, because it is never protruding; but he lends a helping hand daily out of that generous heart of his. You never hear of it. He is supposed to be a moon which has one side dark and the other bright. But the other side, though you don't see it, is not dark; it is bright, and its rays penetrate, and others do see it who are not God.

I would take this opportunity to tell something that I have never been allowed to tell by Mr. Rogers, either by my mouth or in print, and if I don't look at him I can tell it now.

In 1893, when the publishing company of Charles L. Webster, of which I was financial agent, failed, it left me heavily in debt. If you will remember what commerce was at that time you will recall that you could not sell anything, and could not buy anything, and I was on my back; my books were not worth anything at all, and I could not give away my copyrights. Mr. Rogers had long enough vision ahead to say, "Your books have supported you before, and after the panic is over they will support you again," and that was a correct proposition. He saved my copyrights, and saved me from financial ruin. He it was who arranged with my creditors to allow me to roam the face of the earth for four years and persecute the nations thereof with lectures, promising that at the end of four years I would pay dollar for dollar. That arrangement was made; otherwise I would now be living out-of-doors under an umbrella, and a borrowed one at that.

You see his white mustache and his head trying to get white (he is always trying to look like me—I don't blame him for that). These are only emblematic of his character, and that is all. I say, without exception, hair and all, he is the whitest man I have ever known.

Text / Composite, based upon: "Address of Dr. Samuel L. Clemens," Stenographer's Minutes, MTP; "Rogers and Railroads" in *MTS*(10):175–81; and *MTS*(23):389–94.

· 194 ·

Several hundred well-wishers gathered at a testimonial dinner for William Travers Jerome, who had been sharply criticized during his term as district attorney. Mark Twain was one of the committee on arrangements, of which Choate was chairman. Among those present were Alton B. Parker, Depew, Lyman Abbott, Melville Stone, Otto Kahn, Conde Nast, Richard Harding Davis, Charles A. Dana, McKelway, John La Farge, Jacob Ruppert, and S. Stanwood Menken. Mark Twain was introduced as the final authority on public questions and public men.

Dinner Speech

Dinner for William Travers Jerome, Delmonico's, New York, May 7, 1909

Indeed, that is very sudden. I was not informed that the verdict was going to depend upon my judgment, but that makes not the least difference in the world when you already know all about it. It is not any matter when you are called upon to express it; you can get up and do it, and my verdict has already been recorded in my heart and in my head as regards Mr. Jerome and his administration of the criminal affairs of this county.

I agree with everything Mr. Choate has said in his letter regarding

Mr. Jerome; I agree with everything Mr. Shepard has said; and I agree with everything Mr. Jerome has said on his own commendation. And I thought Mr. Jerome was modest in that. If he had been talking about another officer of this county, he could have painted the joys and sorrows of office and his victories in even stronger language than he did.

I voted for Mr. Jerome in those old days, and I should like to vote for him again if he runs for any office. I moved out of New York, and that is the reason, I suppose, I cannot vote for him again. There may be some way, but I have not found it out. But now I am a farmer—a farmer up in Connecticut, and winning laurels. Those people already speak with such high favor, admiration, of my farming, and they say that I am the only man that has ever come to that region who could make two blades of grass grow where only three grew before.

Well, I cannot vote for him. You see that. As it stands now, I cannot. I am crippled in that way and to that extent, for I would ever so much like to do it. I am not a Congress, and I cannot distribute pensions, and I don't know any other legitimate way to buy a vote. But if I should think of any legitimate way, I shall make use of it, and then I shall vote for Mr. Jerome.

Text / Composite, based upon: "Jerome Reviews His Official Years," *Times,* May 8, 1909; "Dinner to Mr. Jerome" in *MTS*(10):160–61; and *MTS*(23):395–96.

Jerome / William Travers Jerome (1859–1934). American lawyer. A Columbia graduate (1884), he was assistant district attorney (1888) who exposed police corruption and opposed Tammany. Elected district attorney of New York County (1901), he warred on gamblers, and set up headquarters on the lower East Side to be near people who needed him. After reelection (1905), his popularity waned, although he made headlines in the sensational Thaw trials (1907–08). He was a brilliant courtroom tactician.

· 195 ·

When Mark Twain went to Baltimore to deliver a short speech at a girls school graduation, he was keeping a promise made to Frances Nunnally, whom he called Francesca, and who was one of his collection of adoring young girls known as the Aquarium Club or Angel Fish. He had met her aboard the Minneapolis *on the way to England in 1907. She called him "grandpa," and, like a good granddaughter, went along with him on social calls in London. The graduation speech was the last public speaking performance of Mark Twain. Feeling the first twinges of the heart ailment that became more painful during the next ten months, he brought to a close his long speech-making career.*

Remarks

The Misses Tewksbury's School Graduation,
Baltimore, Maryland, June 9, 1909

I don't know what to tell you girls to do. Mr. Martin has told you everything you ought to do, and now I must give you some don'ts. There is nothing for me to do but to tell you young ladies what not to do. There are three things that you should never do on any occasion.

First, girls, don't smoke—that is, don't smoke to excess. I am seventy-three and one half years old, and have been smoking seventy-three of them. But I never smoke to excess—that is, I smoke in moderation, only one cigar at a time.

Second, don't drink—that is, don't drink to excess.

Third, don't marry—I mean, to excess.

Now, if you young ladies will refrain from all these things you will have all the virtues that anyone will honor and respect.

Another thing I want to say, and that is that honesty is the best policy. That is an old proverb; but you don't want ever to forget it in your journey through life.

I remember when I had just written *Innocents Abroad* when I and my partner wanted to start a newspaper syndicate. We needed three dollars and did not know where to get it. While we were in a quandary I espied a valuable dog on the street. I picked up the canine and sold him to a man for three dollars. Afterward the owner of the dog came along and I got three dollars from him for telling him where the dog was. So I went back and gave the three dollars to the man whom I sold it to, and I have lived honestly ever since.

Text / Composite, based upon: Baltimore *News,* June 10, 1909; "Advice to Girls," *MTS*(10):107, a misdated text.

MARK TWAIN SPEAKING:

A Chronology

The calendar of speaking performances that follows has been compiled from newspaper reports and memoranda in Mark Twain's notebooks, in which he jotted down dates of a great many dinners and other functions; from his letters to Olivia, Howells, and others; and from invitations in the files of correspondence, MTP: all told, a staggering number of occasions. How many of them he attended and how many speeches he made are uncertainties, to which the editor has applied conjecture, aided by an occasional note of regret from Mark Twain or a notebook comment that he could not attend, or the remark "No speeches" accompanying a dinner date. That he talked volubly in any gathering may be assumed. It is difficult, however, to determine how much of the talk was prepared in advance to be delivered on call from a chairman, and equally difficult to draw the line between a speech and an impromptu conversational monologue. The calendar is undoubtedly incomplete and imprecise, but it shows the prominent role that talking played in the life of Mark Twain. For entries starred with asterisks the editor has found no texts.

1856

January 17 Printers Banquet, Keokuk, Iowa. *Impromptu* *

For an account of this affair, see Fred W. Lorch, "Mark Twain in Iowa," *Iowa Journal of History and Politics* 27, no. 3 (July 1929):420–21; *MTB*,1:107.

1863

July 8 Collins House Opening, Virginia City. *Speech* *

A new hotel called for toasts, proposed by Tom Fitch, Rollin M. Daggett, Colonel Turner, Judge Ferris, and others. According to next day's Virginia City *Evening Bulletin*, "Perhaps the speech of the evening was made by Sam Clemens. . . . He almost brought the house to tears by his touching simple pathos."

October (?) Eagle Fire Company Celebration, Virginia City. *Speech* *

November (?) Meerschaum Presentation, Virginia City. *Speech* *

At a convivial get together, several of Mark Twain's friends gave him a handsome, but fake, meerschaum pipe. Before discovering the hoax, he made an elaborate speech of thanks, which began, said Dan De Quille, "with the introduction of tobacco into England by Sir Walter Raleigh, and wound up with George Washington." See "Reporting With Mark Twain," *California Illustrated* (July 1893):170–78.

December 11 Third House, Carson City. *Remarks as President* *

Unanimously elected president of the Third House, Mark Twain presided at a turbulent session, of which he wrote an account, no doubt exaggerated, for the Virginia *Territorial Enterprise.* See *Mark Twain of the Enterprise,* ed. Henry Nash Smith and Frederick Anderson (Berkeley, 1957):102–10.

1864

January 25 Court House, Carson City. *"Third Annual Message"* *

June 12 Maguire's Opera House, San Francisco. *Presentation Speech*

1866

October 2 Maguire's Opera House, San Francisco. *"Sandwich Islands"*

October 11–November 27 Lecture Tour, California and Nevada: 16 engagements. *"Sandwich Islands"*

December 10 Congress Hall, San Francisco. *"Sandwich Islands"*

1867

March 25–April 9 Midwest Lecture Tour: 5 engagements. *"Sandwich Islands"*

May 6 Cooper Union, New York City. *"Sandwich Islands"*

May 10 Athenaeum, Brooklyn. *"Sandwich Islands"*

May 15 Irving Hall, New York City. *"Sandwich Islands"*

August 25 Yalta, Russia. *"Address to the Czar"*

1868

January 9 Metzerott Hall, Washington, D.C. *"The Frozen Truth"* *

Washington *Morning Chronicle,* January 11, 1868: "The subject of his remarks was the recent trip of a party of excursionists on the steamship *Quaker City* to Europe and points on the Mediterranean, and his descriptions were replete with sparkling wit, to which his slow, deliberate style of speaking gave a peculiar charm."

January 11 Newspaper Correspondents Dinner, Washington, D.C. *"Woman"*

For Mark Twain's entertaining comments on this affair, see his letters from Washington published in the *Alta,* January 28 and February 19, 1868.

February 18 Press Club Dinner. *"Woman," revised* *

Having been reproved by his mentor, Mrs. Fairbanks, for indecorous allusions at the Correspondents Dinner, he told her that for the Press Club he had made the speech "frigidly proper in language and sentiment." See *Mark Twain to Mrs. Fairbanks,* ed. Dixon Wecter (San Marino, 1949):18.

March (?) S.S. *Sacramento,* at sea. *"Charade"* *

April 14–15 Platt's Hall, San Francisco. *"Pilgrim Life"*

April 17–30 Lecture Tour, California and Nevada: 9 engagements. *"Pilgrim Life"*

July 2 Mercantile Library, San Francisco. *"Venice"* *

July 10 S.S. *Montana,* at sea. *"Composition—the Cow"* *

The shipboard program was called "Country School Exhibition." See *The Twainian* 7, no. 6 (November–December 1948):5.

November 17–March 3, 1869 Eastern Lecture Tour: 42 engagements. *"The American Vandal Abroad"*

1869

June 5 Press Club Dinner, New York City. *"Reliable Contraband"*

November 1–January 21, 1870 Lecture Tour: 45 engagements. *"Our Fellow Savages of the Sandwich Islands"*

1870

January 31 Benefit for Father Hawley, Hartford. *"Sandwich Islands"*

1871

October 16–February 6, 1872 Lecture Tour: 77 engagements. *"Uncommonplace Characters," "Artemus Ward," "Roughing It"*

1872

February (?) The Aldine Dinner, New York City. *Dinner Speech*

September 22 Savage Club, London. *Dinner Speech*

September 28 Sheriff's Dinner, London. *"Success to Literature"**

The dinner was given by the new sheriffs of London to the city guilds and liverymen. When one of the sheriffs proposed the health of Mark Twain, he was vociferously applauded, then responded to the toast. The London *Times,* September 30, 1872, called it "an amusing speech." See *LLMT:* 178–79.

October (?) Whitefriars Club, London. *Dinner Speech*

1873

January 31 Benefit for Father Hawley, Hartford. *"Sandwich Islands"*

In a letter to the *Courant,* January 29, 1873, Mark Twain said that charity is "a dignified and respectworthy thing, and there is small merit about it and less grace when it don't cost anything .... We would like to have a thousand dollars in the house; we point to the snow and the thermometer; we call Hartford by name, and we are not much afraid but that she will step to the front and answer for herself.... I am thoroughly and cheerfully willing to lecture here for such an object, though I would have serious objections to talking in my own town for the benefit of my own pocket—we freebooters of the platform consider it more graceful to fly the black flag in strange waters and prey upon remote and friendless communities." All services having been donated, the benefit netted $1,500 for Father Hawley.

February 5 Steinway Hall, New York City. *"Sandwich Islands"*

February 7 Brooklyn. *"Sandwich Islands"*

February 10 Steinway Hall, New York City. *"Sandwich Islands"*

March 31 Monday Evening Club, Hartford. *"License of the Press"*

July 4 Meeting of Americans, London. *Dinner Speech*

October 13–18 Queen's Concert Rooms, London. *"Sandwich Islands"*

October 20, 25 Liverpool Institute, Liverpool. *"Sandwich Islands"*

November (?) Scottish Corporation, London. *"The Ladies"*

November 29 St. Andrews Society, London. *"The Guests"*

December 1–7 Queen's Concert Rooms, London. *"Sandwich Islands"*

December 8–19 Queen's Concert Rooms, London. *"Roughing It"*

December 12 Dinner for the Lord Mayor, London Tavern. *Dinner Speech* *

In a dictation of August 29, 1907, MTP, Mark Twain says that the London Guildhall was crowded with nine hundred diners, who made a terrific clatter. He was ninth and last on the toast list, but when he arose to speak, Sir John Bennett, who made dull speeches nobody listened to, got up uninvited and began a rambling talk. The house objected loudly, but he continued despite shouted protests. Finally they drowned him out by singing "Auld Lang Syne" and smashing their champagne glasses. After that noisy interlude Mark Twain presumably delivered his speech.

December 22 Small gathering, London. *Dinner Speech* *
December 25 Hanover Square Lecture Room, Oxford. *"Magdalen Tower"* *

1874

January 8 Leicester. *"Roughing It"*
January 9, 10 Liverpool. *"Roughing It"*
February 14 Salem, Massachusetts. *Introducing Charles Kingsley*
February 16 Wilkie Collins Dinner, Boston. *Dinner Speech* *

The Boston *Transcript* said, February 17, 1874: "Mark Twain gave a brief description of his reception in England, saying that he was very successful in the object of his visit there, which was to teach people good morals, and to introduce some of the improvements of the present century."

February 17 Press Club Dinner, Boston. *Dinner Speech*
March 3 Unidentified Occasion. *Speech* *
March 5 Unidentified Charity Function. *Speech* *
September 16 Park Theatre, New York City. *Curtain Speech*
October 12 Insurance Men's Dinner, Hartford. *Dinner Speech*
December 15 *Atlantic* Dinner, Boston. *Dinner Speech* *

Howells was toastmaster, and among those present were Aldrich, Holmes, George Cary Eggleston, and Henry James. The Boston *Transcript,* December 16, 1874, calling Mark Twain's speech one of the brightest of the evening, summarized his remarks: "once when sailing on the blue Mediterranean . . . he tried to give the impression that he was a poet. He said no one believed him, and after repeated protestations he rashly laid a wager of ten to one that he could get a poem printed in the *Atlantic.* The poem was forwarded from Gibraltar, the bet was ten dollars to a hundred, which accounts, Mark said, for the fact that he had only three dollars in his pocket when he reached here. A subsequent anecdote related by him and Mr. Osgood jointly, proved that Mark was more at home in a game called 'euchre' than in poetry, and Mr. Osgood assured the company that it was not a safe practice to play cards—with Mark Twain." See Arthur Gilman, "Atlantic Dinners and Diners," *Atlantic Monthly* 100, no. 5 (November 1907):646–67.

December 23 Park Theatre, New York City. *Curtain Speech*

1875

February 15 Monday Evening Club, Hartford. *"Universal Suffrage"*

February 24 Nautilus Club Dinner for Aldrich, Boston. *Dinner Speech* *
March 5 For Father Hawley, Hartford. *"Roughing It"*
May 12 Asylum Hill Church, Hartford. *Introducing Spelling Match*

1876

January 24 Monday Evening Club, Hartford. *"Recent Carnival of Crime in Connecticut"*
September 30 Political Meeting, Hartford. *Speech on Hayes*
November 13 Academy of Music, Brooklyn. *Readings*

Mark Twain read "The McWilliamses and the Membranous Croup," "My Late Senatorial Secretaryship," and "Encounter With an Interviewer." Also on the program were Emma Thursby, a well-known operatic soprano, and a group of singers called the Young Apollo Club. Mark Twain preferred not to share an entertainment with musicians, yet he allowed himself to be talked into doing so a number of times. Then he generally chafed and fidgeted in the wings while soloists held the stage, grumbling to himself when the slightest encouragement sent them back for encores.

November 21 Music Hall, Boston. *Readings* *

Emma Thursby was again on the program, together with the Mendelssohn Quintette.

November 22 Chelsea Academy of Music. *Readings*

Mark Twain read the same pieces he had used in Brooklyn on November 13. Probably musicians were still with him.

November 24 Providence, Rhode Island. *Readings* *

Musicians were there. The several November engagements appear to have been a brief barnstorming tour.

December 22 New England Society Dinner, New York City. *"The Weather"*

Ca. 1876

Asylum Hill Church, Hartford. *Reading from* Tom Sawyer

1877

March 26 Monday Evening Club, Hartford. *"Advantages of Travel"* *
July 31 Fifth Avenue Theatre, New York City. *Curtain Speech*
October 2 Putnam Phalanx Dinner, Hartford. *Dinner Speech*
December 12 Seminary Hall, Hartford. *Introducing Howells* *

Howells was appearing on the Seminary Hall Lecture Course. Of Mark Twain's introduction, the Hartford *Times*, December 13,

1877, gives a fragment: "The gentleman who is now to address you is the editor of the *Atlantic Monthly.* He has a reputation in the literary world which I need not say anything about. I am only here to back up his moral character."

December 17 Whittier Birthday Dinner, Boston. *Dinner Speech*

1878

January 26 Gesellschaft Harmonie, New York City. *Speech* *

February 25 Press Club, New York City. *Speech* *

April 4 Bayard Taylor Dinner, New York City. *Dinner Speech*

June (?) West Middle School, Hartford. *Remarks* *

Mark Twain spoke at the graduation exercises. William Lyon Phelps, who was a pupil there at the time, quotes a fragment in his *Autobiography With Letters* (1939):67: "Boys and girls, the subject of my remarks today is Methuselah. Methuselah lived to be 969 years old; but what of that? There was nothing doing. He might as well have lived to be a thousand. You boys and girls will see more in the next fifty years than Methuselah saw in his whole lifetime."

July 4 Anglo-American Club, Heidelberg. *German-English Speech*

November 30 Artists Club, Munich. *Speech or Story* *

In Notebook 13, October 13, 1878–January 1879, MTP, Mark Twain comments briefly on this "blowout" for Toby Rosenthal, American expatriate painter, chiefly on the speech of Consul Horstmann, who interpolated rhymed doggerel, each stanza ending with "Toby Rosenthal."

1879

Spring Stanley Club Dinner, Paris. *Dinner Speech*

Spring Stomach Club, Paris. *"The Science of Onanism"*

October 16 Republican Meeting, Elmira, New York. *Speech*

November 12 Army Reunion, Haverly's Theatre, Chicago. *Impromptu*

November 13 Reunion Banquet, Palmer House, Chicago. *"The Babies"*

November 14 Founding of Press Club, Chicago. *Speech* *

A letter, A. L. Hardy to Mark Twain, MTP, says that after the reunion banquet at the Palmer House, about fifty men gathered in the underground cafe of Captain Jim Simms on Clark Street. There were sandwiches, wurst, pretzels, beer, ale, Scotch, and a great deal of talk, Mark Twain acting as a sort of chairman at the head of the table. By dawn only seven remained. A note scrawled on the letter by Mark Twain, evidently one of the stayers, says that the Chicago Press Club was founded that night about seven in the morning.

November 14 Breakfast for Mark Twain, Chicago. *Speech* *

The menu, MTP, says that this breakfast was tendered "By a few Chicago Journalists," that the time was 12 noon, and that the bill of fare was: Fruit, Oysters on shell, Broiled Salmon Chateaubriand, with Champignons; French Fried Potatoes, Calves' Sweetbreads with French Peas, Spanish Omelette, Cutlets of Chicken, cream sauce; Broiled Quail on Toast, French Coffee, Cognac. Undoubtedly there were speeches by Mark Twain and others, but they were not reported.

December 3 Holmes Breakfast, Boston. *Speech*

1880

April 5 Monday Evening Club, Hartford. *"Decay of the Art of Lying"*
October 16 Hartford. *Welcome to General Grant*
October 26 Republican Rally, Hartford. *Political Speech*
November 2 Republican Jollification, Hartford. *"Funeral Oration"*
December 20 Tile Club, F. Hopkinson Smith Studio, New York City. *Speech or Stories* *

Francis Hopkinson Smith (1839–1915) was an American engineer, painter, and writer. A building contractor who sketched in charcoal and painted in water colors, he wrote travel books illustrated with his own drawings: *A White Umbrella in Mexico* (1881), *The Arm-Chair at the Inn* (1912), and others. He is best known for his novels, very popular at the time: *Colonel Carter of Cartersville* (1891), and its sequel *Colonel Carter's Christmas* (1903). Bon vivant and clubman, "Hop" Smith was a good storyteller and dinner speaker.

Unknown date Saturday Morning Club, Hartford. *"Plagiarism"* *

Mark Twain organized the Saturday Morning Club about 1875 as a cultural and social aid to young women of Hartford. The club met weekly at his home for programs presented by guest speakers. Among those who appeared to discuss a wide variety of topics were Howells, Warner, James T. Fields, Professor Boyeson, Harriet Beecher Stowe, General Hawley, the Reverend Joseph Twichell, and, of course, Mark Twain himself.

1881

February 24 Papyrus Club Dinner, Boston. *Dinner Speech*
February 26 Twichell's Chapel, Hartford. *"Tar Baby"* *
February 28 West Point. *Readings* *

March 10 Negro Church, Hartford. *Readings* *
June 8 Army of the Potomac Banquet, Hartford. *"The Benefit of Judicious Training"*
November 21 Monday Evening Club, Hartford. *"Phrenography"* *
December 8 Dinner for Mark Twain, Montreal. *Dinner Speech*
December 22 New England Society, Philadelphia. *"Plymouth Rock and the Pilgrims"*

1882

January 31 Fréchette Dinner, Holyoke, Massachusetts. *"On After-Dinner Speaking"*
April 15 Saturday Morning Club, Boston. *"Advice to Youth"*
December 22 New England Society, New York City. *"Woman–God Bless Her"*

1883

February 19 Monday Evening Club, Hartford. *"What is Happiness?"* *
March (?) The Kinsmen, New York City. *Speech* *

The Kinsmen was a club without dues, clubhouse, officers or bylaws, its only purposes being good fellowship and good times. It was instigated by Lawrence Barrett, the name suggested by Laurence Hutton to symbolize practitioners of kindred arts who made up the membership. There were no formal meetings, only casual gatherings, with plenty of food and drink, at studios, each member bringing a guest who automatically became a member. Mark Twain attended as the guest of Hutton in 1883. Other Kinsmen, American and British, were Howells, F. D. Millet, Aldrich, H. C. Bunner, E. A. Abbey, Anthony Hope, Edwin Booth, Matthews, Joe Jefferson, St. Gaudens, Pinero, Bram Stoker, Forbes Robertson, John Singer Sargent, Henry Irving, Julian Hawthorne, Andrew Lang, and Edmund Gosse. See Hutton, *Talks in a Library:* 326–28; Matthews, *The Tocsin of Revolt:* 255.

April 4 Unity Hall, Hartford. *Introducing George W. Cable*
April 4 Supper for Cable, Hartford. *Speech* *

After Cable's program of readings in Hartford, Mark Twain entertained him and the visiting writers—Howells, Aldrich, Gilder, and O'Reilly—at a lively supper at the Hartford Club. Of this late party Cable remarked upon an "abundance of innocent fun. There were a hundred good things said that I suppose I'll never remember." See Hutton, *Talks in a Library:* 416–18.

May 23 Royal Literary and Scientific Society, Ottawa. *"On Adam"*
May 27 Rideau Hall, Ottawa. *Readings* *

1884

February 4 Monday Evening Club, Hartford. *"Southern Literature"* *
April 14 Monday Evening Club, Hartford.
Unfinished Paper to be Completed by Each Member *
April 29 Breakfast for Edwin Booth, New York City. *Speech* *
September 16 or 17 Wheelmen, Springfield, Massachusetts.
Dinner Speech
October (?) Mugwump Rally, Hartford. *"Turncoats"*
October 20 Mugwump Rally, Hartford. *Remarks as Chairman*
November (?) *"The Dead Partisan"*
November 28–February 28, 1885
Speaking Tour with Cable: 103 engagements

1885

March 31 Hutton Dinner, New York City.
"On Speech-Making Reform"
April 9 Actors Fund Fair, Philadelphia. *Remarks*
April 9 Clover Club, Philadelphia. *Dinner Speech* *
April 28 American Copyright League Benefit, New York City.
Reading *
April 29 Authors Readings, New York City. *"Trying Situation"*

At this matinee performance Mark Twain startled everybody by appearing in formal evening dress. As reported by the *World* next day he explained: "I knew it would be night before they reached me, and so I came in evening dress." From Madison Square Garden he went on to a dinner of Cornell alumni at Morelli's.

April 29 Cornell Alumni Dinner. *Dinner Speech* *
May 1 Vassar. *"Trying Situation," "Golden Arm"*
June 5, 6 Art Society Benefit, Hartford.
"King Sollermun," "German Lesson," "Trying Situation," "Short Story"
October 7 Wednesday Morning Club, Pittsfield, Massachusetts.
"Mental Telegraphy"
November 19 White House, Washington, D.C. *Impromptu, Copyright**

In Notebook 20, August 20, 1885–January 20, 1886, MTP, Mark Twain says that, accompanied by Johnson of the *Century* and George Walton Green of the Authors Copyright League, he called on President Cleveland and "wandered into a speech" on international copyright, which evolved into a spirited discussion by all four. The president promised to stress the subject in his next message to Congress.

1886

January 18 Typothetae Dinner, New York City. *"The Compositor"*
January 28, 29 Senate Committee, Washington, D.C. *Remarks on Copyright*
March 22 Monday Evening Club, Hartford. *"Knights of Labor"*
April 3 West Point. *Readings* *
April 22 Authors Club, New York City. *"Our Children"*
May 6 West Point. *Readings* *
July 21 Reformatory, Elmira, New York. *"German," "Whistling," "Trying Situation," "King Sollermun"*
October 11 Monday Evening Club, Hartford. *"A Protest Against Taking the Pledge"*
November 6 Saturday Morning Club, Hartford. *Reading or Remarks* *
November 11 Military Service Institution, Governors Island, New York. *"Yankee Smith of Camelot"*
November 29 Authors Readings, New York City. *Story* *
December 9 Tremont Temple, Boston. *Introducing Stanley*

1887

February 10 Stationers Board of Trade, New York City. *Dinner Speech*
February 26 Monday Evening Club, Hartford. *"Machine Culture"*
March 17 The Kinsmen, New York City. *Speech* *
March 31 Authors Readings for Longfellow Memorial, Boston. *"English as She is Taught"*
April 8 Maryland Veterans Banquet, Baltimore. *"An Author's Soldiering"*
April 13 Supper for John Drew and Ada Rehan, New York City. *Supper Speech*
April 27 Army and Navy Club, Hartford. *Dinner Speech*
November 28 Authors Readings, New York City. *"Fatal Anecdote"*
December 5 Monday Evening Club, Hartford. *"Consistency"*
December 20 Congregationalist Club, Boston. *"Post-prandial Oratory"*
December 31 Authors Club Watch Night, New York City. *Story* *

1888

January 6 Founding of Players Club, New York City. *Speech* *
Prime movers were Edwin Booth and Augustin Daly. Among charter members who gathered at Delmonico's were Mark Twain, William Bispham, Lawrence Barrett, John Drew, Laurence Hut-

ton, Joe Jefferson, Brander Matthews, Stephen H. Olin, and General Sherman.

February 27 Historical Class, Hartford. *Reading or Remarks* *

March 17 Soldiers Home, Washington, D.C. *Reading* *

March 19 Authors Readings, Washington, D.C. *Story* *

In *MTA,* 2:147–51, Mark Twain says that, as usual, the readers ran far overtime. Having been invited to the White House, they finally got there too late to see President and Mrs. Cleveland, who had left for a dinner engagement.

April 27 Supper for Irving and Ellen Terry, New York City. *Speech* *

Augustin Daly, host on this occasion, invited more than sixty guests, among whom were General Sherman, Depew, Matthews, General Porter, William Winter, James Whitcomb Riley, Rose Eytinge, Lester Wallack, Ada Rehan, Effie Shannon, and Lillian Russell. Mark Twain told the "Moses who?" story and talked about international copyright.

April 29 Breakfast for Edwin Booth, New York City. *Remarks* *

Henry Irving was host at this gathering of Kinsmen. Warner was there, Aldrich, Whitelaw Reid, Lester Wallack, and William Winter.

September 11 Reformatory, Elmira, New York. *Readings* *

December 6 For Edith Wilder Smith, Hartford. *"King Arthur and the Yankee"*

1889

January 17 Baltimore. *Readings* *

When the wife of Thomas Nelson Page died suddenly, Mark Twain substituted for him in Baltimore. Also on the program was Malcolm Johnston, to whom Mark Twain gave all the receipts for the evening.

January 21 Smith College, Northampton, Massachusetts. *"Lucerne Girl," "Tar Baby," "Andrea del Sarto," "German Lesson," "Interviewer," "Bluejay," "Baker's Cat," "Golden Arm"*

Mark Twain admitted to his notebook that this long program was too much by at least a half hour.

February 6 Yale Alumni, Hartford. *Dinner Speech*

February 9 South Baptist Church, Hartford. *Readings* *

February 25 Trinity College Alumni, New York City. *Dinner Speech* *

February 27 Athenaeum Club, Boston. *Dinner Speech* *

February 28 Tremont Temple, Boston. *Introducing Nye and Riley*

An unidentified clipping, MTP, described Mark Twain as "a frowsy-headed, round-shouldered man, as gray as a rat, yet still vigorous in spite of his years," who "tottered on to the platform" followed by "two ambiguous-looking orphans in dress suits and goldbowed spectacles."

March 6 Wednesday Morning Club, Pittsfield. *Story or Remarks* *
March 7 Authors Readings, Boston. *Story* *
March 30 Supper for Edwin Booth, New York City. *"The Long Clam"*
April 1 Mrs. Hamersley's, New York City. *Readings* *
April 8 Baseball Dinner, New York City. *"The Grand Tour–1. The Sandwich Islands"*
April 13 Miss Brown's, New York City. *"True Story," "Uncle Remus"*
May 11 Saturday Morning Club, Hartford. *"Isaac Mulĕykeh," "King Arthur," "Interviewer," "Christening"*
May 15 Ology Club, Hartford. *Dinner Speech* *
May 22 Talcott Street Church, Hartford. *"Skinned Man," "Mate and Governor Gardiner," "Whistling," "Interviewer"*
November 12 Press Club, Boston. *Dinner Speech* *
November 15 Fellowcraft Club, New York City. *Dinner Speech*
December 31 Authors Club Watch Night, New York City. *Story* *

1890

January 11 West Point. *Readings* *
January 20 Broadway Theatre, New York City. *Curtain Speech*
April 27 Max O'Rell Dinner, Boston. *"On Foreign Critics"*
May 10 Saturday Morning Club, Hartford. *Remarks* *
July 4 Informal Gathering, Onteora, New York. *"Golden Arm"*
September (?) Druggists Banquet, Washington, D.C. *Dinner Speech*
September 12 Storey Dinner, New York City. *Dinner Speech* *

Moorfield Storey (1845–1929), lawyer and publicist, was a leader of the Mugwumps who opposed Blaine in 1884, and a prominent spokesman of the Anti-Imperialist League, which was opposed to American meddling in the Philippines.

October 9 Roger A. Pryor Dinner, New York City. *Dinner Speech*

1891

March 23 Bryn Mawr. *"Christening," "True Story," "Tar Baby," "Whistling," "Golden Arm"*

According to the Philadelphia *Record,* as reprinted in the Grass Valley, California, *Daily Tidings,* April 21, 1891, Mark Twain said: "I have been elected an honorary member of the class of '94. I feel deeply grateful to my fellow classmates for the compliment they have done me, the more so because I feel I have never deserved such treatment. I will reveal a secret to you. I have an ambition: that I may go up and up on the ladder of education until at last I may be a professor of Bryn Mawr College. I would be a professor of telling anecdotes. This art is not a very high one, but it is a very useful one. One class of anecdotes is that which contains only words. You begin almost as you please and talk and talk until your allotted time and close when you get ready. I will illustrate this by a story of an Irish and Scotch christening." [He told the christening story and others.]

His daughter, Susy, was a student at Bryn Mawr at the time. When her father, who had promised her that he would not tell the story of the Golden Arm, forgot himself and told it, she became much upset and rushed out in tears. See *Susy and Mark Twain,* ed. Edith Colgate Salsbury (1965):287–88; Justin Kaplan, *Mr. Clemens and Mark Twain* (1966):310.

April 22 Authors Readings, New York City. *Story* *

July 14 S.S. *Lahn,* at sea. *Reading* *

In a mock trial, Mark Twain was accused and convicted of unscientific lying. Sentenced to read three hours from his books, he did so, aloud. Probably he did not find the sentence irksome.

December 18 Unidentified Function, Dresden. *"German," "Interviewer," "Blue Jay Yarn," "Duel"*

Ca. 1891 International Copyright Congress, Milan. *Remarks on Copyright* *

1892

January 13 Y.M.C.A. Hall, Berlin. *Readings* *

January (?) Gewerberhaus, Berlin. *Readings* *

May 25 Congregational Chapel, Berlin. *Readings* *

1893

April 6 Carnegie Dinner, New York City. *Dinner Speech* *

November 4 Unidentified Function, New York City. *Readings* *

November 11 Lotos Club, New York City. *Dinner Speech*

November 19 Irving–Ellen Terry Dinner, New York City. *Dinner Speech* *

November 20 St. Andrews Society, New York City. *Dinner Speech* *

November 26 Irving Dinner, New York City. *Dinner Speech* *

November 27 Manhattan Club, New York City. *Dinner Speech* *

December 1 Mackay Dinner, New York City. *Remarks or Story* *

John William Mackay (1831–1902) was one of the four bonanza kings who made fortunes on the Comstock Lode of Nevada in the 1870s. He was an affable, unpretentious, generous man fond of music and the theater. The dinner, given by the Players Club, had somewhat the flavor of miners' fare: soup, raw oysters, corned beef and cabbage. Mark Twain, who arrived about midnight, described the guests as gray-haired veterans of the Pacific Coast, with whom he swapped yarns about old times. He said he did his full share of the talking until about 1:30 A.M. See *MTL,* 2:597.

December (?) Brander Matthews Dinner. *Dinner Speech*

1894

January 13 Mrs. Carrol Beckwith, New York City. *Stories* *

James Carroll Beckwith (1852–1917) was a well-known New York portrait and genre painter, who was born in Hannibal, Missouri.

January 18 Authors Club, New York City. *Remarks* *

January 19 Stanford White Dinner, New York City. *Dinner Speech* *

Stanford White (1853–1906) was an architect who had studied in Europe, then joined the firm of Charles F. McKim and William R. Mead. Preferring the style of the classical and the Renaissance, he designed the Washington Arch on lower Fifth Avenue, New York, and the old Madison Square Garden, modeled after the Giralda Tower of Seville Cathedral. On the Garden Roof he was shot by Harry Thaw, June 25, 1906. In the ensuing trials, persistent defense attempts to besmirch the character of White diverted attention from his merits as an architect, and may still becloud his reputation.

January 25 Authors Readings, Boston. *Story* *

January (?) Musical Evening, New York City.
"Christening," "E. B. Martin and the Etchings"

This party occurred at a house near the Players Club. Some thirty musical ladies and gentlemen were there, also a Hungarian band. After a midnight supper, there was dancing until 4:30 A.M. "By half past four," said Mark Twain, "I had danced all those people down—and yet was not tired; merely breathless." See *MTL,* 2:605.

January 31 Mrs. Gertrude Cowdon, New York City. *Stories* *

February (?) Robert Reid's Studio, New York City. *Stories* *

Robert Reid (1862–1929) was an American painter influenced by the impressionists. He painted murals for the Library of Congress, the Massachusetts State House, and the Appellate

Court House of New York City. At Reid's studio a lively party assembled: Constant Coquelin, Richard Harding Davis, Nikola Tesla, John Drew, Anders Zorn, William H. Chase, and others. Songs, imitations and yarns went on until 4 A.M. Perhaps Mark Twain hoped that night life might be an anodyne for worry over the collapse of his publishing company, and over the bitter truth that the Paige typesetter was a costly failure.

February 17 Charles Hoyt Dinner, New York City. *Dinner Speech* *

Charles Hoyt (1860–1900) was a playwright and manager who had been dramatic critic, sports editor, and columnist on the Boston *Post* (1878–83), then became lessee of the Garrick and Madison Square Theatres. He wrote a number of popular farces, of which the most successful was *A Trip to Chinatown* (1891).

February 22 Town Hall Dedication, Fairhaven, Massachusetts. *"Advice"*

February 26, 27 Reading With Riley and Sherley, New York City. *"Jumping Frog," "Company of Mean Men," "Oudinot"*

March 3 Unidentified Function, New York City. *Story* *

March 4 Aldine Story Tellers Night, New York City. *Story* *

July 22 Oriental Hotel, Manhattan Beach. *"Rev. Sam Jones's Reception in Heaven"*

Samuel Porter Jones (1847–1906) was an American temperance advocate. A Georgia lawyer who drank too much, he was converted to Methodism (1872), and became a famous exhorter of the damnation-and-brimestone variety. He denounced profanity as well as liquor, often so heatedly that his own language became spectacularly profane. See H. L. Mencken, "Hell and Its Outskirts," *New Yorker* (October 23, 1948).

July 25 Oriental Hotel, Manhattan Beach. *"Playing Courier"*

1895

March 25 Cramp's Shipyard, Philadelphia. *Speech*

May 22 Herald Square Theatre, New York City. *Curtain Speech*

July 12 House of Refuge, Randall's Island, New York. *Lecture* *

July 13 Reformatory, Elmira, New York. *Lecture* *

July 15–July 15, 1896 World Speaking Tour: United States, Canada, Australia, New Zealand, India, Ceylon, Mauritius, South Africa: about 140 engagements. *Morals Lecture*

July 23 Reception and Supper, Minneapolis. *Supper Speech* *

July 27 Luncheon, Winnipeg. *Speech* *

July 27 Manitoba Club Supper, Winnipeg. *Supper Speech* *

July 31 Electric Club Supper, Great Falls. *Supper Speech* *

August 1 Supper, Butte. *Supper Speech* *
August 2 Montana Club Supper, Helena. *Supper Speech* *
August 9 Arlington Club Supper, Portland. *Supper Speech* *
August 12 Press Club Supper, Tacoma. *Supper Speech*

The Tacoma *Morning Union* of August 13, 1895, quoted a fragment of Mark Twain's speech: "As a rule a chairman at a banquet is an ass, but your chairman is not an ass. His plan is the best I have ever encountered. It gives the irresponsibles an opportunity to be heard before the guest of the evening is called upon. As a rule the man who is the guest of honor is introduced as the first speaker, and the more he is lauded, the more difficult it is for him to speak. Every compliment ties his tongue."

August 21 Press Club Supper, Victoria. *Supper Speech* *
September 18 Athenaeum Club, Sydney. *Dinner Speech* *
October 3 Yorick Club, Melbourne. *Dinner Speech*
October 12 Late Party, Adelaide. *Speech or Story* *

The Adelaide *South Australian Register* said, October 15, 1895: "Mark Twain had rather a lively and congenial social after his lecture on Saturday night amongst friends with whom wit was rampant and flourished till the 'wee sma' hoors ayont the twal.' "

October 14 Mayor's Reception, Adelaide. *Remarks* *

Of Mark Twain's speech, the *South Australian Register* of above date said: "He was reminded that Adelaide possessed advantages over America . . . in that the city government was honest. He had tried himself to introduce improvements in his own way, but not always with success, but he would like to state that honest civic governments were really the rule in America. There was always a fly in the amber, but which was the particular amber the fly got into was the question; anyway it was the fly that got the amber into discredit." Speaking of the Australian landscape, he said "He recognized the grass, but the trees were new to him. However, Mr. Murphy [C. A. Murphy, American consul] knew all about the trees, and described everything about the country. He did not care whether the information was correct or not, for all he wanted was information and plenty of it."

October 23 Dinner, Bendigo. *Dinner Speech* *
October 27 Journalists Smoke Night, Melbourne. *Four Speeches*
November 15 Savage Club Supper, Christchurch. *Supper Speech*
November 16 Canterbury Club Luncheon, Christchurch. *Remarks* *
December 10 Wellington Club Supper, Wellington. *Supper Speech* *
December 11 Minister for Maori Affairs Dinner, Wellington. *Dinner Speech* *

December 30 Commemoration Luncheon, Glenelg. *Speech*
December 30 Mayor's Reception, Adelaide. *Remarks* *

1896

January 27 Bombay Club Dinner, Bombay. *Dinner Speech* *
February 14 Darjeeling Club Dinner, Darjeeling. *Dinner Speech* *
February 20 Club Supper, Muzaffarpur. *Supper Speech* *
February 22 United Service Dinner, Lucknow. *Dinner Speech* *
March 21 Club Supper, Rawal Pindi. *Supper Speech* *
April (?) Dinner or Supper, Curepipe. *Speech* *
May 12 Savage Club Supper, Durban. *Supper Speech* *

Dr. Samuel Campbell, dinner chairman, said that he prescribed Mark Twain's books as a tonic for convalescing patients. In an undated reminiscence, Natal University Library, Durban, South Africa, Dr. Campbell summarizes Mark Twain's speech: "He commenced his reply by describing how much he admired Durban—what wonderful men they were. He then proceeded to give some of his experiences. . . . he told of how he had been ill in Bombay recently and called in a Doctor, a remarkable man, clever was no name for him, he got right down to the disease and cured it—but left a much worse one behind and passed him on to a Doctor in Calcutta, a wonderful Physician, who cured him of this malignant disease but left a worse one behind. . . . Then he turned his attention particularly to my relationship to him—how soothed he was to hear that he had been so helpful to me in my profession—curing my patients by means of his writing. I was no doubt an honest man, but had it ever occurred to me that I was using his brains to acquire wealth, position, credit. It was surely evident to the simplest intelligence that I owed him something and he would be glad to receive a cheque from me before he left Durban."

May 15 Combined Clubs Dinner, Pietermaritzburg. *Dinner Speech* *
May 20 Mrs. Chapin, Luncheon, Johannesburg. *Remarks* *
May 23 Jail, Pretoria. *Talk to Jameson Raiders*

Mark Twain says (*MTB,* 3:1018): "I made them a speech—sitting down. It just happened so. I don't prefer that attitude. Still, it has one advantage—it is only a *talk,* it doesn't take the form of a speech. . . . I advised them at considerable length to stay where they were—they would get used to it and like it presently; if they got out they would only get in again somewhere else, by the look of their countenances; and I promised to go and see the President and do what I could to get him to double their jail terms."

May 25 Pretoria Club, Pretoria. *Dinner Speech* *
May 28 Dinner or Supper, Johannesburg. *Speech* *
June 1 Press Club Supper, Bloemfontein. *Supper Speech* *
June 6 Club Function, Bloemfontein. *Speech* *
June 16 Queenstown Club, Queenstown. *Dinner Speech* *

1897

January 31 Poultney Bigelow Dinner. *Speech or Story* *
Among guests on this occasion were Lord Young, chief of the Judiciary of Scotland; Sir William Vernon Harcourt, leader of the Opposition, House of Commons; and Herbert Gladstone, son of the former prime minister.
July 1 Supper, London. *Speech or Story* *
October 31 Concordia Festkneipe, Vienna. *"Die Schrecken Der Deutschen Sprache"*

1898

January 2 Dinner and Dance, Vienna. *Speech or Story* *
February 1 Charity Reading, Vienna.
"German and English," "Old Ram," "Golden Arm," "Ornithorhyncus," "Watermelon"
In TS, Notebook 32b (2):55, MTP, Mark Twain wrote an introduction to his program of readings: "Es ist über mein Kraft, das grosse Vergnugen welche mir dies so freundlich Empfangen gibt, in Worte fassen zu können—I could not adequately do it in my own tongue—ich kann nur sagen dass ob ich er vedient habe oder nicht, ich bin Ihnen nichtsdestoweniger aufrichtic dankbar dafür. It is not good German, but the intention is good—better than the clothes it wears."
March 28 Home for English Governesses, Vienna. *"Mexican Plug"*
April 1 Unidentified Dinner. *Four Speeches* *

1899

March 10 Charity Reading, Vienna. *Stories* *
Under the title, "A New German Word" (*MTS*[10]:55), gives a fragment of Mark Twain's introduction: "I have not sufficiently mastered German to allow my using it with impunity. My collection of fourteen-syllable German words is still incomplete. But I have just added to that collection a jewel—a valuable jewel. I found it in a telegram from Linz, and it contains ninety-five letters:

"Personaleinkommensteurschatzungskommissionsmitgliedsreisekostenrechnungserganzungdrevisionsfund.

"If I could get a similar word engraved upon my tombstone I should sleep beneath it in peace."

March (?) Charity Reading, Budapest. *Stories* *

March 23 Hungarian Press Jubilee, Budapest. *Speech*

June 9 Savage Club, London. *Dinner Speech*

June 10 Lord Salisbury's Party, London. *Speech or Story* *

June 12 Authors Club, London. *Dinner Speech*

June 14 Scotch Affair, London. *Speech* *

June 16 Whitefriars Club, London. *Dinner Speech*

June 17 Canon Wilberforce, London. *Remarks* *

June 21 Unidentified Dinner, London. *Speech or Story* *

June 21 Irving Supper, London. *Speech or Story* *

June 25 The Kinsmen, London. *Speech or Story* *

June 28 St. Paul's School, London. *Remarks* *

June 29 New Vagabonds Club, London. *Dinner Speech*

July 3 Unidentified Luncheon, London. *Speech or Story* *

July 4 American Society, London. *"The Day We Celebrate"*

July 5 Campbell-Bannerman Dinner. *Dinner Speech* *

Henry Campbell-Bannerman (1836–1908) was a British parliamentarian of long standing, a leader of the Liberal party who had held posts in the War Office and the Admiralty, and who became prime minister in 1905.

1900

March 23 Moberly Bell Dinner, London. *Dinner Speech* *

Charles Francis Moberly Bell (1847–1911) was a British journalist who had been a London *Times* reporter in Egypt, where he founded an English language paper, the *Egyptian Gazette* (1880). Called to London to manage the *Times* (1890), he reorganized the foreign department, instituted the *Times* book club and *Times Literary Supplement,* published the *Times Atlas,* and republished the ninth edition of the *Encyclopaedia Britannica.*

March 24 Earl of Portsmouth Dinner, London. *Dinner Speech* *

March 26 Gilbert Parker Dinner, London. *Dinner Speech* *

April 3 House of Lords, London. *Remarks on Copyright*

May 2 Royal Literary Fund, London. *"Literature"*

May 9 St. Bartholomew's Hospital, London. *Speech or Story* *

May 30 Canon Wilberforce, London. *"Joan of Arc"*

June 9 Irving Dinner, London. *"The Drama"*

June 10 Magdalen College Luncheon, Oxford. *Remarks* *

June 10 Savage Club, London. *Dinner Speech* *
June 22 The Kinsmen, London. *Stories* *
June 24 Athenaeum Club, London. *Dinner Speech* *
June 29 Lord Mayor's Luncheon, London. *Speech* *
July 4 American Society, London. *Dinner Speech* *
July 7 Savage Club, Mark Twain Chairman, London. *Speeches* *
September 27 Reading Room Opening, London. *Remarks*
October 14 Dockside, New York City. *Travelogue*
October 17 Galveston Orphans Bazaar, New York City. *Speech*
October 27 Woman's Press Club, New York City. *Remarks*
November 10 Lotos Club Dinner, New York City. *Dinner Speech*
November 12 Press Club Reception, New York City. *Three Speeches*
November 15 American Authors Reception, New York City. *Speech*
November 20 Nineteenth Century Club, New York City. *"Disappearance of Literature"*
November 23 Public Education Association, New York City. *Remarks*
December 4 Aldine Association, New York City. *Dinner Speech* *

The dinner for Mark Twain attracted an overflow crowd. Bishop Potter was there, Augustus Thomas, Joe Jefferson, F. Hopkinson Smith, the Reverend Dr. Mackay, John Fox, Jr., Matthews, Bangs, Gilder, Winston Churchill (the American novelist), Owen Wister, George Putnam, Hutton, Charles Scribner, Isador Straus, Major Pond, Captain Joshua Slocum, Frank Doubleday, Colonel Harvey, and many others. The chairman was Hamilton W. Mabie. He and Mark Twain sat within a simulated pilot house, from the corners of which descended streamers of colored lights. On the cornice was *Alonzo Child,* the name of a Mississippi steamboat Sam Clemens had piloted. Hanging moss, oranges and gourds decorated the walls, and there were catfish in glass tanks. Mark Twain found in these adornments the principal themes for his speech, described as "reminiscent and constantly delightful." He had requested that his words not be reported by the press because, he said, public tributes already paid to him fully satisfied the public need.

December 6 St. Nicholas Society, New York City. *"Our City"*
December 11 Meeting of Missourians, New York City. *Speech* *
December 12 Waldorf-Astoria, New York City. *Introducing Churchill*

1901

January 4 City Club, New York City. *"Municipal Corruption"*
January 7 For Mr. Rogers, New York City. *"Ornithorhyncus," "German," "Watermelon," "Dead Man," "Ram," "Mexican Plug," "Christening"*

January 16 Tavern Club, Boston. *Dinner Speech* *
January 20 Hebrew Technical School, New York City. *Speech*
January 24 Thursday Evening Club, New York City. *Story* *
January 28 Bible Class, John D. Rockefeller, Jr. *Story* *
January 31 Churchill Dinner, New York City. *Dinner Speech* *
February 2 University Settlement Society. *Speech*
February 11 Lincoln Celebration, New York City.
Remarks as Chairman
February 18 David Munro Dinner, New York City. *Dinner Speech* *

David Alexander Munro (d. 1910) was general manager of the *North American Review* (1889–96), editor (1896–99), then assistant editor when Harvey bought the *Review* in 1899. Munro compiled a comparative Greek-English New Testament, and collaborated with Dr. Philip Schaff in the preparation of a Companion to a study of the Greek New Testament.

February 27 State Senate Committee, Albany. *Remarks on Osteopathy*
February 28 State Senate, Albany. *Remarks on Water Supply*
March 2 University Club, New York City. *Dinner Speech* *
March 7 Thursday Evening Club, New York City. *Stories* *
March 12 Howells Dinner, New York City. *Dinner Speech* *
March 16 Male Teachers Association. *"Training that Pays"*
March 23 Odell Dinner, New York City. *Dinner Speech*
March 28 Players Club Dinner, New York City. *Speech or Story* *
March 30 Eastman Club, New York City. *Dinner Speech*
April 6 Smith College Luncheon, New York City. *Remarks* *

Mark Twain and Sir Caspar Purdon Clarke were the chief attractions on this occasion. Mark Twain told the story of the tight shoes that refused to go on, then said, according to the *Times*, April 8, 1901: "When I come to a gathering like this, I feel that I should like to be an aspirant for political honors; I should like to be elected the belle of New York so that I could come to these luncheons all the time." The girls gave him a standing tribute of hearty applause and by acclamation elected him "Annual Guest." And a few years later he did become, by general consent, the Belle of New York.

April 29 Mabie Dinner, New York City. *Dinner Speech*
May 9 Student Audience, Princeton.
"Dead Man," "German," "Mexican Plug," "Ram"

MTS(10):422, gives a fragment of Mark Twain's introduction: "I feel exceedingly surreptitious in coming down here without an announcement of any kind. I do not want to see any advertisements around, for the reason that I am not a lecturer any longer. I reformed long ago, and I break over and commit this sin only just this one time this year—and that is moderate, I think, for a person of my disposition. It is not my purpose to lecture any more as long as I live. I never intend to stand up on a platform any more—unless by the request of a sheriff or something like that."

May 10 Harvard-Princeton Debate, Princeton. *Remarks* *

May 11 Normal College Alumnae, New York City. *"German," "Tale of a Fishwife"* *

Fifteen hundred women turned out for this affair. Next day's *Times* said: "In a very formal manner Mr. Clemens was escorted to the platform by Miss Elizabeth Jarrett, M.D., President of the Associate Alumnae. . . . She had begun a little speech complimentary to Mr. Clemens, when he checked her. Gently but firmly he sat her in the chair she had been occupying on the platform, and when the audience had ceased laughing explained that there was no sense in complimenting a man who really deserved it." Then he said: "The President has hardly permitted me to choose whether I will speak or read. I have decided to read. I thought I would tell you about the difficulties I experienced while studying the German language. I owe it an old grudge."

May 27 J. H. Rosenberg's, New York City. *Talk to Boys* *

May 28 Missouri Society, New York City. *Dinner Speech*

August 14 Young People, Bar Harbor. *On Speech-Making*

October 17 Acorns, New York City. *"Edmund Burke on Croker and Tammany"*

October 29 Fusionist Rally, New York City. *Two Speeches*

November 6 Acorns Jubilee, New York City. *Mock Eulogy of Tammany*

November 7 Good Citizenship Association, New York City. *Speech*

November 16 Choate Dinner, New York City. *Dinner Speech*

November 30 St. Andrews Society, New York City. *"Scotch Humor"*

December 19 Debating Club, New York City. *Remarks* *

December 31 Players Club Founding Night. *Speech* *

In Notebook 34, 1901, MTP, Mark Twain outlined a plan for his midnight speech: Joe Jefferson to introduce him and lavishly praise the Players Club, he (Mark Twain) to respond by negating the praise with uncomplimentary remarks about the club.

1902

January 16 Civic Club, Riverdale. *Talk or Reading* *

January 28 Rockefeller Bible Class, New York City. *Stories* *

The *Times* of January 29 gave Mark Twain's concluding remarks: "I am a farmer now. Not a very good farmer yet, but a farmer just the same. So I'll have to go now to be up early in the morning to take care of my crop. I don't know yet what the crop will be, but I think from present indications it will be icicles."

January 31 Yale Alumni, Hartford. *Dinner Speech*

February 14 Public School, New York City. *"Death-Disk," "Tale No. 2"*

February 18 Boys Club, New York City. *Stories* *

March 8 Medical Jurisprudence, New York City. *Dinner Speech*

May 1 For Mrs. Bartholomew, New York City. *Reading* *

May 29 Merchants Exchange, St. Louis. *Speech* *

May 30 Decoration Day, Hannibal. *Chairman, Speeches* *

May 30 High School Graduation, Hannibal. *Speech*

May 31 Labinnah Club, Hannibal. *Remarks* *

May 31 Reception, 1901 Class, Hannibal. *Remarks* *

June 1 Sunday School, Hannibal. *Story*

MTB, 3:1169, quotes Mark Twain as follows: "Little boys and girls, I want to tell you a story which illustrates the value of perseverance—of sticking to your work, as it were. It is a story very proper for a Sunday school. When I was a little boy in Hannibal I used to play a good deal up here on Holliday's Hill, which of course you all know. John Briggs and I played up there. I don't suppose there are any little boys as good as we were then, but of course that is not to be expected. Little boys in those days were 'most always good little boys, because those were the good old times when everything was better than it is now, but never mind that." He told the story of the man, putting in a blast, who got blown up, went out of sight, came down in the same place and went on drilling. Then he concluded: "Little boys and girls, that's the secret of success, just like that poor but honest workman on Holliday's Hill. Of course you won't always be appreciated. He wasn't. His employer was a hard man, and on Saturday night when he paid him he docked him fifteen minutes for the time he was up in the air—but never mind he had his reward."

June 2 Mr. Crookshank's, Hannibal. *Remarks* *

June 3 St. Joseph Academy, Hannibal. *Talk* *

June 3 Phi Beta Kappa Dinner, Columbia. *Dinner Speech* *

The candidates for honorary degrees were guests of honor on this occasion. As reported by the Columbia *Missouri Herald,* June 6, 1902, Mark Twain entertained the audience by making joking remarks about the previous speeches of Messrs. Hitchcock, Wilson, and Galloway. The latter had mentioned a goat. "Mr. Clemens said that he greatly honored the goat, and thought goats ought to be editing half the magazines of the country. When he was young he wrote a very fine article which he carried to every magazine and principal newspaper he could find, carried it twice, and they all refused it. A goat took it at once, and showed himself much wiser than any of the editors. He did not know exactly what a curator was, what he cured, but he was satisfied that the University was being properly managed, and, as an old Missourian, he was proud of it. He said that language could not express his appreciation of the honors the University had conferred upon him. He did not know what he could do, but that as one way of expressing his gratitude he would give the library a set of his books, which he was certain contained everything that was not in any other books." Phi Beta Kappa made him an honorary member.

June 4 University of Missouri Commencement. *Speech*
June 5 Rochambeau Reception, St. Louis. *Remarks* *
June 6 Harbor Boat Christening, St. Louis. *Speech*
June 6 Unveiling Eugene Field Tablet, St. Louis. *Remarks*
June 7 Art Students Association, St. Louis. *Speech on Art*
June 17 Porter Dinner, New York City. *Dinner Speech*
June (?) Alfred Corning Clark Neighborhood House. *Stories* *

Alfred Corning Clark (1815–96) was a philanthropist who used his fortune for humanitarian purposes, like the Neighborhood House, and for assisting struggling artists, one of whom was the young American sculptor, George Grey Barnard.

August 5 250th Anniversary, York, Maine. *Speech* *

A pamphlet, *Two Hundred and Fiftieth Anniversary of the Town of York, Maine,* York Public Library, pp. 119–20, summarizes his speech: "Mr. Clemens [said] . . . that he had come to York to instruct it in its ancient history, to rectify the morals of its inhabitants and to otherwise do valuable things in the way of didactics. He found himself prevented from doing so by the example of another, and noted with surprise that Thomas B. Reed should mistake a desk for a pulpit, especially as the speaker was the one who, in time gone by, had amazed the nations of the world, the human race, and, added Mr. Clemens, 'even myself!' . . . In thirty-seven days he had had no fault to find with the weather as he had stayed strictly at home, and the rain seemed to come only when it thought it could catch one out. For thirty-four of the thirty-seven days he had worked and that was something he never before had been able to do. The climate, he thought, prevented moral deterioration, for he had worked four Sundays without breaking the Sabbath. . . . One of the most serious questions with which he had to contend in York was matches. If he wished to smoke it was next to impossible to get a light. He could buy only a sort of match with a picture of the inventor on each box and labeled 'Safety.' He felt free to say that they are so safe one cannot light them. Even Satan, the inventor and a distant relative of his, can't use them for he has no appliances to make them go, and is utilizing them to build cold storage vaults for such choice morsels as Voltaire, Benjamin Franklin, Alexander VI; and, added the speaker, 'he has a wistful eye on some other notables not yet started, and here present.' Another serious question . . . was the confusion of post offices in this town—York Cliffs, York Beach, York Harbor, York Village, York Corner, and so on. In fact, one cannot throw a brickbat across a thirty-seven acre lot without danger of disabling a postmaster; they are as thick as aldermen in the days of the old city charter. If he stayed here he expected to attend York's tri-centennial in fifty years, for already he had grown younger by many years than he was on his arrival."

October 25 Hutton Dinner, Princeton. *Talk or Story* *

After the inauguration of Woodrow Wilson as president of Princeton University, Hutton assembled a stimulating dinner group: former President Cleveland, Mark Twain, Stedman, Thomas B. Reed, Gilder, Henry Rogers, Colonel Harvey, and others.

November 28 Sixty-seventh Birthday Dinner, New York City. *Dinner Speech*

December 19 Unidentified Dinner, New York City. *Dinner Speech* *

December 20 For Mrs. Bartholomew, New York City. *Reading* *

1903

January 6 Munro Dinner, New York City. *Dinner Speech* *

February 5 Harvey Dinner, New York City. *Dinner Speech* *

February 6 Century Club, New York City. *Dinner Speech* *

February 24 Howells Dinner, Boston. *Dinner Speech* *

March 28 Sidney Lee Dinner, New York City. *Dinner Speech* *

Sidney Lee (1859–1926) was assistant editor of *The Dictionary of National Biography* (1883–90), then became chief editor (1891). An Elizabethan scholar, he published *Life of William Shakespeare* (1898), *Shakespeare and the Modern Stage* (1906), and a twenty-volume edition of Shakespeare (1907–10).

Carnegie was host at the dinner for the British visitor. In *MTE:* 331–38, Mark Twain amusingly describes the extreme shyness of the guest of honor and the hemming and hawing of such practiced speakers as Howells, Carl Schurz, Gilder, and Melville Stone, all of whom seemed affected by Lee's timidity. Brander

Matthews remarks, *The Tocsin of Revolt:* 272, that "When Mark's turn came, he soared aloft in whimsical exaggeration, casually dropping a reference to the time when he had lent Carnegie a million dollars. Our smiling host promptly interjected: 'That had slipped my memory!' And Mark looked down on him solemnly, and retorted: 'Then the next time, I'll take a receipt.' "

April 23 St. George Society, New York City. *Dinner Speech* *

September 6 Associated Press, New York City. *Dinner Speech* *

October 23 Dinner for Mark Twain, New York City. *Dinner Speech* *

Colonel Harvey was host at this farewell dinner for Mark Twain, who was about to sail for Italy with his family. Among guests were Howells, J. P. Morgan, Henry Rogers, William M. Laffan, Henry Mills Alden, Hamlin Garland, J. Henry Harper, Bangs, McKelway, and Melville Stone.

1904

March (?) Benefit, Florentine British Relief Fund, Florence, Italy. *"Italian Without Grammar"* *

According to the English language *Italian Gazette,* n.d.: "The great humorist looked as full of vitality as ever though it was plain that he was labouring under a stress of emotion, and at times he nervously tore the paper he was holding in his hands. At the end of his talk, with a break in his voice, he bade his hearers good-night, and everyone admires his generous courage when it was known that he had left Mrs. Clemens at home seriously ill."

1905

December 5 Seventieth Birthday, New York City. *Dinner Speech*

December 18 Benefit Matinee, New York City. *Speech*

December 21 Society of Illustrators, New York City. *Dinner Speech*

1906

January 3 Dinner for Mark Twain, New York City. *Dinner Speech* *

Because of confusion over payment of dues a few years before, an overzealous management had expelled Mark Twain from the Players Club. In 1906 the club, circumventing by-laws, brought him back into the fold as an honorary member. A small group of his friends celebrated at a dinner of reconciliation. Mark Twain's speech was received so enthusiastically that he responded with an encore, "The Jumping Frog." For his comments on the dinner and the dues controversy, see *MTA,* 1:279–81; 2:227–29.

January 22 Tuskegee Institute Meeting, New York City. *Speech*

January 25 Unidentified Club, Washington, D.C. *Dinner Speech* *

In a dictation of January 23, 1906, MTP, Mark Twain says that for this occasion he thought of giving the old Whittier dinner speech of 1877, but rejected the idea. That he considered resurrecting that controversial burlesque perhaps implies bravado or, since he was now distant from the original scene in space and time and the principals were all dead, his belief that he could carry it off better than he did the first time.

January 27 Gridiron Club, Washington, D.C. *Dinner Speech* *

According to the Washington *Post,* January 28, 1906, the theme was "A Night in Panama." Newspaper wags made game of President Roosevelt and the Panama Canal, Roosevelt himself being present and taking the raillery like a sportsman. Some joker read verses: "Mark Twain once told us there were only seven jokes on earth. / What a shame! / Who's to blame? / The rest are variations on the good old theme of mirth: / All the same / Rather tame. / I've read his books all over with a reverential care / There to view / Something new: / There are seven in the list—but the best ones he has missed— / For he uses only two." Mark Twain, introduced as a Mississippi River roustabout, spoke for twenty minutes, but the Gridiron Club had a rule that speeches not be reported by the press.

January 29 House of Representatives, Washington, D.C. *On Copyright* *

February 7 Manhattan Dickens Fellowship, New York City. *Dinner Speech*

February 14 Alden Luncheon, New York City. *Speech or Story* *

Henry Mills Alden (1836–1919), a graduate of Andover Theological Seminary (1860), was managing editor of *Harper's Weekly* (1863), then editor of *Harper's Magazine* (1869), where he remained thereafter. His policy was to make the fare of the magazine a combination of the scholarly and the popular.

February 14 Keats-Shelley Matinee, New York City. *Remarks* *

This musical entertainment at the Waldorf was given to aid the Keats-Shelley Memorial in Rome. Mark Twain, who sat on the stage with Stedman, Ruth McEnery Stuart, Henry Van Dyke, S. Weir Mitchell, and F. Hopkinson Smith, read a poem. According to Hamlin Hill, *God's Fool:* 164, he said he "took some whiskey, and just enough to bring cobwebs and make him forget the things he was going to say."

February 19 Pilgrims of the U.S., New York City. *Dinner Speech* *

February (?) General Miles Dinner, New York City. *Dinner Speech* *

February (?) Unknown Function, New York City. *Introducing Dr. Van Dyke*

March 4 West Side Y.M.C.A., New York City. *Speech*

March 7 Barnard College, New York City. *Speech*

March 8 Freundschaft Society, New York City. *Dinner Speech*

March 20 Bohemians, Hoffbrauhaus, New York City. *Remarks* *

March 29 Meeting for the Blind, New York City. *Chairman, Speech*

April 2 Vassar Aid Benefit, New York City. *Remarks* *

Three short plays were staged at the Hudson Theatre on behalf of the Vassar Students Aid Society. Twenty-eight white-clad girls greeted Mark Twain, decorated him with a red rose and the pink and gray of Vassar, then escorted him to a lower stage box. That he made a speech is not on record, but he probably said something. Afterward, in an informal reception on the stage, he shook hands and autographed programs, sometimes adding a maxim, such as "Do your duty today and repent tomorrow." To sign programs he rested them on the shoulder of Miss T. V. Dickson, one of the ushers. "A nice quiet little desk," he said, that he wished he could keep. He also kissed a good many of the ladies, especially the young ones. He had such a good time with the Vassar girls that he did not make it to the Museum of Natural History, where the governor general of Canada and other very important persons were anxiously waiting for him to take part in some unknown function.

April 3 Women's University Club, New York City. *Remarks*

April 7 Smith College Alumnae, New York City. *Tight Shoes Story*

April 11 Gorky Dinner, New York City. *Dinner Speech*

April 19 Fulton Monument Benefit, New York City. *Speech*

April 21 San Francisco Relief Meeting, New York City. *Remarks*

April 23 Old Guard's Eightieth Anniversary, New York City. *Story* *

During the speech-making, a concealed versifier composed doggerel about the speakers, and shouted it to the audience through a megaphone. Mark Twain, who arrived late, inspired a satirical jingle about his wild thatch of white hair. He thanked the Old Guard for his fine reception, told a story, and was presented with a bouquet of roses.

April 24 Billiard Exhibition, New York City. *Story*

Summer Informal Club, Dublin, New Hampshire. *Charity Reading* *

The club was a casual affair, mainly for the purposes of eating, drinking, and talking. During the charity speech a lady who kept on knitting while he was talking provoked a Twainian temper tantrum, and he stormed out. See Hamlin Hill, *Mark Twain: God's Fool* (1973):117–18.

September 1 Country Club, Dublin. *Speech-making Experiment* *
September 8 Village, Dublin. *Speech-making Experiment* *
September 19 Associated Press, New York City. *Dinner Speech*
September 22 Clara Clemens Concert, Norfolk, Connecticut. *Remarks*
October 27 Saturday Morning Club, Hartford. *Talk or Story* *
November 8 National Arts Club, New York City. *Speech* *
December 7 Washington, D.C. *Interview*
December 7 Congressional Committee, Washington. *Remarks on Copyright*
December 31 21 Fifth Avenue, New York City. *Burlesque on Temperance*

1907

January 26 Senator Clark Dinner, New York City. *Dinner Speech* *
William Andrews Clark (1839–1925) was a capitalist and politician who made a fortune in Colorado and Montana in mining, banking, and railroads. United States senator from Montana (1901–07), he had a palatial residence on Fifth Avenue and a gallery of art treasures. Mark Twain did not admire Senator Clark. See *MTE:* 70–77.

February 11 Collyer Dinner, New York City. *Dinner Speech* *
Robert Collyer (1823–1912) was a British-born Unitarian clergyman. An abolitionist, active on the Civil War Sanitary Commission, he was afterward pastor of Unity Church, Chicago, then of the Church of the Messiah, New York. He was a great success on the lyceum circuit with his popular lecture, "Clear Grit."

February 14 For Mrs. Gilder, New York City. *Reading* *
February 22 Ladies Tea, Columbia University. *Remarks* *
February 23 Interview, New York City. *"Longfellow and Others"*
March 1 Howells Dinner, New York City. *Dinner Speech* *
March 12 College Women's Club, New York City. *Remarks* *
March 23 Bryce Dinner, New York City. *Dinner Speech* *
April 14 Children's Theatre, New York City. *Curtain Speech*
April (?) Ambassador Tower Dinner, New York City. *Dinner Speech* *
May 4 Tea and Reception, Tuxedo Park. *Talk or Story* *
May 6 Actors Fund Fair, New York City. *Speech*
May 9 Church Benefit, Annapolis. *Speech* *
May 10 Government House, Annapolis. *Dinner Speech*
May 22 Harvey Dinner, New York City. *Dinner Speech* *
June 8 S.S. *Minneapolis,* New York City. *Interview*
June 15 S.S. *Minneapolis,* at sea. *Reading, Autobiography* *

June 19 Society of Women Journalists, London. *Remarks* *
June 21 American Embassy, London. *Dinner Speech* *
June 22 Interview, London. *Royal Garden Party*
June 24 Legion of Frontiersmen, London. *Remarks* *
June 25 Pilgrims Luncheon, London. *"Our Guest"*
June 26 All Souls Luncheon, Oxford. *Remarks* *
June 26 Christ Church Dinner, Oxford. *"Honorary Doctors"* *

On this occasion Mark Twain made the mistake of wearing black evening dress, which was a drab contrast to the scarlet academic garb of other diners. He was chagrined because he had missed a chance to sport his own gaudy Oxford gown. Feeling conspicuous in an unattractive way, he said he felt as out of place as a Presbyterian in hell.

June 28 Rhodes Scholars, Oxford. *Remarks* *
June 29 Army School Pupils, Stratford. *Remarks* *

A by-product of Mark Twain's exasperating afternoon with Marie Corelli was a short talk to boys of the Army School at Stratford. According to the London *Times,* July 1, 1907, he "mentioned that he had once been a soldier for two weeks during the American Civil War, but his experiences were such that he did not care to remember them. Looking upon the budding warriors before him, he sincerely wished them a better liking for their lot than his had been and more of it. The mayor, he understood, had wished to award him civic honours, but his request was that his visit might be considered a personal one to Miss Corelli."

June 29 Lord Mayor's Dinner, London. *Dinner Speech*
July 1 Dominion Day Dinner, London. *Dinner Speech* *
July 2 Henniker Heaton Luncheon, London. *Remarks* *
July 4 American Society, London. *Dinner Speech*
July 6 Savage Club, London. *Dinner Speech*
July 8 Plasmon Luncheon, London. *Talk or Story* *
July 9 House of Commons Luncheon, London. *Remarks* *
July 9 *Punch* Dinner, London. *Dinner Speech* *
July 10 Lord Mayor's Dinner, Liverpool. *"Our Guest"*
July 12 London. *Interview*

The *Times* reported briefly, July 13, 1907: "I have led a violently gay and energetic life here for four weeks, but I have felt no fatigue, and I have had but little desire to quiet down. . . . This is the most enjoyable holiday I have ever had, and I am sorry the end of it has come. . . . For two years past I have been planning my funeral, but I have changed my mind now and will postpone it. I suppose I won't see England again, but I don't like to think of that."

July 20 S.S. *Minnetonka,* at sea. *Stories* *

At the ship's concert Mark Twain was reported to have talked for an hour, in the course of which he told the sock-hunting story and others.

July 22 Dockside, New York City. *Interview*

September 23 Fulton Day, Jamestown. *Speech*

October (?) New York City? *Welcoming British Bishop*

October 15(?) Unidentified Function, Tuxedo Park. *Reading* *

Autumn Players Dinner, New York City. *Stories* *

George C. Riggs was host, and among guests were Howells, Edward Burlingame, David Bispham, Nicholas Biddle, and David Munro. Mark Twain told the story of General Miles and the dog, and probably other anecdotes.

November 11 Homeopathic Society, New York City. *Dinner Speech* *

November 12 Colony Club, New York City. *Speech* *

November 19 Children's Theatre, New York City. *Speech*

November 20 Players Club, New York City. *Dinner Speech* *

December 9 Society of Engineers, New York City. *Dinner Speech*

December 22 Pleiades Club, New York City. *Dinner Speech*

1908

January 10 Collyer Dinner, New York City. *Dinner Speech* *

January 11 Lotos Club, New York City. *Dinner Speech*

January 14 Doe Luncheon, New York City. *Remarks* *

February 11 Doe Luncheon, New York City. *Remarks* *

February 11 Carnegie Dinner, New York City. *Dinner Speech* *

February 13 Clara Clemens Musicale, New York City. *Remarks* *

February 13 Supper and Ball, Sherry's. *Remarks* *

February 19 Whitelaw Reid Dinner, New York City. *Dinner Speech*

March 1 Informal Group, Hamilton, Bermuda. *Reading, Kipling* *

March 3 Benefit, Hamilton. *Speech* *

At this benefit for the Bermuda Cottage Hospital, Mark Twain introduced the performers, and made a speech at the close of the program.

March (?) Benefit Aquarium, Hamilton. *Talk or Reading* *

April 6 Garrison Children, Hamilton. *Cat Story*

April 13 New York City. *Interview*

April 18 Humorists and Cartoonists, New York City. *Speech*

April 23 Children's Theatre, New York City. *Curtain Speech*

May 14 City College Dedication, New York City. *Speech*

May 14 City College Alumni, New York City. *Dinner Speech*

May 20 Publishers and Bussinessmen, New York City. *Speech* *

At a time when muckrakers were flourishing, the Aldine Association sponsored a gathering of publishers and business magnates to encourage better understanding on both sides. Frank Doubleday was host. Mark Twain brought Henry Rogers, who had been heavily attacked as a prominent representative of the Standard Oil Company. John D. Rockefeller, who was also there, gave information about the Rockefeller Institute for Medical Research, to which he had given ten million dollars. Mark Twain made a speech, but it was not reported.

May 20 American Booksellers, New York City. *Dinner Speech*

May 25 British Schools and Universities Club, New York City. *"Queen Victoria–an American Tribute"*

June 7 Howells Luncheon, Lakewood, New Jersey. *Remarks* *

Colonel George Harvey, an enthusiastic arranger of special occasions, chartered two drawing room cars to transport about sixty guests to Lakewood for a farewell luncheon for Howells, who was about to sail for Italy. Kitty Cheatham entertained with recitations, and Denis O'Sullivan, an Irish-American singer, played haunting melodies on Pan-like pipes, and lively tunes on an Irish tin whistle. Principal speakers were Howells and Mark Twain, who had a good time chaffing each other.

June 30 Aldrich Memorial Program, Portsmouth, New Hampshire. *Remarks* *

The occasion honored Thomas Bailey Aldrich by dedicating a memorial museum established by his widow. Mark Twain disliked Mrs. Aldrich, and he had a hot, tiresome journey up to Portsmouth, but he said he would not have missed it. He said that for the ceremony he had prepared a speech, listed last on the program as "Aldrich as Talker and Wit," but that, oppressed by the funereal gloom of speakers who preceded him—among them, Gilder, Higginson, Mabie, and Van Dyke—he discarded his prepared speech in favor of nonsense. According to one observer, he began by mopping his forehead with a large white hankerchief, restoring it to a breast pocket and from another pocket pulling out a fresh handkerchief to dab his face, then a third to pat his throat—all in slow motion and without a word. Finally he said, with a quaver in his voice: "Poor Tom! Poor Tom! I hope—he isn't—as hot—as I am now." See *Mark Twain's Jest Book,* ed. Cyril Clemens (1963):12. For Mark Twain's comments on the Portsmouth excursion, see *MTE:*292–303.

October (?) Stormfield, Connecticut. *Talk to Workmen* *

October 28 Mark Twain Library, Redding. *Speech*

1909

January 20 Medical School, New York City. *"On the Three Great Laws"*
March 17 Lotos Club, New York City. *Dinner Speech*
April 3 Rogers Dinner, Norfolk. *Dinner Speech*
May 7 Jerome Dinner, New York City. *Dinner Speech*
June 9 Misses Tewksbury's School, Baltimore. *Remarks*
September 21 Concert, Stormfield. *Remarks*

At this afternoon concert for the benefit of the Mark Twain Library, Mark Twain acted as master of ceremonies. He introduced the artists: Ossip Gabrilowitsch, pianist; David Bispham, singer; Clara Clemens, contralto. Of his daughter he said, "My daughter is not so famous as these gentlemen, but she is ever so much better looking." Tickets were fifty cents, seventy-five cents, and one dollar. An audience of more than five hundred contributed $372 to the building fund. See *MTB,* 4:1521–22.

Index

Abbey, Edwin Austin: 127, 193, 338, 655
Abbott, Lyman; 381, 506, 643
Actors Fund Fair: 194, 548, 656, 676
Adam: 7, 117, 130, 178–80, 249, 284, 386, 488, 655
Albany, New York: 384, 389, 588, 668
Alden, Henry Mills: 453, 673, 674
Aldrich, Thomas Bailey: 176, 177, 349, 393, 427, 535, 651, 652, 655, 658, 679
Alexander, King of Macedon: 255, 286, 566
Anne, Queen of England: 536, 537, 539–40
Army of the Potomac: 3, 151, 655
Army of the Tennessee: xxiv, 130, 653
Arnold, Matthew: 225 *passim*, 237, 257, 259, 260, 305, 322
Ascot Cup: 560, 564, 567, 572, 577, 585
Associated Press: 522, 523, 527, 639, 673, 676
Atlantic Monthly: 87, 110, 134, 177, 545, 605, 651, 653
Authors Club: 210, 322, 323, 657, 659, 661, 666
Authors Copyright League: 206, 207, 656
Authors Readings: 544, 545, 656 *passim*

Baltimore, Maryland: 219, 554, 645, 657, 658, 680
Bangs, John Kendrick: 349, 356, 453, 456, 461, 667, 673
Barnard College: 495, 513, 675
Barnum, Phineas Taylor: xv, 224, 238, 240
Barrett, Lawrence: 240, 655, 657
Barrymore, Ethel: 549, 611
Beard, Daniel Carter: 472, 473, 476, 596, 630, 631
Beecher, Henry Ward: xv, 63
Berlin, Germany: 342, 355, 660
Bernhardt, Sarah (Henriette Rosine Bernard): 468, 469, 471–72
Bigelow, Poultney: 324, 385, 388, 596, 665
Billings, Josh (Henry Wheeler Shaw): xv, 424, 425
Birrell, Augustine: 558, 560, 562, 563, 567, 573
Bispham, David: 657, 678, 680
Blaine, James Gillespie: 182 *passim*, 659
Bombay, India: 312, 342, 365, 434, 664
Booth, Edwin: 240, 243, 655 *passim*
Borgia, Lucrezia: 21, 22, 798
Boston *Advertiser:* 87, 110, 114
Boston, Massachusetts: 44, 48, 110, 136, 148, 163, 176, 230, 233, 234, 310, 327, 513, 543, 544, 582, 609, 651, 652, 654, 655, 657, 658, 661, 668, 672
Boston *Transcript:* 185, 187, 215, 369, 651
Boxers, Chinese insurgents: 352, 361–62, 363, 369, 399
Boyce, Rubert William: 577, 578, 583
Bryan, William Jennings: 372, 373, 624
Bryce, James: 621, 622, 676
Bulwer, William Henry Lytton: 226, 228–29
Bunker Hill: 43, 106, 448
Bunyan, John: 42, 343, 347
Burke, Edmund: 406, 409, 410, 411, 413
Burton, Nathaniel Judson: 94, 427, 428

Bushnell, Horace: 427, 428, 444–45, 446
Butler, Nicholas Murray: 478, 506, 527, 567
Butte, Montana: 287, 292, 343, 663

Cable, George Washington: xviii, 176, 177, 188, 393, 427, 453, 655
Caesar, Julius: 125, 249, 255, 286, 401, 625, 640
Calcutta, India: 342, 404, 405, 664
Cape Cod: 162, 165, 488
Carnegie, Andrew: 265, 381, 391, 392, 398, 420, 421, 423, 425, 472, 474, 475, 482, 507, 511, 525, 527, 596 *passim,* 604, 606, 612, 637, 638, 639, 660, 672, 678
Carson City, Nevada: 51, 53, 63, 487, 648
Century Magazine: 109, 177, 419, 424, 656
Chicago, Illinois: xxiv, 130, 493, 569, 588, 618, 653, 654
Chicago *Tribune:* 63, 130, 133, 147
Children's Theatre: 546, 596, 620, 632, 676, 678
Choate, Joseph Hodges: xix, 100, 173, 324, 326, 329, 333, 338, 340, 420, 421, 422, 464, 478–79, 481, 506, 510, 567, 612, 613, 614, 621, 643, 669
Christchurch, New Zealand: 302, 303, 663
Churchill, Winston Leonard Spencer: 367, 368, 667, 668
City College of New York: 621, 623, 678
Clarke, Arthur Purdon: 472, 473, 476, 668
Clemens, Clara: 269, 287, 300, 301 344, 528, 541, 546, 561, 611, 615, 676, 678, 680
Clemens, Olivia: xvii, 36, 37, 83, 194, 267, 269, 270, 271, 287, 300, 313, 330, 396, 458, 459, 462, 502, 543, 546, 561, 581, 641–42, 647, 673
Cleveland, Grover: 177, 182, 186, 188, 263, 307, 342, 510, 587, 641, 656, 658, 672
Cleveland *Herald:* 36, 37, 71
Cleveland, Ohio: 31, 36, 37, 44, 123, 124, 279
Collins, William Wilkie: 74, 543, 544–45, 651
Collyer, Robert: xv, 513, 621, 676, 678
Columbus, Christopher: 28, 214, 638
Connecticut Yankee in King Arthur's Court: 211, 252, 473, 477, 531
Conway, Moncure D.: 69, 71, 349
Cook, James: 6, 10, 15, 324
Cooper Union: xvi, 64, 486, 487, 648
Croker, Richard: 366, 371, 372, 404 *passim,* 414, 415, 416
Curtis, George William: xv, 100, 134, 184, 186, 209
Curzon, George Nathaniel: 566, 584, 594

Daly, Augustin: 222, 223, 224, 240, 611, 657, 658
Dana, Charles Anderson: 184, 265, 266, 268, 455, 456, 582, 583, 609, 615, 643
Darwin, Charles: 120, 126, 359, 559, 563
Davis, Richard Harding: 596, 643, 662
Declaration of Independence: 568 *passim,* 588
Depew, Chauncey Mitchell: xix, 173, 232, 234, 240, 243, 244, 263, 324, 326, 333, 349, 351, 392, 393, 420, 453, 454, 558, 596, 643, 658
Dickens, Charles: xxv, 81, 482, 545
Disraeli, Benjamin: 80–81, 226, 228
Dodge, William E.: 363, 381, 420, 423
Drew, John: 222, 651, 657, 662
Durand, Mortimer: 556 *passim*

Eddy, Mary Baker: 388, 532, 548
Edison, Thomas Alva: 488, 606
Educational Alliance: 546, 547, 620
Edward, Prince of Wales: 306, 321, 453, 477
Edward VII of England: 556, 557, 585, 586, 594, 607
Eliot, Charles William: 359, 360, 596

Elmira, New York: 36, 37, 128, 180, 653, 657, 658, 662
Emerson, Ralph Waldo: 110 *passim,* 134, 535, 543, 605
Eve: 7, 21, 79
Everett, Edward: xvi, 46, 47–48

Fairbanks, Mary Mason: 37, 72, 649
Fairhaven, Massachusetts: 271, 272, 469, 662
Fellowcraft Club: 247, 449–50, 659
Field, Eugene: 442, 671
Fields, James Thomas: 543, 545, 654
Florence, Italy: 32, 342, 673
Fourth of July: 12, 74–75, 76, 121, 333, 334, 567 *passim,* 587, 588
Franklin, Benjamin: 75, 125, 200, 216, 226, 488, 672
Fréchette, Louis Honoré: 158, 160, 166, 167, 655
Frohman, Daniel: 256, 257, 546, 548, 549
Fry, James Barnet: 211, 226, 229
Fulton, Robert: 488, 515, 516, 518, 587, 588, 589, 675, 678
Fusion party: 373, 404, 413, 414, 415, 669

Gabrilowitsch, Ossip: 344, 680
Galen, Claudius Galenas: 126, 127, 635
Galloway, Beverly Thomas: 435, 437, 439, 670
Galveston, Texas: 341, 344, 667
Garfield, James Abram: 138, 146, 147
Garland, Hamlin: 453, 673
Gilded Age: 77, 87, 89, 92, 267, 485, 626
Gilder, Richard Watson: xxi, xxvii, 176, 177, 247, 265, 377, 398, 400, 427, 450, 453, 527, 637, 639, 655, 667, 672, 679
Gorky, Maxim: 513, 514, 675
Gould, Jay: 75, 77, 477
Grant, Frederick Dent: 515, 518, 612
Grant, Ulysses Simpson: 87, 128, 131, 133, 136, 152, 173, 209, 218, 225 *passim,* 235, 268, 345, 382, 397, 402, 424, 654
Greeley, Horace: xv, 613–14, 615, 628
Greenbacks: 2, 3, 13, 375
Griffin, Lepel Henry: 257, 259, 260
Grout, Edward Marshall: 413, 503, 505
Gutenberg, Johann: 200, 204, 206

Hale, Edward Everett: 100, 533, 534, 536
Hannibal, Missouri: 63, 106, 431 *passim,* 437, 457, 552, 661, 670
Hapgood, Norman: 472, 558
Harper's Magazine: 15, 193, 209, 267, 311, 320, 674
Harper's Weekly: 412, 442, 459, 461, 467, 527, 557, 562, 674
Harte, Francis Bret: 103, 338, 615
Hartford, Connecticut: 83, 89–90, 92, 94, 97, 106, 136, 138, 146, 151, 176, 183, 184, 186, 222, 228, 235, 250, 251, 276, 295, 311, 341, 374, 376, 418, 426, 427, 444, 446, 469, 474, 494, 497, 502, 508, 559, 605, 649 *passim,* 670, 676
Hartford *Courant:* 14, 87, 89, 91, 94, 96, 99, 109, 114, 118, 129, 138, 144, 151, 154, 157, 160, 166, 175, 186, 187, 202, 213, 218, 225, 227, 237, 263, 264, 267, 336, 388, 415, 426, 427, 650
Harvard University: 48, 172, 236, 359, 360, 482, 559, 563, 596
Harvey, George Brinton McClellan: xxi, xxii, 349, 453, 455, 456, 459, 460, 462, 596, 667, 668, 672, 673, 676, 679
Hastings, Warren: 404 *passim*
Hawkins, Anthony Hope: 337, 338, 558, 655
Hawley, D. "Father": 374, 376, 564, 565, 649, 650, 652
Hawley, Joseph Roswell: 98, 99, 128, 129, 151, 180, 186, 187, 206, 207, 208, 267, 376, 654
Hay, John: 265, 402, 453, 454, 456, 457, 458, 613, 614
Hayes, Rutherford Burchard: 97, 98, 99, 652
Heaton, John Henniker: 556, 579, 583, 584, 677

Heidelberg, Germany: 120, 508, 653
Higbie, Calvin H.: 56, 57, 63
Higginson, Thomas Wentworth: 110, 527, 543, 679
Hitchcock, Ethan Allen: 435, 436, 439, 670
Holmes, Oliver Wendell: 44, 45, 110 *passim,* 134, 135, 136, 535, 543, 605, 651, 654
Homer: 125, 255, 566
Hotten, John Camden: 69, 253
House of Lords: 335, 535, 536, 666
Howells, William Dean: xix, xxii, xxv, 110, 116, 131, 160, 176, 177, 228, 265, 320, 349, 367, 393, 398, 400, 427, 453, 454, 456, 459 *passim,* 494, 513, 532, 533, 535, 543, 545, 546, 559, 605, 647, 651, 652, 654, 655, 668, 672, 673, 676, 678, 679
Howland, Henry M.: 244, 420, 423
"How to Tell a Story": 155, 156, 240
Huckleberry Finn: xxv, 195, 199, 308
Hughes, Charles Evans: 467, 596
Hutton, Laurence: xxi, 177, 190, 193, 222, 507–8, 655 *passim,* 667, 672

Ingersoll, Robert G.: xv, 185
Innocents Abroad: xvi, xvii, 3, 23, 27, 36, 49, 72, 83, 135, 171, 474, 476, 532, 601, 626, 627, 645
Irving, Henry (John Henry Brodribb): 69, 322, 338, 339, 340, 565, 566, 655, 658, 660, 666

James, Henry: 120, 651
Jameson raiders: 343, 347, 664
Jefferson, Joseph: 263, 276, 278, 655, 658, 667, 669
Jerome, William Travers: 413, 594, 595, 596, 643, 644, 680
Joan of Arc: 21, 79, 472, 473, 476, 642
Johnson, Samuel: 226, 413, 625

Kanaka: 6 *passim,* 15
Keats, John: 566, 674
Keller, Helen: 348, 460, 506, 507, 510, 642
Keokuk, Iowa: xv, 200, 647
Kingsley, Charles: 69, 83 *passim,* 322, 651
Kinsmen: 655, 657, 658, 666, 667
Kipling, Rudyard: 322, 323, 466, 485, 522, 678
Kruger, Johannes Paulus: 342, 343, 344

La Salle, Robert Cavelier de: 440–41, 604
Lawrence, Frank Richard: xxi, xxii, 267, 392, 447–48, 603, 604, 606, 637, 638
Letters From the Earth: 513, 527
Lincoln, Abraham: 128, 145, 177, 228, 243, 381, 382, 383, 402, 424, 486, 488, 570, 571, 591, 625, 668
Lipton, Thomas Johnstone: 558, 571, 595
Liverpool, England: xvii, 48, 78, 83, 577, 580, 581, 609, 650, 651, 677
Livingstone, David: 73, 74, 215, 325, 573, 628
London, England: xvii, 45, 48, 69, 78, 86, 106, 252, 258, 275, 304, 321, 322, 324, 325, 330, 333, 343, 365, 377, 385, 404, 419, 430, 508, 554, 555, 556, 558, 575, 586, 607, 612, 645, 649, 650, 666, 667, 677
London *Times:* 335, 610, 650, 666, 677
Longfellow, Henry Wadsworth: 75, 110 *passim,* 134, 543, 544, 657
Lotos Club: 265, 267, 304, 349, 392, 420, 447, 452, 603, 637, 638, 660, 667, 678, 680
Louisiana Purchase Exposition: 401, 441, 476
Love Letters of Mark Twain: 84, 194, 235, 267, 271, 650
Lowell, James Russell: 44, 115, 148, 545, 563, 605
Low, Seth: 265, 266, 268, 377, 409, 413, 414, 416, 417, 423, 612

Mabie, Hamilton Wright: 398, 399, 453, 596, 604, 667, 668, 679
MacAlister, John Young Walker: 321, 322, 584
Macaulay, Thomas Babington: 226, 305, 405, 413, 538, 540

Mackay, Donald Sage: 363, 366, 667
Mackay, John William: 482, 660–61
MacVeagh, Isaac Wayne: 453, 455,456, 460
Madison Square Garden: 381, 520, 594, 656, 661
Mark Twain: A Biography: 14, 19, 180, 187, 321, 336, 383, 442, 487, 557, 563, 572, 611, 631, 647, 664, 670, 680
Mark Twain in Eruption: xxiv, xxv, 292, 392, 484, 564, 599, 672, 676, 679
Mark Twain's Autobiography: 63, 89, 182, 495, 511, 545, 658, 673
Mark Twain's Letters: xxiv, 131, 661
Mark Twain's Notebook: xxiv, 260
Mark Twain, storyteller: 62–63, 66–67, 110–14, 122–24, 155–56, 195–99, 211–13, 254–55, 261–62, 272–73, 279 *passim,* 289–92, 303, 308–11, 331–32, 378–79, 419, 424, 438–39, 469–71, 482–83, 497 *passim,* 508–10, 512, 516–17, 520–21, 539, 547, 552–54, 565–66, 579–80, 601–2, 616–17, 624–25, 656, 658 *passim,* 665 *passim,* 675, 678; curtain speeches, 87–88, 92–93, 103–5, 256–57, 276–78, 546–47, 596–97, 620, 651, 652, 659, 662, 676, 678; political speeches, 97–99, 128–29, 138–44, 146–47, 182–84, 186 *passim,* 404–12, 414–16, 653, 654, 656, 669; on copyright, 158, 206–9, 235, 251–52, 335–36, 530, 532 *passim,* 656, 657, 660, 666, 674, 676; on behalf of causes, 194, 344–46, 384–88, 468–71, 478–81, 506–10, 513 *passim,* 522–26, 548–49, 656, 667, 668, 674, 675, 676; interviews, 251–53, 287–88, 312–13, 342–43, 530–32, 543–44, 554–57, 585–86, 617–18, 667, 676, 677, 678
Matthews, James Brander: xxii, 250, 269–70, 393, 398, 453, 511, 527, 596, 655, 658, 661, 667, 672–73
McAleer, Patrick: 494, 502, 546
McClellan, George Brinton: 2, 3, 150
McKelway, St. Clair: xix, 265, 266, 268, 349, 370, 392, 453, 456, 637, 638–39, 643, 673
Melbourne, Australia: 292, 298, 663
Miles, Nelson Appleton: 151, 381, 601, 602, 674, 678
Millet, Francis David: 193, 244, 533, 655
Milton, John: 42, 226, 321, 332
Minneapolis, Minnesota: 287, 292, 343, 662
Mississippi River: 275, 294, 297, 349, 362, 431, 440, 457, 499, 578, 604, 617, 674
Monday Evening Club: 150, 426, 427, 428, 650, 651, 652, 654 *passim*
Montreal, Canada: 157, 158, 159, 161, 166, 180, 655
Morgan, John Pierpont: 173, 381, 612, 613, 614–15, 673
Mugwump: 97, 182 *passim,* 224, 267, 351, 372, 392, 404, 656, 659
Munro, David: 668, 672, 678

Nansen, Fridtjof: 321, 327, 329, 556
Napoleon: 81, 152, 153, 255, 286, 566, 640
Nasby, Petroleum Vesuvius (David Ross Locke): xv, 167, 168
Nelson, Horatio: 70, 72, 159, 619
New England Society of New York: 100, 173, 652, 655
New Orleans, Louisiana: 63, 176, 297
Newton, Isaac: 66, 210, 211
New Vagabonds Club: 330, 332, 666
New York City: xvi, xviii, xxi, xxii, 23, 44, 45, 59, 103, 176, 184, 275, 344, 345, 355, 364–65, 366, 375, 389, 405 *passim,* 414, 456, 486, 504, 515, 531, 543, 585, 597, 621, 648 *passim,* 656, 667, 668, 676, 678
New York *Herald:* 64, 74, 244, 256, 257, 278, 348, 510
New York Press Club: 38, 40, 353, 357
New York *Sun:* xviii, 184, 247, 268, 459

New York *Times:* 92, 93, 99, 100, 103, 105, 109, 124, 129, 144, 148, 150, 154, 160, 166, 240, 251, 253, 267, 274, 276, 278, 311, 340, 343, 352, 355, 357, 362, 365, 367, 372, 376, 380, 383, 384, 388, 390, 391, 394, 397, 399, 402, 412, 416 *passim,* 422, 425, 426, 430, 439, 441, 452, 459, 460, 467, 471, 472, 481, 486, 494, 505, 510, 512, 514, 518, 520, 532, 539, 541 *passim,* 547, 549–50, 554, 555, 557, 576, 585, 586, 594, 599, 602, 610, 617, 618, 619, 621, 622, 623, 625 *passim,* 639, 644, 668, 669, 677
New York *Tribune:* 118, 138, 268, 311, 415, 416, 419, 549, 610, 613, 615
New York *World:* 68, 88, 268, 336, 340, 348, 357, 362, 395, 460, 467, 511, 512, 532, 586, 597, 614, 620, 656
North American Review: 229, 399, 400, 456, 460, 544, 563, 668
Norton, Charles Eliot: 110, 559, 563
Nye, Edgar Wilson "Bill": 238, 239, 436, 448, 658
Nye, James Wilson: 64, 240, 487

O'Connor, Thomas Power "Tay Pay": 324, 337, 558, 567, 577, 578, 579, 581, 583, 584
Odell, Benjamin Barker: 349, 351, 353, 392, 394, 668
Ogden, Robert Curtis: 381, 478, 482
Olin, Stephen Henry: 240, 377, 658
Onteora, New York: 501, 502, 659
Order of Acorns: 404, 414, 415, 669
O'Reilly, John Boyle: 148, 176, 177, 655
O'Rell, Max (Leon Paul Blouet): 257, 260, 324, 659
Ottawa, Canada: 178, 558, 655
Outlook: xxvii, 398, 399, 400, 604
Oxford University: 227, 554, 558, 564, 566, 574, 579, 582, 584, 585, 587, 593, 603, 605, 607, 609, 610, 612, 621, 622, 651, 666, 677

Paine, Albert Bigelow: xx, 182, 605
Paris, France: 29, 122, 125, 174, 313, 329, 355, 362, 400, 402, 445, 449, 653
Parker, Gilbert: 558, 584, 666
Philadelphia, Pennsylvania: 63, 162, 194, 216, 274, 485, 492, 495, 570, 639, 655, 656, 662
Pinero, Arthur Wing: 338, 339, 340, 655
Pittsburgh, Pennsylvania: xvi, 31, 36, 493
Platt, Thomas Collier: 371, 372, 373
Players Club: 193, 224, 240, 548, 657, 661, 668, 669, 673, 678
Plymouth Rock: 100, 162, 165
Pond, James Burton: xviii, 215, 238, 247, 286, 344, 450, 667
Porter, Horace: xxi, 151, 173, 222, 240, 265, 266, 268, 447, 448, 449, 451, 452, 604, 658, 671
Porter, Robert Percival: 584, 607, 610
Potter, Henry Codman: xxi, 363, 365–66, 370, 372, 551, 612, 667
Prince and the Pauper: 157, 256, 257, 546, 596
Pryor, Robert Atkinson: 263, 264, 659
Public Education Association: 360, 362, 667
Pudd'nhead Wilson: 276, 278, 342, 503, 541
Punch: 563, 584, 608, 610, 611, 677
Putnam, George Haven: 263–64, 264–65, 504, 667

Quaker City: xvi, 4, 18, 23, 27, 35, 36, 37, 648
Quebec, Canada: 158, 159, 160, 161, 166

Raymond, John T. (John O'Brien): 87, 88, 89, 92
Redding, Connecticut: 625, 630, 632, 633, 679
Reed, Thomas Buchanan: xix, 349, 350, 352, 420, 453 *passim,* 458, 671, 672
Rehan, Ada: 222, 657, 658
Reid, Whitelaw: 381, 567, 584, 612 *passim,* 658, 678

Riley, James Whitcomb: 238, 239, 240, 658, 662
Rockefeller, John Davison, Jr.: 483, 484, 668, 669
Rogers, Henry Huttleston: 271, 348, 349, 453, 455, 459–60, 520, 558, 587, 617, 619, 640 *passim*, 667, 672, 673, 679, 680
Rome, Italy: 27, 29, 32, 174, 250
Roosevelt, Theodore: 244, 307, 351, 353, 373, 392, 417, 460, 527, 548, 594, 614, 674
Roughing It: xvi, xvii, 25, 41, 63, 69, 93, 145, 224, 240, 289, 308, 529, 626, 627, 629

St. Andrew's Society: 423, 660, 669
St. Gaudens, Augustus: 193, 240, 614, 655
St. Louis, Missouri: 7, 63, 287, 295, 297, 298, 401, 440 *passim*, 573, 670, 671
Sandwich Islands: xvi, 5, 8, 12, 13, 135, 244–46, 531, 616
San Francisco *Alta California:* 2, 17, 20, 23, 26, 649
San Francisco, California: xvi, 1 *passim*, 16, 20, 23, 25, 59, 104, 278, 342, 343, 378, 380, 493, 517 *passim*, 528, 529, 538, 579, 599, 629, 648, 675
Satan: 40, 118, 276, 672
Saturday Morning Club: 237, 654, 657, 659, 676
Savage Club: 69, 71, 302, 304, 321, 564, 572, 575, 649, 663, 664, 666, 667, 677
Schiller, Johann Christoph Friedrich von: 315, 316, 318
Schurz, Carl: 184, 186, 187, 377, 423, 478, 672
Scott, Walter: 80, 226, 324, 358, 359
Shakespeare, William: 86, 226, 255, 257, 307, 321, 526, 566, 573, 597, 672
Shepard, Edward Morse: 409, 410, 413, 414
Sherman, William Tecumseh: xxi, xxiv, 130, 131, 151, 152, 154, 211, 222, 226, 228, 240, 263, 658
Siamese twins: 238, 240, 276–78, 541–42
Sickles, Daniel Edgar: 151, 263, 381
Smith College: 658, 668, 675
Smith, Francis Hopkinson: xxi, 398, 453, 654, 667, 674
Smith, John: 210, 211, 589
Society of Illustrators: 472, 476, 673
Southampton, England: 46, 48, 314, 343
Stanley, Henry Morton: 69, 73, 74, 214, 215, 288, 321, 322, 573, 628, 657
Stanton, Elizabeth Cady: xv, 21, 22
Stedman, Edmund Clarence: 65, 134, 265, 393, 395, 672, 674
Stoddard, Richard Henry: 65, 68, 110, 614
Stoker, Bram Abraham: 254, 565, 566, 624, 655
Stone, Melville: xxi, xxii, 522, 643, 672, 673
Stowe, Harriet Beecher: 535, 588, 654
Sydney, Australia: 342, 600, 663

Tammany Hall: 356, 366, 372, 404 *passim*, 408 *passim*, 413 *passim*, 481, 644
Taylor, James Bayard: 65, 116, 118–19, 615, 653
Tennyson, Alfred: 265, 477, 574, 589
Terry, Ellen: 340, 556, 658, 660
Thaw, Harry Kendall: 592 *passim*, 644, 661
Thomas, Augustus: 349, 401, 621, 667
Tilden, Samuel: 97, 264, 383
Tile Club: 190, 193, 654
Tom Sawyer: 391, 626, 627, 652
Tower, Charlemagne: 637, 638, 639, 676
Train, George Francis: xv, 21, 22
Tramp Abroad: 120, 121, 308
Trinity College: 235, 237, 427, 428, 658
Tuskegee Institute: 478, 479, 480, 482, 674
Tweed, William Marcy: 75, 76, 372
Twichell, Joseph Hopkins: 84, 94, 96, 120, 177, 185, 309, 310, 311, 418, 426, 427, 454, 458–59, 460, 508, 509, 510, 559, 560, 654

University of Missouri: 431, 432, 435, 436, 439, 671

Vancouver, B.C.: xviii, 287, 292, 342, 343
Van Dyke, Henry: 367, 398, 453, 459, 461, 487, 543, 674, 675, 679
Van Rensselaer, Mrs. Schuyler: 360, 362, 377
Venice, Italy: 29, 30, 31, 32, 174, 329, 444
Vesuvius: 12, 32, 547
Victoria, Queen of England: 74, 78, 160, 477, 628, 629
Vienna, Austria: 314, 318, 319, 320, 343, 402, 449, 665
Virginia City, Nevada: 2, 520, 647, 648
Virginia City *Territorial Enterprise:* 57, 58, 240, 518, 648

Ward, Artemus (Charles Farrar Browne): xvii, 41 *passim,* 62, 71, 72, 78, 168, 425
Warner, Charles Dudley: 77, 99, 110, 116, 134, 138, 187, 265 *passim,* 654, 658
Washington, Booker Taliafero: 349, 478, 481, 482
Washington, D.C.: 20, 24, 64, 77, 103, 206, 207, 235, 251, 261, 477, 530, 531, 533, 601, 602, 612, 648, 649, 656 *passim,* 674, 676
Washington, George: 21, 60, 75, 271, 273, 332, 345, 383, 401, 420, 421, 424, 438, 483, 488, 498, 553, 648
Waterloo: 79, 137, 153, 171
Wellington, Arthur Wellesley, Duke of: 70, 72, 137, 153
West Point: 152, 153, 154, 654, 657, 659
Whitefriars Club: 69, 72, 73, 324, 325, 326, 584, 650, 666
Whittier, John Greenleaf: 110, 115, 134, 535, 543, 544, 605, 653, 674
Wilberforce, Albert Basil Orme: 333–34, 560, 584, 666
Wilson, James: 435, 436–37, 439, 670
Wilson, Woodrow: 373, 672
Winter, William: 222, 240, 658
Wood, Fernando: 139, 140, 142, 144

Yale University: 235, 393, 426, 427, 428, 435, 436, 658, 670